# NEOPLATONISM AND JEWISH THOUGHT

# NEOPLATONISM AND JEWISH THOUGHT

*edited by*

Lenn E. Goodman

*INTERNATIONAL SOCIETY FOR NEOPLATONIC STUDIES*

Volume 7 in *Studies in Neoplatonism: Ancient and Modern*
R. Baine Harris, General Editor

STATE UNIVERSITY OF NEW YORK PRESS

Published by
State University of New York Press, Albany

© 1992 State University of New York

All rights reserved

Printed in the United States of America

For information, address State University of New York Press,
State University Plaza, Albany, N.Y., 12246

Production by Marilyn P. Semerad
Marketing by Theresa A. Swierzowski

**Library of Congress Cataloging-in-Publication Data**
Neoplatonism and Jewish thought/edited by Lenn E. Goodman.
    p. cm. — (Studies in Neoplatonism; v. 7)
    Includes bibliographical references and index.
    ISBN 0-7914-1339-X (hardcover). — ISBN 0-7914-1340-3 (pbk.)
    1. Neoplatonism—Congresses.  2. Philosophy, Jewish—Congresses.
    3. Judaism and philosophy—Congresses.  4. Philosophy, Comparative-
    -Congresses.  I. Goodman, Lenn Evan, 1944-   .  II. Series.
    B517.N456 1992
    181′.06—dc20
                                 92-8369
                                     CIP

10  9  8  7  6  5  4  3  2  1

# CONTENTS

List of Abbreviations . . . . . . . . . . . . . . . . . . . . . . . . . . .  viii

Preface
    R. Baine Harris . . . . . . . . . . . . . . . . . . . . . . . . . . .  ix

Editor's Introduction:  Thematizing a Tradition
    L. E. Goodman . . . . . . . . . . . . . . . . . . . . . . . . . . .  1

Philo's Conception of the Divine Nature
    David Winston . . . . . . . . . . . . . . . . . . . . . . . . . . .  21

Solomon Ibn Gabirol's Doctrine of Intelligible Matter
    John M. Dillon . . . . . . . . . . . . . . . . . . . . . . . . . . .  43

Parallel Structures in the Metaphysics of Iamblichus and Ibn
    Gabirol
    C. K. Mathis II . . . . . . . . . . . . . . . . . . . . . . . . . . .  61

Ibn Gabirol:  The Sage among the Schoolmen
    Bernard McGinn . . . . . . . . . . . . . . . . . . . . . . . . . . .  77

From What is One and Simple only What is One and Simple
    Can Come to Be
    Arthur Hyman . . . . . . . . . . . . . . . . . . . . . . . . . . .  111

Maimonides and Neoplatonism: Challenge and Response
Alfred L. Ivry ........................... 137

Maimonidean Naturalism
L. E. Goodman .......................... 157

The Virtue of Faith
Menachem Kellner ....................... 195

Why Not Pursue the Metaphor of Artisan and View God's
Knowledge as Practical?
David B. Burrell, C.S.C. ................... 207

Matter as Creature and Matter as the Source of Evil:
Maimonides and Aquinas
Idit Dobbs-Weinstein ..................... 217

Divine Unity in Maimonides, the Tosafists and Me'iri
J. David Bleich ......................... 237

Platonic Themes in Gersonides' Doctrine of the Active
Intellect
Seymour Feldman ....................... 255

Utterance and Ineffability in Jewish Neoplatonism
Steven T. Katz ......................... 279

Self-Contraction of the Godhead in Kabbalistic Theology
David Novak .......................... 299

Jewish Kabbalah and Platonism in the Middle Ages and
Renaissance
Moshe Idel ............................ 319

Love and Intellect in Leone Ebreo: The Joys and Pains of
Human Passion
Hubert Dethier ......................... 353

Spinoza, Neoplatonic Kabbalist?
*Richard Popkin* . . . . . . . . . . . . . . . . . . . . . . . . 387

The Psychodynamics of Neoplatonic Ontology
*Robert B. McLaren* . . . . . . . . . . . . . . . . . . . . . . 411

Bibliography . . . . . . . . . . . . . . . . . . . . . . . . . . . . 427

The Contributors . . . . . . . . . . . . . . . . . . . . . . . . . . 435

Index . . . . . . . . . . . . . . . . . . . . . . . . . . . . 439

# LIST OF ABBREVIATIONS

| | |
|---|---|
| AJS | Association for Jewish Studies |
| B. | Babylonian Talmud (*Bavli*) |
| DK | H. Diels and W. Kranz, *Fragmente der Vorsokratiker* (Berlin, 1934-54) |
| HUCA | *Hebrew Union College Annual* |
| IJMES | *International Journal of Middle Eastern Studies* |
| JAOS | *Journal of the American Oriental Society* |
| JHP | *Journal of the History of Philosophy* |
| JJS | *Journal of Jewish Studies* |
| JPS | Jewish Publication Society |
| JQR | *Jewish Quarterly Review* |
| JTS | Jewish Theological Seminary of America |
| LCL | *Loeb Classical Library* |
| LXX | *The Septuagint* |
| M | Mishnah |
| PAAJR | *Proceedings of the American Academy for Jewish Research* |
| REI | *Revue des Études Islamiques* |
| REJ | *Revue des Études Juives* |
| SUNY | State University of New York |
| SVF | H. von Arnim, *Stoicorum Veterum Fragmenta* (Leipzig, 1903-24) |
| Y. | Jerusalem Talmud (*Yerushalmi*) |

# PREFACE

R. Baine Harris

Religion can never be completely free from philosophy. Although it might be possible to construct a philosophy that would be free from any religious meanings, philosophical concepts and opinions are essential elements in religion; and they are found in all religions.

Philosophy is a fundamental human activity—even more fundamental than religion. It is an effort to inquire into the origin and nature of everything we encounter, an inquiry that no individual capable of reflection can avoid, but one that can be responded to in a number of ways, some of which are religious.

Philosophy in its early stages is an intellectual analysis of everything we can know or think about in some way. It may or may not move on to a rational synthesizing of our knowing experiences, and to an intellectual commitment to some logical way of systematizing them. Religion, in contrast, is always a statement of belief about the nature of whatever the believer believes to be ultimately real and of ultimate importance. Religion usually involves some form of personal commitment either to an identifiable being or to some teaching about the ultimate nature of reality—a commitment which cannot occur without making some philosophical assumptions. It is a response that is affected to some extent by the nature of the original philosophical inquiry.

Religions usually begin with the vision of a founder around which, as time goes on, are constructed additional teachings and interpretations by its various proponents. The original vision soon becomes encased in a superstructure of organized doctrines, as interpreters attempt to explain and even expand the significance and larger meaning of the views of the founder. Although the original visions of the founders of religions are often emotionally intense and profound in their insight into human nature and human behavior, they are not always philosophically profound. A notable exception is the vision of the Buddha. This is not to say, however, that these visions are philosophically uncommitted, for they are given and developed in languages which are themselves historical, and as such, are dependent upon some concepts of reality that are the products of someone's philosophical reflection.

Even though the original vision may not be clear in its ontology, consistent in its logic, or rich in its epistemological options, the basic components used by the founder and the concepts used by those who interpret the vision are themselves products of history, and, as a consequence, are philosophically laden. However timeless and universal the original vision of the founder of a religion may be, it is a product of the philosophical outlook of its age. This is why religions are always in need of new interpreters to update the vision, translate it into terms and concepts that are meaningful in the new age, and at the same time revive the ancient meanings of the religion in some way that is amenable to some contemporary philosophical outlook. These two objectives are not always compatible. One of the dynamic tensions that seems to run throughout the history of most of the world's great religions is whether the main focus of the religion is to be upon the simple interpretation of the vision of the founder or upon the more elaborate and sophisticated philosophical ramifications of it that have evolved over the years.

Religions are much more complex than they appear to be. Not only is there a philosophical factor involved in their internal growth and development, but their interpreters must also make intellectual adjustments in their theology along the way as they encounter certain well-developed and established philosophies of challengingly similar or rival content. One instance of such an encounter is the main theme of this book, most of the essays of which chronicle the historical encounter from the First through the 17th centuries of an old established religion, which we now call Judaism, with a very sophisticated and Romanized form of late Platonic thought which grew to become what we now call Neoplatonism. Serious Jewish thinkers had to deal with Neoplatonism, both because they were wise enough to see that no religious thinkers can afford to ignore any well-ordered philosophy contemporary to them and because they saw in the speculations of certain Neoplatonic philosophers epistemological and metaphysical notions that were quite compatible with their own historical and traditional attempts to characterize the nature of God and his relation to nature and man.

It was of no great importance to them that Roman Neoplatonism, in addition to being a philosophy, was also a way of life, and even practiced as a religion by a few elitist philosophers. They had no need of it as a philosophy of life or as a form of religious commitment, since they already had quite satisfactory forms of both in Judaism. They were interested in it mainly for its utility in developing a religious epistemology and metaphysics, a main concern of the many Jews, Christians and Muslims down through the centuries and even in the present time who have been seriously interested in Neoplatonic thought.

Not all Jewish thinkers were enthusiastic supporters of Neoplatonism. Some strongly opposed it in favor of some other philosophical approach; and the larger history of Judaism in the Late Hellenistic, Roman, and Medieval Periods must include those who reacted to Neoplatonism as well as those who advocated it. But it would not be an exaggeration to say that Neoplatonism was the philosophy that was most influential upon the formation of Jewish thought during these periods. It played a significant role, if not the dominant role, in the whole development of modern Jewish thought.

The essays in this volume should be of interest to modern Jewish intellectuals who wish to have a deeper understanding of the actual historical philosophical elements in their own religious tradition. But they also have an importance much broader than Jewish cultural self-definition. This is because they generally deal with those larger intellectual issues that are involved whenever the thinkers and scholars of a religious tradition attempt to become philosophical about their religion, namely, when they attempt to translate sacred meanings into metaphysical meanings with the aid of a critical epistemology.

These larger intellectual issues, such as the definition of the divine, man, and nature, their proper relations, the meanings of time, history, and worship, are remarkably similar in the great religions, although their metaphysical formulations may differ radically. The essays in this volume show how major Jewish thinkers dealt with some of these issues. But the intellectual issues are universal and reflect concerns held in common with many religious traditions, and especially with Hinduism, Christianity, and Islam, all of which in the course of time have had their own scholars who have considered some of the same issues, and in some instances provided responses similar to those provided by the Jewish philosophers.

These essays should be of special interest to modern Christian and Muslim scholars. The monotheistic faiths are still struggling today with the same basic problem dealt within most of them, namely, that of making monotheism metaphysically meaningful. They should be of interest to anyone who does not think that monotheism can be completely divorced from philosophy and wishes to establish some connection between the God of Abraham and the God of the philosophers.

Although the idea for a conference on "Neoplatonism and Jewish Thought" was my own, its development and execution into reality was the work of one man, Professor Lenn E. Goodman, of the Philosophy Department of the University of Hawaii. He not only organized the conference, but also secured the funding for its support and edited the papers contained in this work, spending hundreds, if not thousands of hours of his time on the project. His devotion and scholarly professionalism have been an inspiration to me during these past five years. I can only say of him what Leigh Hunt says of Abou Ben Adhem, "May his tribe increase!"

My deep thanks are extended to President Albert J. Simone of the University of Hawaii at Manoa, the host institution, for his strong support of the project. Appreciation is also expressed to the sponsors of the conference, namely, the Department of Philosophy, the Department of Religion, the Department of European Languages and Literatures, the College of Continuing Education and Community Service, Temple Emanu-El and the Hawaii Council of Churches. To the Matchette Foundation, the University of Hawaii Foundation, the Hawaii Committee for the Humanities, the Office of the University of Hawaii Vice-President for Academic Affairs, and the American friends of the Hebrew University my deep appreciation is also given for their financial contributions, without which the conference would not have been possible. My gratitude is also given to Old Dominion University for its seventeen year support of all the numerous enterprises of the International Society for Neoplatonic Studies, including the production of this volume. Kudos are especially extended to Elaine Dawson of the Arts and Letters Office of Research Services at Old Dominion University, for her excellent work in preparing the final copy of the manuscript.

August, 1990                                   Department of Philosophy and
                                                         Religious Studies
                                                   Old Dominion University

# EDITOR'S INTRODUCTION :
# Thematizing a Tradition

One benefit of studying texts from another age is the access they afford us to alternative problematics and thus to crosschecks of our own speculations and assumptions. In the great tradition of philosophy that extends from Philo, the intellectual godfather of Neoplatonism, to Spinoza, who restructured the by then classic Neoplatonic mode of thought, it was not the existence of God or even the reality of minds or universals that principally exercised philosophic minds. Rather the great issues were those of relating the ineffable indefiniteness of the One with the finite and intelligible specificity of the many, the absoluteness of divine power and perfection with the seemingly arbitrary particularities of practical experience and choice. Minds and universals were not problems but parts of the solution of this single problem that loomed so much larger than any difficulty the bare fact of consciousness or notion of intelligibility might sometimes seem to pose: the problem we can identify under the shorthand title of the many and the One. If that name scarcely seems for us to designate a problem at all, it is only because we may not have assigned quite the role and function to the One and quite the rigorously construed alienness to the many that the schemes of philosophy ancestral to our own traditionally assigned.

The philosophic method founded by Plato and forged into a system by its synthesis with the thought of Aristotle provided philosophers in antiquity and throughout the Middle Ages not only with an explanation of the possibility of knowledge but also with an exposition of the content of that knowledge. It was clear why and how God was real, if reality and value were coextensive, so that the highest value was the highest reality. It was clear as well how God could be known, if what was most real was also most beautiful and most intelligible in itself, and if the knowledge of all specificities came through the knowledge of the absolute truth Itself, the Source of all that is real, constant, or intelligible among changing things. It was clear how living beings are animated and how consciousness is possible, if reality and thought are gifts from the highest reality and pure thought is pure actuality. For it was clear that the loss of form and rationality betokens as well loss of reality. When amorphousness and indefiniteness are complete only the utter limit of non-being remains.

What was not clear and not agreed among Neoplatonists was why and how the One, or God, the Unconditioned, would compromise Its absoluteness. The problem was not how being was possible, for it was clear that being was actual. Nor was the problem how the Absolute was possible. For the Absolute was necessary in and of Itself. Rather the problem was how the Unconditioned could give rise to the conditioned. The problem of creation, the problem of evil, the problem of revelation, the problem of specifying the doable good in relation to the demands of absolute Perfection, were all conceived as special cases of the general problem of relating the finite to the Infinite, the many to the One.

In the Middle Ages varieties of Neoplatonic Aristotelianism afforded the overarching philosophic framework for most thoughtful Muslims, Jews and Christians who believed that they required a philosophic framework at all, and for many who believed that they did not. The cliche is that it was an age of faith. If this means that communities of faith defined the alignments of society, the cliche is probably true. But it is certainly false if it is taken to mean that philosophers in the Middle Ages were more dogmatic or less critical than philosophers of other epochs. And it is certainly false if it is taken to mean that the philosophers of Neoplatonic-Aristotelian persuasion took refuge in fideism from the problems of critical thinking. Such a description is a romantic projection, seeking comfort and escape in an illusory, idealized past from intellectual difficulties that were just as alive then as they are today, only confronted with different tools and perhaps tackled from a different end or aspect, as climbers might concentrate now on one face, now on another, of the same peak or summit. When Philo made philosophy the handmaiden of theology, what was important was not merely that he gave philosophy a seemingly subordinate role, serving theology, but that it was philosophy he gave that role. When Origen reasoned that God's perfection requires that in the end even Satan will be reconciled and brought back to union with God, he found the proof-texts in Christian scripture, but they were used to bear out what reason had demonstrated must be so.

When Augustine molded Christian faith out of Platonic *pistis*, Ciceronian *fides*, and Stoic assent or appropriation, and spoke of faith seeking understanding, he made faith the means but understanding the end. Likewise when Saadiah set forth his beliefs and convictions in treatise form, he qualified their description in the title of his book with the designation 'Critically selected' and organized the book around the arguments that vindicated each of his theses *vis-à-vis* its alternatives. When al-Ghazālī appraised the character that had made him a thinker, he mentioned an innate curiosity and an inability to accept dogmas on blind faith; he said that if critics expected him to refute a position he had not first assayed for its merits, they were expecting the wrong task from the wrong person; and he sustained all his criticisms of the established traditions in philosophy with detailed philosophic argumentation, rejecting only those theses that could not withstand such scrutiny. Maimonides too held that if scripture clashed with reason, scripture could and must be allegorized, adjusting our reading of its meaning to preserve its truth. And Thomas, in his mighty Summas, always states objections first, in the manner of the Arabic *kalām*, and follows his thesis with its Euclidean proof and then the answers to the objections. Sacred and authoritative texts are quoted only to establish the authenticity as Christian, traditional doctrine of the theses sustained by argument. The same is true with the proof-texts used by the Muslim and Jewish philosophers. All see a congruence and complementarity of reason and revelation, where tradition supplies the bond uniting the two— reconciling insight with insight by way of dialectic and so making possible the coherence of a community that endures from moment to moment and from epoch to epoch.

Modern historians of ideas who write of medieval philosophy as though it were a battleground between reason and revelation are projecting their own unease about the sacred and the secular, the ancient and the modern, left and right, red and black, fathers and sons, onto domain where such a conflict does not enter the terms of reference. Scholars play this game of old and new, reason and faith, only by refusing to allow the philosophic texts to speak for themselves and define their own concerns. For the primary food for any philosophy is the corpus of texts bearing the critical thinking of past generations; and the primary test of the scholarship that profits from those texts is its willingness to allow them to thematize themselves. Only the scholarship that is willing in this way to listen to the great thinkers is qualified to judge their critical achievement, and only through such judgment can our own thought become critical and in some measure transcend the boundaries of its generation.

Ennui is the great enemy of scholarship, and it takes many guises—not only literal boredom with the musty tomes, but fear of readers' boredom and a resultant desire to make old texts palatable or relevant by reducing them to pawns or players in some contemporary contest or struggle. Such reductionism is both self-aggravating and self-defeating. It buries the insights of past thinkers beneath concealing projections and muffles the voices of their advocates, stifling the freshness they might bring us from another age and thus perpetuating ennui by confronting a vision as yet unfocused with an apparent wall of opacity and the temptation merely to silver that wall, on the cynical assumption that scholarship must always be about ourselves. Intellectuals who believe that the texts they study will tell them nothing that does not resolve to partisan advocacy of contemplation or praxis, autonomy or heteronomy, individual or society, universality or particularity, or any other preconceived polarity, are not prepared to glean more from the texts they con than what they have already brought with them—least of all are they prepared to profit from the discovery of alternative problematics.

One who supposes that medieval thought revolves around a conflict between reason and revelation operates as though reason and revelation were products rather than processes, and as though it were already known, before scholarship or philosophy, or the dialectic between them, has begun its work, what will be the outcome and content of each. But if there is any truth in saying that the Middle Ages were an age of faith, that truth lies in the fact that the great issues of the day, for so many, could be summed up in the question: What ought to be the content of faith?

The present volume brings together the papers presented at the International Conference on Neoplatonism and Jewish Thought held in Honolulu November 30-December 3, 1987. If there is merit in these papers it arises in each author's probing of a particular text or body of texts for its Neoplatonic themes and their intellectual relevance, allowing the texts to speak for themselves. The striking finding, if we may use a somewhat scientific-sounding word, is that independent scholars, writing independently about figures who worked in different periods and languages, albeit in a common religious confession and philosophic construction, alighted repeatedly on the issue of mediation, the central Neoplatonic concern with the means by which the Absolute can be related to the here and now. This became the unifying theme of the conference and of this volume, linking the diverse approaches adopted by the thinkers studied and the diverse methods of the scholars, theologians and philosophers who took part, as a spontaneous but recurrent focus. Arranged in a rough chronological sequence, the papers afford a striking historical sampler of the ideas, achievements, difficulties and philosophic struggles of a group of men who worked not quite at one another's sides, nor wholly in isolation, to form a tradition of intellectual exploration that grew out of the philosophic work of antiquity and late antiquity. Readily bridging the gap that separates pagans from monotheists and rival confessions and sects from one another, this tradition, sustained by common theological values and philosophical concerns, continued for centuries to aid thinkers in confronting problems in a wide variety of contexts, fostering a common conceptual vocabulary and indeed a common philosophical aesthetic for mystics, rationalists, and empiricists, Jews, Christians, and Muslims—a philosophic source whose vitality is not yet exhausted.

David Winston, a specialist in the thought of Philo of Alexandria, the great Hellenistic Jewish thinker of the first century B.C., opens the volume with reflections on the very Maimonidean, Rabbinic, and indeed universal problem of naming or describing God. He shows how Philo availed himself of Stoic strategies to prevent the idea of divine transcendence, say, of the passions, from strangling discourse about the divine altogether, discovering and exploiting affective terms that do not imply passivity, and so licensing and rendering coherent with the Biblical idea of divine transcendence the seemingly incompatible usage that conceives of God in terms of compassion, joy or will. The idea of divine joy becomes an important theme for mystics, including philosophic mystics; the idea of divine will becomes the common focus of all monotheistic thinkers in the Middle Ages in responding to the Neoplatonic theme of emanation.

John Dillon addresses the *Fons Vitae*, or *Fountain of Life* of Solomon Ibn Gabirol, a remarkable work of almost pure Neoplatonic metaphysics, which, as Dillon, Mathis and McGinn show, is rooted in the late ancient theories of Greek Neoplatonism and spreads its influence far beyond its own time and place to become a point of departure and dialectical response to Christian continuators of the philosophic tradition of natural theology. It is commonly said that the chaste dialogue of the *Fons Vitae*, which survives in full only in a Latin translation of the Arabic original, is devoid of Biblical allusions or other distinctive marks of its Jewish origin—so that the schoolmen who used it could not tell if the author was Muslim or Jewish. Indeed, it was not until Rabbi Salomon Munk of Paris in 1845 discovered quotations from the work in a text by Shem Tov Ibn Falaquera that scholars knew that Ibn Gabirol, the well-known Hebrew poet of sacred and secular themes, was identical with the "Avicebrol" of the *Fons Vitae*. But in fact, the work bears in its title an allusion to the beautiful lines from the Psalms: "For with Thee is the Fountain of Life; by Thy light do we see light." It was this poetic equation of life with light, the principle of being with that of understanding, that convinced many Jewish neoplatonists of the underlying harmony between Biblical and Neoplatonic theism: At bottom the Torah and the philosophers were saying the same thing in different ways—thus the insights of either tradition could shed light on the problems of the other.

Newcomers who came to Plato's Academy to hear his famous Lecture on the Good were shocked to find that instead of a discussion of the good life, Plato was exploring the most basic problem of arithmetic, the relation between the numbers one and two. But for Plato this issue had become the final undissolved residue of philosophy. If it could be explained how the pure simplicity of the One, or the Good, gave rise to that first otherness of "the Indefinite Dyad," of "the great and the small," then the emergence of the cosmos, of matter from idea or spirit, of time from the eternal, of change from changelessness, and of specificity from pure generality, would seem easy. The key to Plato's problem, Ibn Gabirol thought, lay in the recognition that thought has an objective, thus obectifying aspect to it: Thought itself is like matter, a principle of differentiation or otherness and thus the first precipitate of emanation—the first matter.

Dillon shows how Ibn Gabirol drew his striking idea of a material nature in the spiritual realm of the divine from a well developed Neoplatonic tradition of thinking about "intelligible matter," applying that idea, as earlier Platonists had done, to preserve divine transcendence—mediating but not compromising the absoluteness of God's oneness and perfection. He shows how Ibn Gabirol responds, much in the manner of Plotinus, the founder of Neoplatonism, and Iamblichus (fourth century), to difficulties about the notion of intelligible matter, drawing upon our familiarity with the anatomy of thought to assign to intelligible matter the hybrid character it will need if it is to function successfully as the vehicle of the mind's access to the divine world and of God's access to nature.

Carl Mathis pursues the parallel between Ibn Gabirol and Iamblichus, exposing more fully the motive of preserving the absolute transcendence of the One while conceptually allowing the traffic between God and nature, without which the most transcendent God becomes a metaphysical irrelevancy. In Iamblichus, as in Ibn Gabirol, Mathis finds a "doubling" of the One, which allows God both to remain in "unspeakable splendor" and to "unfold Himself" into principles that give rise to nature and diversity as we know it. Here Ibn Gabirol is seen continuing work on the problem that was racking Plato's mind in the years before his death in much the way that Einstein, in his last years, was seeking a unified field theory. The same motives and values and often the same strategies are at work later in the Kabbalistic thinkers, as we see in the papers of Novak, Katz, Idel and Popkin—the need to preserve divine transcendence, yet to allow access of God to the world and of the human mind and heart to God.

Bernard McGinn takes us to an endgame of Ibn Gabirol's gambit in philosophy, showing how problems in the idea of intelligible matter—for example, about the unity of the human person—made that idea less helpful than Ibn Gabirol had hoped, even for thinkers who took his approach far more seriously than did the mainstream Jewish philosophical tradition. At the same time, he takes us deeper into the architecture of Ibn Gabirol's intellectual universe (to borrow A. H. Armstrong's phrase), revealing the central role of divine will (*Voluntas*), a theme preserved in all the later Jewish philosophers and in the Kabbalists. Indeed the centrality of Will becomes a hallmark of Jewish Neoplatonism, in a way curtailing or redefining the commitment to Neoplatonic thinking. God's will becomes a Neoplatonic hypostasis or is identified with the Ineffable highest Unity that Neoplatonism taught Jewish thinkers how to conceptualize without reduction, and so, in their own distinctive ways, to address without compunction (despite its utter transcendence) and even (in the case of some Kabbalists) to engage with in the expectation of a response.

It is Will for Ibn Gabirol that brings matter and form together and so makes creation possible. Creation is thus in some way a free act of God. It is not a mere timeless flowing forth of necessity, a freezing of the event within the eternity of God, as though nature somehow remained embedded within God and never actually acquired its own reality. This idea, the reality of creation—symbolized by the thesis that nature had an origin and epitomized in the affirmation of divine volition, God's freedom to act or not to act, according to his grace and pleasure—becomes the great theme of medieval Jewish philosophy and the great thesis to be defended. Human freedom, the contingency and openness of the future, are just two of the corollaries of this response to what was seen as the constraining necessitarianism of the intellectualist, determinist reading of Neoplatonic emanation theory. It is here that Arthur Hyman's paper introduces the challenge that scriptural monotheists consistently threw down at the feet of the more strictly intellectualist and deterministic exponents of emanation: How can what is one and simple (as the Neoplatonic God is supposed to be, if God is to be absolute, indestructible, necessarily existent, unique and unrivaled) give rise to anything but what is one and simple? That is, even assuming the success of some Neoplatonic strategy of mediating the gap between the One and its product, through a series of Neoplatonic-Aristotelian disembodied intellects, how can any outcome emerge but a series of such presumably "simple" beings—not a world of multiplicity and change, but simply an indeterminately long sequence of undifferentiated and therefore undifferentiable theoretical beings. The answer, as Ibn Gabirol clearly anticipated and as Jewish philosophers of many backgrounds and persuasions were to underscore, with aid from Muslim predecessors who had raised the same question, was that only divine will could make a difference where none was given at the outset.

Hyman shows how the tension between divine simplicity and the world's multiplicity and complexity was addressed by Plotinus, Avicenna, al-Ghazālī, Isaac Israeli, Ibn Gabirol, Ibn Daud, Maimonides, Averroes, Ibn Falaquera, Narboni, and Albalag. He follows the principle that the simple can give rise only to the simple from its origins in Neoplatonic philosophy to its use in the critique of that philosophy by al-Ghazālī and Maimonides and its eventual refinement, qualification or abandonment by Jewish Averroists, under pressure from adversaries who sought to restructure emanationism in a more voluntaristic, less mechanical direction.

Alfred Ivry questions the success of Maimonides in fusing emanationism with the idea of creation, insightfully glossing Maimonides' emphatic strictures against polytheism as veiled attacks on the Neoplatonic-Aristotelian scheme of celestial intelligences associated with the spheres and mediating God's governance over the sublunary world. Maimonides saw the ultimately pagan roots of this scheme, Ivry argues, but rather than reject a solution to the problem of the many and the One that was at its root "inimical to monotheism," he sought to tame it by emphasizing the createdness of the intelligences. In inveighing against an Aristotelian view that seemed to make God *"primus inter pares,"* first among His peers, "Maimonides is protesting against a world view in which God plays essentially a mechanistic role." Critically exploring the somewhat neglected Neoplatonic side of Maimonidean thought and its backgrounds in the philosophy of Ibn Sīnā, Ivry finds that the Avicennan philosophy had failed to resolve its problem of the many and the One: "Perhaps Maimonides realized this and therefore drew back from utilizing the distinction between essence and existence more than he did." But Maimonides' ambivalence between commitment to Neoplatonic solutions and sensitivity to Neoplatonic deficiencies remains unresolved, in Ivry's view, a source of continuing difficulties in his philosophy, which are concealed by his reticence.

My own paper takes a more favorable view of the success of Maimonides' neoplatonizing project, although within the framework of the assumption that no work of philosophy, as a human enterprise, can achieve perfect coherence and resolve all tensions. The paper focuses on Maimonides' bold effort to interpret the Biblical imagery of angels as divine messengers, with the help of Neoplatonic and Aristotelian philosophy, in a manner that will preserve both the naturalism of the sciences (and his own art of medicine) and the Biblical axiom that God is the ultimate author of all events. Here again we see our theme of the mediation between God's absoluteness and the conditional realm of the ephemeral and empirical. Maimonides sharply attacks "those men who purport to be the Sages of Israel" for superstitiously believing that God sends an angel, a being one-third the size of the physical world, to form the foetus in the womb, and failing to understand what Rabbinic usage about angels plainly indicates: that angels are natural forms and forces imparted by God through the Active Intellect—that this is "the real meaning of greatness and power" in God's act. Maimonides glosses the midrashic equation of angels with the third part of the world as proposing a tripartite ontology in which Platonic forms, classically conceived as thoughts of the supernal intelligences, play a critical mediating role. After laying out the anatomy of this scheme, my essay seeks a philosophical significance for it in an era after the Ptolemaic spheres have fallen.

Menachem Kellner explores the idea that faith can be a virtue and shows that this virtue is not to be understood in strictly intellectualist terms. The problematic of his paper is expressive of the longstanding Maimonidean/Ghazalian protest against the intellectualism of that strand of Neoplatonic-Aristotelian philosophy that was taken up and pushed to deterministic extremes by Jewish and Muslim philosophers of Averroistic inclination. David Burrell, in a different way, takes up the same theme. A theologian whose background is informed by Avicennan and Ghazalian studies as well as the Thomistic tradition, he brings a Whiteheadian and perhaps also Bergsonian slant to his inquiry when he asks why Maimonides did not more fully pursue the idea that God's knowledge is practical rather than strictly cognitive. He asks further whether theologians today should not follow up on this approach, which Thomas, for one seemed to regard as promising in terms of preserving both divine and human freedom.

Idit Dobbs-Weinstein, like Ivry, stresses the tensions between Neoplatonic and Aristotelian elements in Maimonides' philosophy. Such an exercise always runs the risk of submerging the synthetic achievements of a philosopher who sought to reconcile what others might conceive as incompatible ideas. But the feminist slant of Dobbs-Weinstein's writing vividly highlights an ancient Neoplatonic difficulty which Maimonides himself pinioned as the Achilles heel of Neoplatonism: its desire to treat matter both as the explanation of all evil and as a mere "receptacle" or condition of otherness, with no positive being or character of its own. In Maimonides' exegeses, matter is personified both as the married harlot of the Book of Proverbs, always changing forms, never content with just the form it has; and as the good woman (the so-called Woman of Valor, in the familiar mistranslation) of the same book. Maimonides seeks to reconcile these two images by arguing that matter itself is neutral and that whether it becomes good or evil depends on what is done with it. It is not evil in itself; yet, as a condition of otherness and privation, it is the basis of evil. But Dobbs-Weinstein discovers unresolved tensions within Maimonides' accounts of matter as created and physical or as metaphysical and notional; and she finds similar problems in his accounts of evil, which sometimes seek to relativize, sometimes to objectify it. Maimonides, she argues, "deliberately declines to give matter an essential role in human perfection." Dobbs-Weinstein finds a resolution of such tensions in the philosophic synthesis of Aquinas, which "succeeds in dissociating matter from evil and overcomes the tension between sub- and supralunar existence."

Whether it is true that Maimonides' sometimes magisterial dicta and sometimes Puckish silences about matter and evil conceal unease and bad faith or a profound insight into the strengths and weaknesses of Neoplatonism will continue to be debated well beyond the confines of this volume, but Dobbs-Weinstein's engaging paper, as the very least of its merits, may attract some students of Maimonidean and post-Maimonidean philosophy away from endless and usually ill-conceived debates over the preferability of the intellectual or the practical life and encourage them to address the question whether Neoplatonic or Aristotelian approaches, or some hybrid or synthesis of the two, can aid us in addressing the question of our embodiment and the ambiguities of our status as creatures who live, as Dobbs-Weinstein puts it, in both realms, the intellectual and the physical.

David Bleich's paper is a Talmudic *shi'ur* and in some measure a *jeu d'esprit*, arising from the endeavor to explain the efforts of such medieval rabbis as Me'iri to disallow the claim that Christians were idolators. Cutting away from socio-economic explanations, Bleich sifts the record of Christian dogmatics for evidence of early Christian heretics whose doctrines of the Trinity may have provided a theological basis for Me'iri's ruling. The focus of his study, which follows in the traces of Harry Wolfson's survey of the teachings of the Church Fathers, call to mind one of the central findings of Wolfson's work in the history of ideas: that while Jews and Muslims may reject trinitarianism, its central metaphysical ideas are not exclusively of Christian interest but arise precisely from the Platonic problematic of the One and the many and were pioneered by Philo before the founding of Christianity, and thoroughly explored by the Muslim theologians of the *kalām* in dialogues and debates that laid the basis of the philosophic claim for the radical simplicity of the divine nature and thus for the central themes of medieval natural theology in Ibn Sīnā, al-Ghazālī, Maimonides, Thomas, and other Western thinkers down to and including the argumentation of Spinoza.

With Seymour Feldman's paper we turn to Gersonides and the juxtaposition of his views about epistemology with the corresponding arguments and theses in Plotinus, Alexander of Aphrodisias, and Themistius. Gersonides' reliance on an external and hypostatic Active Intellect, Feldman argues, jeopardizes empiricism, carrying rationalism to the point of regarding all knowledge as essentially inspired. If sensory data are needed at all on such a scheme, he argues, it will only be as cues, Platonic "reminders," not of what we know eternally, but of what our limited, material intellect is given to know by the Active Intellect. Like Dobbs-Weinstein, Feldman finds a fuller resolution to the difficulties he raises in the philosophy of Thomas, where the Active Intellect is dethroned from its hypostatic state and restored to an immanent position as an aspect of the human mind. Averroes pioneered this more naturalistic approach, shying away from a hypostatic formgiver, in reaction to what he came to see as the excesses of Avicennan Neoplatonism. But Gersonides did not follow Ibn Rushd here, evidently less convinced of the adequacy of a reductionistic account of the informing of the human mind and the natural world at large.

Jewish mysticism does not abandon the positions and problematics of Jewish philosophy in general or of Neoplatonism in particular. Rather, it is attracted to the Neoplatonic device of dispatching hypostatic beings to mediate between divine infinity and the compromised world of the here below. The inspiration may be gnostic at times, as Kabbalists view the world with deepening anguish, but the element of hope is never wholly beneath the surface, and the most demonically infested Kabbalistic visions are still animated by the ancient Biblical conviction that this world can be redeemed by human action in concert with the purposes of God. Mythic masks may obscure the features of the Kabbalistic surrogates for argument, but all of the most sophisticated cosmographers of the Kabbalah remember the philosophic problems which the figures they evoke are meant to resolve; and, as the papers of Dethier, Idel, and Popkin reveal, founding figures of the Renaissance and the Enlightenment like Leone Ebreo (Isaac ben Judah Abarbanel, 1437-1508) and Spinoza reclaim what is distinctively philosophical from the creative achievements of the Kabbalah.

Steven Katz, paralleling Winston's paper on Philo, shows how the apophatic or negative theology of pure transcendence was not allowed, in the name of consistency, to exclude all characterizations of the divine. Rather, from Philo to Isaac Israeli, Ibn Gabirol, Bahir, Cordovero, Luria, Azriel of Gerona, Moses de Leon (the author of the *Zohar*) strategies of mediation and qualification were devised both to allow characterization of the divine by man and to ensure that access to creation was not denied to its creator, ruler and judge. Moshe Idel and David Novak develop these themes in detail.

Idel shows how Kabbalistic thinkers took up the idea of God's inner knowledge of the forms of all things and made this the basis of the scheme by which the *Sefirot*, dynamic Kabbalistic hypostases, mediate between God and creation. He also examines the Kabbalists' reliance on other mediating entities and images, surveying the contributions of Ya'akov ben Sheshet, Isaac the Blind, Menaḥem Recanati, Shem Tov ben Shem Tov, Azriel of Gerona, Naḥmanides, Isaac Abravanel, Alemanno, Luzzato, Cordovero, Herrera and others in their responses to the philosophic tradition and its problems.

Novak complements this exposition with a detailed anatomy and dynamic of one of the most original conceptions of the Kabbalah, the idea of *zimzum*, divine self-contraction, as a means of reconciling emanation with the Biblical ideas of divine creation and human freedom. As he shows, *zimzum* was intended to make clear not only how God allows room for creation and affords freedom and existence to lesser beings, but also how the revelation of the Torah and the delegation of its interpretation and elaboration to human minds and hands is a mark of divine favor, withdrawing somewhat from the creaturely realm to afford authenticity to creation in its own right. As Novak writes, "For Kabbalists there is no real difference between creation and revelation. Creation is itself an act of revelation." And the impact of this equation is twofold. Not only was the world an epiphany, as it had always been for serious theists of all persuasions, but the Torah, as the articulate expression of God's will, became our means of participating in the life of God and helping to bring about the cosmic reconciliation which was the great theme of the Kabbalistic version of Neoplatonic eschatology.

Hubert Dethier closely follows the Italian text of the Renaissance Jewish Neoplatonist Leone Ebreo to show how Leone took up Kabbalistic ideas to develop what would become one basis for Spinoza's idea of the intellectual love of God. God imparts His own perfection to creation, and "human sin may adversely affect God himself. . . . It is love that imparts the unity at each level and thus explains the existence and active functioning of each thing in the universe and each level of the celestial hierarchy. . . . Although God is perfectly one and simple, a mysterious multiplication occurs within Him [a theme we have seen in Iamblichus, Ibn Gabirol and the Kabbalah]:  Just as Eve is said to have sprung from the body of Adam, the original active entity, God's beauty or simply essence, produces a feminine entity. . . . Beyond his original, intrinsic love, God also loves extrinsically. For, in loving himself, God also desires to reproduce his beauty. . . . The divine Intellect contemplates itself as well as God, and from this contemplation a female entity is produced. . . . From their mutual love emerges all generation."

Richard Popkin completes the arc from Philo to Spinoza by showing why the first readers of Spinoza saw him as a crypto-Kabbalist. Popkin uncovers the sources of the Kabbalistic ideas that formed a vital part of Spinoza's thinking, despite his rejection of the cosmographical and exegetical excesses of the millenarian Kabbalah of his day. Herrera in particular, in the metaphysical portions of his *Puerta del Cielo*, provides the unifying structure that Spinoza would call to his aid in responding to the dualism of Descartes. And the early responses to Spinoza by such figures as Moses Germanus rightly noted the connection. When the French Huguenot Jacques Basnage ascribed Spinoza's monism to a commitment on his part to the "Kabbalistic" principle *ex nihilo nihil fit,* he was not speaking nonsense, but was rightly perceiving, if rather crudely stating, the Neoplatonic basis of Spinoza's treatment of matter and thought as attributes of God. If the world was not to be sundered by the Cartesian epistemological turn, into corporeal substance and spiritual or intellectual substance, with no possible connection between them, either in the case of human perception and voluntary movement or in the case of divine creation and governance—or love—then matter (even Cartesian matter, as it now was, no longer the intellectual stuff of Ibn Gabirol or the curious "otherness" of Ibn Sīnā and Maimonides) would have to be given back somehow to God, no longer alienated from Him. If nothing comes from nothing, then the materiality in nature cannot "come from" what in itself contains no materiality: Matter must be one manifestation or "attribute" of God (using Maimonides' interpretation of the word 'attribute' as an aspect under which we apprehend divinity). If God is everywhere, then God is in matter too; if the highest monotheism, as al-Ghazālī put it, sees God in everything, then matter is not exempt; and if dualism is untenable and renders matter inaccessible to God or the mind, then the idea of emanation must be revised to reveal not a penetration of alien matter by the pure light of form—the female by the male—but a coordinate authenticity of extension and idea, as each other's representations, conjoint manifestations of the infinite essence of the Divine.

In the final conference paper, Robert McLaren surveys Neoplatonism as a whole and Jewish Neoplatonism in particular with a view to discerning the psychodynamical needs and theological conundrums which the recurrent Neoplatonic epochs in Western philosophy may address. His appraisal does not (in the manner of Freud's classic dismissal of the religious quest) simply dismiss Neoplatonism, or the religious impulses it expresses, as a delusion, on the ground that it answers questions of the heart; but equally it does not seek in the manner of pop theology to validate Neoplatonism on those same grounds, as if the service of the needs of the heart were sufficient vindication of an idea's veracity. For if our age can learn anything from the thinkers of the past it is that religion in general and religious philosophy in particular are not elevated by being treated as a consumer commodity. To a wiser sensibility like that of Bahyā ibn Paquda, the service of the heart means not service *to* but service *by* the heart.

McLaren seeks sympathetically to explicate, in psychodynamic terms, the same crosspressures that the classic thinkers studied in this volume sought to reconcile philosophically. One is reminded of Maimonides' comment, echoing Saadiah as he so often does, that the Ash'arites and occasionalists of the *kalām* are not to be scorned but respected for their endeavors to struggle with great issues, and for the honesty, clarity and consistency of their respect for the values we still find enshrined within their philosophies, even where those philosophies do not succeed in making all coherent but leave the threads and crossthreads imperfectly disentangled.

Expositors, here in this volume and in the past, have sought to tease out some of those threads, sometimes to weave them into a more durable fabric, sometimes simply to show them to be hopelessly snarled or at risk of unraveling completely if handled any further. The names of the great thinkers whose work informs the matter of this volume are thus themselves intertwined in the notes and bibliography with the names of scholars of their work whose thoughts were never far from the minds of our symposiasts and whose writings underlie much of what is written here: Alexander Altmann, M.-M. Anawati, A. H. Armstrong, W. Bacher, Abdur-Rahman Badawi, Zvi Baneth, Clemens Baeumker, Maurice Bouyges, Émile Brehier, Fernand Brunner, Hermann Cohen, Israel Efros, J. N. Findlay, Louis Gardet, Étienne Gilson, Louis Ginzburg, A.-M. Goichon, Julius Guttmann, P. Henry, A. J. Heschel, George Hourani, Isaac Husik, Louis Jacobs, J. Kafah, David Kaufman, S. Landauer, R. J. McCarthy, Ibrahim Madkour, Muhsin Mahdi, Henry Malter, Philip Merlan, P. Moraux, Salomon Munk, David Neumark, Joseph Owens, Shlomo Pines, Fazlur Rahman, Franz Rosenthal, W. D. Ross, Cecil Roth, Joseph Sarachek, Shmuel Sambursky, Solomon Schechter, Gershom Scholem, Steven Schwarzschild, H. Schwyzer, Leo Strauss,

Samuel Stern, Leo Sweeney, Georges Vajda, Simon Van Den Bergh, Richard Walzer, Zwi Werblowski, John Wippel, Stephen Wise, Harry Wolfson, A. S. Yahudah, and a handful of others. Their influence is pronounced, not only here, but in the writings of many of our colleagues cited frequently in these pages: Edward Booth, Pierre Cachia, Vincent Cantarino, Herbert Davidson, Majid Fakhry, Stephen Gersh, Dimitri Gutas, David Hartman, Raphi Jospe, Barry Kogan, Joel Kraemer, Michael Marmura, Dominic O'Meara, Eric Ormsby, Ian Netton, F. E. Peters, Shalom Rosenberg, Everett Rowson, Tamar Rudavsky, Norbert Samuelson, Jacques Schlanger, Kenneth Seeskin, Yirmiyahu Yovel, and others recurrently cited in the notes to our papers.

Philosophy, like Penelope's web, is torn down in the night but rewoven every morning, not out of mere doggedness or temporizing, but in a continual effort to capture adequately and in the perfect balance of its natural colors a single subtle but elusive pattern that will be emblematic of all reality. In the course of our studies of that weaving and unweaving, we may catch traces of the design that animates the ancient craft, and may seek to describe it to one another, or perhaps ourselves to take our places in the weaver's chair and touch our fingers to the clews.

*** 

Our conference was the Seventh Congress of the International Society for Neoplatonic Studies. R. Baine Harris, the president of that society, deserves special acknowledgment for his many years of service to Neoplatonic studies and for first suggesting the conference whose deliberations are represented here. He had long felt the need for a conference exploring the achievements of Jewish Neoplatonism, the responses of Jewish thinkers to Neoplatonic philosophy, and the impact of that philosophy on Jewish thought. He invited me to organize such a meeting; and, finding a warm response from prospective scholarly participants, academic sponsors, and funding agencies, I was glad to do so. The conference was sponsored by the University of Hawaii Department of Philosophy, which has a history of commitment to comparative philosophic studies that goes back over fifty years. Our meeting was aided with generous grants and in kind support from the University of Hawaii, the Matchette Foundation, the Hawaii Committee for the Humanities, a state-based program of the National Endowment for the Humanities, the American Friends of the Hebrew University, the Jewish Federation of Hawaii, Temple Emanu-El of Honolulu, and the Hawaii Council of Churches.

Special thanks are due to F. Glen Avantaggio for giving freely of his time to prepare the index of this volume, to John Casey for his graphic design work and photography at the conference, and to Guy Axtell, Ray Steiner and their fellow members of the Philosophy Students' Association at the University of Hawaii for driving the conference vans and facilitating the meeting in many other ways. Ours was the first Jewish studies conference to be held in Hawaii and the first conference to bring together the unique constellation of scholars represented in this book, many of whom had never met before. In addition to its formal academic proceedings, which are represented here, the conference also involved an ecumenical scholar-in-residence weekend, a public lecture series, a University of Hawaii mini-course for the academic and lay community on Neoplatonism and the Kabbalah, and publication of an adult education Interpretive Guide for the benefit of the host community. The scholars and I join in thanking the sponsoring bodies and the communities locally, nationally, and internationally, from whom they draw their support, for the opportunity they gave us to work together and the occasion for which we produced the body of work represented in this volume.

We met in true conference style, seated like the members of an orchestra, with our music before us, at the concentric tables of the Asia Room in the East West Center on the University of Hawaii campus. The papers as presented here cannot reproduce the full liveliness of the exchanges that took place, although most of them profited from those exchanges, often in ways now imperceptible. The twinkling eye of Bernie McGinn, the jovial laughter of Menachem Kellner, the hearty earnestness of David Novak, and Dick Popkin's delightfully low-key narrative style as he reported the forgotten or hitherto unknown comings and goings of Renaissance and Enlightenment figures—the general tone of anticipation and delight as each of us warmed to his topic and sparked off one another's observations, cannot be recorded here. But it was when the players took up their instruments in earnest that the real event began—the light, airy allegro of David Winston, introducing Philo's theme in the flutes and piccolos, against a background of Greek woodwinds, followed by the extended andante passages of Ibn Gabirol in the cellos of Dillon, Mathis, and McGinn; the stately adagio of Maimonides in the strings, offset by reedy counterpoints of Islamic rhythms and Thomistic counterstatements in the basses, and by Ivry's and Dobbs-Weinstein's querulous oboe and clarinet solos; the intricately patterned Kabbalistic largo, and the brilliant scherzo and finale in which the new themes of Leone and Spinoza are heard in counterpoint with the now familiar material of the earlier presentations, and the whole brought together, rousingly, pleasingly but quizzically in McLaren's brassy and tympanic coda. Some of this effect is recorded here. The significance of none of the materials touched on is exhausted, but if this volume leads some of its readers to delve further into the texts themselves and the intellectual questions they subtend, it will have fulfilled its purpose.

Lenn E. Goodman<br>Honolulu

# Philo's Conception of the Divine Nature

David Winston

## The Divine Transcendence

Philo's doctrine of the transcendent character of God undoubtedly derives from the Middle Platonic and Neopythagorean traditions that had postulated a supranoetic First Principle above a pair of opposites, the Monad, representing Form, and the Dyad, representing Matter. Philo seems to be referring to such predecessors when he writes: "Others maintain that the Unoriginate resembles nothing among created things, but so completely transcends them, that even the swiftest understanding falls far short of apprehending Him and acknowledges its failure."[1] As is often the case with Philo, we have here an example of the convergence of his Jewish inheritance with his Greek philosophical antecedents. The prophetic teaching of the incomparability and unnameability of God reinforced Philo's philosophical convictions and led him to espouse an emphatic doctrine of extreme divine transcendence. It was his philosophical commitment, however, that (pace Wolfson) was clearly the decisive element in his sharp distinction between God's essence and his existence, and his insistence on man's absolute inability to know the former. For such metaphysical categories were completely alien to the Biblical and Rabbinic traditions.[2]

Philo states repeatedly that God is absolutely *apoios*, qualityless (*LA* 3.36, 51, 3.206; *Deus* 55-56; *Cher.* 67). Drummond and Wolfson have shown that this means that God is without accidental

21

quality, but also implies that in God there is no distinction of genus and species. God is *to genikotaton*, the most generic (*Gig.* 52). And, since He belongs to no class, we do not know what He is.[3] All God's predicates are, strictly speaking, properties (*idiotetes*). They are derivative of His essence but, unlike definitions, do not indicate that essence itself and, unlike qualities, are not shared with others. Further, since the essence of God is one and single, whatever belongs to it as a property must be one and single. Thus Philo reduces all divine properties to a single one, that of acting (*Cher.* 77).[4]

In Philo's hierarchy the essence of God, although utterly concealed in its primary being, is nevertheless made manifest on two secondary levels: the intelligible universe of the Logos, which is God's image (*Som.* 1.239; *Conf.* 147-48), and the sensible universe, which in turn is an image of that Logos (*Op.* 25). Although the essence of God in itself remains forever undisclosed, its effects, images or shadows (or, to use a Plotinian term not employed by Philo, traces: *Enneads* VI 7.17) can be perceived. Philo attempts to delineate the dynamics of the Logos' activity by defining and describing its two constitutive polar principles: Goodness or the Creative Power (*poietike dynamis*) and Sovereignty (*exousia*), the Ruling Power (*basilike dynamis*) (*Cher.* 27-28; *Sac.* 59; *Her.* 166; *Abr.* 124-25; *QE* 2.68; *Fug.* 95). It is not difficult to recognize in these two powers the *apeiron* and *peras*, the Unlimited and Limit, of Plato's *Philebus* (23C-31A).[5] These reappear in Plotinus' two moments in the emergence of Nous. Undefined or unlimited Intelligible Matter proceeds from the One and then turns back to its source for definition (II 4.5.5; V 4.2; VI 7.17; cf. Proclus *Elements of Theology*, Props. 89-92, 159). The various positive properties attributed to God by Philo are all subsumed under one or the other of these two polar forces, and are therefore all expressions of the Logos, manifesting God as thinking/acting (*Prov.* 1.7; *Sac.* 65; *Mos.* 1.283).

At the summit the powers of the Logos are grasped as constituting an indivisible unity. But at lower levels there are those who know the Logos only as the Creative Power, and those beneath them who know it as the Ruling Power (*Fug.* 94 ff.; *Abr.* 124-25). Lower still are those who are sunk in the mire of sensible being and unable to perceive the intelligible realities steadily (*Gig.* 20). At each lower level of knowledge the image of God's essence grows more dimmed or veiled.

Since God's essence in itself is beyond human experience or cognition, even beyond mystic vision, the only attributes applicable to Him in His supreme concealment are those of the *via negativa* (e.g., *agenetos, adekastos, akataleptos, akatonomastos, aoratos, aperigraphos, arrhetos, asygkritos*) (*Mut.* 7-15), or of the *via eminentiae*.[6] Although Philo sometimes speaks of God as a Monad and as good, blessed, or benevolent (*LA* 2.2; *Deus* 26; *Cher.* 86; *Det.* 146; *Abr.* 203; *Mut.* 129), he also emphasizes that God is actually "better than the Good, more beautiful than the Beautiful, more blessed than Blessedness, more happy than Happiness itself, and anything there may be more perfect than the aforementioned."[7] He says that God is "more venerable than the Monad, and purer than the Unit" (*Praem.* 40; *Cont.* 2), and that He alone has veritable being,[8] truly acts, is the true Peace or Repose, and is free and joyful.[9] God's superiority to such attributes undoubtedly signifies for Philo that they are applied to Him only equivocally.

## Scriptural Anthropomorphism

While sternly opposed to all anthropomorphic and anthropopathic descriptions of the Deity,[10] Philo is sensitive to the human weaknesses that induce them:

> Since we are for the most part mortal, we are incapable of conceiving anything independently of ourselves and have not the strength to sidestep our defects. We crawl into our mortal shell like snails and like hedgehogs curl up in a ball, entertaining ideas about the blessed and the imperishable identical to those about ourselves. In words we shun indeed the extreme notion that the Godhead is of human form. But in fact we commit ourselves to the impiety that he possesses human passions. So in addition to hands and feet, entrances and exits, we invent for him enmities, aversions, estrangements, anger, parts and passions unfitting the Primal Cause.[11]

The anthropomorphic language used in Scripture is for the admonition of the masses, who could not otherwise be brought to their senses:

> For among the laws which consist of commands and prohibitions, laws, that is, in the strict sense of the word, two ultimate summary statements are set forth concerning the First Cause, one that 'God is not like a man' (Numbers 23:19), the other that he is as a man. But although the former is guaranteed by absolutely secure criteria of truth, the latter is introduced for the instruction of the many. Wherefore it is also said of him, 'like a man he shall discipline his son' (Deuteronomy 8:5). Thus it is for education and admonition,[12] not because God's nature is such, that this is said of him. . . . The companions of soul, in contrast to the lovers of body, do not compare the existent to any form of created things. They have excluded him from every quality. For one of the things that pertains to his blessedness and supreme felicity is that his existence is apprehended as simple, without any other distinguishing characteristic. So they have allowed a representation of him only in respect of existence, not endowing him with any form. . . . Those, on the other hand, who are of a dull and obtuse nature, who have been ill-served in their early training, incapable as they are of keen vision, need overseeing physicians to devise the proper treatment for their condition: Ill-bred and foolish slaves too are profited by a master who frightens them. In dread of his threats and menaces, they cannot help but fearfully accept reproof.[13] Let all such learn the lies that will benefit them, if they are unable to become wise through truth. The most esteemed physicians do not dare tell the truth to those dangerously ill in body, since they know that they will become disheartened as a result and their sickness will not be cured, whereas with the consolation of the opposite approach they will bear their condition more lightly and their illness will abate.[14]

### God's *Apatheia/Eupatheia*

The absolute rationality of God entails for Philo His insusceptibility to *pathos*, an irrational impulse of any kind (*Deus* 52; *Abr.* 202). The Stoics had similarly insisted that the wise man must be wholly *apathes*, clearly implying that he thus assimilates himself to God, who is perfect rationality. "The wise man's soul ought to be such as would be proper for a god," writes Seneca (*Ep.* 92.4). "Just as it is the nature of our bodies to stand erect and look upward to the sky, so the soul, which may reach out as far as it will, was framed by nature to this end, that it should desire equality with the gods" (ibid. 30). Epictetus declares more boldly: "Let one of you show me the soul of a man who wishes to be of one mind with God . . . to be free from anger, envy and jealousy—but why use circumlocutions?—a man who has set his heart upon changing from a man into a god, and although he is in this paltry body of death, does none the less have his purpose set upon fellowship with Zeus" (2.19.26-27; 2.14.11-13). The Old Stoa preferred to speak of the wise man's "living in complete agreement with Nature" (*SVF* 2.127; 3.12, 16) rather than of *homoiosis to theo* like the Platonists (*Theaetetus* 176B). But the Middle and Late Stoa made Plato's formula their own.[15]

Moreover, in reinterpreting popular myth, the Stoics were constrained to criticize both anthropomorphic and anthropopathic descriptions of the divine:

> The perversion has been a fruitful source of false beliefs, crazy errors and superstitions hardly above the level of old wives' tales. We know what the gods look like and how old they are, their dress and their equipment, and also their genealogies, marriages and relationships—and all about them is distorted into the likeness of human frailty. They are actually represented as liable to passions and emotions—we hear of their being in love, sorrowful, angry. According to the myths, they even engage in wars and battles.[16]

As an exegete of Scripture, Philo faced a similar problem. We have seen the pains he took to neutralize Biblical verses that appeared to contradict his philosophical convictions about the divine nature. His efforts were considerably facilitated by the Stoic doctrine of *eupatheiai*, good or rational emotions. This aspect of Stoic theory will help us to understand Philo's readiness to ascribe certain emotions to God.

According to Stoic theory, *hormai* or impulses of various kinds are generated in the *hegemonikon* or commanding faculty of an individual as a result of the stimulus of various *phantasiai* or impressions conducted to it from the excited sense organs by way of tensile motion.[17]   If the *hegemonikon* is in a healthy state, a condition of right reason, the impulses released through its acts of assent will be rational or wholesome *eupatheiai* and express correct judgments (*SVF* 3.169-77).  But if it is diseased or irrational, the impulses released will be excessive and will constitute *pathe*, erroneous judgments.[18]   The sage's perfect *hegemonikon* spontaneously makes correct judgments, wholly eliminating the *pathe* and generating only *eupatheiai*, purely rational impulses.[19]

The three canonical *eupatheiai* are *boulesis* (willing), *eulabeia* (watchfulness or caution), and *chara* (joy),[20] and it is clear that Philo was in no way embarrassed to apply at least two of these to God.  He frequently employs the verb *boulomai* and the noun *boulema* of God,[21] and if the reports of Diogenes Laertius and Plutarch are accurate, it would appear that the Old Stoa spoke of "the will (*boulesis*) of him who orders the universe."[22]   Similarly Philo had no difficulty in describing God not only as beneficent but also as benevolent and kind (*Op.* 81; *Mut.* 129; *Abr.* 137).  He was aided by the fact that benevolence (*eunoia*) was classified by the Stoics as a variety of *boulesis.*   Antipater of Tarsus characterizes God as beneficent (*eupoietikon*), not benevolent, towards men.[23]   But Seneca adds that the gods are "ever gentle and kindly (*placidi ac propitii*), and bear with the errors of our feeble spirits."[24]  *Chara* too was accounted a *eupatheia* by the Stoics. So it comes as no surprise that this attribute also was ascribed by Philo to the daemons or disembodied rational souls (which he also called 'angels'), to the world, which he describes as "a rational and virtuous living being, philosophical by nature,"[25] and to God himself.  He notes with evident approval:

> It is said that even the Father and Creator of the universe continually rejoices in his life and plays and is joyful, finding pleasure in play which is in keeping with the divine and in joyfulness. And he has no need of anything, nor does he lack anything, but with joy he delights in himself and in his powers and in the worlds made by him. . . . Rightly, therefore, and properly does the wise man, believing his end to consist in likeness to God, strive so far as possible, to unite the created with the uncreated and the mortal with the immortal, and not to be deficient or wanting in gladness and joyfulness in his likeness. For this reason he plays this game of unchangeable and constant virtue

with Rebeccah, whose name is to be interpreted in the Greek language as 'Constancy' (*QG* 4.188, tr. Marcus).

The wise man's *chara*, however, is not the equal of God's. The limited capacity of finite creatures denies us the unbroken continuity that marks the divine archetype of our happiness. In *Abr.* 201-07 Philo expands on this theme:

> The intended victim is called in Chaldean Isaac, but when translated into Greek, Laughter. But laughter here is not taken as the laughter which arises in the body when we are engaged in play, but the rational emotion of the understanding, joy. Thus the wise man is said dutifully to sacrifice to God, showing through a symbol that rejoicing is most appropriate to God alone. For mankind is troubled and very fearful of evils either present or expected. . . . But the nature of God is without distress or fear and free from all passion, and alone partakes of perfect happiness and bliss. To the temper of mind that has made this true acknowledgment, God, in his goodness and benevolence, having driven away envy from his presence, returns the gift according to the measure of the recipient's capacity. And, in effect, he delivers the following oracle: The full gamut of joy and the act of rejoicing I know well are the possession of none but me alone, the Father of All. Yet, although in possession of this good, I do not begrudge its use by those who are worthy. . . . Let no one assume, however, that joy descends from heaven to earth undiluted and free from admixture of distress. It is rather a mixture of bliss and suffering, although the better component is predominant. . . . This was the reason, it seems to me, that Sarah, who is named after virtue, first laughs and then denies her laughter in response to the questioner. She feared lest she usurp the joy that belongs to no created being but to God alone. Holy Writ therefore encourages her and says: 'Have no care; you did indeed laugh and you have a share in joy.' For the Father did not permit the human race to be borne amid griefs and pains and irremediable burdens, but mixed with them something of the better nature and judged it right that the soul should at times enjoy calm and fair weather. As for the soul of the wise, he willed that it should pass the greater part of its life in the joy and cheer of the spectacles offered by the universe.[26]

Although here Philo attributes perfect joy to God alone, in *QG* 4.188 he allows the angels, the stars, and the universe as a whole, a portion of eternal joy unmixed with sorrow. Most likely, when he attributes perfect joy to God alone, he intends only to restrict that attribute to the heaven at large, and sees earth as the abode of mixed realities. It is not clear, however, how the Philonic attribution of joy to God is related to the Stoic position. For the earliest explicit testimony for the Stoic assignment of *chara* to God is found in Seneca. "The effect of wisdom," he writes, "is a joy unbroken and continuous. The mind of the wise man is like the firmament beyond the moon. Eternal calm pervades that region. . . . The joy which attends the gods and those who imitate the gods, is not broken off, nor does it cease."[27]

To understand Seneca's assertion, we must recall an early controversy between Cleanthes and Chrysippus. Cleanthes argued that since virtue can never be lost and the good man is always exercising his mind, the wise man's virtue is exercised continually. He enjoys an unbroken state of *chara*. Chrysippus believed that virtue can be lost through drunkenness, 'melancholy,' heavy drowsiness, lethargy, and drugs. So he would deny an uninterrupted *chara*.[28] In line with Chrysippus' position, Diogenes Laertius writes (7.98) that *chara*, like walking exercise, is not a permanent good; the wise man does not enjoy it continuously.[29] But Seneca, like Cleanthes, must have believed that once a man becomes wise, he has achieved a state of uninterrupted virtue, so that the rational elation of *chara* attendant on the exercise of virtue (D.L. 7.94) continues at least to his death. God, whose rationality is unchanging,[30] must forever be in a state of *chara*, his *pneuma* characterized by the perfect *tonos* (*eutonia*, SVF 3.47) that the wise man's psyche attains or expands into only on his conversion to the life of virtue. It is not inconceivable, therefore, although there is no explicit evidence for it, that the early Stoa too held that the perfect rationality of God is continuously accompanied by joy. While agreeing with Seneca that God enjoys continuous *chara*, Philo diverges from him and appears to approximate the position of Chrysippus in denying a like condition to the wise man.[31]

There are some further hints in the surviving texts that the attribution of joy to God was already a characteristic of Middle Stoic teaching, and possibly of early Stoic doctrine as well. Cicero's Stoic spokesman Balbus asserts that "the nature of the world has all the

movements of volition, impulses and desires which the Greeks call
*hormai*, and exhibits the actions in agreement with these in the way
that we ourselves do who are moved by emotions and sensations"
(*ND* 2.58, tr. Long). "As body-soul compounds," writes Long, "we
humans are microcosmic beings, and attributes that we possess in
virtue of having rational souls are features of the world."[32] A
similar ascription of impulses to God is found in Epictetus, who
speaks of our observing the impulses of God and his governance
(4.1.100; cf. 4.1.89), and boldly declares: "I shall attach myself to
God as a servant and follower, my impulse is one with His
(*synormo*), my desire one with His (*synoregomai*), my will is one
with His will (*synthelo*)."[33]

The third *eupatheia*, *eulabeia* is never ascribed by Philo to God
directly. But there may have been no theoretical difficulty in his
doing so. *Eulabeia* is the rational avoidance of evil (Cicero, *Tusc.*
4.15; Plutarch, *Stoic. Repug.* 1037F; cf. Philo *Det.* 45; *Som.* 2.82),
and it could be said that the Divine Logos is continuously
characterized by such a spontaneous avoidance. Indeed, the Stoics
come close to saying as much when they state that the deity is a
living being "admitting nothing evil into him" (*kakou pantos
anepidekton*).[34] For Philo, God's *eulabeia* could readily be
subsumed under the *basilike dynamis*, his power of delimitation
which rejects and punishes evil.[35]

For Philo, *chara* is the best of the *eupatheiai* (*Mut.* 1.131; *Cong.*
36; *Praem.* 31), and it is quite possible that, like the early Stoics, he
would have shrunk from ascribing either *boulesis* or *eulabeia*
explicitly to God, since, strictly speaking, the Deity could not be
characterized by want of any kind. *Chara*, as an *epigennema* (D.L.
7.94; cf. Aristotle *EN* X 1174b32; Philo *LA* 3.86), was exceptional in
that it involved no imputation of want to its subject and was therefore
designated by Philo as the best of the *eupatheiai*. On the other hand,
Philo's use of terms like *boulema* and *boulomai* in relation to God
can readily be seen as a concession to ordinary linguistic usage (cf.
Cicero, *De officiis* 2.35). But since *chara* in relation to God does not
involve an *eparsis*, it should not strictly be called a *eupatheia* at all.
The term accurately describes a psychic state only in man. In
enjoying *chara* God may be said to be characterized by a state which
in man is designated as a *eupatheia*, that is, the *eupatheia* of *chara*

is assigned to God only equivocally. If the above interpretation is correct, we should conclude that Philo ascribes to God neither *pathe* (with the possible exception of *eleos*) nor *eupatheiai*, but only a perfect *eudaimonia*, his objective state,[36] and a subjective *chara*, which in view of the fact that in God it involves no change whatever, is strictly not accounted a *eupatheia*.

Turning from the *eupatheiai* to the *pathe* proper, we find Philo in complete accord with the Stoics in rejecting anger (*thymos*) as a feeling inapplicable to God (cf. Pseudo-Aristeas 254). He is quite willing to stand Scripture on its head to avert such an attribution. After indicating that the description of God as wrathful was necessary for the duller folk who need to be schooled by fear,[37] he offers a forced interpretation of the troublesome verse in Genesis 6:7: "I was wroth in that I made them." Philo suggests that perhaps the intent of the verse is to indicate that the wicked are so through God's wrath, i.e., through the wrath that comes from God; and the righteous by his grace, since the next words are "but Noah found grace with Him" (Gen. 6:8). He squeezes out of the fact that the word-order is "I was wroth in that I made them," rather than the reverse, "because I made them, I was wroth," the notion that these words are only a figure to convey the meaning that it was through wrath that God made or caused their blameworthy actions. Scripture's meaning, then, is that those human actions which result from any of the four primary passions or their derivatives are blameworthy, whereas those which are the product of right reason are worthy of praise.[38]

Having rendered innocuous a troublesome verse, Philo finds in the statement that Noah found grace with God, an allusion to God's saving mercy (*soterion eleon*). Were God's judgment not tempered by mercy, we should find, he says, that the human race could not endure, since sin is unavoidable:

> For if God should will to judge the race of mortals without mercy (*eleon*), His sentence would be one of condemnation, since there is no man who self-sustained has run the course of life from birth to death without stumbling. . . . So then, that the race may subsist, though many of those which go to form it are swallowed up by the deep, He tempers His judgment with the mercy which He shows in doing kindness even to the unworthy. And not only does this mercy follow

His judgment (*ou monon dikasas eleei*) but it also precedes it (*kai eleesas dikazei*) (*Deus* 74-76).

In ascribing pity (*eleos*) to God,[39] Philo decisively parts company with the Stoics, who had classified pity as a species of *lype* or distress, one of the four primary passions (*SVF* 1.213; 3.394, 413-134, 416; cf. Seneca *Clem.* 2.4 ff). He might have avoided the overt break without yielding too much on the issue of God's mercy had he simply substituted the terms *philanthropia* and *epieikeia* for *eleos*.[40] Thus Seneca sharply distinguishes *misericordia*, or pity, (a form of *aegritudo* or distress) from *clementia*, or mercy.[41] He recommends the latter as the action of "an unruffled mind and a countenance under control" (*Clem.* 2.6.2-3). The Old Stoa had made no such distinction. Their doctrine was that the wise "are not pitiful and make no allowance for anyone; they never relax the penalties fixed by the laws, since indulgence and pity (*eleos*) and even 'equity' (*epieikeia*, a sense of fair play going beyond the rigid line of the law) are marks of a weak mind, which affects kindness in place of chastising."[42] But the Middle Stoa may have modified the Old Stoic view of *epieikeia* in the direction of Seneca's theory.[43] We have evidence that the Stoics were attacked for their severity in rejecting pity as a vice. They may have been compelled to emend their unpopular position. Cicero clearly reflects one line of defense:

> It is urged too that it is useful to feel rivalry, to feel envy, to feel pity. Why pity rather than give assistance if one can; or are we unable to be open-handed without pity? We are able. For we ought not to share distresses ourselves for the sake of others, but we ought to relieve others of their distress if we can. (*Tusc.* 4.56)[44]

In elaborating his doctrine of *clementia* Seneca too refers to the sharp critique leveled against the old Stoic view:

> I am aware that among the ill-informed the Stoic school is unpopular on the ground that it is excessively harsh and not at all likely to give good counsel to princes and kings; the criticism is made that it does not permit a wise man to be pitiful, does not permit him to pardon. (*Clem.* 2.5.2)

In the light of the later Stoic doctrine of *clementia*, it may be asked why Philo did not restrict himself to the Middle Stoic *philanthropia/epieikeia* formula in his description of God's mercy. Had Greek possessed a word precisely equivalent to *clementia*,[45] Philo might well have been happy to adopt it as a substitute for *eleos*. But in the absence of such a convenience, he undoubtedly felt constrained by the stress laid upon God's attribute of mercy in his native tradition.[46] It seemed incumbent to ascribe *eleos* not only to the wise man (*Sac.* 1.5221; cf. *Ios.* 82; *Spec.* 2.115, 138; *Virt.* 144), but also to God.[47] There is an occasional slip in Seneca,[48] but Philo's frequent indulgence in the ascription of pity to God and on occasion even anger (*Som.* 2.179; *Op.* 156), which he had labored so mightily to remove from him in *Deus* 70-73, is considerably more jarring. We may conclude that it was the frequent application of *eleos* to God in the Septuagint, Philo's canonical text, that made it so difficult for him to avoid the philosophically problematic attribution.[49] Yet in ascribing *eleos* to God, he undoubtedly had in mind a rational form of the emotion, like Seneca's *clementia*.

The Old Academy and the Middle Platonists generally adopted the Peripatetic ideal of *metriopatheia*, measured or moderate emotions, in lieu of the more rigorous Stoic goal of *apatheia/eupatheia*, freedom from emotions, at least of the 'negative' sort.[50] But Philo apparently was sufficiently attracted by the Stoic model to adopt it in preference to the Platonic mean—in spite of the difficulties and modifications this choice entailed.[51] The ideal of *eupatheia* so intrigued him that, not only did he ascribe it to the wise man but, in a way, to God himself—although the Stoics may have anticipated him in this. Philo's rare references to divine anger may be regarded as occasional slips. The major deviation from Stoic theory in his description of God is his insistence on attributing *eleos* to the Deity. In doing so he was clearly acting under the influence of Jewish teaching.

## Notes

1.  *Som.* 1.184, tr. Colson. Cf. *Anon. Comm. Parm.* 4.22-26 (see n. 8 below); 2.10-14; 9.7: the *Chaldean Oracles* would not even designate God as 'one'; *Corp. Hermet.* 4.9; 11.5. Philo cites Philolaus (DK 44 B. 20), "Himself like unto Himself, different from all others" (*Op.*

100). For Eudorus' supranoetic 'One,' see Simplicius *In Phys.*, 181.17 ff. Diels. See John Whittaker, *Studies in Platonism and Patristic Thought*, essays IX, XI. The claim that Speusippus' 'One' was *hyperousion* was made by Philip Merlan, Walter Burkert, H. J. Krämer, Eduard Zeller, Louis Robin, H. J. Armstrong and H. R. Schwyzer, but has been denied by Leonardo Tarán, *Speusippus of Athens* (Leiden: Brill, 1981), 338-39. See the detailed discussion by John Dillon, "The Transcendence of God in Philo: Some Possible Sources," Colloquy 16 of the Center for Hermeneutical Studies, ed., Wilhelm Wuellner (Berkeley, 1975), and the extensive treatment by A. J. Festugière, *La Révélation d'Hermès Trismégiste* (Paris: Gabalda, 1954) **4**: *Le Dieu Inconnu et la Gnose*; Philip Merlan, *From Platonism to Neoplatonism*, 97, 105; H. J. Krämer, *Der Ursprung der Geistmetaphysik* (Amsterdam: Grüner, 1967), 207-18, 351-58; H. Happ, *Hyle* (Berlin: De Gruyter, 1971), 208-41.

2. See H. A. Wolfson, *Philo*, 2.94-101.

3. Although Philo generally affirms that God is *asomatos* and *apoios*, at *LA* 3.206 he asserts that we cannot even make negative statements of God. Heinemann thinks that he is here echoing the Skeptics, but he may be reflecting a Middle Platonic formulation seen later in Albinus: *Epit.* 10.4 Louis: *oute poion oute apoion*, i.e., beyond such categories altogether. Cf. Proclus *In Parm.* 7.67-76; *Platonic Theology* 2.109.

4. See James Drummond, *Philo Judaeus* (London, 1888; repr. Amsterdam: Philo Press, 1969) **2**.17-34; Wolfson, *Philo* **2**.94-164.

5. Cf. *Philebus* 27BC: "The first then I call the Unlimited, the second the Limit, and the third the being that has come to be a mixture of these two." A similar triadic configuration reappears in the Zohar. The *sefirot* of Wisdom and Intelligence represent the Logos, while those of Love and Stern Judgment are its dynamic polar principles, the Unlimited and Limit. The two in this case are balanced and anchored in the *sefirah* of Compassion.

6. Wolfson rightly pointed out that "though Philo used many negative descriptions of God, he does not say outright that, as a result of the unknowability and ineffability of God, He is to be described by negations. Nor does he apply the principle of negation as an interpretation of those predicates in Scripture that are couched in positive form." *Studies in the History of Philosophy and Religion*, **1**.117. Philo did not need to do so, since in his view these predicates indicate only God's properties and not his absolute essence. Philo also seems to hint in *Deus* 55-56 at another way of speaking of God: the analytical process of *kat' aphairesin*, depriving the object of knowledge of any sensible attribute; cf. Albinus, *Epit.* 10.5, Louis:

"We shall achieve the first idea of God by making successive abstractions, just as we get the conception of a point by abstraction from what is sensible, removing first the idea of surface, then that of line, till finally we have a point," tr. Chadwick in *Origen Contra Celsum* (Cambridge: at the University Press, 1965), 429, n. 4. See Whittaker, *Studies*, IX; S. R. C. Lilla, *Clement of Alexandria* (Oxford: Oxford University Press, 1971), 221.

7. *Legat.* 5. At *Spec.* 2.53, Philo writes that God "is filled with perfect forms of good, or rather, if the real truth be told, Himself the good." Cf. J. R. Harris, *Fragments of Philo Judaeus* (Cambridge: at the University Press, 1886), 24: *mallon de makariotetos autes hyperano.* Although Philo sometimes speaks of the Ever-living God, and of the Father and Creator who continually rejoices in his life (*QG* 4.188), at *Fug.* 198 he says, "God is something more than Life, an ever-flowing spring of living."

8. At *Det.* 160 Philo says: "Things posterior to God (*met' auton*) have no real being, but are believed to exist in imagination only." We find precisely the same notion later in the anonymous commentator (Porphyry?) of Plato's *Parmenides*, fr. 2 (fol. 4, ll. 19-28): "For it is not He who is non-existent and incomprehensible for those wishing to know Him, but it is we and all existing things who are nothing in relation to Him. And this is the reason it has been impossible to know Him, because all other things are nothing in relationship to Him, whereas acts of knowing perceive the similar through the similar. It is therefore we who are the nothing in relationship to all things that are posterior to Him (*ta met' auton*)." See Pierre Hadot, *Porphyre et Victorinus* (Paris: Études Augustiniennes, 1968) 1.119; 2.76.

9. *Det.* 160; *Cher.* 77-78; *Post.* 27-28; *Som.* 2.253; *Cher.* 86; *Abr.* 201-07; *Spec.* 2.54-55; *QG* 4.188.

10. Cf. the Stoic opposition to anthropomorphism, SVF 2.1076 (=Philodemus, *De Pietate* 11); Cicero, *De Natura Deorum* 2.45; Diogenes Laertius 7.147.

11. *Sac.* 95; cf. *QG* 1.42: "God gives the impression of walking without actually walking, indeed without moving at all."

12. Philo understands the LXX *paideuo* (where it is used in the "vulgar" sense of "to discipline," translating Hebrew *yasser*) in the classical sense of "educate."

13. Cf. Seneca, *NQ* 2.42.3: "Being very wise [the ancients] decided that fear was necessary for coercing the minds of the ignorant. . . . It was useful, in times of such insolent crime, that there exist something against which no one might consider himself powerful enough. And so to terrify men who find nothing attractive in good behavior unless

it is backed up by fear, they placed an avenger overhead, and an armed avenger at that." Cf. also *Ep.* 47.18-19; and Critias, *Trag. Graec. Frag.* 43F 19.16 ff.

14. *Deus* 53-55, 63-65; cf. *Som.* 1.237; *QG* 2.54. For the physician analogy, cf. *Cher.* 15; Plato, *Republic* 389B; *SVF* 3.554-55; **2**.132. See F. Wehrli, "Der Arztvergleich bei Platon," *Museum Helveticum* 8 (1951): 177-84.

15. See Cicero, *De Natura Deorum*, 2.37-39, 153; *Tusc.* 4.57; Musonius, fr. 17; Epict. 2.14.11; Seneca, *De Ira* 2.16; *Prov.* 5.4; Marcus Aurelius 10.8. See also H. Merki, *Homoiosis Theo* (Freiburg: Paulus Verlag, 1952), 8-17; A. C. van Geytenbeek, *Musonius Rufus and Greek Diatribe* (Assen: Van Gorcum, 1962), 22-24.

16. Cicero, *De Natura Deorum*, 2.70; cf. Seneca, *Hippolytus* 195; Plutarch, *Amat.* 757C; Pericles 39; *SVF* 3. Diogenes of Babylon 33; Diogenes Laertius 7.147. See also Aristotle, *Metaphysics*, 1073a, 11; Epicurus *K.D.* 1; Cicero, *De Officiis*, 3.102: "It is the universally accepted view of all philosophers that God is never angry, never hurtful." See Max Pohlenz, *Vom Zorne Gottes* (Göttingen: Vandenhoeck and Ruprecht, 1909), 1-9.

17. For tensile motion, see A. A. Long and D. N. Sedley, *The Hellenistic Philosophers* (Cambridge: at the University Press, 1987) **1**.288. Impressions in mature human beings are envisaged to have a propositional content; we assent to them by assenting to their corresponding *lekta* or propositions. "Rationality presumes that the mind's stock of conceptions is immediately activated when a sense-impression is received, with the result that the impression presents its object in a conceptualized form." See Long and Sedley 1.240.

18. Zeno held that a temporal sequence was involved, in which first a judgment is made by the *hegemonikon*, and then rationality or irrationality leads to a *eupatheia* or a *pathos*. For Chrysippus, however, the emotional effects are constitutive to the judgment itself, and there is no such thing as a purely emotionless act of thought. See J. M. Rist, *Stoic Philosophy*, 22-36.

19. See F. H. Sandbach, *The Stoics* (London: Chatto and Windus, 1975), 59-68; Brad Inwood, *Ethics and Human Action* (Oxford: at the University Press, 1985), chs. 3-5; Long and Sedley, 1.410-23; Pohlenz, 1.151-58; Ernst Holler, *Seneca und die Seelenteilungslehre und Affektpsychologie der Mittelstoa* (Diss., Munich; Kallmünz: Lassleben, 1934); David Winston, "Philo's Ethical Theory," in Wolfgang Haase, ed., *Aufstieg und Niedergang der römischen Welt, Principat* 2.21.1 (Berlin: de Gruyter, 1984), 400-05; N. P. White,

"Two notes on Stoic Terminology," *American Journal of Philology* 99 (1978), 115-19.

20.  Diogenes Laertius 7.116: The Stoics "say that there are three good feelings: joy, watchfulness, wishing. Joy, they say, is the opposite of pleasure, consisting in well-reasoned swelling [elation] (*eulogon eparsin*); and watchfulness is the opposite of fear, consisting in well-reasoned shrinking (*eulogon ekklisin*). For the wise man will not be afraid at all, but he will be watchful. They say that 'wishing' is the opposite of appetite, consisting in well-reasoned stretching [desire] (*eulogon orexin*). Just as certain passions fall under the primary ones, so too with the primary good feelings. Under wishing: kindliness (*eunoian*), generosity (*eumeneian*), warmth (*aspasmon*), affection (*agapesin*). Under watchfulness: respect (*aido*), cleanliness (*hagneian*). Under joy: delight (*terpsin*), sociability (*euphrosynen*), cheerfulness (*euthymian*)," tr., Long. Cf. *SVF* 3.432-42.

21.  *Op.* 16, 44, 77; *LA* 1.35; *Deus* 75; *Post.* 73; *Her.* 272; *Abr.* 204; *Mos.* 1.287, etc.

22.  D. L. 7.88; Plutarch *Comm. Not.* 1076E. Cf. Plato, *Timaeus* 29E, 30A, 41B5, cited by Philo *Aet.* 13. Cf. Epictetus 1.17.14; 2.17.23; 3.5.9; 4.7.20; 4.1.99; *Encheiridion* 26; Seneca *NQ* 3.15.3; 7.27.6; *Ep.* 66.39; 76.15-16; Aetius, *Plac.* 1.6.1: God is a *pneuma noeron . . . metaballon de eis ho bouletai*, Diels, *Dox. Graec.*, 292. Note that for the Stoics (certainly at least for the Middle and Late Stoa) God is not an impersonal force, but "a living being, rational, perfect or intelligent in happiness, admitting nothing evil into him, taking providential care of the world, although he is not of human shape," D. L. 7.147; cf. Epictetus 3.13.7; Seneca *Ep.* 92.27. See A.-J. Voelke, *L'Idée de Volonté dans le Stoicisme* (Paris: Presses Universitaires de France, 1973), 105-12; Plutarch *Stoic. Repug.* 1051F.

23.  The first of Plato's canons of theology (*typoi peri theologias*) is that God is good, and the good is beneficent (*Republic* II 379AC). According to Musonius Rufus 17, Lutz, God is *euergetikos* and *philanthropos*. Cf. Plutarch *Stoic. Repug.* 1051E, where it is said that Chrysippus bases his attack against Epicurus upon our conceptions of the gods as beneficent and humane (*euergetikous kai philanthropous*).

24.  *De Ira* 7.31.4; cf. 2.27.1. There seems to be no evidence prior to Seneca that the Stoics attributed benevolence to God.

25.  See Plato, *Timaeus* 30B; Cicero, *De Natura Deorum* 2.36.

26.  Cf. *Spec.* 2.54-55; *Cher.* 85-86. For the contrast between God's perfect *chara* and the imperfect form enjoyed by man, cf. Hippodamas, ap. Stob. 4.39.26, cited by E. R. Goodenough, *By Light, Light* (New

Haven, 1935; repr. Amsterdam: Philo Press,1969), 141, n. 106; Aristotle, *Nicomachaean Ethics* X 1178b25: "The gods enjoy a life blessed in its entirety; men enjoy it to the extent that they attain something resembling the divine activity"; cf. Seneca, *Ep.* 102.27.

27. *Ep.* 59.16, 18; cf. 50.8; *Vita Beata* 44; *Const.* 9.3. And cf. Epictetus 3.5.16: "Always to wear the same expression on one's face, whether one is coming out or going in"; 1.26.31: "That is why Socrates always wore the same expression on his face"; Cicero, *Tusc.* 3.31; Seneca, *De Ira* 2.7.1. With Philo *Det.* 137, cf. Seneca *Ep.* 23.2-3. See Adolf Bonhöffer, *Epictet und die Stoa* (Stuttgart: Friedrich Fromann Verlag, 1890), 297-98. But Plato denied that the gods feel either joy or its opposite (*Philebus* 33B; *Ep.* 3.315C; but cf. *Timaeus* 37C).

28. D.L. 7.127-28, where only drunkenness and melancholy are mentioned—but Simplicius, *In Cat.*, 401, 35, 402, 25 ff., Kalbfleisch (*SVF* 33.238), naming no particular Stoic teacher, adds the other conditions. All these states, as Rist (*Stoic Philosophy*, 16-17) has pointed out, were regarded by the ancients as physical disorders. The wise man's actions under their influence might well be irrational. Epictetus refers to some of these states but seems to leave the issue open, suggesting only that one who could overcome such states could indeed be regarded as an invincible athlete (1.18.23; 2.17.33).

29. According to a report in Stobaeus 2.68.24 (SVF 3.103), not only is joy not necessarily continuous, but neither does every wise man enjoy it. It is difficult, however, to make sense of this report.

30. Cf. Aristotle's Unmoved Mover, *Nicomachaean Ethics* VII 1154b 25; *Metaphysics* VII 1072b 16. For Aristotle's notion that pleasure is an *epigennnema*, see *EN* 1174b 32.

31. At *Praem.* 35, however, Philo assigns to Isaac, the sage who has gained virtue through Nature, a life that has no share in anxiety or depression, and is free from distress and fear (*alypon te kai aphobon*): "The hardships and squalor of life never touch him even in his dreams, because every spot in his soul is already tenanted by joy."

32. See Long and Sedley, *Hellenistic Philosophers* 1.319.

33. Epictetus, 4.7.20. Epictetus also refers to God's perception (*aisthanetai*) of the motions of human souls, inasmuch as they are portions of his own being (1.14.6,9). In the same vein, Marcus Aurelius declares that all things happen neutrally "by some primal impulse of Providence (*horme tini archaia pronoias*), in accordance with which She was impelled by some primeval impulse to this making of an ordered universe, when She had conceived certain principles for all that was to be" (9.1.4; cf. 9.28; 10.21). See also Albinus, *Did.* ch. 25: The souls of the gods contain a part called

*hormetikon* corresponding to the human *thymoeides*. Cf. John Dillon, "*Metriopatheia* and *Apatheia*: Some Reflections on a Controversy in Later Greek Ethics," in *Essays in Ancient Greek Philosophy*, ed. J. P. Anton and A. Preus (Albany: SUNY Press, 1983) 2.508-17.

34.  D.L. 7.147. In *Op*. 73, Philo similarly asserts that the stars, which he believes are thoroughly rational, are insusceptible of any evil (*pantos anepidektos kakou*). Cf. D. Winston, *Logos and Mystical Theology*, 33.

35.  Cf. Dillon, in David Winston and John Dillon, *Two Treatises of Philo of Alexandria* (Chico: Scholars Press, 1983), 225.

36.  See Sandbach, *The Stoics*, 40-41. God's essence as it is in itself is, of course, beyond blessedness and happiness. *QG* 2.54; *Legat.* 4-6; cf. n. 7.

37.  *Deus* 51-68. Cf. Origen, *Contra Celsum* 4.71: "After this because Celsus failed to understand them, he ridicules passages in the Bible which speak of God as though He were subject to human passions, in which angry utterances are spoken against the impious and threats against people who have sinned. I reply that, just as when we are talking with little children we do not aim to speak in the finest language possible to us, but say what is appropriate to the weakness of those whom we are addressing, and, further, do what seems to us to be of advantage for the conversion and correction of the children as such, so also the Logos of God seems to have arranged the scriptures, using the method of address which fitted the ability and benefit of the hearers . . ."; 72: "When we speak of God's wrath, we do not hold that it is an emotional reaction on His part, but something which He uses in order to correct by stern methods those who have committed many terrible sins," tr. Chadwick.

38.  *Deus* 70-73. For similar deductions from word-order, see *LA* 2.78; *Mig.* 140; *Conf.* 103. Cf. the rather more straightforward exegesis of *QG* 1.95, where the possibilities of juggling the *hoti* clause have not yet occurred to Philo.

39.  Cf. *Sac.* 42: "for on God's mercy (*eleo*), as a sure anchor, all things rest"; *Her.* 112; *Fug.* 95; *Mut.* 133; *Som.* 1.93, 112, 147, 2.149; *Ios.* 255; *Mos.* 1.86; *Spec.* 1.308; 4.180; *Praem.* 39, 117; *Legat.* 367.

40.  Compare *Mos.* 1.198, where Philo begins the sentence with a reference to God's *epieikeia* and *philanthropia*, but ends by applying to Him the verb *eleeo*: "God moved partly by the clemency and benevolence to man which belongs to His nature (*dia ten symphyton epieikeian kai philanthropian*), partly too by His wish to honor the ruler whom He had appointed . . . took pity on them (*eleesas*) and healed their sufferings." Cf. also *Praem.* 166, where Philo refers to "God's

clemency and kindness (*epieikeia kai chrestoteti*)"; *Spec.* 2.110; *Praem.* 166. Both Cleanthes and Chrysippus called the gods *philanthropoi* (*SVF* 2.1115). Cf. Plato *Laws* 713D (*ho theos philanthropos on*); Wisdom of Solomon 12:18: "But while disposing of might, you judge in fairness (*en epieikeia*)."

41. "Clementia," says Seneca, "means restraining the mind from vengeance when it has the power to take it, or the leniency of a superior towards an inferior in fixing punishment" *Clem.* 2.3.1. For *misericordia*, cf. Cicero *Tusc.* 3.20-21. The nearest Greek equivalents to the Roman concept of *clementia* in its various aspects are *philanthropia*, *epieikeia* and *praotes*. See F. Weidauer, *Der Prinzipat in Seneca's Schrift de Clementia* (Diss., Marburg, 1950), 106-09; M. T. Griffin, *Seneca, A Philosopher in Politics* (Oxford: at the University Press, 1976), 149.

42. D.L. 7.123. Cf. Aulus Gellius, *Noctes Atticae* 14.41, quoting Chrysippus: Justice "has the title of virgin as a symbol of her purity and an indication that she has never given way to evil-doers, that she has never yielded to words of blandishment (*tous epieikeis logous*, words involving indulgence), to prayers and entreaties, to flattery, nor to anything of that kind"; and cf. Plutarch, *Cato Minor* 4.1.

43. See M. Fuhrmann, "Die Alleinherrschaft und das Problem der Gerechtigkeit," *Gymnasium* 70 (1963): 514, n. 34; Griffin, *Seneca*, 166. Cf. Cicero *De Officiis*, 1.88; 2.18. "If Knoellinger's reconstruction of Cicero's treatise *De Virtutibus* from a fifteenth-century French work could be accepted with confidence," writes Griffin, "it would provide evidence that before Seneca, the Stoics, whose doctrines clearly infuse the material, had accepted *clementia* as a virtue distinguished from *misericordia*, and had admitted it into the administration of justice with the definition: iustitia humane et liberaliter exercitata (Fr. 8)," *Seneca*, 167. See W. S. Watt, Review of the 1949 Teubner edition of Cicero's *De Virtutibus* by W. Ax, *Journal of Roman Studies* 41 (1951): 200.

44. Cf. Seneca *Clem.* 2.6.2; *Tranq.* 468D; W. Dittenberger, *Sylloge Inscrip. Graec.* (Leipzig, 3rd ed., 1915-24), 814.21: *ou di' eleon hymas, alla di' eumeneian euergeto* (Nero's proclamation to the Greeks). Spinoza, in condemning pity as a passion, similarly insists that he is "speaking expressly of a man who lives under the guidance of reason. For he who is moved neither by reason nor pity to help others is rightly called inhuman, for he seems to be dissimilar to man" *Ethics* IV, Prop. 50. Cf. Philo *Virt.* 144; *Ios.* 82. Hasidic teaching was similar—that one should help one's fellow not out of pity but out of love. "Thus it is told of one zaddik that when a poor person had excited his pity, he

provided first for all his pressing needs, but then, when he looked inward and perceived that the wound of pity was healed, he plunged with great, restful and devoted love into the life and needs of the other, took hold of them as if they were his own life and needs and began in reality to help." See M. Buber, *Hasidism and Modern Man* (New York: Harper and Row, 1958), 120-21. Cf. Maimonides, *Guide* I 54, 126 (tr., Pines): "Sometimes, with regard to some people, he should be merciful and gracious, not out of mere compassion and pity, but in accordance with what is fitting." See Herbert Davidson, "The Middle Way in Maimonidean Ethics," *PAAJR* 54 (1987): 31-72. Nietzsche similarly wrote: "Ich will sie das lehren, was jetzt so wenige verstehen und jene Prediger des Mitleidens am wenigsten: —die Mitfreude"—"I wish to teach you, what so few now understand, and the preachers of pity least of all, namely to share in joy," *Fröhliche Wissenschaft*, 44.338, in *Sämtliche Werke*, ed. G. Colli and M. Montinari (Berlin: de Gruyter, 1973) 5.2, 248. See Walter Kaufmann, *Nietzsche* (Princeton: Princeton University Press, 4th ed., 1974), 364-71.

45. For a full discussion of Seneca's doctrine of *clementia*, see Griffin, *Seneca*, 129-71; and J. Rist, "The Stoic Concept of Detachment," in *The Stoics*, 259-72.

46. See Exodus 33:19; 34:36; Numbers 14:18; Psalms 145:19: Ben Sira 6:11; 2:7-11; 18:5-14; Tob. 11:14; Pseudo-Aristeas 192, 208; Wisdom of Solomon 11:23; 15:11. Philo's acute awareness of the centrality and ubiquity of the quality of mercy in Jewish tradition is clearly evident in *Spec.* 4.72: "And this [not to show pity to the poor man in giving judgment] comes from one who has filled practically his whole legislation with injunctions to show pity and benevolence (*eleon kai philanthropian*)." Cf. *Virt.* 141: "After this let those clever libellers continue, if they can, to accuse the nation of misanthropy and charge the laws with enjoining unsociable and unfriendly practices, when these laws so clearly extend their compassion to flocks and herds, and our people through the instructions of the law learn from their earliest years to correct any wilfulness of souls to gentle behavior"; 144: "and since milk is so abundant, the person who boils the flesh of lambs or kids or any other young animal in their mother's milk, shows himself cruelly brutal in character and gelded of compassion, that most vital of emotions and most nearly akin to the rational soul," tr. Colson.

47. Philo's philosophical position emerges momentarily in *Spec.* 1.116, where it is said that the High Priest will put himself above pity (*kreitton oiktou*) and continue free from distress, since his nature must approximate to the Divine.

48. *Vita Beata* 24.1; *Ben.* 6.29.1; cf. Marcus Aurelius, 2.13. See also Bonhöffer, *Epictet und die Stoa*, 305-06.

49. In the LXX *eleos* is normally used for *hesed* and less frequently (six times) for *rahamim*; *Theological Dictionary of the New Testament*, ed. G. Kittel (Grand Rapids: Wm. B. Eerdmans, 1964) **2**.479.

50. See Cicero, *Acad. Pr.* 2.131; Plutarch *Virt. Mor.* 443C, 444B, 451C; Albinus *Did.* 30.5-6 Louis; Gellius *NA* 1.26.11; Maximus of Tyre *Or.* 1.19b; 27.116b. Apuleius seems to be the only exponent of Middle Platonism who openly adopted *apatheia* instead of *metriopatheia*. See Lilla, *Clement of Alexandria*, 99-106.

51. We find, for example, that Philo ascribes *metameleia* and *eleos*, two subspecies of *lype*, to the wise man (*Fug.* 157; *Sac.* 121), as also *epithymia* in the form of its subspecies *orge* and *misos* (though the latter are limited to *orge dikaia* (*Fug.* 90; *Som.* 1.91; 2.7; *Mos.* 1.302; *Spec.* 4.14; cf. Aristotle *EN* 1125b, 31-35) and *misoponeria* (*Mos.* 2.9, 53; *Decal.* 177; *Spec.* 1.55; 4.170; cf. Ps-Aristotle *Virt. et Vit.* 1250b, 23-24; Plutarch *Stoic. Repug.* 1046C). As for *misoponeria*, he even ascribes it to God at *Her.* 163, where he says that God hates and abominates injustice. When Seneca wishes to speak of a proper form of anger, he uses the terms *vis* and *impetus* (*De Ira* 2.17.2; 1.9.1). See Holler, *Seneca*, 29, n. 84. Moreover, at *Abr.* 257, we are told that at the death of Sarah, Abraham chose not *apatheia*, but *metriopatheia*, moderating his grief instead of extirpating it. Strictly, by Stoic theory, Philo should have described Abraham's grief and tears, since Abraham was a sage, as a sort of "sting and slight convulsions of the soul (*morsus et contractiunculae quaedam animi*)" Cicero *Tusc.* 3.82, as he does, for example, in *QG* 4.73, Greek frag., Marcus, **2**.220, where we are told that Abraham experienced not a *pathos* but only a *propatheia* (cf. Aristotle *De Motu Anim.* 703b 5-20; *De Anima* III 99). The term *propatheia* is elsewhere found only in Origen on Psalms 4:5 and 38:4 (*Patrologia Graeca* **12**.560 and 689) and on Matthew 26:37 (*G. Chr. Schr.* **11**.206k1) and Hieronymus *Ep.* 79.9, **22**.506. It appears to have its origin in the medical literature (Plutarch, *Sanit. Praec.* 127D-129A). See Pohlenz, *Die Stoa* **2**.154. Although the Stoics did not consider *degmos* (biting, sting) to be a *pathos*, neither did they consider it a *eupatheia*, but placed it rather in the category of an automatic bodily reaction such as pallor, shuddering, or contraction of the brow; Epictetus, fr. 9 (180); Seneca *De Ira* 2.2.3; *Ad Polyb.* 17.2; *Ep.* 57.3; 71.299; 99.15. The Stoics were frequently attacked on this account for fudging and resorting to linguistic quibbles in order to escape from reality (Plutarch *Virt. Mor.* 449A). But Philo classified *degmos* as a

*eupatheia* (*QG* 2.57). He was either following some minor Stoic sensitized by the criticism, or he simply did this on his own: He could therefore describe Abraham's grief as *eupatheia*, but the technicalities of such an explanation may have deterred him. He preferred to use the Peripatetic ideal instead. See Plutarch *Ad Apoll.* 102D; Cicero *Tusc.* 3.12; cf. Plato *Republic* 603E; D.L. 10.119; Plutarch *Non Posse Suav.* 1101A. Seneca himself, who generally follows a strict Stoic line in this matter, does on occasion yield to the Peripatetic *metriopatheia*: "For Nature requires from us some sorrow, while more than this is the result of vanity. But never will I demand of you that you should not grieve (*maereas*) at all. I well know that some men are to be found whose wisdom is harsh rather than brave, who deny that the wise man will ever grieve (*doliturum*). But these, it seems to me, can never have fallen upon this sort of misfortune. If they had, Fortune would have knocked their proud philosophy out of them. . . . Reason has accomplished enough if only she removes from grief (*ex dolore*) whatever is excessive and superfluous; it is not for anyone to hope or to desire that she should suffer us to feel no sorrow at all. Rather let her maintain a mean which will copy neither indifference nor madness, and will keep us in the state that is the mark of an affectionate, and not an abandoned, mind. Let your tears flow, but let them also cease, let deepest sighs be drawn from your breast, but let them also find an end," *Ad Polyb.* 18.5.6, tr. Basore; cf. *Ad Helv.* 16.1; *Ad Marc.* 7.1. In *NQ* 2.59.3, Seneca says that we can be unconquered but not unshaken, "and yet the hope occasionally arises that we can also be unshaken (*inconcussos*)." See Eduard Zeller, *Die Philosophie der Griechen* (repr. Hildesheim: Georg Olms, 1963) 2.1.1047, n. 7.

# Solomon Ibn Gabirol's Doctrine of Intelligible Matter

## John M. Dillon

## I

The concept of matter has a long and fascinating history in Greek philosophy,[1] but only one aspect of that history is of relevance to my theme. That theme is the search for sources of the striking dominant motif in the eleventh-century philosopher Solomon Ibn Gabirol's *Fons Vitae*: the remarkable theory of the primacy among created things of Universal Matter and Universal Form.[2]

The term 'matter' (*hyle*), of course, we owe to Aristotle, but the concept is found in Plato, under the name of the 'receptacle' (*hypodoche*) of the *Timaeus*. Aristotle himself does not hesitate to refer to this as 'matter' (*Physics* IV 2, 209b 33 ff.). Many scholars today feel that Aristotle was quite mistaken in this identification. Harold Cherniss is particularly clear about this,[3] especially since Aristotle further identifies the Receptacle of the *Timaeus*, as a material principle, with the Indefinite Dyad, or 'the great and small' of Plato's unwritten philosophy (*Physics* 187a 16-20; 192a 11-14).

Clearly Aristotle and Plato need not mean the same thing by matter. But, although I accept the possibility that Aristotle's reading of Plato here is profoundly polemical, I find it inconceivable that he would misinterpret Plato as radically as Cherniss would claim. But whether or not Aristotle is misinterpreting Plato, he has put his finger

43

on an important aspect of the Platonist concept of matter, an aspect which comes into prominence especially in the Neopythagorean tradition stemming from Plato's successors Speusippus and Xenocrates, and which is crucial for the Neoplatonists[4], and ultimately for Ibn Gabirol, namely the doctrine that a 'material' principle operates at the highest as well as the lowest level of the universe, as the immediate correlate of the unitary first principle as well as the ultimate substratum of the system of Forms in the physical realm.

What we need to clarify for ourselves at the outset, since this will in turn make sense of the various equivalences that we will see being drawn, is what role this entity 'matter' is intended to play in Neoplatonic ontology. As we can see from the later chapters (6-16) of Plotinus' tractate On the Two Kinds of Matter (*Enneads* II 4), later Platonism accepted Aristotle's analysis of matter in the material world as the substratum that necessarily underlies opposite qualities and survives their change. Primary matter is that which underlies all sets of opposites, or all form. What later Platonists were prepared to do (against Aristotle's objections) was to place in this role of substratum that entity inherited from Pythagoreanism, the Indefinite Dyad.[5] These later Platonists may have been encouraged to this view by a tendentious interpretation of an interesting usage of Aristotle's. In four passages of the *Metaphysics* (Z 10, 1036a 9-12; Z 11, 1037a 4-5; H 6, 1045a 33-37, and I 8, 1058a 23-24), he talks of *hylé noété*, 'intelligible matter.' What Aristotle seems to intend by this expression, as becomes clearest from the third and fourth passages, is the part of a definition which sets a particular species in a wider genus, e.g., 'plane figure' in the sentence, 'a circle is a plane figure.' This is certainly not what Plotinus, for one, wants to mean by 'intelligible matter,' but the idea that there is a common substratum to particular Forms is one that I think a Platonist could pick up and run with.[6]

Nor should a third source of stimulation be overlooked, that of Speusippus—insofar as he can be distinguished from the Neopythagorean tradition he did so much to inaugurate. Speusippus does seem to me to contribute to the concept, worked with later by Moderatus of Gades, that the same entity manifests itself on successive levels of reality.[7] For Speusippus, Multiplicity (*plethos*) already appears at the level of the One "as a completely fluid and pliable matter." It continues to manifest itself at each successive level of reality: arithmetical, geometrical, psychical, physical—until it appears as matter proper.

## II

What we find, then, in the doctrine of Plotinus is the concept of a 'material' element present from the outset in the intelligible world. I want now to look more closely at the arguments Plotinus employs in *Enneads* II 4.2-5 to establish the necessity of such a material element in the realm of forms. These arguments prove to bear an interesting resemblance to those used by Ibn Gabirol. Plotinus begins in chapter 2 by presenting objections to the existence of intelligible matter:[8]

1. If something such as matter must be undefined and shapeless, and there is nothing indefinite (*aoristos*) or shapeless among the beings There, which are the best, there would not be matter There.

2. If every intelligible being is simple (*haploun*), there would be no need of matter, so that the composite being (*syntheton*) might come of it and from something else.

3. There is need of matter for beings that come into existence and are made into one thing after another—this was what led people to conceive the matter of sense-objects—but not for beings that do not come into existence.

4. Where did matter come from, and whence did it take its being? If it came to be, it was by some agency; but if it was eternal, there would be several principles, and there would be an element of chance in the activity of the primary beings.[9]

5. If form comes to matter, the composite being will be a body, and so there will be body There also.

This is a pretty comprehensive schedule of objections, originating from the argumentation of both Peripatetics and earlier Platonists. As we shall see, Ibn Gabirol reproduces them and deals with them in much the same terms as does Plotinus.

In chapters 3-5, Plotinus responds. First, he points out, not everything indefinite and shapeless is to be despised. If it is prepared to submit to ordering by form, as Soul,[10] for instance, is prepared to submit to ordering by Intellect and logos (3.1-6), it is a positive entity. Secondly, it is not true that every intelligible being is simple, although compositeness in the intelligible realm is of a different sort than that of bodies. *Logoi* are composite and through their compositeness make composite the natural objects which they bring to actuality (3.6-9). More to the point, surely, although Plotinus does not say it here, is that forms themselves are composite, in the sense expounded e.g. in the later tractate VI 7 (especially chapters 10-15), that each of them in a way contains all the others. This is not a point made by Ibn Gabirol, so we need not dwell on it.

Plotinus' reply to the third argument is simply to point out that just because the intelligible realm is comprised of eternal objects, and so has no coming to be and passing away into and out of an underlying matter, that does not mean that there is no role for matter there. It means only that "in the intelligible world matter is all things at once; so it has nothing to change into, for it has all things already. Therefore, matter is certainly not ever shapeless There, for even matter here is not, but each of these matters has shape in a different way" (3.13-17). This argument does not, of course, prove that intelligible matter exists. But it does counter the opposing argument that it need not exist because it is only required as a substratum for changing qualities.

The fourth question, about the origin of this matter, Plotinus postpones to chapter 5; but we may deal with it now. He postpones it because it needs some leading up to, as it involves the obscure question of the derivation of Intellect from the One. Matter, as we learn in chapter 5, is the basis of primal Otherness and Motion, two of the five 'categories' of the noetic world, which come forth from the One to form Intellect: "The Motion and Otherness which came from the first are undefined (*aoriston*) and need the First to define them; and they are defined when they turn to it" (5.32-4). Matter is here identified with the initial, undefined stage of the (timeless) production of Intellect, and its connection with the Indefinite Dyad is made unusually clear. But this is only one aspect of Matter in the noetic realm, and not even the main one. Ibn Gabirol refers to it only incidentally in the *Fons Vitae*, since he is not primarily concerned there with the derivation of all things from God,[11] but rather with the structure of intelligible reality.

When Plotinus turns to counter the final objection, that the introduction of Matter into the noetic world seems to involve the introduction of body into that world, he deals with it, in chapter 4, not directly, but rather by describing the necessary role Matter does play:

> If, then, Forms are many, there must be something in them common to them all; and also something individual, by which one differs from another. Now this something individual, this separating difference, is the shape (*morphe*) that belongs to each. But if there is shape, there is that which is shaped, of which the difference is predicated. Therefore, there is matter, which receives the shape and is the substrate (*hypokeimenon*) in every case.
>
> Further, if there is an intelligible world (*kosmos noetos*)[12] There, and this world is an imitation of that, and this is composite, then there must be matter There too. Or else how can you call it a 'world' except with regard to its form? And how can you have form without something on which the form is imposed? (4.2-11)

For Ibn Gabirol these last two arguments are the most important, as we shall see: first, that the multiplicity of the forms necessitates a common substrate, and second, that, since this world is an image of the intelligible, and this one is a composite of form and matter, then so must that be. There is nothing in the sensible realm that is not already present in the intelligible.

The mid-portion of Plotinus' treatise (chapters 6-12) is devoted to an analysis of the concept of matter in the physical realm, based largely on Aristotle's *Physics* and *Metaphysics*, and so is not relevant to our present purpose. But in the last part of the treatise (chapters 13-16), in analyzing what Matter in general is not (Quality, Unlimitedness, Otherness), Plotinus says a number of pertinent things. In chapter 15 he is inquiring as to the possible relationship of Matter to 'the unlimited' (*to apeiron*) and 'the indefinite' (*to aoriston*) and once again makes clear the essential identity between Matter at the intelligible level and the concept of the Indefinite Dyad and the Unlimited of the *Philebus*, as a substratum for the multiplicity of forms and also as a reason for generation in general. The forms as a whole, says Plotinus (15.3 ff.), constitute Limit (*peras*). Matter, which they set in order, is *to apeiron*. He goes on (15.18 ff.) to refer to Matter's relation to the One:

> For in the intelligible world, too, Matter is the Unlimited, and it would be produced from the unlimitedness (*apeiria*) or the potency or the everlastingness of the One; not that unlimitedness is in the One, but the One produces it.

This linkage with the pair of *peras* and *apeiron* seems to me important. Plotinus never hypostatises these entities; but his successors do, from Iamblichus on, and it seems possible to me, as I shall explain, that something of Proclus' treatment of *peras* and *apeiron* filtered down, through the Arabic tradition, to Ibn Gabirol.

I turn now to Ibn Gabirol's chief arguments for the existence of intelligible matter, and will then discuss the troublesome question of sources and possible lines of influence.

## III

The main purpose of the *Fons Vitae*, as is generally agreed,[13] is to investigate the nature of reality, and specifically to prove that the universe at all levels, intelligible as well as physical, is made up of Matter and Form. God Himself, Ibn Gabirol declares at the outset (*Fons Vitae* I 5), is unknowable in His essence, and known only through His works. It is the totality of these works that Ibn Gabirol will confine himself to examining. For our purposes here, it is Book IV of the work that is of primary importance. It follows a long discussion, comprising Book III, intended to prove the existence of intelligible substances, as a necessary middle term between the First Principle and bodily substance. Ibn Gabirol then turns to the proof that intelligible substances, like bodily ones, are necessarily composed of form and matter. This leads us back to what was said in Book II about bodily substance. In chapters 1 to 3 of that book, Ibn Gabirol asserted that, even as body is 'matter' for the forms it contains—the shapes, colors and other accidental qualities present in it—so there is a non-sensible substance which serves as 'matter' for corporeal nature, and for which corporeal nature is 'form.'[14] In chapters 6-8, we are told that the universal matter which acts as substratum for sensible entities is the substance which acts as substratum for the nine categories (i.e., the Aristotelian categories other than Substance itself), and they constitute its form. This substance is the limit which separates the sensible from the intelligible, and it is here that we must begin the study of intelligible reality. In fact, because the lower derives from the higher and is its image, one attains knowledge of the higher by studying the lower. Therefore, one can compare the substance of the categories with the absolutely universal primal matter.

The terms 'matter' and 'substance' in fact designate the same entity, we are told in chapter 11. This entity is to be viewed as matter when it is imagined as not yet having received the form proper to it, and as substance when it is seen as being already informed. In fact, of course, matter is never found without form, or form without matter, either in this realm or among the intelligibles.

In Book IV, then, we turn to the consideration of matter and form in simple (intelligible) substances. Ibn Gabirol begins by reasserting that these intelligible substances, like composite (physical) substances, are composed of matter and form. In support of this thesis he produces two of the arguments of Plotinus. First, as he already urged in Book II, If the lower emanates from the higher, all that is in the lower must be in the higher (IV 1, 211, 13-14). When the pupil asks for evidence (*signum*) of this, Ibn Gabirol answers:

> The proof of this is that spiritual substances are common in matter but diverse in form, that is, since their effects are diverse, there can be no doubt that their forms are diverse, and it is not possible that the matters of these substances be diverse, because they are all simple and spiritual, and diversity derives only from form, and simple matter does not have form in itself (212, 2-9).

This is Plotinus' fifth and central argument for the existence of intelligible matter, as set out in *Enneads* II 4.4. There must be a common substratum to account for the unity of the intelligible realm, where the individual forms provide the diversity.[15]

Ibn Gabirol's second argument corresponds exactly to that presented by Plotinus at the beginning of *Enneads* II 4.4: If simple substances were solely matter, there would be no basis for their difference from each other; but if they were composed of form alone, they would lack any substratum (IV 1, 212, 18 - 213, 13). This argument provokes the Pupil to ask how spiritual substance can be composite while being also spiritual (IV 2, 213, 21-22), an objection, as we recall, also raised in *Enneads* II 4.2. But Ibn Gabirol's solution is rather different from what we find there. He points out that there are various levels of spiritual substance. This at least is a sign of complexity. The distinctions among the levels of soul, for example, and those between soul and intellect, show that these substances possess a diversity of forms. Yet it remains to be explained how there can be a diversity of levels of form, if one wishes to maintain, as Ibn Gabirol does, the basic unity of form:

> What you must imagine about spiritual forms is this, that they are all one form, and that there is no diversity among them of themselves, because they are purely spiritual, and diversity is not a property of theirs except on account of the matter which supports them. The more it is near to perfection, the more subtle it will be, and the form which is supported by it will be at the extreme of simplicity and spirituality, and vice versa. Take as a comparison the light of this sun of ours: Its light in itself is one, and if it comes up against subtle and clear air, it will penetrate it and will appear in a different guise to what it will appear in air that is thick and not clear. The same must be said of form.

So the root of diversity is put back onto matter! Form is just the agency provoking this diversity. Evidently in Ibn Gabirol's mind differing degrees of 'opacity' do not conflict with the underlying formlessness of matter.

With all its problems, Ibn Gabirol's account of the different degrees of being in the universe does not correspond to anything in Plotinus. It is curiously reminiscent, however, of the theory of the manifestation of matter at different levels of reality, which appears in chapter 4 of Iamblichus' *De Communi Mathematica Scientia* (attributable almost certainly, I feel, to Speusippus[16]).

But the answer Ibn Gabirol offers here deals only with the diversity among the levels of spiritual substance. Under further prodding from his pupil, Ibn Gabirol goes on to claim that there is complexity *within* a given spiritual substance, namely, the soul (IV 3, 216, 12 ff.). His argument is that the soul, although an immaterial entity, has capacities for changing its nature for better or for worse, and that from its own resources. This argument is reminiscent of Plotinus' second, about the complexity of *logoi*, although not identical with it. The *logoi*, like the soul, contain the possibility of many different manifestations.

## IV

On the whole, our comparison of Ibn Gabirol with Plotinus supports a conclusion one would be forced to reach on other grounds as well: that while there are interesting parallels, there is no evidence of a direct connection between the two thinkers. What we seem to have, rather, is two incisive and highly original minds working within the same tradition and reaching similar conclusions about the structure of the universe. This, I think, is a more interesting result than any proof of direct dependence. Mere dependence would diminish the stature of Ibn Gabirol as a creative thinker; but it would also pose a serious problem in the history of the transmission of texts. For so far as we know there was no Arabic translation of the first three *Enneads* of Plotinus, although the last three were extensively drawn upon for the *Theology of Aristotle*, the *Letter on Divine Science*, and the *Sentences of the Greek Sage*, all texts which seem to have been available to Ibn Gabirol.

But if Ibn Gabirol did not derive his doctrine of intelligible matter directly from Plotinus, what plausible sources or backgrounds to his reasoning present themselves? His was certainly not an obvious doctrine for a thinker of his era to propound, even if it was authentically rooted in the Neoplatonist tradition. Yet there certainly were allied doctrines available from the accessible materials of the Greek tradition that could stimulate a creative thinker to develop such a theory.

As a preliminary to asking what these may have been, let us briefly set Ibn Gabirol's doctrine of intelligible matter in context conceptually. The *Fons Vitae* posits a completely unitary and ineffable First Principle, knowable only by his activities and products. The first of these is his Will, of which we hear much in Books I and V. The Will may be compared to the Stoic (and Philonic) Logos, in that it permeates and informs the universe. But it is even more closely analogous to the Will of the Father in the Chaldaean Oracles,[17] a source not available as such in Arabic, but which influenced many documents that were. This hypostatic Will, issuing forth from the One, strikes upon a primal Otherness and Indefiniteness, which is matter. Matter, declares Ibn Gabirol (*FV* V 32), must be conceived to be in a sort of movement consequent on its desire for the One—specifically, for being informed by the One. The response to this movement is the emanation of God's will, which imposes itself on matter as form. Thus form is really only an actualization of will in matter.

All this activity, of course, is differentiable only through analysis. It is not a temporal sequence. In fact, as Ibn Gabirol assures us (e.g. IV 4, 219, 3), there was never a time, not the twinkling of an eye, when form was not united to matter. But for the sake of theory we are driven to postulate a succession of stages, beginning (a) with matter somehow present "in the knowledge of the Eternal One" (V 10, 274, 20-22), in a state of potential being, but then (b) having a shadowy existence outside the First Principle, moving in anticipation of receiving form from God's will, and finally (c) united to form to constitute substance.

Ibn Gabirol is wrestling here with mysteries like those that surround the emergence of Intellect from the One in the philosophy of Plotinus. He cannot be expected to come away with any more satisfactory conclusions than Plotinus does. Nous for Plotinus emerges as a formless entity, rather like matter, "before" it becomes Intellect by reflecting back on the One (e.g., *Enneads* V 1.6, V 6.5, VI 7.16-17). Indeed, the initial, processive aspect of Nous is that same intelligible matter that Plotinus is discussing in *Enneads* II 4.5.

But if we are concerned with sources rather than mere conceptual analogies, we must look beyond Plotinus. I have suggested that Ibn Gabirol seems to be drawing on some form of the later Neoplatonic doctrine, attested in Iamblichus,[18] of a pair of principles following upon the One and structuring the universe, Limit and Unlimitedness, a scheme developed by the later Neoplatonists out of what Plato says in the *Philebus* (17C ff.). There is still a problem, of course, as to how Ibn Gabirol might have become acquainted with this doctrine. But there are a number of reasonable hypotheses.[19]

First of all, we may note the doctrine of "Empedocles" as reported in the *Book of Five Substances*, a text probably available to Ibn Gabirol,[20] and described also in Shahrastānī's *Kitāb al-Milal wa'l-Nihal* (II 2, ch. 1).[21] Empedocles is reported by Shahrastānī to have held that:

> Prime matter is simple, as is the essence of intellect, which is other than it, but not of an absolute simplicity. That is to say, it is not absolutely one, like the essence of the First Cause; for there is no effect which is not composite, whether it be of intelligible or sensible composition. Matter, in its essence, is composed of Love and Strife, and from these two principles are produced both simple, spiritual substances and composite, corporeal substances, in such a way that Love and Strife constitute two attributes or indeed two forms for substance, two principles for the totality of existent things.

The doctrine of "Empedocles" set out here certainly does not quite square with that professed by Ibn Gabirol. In particular, it makes matter a composite of Love and Strife, rather than one of the two elements making up all substance. But such a report as this could have given a creative mind like Ibn Gabirol's some inspiration and impetus towards his own doctrine. Love and Strife, after all, can be seen as simply poetic representations of the more properly philosophical pair Limit and Unlimitedness, which in turn can be assimilated to the more Aristotelian pair of form and matter.

The *Book of Five Substances* again presents some interesting "Empedoclean" doctrines.[22] The Creator creates, first, matter, in which are found in embryo all the forms of the universe. After creating matter, he creates intellect, and extends over it life, through the intermediacy of matter. Intellect, then, since it draws its life from matter, turns its attention towards the forms in matter, and draws from them the beauty of form which is in it. It then comes to possess intelligible forms, which, by combining with matter, produce soul. Here we have all the constituents of Ibn Gabirol's universe, although arranged slightly differently. Once again, however, one can see how such speculations could lead him to his own solutions.

The most striking analogy to Ibn Gabirol's doctrine of matter and form, however, and indeed its probable immediate source, is the doctrine of Isaac Israeli,[23] who was active in Egypt in the first half of the tenth century, and who is in turn indebted for his doctrine of matter and form to a source whom Stern calls 'Ibn Hasday's Neoplatonist,' since his doctrine is to be found in a philosophical excursus in chapters 32-35 of the twelfth-century writer Ibn Hasday's *The Prince and the Ascetic*.[24] The most tellingly pertinent passage occurs in Israeli's *Book of Substances*,[25] of which only fragments survive. In Frg. 4 he embarks on a proof that "the first of created things are two simple substances, out of which is established the nature of the intellect." He proves this by an 'ascent' from the lowest form of soul (vegetative), through animal and rational soul, to intellect, which he declares to be "most particularly affected by the action, without mediation, of the power and the will." It is composed of matter and form.

Israeli dwells on the comparison of the intellect to light and to levels of light corresponding to levels of being (cf. Ibn Gabirol's distinctive response to the student at *FV* IV 2, quoted above):

> Regarding the quality of the emanation of the light from the power and the will, we have already made clear that its beginning is different from its end, and the middle from both extremes, and this for the following reason: When its beginning emanated from the power and the will, it met no shade or darkness to make it dim or coarse, while its end met various imperfections and obscurities which made it dim and coarse; the middle partook of both extremes.

The reason for the variations is the varied receptivity of matter.

It is fairly clear, then, I think, that we can trace the chain of influence back to Israeli, and beyond him to the source of Ibn Hasday (which is also the source of the longer version of the *Theology of Aristotle*). But when one tries to reach back beyond these probable proximate sources the problems become greater. What Greek Neoplatonic sources may lie behind the pseudo-Empedoclean doctrine is not easy to unravel. Certainly for Proclus, Empedocles' Love and Strife are cosmic forces analogous to Limit and Unlimitedness. At *In Tim.* II 18, 6 ff., for example, he links 'Empedoclean Strife' with Otherness and Unlimitedness as belonging to the realm of Becoming, but producing along with Love a synthesis or bond (*desmos*) whose product is the physical world. Later, at II 69, 23 ff., Love is presented as the mode of being proper to the intelligible world, while Strife is proper to the physical world, although, in truth, they must both operate at both levels.[26] But Proclus' commentaries do not seem to have been available in Arabic, so other intermediaries remain to be sought. All I can do here is attest to the naturalization of Empedocles within the tradition of Neoplatonism and leave further investigation to others.

I can make one further contribution, however, to a field of inquiry in which no doubt there is much still to be discovered. The Arabic *Liber de Causis*, as we know, is a compilation from Proclus' *Elements of Theology*. Yet it happens that the doctrine of intelligible matter does not figure in the propositions from the *Elements* which are included in the Arabic work, although a number of other doctrines do that are relevant to Ibn Gabirol's system, such as the Procline doctrine of receptivity, for example.[27] But in 1973 the German Arabist Gerhart Endress published for the first time the text of twenty propositions from the *Elements*,[28] one of which is Proposition 72, which lays down the principle that everything which serves as a substratum (*hypokeimenon*) to something else proceeds from more complete and more universal causes (sc. than that which informs it). This yields the corollary that "matter, taking its origin from the One, is itself devoid of form. For matter, which is the substratum of all things, proceeded from the cause of all things." The same, Proclus adds, is the case with body in relation to soul.

Proclus' Proposition 72 is transmitted in the Arabic in a rather truncated form—yet with some material added. The whole passage is highly relevant to Ibn Gabirol's doctrine of matter, and I present it here in full:

> Every substratum which has the capacity to underlie a great number of things proceeds from a more universal and perfect cause. Every cause which is a cause of more things is more universal, stronger and nearer to the ultimate Cause than a cause which causes less and less important things. If this is as we have set out, and if the first substratum can underlie all things, and the first agent can effect all things, then the first agent must actualize and produce the first substratum, namely matter, which embraces all things. It is clearly proved, then, that the first substratum, that is, matter, underlies all things and that it is an intelligible substratum, even as the first agent actualizes it, because it is the agent of all things.

Here we have matter presented as an intelligible entity deriving from the First Principle, and, with form,[29] bringing all substance into being. This is Ibn Gabirol's doctrine in a nutshell. The passage would certainly have provided food for thought for Ibn Gabirol, if he had this text available to him. Unfortunately, we can demonstrate no such thing. But we see here that there were more Neoplatonic texts available in Arabic than we used to think, and there may well be more still to be discovered.

## V

As I said at the outset, the concept of matter in Platonism is a complex one, based on Plato's Receptacle in the *Timaeus*, but affected by Aristotle's doctrine of matter and form, the Pythagorean pair of One and Indefinite Dyad (appearing also in the Limit and Unlimitedness of the *Philebus*), and even the Stoic *ousia*, 'essence' or substance, construed as matter, the passive element in the universe. Ibn Gabirol, in eleventh-century Saragossa, is the heir to all this complexity, and out of it he weaves a theory worthy of his great intellectual ancestry as a Platonist.

What I think we find in examining Ibn Gabirol's philosophy in general and in his doctrine of intelligible matter in particular, is a thinker steeped in the Neoplatonic tradition relayed to him by a variety of Arabic sources, but also possessed of an incisive and logical mind, capable of working out solutions of his own that are harmonious with the themes of the tradition as it reached him. The method of work, indeed, is very much like that of Plotinus himself. The role Ibn Gabirol gives to matter in his universe and the arguments with which he supports his theory bear a notable resemblance to those of Plotinus; and the development of the nuances of the theory in a distinctive way follows the tenor of the Plotinian tradition as it unfolded. But there is no need, I think, to postulate a direct dependence on Plotinus, or to seek an immediate source to be copied by Ibn Gabirol, rather than to provide a hint or stimulus to his own problem solving. Better to see here a case of great minds thinking alike.

# Notes

1. See Clemens Baeumker, *Das Problem der Materie in der griechischen Philosophie* (Münster, 1890)—the same who produced the only text of the *Fons Vitae*; see also Heinz Happ, *Hyle: Studien zum aristotelischen Materie-Begriff* (Berlin, 1971).

2. Ibn Gabirol was born of Jewish parents in Malaga around 1021/2 and was educated in Saragossa, where he spent most of his life. He died in Valencia about 1058, still only in his late thirties. There is little or no external mark of a distinctively Jewish origin in his main philosophic work, *The Fountain of Life*, composed originally in Arabic, but now available only in a Latin translation. But he is also well known for his poetry, both religious and personal, which is composed in Hebrew and clearly Jewish in inspiration. Indeed, for a long time the author of the *Fons Vitae* was not identified with the poet, as Bernard McGinn's paper details. Ibn Gabirol's poetry reveals a lively and headstrong character, frequently at odds with his contemporaries, including even his patron, the Jewish statesman, Samuel ha-Nagid, vizier of the King of Granada.

3. *Aristotle's Criticism of Plato and the Academy* (Baltimore: Johns Hopkins University Press, 1944), 83-96.

4. Plotinus, in chapter 11 of his tractate On the Two Kinds of Matter (II 4 [12] 11.33-35) accepts the validity of this equating of matter with the 'great-and-small,' and puts it to work in his own theory. We shall have more to say about this presently.

5. As we can see from Porphyry's references to him in his treatise On Matter (quoted, in turn, by Simplicius, *In Phys.* 230, 34 ff. Diels), the Neopythagorean Moderatus of Gades envisaged a role for matter at all levels of the universe: Physical matter was simply a reflection of what he terms 'quantity' (*posotes*) at the noetic level, this 'quantity' being the indefinite substratum left if one mentally 'withdraws' the One from the process of production of forms or logoi. Moderatus' theory must have had a considerable influence on Plotinus, although Plotinus does not approve of *posotes* being given the role of intelligible matter; see *Enneads* II 4.9.

6. See Happ, 639-49. For Aristotle, of course, the only incorporeal beings are pure forms, not composites of form and matter; see *Metaphysics* XII 6, esp. 1071b 20: *eti toinun tautas dei tas ousias aneu hules.*

7. That is, if we accept Philip Merlan's identification of chapter 4 of Iamblichus' *De Communi Mathematica Scientia* as essentially Speusippan, as I argue we should, in "Speusippus in Iamblichus," *Phronesis* 29 (1984): 325-32.

8.  Tr. after A. H. Armstrong. See the useful discussions in Thomas Szlezk, *Platon und Aristoteles in der Nuslehre Plotins* (Basel/Stuttgart: Schwabe, 1979), 72-79, and J. M. Rist, "The Indefinite Dyad and Intelligible Matter in Plotinus," *Classical Quarterly* 12 (1962): 99-107.

9.  I.e., there would be an unexplained factor in the coming together of the two first principles; or, perhaps, matter itself would introduce an element of chance into the process.

10. This suggestion that Soul is in a way 'matter' for Intellect is interestingly reflected in a suggestion of the Pupil at *Fons Vitae* IV 1, 212, 9-10: "What will you reply if I say that the substance of Soul is matter, and the substance of Intellect is form?"

11. The notion of matter as 'otherness' does seem to come up at IV 6, 222, 24-28 , where Ibn Gabirol argues, as a further proof that intelligible substance is composed of matter and form, "the creator of all must be one, and what is created must be different (*diversum*) from him. Hence if what was created had been matter alone or form alone it would have been assimilated to the One, and there would be no mediating element (*medium*) between the two of them, (as there is) because there are two after the One." Here, matter seems really to provide the necessary element of 'otherness.' Also, Ibn Gabirol has a theory of the motion of matter, as a consequence of its desire to receive form (V 32). See further below, p. 51. And for the issue of the *medium*, Bernard McGinn's discussion in the present volume.

12. In the sense of an ordered whole.

13. I am chiefly indebted in this part of the paper to Jacques Schlanger, *La Philosophie de Salomon Ibn Gabirol*. I have also consulted Jakob Guttmann, *Die Philosophie des Salomon Ibn Gabirol* (Göttingen, 1889), and D. Kaufmann, *Studien über Salomon Ibn Gabirol* (Budapest, 1899).

14. This notion that a higher principle may serve as 'matter' for a lower one is taken further in IV 8 (229, 22-24): "So on this account we must conclude that what is more corporeal is form for the more simple (substance), until our analysis attains absolutely simple matter." The doctrine that reality becomes increasingly complex as one descends the scale of being would be accepted by Plotinus, e.g. II 9.6.28 ff., VI 7.8.17 ff.: *to gar plethos en elleipsei* (l. 22), and is formalized by Proclus, *Elements of Theology*, Props. 61-62.

15. This, incidentally, creates a difficulty for Ibn Gabirol's postulation of universal form as a single entity, which he gets around (as Plotinus does) by taking Intellect to be the universal form that holds together all the particular ones: IV 12, 238, 16-22.

16. Cf. n. 7 above.

17. E.g., Fr. 37, 1-3, Des Places: *Nous patros erroizêse noêsas akmadi boule/pammorphous ideas, peges de mias apo pasai/exethoron. patrothen gar een boule te telos te.* Here the basic entity is the *Intellect* of the Father, but it issues as an act of will (*boule*). Its 'leaping forth' generates the Ideas. The surviving fragments of the Oracles do not bring this Intellect or Will into direct contact with matter. But matter, as we gather from Fr. 34, also springs forth from the Father, as it does for Ibn Gabirol (V 10).

18. Ap. Damascius, *De Primis Principiis*, ch. 51, I 103, 6 ff. Ruelle. See my discussion in *Iamblichi Chalcidensis Fragmenta* . . . (Leiden: Brill, 1972), 31-33.

19. The possibilities are set out usefully by Schlanger in ch. 4 of his monograph, 52-109.

20. Shem Tob ibn Falaquera, in the introduction to his collection of extracts in Hebrew of the *Fons Vitae*, tells us that in this work one finds opinions very close to those of Ibn Gabirol; see Schlanger, 88.

21. Schlanger, 76-79. For "Empedocles" as an authority in Arabic philosophy, see S. M. Stern, in *Encyclopedia of Islam*, s.v. "Anbaduklis," I 483-84.

22. D. Kaufmann published the surviving fragments in "Pseudo-Empedokles als Quelle Salomon Ibn Gabirol," in his *Studien über Salomon ibn Gabirol* (Budapest, 1899; repr. London, 1972). See 19, para. 8.

23. I am indebted here to A. Altmann and S. M. Stern's excellent *Isaac Israeli*.

24. See also S. M. Stern, "Ibn Hasdāy's Neoplatonist."

25. The work is in the *kalām* form of problems and solutions, the format adopted by Ibn Gabirol.

26. Cf. also *In Parmenidem*, 723, 22 ff., Cousin, where the same contrast is made.

27. *Liber de Causis*, para. 23 = *Elements of Theology*, Prop. 142. Ibn Gabirol could certainly have derived his conception of the varying degrees of 'opacity' of matter from this source.

28. *Proclus Arabus: zwanzig Abschnitte aus der Institutio Theologica in arabischer Übersetzung*, (Beirut: Steiner, 1973). The full collection of 20 is found only in one manuscript, but a number of other mss. contain some of them.

29. The Arabic author avoids mention of form here, talking rather of *al-fā'il*, 'the creator' or 'agent,' thus confusing form with the first principle, but both elements are inevitably involved and need to be distinguished.

# Parallel Structures in the Metaphysics of Iamblichus and Ibn Gabirol*

## C. K. Mathis II

This communication has a purpose both novel and modest. Its novelty resides in its being the first suggestion that striking parallels exist between the metaphysical system of Iamblichus (d. ca. 320) and that of Solomon Ibn Gabirol (died ca. 1058). With the exception of one casual remark by Fernand Brunner, I have found no previous mention of a parallel between these two thinkers.[1] The aim here is solely to advance the claim that such parallels exist. No attempt is made to show a line of filiation. Neither is the claim advanced that the systems of these thinkers are identical, even though the structural parallels, at the hypernoetic levels, are exact. Divergences surely exist—historical, cultural and linguistic—that are palpable and that could not be ignored in a full treatment. I do not hold that by adducing these parallels the many problems we all have with the text and thought of Ibn Gabirol disappear—problems, to take but one key example, such as those regarding his concept of matter.

The terminology of our two thinkers differs not merely because the one man wrote in Greek and the other in Arabic. Iamblichus was

* An earlier version of this paper was presented at the Patristic, Medieval and Renaissance Conference at Villanova University in October, 1987, where I benefitted from the comments of Kevin Corrigan and Father Leo Sweeney. Special thanks for the patient editing of Lenn Goodman.

doing philosophy in the context of a pagan culture, beleaguered but still vital. Ibn Gabirol wrote in the context of an ancient, monotheistic faith, enveloped in the culture of another monotheism, then in the full bloom of its spiritual outburst and imperial strength. But both thinkers were Neoplatonists, committed to a philosophy that would be responsive to its cultural and historical context but retain its inner coherency and integrity. As a standard of the challenge for such a philosophy, I refer you to Father Leo Sweeney's succinct and useful three-point test for determining the Neoplatonic status of a thinker.[2]

Iamblichus and Ibn Gabirol share a common perspective, nuanced by the differences of time and place. Both seek solutions to a perennial problem for that perspective, and their meditations intend a commonly experienced reality. Their symbolic structures show remarkable parallels. Both authors posit a quiescent first principle followed by an active second principle, which engenders a third pair productive of a hypostasis that is noetic.

The argument of this paper unfolds through three moments. First, I shall identify the Neoplatonic spiritual aporetic that animates the efforts of both Iamblichus and Ibn Gabirol. Second, I will display the principal known features of the Iamblichean system—as far as it can be reconstructed. And finally, I will offer the texts from Ibn Gabirol that demonstrate the parallels.

## I

Damascius, with unaccustomed succinctness, states the problem: *oti zeteitai pos aph' henos ta polla proelthen*: "The question is how plurality has proceeded from unity."[3] Neoplatonists characteristically approach the Divine through a monistic symbolism. The One escapes every attribute, is above all other realities, and is the source of all that has real existence. The noetic and psychic realms are real, and the somatic realm, which participates in these principles, also has a kind of reality. But each thing below the hypernoetic realm has its reality only because of the One that is in it. Here is the root of the problem. The One in Plotinus does too much—covers too much symbolic ground. Somehow it is simplicity or unity, needing nothing. But at the same time it is the cause of the unity-in-multiplicity that is Nous. Some later Neoplatonists were less sure that the reality they experienced could be symbolized adequately in this manner. They clearly were unhappy about the proximity of the ultimate simplicity of the One to the busy-ness of producing the many.

If Plotinus' conception of the nature of the One was fraught with problems for his successors over the tension between the unity and the fecundity of the One, the situation did but mimic that of the earlier followers of Plato.[4] Passages in the *Republic, Cratylus*, the *Seventh Letter* (whether by Plato or a colleague), and, of particular interest for us, the *Philebus*, leave the nature, status and function of the Good in considerable ambiguity. Speusippus surely opts for a dualistic solution. His two principles are above being and non-being and are productive through their interaction.[5] It is not until the first century B.C. that a clearly monistic approach to the problem is articulated. Eudorus of Alexandria posits the One as a supreme principle, below which he discerns a pair called the monad and the dyad, which represent form and matter respectively.[6] Others with a similar view abound, such as Pseudo-Archytas and Brotinus. Pseudo-Archytas developed a metaphysics embracing three principles: matter, form and God. Very suggestively of Ibn Gabirol, he says (in John Dillon's translation), "It is not possible for matter to partake of form of its own volition, nor for form to come together with matter, but it is necessary for there to be some other cause which will move the substance of things toward form."[7] This scheme is particularly interesting because Archytas is emphatic that his first principle is hypernoetic. He is seconded in this, according to a passage in Syrianus, by Philolaus, Archaenetus and Brotinus.[8]

In his studies of Neopythagorean influences on the Platonic tradition and on the idea of self-generation, John Whittaker tells us that for Philo, "An act of generation is incompatible with the immobility and impassability ascribed to the Supreme Deity."[9] Philo says twice in his writings that the Supreme God is neither generated nor a cause of generation. How then does the world originate? One answer was to make the second principle (variously conceived by different thinkers) a "self-generating" principle that creates itself out of the quiescent first principle. One finds this solution adapted in various ways in the *De Mundo*, Numenius, the *Codex Brucianus*, the Peratae, and the *Chaldaean Oracles*.[10]

## II

The reputation of Iamblichus as a philosopher has been rising in the past two decades.  In the 1970s B. D. Larsen[11] and John Dillon[12] became the prime exponents of this rise in stature.  The studies by John Finemore[13] and especially by Gregory Shaw[14] in the 1980s, have greatly advanced the process of rehabilitation.  The system of Iamblichus' First Principles can be reconstructed from two main sources.  John Dillon accomplished the task with reports from Damascius in his *De Primis Principiis*.  Damascius tells us, in chapter 43, that Iamblichus posits two first principles in his commentary on the *Chaldaean Oracles*.[15]  The first of these Iamblichus calls the *pantelos arrheton*, the Utterly Ineffable.  The second, we learn from chapter 50, is *ho haplos hen* or the Simple One.  Between this second principle and *to hen on*, the One-Existent (simultaneously the last moment of the realm of the One and the first moment of the noetic realm) is a dyad.  From chapter 51 we learn that this dyad is composed of principles that Damascius says may be called the Limit and the Unlimited or the One and the Many.

Iamblichus uses the Pythagorean terminology of Peras/Apeiron, where Ibn Gabirol uses the "Aristotelian" language of form and matter.  But both Damascius, reporting the views of Iamblichus, and Proclus, developing them, repeatedly make it clear that the names of this dyad are conveniences.[16]  They can be called Limit and Unlimited, One and Many, or Orphically "Aether" and "Chaos." Syrianus calls them Monad and Dyad.[17]  But Proclus identifies them with Form and Matter.[18]  Jean Trouillard has written convincingly about Proclus' hylomorphism, showing that he equates form and matter with the Iamblichean *peras* and *apeiron*.[19]  Iamblichus himself, in a report by Simplicius, seems, in a commentary on a passage of the *Philebus*, to relate form and matter to *peras* and *apeiron*, calling them auxiliaries (*sunaitia*) to the Cause (*Aition*).[20]

The passage that helps us reconstruct Iamblichus' system is *De Mysteriis* VIII 2-3, which expresses the same system in religious rather than philosophical terms.  Here we learn that prior to what is regarded as the first God and King (*to haplos hen*) is a God who is immovable and "abiding in the solitude of His own unity." This ineffable is (somehow) the paradigm of the second principle, and is like a Fons Vitae—"for He is . . . the fountain of all things, and the root of the first intelligible forms."[21] Iamblichus splits or, to express it better, doubles the One.

About *to haplos hen* we learn that He is the father of Himself, Self-begotten, the Father alone, and the truly good, also that he is a God sufficient to Himself and (significantly) that He unfolds Himself into light. He is the God of Gods. Simplicius, in his commentary on Epictetus' *Enchiridion*, says that it is this God of Gods who creates everything.[22] We learn in *De Mysteriis* that he is a monad from the One, and that he is prior to essence and is its Principle. Finally we learn that from this God of Gods are derived two things: entity and essence. That these may perhaps be equated with *peras* and *apeiron* is adumbrated in the next chapter (chapter 3). There we are told, "Everywhere an indefinite nature is under the dominion of a certain definite measure and under the supreme uniform cause of all things."[23] Damascius tells us that the production of plurality out of unity is via the intermediate stage of duality, that is, *peras* and *apeiron*, and that "only a symbolic value can be attached to the distinction between the two principles."[24]

The relation of the creative simple one to the dyad and of both of these to *to hen on* for Iamblichus is admirably summarized by Dillon: "On this scheme the *to hen on* or *aei on* at the summit of the noetic realm, will be the *mikton* (mixture) resulting from the concerted action of these two principles (the dyad), the *second one* serving as the mixing agent, while the *first one* sits in unspeakable splendor above all this."[25] This terminology of the *second one* as mixing agent, of the dyad as the ingredients, and the head of the noetic realm as the mixture (all drawn from the *Philebus*) will be most significant when we turn to the *Fons Vitae*. Gregory Shaw explains the importance of the dyadic principles for Iamblichus most effectively as "transforming the conflict of good and evil into the generative principles of the cosmos, expressed as *peras/apeiron*, the first derivations of the One and the Good." In this sense, "every expression within the Whole contains the Whole in a different manner *and measure* of the *peras/apeiron* formula."[26]

Iamblichus' doubling of the One seems to be a response to the intense experience of the (to repeat Dillon's words) "unspeakable splendor," the superabundance itself, of this Fountain of Life and every other good. Iamblichus will not profane the Source by making Him even the first moment in the process of reality. This is why *ho haplos hen "unfolds Himself"* into light to be the creative God of Gods. I take the second principle to be the initial and hence pure overflow of the superabundant Ineffable from whom the process of reality proceeds. Doubling the One expresses the Divine in both of the experienced relations as *aition* and as *telos*. The symbolism addresses what Eric Voegelin calls the problem of the Beginning and its Beyond.[27]

# III

Ibn Gabirol's system of first principles leaves everyone who studies the *Fons Vitae* with more questions than answers. There are three major factors (and many minor ones) in this situation. Most obviously there is the problem that we lack the original text. Apart from a few fragments, the Arabic original is lost. The Hebrew epitome that survives from the pen of Shem Tov Ibn Falaquera is in a different shape than the dialogue form of the Latin text.[28]

A second problem is the nature and number of Ibn Gabirol's works. The pronounced differences in the style and content of his various works makes it hard to relate ideas from one work to another. His poetry runs from the profoundly religious (and explicitly Jewish) in theme through the affecting artistry of the panegyric to the equally profoundly sensual, erotic poetry, both heterosexual and homosexual in focus. His work on psychology, *On The Improvement of Moral Qualities*, deals principally with the animal soul. It does allude to and quote scripture but shuns reference to the Rabbinic traditions of interpretation.[29] And the *Fons Vitae* itself makes no direct mention of any identifiable source or authority. The only name briefly mentioned is that of Plato. The question of lost works by Ibn Gabirol has been disposed of by Heinrich Simon, who effectively reduces these tomes to the ghostly status they deserve. The Witch of Endor was more successful in conjuration than the proponents of these ectoplasmic pages.[30]

The third problem, that of sources, has involved the greatest spilling of ink. Various possibilities have been proposed, singly and in combination. Doubtless many, if not most, of the major candidates could have served as ingredients in the mixture that coalesces as the teaching of the *Fons Vitae*. The principal candidates put forward include Isaac Israeli, Pseudo-Empedocles, *The Theology of Aristotle* (long version), "Ibn Hasday's Neoplatonist," and even Eriugena. The problem seems to stand where it did more than twenty-five years ago when Alexander Altmann surveyed the question of will in Ibn Gabirol.[31]

Recent scholarship shows that the philosophy of Iamblichus and Damascius (who is the main source for our knowledge of Iamblichus' system and an adherent of it) *may* have survived in the Islamic world in forms other than merely doxographic. Harry Wolfson showed that Ibn Ḥazm (994-1046) probably had knowledge of Damascius' idea of the senses of the souls of the spheres.[32] Everett Rowson shows a definite influence on al-Āmirī in the tenth century from the *Phaedo* commentaries of Olympiodorus and Damascius.[33] J. C. Bürgel has shown the same influence in a Persian version of the *Phaedo*.[34] And Michel Tardieu has recently made a strong case that Damascius and the seven philosophers exiled by Justinian returned from their sojourn in Persia in 532, not to Athens or Alexandria but to Harran, in what is now eastern Turkey. He believes that these seven (strongly influenced by Iamblichus) contributed the Hellenic component of the mysterious culture of the so-called Sabians of Harran.[35] At this point these facts are but faint clues (or will-o-the-wisps) that someone trained in Arabic studies can better pursue.

The principal elements of Ibn Gabirol's system include God, the *Primum Esse* (also called *Deus Excelsis et Sanctus, Essentia Prima et Sancta*, and *Factor Primus Excelsis et Sanctus*).[36] Below Him is *Voluntas*, followed by *Prima Forma*, and *Prima Materia*, and lastly *Intellectus*. For brevity's sake I will refer to these as God, Will, Form, Matter and Intellect. The system clearly parallels that of Iamblichus—but is this parallelism structural or decorative? The first principles of Iamblichus have definite functions to serve. Do the principles of the *Fons Vitae* serve the same functions? Let us reverse Ibn Gabirol's order and travel down from the top to find our parallels.

We must remember that for Iamblichus, Proclus and Damascius, Form and Matter are among the names always applicable to the dyad.

Medieval Christian thinkers understood the terminology of the Latin translation of Ibn Gabirol's work in the context of their study of Aristotle; they justified or damned "Avicebrol" by showing him to be a successful or unsuccessful student of the Philosopher. But like John Goheen, Vincent Cantarino and Joseph Blau, I find no direct importance in the use of Aristotelian terminology in the translation. General similarities of terminology, in any case, cannot be considered determinative of the meaning of concepts. One could, for instance, adduce the commonplace statement of Iamblichus' so-called "Law of Mean Terms" at *Fons Vitae* I 7 and V 15 to prove Ibn Gabirol an Iamblichean. The terminology of the work is indeed of Aristotelian coinage; but the meaning and function of the principles these terms name is consistently in the mode of later Neoplatonism, itself thoroughly impregnated by the Aristotelian concepts and terms.[37] We can be much more concrete and specific however.

At the summit of Ibn Gabirol's system stands God. *Deus*, however, is not the most common term here for the highest reality. Like the *Pantelos Arrheton* of Iamblichus this highest principle is little described and given no action to perform. At V 39 a distinction (albeit partial and ambiguous) is made between God and Will. The radical immobility of God (cf. *De Mysteriis*, VIII 2) is emphasized by the fact that even his hypostatic Will is immobile, and it "pervades all without change and prompts all without temporality."[38]  That God is indeed the Fons Vitae (like the ineffable font of everything at *De Mysteriis*, VIII 2) is seen in the passages such as this (V 19): "The Supreme and Holy God contains Will, and whatever Matter and Form is in it, uniquely and incomparably." God in Himself remains strictly unknowable; and Will is scarcely to be known: "To ascend to the primary essence on high is impossible; and the ascent to that which follows it (Will) is exceedingly difficult" (V 35).

Ibn Gabirol tells us that Will can be considered from two standpoints: in itself or as creator. In itself it is inactive, and its function need not be considered. Considered as the ultimate cause, the "active unity," Will is intermediary between the simplicity of God and the duplicity of the dyad, and it is creative. Other texts, such as V 43, affirm this intermediary status of Will. In some passages (such as IV 19) Will is spoken of as engendering only Form. But a number of texts derive both Form and Matter from Will. At II 13 it is baldly stated that, "Will is the creator of Form and Matter, and moves them" (and see IV 19).

The unescapable tension in Neoplatonic ontologies between acceptance of God as ineffable mystery and experience of Him as Creator or Father of Being has survived many attempted dissolutions. The Neoplatonists used various symbolizations as we have seen, often positing a dyad after a monad. Iamblichus, Damascius and Ibn Gabirol seem almost alone in attempting to resolve the tension with a symbolism that doubles the One Itself (or, if you judge that effort erroneous, of splitting the One). But in the work of Marius Victorinus we find a Christian Neoplatonic solution with at least some parallels. In his work against the Arians Victorinus distinguishes the Father and the Son with language not uncongenial to that of Iamblichus and Ibn Gabirol. The Father for Victorinus is pre-intelligence and pre-existence, "dwelling within itself, alone in the alone."[39] The Son, Victorinus describes as leaping forth and as the power through which act is actuated.[40] Here in a Christian idiom is the common aporetic context that exercises our two Neoplatonists and moves them toward their commonly structured symbolisms.

In the Islamic philosophical milieu within which Gabirol wrote, spiritual thinkers labored with no less concern to protect the ineffability of the ultimate reality from compromise with multiplicity and change. In the century prior to Ibn Gabirol, the Ismāʿīlī Abū Yaʿqūb al-Sijistānī argued that the ineffable God has the attribute of power but not of force.[41] God is a *source* of power, but not, *sensu strictu*, the Creative Force that makes things be. Al-Sijistānī could hardly adopt the symbolism of two Gods; but he accomplishes the Neoplatonists' intention by having his second hypostasis, Intellect, provide the attributes of God's creative command and goodness—the only things knowable about God. Al-Sijistānī's God is not a Cause, nor even (as in the *Theology of Aristotle*) a Cause of Causes. So Al-Sijistānī does distinguish between God as ineffable and God as Creator. Attributes can be applied to God only as the Creator, not to the ineffable highest reality. This is not unlike Will in Ibn Gabirol— indistinguishable from God except when looked upon as Creator.

In Ibn Gabirol the same protection is extended in the relation of God to Will and of Will to Form and Matter. In Falaquera, where the word is Unity, we read that Will is superior to Form and Matter, "because the unity of Form and Matter only exists by reason of the imposition of unity in them. And since between one and two there exists no intermediary, you must realize from this that there is no intermediary between unity and Form and Matter."[42] Furthermore this creation by imposition of unity is a process of emanation—Ibn Gabirol uses the Plotinian metaphor of the flow of water from its source. The flow is uninterrupted but the source is without loss or change.[43] Ibn Gabirol even suggests that the emanative flow from Will must be *through* the dyad (V 41). The dyad thus performs an auxiliary function that parallels the Iamblichean function of Limit and Unlimited as *synaitia*. In one passage (V 19) Ibn Gabirol graphically likens Will to the writer, Form to the act of writing, and Matter to the parchment or wax tablet, an Islamic topos that serves his purpose well.

A variety of texts describe the relation of Will to Form and Matter, and these in turn to Intellect. The relation parallels that of the One to the dyad and the noetic One-Being as cause, auxiliaries and mixture in Iamblichus (V 7; cf. IV 14; V 2, 8, 9, 10, 21, 31, 38). To take but one of the ten texts I find that cover this point, consider this exchange between the Pupil and the Master:

> P: What idea is understood regarding matter and form when they are joined?
> M: It is intellect, constituted of matter and form.
> P: By what means do we know that intellect is constituted from these?
> M: When you realize that intellect gathers together all form, then you will know that its form is universal matter. (V 7)

Form for Ibn Gabirol is the active partner of the dyad. We saw earlier, at V 19, that Form is directly identified with the Will in its aspect of unity and power. Ibn Gabirol explicitly attributes to Form the power of imposing itself on Matter. We read that Form as a secondary unity is capable of multiplicity and division: "The cause here, however, is that this same unity envelops Matter and is alienated from the source of unity" (IV 19). Repeatedly Ibn Gabirol returns to this sharing and limiting function of Primary Form on Primary Matter with the metaphor of sunlight penetrating the air (IV 14).

Matter as the substance out of which Intellect is engendered by the limiting power of Form is *Materia Intelligibilis*. The texts indicating this are listed in Clemens Baeumker's edition of the *Fons Vitae* in the *Index Rerum* (p. 485). Matter's passive reception of Form was of great interest to John Goheen in his book on Aquinas' *De Ente et Essentia*. In a discussion of the difficulty many have had from the time of Aquinas (and even Ibn Daud) with the conflicting statements that Matter exists prior to union with Form and that it exists only in its union with Form, Goheen points out that Matter is described by Ibn Gabirol as *occulta*, whereas Form is *manifesta*: Form perfects Matter, the Platonic "receptacle."[44]    Matter's receptivity is not seen by Ibn Gabirol as sterile but as the fullness of potentiality from which all things arise. In fact, Ibn Gabirol calls the independent existence of Matter "potential existence," contrasted with the concrete existence of Form—another indication that the usage here (e.g. IV 14) is Neoplatonic. Syrianus, developing the *peras/apeiron* concept of Iamblichus, analogously speaks of the *apeiron* (as an aspect of the dyad) as *apeirodynamos*, which Ann Shephard renders "infinite in power," but which John Rist, perhaps more faithfully for our purposes, understands as "of unlimited potentiality."[45]

There are a number of texts of particular interest that deal with the relation of Form and Matter. Both are eternal: "Matter never existed apart from Form for an instant as noncreated and not having existence" (V 42). The same passage and two others affirm that Form may be seen as the unity and Matter as the infinity of God.[46] The parallel here with the Iamblichean system is apparent. Proclus, building on Iamblichus, tells us in his *Elements of Theology* (Props. 87-92) about *autoperas* and *he autoapeiria*. E. R. Dodds explains that Limit itself is the expression of the unity of the One (like Will in Ibn Gabirol) while the Unlimited Itself is the expression of the One's infinity (correlate to Ibn Gabirol's God).[47] For Ibn Gabirol the entities interact (V 23) yet remain separate (V 2). Evidently, we are expected by Ibn Gabirol to understand Form and Matter as distinguishable, but not exactly discrete, entities. And we have already seen that Damascius, following Iamblichus, finds the distinction between the two elements of the Dyad only symbolic. Thus both Iamblichus and Ibn Gabirol want the components of their dyads to be a two-ness that proceeds from the One-ness of the Cause and to be the fecund mixture out of which all plurality (beginning with the unified plurality of Nous) flows. Theon of Smyrna succinctly expressed the same insight centuries earlier when he said, "The first increase, the first change from unity, is made by the doubling of unity which becomes Two, in which are seen matter and all that is perceptible, the generation of motion, multiplication and addition, composition and the relationship of one thing to another."[48]

Alexander Altmann held fast to the thesis stated in the translation and study of Israeli's work that he co-authored with S. M. Stern that Israeli distinguishes between two forms of causality within the various hypostases.[49] He contends that for Israeli Form and Matter are produced by a creative act, while the spiritual realities below Intellect flow from it by a necessary emanative process. Altmann acknowledges that this distinction is not present in Ibn Gabirol's system. I am unconvinced by his arguments for seeing this distinction in Israeli's work. It seems to me that the same problem, of accounting for Unity's production of plurality, is receiving in Israeli essentially the type of solution sought by Iamblichus and Ibn Gabirol. Form and Matter for Israeli are hypernoetic principles and therefore hyperousian also. They are a power of duality; they oscillate and interpenetrate and so produce Intellect as a unified plurality like a Plotinian One/many—a mixture from which the lower levels, if it is permissible to speak thus, bubble up into being.[50]

Ibn Gabirol says of Form and Matter, "Each of them differs from the other in itself. And I do not mean here a difference of convenience, but I mean a difference of opposition and of true contrariety." Iamblichus in a fragment (Frg. 7) preserved in Proclus' commentary on the *Timaeus*, similarly describes the opposition within composite things as ranging even up to the level of the dyad. Here again Iamblichus and Ibn Gabirol seem both to be concerned to protect their highest principles from effortful activity by allowing the effortless flow of essence to descend in an overflow to successively lower fonts from the Fountain of Life Himself. Ibn Gabirol is emphatic (V 21) about the interaction of Matter and Form: "Primary transcendent Form must absolutely operate in everything; but the evidence of this operation differs according to the distance from the source." He describes Form and Matter as the ingredients, whose amalgamation produces the mixture that is the first Intellect: "Out of the amalgamation of Matter and Form another substance or nature comes into being compounded from them, which was not previously in either of them as itself . . . but of their blending and combining a concept arises which was not previously in either of them alone" (V 9; cf. V 8). Ibn Gabirol also treats Form and Matter as the One and the Many; a name for the dyad which we saw from Damascius and Proclus as an alternative to the language of *peras* and *apeiron*. In a key passage (IV 12) too long to be quoted here, but of particular interest, Ibn Gabirol names the Form of the dyad "the One" and its matter as "the Two" (IV 12). This is reminiscent of Syrianus, who in his commentary on the *Metaphysics* calls Limit the monad and Unlimited the dyad.

The hypostatic of Intellect in the *Fons Vitae* parallels the Iamblichean *to hen on*. We have seen that Intellect for Ibn Gabirol (e.g. V 7) is the product of the mixing of Form and Matter. Goheen's analysis shows the "universal intelligence," as the first emanation from God by the union of Universal Form with Universal Matter. Of this intellect, Goheen observes, "it is correct to speak of it as the World Intelligence, moreover, because within it are contained the form of all things. It knows all. Not only are all forms conceived in this intelligence, but they are conceived 'non-loco' and 'non-tempore' in their positive fullness."[51] Thus, Ibn Gabirol's *Intellectus*, like Iamblichus' *to hen on*, is engendered in the very interaction of the dyad, contains all of the forms, and is the existence in which the lower compounds, both spiritual and corporeal, participate.

The texts adduced here do not exhaust the parallels, but I trust they suffice to authenticate the central contention of this paper: The Neoplatonists Iamblichus and Ibn Gabirol, living seven centuries apart and in quite different cultural milieus, developed strikingly parallel answers to a common problem. Both sought to understand how the ineffable highest reality could be what they conceived Him as being—perfect, yet productive; abiding in the aloneness of His unity, yet the Fons Vitae. They differ in an immense number of details, yet their answers are structurally identical because they intend an identical reality. Thus, they proffer us equivalent symbols.

**Notes**

1.  *De Jamblique a Proclus*, 31-32. But see now John Dillon's paper in this volume.
2.  Leo Sweeney, "Are Plotinus and Albertus Magnus Neoplatonists?" In Lloyd Gerson, ed., *Graceful Reason, Studies in Honor of Joseph Owens* (Toronto: Pontifical Institute of Medieval Studies, 1983).
3.  Damascius, *Lectures on The Philebus*, L. G. Westerink, ed., (Amsterdam: North Holland, 1959), 47.
4.  What follows is indebted to R. T. Wallis, "The Importance of not Knowing," in A. H. Armstrong, ed., *Classical Mediterranean Spirituality*, 464-77.
5.  Philip Merlan, *From Platonism to Neoplatonism*, 115-16.
6.  John Dillon, *The Middle Platonists*, 126. See also Theon of Smyrna, *Mathematics Useful For Understanding Plato*, tr. after J. Dupuis by R. and D. Lawlor (San Diego: Wizard's Bookshelf, 1979), 13.
7.  *The Middle Platonists*, 3.
8.  For the Syrianus and parallel (and likely affiliated) developments in Philo and Plutarch, see Dillon's *Middle Platonists* and David Winston's *Logos and Mystical Theology In Philo of Alexandria*.
9.  *Studies In Platonism and Patristic Thought*, 180.
10. Whittaker, 182-83.
11. *Jamblique De Chalcis:     Exegete et Philosophe* (Aarhus: Universitetsforlaget, 1972).
12. In his edition of *Iamblichi Chalcidensis, In Platonis Dialogos Commentariorum Fragmenta* (Leiden: Brill, 1973).
13. *Iamblichus and the Theory of the Vehicle of the Soul* (Chico: Scholars Press, 1985).
14. See his 1987 dissertation at U.C. Santa Barbara, *Theurgy, the Language of the Embodied Soul*; also "Theurgy: Rituals of Unification in the Neoplatonism of Iamblichus," *Traditio* 41 (1985); and his paper at the American Academy of Religion Conference, Anaheim, 1985, "Philosophus Hieraticus."
15. Dillon, *Fragmenta*, 29. Dillon's reconstruction is given strong support by Iamblichean fragments recovered from two works of Psellus by Dominic O'Meara in his *Pythagoras Revived, Mathematics and Philosophy in Late Antiquity* (Oxford, 1989), 81-85, 226-27.
16. Damascius, 47; Proclus, *Commentaries on the Timaeus of Plato*, I, tr., Thomas Taylor (London, 1820), 140-44.
17. *The Middle Platonists*, 32.

18. Proclus, *On the Timaeus*, 221; cf. Proclus *On The Platonic Theology*, Book 3, 169; and *Ten Doubts Concerning Providence and a Solution of those Doubts and on the Subsistence of Evil*, tr. Thomas Taylor (Chicago, 1980), 129.

19. *Le Un et L'Âme selon Proclus* (Paris: Belles Lettres, 1972), 69-89.

20. Simplicius, *In Categorias*, ed. C. K. Kalbfleisch (Berlin: C.A.G. 8, 1907), 327.

21. Iamblichus, *On the Mysteries*, tr., Alexander Wilder (London: Chthonios, 1989), 301.

22. See Richard Sorabji, *Time, Creation and the Continuum* (Ithaca: Cornell University Press, 1983), 306.

23. Translated by Gregory Shaw, in *Philosophus Hieraticus*, Quotation 1b.

24. Dillon, *Fragmenta*, 46, 48.

25. *Fragmenta*, 32.

26. Shaw, "Theurgy," 28, 21.

27. See Eric Voegelin, "Equivalences of Experiences and Symbolization," in *Eternita e Storia* (Florence, 1970), 10-11.

28. Collette Sirat, *A History of Jewish Philosophy in the Middle Ages*, 69.

29. See Ibn Gabirol, *The Improvement of the Moral Qualities*, tr., Wise.

30. H. Simon, "Lost Treatises of Ibn Gabirol?" *Proceedings of the Second International Conference on Studies on Cultures of the Western Mediterranean* (Algiers, 1978), 264-68.

31. See his "Problems of Research in Jewish Neoplatonism," *Tarbiz* (1961); but now see John Dillon's careful paper in this collection for suggestive possibilities.

32. *Studies in the History of Philosophy and Religion*, 1.45.

33. *A Muslim Philosopher on the Soul and its Fate: al-Āmirī's K. al-Amad 'alā 'l-abad.*

34. J. C. Bürgel, "A New Arabic Quotation from Plato's *Phaedo* and its Relation to a Persian Version of the *Phaedo*," *Actas do IV Congresso de Estudios Arabis e Islamicos, Lisbon, 1968* (Lisbon, 1971).

35. Michel Tardieu, "Sabiens Coraniques et 'Sabiens' de Harran," *Journal Asisatique* (1986).

36. Vincent Cantarino, "Ibn Gabirol's Metaphysics of Light," *Studia Islamica* 26 (1967): 56, n. 1.

37. See John Goheen, *The Problem of Matter and Form in the De Ente et Essentia of Thomas Aquinas*, esp. 17-19; Joseph Blau, "On the Supposedly Aristotelian Character of Ibn Gabirol's *Keter Malkhut*," in *Salo Baron Jubilee Volume* (Jerusalem, 1974) esp. 1.224-25.

38.  Unless otherwise noted, all quotations are of Ibn Gabirol, *The Fountain of Life*, tr., Alfred G. Jacob (Philadelphia, 1954), with my corrections of terminological awkwardnesses.

39.  Marius Victorinus, *Theological Treatises on the Trinity*, tr., Mary T. Clark (Washington: Catholic University of America Press, 1981), 172. Lenn Goodman has pointed out to me the echoes here of Plotinus and the *Psalms*, such as 27:10 and 113:5.

40.  *Theological Treatises*, 175.

41.  Paul Walker, "An Ismaili Answer to the Problem of Worshipping the Unknowable Neoplatonic God," *American Journal of Islamic Studies* 2 (1979): 15-16.

42.  II 13; cf. V 31. Iamblichus uses the same kind of analogy in his *Theology of Arithmetic*, tr., Robin Waterfield (Grand Rapids: Phanes, 1988), 36, 38, 40 = Falco's edition 2, 4, 5, 7.

43.  V 31. Clearly, the aim of Ibn Gabirol here parallels that of Iamblichus, to exclude from the highest reality any need or effort to act or be anything other than the superabundant source of reality and life that He is.

44.  Goheen, 17-19, esp. n. 39.

45.  A. Sheppard, "Monad and Dyad as Cosmic Principles in Syrianus," in H. J. Blumenthal and A. C. Lloyd, eds., *Soul and the Structure of Being in Late Neoplatonism* (Liverpool: Liverpool University Press, 1982), 3; Rist's comments, op. cit., 15.

46.  See IV 10, IV 11. A perception that seems not unlike Syrianus calling the Unlimited, *apeirodynamos*.

47.  Proclus, *Elements of Theology*, 247-48. Cf. Iamblichus ap. Simplicius on the *Categories* 135.10 ff.

48.  Theon of Smyrna, 66.

49.  A. Altmann, "Creation And Emanation In Isaac Israeli:   A Reappraisal."

50.  My metaphor is drawn from Damascius, *Dubitationes et Solutiones*, ed. C. E. Rolle (Paris, 1889) 1.195.7-8; where he says that the life (*zoe*) of each essence is its boiling (*zeon*).

51.  Goheen, 32; cf. 28-30.

# Ibn Gabirol: The Sage Among the Schoolmen

To the memory of Alexander Altmann (1906-1987),
superb scholar and inspiring teacher

Bernard McGinn

Philosophy was the first form of ecumenism in Western history. Communities that for centuries had nothing good to say about each other from the religious point of view, and that easily found excuses for persecution when the possession of power allowed them to put their prejudices into practice, still found it important to study the philosophical writings of their religious opponents, and, even when disagreeing, to treat them with a grudging respect. This paper investigates one historical example of the interaction between philosophers and philosophical theologians of different faiths.

From the time of Philo the ancient tradition of Greek philosophy has played a significant role in the intellectual exposition of monotheistic faith in the West, first in Judaism, later in Christianity, and eventually also in Islam. Although no one has ever been defined as a Jew or Christian or Muslim simply because of adherence to some particular philosophical understanding of what the community's beliefs entail, Jewish, Christian and Muslim thinkers have often felt constrained to provide philosophical explanations and defenses of their creeds both to coreligionists and to adversaries. What were these defenses intended to do? How do they relate to the classical philosophical tradition which Jews, Christians and Muslims used in the exposition of their beliefs? What do they tell us about the relations among religions in pre-modern Europe? A consideration of Solomon Ibn Gabirol provides an interesting test case.

Ibn Gabirol, like all medieval philosophers, received the classical philosophical tradition via an ecumenical route. The early Muslim philosophers obtained much of their knowledge of Greek thought through translations made by Syrian Christians. Medieval Jewish philosophers in turn absorbed this complex and developing tradition through the writings of the Muslim *falāsifa*. And beginning in the early twelfth century the philosophically undernourished West went on a veritable translation binge to sate its speculative hunger. The appetite for new learning and insight was as often satisfied from Jewish and Arabic sources as from Greek texts.[1]

The influence of Ibn Gabirol's own works, especially his central philosophical text, the *Mekor Hayyim*, is illustrative of the ecumenical nature of medieval philosophy.[2] Originally written in Arabic, it was translated in Latin as the work of "Avicebron" or "Avencebrol" under the title *Liber Fontis Vitae*, probably in the second half of the twelfth century by Dominicus Gundissalinus and Johannes Hispanus.[3] Ibn Gabirol's philosophical economy called for no mention of the Hebrew Scriptures or other overt indications of the philosopher's Jewish sources, so his many Christian readers thought that Avicebron was either a Muslim philosopher or a Christian Arab. The partial Hebrew translation of the work by Shem Tob ibn Falaquera in the thirteenth century seems not to have been widely read, although it would be incorrect to say that Ibn Gabirol's metaphysical thought was without influence in the history of Jewish philosophy and mysticism. It was not until 1845, when Solomon Munk correctly identified Avicebron as identical with the well-known Hebrew poet Ibn Gabirol, that this major philosophical mind began to receive his due.

My intention is to examine Ibn Gabirol's Neoplatonism and its reception by the Christian Schoolmen. These remarks must be partial ones. While Ibn Gabirol is traditionally said to be the greatest of the Jewish Neoplatonists,[4] his investigators frequently note that his thought is complex and perhaps not always fully coherent. Some aspects of his influence on medieval Scholasticism have been studied, but we have no complete treatment. Avicebron is mentioned by many of the Schoolmen, but his work appears to have been closely studied by few. It may be an ecumenical anomaly, or a deeper truth worth pondering in our age of frantic search for easy agreement, that those Christian *magistri* who took Ibn Gabirol most seriously and pondered his arguments most closely were usually not his friends but his critics.

## I. The Character of Ibn Gabirol's Neoplatonism.

One difficulty in commenting on Ibn Gabirol's Neoplatonism is that the *Fons Vitae* does not give us a full account of his system. Early in this austerely argued philosophical dialogue, the Master tells the Disciple, "There are three parts of science as a whole:  the science of matter and form, the science of the Will, and the science of the First Essence."[5] The five treatises or books of the *Fons Vitae* deal in detail only with the first part of science, although there is some discussion of the *Essentia Prima* or *Factor Primus*,[6] and even more of the *Voluntas*.[7] At least some of the obscurities and seeming contradictions in Ibn Gabirol's thought must be laid to the fact that we do not have a full exposition of all three parts.

But why should philosophy have three parts at all?  Obviously, because the nature of reality is threefold.  When we ask why reality is threefold, we immediately confront one of the central laws that governs Gabirol's system and that shows how deeply rooted he is in Neoplatonism.  In response to the Disciple's question, "What is the reason why only these three things exist?" the Master says, ". . . for every created thing there must be a cause and something intermediate between them.  The cause is the First Essence, the created thing is matter and form, what mediates between them is the Will."[8]  In a famous passage in the *Timaeus* (31C) Plato had insisted on the necessity for such a third thing, or medium:  "But two things alone cannot be satisfactorily united without a third; for there must be some bond between them drawing them together.  And of all bonds the best is that which makes itself and the terms it connects a unity in the fullest sense."[9]

Rooted in the Platonic conception of the essential duality of the spiritual and material realms, the law of mediation (as I shall call it) was one of the central philosophical principles in the history of Platonism.  More implied than explicitly invoked in the thought of

Plotinus, it was richly developed in the Iamblichan-Proclean tradition of Neoplatonism.[10]   The proliferation of horizontal and vertical triadic structures in Proclean metaphysics cannot be understood apart from this fundamental dynamic principle.  Proclus's *Elements of Theology* clearly articulates the metaphysical need for such a principle: "For that which has its existence embraced by time is in all respects temporal, since *a fortiori* it has a temporal activity; and the fully temporal is altogether unlike the fully eternal; but all procession is through terms (Prop. 29): therefore there exists an intermediate principle."[11]

The law of mediation operates on all levels of Ibn Gabirol's universe. Every mode of being is fundamentally mediational. Ibn Gabirol describes the levels of reality in a bewildering, but coherent, variety of ways throughout the *Fons Vitae*.  The basic threefold structure is expanded from several perspectives as the philosopher proceeds with his analysis of created reality.  In the second treatise he speaks of nine levels of subsistence by which the *"forma loci"* descends from the superior to the inferior levels:

> First is the subsistence of all things in the Creator's knowledge; second, the subsistence of universal form in universal matter; third, the subsistence of simple forms in each other; fourth, the subsistence of the accidents of simple substances in simple substances; fifth, the subsistence of quantity in substance; sixth, the subsistence of surfaces, lines and points; seventh, the subsistence of colors and figures in surfaces; eighth, the subsistence of parts of bodies in other parts; and ninth, the subsistence of some bodies in others.[12]

Other passages analyze seven kinds of simple substances.[13]   Still others set out the parallels between spiritual and corporeal substances.[14]   Both fourfold and threefold divisions of matter are studied.[15]  The divisions of form are even more complex.

The different types of form are helpful in providing a simplified, but I hope generally accurate, picture of the levels of reality in Ibn Gabirol's universe. In good Neoplatonic fashion, Ibn Gabirol always insisted *"omne esse rei ex forma est,"* that is, the being of something (that by means of which we can conceptualize its existence) comes from its form.[16]   So an analysis of the kinds of form can provide a conceptual map of reality. There are three general types of form: the form of things which is found in the *essentia voluntatis* (which is form only in an equivocal sense); the form joined to matter in act (that is, the form of the *intelligentia universalis)*, and the form joined to matter in potency. All "other forms are contained under the universal form,"[17] that is, the form joined to matter in act. They descend according to the following levels:[18] Directly under the *forma intelligentiae*, the universal form containing all others, is the *forma animae*, Ibn Gabirol's equivalent to the Plotinian World Soul. This is frequently spoken of as a single unified principle,[19] but because it precontains on a higher level all the lower operations of soul, it is also discussed in terms of the tripartition of soul into its vegetative, animal and rational functions.[20] The lowest of the simple substances, that is, those that consist of a combination of higher form and matter, is the *forma naturae*, or *forma mundi.*[21] On the level of corporeal substances, that is, those beings made up of combinations of lower matter and the *forma quantitatis*, the root of all corporeality, we have parallel levels which Ibn Gabirol describes in different ways at different times. From the formal perspective we can say that the lower level consists of the *forma substantiae*, the *forma corporis* and the *forma figurae et coloris*,[22] while from the perspective of existing substances, the corporeal world contains heavenly bodies, human beings, animals, plants and elements.

Our interest is not so much in the exact portrayal of all these levels as in the dynamic laws of the system that generates them. The most prominent of these is our principle of mediation. According to this law, not only is *voluntas* a necessary medium between God and the created world, as we have seen, but form itself also serves as a medium between *voluntas* and *materia.*[23] In arguing for the necessity of a *substantia media* between God and bodies in the third treatise, Ibn Gabirol's dependence on the principle of mediation becomes almost tiresome. His famous fifty-six proofs for the existence of simple substances ring the changes on the theme of mediation in order to protect God's transcendence above material reality. "If there were no medium between the essence of the First Maker and the substance which sustains the predicates, the essence of the First Maker would be joined to that substance."[24] Thus, for Ibn Gabirol as for Avicenna, the transcendence of God excludes His creating lower substances directly.[25] A subsequent passage applies the principle to all the levels of substance found in the corporeal world.[26]

But what mediates between universal matter and universal form themselves, we might ask? Is this an exception to the principle of mediation? The answer appears to be yes and no, perhaps because of the mingling of Aristotelian elements into Ibn Gabirol's Neoplatonic metaphysics.[27]   Universal matter and form are not opposites or extremes in the way that God and the world or spiritual and corporeal reality are in Neoplatonic metaphysics.  Rather, they appear to be correlatives.  The Jewish sage always insists that matter and form are essentially coordinate and cannot exist apart from each other.[28]   Yet they do need the action of *Voluntas* to bring them together—"form receives from the Will the power of holding on to matter."[29]   Thus in a sense Will may be said to be their medium.

Taken by itself, the principle of mediation might suggest static levels of reality insulated from each other.  But this, of course, is just the opposite of what Neoplatonic systems intend, as can be seen especially when the principle of mediation works together with a second principle of Neoplatonic metaphysics, which we can call the principle of coinherence.  Plotinus put it succinctly in *Enneads* V 5.9: "Everything which is brought into being by something else is either in that which made it or in another thing, if there is something after what made it; for in that it is brought into being by something else and needed something else for its coming into being, it needs something else at every point. . . . But the Principle [i.e., the One], since it has nothing before it, has not anything else to be in; but since it has nothing else to be in, and the other things are in those which come before them, it encompasses all the other things.  But in encompassing them it is not dispersed into them and it possesses them without being possessed."[30]   Briefly put, all things are in their superiors by way of what we might call "precontainment," while the omnipresent Highest Principle is both in and not in all the lower things, possessing, but not possessed.

Middle Platonists, such as the second-century Numenius of Apamea, in speaking of the intelligible substances, used the formula "all in all, but in each according to its nature."[31]   In the development of Neoplatonism this principle was expanded eventually beyond the intelligible realm to suggest how the whole of reality is bound together by a dynamic coinherence.[32]   Not all Neoplatonists understood this mutual involvement of "all in all according to what is proper to each" in the same way. But there is a community of thought behind the various expositions of the principle. Ibn Gabirol's version of the principle of coinherence is crucial to the understanding his philosophy. It underlies one of the longer and more vexed parts of the *Fons Vitae.*

Shortly after exasperating his readers with fifty-six proofs of the necessity of a *substantia media* between God and bodies, Ibn Gabirol tries them still further with no less than sixty-three proofs that corporeal substances come from and depend upon spiritual ones.[33] This plethora of proofs rests on the underlying principle of coinherence. The central theme is perhaps best expressed in Proof 45: "Therefore, inferior forms must exist so that they may all be present in the superior forms, grade by grade up to the universal form, in which all forms are gathered. But there the forms are not in a place, here they are. There they are united in the union of spiritual substance; here they are scattered in the dispersal of corporeal substance."[34]

The dynamism that the Neoplatonic principle of coinherence introduces into Ibn Gabirol's thought is evident throughout the *Fons Vitae.* The Jewish sage is especially interested in what we might call the "precontainment" aspect of coinherence, that is, the way in which all lower levels of reality are contained in, or find their true "place" in the level of reality immediately above them. He summarizes as follows: ". . . form contains matter, just as Intelligence contains soul and soul contains body. Will contains form, just as each one of these contains the other; and God, holy and exalted, contains Will and whatever exists in Will of matter and form, although in an incomparable manner."[35]

The principle of coinherence means not only that the forms imitate the *Factor Primus* in diffusing themselves and their powers insofar as they are able,[36] but also that everything in the lower forms must be precontained in the higher,[37] so that lower forms exemplify higher ones.[38] Accordingly, a primary mode of philosophical argumentation is from the lower to the higher.[39] As in all Neoplatonic systems, however, the dialectic is not fully reversible. In Ibn Gabirol's words, "It follows that whatever exists in lower substances also exists in higher ones, but not that whatever exists in higher ones exists in lower. For example, growth and generation exist in the animal soul, but sensation and motion are not present in the vegetative soul; and sensation and movement are in the rational soul, but rationality and knowledge are not present in the animal soul."[40]

The coinherence principle helps us to understand the view of causality found in the writings of the Jewish philosopher. We must note at the outset the critical distinction Ibn Gabirol makes between God's mode of causing, *creatio ex nihilo*, and all other causation. "*Creatio est acquisitio essendi*," and it belongs to God alone to give being.[41] To be sure, creation can be described in the language of emanation as the "coming forth (*exitus*) of form from the First Source, that is, the Will, and its infusion (*influxio*) on matter,"[42] and there are passages that draw out the analogies between the divine causality of creation and causality here below. But an essential difference always remains. All lower causation is the *impressio* or *influxio* in matter of what is found or located in the essence of the higher substance; God alone creates matter and form, that is, makes something that is other than his essence. "If the simple substance were to imprint what is not in its essence, its action would not be an impression, and it would be a creator from nothing. But there is no creator from nothing other than the First Maker, holy and exalted."[43] We might say that God alone can give what he does not have, namely, created being.

What is the nature of the *impressio* and *influxio* that is the essence of causality here below? Fundamentally, it is the active diffusion of all the forms present in the *Intelligentia* or *Intellectus*, the first created reality composed of universal matter and universal form. Since all lower levels of both simple and corporeal substances are specifications of universal matter by more particular forms that are precontained in *Intelligentia*, their realizations are exemplifications of the principle of coinherence, that is, they can be impressed upon or flow into matter because they pre-exist in a higher essence that has the power to impart them.

The notion of the *vis* or *virtus agendi* is central here. "It is necessary that what is acted upon by the First Maker without a medium receive the power of acting (*virtus agendi*). And what receives the power of acting is an agent."[44] A later passage explains this in more detail: "This is still clearer proof that a form proceeds from the First Maker and is submissive to Him in that it is compelled in its nature to give itself and to confer its form when it finds matter to receive it. And because it was the first thing made and the first activity, it was necessary that this thing and activity should penetrate through everything until it could no longer be received."[45] What flows forth by way of generation from this highest substance and from all subsequent substances in their proper ranks is not their essence itself, but their power (*vis*) of formation. That is why the essences of the higher substances, and *a fortiori* the *Prima Essentia*, are never diminished by their causal action.[46] Light is Ibn Gabirol's constant metaphor when speaking of causality as *fluxus*. Just as light remains essentially within the sun, but radiates out through the air and becomes visible when it encounters a body, so too the *Intelligentia* sends forth the rays that are the simple substances into apt matter, spiritual or corporeal.[47]

If the twin principles of mediation and coinherence place Ibn Gabirol firmly in the Neoplatonic tradition, certain aspects of his teaching on creation demonstrate the distinctive and, it may be suggested, Jewish character of his Neoplatonism. Recent studies have emphasized the shifts Neoplatonic themes underwent as the philosophy was being accepted as a "co-determinant" along with Church teaching in the systematic and speculative exposition of Christian belief.[48] Just as Thomas Aquinas' use of Aristotelian philosophy as a tool for the systematic exposition of *sacra doctrina* led to profound inner transformations of Aristotelianism, so too Augustine, Pseudo-Dionysius, Boethius, and a host of successors transformed Neoplatonism in the service of Christian theology. The textual record is sparser in Jewish Neoplatonism, but the case of Ibn Gabirol shows that a parallel process was under way in Judaism.[49] Two central topics in Ibn Gabirol's thought reveal this transformative process at work: Ibn Gabirol's discussion of the relation of unity to duality and his treatment of the Divine Will.

In Plotinus and in earlier Neoplatonism in general the One, which is beyond being, produces a second, Being or Nous, which is a transcendental unity in multiplicity, a "one-many." Insofar as Nous turns towards and contemplates the One, it is united with it; but Nous is unable fully to capture the simplicity of the One. The most it can achieve is to "think" the super-intellectual One as a single and simultaneous multiplicity of forms (see *Enneads* V 3.0-11; VI 7.15).

Through this activity Nous becomes the productive source of all the lower, differentiated stages of reality. "But this one thing is two things: Intellect and Being and thinking and thought—Intellect as thinking and Being as thought. For there could not be thinking without otherness and also sameness."[50] The axiom that what is produced by the Absolute One must itself be one, although in some derived and less perfect way, is characteristic of Neoplatonism. In the words of Alexander Altmann, "In all Neoplatonic systems the principle prevails that from the One only one substance can proceed."[51] In its Avicennan form, in which it was used to derive the origin of differentness and multiplicity in the universe from the First Intelligence and not from God, it had a crucial role in the history of medieval thought in Islam, Judaism and Christianity.[52]

Ibn Gabirol's stance toward this fundamental principle reveals much about his thought. Ermenegildo Bertola's claim that he "substantially accepted" it[53] is misleading in view of the highly qualified way in which this basic law of Neoplatonism appears in the *Fons Vitae*. Pressing the distinction between the transcendent Creator God and His creation, Ibn Gabirol insists that the Absolute One can produce only *what* is *two*. The principle is briefly announced in IV 6: "The Creator of all things ought to be one only, and the created should be different from him. Hence, if the created were only matter or only form, it would be assimilated to him and there would not be a medium between them, for two is after one."[54] This general thesis is followed by a careful argument showing that all creation cannot be resolved into one root, or into more than two, but must be traced back to the duality of matter and form, so that "everything that exists from the beginning first point of the ultimate highest down to extreme lowest point is also composed of matter and form."[55] Critics of Ibn Gabirol like Albert the Great were to seize on this denial of what they considered a universally accepted philosophical principle as evidence of the problems of his thought, as we shall see.

It might be thought that Ibn Gabirol's Divine Will functions like the "one-many" of the Plotinian Nous, but the differences are more evident than the similarities. In addressing the underlying problem of the origin of multiplicity from unity, the *Voluntas* is both creative (the *Factor Primus* precisely as Creator) and ultimate unity (*prima unitas*). It is the origin of subsequent multiplicity insofar as it is simply one, not insofar as it is a one that is potentially many, like

Plotinus' Nous and Avicenna's First Intelligence. It is true that Ibn Gabirol accepts a modified version of the traditional axiom of the one giving rise only to one in the passages where he speaks about the relation of the *prima unitas*, or *unitas agens* (i.e., the Will) to the *unitas creata*, or *unitas patiens*, i.e., the First Intellect composed of universal form and universal matter.[56] But, unlike Avicenna's First Intelligence, this entity is actually and not merely potentially two, a metaphysical composition of form and matter.

Ibn Gabirol's insistence on the necessary duality of creation appears to spring, at least in part, from a fundamentally Jewish concern with protecting divine transcendence. The same fundamental value grounded his most famous philosophical doctrine, universal hylomorphism, that is, the ascription of matter and form to all created reality. The beginning of creation for the Jewish sage is precisely the commencement of the union of matter and form.[57] An analysis of Ibn Gabirol's understanding of the roles of universal matter and universal form in the constitution of created being will help explain why.[58]

Aristotle had understood matter as what is needed to explain physical change in a universe that is eternally given. For Ibn Gabirol, who, like all monotheistic Neoplatonists, was fundamentally interested in why there was a universe at all, matter is much more. More than the root of the possibility of physical change, matter is the root of all possibility. Whatever might not have been must be material.[59] This can be seen in a text from the same *resolutio* argument cited above: If there were one root to creation, "it would be necessary that the one root be either only matter or only form. If it were only matter, it would not be possible for forms to come to be through it, and if forms were not, beings would not have *esse*. And if it were only form, it would not have *existere per se*, nor likewise would it be possible that various kinds of matter could come to be through it."[60]

Ibn Gabirol discusses the properties of universal matter and universal form early in the *Fons Vitae*. Universal matter is described as what is *per se existens*, of one essence, sustaining diversity, and giving essence and name to all things. Universal form subsists in another (i.e., in universal matter), perfects the essence of that in which it is, and gives it *esse*.[61] In order to understand these properties we need to grasp Ibn Gabirol's rather unusual use of such terms as *esse, essentia, existentia*, and the like, and here we can be helped by his discussion of key philosophical terms in *Fons Vitae* V 7-8.[62] Although his use of these metaphysical terms may not always be consistent, many apparent problems are resolved when we recognize that Ibn Gabirol's basic philosophical vocabulary is essentially relational. Because created reality is always a composition, we need to analyze how each term expresses composition in order to grasp its meaning.

While it may be puzzling initially to hear that matter is *per se existens*, a subsequent passage explains that this does not mean that matter can ever exist by itself, but rather that it is the principle of reality which receives, or "sustains," form. In other words it is that without which form could never have a more than ideal reality.[63] This is why matter for Ibn Gabirol is the source of substantiality and why he claims that the same reality is called matter in reference to form and substance insofar as it stands on its own.[64] The term *essentia* signifies the formality under which we understand things, and it seems to be used in two perhaps equivocal ways by Ibn Gabirol. First, generally, as the *essentia materiae*, that by which anything can be said to be a substance; and second, more properly, as the equivalent of form, namely, that by which *something* is what it is—"*forma constituit essentiam eius in quo est.*"[65] *Esse* is the most relational of all the terms. Since creation is the "*acquisitio essendi*," *esse* in the true sense is what eventuates when matter and form come together through God's action, the "*existentia formae in materia.*"[66] Matter conceived in itself possesses only *esse in potentia*, that is, the power to sustain form; form possesses *esse in actu*, and this is why Ibn Gabirol can make use of the traditional Neoplatonic formula "*omne esse ex forma est.*" But without matter's sustaining power, form would only serve to demarcate an unsubstantial ideal or mental reality.[67] The sage summarizes the respective roles of universal form and universal matter thus: "It is necessary that this be the form which gives every form *esse* and *quod est (essentia)*, just as matter is that which gives all substantiality."[68]

Two important implications of universal hylomorphism need to be mentioned before we pass on to the other innovative aspect of Ibn Gabirol's Jewish Neoplatonism, his view of the Divine Will. The first is the well-known issue of the plurality of forms; the second, the related question of primacy between matter and form. Ibn Gabirol has been controversial both among the Schoolmen and among modern scholars for his doctrine of the plurality of forms in each existing subject. From the viewpoint of his Neoplatonic metaphysics, this teaching is no more than a necessary implication of a coinherent universe composed of matter and form on every level. All existing substances from the First Intellect down to the lowest bodies are not only based upon the fundamental combination of universal matter and universal form, but also composed of the kinds of matter and form appropriate to their substantial level in the spiritual or corporeal realms.[69] Other Neoplatonists share this perspective, although they spell it out in different ways.

More revealing of the uniqueness of Ibn Gabirol's thought is his conception of the priority of matter to form. It is no secret that in Aristotle's world form is king. In Ibn Gabirol's world we might say that matter is king, but it is a constitutional monarch. Because it is matter that provides substantiality to all created things, Ibn Gabirol can describe *materia prima*, rather than being as the *genus generalissimum*.[70] Viewing created reality from the perspective of substantiality leads the Jewish philosopher to passages in which the traditional Great Chain of Being comes to sound more like a Great Chain of Matter. A good example is in *Fons Vitae* V 29, where we read: "Understand that matter has as it were two extremes, the one ascending to the limit of creation, namely, the beginning of the uniting of form and matter, the other descending to the goal of rest."[71] Yet, from another perspective, that of the modalities by which we come to understand what God has established in the realm of substance, forms still possess an intellectual if not a real priority.[72]

The final area I wish to examine is that of the Divine Will. In Plato's intellectualist metaphysics the Forms or Ideas are outside the maker of the universe, the Demiurge (*Timaeus* 28a, 29a). The multiplicity and "extradeical" position of the Ideas created difficulties for later Platonists, since the transcendental source must be a unity. The solution was the creation of an intradeical interpretation of the Ideas: The Ideas form a unity in the mind of God. Philo is our earliest witness to the intradeical view, but it seems to go back well before him.[73] Plotinus identified the Nous with the world of Ideas in *Enneads* V 9.9 and elsewhere; his view may be called intradeical insofar as the Nous is a god. But the multiplicity implied in thinking and thought exclude Nous from the highest divine realm, that of the One. For Christian Neoplatonists, especially St. Augustine, the Ideas form a unity in the Divine Mind, understood as the coeternal Logos, the second Person of the Trinity.[74] Speculation on the status and role of the Divine Ideas was one of the central themes in medieval Christian thought.

From this perspective, the restricted role of the Ideas in Ibn Gabirol's thought, at least as it comes down to us, is initially surprising. True, he insists that "form *per se* existed in the knowledge of God (*scientia dei*), exalted and great,"[75] and even that the first subsistence is that of all things in the Creator's knowledge;[76] but speculation on what the nature of the "*scientia factoris primi*" might be and what role the Ideas play in it is noticeably lacking.[77] Its place is taken by Ibn Gabirol's teaching on the Divine Will.[78]

We have already seen *Voluntas* as the necessary medium between God and creation; we must now investigate how it relates to God, the *Essentia Prima*, as well as to matter and form.[79] Ibn Gabirol describes *Voluntas* from two perspectives: first, as not acting, in which case it is infinite and identical with the Divine Essence; and second, as actually producing universal form and matter,[80] in which case it is finite and thus less than God. Given Ibn Gabirol's insistence, like that in Maimonides after him, that the First Essence is absolutely unknowable, positive predicates such as willing cannot be really ascribed to the divine as it is in itself. The role that Ibn Gabirol assigns to the divine "hypostasis" of *Voluntas* attempts to qualify this fundamental apophaticism yet remain faithful to the traditional Jewish understanding of the centrality of the divine command in cosmology and ethics.[81]

*Voluntas* is both united to and separated from the absolute *unitas* of the First Essence.[82] "When you remove action from the Will it is the same as the Essence; when it is taken with action, it will be different from the Essence," as we read towards the end of the fifth treatise.[83] The *Voluntas*, as God's transcendent *virtus* or *vis agendi*, is described as the "*virtus unitatis*,"[84] or "the power of God the Holy penetrating all things, existing in all things, acting in all things outside of time."[85]   However, the Divine Will acts in different things in different ways, as we shall see.

When we look at the relation between the Will and the world it creates, we see a pattern both like and unlike Neoplatonic Christian views of the Logos as Creator. Ibn Gabirol's *Voluntas* is creative, but with two important differences from the Logos. The first and essential difference is that for the Jewish sage the dual creation is rooted, at least according to many texts, in different aspects of the divine being. "Concerning matter the same can be said as for form, namely that matter is created by the Essence, and form is from the property of the Essence, that is, from Wisdom or Unity (i.e., the Will), although the Essence is not made proper by some property extrinsic to it."[86] This is one of the most ambiguous areas in Ibn Gabirol's thought, especially because other texts link both form and matter to the Divine Will, as when the reader is encouraged to attain the knowledge of ". . . how there is a subsistence of all forms in universal matter and how there is a subsistence of universal matter and universal form with everything it contains in the Will of the First Maker, holy and exalted."[87] Ibn Gabirol seems to want to have his cake and eat it too. Rooting matter and form in two aspects of God explains their essential difference, but it also highlights the unresolved problems in Ibn Gabirol's thought about the relation of the Divine Essence and the Divine Will. Locating the source of both matter and form in the Divine Will may provide a clearer solution, but creates difficulties for those texts that either point to a dual origin or insist that form too, and not just matter, is found in the *scientia dei excelsi et magni*, that is, in the Divine Essence.[88] This nest of problems is certainly among the most difficult facing interpreters of the philosopher's thought.

A second difference concerns the kinds of causality ascribed to the Divine Will. *Voluntas* is described as the *verbum agens* of the entire creative process.[89] This might seem to bring *Voluntas* close to Christian understandings of the creative Logos or *Verbum*, but a closer perusal of the mode of activity of Ibn Gabirol's Divine Will shows some important differences. Not only is the Christian Logos coessential with the Father in every way, but He also acts directly and immediately on all levels of created reality. Ibn Gabirol's Divine Will works on the different levels of creation in diverse ways—as *verbum* in spiritual substances, and as *motus* in corporeal ones.[90]  In describing how the forms of all things exist in the Divine Will, however, Ibn Gabirol is closer to some of the patterns found in Christian discussions of the pre-existence of all things in the Logos. The forms of all things can be said to exist in the essence of the Will because they are caused by it, not because they have some intrinsic relation to it (the traditional Latin *via causalitatis*).[91]  Some passages also seem close to Logos speculation on the *via eminentiae* in claiming that all the forms exist in the Will in a more perfect, more ordered and full way.[92]

In the brief treatise on the Will that closes the *Fons Vitae*, Ibn Gabirol identifies the *Voluntas* with the scriptural *"sapientia essentiae primae"* (see Proverbs 8),[93] hinting at the religious roots of his transformation of Neoplatonism. From this perspective, Ibn Gabirol's complex and elusive teaching on the Divine Will can take its rightful place alongside other attempts in Jewish religious philosophy to emphasize a voluntaristic approach to the doctrine of God that remains fully respectful of the divine mystery.[94]  At this supreme point of philosophical speculation we are left with several puzzling problems, not only about the relation of the two aspects of the *Voluntas*, but also about the relation of the *scientia dei* in which all things in some way pre-exist and the active *sapientia dei* by which the world is created.  One passage seems to treat them as equivalent,[95] but we are given no indication of how this is the case and no description of how the Ideas themselves might function as primordial causes (one of the key themes in Christian Logos speculation).  This is not to try to judge Ibn Gabirol by a Christian yardstick; it is merely meant to emphasize how different the sage's brand of Jewish "voluntaristic" Neoplatonism is from the Logos speculations of his Neoplatonic Christian predecessors, contemporaries and successors.

## II.  Some Scholastic Reactions to Solomon Ibn Gabirol.

The *Fons Vitae* was widely read by the Latin Schoolmen.  It was influential, within important limits, and vigorously debated.  The full history of Ibn Gabirol's influence on the Masters of the Schools has yet to be written, although there are some useful studies.[96] It will not be possible here to do more than sketch a broad picture, illustrated by a few details, as a way of highlighting the real achievements, as well as the significant limitations, of medieval philosophical ecumenism.

Ibn Gabirol's powerful but in some ways idiosyncratic system became available to Latin Christian authors at a propitious moment. The late twelfth century was a period that would be difficult to describe as other than eclectic, as long as we are prepared to admit that "eclecticism," understood as creative openness to new ideas and systems without undue concern for ultimate systematic coherence, can have positive values. Ibn Gabirol's special form of Neoplatonism contained elements compatible with important themes in Augustine and Boethius, two of the major Christian Neoplatonic authorities. It also complemented the forms of twelfth-century Platonism connected with what has been called the "School of Chartres." These complementarities and the nonsectarian religious tone of the *Fons Vitae* assured it a role in the thought of High Scholasticism.

The work was translated when Latin Christian philosophy and theology were just beginning to sense the possibility of separate but intertwined academic existences. This element of timing may help explain the power of its early influence. It appeared on the scene when distinctions between philosophical and theological positions were still fluid and when Augustine was still the master of truth in both realms. At the end of the twelfth century, whatever served to complement and explain what was thought of as Augustine's philosophy was welcomed and promptly put to use.

Dominicus Gundissalinus, the Spanish archdeacon who translated the *Fons Vitae*, was also responsible for mixing Ibn Gabirol's views into the philosophical stew of the time. The Spaniard was the most "Gabirolean" of all Latin thinkers, but his eclectic thought uses much from Augustine, Boethius and Avicenna too, and at times advances contradictory positions in different works. Gundissalinus's small treatise *De unitate et uno* is an odd mixture of Boethius, Augustine and Ibn Gabirol. Since it circulated under the name of Boethius, it gave a Boethian cachet to such Gabirolean doctrines as universal hylomorphism[97] and the existence of both a *"prima et vera unitas"* (i.e., God) and an *"unitas creata . . . omnino diversa . . . et quasi opposita.*" It gave an aura of acceptability and familiarity to an understanding of creation that is clearly under the impress of the Jewish philosopher's fundamental principle that only what is dual can come from the One.[98] In another treatise, the *De processione mundi*, Gundissalinus explicitly advances that principle, paraphrasing a passage from the *Fons Vitae*: "Everything created must be different from the Creator. Since the Creator is truly one, unity ought not belong to creatures. . . . Since the Creator is truly one, the creature which comes after him must be two."[99] The overall metaphysical picture in these two treatises, the discussion of the nature and kinds of matter and form, and the insistence on the plurality of forms, are clear marks of the influence of the Jewish philosopher.[100]

On the plurality of forms, however, Gundissalinus stands at the head of two opposing traditions. Universal plurality of forms throughout the created universe implies substantial plurality in the human person, especially the plurality of the three Aristotelian souls—vegetative, animal and rational. Ibn Gabirol held this view and Gundissalinus echoes it. Avicenna, however, while admitting that a form of corporeity (*forma corporeitatis*) combines with other forms in constituting bodies, insisted that there is only one soul in each living being. The Spanish archdeacon translated Avicenna's psychology (the famous *Liber sextus naturalium*), and adhered to this position in his own *De anima*.[101]

Much has been written about the twin issues with which the history of Ibn Gabirol's influence on the Schoolmen of the thirteenth century has often been linked—universal hylomorphism, the teaching that all creation is composed of matter and form,[102] and the separate but related issue of the plurality of forms, that is, whether in one and the same individual there are many substantial forms or only one.[103] It was possible to affirm one of these two theses and not the other. William of Auvergne (ca. 1180-1249), who praised Ibn Gabirol as "*unus omnium philosophantium nobilissimus,*"[104] held to the plurality of forms but denied the existence of spiritual matter. Later, Bonaventure accepted universal hylomorphism (although he never cites Ibn Gabirol) but denied plurality of forms.[105]

The existence of intellectual or "spiritual matter" (*materia spiritualis*) had enjoyed a long history among pagan Neoplatonists.[106] More important for thirteenth-century Christian thinkers, it also found a clear foundation in Augustine in texts both authentic and pseudonymous, and in the writings of many Augustinian theologians of the twelfth century.[107] The exact extent of Ibn Gabirol's influence in spreading this view is not easy to determine and has been evaluated differently by various investigators. He is not mentioned explicitly as often as one might expect. But the fact that he developed the arguments for this position in far greater detail and with more rigor than any of the other sources known to the Christian *magistri* indicates that, despite sparse citation, he was of considerable importance in furthering this view and the related position of the plurality of forms. Maurice de Wulf, criticizing Étienne Gilson's description of the reigning philosophical complex of the early thirteenth century as an "augustinisme avicennisant," suggested that we might as legitimately speak of an "augustinisme avicebrolisant."[108] Such awkward, hybrid terms do not really give a very satisfactory picture of a complex situation. We can agree with the recent evaluation of James Weisheipl that "Avicebron rather than Augustine is the source of what appeared to the vast majority of thirteenth-century theologians as the traditional and sound doctrine."[109] But we should remember that it was the compatibility of these doctrines to passages found in Augustine's writings and to themes in the history of Augustinianism that made them so widely acceptable.

What was at issue was the best way to protect divine transcendence. As William de la Mare, one of Thomas Aquinas' opponents on this issue, later put it: "If an angel does not have matter it is altogether immutable and hence God."[110] William, like Ibn Gabirol, identified matter with contingency, composition and the possibility of change. So he and his predecessors, both Dominicans and Franciscans, were convinced that some form of matter must characterize all created being.

Up to the third decade of the thirteenth century, most Scholastics, following the lead of Gilbert of Poitiers and Peter Lombard, had denied that spiritual substances, such as angels, were composed of matter and form, basing their composition on some other ground, such as the Boethian distinction between the *id quod est* and the *id quo est*. Around 1230, however, we find Roland of Cremona, the first Dominican Master at Paris, affirming that the angels are composed of form and spiritual matter, a position also put forth by Alexander of Hales, the first Franciscan Master, around the same time. During the next decade opposition to this view is also found, both among secular masters, such as William of Auvergne and Philip the Chancellor, and Mendicants, such as the Franciscan John of La Rochelle and the Dominicans Hugh of St. Cher and later Albert the Great. While support of universal hylomorphism was to become a hallmark of Franciscan attacks on Thomas Aquinas, the early picture is more complex than a simple split between Dominicans and Franciscans.

The question of plurality versus unity of substantial form shows a similar confused development. The judgment of the best modern scholarship, such as that of D. A. Callus and Fernand van Steenberghen, has continued to emphasize the importance of Ibn Gabirol in furthering the doctrine of plurality.[111] When the issue surfaced in the first decade of the thirteenth century among figures like Alfred of Shareshal and John Blund it was unity that held the field. This view continued to find strong support among the Dominicans in the line that stretches from Roland of Cremona, through Albert, to Thomas Aquinas. But in the middle decades of the century some theologians began to shift to plurality. The real debate, however, was only to erupt in the wake of Aquinas' support of the unity of substantial form in his attack on Ibn Gabirol in the *De substantiis separatis* and throughout his writings.

The two Schoolmen who have the most to say about "Avicebron," Albert the Great and his pupil Thomas Aquinas, disagreed strongly with him on these and other issues. Thomas' critique has been treated by a number of scholars.[112] Albert's reaction is not as well known but is particularly revealing,[113] because he disagreed with the Jewish philosopher not just on universal hylomorphism and plurality of forms, but on even more fundamental metaphysical principles. The roots of Albert's critique are most evident in his *De causis et processu universitatis*, a paraphrase, commentary and expansion on the *Liber de causis* that he wrote between 1267 and 1271. Book I devotes three full chapters and other comments to the Jewish philosopher.

Albert clearly had read the *Fons Vitae* carefully, and his condescending remarks about it as the product of "some undergraduate" (*quidem sophistarum*) are in conflict with the attention he gives it. The Dominican recognized the importance of the principle of mediation in Ibn Gabirol's thought, especially with regard to the role of the *Voluntas* in the creation of the *binarium famosissimum*, the primal duality of universal matter and form.[114] He resolutely opposed this principle, at least with regard to divine activity. Analyzing the notion of an infinite First Principle, he affirms: "A thing said to be infinite in this way is absolutely perfect and has no need of a medium,"[115] a position in accord with the revised Neoplatonic metaphysics he developed out of Pseudo-Dionysius and the *Liber de causis*.[116] The "doctor universalis" also disagrees with what we have called the principle of coinherence, at least insofar as he sees it positing an essential "flow" (*fluxus*) of the First Principle into all things by way of penetration. In this critique Albert can be accused of misreading Ibn Gabirol's intention from the perspective of his own Dionysian Neoplatonism based upon the universal diffusion of the Highest Good.[117]

Even more interesting are the Dominican's reactions to Ibn Gabirol's distinctive insistence that only two can come from what is one and that the Will mediates between God and creation. Citing Aristotle, al-Fārābī, Avicenna, and Averroes, he most strenuously objects (*fortissime objicitur*) to Ibn Gabirol and defends the axiom "Only what is one can come from the Simple One."[118] The contrary is a position that "Avicebron" alone among the philosophers has upheld.[119] Much of the Dominican's argument against the Jewish philosopher, both here and elsewhere in his vast *corpus*, is devoted to a detailed refutation of the most problematic philosophical corollary of created duality, the doctrine of universal hylomorphism.[120]

Ibn Gabirol's emphasis on the divine *Voluntas creatrix* had been much valued both by Gundissalinus and by William of Auvergne, two of his most fervent Christian admirers, perhaps because they saw this doctrine as an answer to the necessitarianism of the Arabic philosophers.[121] But Albert the Great will have none of it. He mounts his attack on Ibn Gabirol's voluntaristic Neoplatonism in the name of traditional Christian Logos speculation centered on the intradeical interpretation of the Ideas.

Albert begins by noting how Ibn Gabirol's description of the derivation of the universe is basically Platonic, with the exception of his stress on the Divine Will.[122] The importance he accords to this deviation is shown by his two lengthy attacks on the error of having Will rather than Intellect as the medium between God and creation— if a medium is really needed![123] In chapter 6 of the first treatise he offers five related reasons why "the First acts through itself and its essence without anything that determines it to act."[124] In the fourth chapter of the third treatise he gives a detailed refutation based upon the Aristotelian principle that the will is always specified to action by the intellect. His arguments on the relation of intellect and will are scarcely as detailed and profound as those of Thomas. But they are central to his disagreement with the Jewish philosopher. Neither Albert nor Thomas, however, was able to prevent the priority of the Divine Will from winning the day among many Scholastics in the century to come.

Albert the Great attacked the metaphysical roots of Ibn Gabirol's Neoplatonism more directly and effectively than any other Scholastic author. His student, Thomas Aquinas, also disagreed with the Jewish sage; but an investigation of just how Thomas took issue with Ibn Gabirol lies beyond the scope of this paper. In reading the Angelic Doctor's detailed critiques of Ibn Gabirol's universal hylomorphism and plurality of forms, it is difficult not to say that he won out in the technical argument.[125] But this does not negate the value of Ibn Gabirol's thought, nor does it preclude the possibility of a "revised" Neoplatonic response to at least some of Thomas's objections.[126]

Many historians of thought have commented on the relations between Maimonides and Aquinas. Thomas had read the *Guide* with care. He cites Rabbi Moses often and with respect, even when he disagrees with him. Fewer scholars have studied the fascinating relations between Maimonides and Meister Eckhart, a student of both Albert and Aquinas. It would probably be too much to call Eckhart a Latin Maimonidean, since he is so much his own man in many ways. But Eckhart uses Maimonides extensively throughout his Latin works and never expresses disagreement with him.[127] His habit of quoting or paraphrasing large chunks of Maimonides led to one of the curious paradoxes of ecumenical thought in the Middle Ages. The twenty-third of the propositions for which Eckhart was condemned in the papal bull of 1329 actually comes from the *Guide* I 51; so Maimonides has the unique distinction of being the only Jewish thinker condemned as "suspect of (Christian) heresy."

Solomon ibn Gabirol offers us another case of a philosophical encounter in the era of High Scholasticism, one perhaps more indicative of the limits of ecumenism in the Middle Ages. In the case of Maimonides, his closest student, Meister Eckhart, was also his sincerest admirer. Ibn Gabirol had many Christian admirers, and his thought was of real influence in developing two of the themes that came to characterize the Augustinian reaction to Thomism in the latter part of the century. But it appears that Ibn Gabirol's closest students were his most strenuous opponents, Albert the Great and his pupil, the greater Thomas. Perhaps this can serve to remind us that true ecumenical discussion in our own age must be as honest about differences as it is hopeful for discovering shared truths.

### Notes

1. On the role of Arabic translations in medieval scholastic philosophy, see John F. Wippel, "Latin Translation Literature from Arabic," *New Catholic Encyclopedia* (New York: McGraw-Hill, 1967) 14.254-56. For the translations into Arabic, see L. E. Goodman, "The Greek Impact on Arabic Literature," *Cambridge History of Arabic Literature*, 1.460-82.

2. The two most recent monographs on Ibn Gabirol are those of Ermenegildo Bertola, *Salomon Ibn Gabirol (Avicebron): Vita, Opere e Pensiero* (Padua: Cedam, 1953); and Jacques Schlanger, *La philosophie de Salomon Ibn Gabirol: Étude d'un Neoplatonisme.*

3. See M.-T. d'Alverny, "Dominic Gundisalvi," *New Catholic Encyclopedia*, 4.966-67.

4. A. Altmann and S. M. Stern, *Isaac Israeli*, xiii.

5. All citations will be from the edition of Clemens Baeumker, by book and chapter with page and line number where necessary. For this passage, I 7, 9, 24-26: *Partes scientiae omnis tres sunt, scilicet scientia de materia et forma, et scientia de voluntate, et scientia de essentia prima.* Cf. V 36, 322-23.

6. Significant passages on the *Essentia Prima* are scattered through the work; see especially the discussions of the differences between the *Factor Primus* and his creation in III 2-5, 75-88; and III 6-8, 90-95. For the various names of the *Factor Primus*, see Bertola, 83.

7. Major texts discussing the *Voluntas* are found in II 13, 46-47; III 15-16, 111-13; III 57, 205-06; IV 19-20, 252-56; V 17, 288-89; V 31, 314; and especially V 36-39, 323-36. For a fuller list, see Bertola, 95.

In V 4, 330, 10-12, Ibn Gabirol mentions having written a book treating "de scientia voluntatis." This has not survived.

8. I 7, 10, 1-4: D. *Quid causae est quod in esse non sunt nisi haec tria?* M. *Causa in hoc haec est, quod omni creato opus est causa et aliquo medio inter se. causa autem est essentia prima, creatum autem materia et forma, medium autem eorum est voluntas.*

9. Tr., F. M. Cornford in *Plato's Cosmology* (New York: Bobbs Merrill, 1957), 44.

10. See R. T. Wallis, *Neoplatonism*, 130-32. Wallis calls it the "Law of Mean Terms."

11. Proclus, *Elements of Theology*, ed., Dodds, 95, Prop. 106. Cf. Props. 28, 29, 132, 148, etc.

12. II 14, 48, 11-24.

13. III 27, 143-44; cf. III 47-48, 184-88; and IV 17, 250.

14. E.g., III 56, 203-04; and IV 4, 217.

15. For a fourfold division of matter parallel to four divisions of form, see I 17, 21; and II 2, 26-27; for a threefold division, see IV 8, 229. Colette Sirat, *A History of Jewish Philosophy in the Middle Ages*, 76, lays out a fivefold general division.

16. E.g., III 39, 168, 24; IV 5, 221, 11-12; and V 8, 271, 8. Cf. Boethius's equivalent formula *"omne namque esse ex forma est"* in *De Trinitate* 2, in *The Theological Tractates* (Cambridge: Harvard University Press, *LCL*, 1952), 8.

17. IV 20, 255-56.

18. See especially V 20, 295; III 27, 143-44; and V 34, 319-20.

19. E.g., II 24, 70; III 15, 111; III 23, 132-33; III 26, 142; III 51, 194; III 57, 207.

20. E.g., III 47-48, 184-86; III 54, 199; IV 17, 250.

21. On the *forma naturae*, see III 27, 143-44; IV 13, 239; V 20, 295. On the *forma mundi* and its relation to *materia vel hyle*, see II 9-14, 40-49.

22. See V 20, 295; and IV 17, 217. On the proportionality between the realms of simple and corporeal substances, see II 8, 38-39.

23. V 39, 328.

24. See III 9, 97, 2-5: *Si inter essentiam factoris primi et substantiam quae sustinet praedicamenta non esset medium, essentia primi factoris esset iuncta substantiae quae sustinet praedicamenta.* The fifty-six proofs are found in III 2-10, 75-102.

25. The Disciple had already asked why there might not be only God the creator and lower substance in II 12, 44. The Master's response was to tell him to wait for the fifty-six proofs.

26. III 51, 194. See also II 1, 24; III 1, 73-74; IV 8, 229; V 15, 284-85.

27. T. M. Rudavsky, "Conflicting Motifs in Ibn Gabirol's Discussion of Matter and Evil," esp. 57-58, has argued that there is a fundamental imbalance between the Aristotelian and Neoplatonic elements in Ibn Gabirol, but she may overemphasize the distinctively Aristotelian elements.
28. See IV 5, 221; IV 10, 234; V 31-34, 315-20.
29. V 39, 327, 24: *forma suscepit a voluntate virtutem qua retinet materiam.* Cf. III 16, 113, 19-20.
30. Tr., Armstrong, **5**.181-83.
31. Numenius, *Fragments*, ed. E. des Places (Paris: Les Belles Lettres, 1973), 90, Fr. 41.
32. E.g., *Enneads* IV 4.2, 9.5, V 8.4, VI 5.7; *Elements of Theology*, Prop. 103; Dodds, n. 254.
33. III 17-24, 114-38.
34. III 23, 133, 17-23: *ergo formae inferiores debent esse ut omnes sint in formis superioribus, gradu post gradum, donec perveniatur ad formam universalem in qua est collectio omnium formarum; excepto hoc quod illae formae sunt in non-loco, istae vero in loco, illae sunt unitae unitione substantiae spiritualis, et istae sunt dispersae dispersione substantiae corporalis.*
35. V 19, 293, 6-11: . . . *quod forma continet materiam, sicut intelligentia continet animam, et anima continet corpus; et voluntas continet formam, sicut unaquaeque harum continet aliam; et deus excelsus et sanctus continet voluntatem et quicquid materiae et formae est in ea sine comparatione et exemplo.*
36. III 13, 107, 10-20.
37. IV 1, 211, 13-14.
38. This is one of Ibn Gabirol's most frequently invoked principles, e.g., II 7, 37; II 24, 70; IV 16, 247; V 17, 289-90.
39. E.g., II 24, 70; III 50, 191-93; III 56, 203.
40. III 49, 188, 25 - 189, 3: *Sequitur hoc quod quicquid est in substantiis inferioribus, est et in superioribus; sed non quicquid est in superioribus, est et in inferioribus, sicut vegetatio et generatio sunt in anima animali, sed sensus et motus non sunt in vegetabili, et sicut sensus et motus sunt in anima rationali, sed rationalitas et cognitio non sunt in anima animali.*
41. V 42, 334, 7.
42. V 41, 33, 17-21: *Dico ergo quod creatio rerum a creatore alto et magno, quae est exitus formae ab origine prima, id est voluntate, et influxio eius super materiam, est sicut exitus quae emanantis a sua origine et eius effluxio quae sequitur alia post aliam . . .*

43. III 25, 139, 22-25: *Si substantia simplex imprimeret quod non est in sua essentia, non posset eius actio esse impressio; et esset creatrix ex nihilo. sed creator ex nihilo non est nisi factor primus altus et sanctus.* See also II 9, 40, 21-22: *Omnis auctor, excepto primo auctore, in suo opere indiget subiecto quod sit susceptibile suae actionis.* Similarly, II 3, 79, 18-20; IV 13, 240, 16-23. On the basis of such passages, one can well take issue with Julius Guttmann's claim that ". . . in Gabirol's system even the divine activity is subordinated to the general categories of action," *Philosophies of Judaism,* 114. Bertola, 83-85, has stressed Ibn Gabirol's creationism.

44. III 4, 82, 23-25: *Necessarium est ut patiens a primo factore sine medio sit recipiens virtutem agendi. et quod est recipiens virtutem agendi, agens est.*

45. III 14, 108, 23 - 109, 3: *et hoc est evidentius signum quod forma processit a factore primo et est obtemperans illi, eo quod compellitur in natura sua ad dandam se et ad conferendum formam suam, cum invenerit materiam receptibilem sui. Et etiam, quia erat factura prima, et actio similiter, fuit necesse ut haec factura et haec actio esset penetrans per omne usque ad defectum receptibilis sui.*

46. See the important passage in III 52-55, 195-202; cf. IV 17, 249-50; V 15-16, 285-87; V 18, 290.

47. For the light metaphor, see, e.g,, III 16, 112-13; III 25, 141; III 35, 160-61; III 45, 181; III 52, 195-96; III 54, 200; IV 14, 241, and 244-45. In a striking metaphor Ibn Gabirol compares the existence of corporeal substances within the ambience of spiritual substances to the flight of a bird in the air—V 30, 311, 13-15. Vincent Cantarino, "Ibn Gabirol's Metaphysic of Light," argues for a much larger role for *Lichtmetaphysik* than I believe the text allows.

48. See, e.g., Stephen Gersh, *From Iamblichus to Eriugena: An Investigation of the Prehistory and Evolution of the Pseudo-Dionysian Tradition* (Leiden: Brill, 1978); Bernard McGinn, "Meister Eckhart on God as Absolute Unity," in Dominic O'Meara, ed., *Neoplatonism and Christian Thought,* 128-39.

49. Cf. Isaac Israeli and the texts and discussions in Altmann and Stern.

50. *Enneads* V 1.4, after Armstrong, 5.25; cf. VI 2.21.

51. Alexander Altmann, "Creation and Emanation in Isaac Israeli: A Reappraisal," 20. On the history of this axiom, see the paper by Arthur Hyman in this volume.

52. Avicenna, *Metaphysics* 9.4 in *Opera Philosophica* (Venice, 1508; repr. Louvain, 1961), ff. 104v-105r. See the responses by Thomas Aquinas, *Summa theologiae* Ia, 47, 1; and Meister Eckhart, *Comm. in Gen.* n. 10, and *Comm. in Sap.* n. 36. For Averroes's rejection of the principle

in his later writings, see Barry Kogan, "Averroes and the Theory of Emanation."

53. Bertola, 100.

54. IV 6, 222, 25-28: . . . *quia creator omnium debet esse unus tantum, et creatum debet esse diversum ab eo. unde si creatum esset materia tantum aut forma tantum, assimilaretur uni, et non esset medium inter illa, quia duo sunt post unum.*

55. IV 6, 224, 15 - 226, 7. The passage cited is found on 226, 5-7: *constat per hoc quod totum quod est ab initio extremi superioris usque ad extremum infimum est etiam compositum ex materia et forma.* For other texts on this central theme, see I 6, 9, 12-14; V 12, 279, 3-19; V 25, 304, 10-15; and V 42, 333, 3-17. On Ibn Gabirol's view of unity, see A. J. Heschel, "Der Begriff der Einheit in der Philosophie Gabirols," *Monatschrift für Geschichte und Wissenschaft des Judentums* 82 (1938), 89-111.

56. E.g., II 20, 61-62; IV 14, 240; and IV 19, 252.

57. See V 30, 311, 19.

58. These issues have been much discussed in the literature. See Bertola, 106-22; Schlanger, 216-72; and Fernand Brunner, "La doctrine de la matière chez Avicebron," *Revue de théologie* 6 (1956): 261-79.

59. See Brunner, 268.

60. IV 6, 224, 20-25: *Et etiam necesse est ut ipsa una radix aut esset materia tantum, aut forma tantum. si esset materia tantum, non esset possibile ut formae fierent per eam; et si formae non fierent, non haberent esse. si autem fuerit forma tantum, non posset existere per se; similiter nec esset possibile ut materiae fierent per eam.*

61. On matter, see I 10, 13, 14 - 14, 5; on form, I 13, 16, 9-19.

62. V 7-8, 269-77.

63. V 25, 304, 12-13: *existens autem per se sit sustinens, non existens per se sustentatum.*

64. V 7, 269, 17-21.

65. IV 11, 235, 23-24; cf. 236, 22-23; V 9, 272, 26 - 273, 3.

66. V 10, 274, 19.

67. On *esse in potentia (esse materiale)* and *esse in actu seu effectu (esse formale)*, see V 8-11, 271-77; and I 3, 16, 21-24.

68. V 16, 286, 15-17: *oportet ut haec forma sit quae dedit omni formae esse et quod est, sicut materia est quae dedit omnem substantialitatem.*

69. On the plurality of forms, see I 11, 14; II 2, 26-27; III 46, 181-82; IV 3, 215-16; V 20, 295; V 34, 320.

70. V 8, 270, 4-5.

71.  V 29, 310, 14-17: *Intellige materiam quasi habeat duo extrema, unum ascendens ad terminum creationis, scilicet principium unitionis materiae et formae, aliud descendens ad finem quietis.*

72.  Cf. II 20, 61; V 23, 300; V 42, 335; etc.; Brunner, 272-79.

73.  E.g., *De opificio mundi* 20. See H. A. Wolfson, "Extradeical and Intradeical Interpretations of Platonic Ideas," in *Religious Philosophy: A Group of Essays*, 27-68.

74.  Augustine's classic treatment is in *De diversis quaestionibus* q. 46.

75.  V 27, 306, 7-8: M. *Forma erat in scientia dei excelsi et magni per se.* Matter also pre-exists in the *scientia dei*, cf. V 10, 274, 20-22.

76.  II 14, 48, 13-14: *primus eorum est subsistentia omnium rerum in scientia creatoris.* Cf. III 57, 207-08; and V 30, 312-13.

77.  On *scientia dei* in Ibn Gabirol, see Schlanger, 275-77. For the sparse references, see the "Index rerum" in Baeumker, 513.

78.  On the Divine Will in Ibn Gabirol, see Bertola, 94-105; Schlanger, 277-84; cf. Guttmann, 114-17.

79.  In V 40, 329, 9-10 we read *perfectio sapientiae est scientia de voluntate.* This, of course, is because there can be no *sapentia* concerning the *essentia prima.* On the two modes of knowing the Divine Will, see V 43, 388, 10-15.

80.  On the dependence of matter and form on the Will, see II 13, 46-47; IV 20, 254-56; V 28, 308; V 31, 314.

81.  *Voluntas* is more than an attribute or quality of God, as Schlanger notes, 277.

82.  See V 40, 329, 27 - 330, 1.

83.  V 37, 325, 23-24: . . . *quia voluntas, remota actione ab ea, ipsa et essentia sunt unum, et considerata cum actione, erit alia ab essentia.* See especially III 57, 205, 23 - 206, 5; IV 19, 252, 18 - 253, 18.

84.  V 37, 315, 16.

85.  III 15, 111, 25-26: . . . *virtus dei sancti penetrans omnia, existens in omnibus, agens in omnibus sine tempore.* Cf. V 38, 326, 3-19; V 39, 327, 14-17; 328, 11-17.

86.  V 42, 333, 3-5: *De materia hoc idem dicitur de forma, scilicet quod materia est creata ab essentia, et forma est a proprietate essentiae, id est sapientia et unitate, etsi essentia non sit propriata ab ea extrinsica.* Also in V 42, see 334, 4-5; and 334, 24 - 335, 11. In IV 19, 252, 21 - 253, 3, form alone flows from the Will.

87.  III 32, 153, 5-9: *et inde eriges te ad sciendum quomodo est subsistentia omnium formarum in materia universali, et, quo modo est subsistentia materiae universalis et formae universalis cum omni quod continetur in voluntate factoris primi sancti et excelsi.* Cf. V 38, 326, 4-5, where Will makes and joins both matter and form. On these two

diverse formulations, see Bertola, 97-98; Schlanger, 282-83; and Sirat, 76.

88.  E.g., V 27, 306, 7-9.

89.  E.g., V 36, 322, 22 - 323, 20.

90.  V 36-37, 323-25. Important in this regard are the two metaphors that Ibn Gabirol uses to illustrate the relation of *voluntas* to *materia* and *forma*: the image of matter receiving form from Will as a mirror receives an image from the onlooker (e.g., V 41, 331, 1-3), and matter as the seat of the One (*cathedra unius*) in which Will as the giver of form sits and rests (V 42, 335, 22-24).

91.  IV 20, 256, 11-16.

92.  V 17, 289, 13-24: *et secundum hoc oportet ut formae sint in voluntate prima perfectius, quoad esse potest, et ordinatissime et plene.* Cf. V 20, 308. For more on the relations of *voluntas, materia* and *forma*, see V 38, 326-27.

93.  V 42, 333, 1: *sapientia essentiae primae.* Cf. V 41, 331, 10-11.

94.  In this connection, see the remarks of Alexander Altmann on the role of power and will in Isaac Israeli's understanding of creation: "Creation and Emanation in Isaac Israeli: A Reappraisal," 25-26. Note also Maimonides' well-known interpretation of God's speaking as God's willing in *Guide* I 65.

95.  V 10, 274, 19 - 25: *similiter etiam materia non est privata absolute, quia habet esse in se in potentia, scilicet illud quod habebat esse in scientia aeterni, excelsi et magni, non composita cum forma.* D. *Declara mihi hunc intellectum amplius, scilicet esse materiae sine forma in sapientia creatoris excelsi et magni.*

96.  The most useful works are Michael Wittmann, *Die Stellung des hl. Thomas von Aquin zu Avencebrol (Ibn Gebirol) (Beiträge zur Geschichte der Philosophie des Mittelalters* 3.3. Münster: Aschendorff, 1900); Jacob Guttmann, *Die Scholastik des dreizehnten Jahrhunderts in ihren Beziehungen zum Judenthum und zur jüdischen Literatur* (Breslau: Marcus, 1902); Fernand Brunner, *Platonisme et Aristotelisme. La critique d'Ibn Gabirol par saint Thomas d'Aquin*; and most recently James A. Weisheipl, "Albertus Magnus and Universal Hylomorphism: Avicebron," *Albert the Great Commemorative Essays*, ed., Francis J. Kovach and Robert W. Shahan (Norman: University of Oklahoma Press, 1980), 239-60.

97.  Paul Correns, *Die dem Boethius fälschlich zugeschriebene Abhandlung des Dominicus Gundisalvi De Unitate (Beiträge zur Geschichte der Philosophie des Mittelalters* 1,1. Münster: Aschendorff, 1891), 3, ll. 10-12, etc.

98.  Correns, 5, ll. 15-21.

99. See the edition in Menendez Pelayo, *Historia de los Heterodoxos Espanoles* (Madrid, 1880), 1. 698: *Omne creatum a creante debet esse diversum. Cum igitur creator vere unus sit, profecto creaturis non debuit esse unitas; . . . cum igitur creator vere sit unus, profecto creatura que post ipsum est debet esse duo.* Cf. *Fons Vitae* IV 6, 222, 24-28.

100. E.g., *De unitate*, ed. Correns, 8, ll. 1-10.

101. On this issue, see Daniel A. Callus, "The Origins of the Problem of the Unity of Form," *The Dignity of Science: Studies in the Philosophy of Science presented to William Kane, O.P.*, ed. James A. Weisheipl (Washington: The Thomist Press, 1961), 126-32. See *Avicenna's Psychology (Najat* II vi), tr., Rahman, 64-68.

102. The issue was most often posed in relation to spiritual substances, especially the angels. See Erich Keineidam, *Das Problem der hylomorphen Zusammenhang der geistigen Substanzen im 13. Jahrhundert behandelt bis Thomas von Aquin* (Breslau: Universität, 1930); D. O. Lottin, "Le composition hylémorphique des substances. Les débuts de la controverse," *Revue néoscolastique de Philosophie* 34 (1932): 21-41; and Paul Bissels, "Die sachliche Begrundung und philosophiegeschichtliche Stellung der Lehre von der materia spiritualis in der Scholastik," *Franziskanische Studien* 38 (1956): 241-95.

103. Besides the article of Callus mentioned above, see Gabriel Théry, "L'Augustinisme médiéval et le problème de l'unité de la forme substantielle," *Acta Hebdomadae Augustinianae-Thomisticae* (Turin-Rome, 1931), 140-200; D. O. Lottin, "La pluralité des formes substantielles avant saint Thomas d'Aquin," *Revue néoscolastique de philosophie* 34 (1932): 449-67; Roberto Zavalloni, "La metaphysique du composé humain dans la pensée scolastique préthomiste," *Revue philosophique de Louvain* 48 (1950): 5-36; and especially his *Richard de Mediavilla et la controverse sur la pluralité des formes. Textes inédits et étude critique* (Louvain: Institut superieur de Philosophie, 1951).

104. William of Auvergne, *De Trinitate*, ed., Bruno Switalski (Toronto: Pontifical Institute of Mediaeval Studies, 1976), chap. 12, 77-78.

105. See John Quinn, *The Historical Constitution of St. Bonaventure's Philosophy* (Toronto: Pontifical Institute of Mediaeval Studies, 1973), 219-319, and 845.

106. The term "materia spiritualis," while rare in the *Fons Vitae*, is found in III 24, 135, 22. See the paper by John Dillon in this volume for the background.

107. The primary texts in Augustine affirming spiritual matter are to be found in Book 7 of the *De genesi ad litteram*, e.g., 7.5.7, 7.6.9, 7.17.39, 7.19.25. Frequently cited also was the pseudo-Augustinian *De mirabilibus sacrae scripturae* (see *Patrologia Latina* 35, cc. 2149-2200), a seventh-century Irish text. Among the twelfth-century theologians supporting this view were Honorius Augustodunensis and Hugh of St. Victor. See Bissels, 238-52.

108. Étienne Gilson first advanced the term in two important articles: "Pourquoi saint Thomas a critique saint Augustin," *Archives d'histoire doctrinale et littéraire du moyen age* 1 (1926): 5-126; and "Les sources gréco-arabes de l'augustinisme avicennisant," *Archives . . .* 4 (1930): 5-107. Maurice De Wulf responded in *Revue néoscolastique de philosophie* 33 (1931): 1-39; see 32-33 for "augustinisme avicebrolisant."

109. Weisheipl, 241. Compare Weisheipl's five characteristics of thirteenth-century Augustinianism (voluntarism, universal hylomorphism, plurality of substantial forms, Avicennan interpretation of divine illumination, and identity of the soul with its powers, 242-43) with the seven themes identified by De Wulf in his 1931 article (17-18): plurality of substantial forms, universal hylomorphism, theory of *rationes seminales*, identification of perfection of corporeity with light, plurality of forms used to defend the substantial independence of soul from body, identity of soul with its powers, and necessity for creation of world in time.

110. See P. Glorieux, *Les prémiers polémiques thomistes. I. Le correctorium corruptorii Quare* (Paris: Le Saulchoir, 1927), 50.

111. See Callus, 133-36, 146; and F. van Steenberghen, *La philosophie au XIIIe siècle* (Louvain-Paris: Beatrice-Nauwelaerts, 1966), 491-92, responding to R. Zavalloni's attempts to minimize Ibn Gabirol's role here.

112. Besides the studies of Wittmann and Brunner mentioned in note 96, see John Goheen, *The Problem of Matter and Form in the "De Ente et Essentia" of Thomas Aquinas.*

113. See Jacob Guttmann, *Die Scholastik . . .*, 60-85; and J. A. Weisheipl. The extent of Albert's Neoplatonism has been evaluated in different ways by recent studies. Leo Sweeney, S.J., in his article "Are Plotinus and Albertus Magnus Neoplatonists?" in *Graceful Reason: Essays in Ancient and Medieval Philosophy Presented to Joseph Owens, CSSR*, ed. Lloyd P. Gerson (Toronto: Pontifical Institute of Medieval Studies, 1983), 177-202, shows important differences between Plotinus and Albert, but in adopting too rigid a view of Neoplatonism does not resolve the question of whether Albert can be judged a Neoplatonist

on broader grounds. Edward Booth in *Aristotelian Aporetic Ontology in Islamic and Christian Thinkers* (Cambridge: at the University Press, 1983), ch. 5, demonstrates the great weight that Proclean and Dionysian Neoplatonism had in Albert's metaphysics.

114. See *Liber de causis et processu universitatis*, Liber I, tr. 1, cap. 5, in *Beati Alberti Magni Opera Omnia*, ed. Auguste Borgnet (Paris: Vives, 1891), 10. 371a.

115. *Liber de causis*, Liber I, tr. 3, cap. 4: *Taliter autem vocatum infinitum, perfectissimum est, et nullo indiget medio* (Borgnet, 10. 406b); cf. tr. 1, cap. 6, on God's direct action on all things (373b).

116. See Booth, 180-85, 195, and 202-04.

117. *Liber de causis*, Lib. I, tr. 4, ch. 3 (Borgnet, 414a-15b). Albert's position centers on his claim: *Per hoc enim quod dicamus primum principium penetrare per omnia propter sui simplicitatem, non determinatur ratio qua ostenditur qualiter bonitas fluens ab ipso efficitur in alio.*

118. Liber I, tr. 1, cap. 6, 372b.

119. Liber I, tr. 4, cap. 8, 428a. Yet in his response to authorities defending the origin of matter and form from the First Principle Philip the Chancellor had included a text he claimed to find in the Pseudo-Dionysius: *Item. Post monadem sequitur dyas, secundum Dyonisium. Ergo cum prima substantia non sit angelus, sub dyade cadit. Set prima duas est materie et forme. Ergo habet materiam et formam.* See D. O. Lottin, "La composition hylémorphique des substances spirituelles," 27.

120. The major arguments in the *Liber de causis* are advanced in Liber I, tr. 1, cap. 6, 372a-74a; but cf. tr. 4, cap. 8, 430b. For other passages, see *In II Sent.*, d. IA, art. 4 (ed. Borgnet, 27. 14b); and *Metaphysica* XI, tr. 2, caps. 8 and 16.

121. See Weisheipl, 244.

122. *Liber de causis*, Liber I, tr. 1, cap. 5, 371b.

123. Liber I, tr. 1, cap. 6, 372b-73a, giving five reasons; and tr. 3, cap. 4, 405b-407a, with four reasons. Cf. *Summa theologiae* II, tr. 1, q. 4, m. 1, art. 2, p. 2 (ed. Borgnet, 18. 37).

124. 372b: *de ratione enim primi est per se et per essentiam determinet ipsum ad actionem . . .*

125. Aquinas's major attacks on universal hylomorphism can be found in *In II Sent.* d. 3, q. 1, a. 1; *De ente et essentia* 5; *De substantiis separatis* 5-8; *De spiritualibus creaturis* a. 3; *Summa theologiae* Ia, q. 50, a. 2, ad 2, and q. 66, a. 2; and *Summa Contra Gentiles* II, 50. The issue of plurality of forms is treated in *In II Sent.* d. 12, q. 1, a. 4; *De sub. sep.* 6; *De spir. creat.* a. 1, and a. 3; *Quodlibet* XI, q. 5, a. 5; *STh*

Ia, q. 66, a. 2; *De anima* q. 6; *In II de Anima*, lect. 1; and *In I de generatione et corruptione*, lect. 10.8.

126. See Brunner, *Platonisme et Aristotelisme*, for an attempt at to look at Ibn Gabirol with "une autre objectivité."

127. For the relation between Eckhart and Maimonides, see *Meister Eckhart: Teacher and Preacher*, ed., Bernard McGinn (New York: Paulist Press, 1986), 15-30.

# From What is One and Simple only What is One and Simple Can Come to Be[*]

## Arthur Hyman

In an article entitled "Maimonides on Causality"[1] I undertook to show, in part, that Maimonides uses the theory of emanation to explain how incorporeal intelligences can causally affect other incorporeal intelligences and bodies as well, but rejects emanation as a cosmogonic theory. One of his major arguments against the emanationists, who hold that the world proceeds from God by necessity, is that they accept the principle that "from what is one and simple only what is one and simple can come to be,"[2] yet at the same time hold that a world of multiplicity necessarily emanates from a principle that is one and simple in all respects.

Maimonides attributes the emanationism he criticizes to Aristotle and his followers; but, more accurately, it is a theory proposed by al-Fārābī and Avicenna.[3] According to the Farabian version, from God, the First, who is one and simple, there necessarily emanates an incorporeal intelligence which is also one and simple. This Intelligence thinks itself, but also its cause. As a result of thinking

* This article was completed while I served as Lady Davis Visiting Professor at the Hebrew University of Jerusalem in the Spring of 1988. I wish to thank the Hebrew University for its hospitality and the Lady Davis Fellowship Trust for its support. I also thank Professors S. Pines, M. Idel and S. Rosenberg for their helpful comments.

its cause there emanates from it a second intelligence, while as a result of thinking itself there emanates from it the first celestial sphere. This dyadic emanative process continues until it comes to an end with the Agent Intellect and the sublunar world.[4]

The Avicennian version is somewhat more complex, since it rests on Avicenna's schematism of necessary and possible existence. From God, who is one and simple, there necessarily emanates a first incorporeal intelligence which is also one and simple. But while God is necessary through Himself, the emanated intelligence is possible through itself, necessary through its cause. Reflecting upon God, its cause, the first intelligence emanates a second intelligence; reflecting upon itself as necessary, it brings forth the soul of the first celestial sphere; and, reflecting upon itself as possible, it produces the body of the first celestial sphere. This now triadic process continues until, once again, it comes to an end with the Agent Intellect and the sublunar world.[5]

It will be helpful to examine the texts in which Maimonides discusses our principle and presents his critique:

> A proposition universally agreed upon, accepted by Aristotle and by all those who have philosophized, reads as follows: It is impossible that anything but a single simple thing (al-shay al-basīt, ha-davar ha-pashut) should proceed from a simple thing. If the thing is composite, there may proceed from it several things according to the number of simple things of which the compound is composed.[6]

Having provided some illustration for the latter point, he concludes:

> In accordance with this proposition, Aristotle [sc. al-Fārābī and Avicenna] says that what first proceeded from God was constituted by a single simple intellect only.

Maimonides' critique is lengthy, but two objections indicate its direction and are crucial to our investigation:

> [1] With regard to Aristotle's statement that the first intellect is the cause of the second, the second of the third and so on—even if there were thousands of degrees, the last intellect would indubitably still be simple. How then can composition [that is, multiplicity] have come to exist, the composition existing—as Aristotle believes—in beings in

virtue of necessity? . . . [2]  But even if we grant him his guess and conjecture, how can the intellects be a cause of the procession of the spheres from them?

Who are the philosophers that accept the principle "from what is one and simple only what is one and simple can come to be" yet hold that it can form the basis of a valid cosmogonic theory, and who are their opponents?  What are the models and arguments of each group?  What is the history of this issue within medieval Jewish philosophy?  Some of these questions have been discussed by Herbert Davidson and Barry Kogan, and I acknowledge my indebtedness to their studies.[7]

## I

Our problem had its origin in Plotinus.  Dissatisfied with a cosmogony that explains the origin of the world on the analogy of the production of an artifact by a craftsman,[8] Plotinus formulated the theory of emanation: The world proceeds from an ultimate principle, the One or the Good, like streams of water from a spring or like sunlight from the sun, like heat from fire, like cold from snow, or like perfume from something scented.[9]  The One is absolutely transcendent and beyond the capacities of the human mind.[10]  This thought is expressed in a passage from Plato's *Republic* (509B, 8-10) which reads, "the Good is not being (*ousia*), but is beyond it in dignity and surpassing power," which Plotinus often echoes.[11]  The One is unconditioned and unlimited.  Itself uncaused, it is the cause of things.  The categories of space and time do not apply to it.  It is not form nor definable.  It is not subject to motion or contingency, and it is ineffable.  "We must be forgiven for the terms we use," writes Plotinus in a characteristic passage, "if in speaking about Him in order to explain what we mean, we have to use language which we, in strict accuracy, do not admit to be applicable. *As if (hoyon)* must be understood with every term."[12]  Above all, the One is simple in all respects, admitting of no multiplicity.

The world, however, is manifold, and Plotinus must explain how multiplicity can proceed from something absolutely one.[13]  Even before this he must ask how anything at all can come to be from a principle that is self-sufficient, without needs or desires.  Invoking what has been called "the Principle of Plenitude" and what might be called "the dynamism of existence," Plotinus holds that whatever is perfect produces something other than itself.[14]   Thus, the One produces Intelligence (*nous*) as a hypostasis.   Like the One, Intelligence is one, yet at the same time it also contains multiplicity:

> Intellect is all things together and also not together, because each is a special power.  But the whole Intellect encompasses them as a genus does a species and a whole its parts.  The powers of seeds give a likeness of what we are talking about:  for all the parts are undistinguished in the whole, and their rational forming principles (*logoi*) are as in a central point. (*Enneads* V 9.6; cf. V 4.2.)

Turning to the question that concerns us most directly here, Plotinus asks "how from the One, if it is such as we say it is, anything else, whether a multiplicity or a dyad or a number, comes into existence . . ." (*Enneads* V 1.6).   He answers that what is produced must be inferior to its source and this inferiority is manifest in multiplicity.   But why does Intelligence proceed from the One? Plotinus answers that the First Intelligence is an image of the One (*Enneads* V 1.7).   To be sure the One does not think in the conventional fashion, but in its self-quest it has vision, and this vision is imitated by Nous.[15]   As intelligence, Nous requires intellectual objects.   As objects of thought, these are many, as belonging to the First Intelligence they are one:

> Intellect is not simple but many; it manifests a composition, of course an intelligible one, and already sees many things.  It is certainly also itself an intelligible [it is an object of thought], but it thinks as well [it is an intellect]:  so it is already two. (*Enneads* V 4.2; cf. III 8.9)

So the emanative process is the cause of multiplicity.   Like its source, the First Intelligence is one; but, having emanated and being intellect, it differs from its source in that it contains multiplicity within itself. This thesis became the mainstay of those who held that necessary emanation is compatible with the principle that "from what is one and simple only what is one and simple can come to be."

The Plotinian theory found a subsequent expression in Proclus'

*Elements of Theology.* While Plotinus' *Enneads* are rather associative, Proclus presents his views in geometric fashion, in propositions and proofs. Like Plotinus, he holds that the world proceeds from the One or Good and that the One is absolutely transcendent. The question of how multiplicity can come from what is absolutely one engages his attention at the very beginning of the *Elements.* Starting with the observation that the world is a multiplicity, Proclus begins with the propositions that "every manifold in some way participates in unity" (Prop. 1) and that "all that participates in unity is both one and not-one" (Prop. 2). With characteristic dialectical subtlety he argues: Since the manifold proceeds from the One it must somehow manifest the principle from which it comes, that is, it must be one; but since it is also derived from the One it *participates* in the One, that is, it is also not-one, that is, multiple. Proclus compares the One and what emanates from it to a root and its branches (Prop. 11; cf. *Enneads* II 8.3). As with Plotinus, "the dynamism of existence" is the cause of emanation (Props. 7 and 25). But Proclus differs from Plotinus in that he interposes henads or gods between the One and the First Intelligence (Props. 113-65, esp. 115).[16]

Like Plotinus, Proclus uses thought as a model to show how Nous can be both one and many: In every cognitive act, he argues, there is a knower that is one and objects of knowledge that are many. But since the First Intelligence is its own object of cognition, it is both one and many: "Every intelligence has intuitive knowledge of itself; but the First Intelligence knows itself only, and the intelligence and its object are here numerically one" (Prop. 167).

Neoplatonic theories came to the Islamic and Jewish worlds through Arabic translations of excerpts from Neoplatonic works. Among the key collections: *The Greek Sage, The Letter Concerning the Divine Science,* and, most important, the *Theology of Aristotle* (which circulated in two recensions) and *Concerning the Pure Good,* known in its Latin version as *Liber de Causis.* The *Theology* was a paraphrase of books 4, 5 and 6 of Plotinus' *Enneads.* The *Book of the Pure Good* comprised excerpts from Proclus' *Elements of Theology.*[17] Neoplatonism found a further line of development in the *Epistles of the Sincere Brethren*[18] and in the Neoplatonizing Aristotelianism of al-Fārābī and Avicenna.

The self-conscious human intellect is at the root of Avicenna's metaphysical and cosmogonic speculations (al-Shifā, De Anima, I 1).[19] This intellect has an immediate intuition of being and a concomitant intuition of the distinctions between essence and existence, and necessary and possible existence. That which is necessary through itself is its own cause, that which is possible through itself requires a cause in order to exist. From a world of possible existences Avicenna argues to the existence of a being necessary through itself and one and simple. This being is God (al-Shifā', Metaphysics, I 6 and 7).[20]

To explain how the world came to be—in Scriptural language, how it was created—and how a world of multiplicity can derive from a being that is one and simple, Avicenna turns to the Neoplatonic theory of emanation, interpreted in accordance with his own metaphysical scheme. As in the Greek Neoplatonists, God, the One, is absolutely transcendent, and the world emanates from Him by necessity. Reflecting upon Himself with a reflection wholly different from human thought, ruled by His own goodness, God emanates a first substance which is one. This substance cannot be composed of matter and form. It must therefore be an intelligence. Reflecting upon itself, this First Intelligence produces multiplicity. As we have already seen, reflecting upon its necessary cause, the First Intelligence emanates the intellect of the second celestial sphere, reflecting upon itself as necessary it produces the soul of the first celestial sphere, and reflecting upon itself as possible it brings forth the body of the first celestial sphere. It is here that Avicenna combines the notions of necessary and possible existence with the theory of emanation to explain how a world of multiplicity can come to be from a being totally one.[21]

The Avicennian (and Farabian) emanationist scheme found its critic in al-Ghazālī. In his Incoherence of the Philosophers (Tahāfut al-Falāsifa)[22] he offers one general and five specific arguments against it.[23] The burden of his proofs is to insist that the principle "from what is one and simple only what is one and simple can come to be" must be construed strictly. It follows that the Avicennian scheme cannot explain the origin of multiplicity. Of al-Ghazālī's arguments against necessary emanation, let us consider the two that are reflected in the Maimonidean critique.

According to the view of the Philosophers, the first argument goes, multiplicity can come to be in one of four ways: (1) through a difference in acting powers—a man, for example, commits one kind of act through the power of passion and another through the power of anger; (2) through a difference in the matters on which an agent acts—the sun whitens a garment, blackens the face of a man, melts certain substances and hardens others; (3) through a difference in instruments—the same carpenter performs different acts with a saw, an ax and an awl; or (4) through mediation (*tawassuṭ*), that is, by the interposition of an intermediary between agent and object. The first alternative is inapplicable to God, since His unity precludes a differentiation of powers within Him. The second and third are impossible, since they place matters or instruments on a par with God. This leaves mediation. But even this is impossible. For if the philosophers are correct in holding that "from something one and simple only something one and simple can come to be" it would follow that the world consists of unitary beings, not of anything composite. But this conflicts with the philosophers' thesis that within the world bodies are composed of form and matter, men and even celestial beings of soul and body (*Tahāfut*, Bouyges, 110; cf. Van Den Bergh, 104).

Another of al-Ghazālī's arguments important for the Maimonidean critique is that an act of thinking cannot produce a material substance. Let us perform a thought experiment. Assume that there exists a certain man who knows himself and his Creator. If a material substance can follow from an act of thought, it would be possible that in thinking of himself as possible this man could bring forth a celestial sphere, another intelligence, and a soul. But who would subscribe to such a conclusion? (*Tahāfut*, Bouyges, 129-30; cf. Van Den Bergh, 150). These and other arguments bring al-Ghazālī to the conclusion that only a volitional being can be a cause of multiplicity—a point on which Maimonides seems to agree, at least in part. With these backgrounds in mind, let us now consider the influence on medieval Jewish philosophy of our principle and its critique.

## II

Neoplatonism had at least a threefold history within medieval Jewish philosophy. Some writers, like Isaac Israeli and Solomon ibn Gabirol, developed their philosophy along more or less strict Neoplatonic lines. Others, like Abraham ibn Daud, accepted the Neoplatonic Aristotelianism of al-Fārābī and Avicenna. And still others—Maimonides belongs here—followed al-Ghazālī in his critique. Many Jewish philosophers were troubled by the necessitarian aspects of Neoplatonism. To remove this difficulty some introduced the divine will within the emanationist scheme, although it is not always clear how a given philosopher understood this will. Other Jewish philosophers relied on the so-called Pseudo-Empedoclean writings and a work by an unknown author, whom Alexander Altmann and Samuel Stern called "Ibn Hasdāy's Neoplatonist."[24]　These works interposed universal matter, or universal form and universal matter, between God and Intellect.

Isaac Israeli (d. 955) was the first medieval Jewish Neoplatonist. His views, scattered throughout his writings, are not always clear. Altmann and Stern published some new texts and translated and systematized his writings,[25] showing that he was primarily influenced by al-Kindī and Ibn Hasdāy's Neoplatonist.[26] Committed to the Scriptural account of creation, Israeli describes God[27] as the "Creator" (al-bāri') and argues for creation out of nothing. In characteristic Neoplatonic fashion, Israeli holds that God is transcendent, not comprehensible by the human mind. Yet, as Altmann pointed out, negative theology seems to be absent from Israeli's account. Acting without needs or desires, God, through his goodness and love, created the world. In a departure from the Neoplatonic scheme and apparently to counter its necessitarian aspect, Israeli ascribes the creation of the world, at least its first stage, to the "power and the will" of God (Book of Substances IV 5r, 86). Affirming creation out of nothing, Israeli ascribes the creation of universal matter and form (wisdom) and of the Intellect to the "power and will" (qudra and 'irāda) of God. For Israeli, unlike Ibn Gabirol later on, power and will are attributes of God, not separate hypostases. But the world subsequent to the First Intellect proceeds from it not by free creation but by necessary emanation.

Clearly Israeli tries to strike a balance between volitional creation and necessary emanation. Under the influence of Ibn Hasdāy's Neoplatonist and the Pseudo-Empedoclean writings, he modifies the Plotinian and Proclean schemes.[28] Intellect is no longer the first hypostasis proceeding from God; universal matter and form emanate first. Alluding to the problem of many out of one, Israeli describes universal, or first matter as "the first substance which subsists in itself and is the substratum of diversity" (*Mantua Text* 1, 119). Such matter is "the universal substance which is one in number, exists by itself and is the substratum of diversity absolutely" (*Book of Substances* IV 5v, 86). Diversity is provided by universal form, which Israeli identifies with perfect wisdom, the pure radiance and clear splendor (*Mantua Text* 1, 119) or "the light created by the power of God without mediator" (*Book of Definitions* 2, 25-26). In some passages it appears that universal matter and form are constitutive principles of Intellect as first hypostasis; but on balance Israeli seems to hold that they precede Intellect in the cosmogonic scheme.

In maintaining that universal matter and form are the first emanated hypostases, Israeli and others like him provide an alternative model for the emanation of multiplicity from what is one and simple. The new model is based on a reworking of Aristotle's conception of substance. According to Aristotle, primary substances in the sublunar world are one and individual and are composed of form and matter. Form makes a substance what it is, while matter serves as substratum of the form and principle of individuation. Israeli and his sources reverse this scheme. It is now the matter that gives a thing its determinate nature, while form is incidental to matter and serves as the principle of diversification: The bronze statue is bronze that happens to be a statue not a statue that happens to be bronze. With universal matter and form present as first hypostases, created by God's free act, Israeli seems to feel that there need be no difficulty in accounting for the origin of diversity.

There is no conclusive evidence that Solomon ibn Gabirol (d. 1058), the Avicebron of the Latins, knew the writings of Israeli, but it is clear that he was heir to the same Neoplatonic tradition upon which Israeli relied. Ibn Gabirol presented his ideas not only in his famous philosophic work, *Fons Vitae*, but also in a religious poem, *The Kingly Crown*.[29] There are differences between the two works, but their cosmogonic scheme is essentially the same. Ibn Gabirol affirms the transcendence of God; but, unlike Israeli, he holds that God is known through negation, as is clear from a number of stanzas dealing with God's attributes in the *Kingly Crown*. Thus:

> Thou art One and in the mystery of Thy Oneness the wise of heart are astonished, for they know not what it is.
>
> Thou art One and Thy Oneness neither diminishes nor increases, neither lacks nor exceeds.
>
> Thou art One, but not as the One that is counted or owned, for number and change cannot reach Thee, nor attribute nor form . . . (p. 28)

Ibn Gabirol differs again from Israeli in that he posits a first hypostasis (perhaps two) between God—called in *Fons Vitae, essentia prima*—and universal matter and universal form. He variously calls this hypostasis "Wisdom" (*sapientia*) or "Logos" (*verbum*) or "Will" (*voluntas*). In the *Kingly Crown*, "wisdom" (*hokhmah*) and "will" (*hefez*) are distinct, successive hypostatic emanations:

> Thou art Wise, and wisdom, the source of life, flows from Thee (*mimekha noba'at*), and every man is too brutish to know Thy wisdom.
>
> Thou art Wise, prior to all pre-existence, and wisdom was with Thee as a nurseling.
>
> Thou are Wise, and from Thy wisdom Thou didst send forth (*'ozalta*) a predestined will (*hefez mezuman*) and made it as an artisan and craftsman to draw the stream of being from the void [nothing]. (32-33)

In the religious poem at least, Ibn Gabirol appears to maintain voluntary creation out of nothing. But the relation between "Logos," "Wisdom" and "Will" is less clear in *Fons Vitae*. In most passages Ibn Gabirol places "Will" between the First Essence and universal matter and form. For example, when the student inquires concerning the objects of knowledge, the master informs him that they are: (1) matter and form, (2) Will, and (3) the First Being (I 7). Similarly, toward the end of the Fifth Treatise, Ibn Gabirol speaks largely about will (V 36-40; cf. I 2). But there are other passages where he identifies "will" with "acting logos" (*verbum agens*) or "wisdom."

Thus, speaking once again of the three kinds of knowledge, he now describes the second as "knowledge of the acting logos, that is, will" (V 36). In another passage he speaks of "will, that is, wisdom" (V 42). So it is not too clear how Ibn Gabirol conceives of creation in *Fons Vitae*. He speaks of creation by will in several places (e.g., V 36-40), suggesting that creation took place through a volitional act. Yet he also uses models for creation like the flowing forth of water from a fountain, the reflection of light in a mirror, and the issuance of human speech (V 41, 43), suggesting that creation should be understood as necessary emanation. Whatever the solution, it is clear for our purposes, that Ibn Gabirol posits "will" (and/or "wisdom") and universal matter and universal form as intermediaries between God ("the First Essence") and Intellect in order to explain how multiplicity can come to be from a unitary being.[30]

Abraham Ibn Daud (d. ca. 1180), generally considered the first Jewish Aristotelian, brings the Avicennian solution into Jewish philosophic thought, devoting to it a chapter of his *The Exalted Faith*.[31] Ibn Daud maintains that God is absolutely one and identifies Him with Avicenna's necessarily existent. He holds that divine attributes must be understood in terms of negations. Invoking the schematism we have already met in al-Ghazālī's critique of Avicenna, Ibn Daud considers the four ways in which multiplicity might come to be from a unity and concludes that the world's multiplicity must arise through mediation. Following the approach developed by Avicenna, Ibn Daud reasons that Intellect, called "angel" in the Torah, proceeds from God "without an intermediary" (*beli 'emza'i*) (152, 9-11). Like its source, this universal Intellect is one, but "its oneness is not like the oneness of the First" (152b, 12). The First is necessarily existent through Himself, but Intellect is only possibly existent through itself (152b, 12-153a, 2). Possible through itself, necessary through another, Intellect is composed of something *like* matter and form. Its possible existence is *like* matter, its necessary existence from another is *like* form (153a, 2-5). But although he holds that Intellect is composed of something *like* matter and form, Ibn Daud distances himself from Ibn Gabirol. He does not interpose universal matter and universal form between God and Intellect or hold that even incorporeal beings are composed of matter and form. Probably influenced by the Aristotelian teaching that

incorporeal intelligences cannot be composed of matter and form, he
writes:

> Ibn Gabirol, in the fifth treatise of his book, tried to establish the
> existence of hyle [matter] and form [in the incorporeal intelligences].
> He did not explain that [what] they have is something like hyle and
> something like form. Rather, he ordained that they have matter and
> form, and when he tried to establish this, he could not. (153a, 6-9)

Ibn Daud continues in the Avicennian mode by holding that from the
First Intellect there emanates another, as well as the body and soul of
the first celestial sphere, and so forth until the procession ends with
the Agent Intellect and the sublunar world.

This brings us back to Maimonides. His critique is clearly
indebted to al-Ghazālī's *Incoherence of the Philosophers*.[32] He
adopts al-Ghazālī's argument that even if it is admitted that other
substances emanate from God, it follows that these substances are
simple, so that, at best, the universe is an aggregate of simple
substances. Similarly, Maimonides' argument that a material
substance cannot result from intellectual reflection is the fifth of al-
Ghazālī's more specific arguments.[33]

If necessary emanation cannot explain how a world of
multiplicity can come to be from a being absolutely one and simple,
is there a theory that can provide an adequate account? Agreeing in
part with al-Ghazālī, Maimonides turns to volitional causality for a
solution. He writes: "Every agent, acting in virtue of purpose and
will and not in virtue of its nature, accomplishes many different acts"
(*Guide* II 22, 317). But Maimonides does not have in mind a divine
will like the human will. In his discussion of divine attributes he
rules out the view that will in God is a disposition.[34] To hold that
God created the world through his volition solved the problem that
those who believed in necessary emanation were unable to solve. But
it must be added that Maimonides also differed from al-Ghazālī. For
al-Ghazālī denied the principle of necessary causality altogether,
admitting divine volition as the only cause, while Maimonides
followed the Aristotelian tradition in holding that necessary causes
are operative in the sublunar world.[35]

## III

One more opinion concerning our problem must engage our attention, that of Averroes (d. 1198), Maimonides' Muslim contemporary. As Davidson[36] and Kogan[37] have shown, Averroes, in his Epitome of the *Metaphysics*, accepted a modified version of the emanationism of al-Fārābī and Avicenna, but—possibly as the result of having read al-Ghazālī's *Incoherence*—revised his opinion in the annotations to the Epitome, and in the Middle and Long Commentaries on the *Metaphysics*. He now abandoned the theory of emanation; and instead of distinguishing between God and the mover of the outermost celestial sphere, he now identifies the two.

Through the Hebrew translations of his works,[38] Averroes' opinions became widely known in Jewish philosophic circles. In fact, next to Maimonides himself, he became the most important philosophic authority during the post-Maimonidean period. In the discussion of our problem his critique of al-Fārābī and Avicenna as well as his own views play an important role. Whatever other Averroean sources may be at work, it is clear that the Third Discussion of the *Incoherence of the Incoherence* was central. Here only a sampling from three of the major participants in the discussion can be presented.

Shem Tov ben Joseph ibn Falaquera (d. 1295) addresses the issue in his *Moreh ha-Moreh*[39] (completed in 1280), and his account is taken over verbatim by Joseph ibn Kaspi (d. 1340) in his *'Amudei Kesef.*[40] Both works are commentaries on the *Guide*; and the occasion for the discussion is *Guide* II 22, the chapter we have already highlighted. Ibn Falaquera investigates the origin of our problem, what he takes to be a Farabian-Avicennian misunderstanding, and the correct solution proposed by Averroes. Citing Porphyry,[41] Ibn Falaquera traces the origin of our problem to the philosophers of Greece. Having observed that whatever comes to be requires a cause and that whatever is moved requires a mover, they came to the conclusion that there must exist a unitary being that is the ultimate cause of all that comes to be and the ultimate mover of everything moved. But having agreed on the principle, they disagreed concerning its interpretation. Aristotle and his follower Averroes understood it correctly; Porphyry, al-Fārābī and Avicenna understood it incorrectly. Invoking the authority of Averroes, Ibn Falaquera explains that the error of al-Fārābī and Avicenna arose because the two attempted to accommodate the opinion of the philosophers to that of the masses. Holding that the philosophic view that the world is eternal and that the mover of the outermost sphere is the First Principle is incompatible with the belief that the world was created by God, al-Fārābī and Avicenna tried to effect a compromise by differentiating between God and the mover of the outermost sphere. Having made this distinction, they explained creation by holding that the world came to be from God by means of emanation. But with the acceptance of this theory, the Ghazalian critique applies: how can multiplicity come to be from what is absolutely one and simple? Moreover, the Farabian-Avicennian account deprives God of one of His noblest attributes, as the cause of motion.

In identifying God with the mover of the outermost celestial sphere, Averroes provides the correct account. The theory of emanation is now no longer needed. By the Averroean account the world is eternal and self-contained and "creation," correctly understood, becomes an account of how God, the mover of the outermost sphere, is the ultimate cause of the changes and motions within the world. Averroes and his Jewish followers do not seem to be troubled by these conclusions since, as they see it, they contain the true, that is, philosophic interpretation of the Scriptural motif of creation. The Averroean scheme provides the correct solution:[42] The world consists of incorporeal intelligences that are one and simple and of bodies composed of matter and form. The incorporeal intelligences "ascend to" (ya'alu el), i.e., are causally dependent on the unitary intellect that moves the outermost sphere; bodies within the world "ascend to" the composite celestial body. Thus, from what is one and simple only what is one and simple comes to be; what is composite comes only from what is composite.

Isaac Albalag (late thirteenth century) translated al-Ghazālī's *Opinions (Intentions) of the Philosophers* from Arabic into Hebrew and added critical notes entitled, rather tellingly, *Correction of the Opinions* (1292) to his translation.[43] Albalag contends that al-Ghazālī intended to present the opinions of the philosophers (sc. Avicenna) in order to refute them afterwards, but in the end accepted them (5:5-9; 21). Albalag's discussion of the origin of our problem is more extensive than Ibn Falaquera's and contains views not found in the *Moreh ha-Moreh*: Ignorant of the methods of demonstration and employing dialectical arguments, ancient thinkers held that the world is governed by two principles, good and evil. They reasoned that good and evil are opposites and cannot come from the same principle. Subsequently, however, philosophers began to realize that everything, including good and evil, is derived from a unitary principle, that is, from God. Having acknowledged that the world depends on an ultimate being that is one, and recognizing that the world is multiple, Aristotle and the Sages of Israel alike[44] agreed that from something one and simple a world of multiplicity comes to be (59:24-60:3; 204).

The notion that "from what is one and simple only what is one and simple can come to be" was introduced by some unnamed ancient "philosophizers" through an error of logic. Noting that a unitary effect can come only from a unitary cause, these "philosophizers" erroneously thought that this proposition is convertible: that what is multiple cannot come from what is one and simple. It was this error that presented them with their problem (60:3-10; 205). For a solution they turned to the theory of emanation. The "philosophizers" did not distinguish between an agent that acts through its essence and an agent that acts through an attribute added to its essence. An agent of the latter kind can produce only one effect: heat as an attribute added to the essence of fire can only produce heat. But an agent of the former kind—an intellect for example—can produce many effects (55:17-21; 198).

Albalag mentions in passing that al-Ghazālī raised many questions concerning our principle in *The Incoherence of the Philosophers* (Albalag calls it *Shibush ha-Pilosophim*), but his arguments differ from those of al-Ghazālī mentioned earlier in this paper.[45] Albalag finds contradictions in al-Ghazālī's views as presented in the *Opinions of the Philosophers*. Al-Ghazālī accepts the principle that "from what is one and simple only what is one and simple can come to be," yet holds that multiplicity can come to be from something one and simple. For example, God knows the species of existing things in unitary fashion, yet from this divine knowledge the multiplicity of species existing in the world comes to be. Again, the proponents of the principle deny that multiplicity can come from God, yet admit that a multiplicity of forms can come to be from the Agent Intellect or Giver of Forms—which, however different from God, is still a unitary intellect. Even if it is admitted that from the forms residing in the Agent Intellect there proceed the embodied forms existing in the sublunar world, it can still be asked how from a single form in the Agent Intellect there proceeds the multiplicity of forms of individual substances belonging to a given species (55:2-16; 197-198).

Albalag, like Averroes, identifies God the Creator with the mover of the outermost celestial sphere (29:9-10; 132 and 61:17-19; 30) and interprets creation as an eternal act. Creation without beginning or end, he argues, is superior to creation that has a beginning in time, and for this reason should be ascribed to God. To create, in its most proper sense, he argues, means to bring something from potentiality to actuality—and potentiality requires an underlying matter. Since matter exists only in the sublunar world, God can be said to be the Creator only insofar as He is the ultimate cause of the changes that take place within that world (62:10-18).

While Ibn Falaquera still tries to find some interpretation of our principle, Albalag rejects it altogether. So he has only to show how a unitary principle can be the cause of multiplicity. This he does in several ways, all based on the supposition that the world is eternal. Since all the corporeal effects (motions) within the world are dependent on the motion of the outermost sphere, one such argument goes, and God is the cause of the motion of that sphere, God can be said to be the cause of the many motions within the world (29:9-12; 132). According to another argument, the essences of the incorporeal intelligences consist of what each intelligence knows of God. As the unitary object of the thoughts of these intelligences, God is their cause (63:7-16; 99). According to still another argument, God, as the form of the world, may be compared to the form that makes a man what he is. Just as each of the limbs and organs of man has its own structure and motion, yet each is dependent on the human form, so each of the celestial spheres has its own structure and motion, yet all are dependent on God, the form of the world (96:14-97:9; 95-96). From these and similar arguments it follows that God is the first efficient, formal and final cause of the world (92:8-11; 102).

Of the three post-Maimonideans, or post-Averroeans, considered in this paper, Moses of Narbonne, known as Narboni (d. 1362), most closely follows Averroes in discussing our problem. Most of what he has to say in his Commentary on *Guide* II 22 consists of quotations from, paraphrases of, or elaborations on the Third Discussion in the *Incoherence of the Incoherence*.[46] He tells his reader: "And I saw fit to collect in this place whatever words of Averroes in the *Incoherence of the Incoherence* are appropriate, and I shall expand the explanation" (34b, 36-37).

Narboni's account of the origin of our problem is, with one addition[47] and some deletions,[48] an almost literal translation of a passage in Averroes' *Incoherence of the Incoherence*: Ancient Greek thinkers at first supposed that there are two ultimate principles, those of good and evil, but through dialectical arguments they came to realize that there must be one ultimate principle, since all things tend toward an end, the order existing in the world. This order is like that which an army receives by having a single leader or like that which a state receives by having a single ruler (34b, 37-51).[49] Having accepted that there is one ultimate principle and holding additionally that from something one and simple only something one and simple can come to be, the ancient philosophers wondered how this unitary principle can be the cause of multiplicity. The question was answered in three ways: Anaxagoras held that multiplicity comes to be through matter; some unnamed philosophers believed that it comes to be through instruments; and Plato affirmed that it comes to be through intermediaries. While among these opinions that of Plato is the most adequate, it still cannot explain how from an incorporeal intelligence matter can come to be (34b, 51-35a, 6).[50]

The difficulty arose, continues Narboni, because the ancient philosophers and their Muslim followers, al-Fārābī and Avicenna, believed that God, the First Agent, acts like a simple, unitary agent in the perceptible world. To be sure, a simple agent in the perceptible world can only have one effect, but the First Agent can have many effects. One who distinguishes correctly between the perceptible, material world and the intelligible, immaterial world will understand that bodies composed of matter and form "ascend to" (*ya'alu el*), that is, are causally dependent on the (composite) celestial body,[51] while the incorporeal intelligences "ascend to" the unitary First Principle which is their formal, final and efficient cause (35a, 6-11).[52]

Narboni is primarily concerned with explaining how multiplicity can come to be from a unitary principle, but he takes account of the rival opinions by showing that the principle "from what is one and simple only what is one and simple can come to be" correctly understood is valid and that matter, instruments and intermediaries all have some role in the origin of multiplicity. To explain how multiplicity can arise from a unitary principle he turns to an Averroean argument. There exist in the world composite substances such as those composed of matter and form or of the four elements, whose existence comes to be through the conjunction of their component parts. The bestower of conjunction is, therefore, also the bestower of existence. But since everything conjoined is conjoined only through a unity within it and this unity is ultimately dependent on a unitary First Principle, it follows that this principle is the cause of both unity and multiplicity. It is the cause of unity insofar as the unities existing in the world are dependent on it, and it is the cause of multiplicity insofar as these unities receive it in accordance with the diversity of their component parts (35a, 30-40).[53]

Refining this analysis and, once again, using an Averroean source, Narboni undertakes to show how the various multiplicities in the world come to be with the aid of intermediaries, matter and instruments.[54] Each incorporeal intelligence is a unitary substance, but each, in accordance with its rank, has a different understanding of the First Principle. This difference accounts for their multiplicity. The differences among the celestial spheres result from their having different causes. Each sphere has its own mover (efficient cause), its own form, its own matter and, through its acts in the world, its own purpose. Here the reliance is on instrumentalities. Cautiously Narboni adds that if the celestial body possesses matter, it is a matter of a special kind,[55] and that the philosophers did not believe that the celestial bodies existed for the sake of their effects in the sublunar world.[56] Turning to the sublunar world, Narboni, still following Averroes, finds that the differences among the four elements depend on the differences in their matter and on their closeness to or remoteness from the celestial bodies, their movers.[57] Generation and corruption, of course, depend on the motion of the sun along the ecliptic. When the sun approaches the sublunar world it causes generation; when it recedes it causes corruption.[58]

Summarizing how multiplicity comes to be in the sublunar world and attempting to do justice to the alternative accounts, Narboni states that differences in that world arise from four causes: difference of agents, difference of matter, difference of instruments, and difference of intermediaries. These intermediaries (the heavenly bodies) transmit the acts of the First Agent without its direct interference. Apparently somewhat hard pressed to find room for instruments in this scheme, Narboni states that intermediaries are similar to instruments. To illustrate how differences can arise through differences in the recipients and how some differentiated things can be the cause of others, Narboni invokes the example of color. Color in the air differs from color in the eye, and again from color in the common sense, in the imagination, and finally in the memory (35b, 2-17).[59]

## Notes

1. In S. Pines and Y. Yovel, eds., *Maimonides and Philosophy*, 157-72. See also, A. Hyman, "Maimonides on Creation and Emanation," in *Studies in Medieval Philosophy*, ed. J. F. Wippel (Washington: Catholic University of America Press, 1987), 59-61.

2. The principle is found in two versions: (1) "from what is one only what is one can come to be," and (2) "from what is simple only what is simple can come to be." Except for direct quotations, I have combined the two versions in this paper.

3. Maimonides' account and critique applies to both philosophers, but there is evidence that it is primarily directed against Avicenna: (1) while he rejects Avicenna's account of emanationism as a cosmogonic theory, he accepts his cosmology in preference to that of al-Fārābī (*Guide* II 4); (2) he accepts the Avicennian distinction between necessary and possible existence (*Guide* II, Introduction, Props. 19 and 20; II 1); (3) the Ghazalian critique of necessary emanation, to which Maimonides is indebted, aims primarily at the Avicennian version; (4) Shem Tob writes in his commentary on *Guide* II 22: ". . . and the Master thought that concerning these matters the opinion of Avicenna is that of Aristotle"; *Guide* (Warsaw, 1872; repr. Jerusalem, 1959-1960) 2.49r.

4. *Al-Farabi on the Perfect State*, II 3, 100-05, 362-67; *Al-Fārābī's The Political Regime (Al-Siyāsa al-Madaniyya)* ed., F. M. Najjar (Beirut: Catholic Press, 1964), 52 l. 5 - 55 l. 5. The German tr. in *Die Staatsleitung von Alfarabi*, eds., F. Dieterici and F. Brönnle (Leiden: Brill, 1904), 28-32, is based on an inferior text. See also A.-R. Badawi, *Histoire de la philosophie en Islam* (Paris: Vrin, 1972) 2.538-45; Herbert Davidson, "Alfarabi and Avicenna on the Active Intellect

in the *Cuzari* and Hallevi's Theory of Causality," *Revue des Études Juives* 131 (1972): 354-57; "Averroes on the Active Intellect as a Cause of Existence," 195; *Proofs for Eternity*, 206-07; T. A. Druart, "Alfarabi and Emanationism," in J. F. Wippel, ed., *Studies in Medieval Philosophy* (Washington: Catholic University of America Press, 1987), 23-43; M. Fakhry, *A History of Islamic Philosophy* (New York: Columbia University Press, 1970), 136-38. The account given here is from *Al-Farabi on the Perfect State*. But in a more refined analysis in the same work (III 7) he holds that each celestial sphere has its own form, variously described as intellect or soul, which is distinct from the incorporeal intelligence governing the sphere (120-25, 376-77). But this does not change the dyadic character of the scheme. According to al-Fārābī's cosmology, God is followed by ten incorporeal intelligences, governing, in descending order, the spheres of the diurnal motion (the all-encompassing sphere), the fixed stars, Saturn, Jupiter, Mars, the Sun, Venus, Mercury, and the Moon; the tenth, the Agent Intellect, governs the sublunar world.

5.　See S. M. Afnan, *Avicenna: His Life and Works* (London: Allen and Unwin, 1958), 132-35; Badawi, *Histoire* 2.648-56; Fakhry, 172-77; A.-M. Goichon, *La distinction de l'essence et de l'existence d'après Ibn Sīnā*, 201-59; B. S. Kogan, "Averroes and the Theory of Emanation," 384-87; *Averroes and the Metaphysics of Causation*, 248-49; S. H. Nasr, *An Introduction to Islamic Cosmological Doctrines*, rev. ed. (Boulder: Shambala, 1978), 197-214. Avicenna's order of the celestial spheres is the same as al-Fārābī's, except that he places Venus and Mercury above the Sun. For the controversy over the two planets' positions, see Maimonides, *Guide* II 9.

6.　*Guide* II 22, 317. The following versions of the *Guide* were used: Arabic: ed. I. Joel (Jerusalem, 1930-31); Hebrew tr., Samuel Ibn Tibbon, ed., Y. Even Shemu'el (Jerusalem: Mossad Harav Kook, 1981-82). Page references here are to the Pines translation.

7.　See notes 4 and 5 above.

8.　See A. H. Armstrong, "Plotinus," in *The Cambridge History of Later Greek and Early Medieval Philosophy*, 239-41; D. J. O'Meara, *Structure hiérarchique dans la pensée de Plotin*, 68-69, 71-73, 78-79; R. T. Wallis, *Neoplatonism*, 63.

9.　*Enneads* III 8.10; V 1.6; cf. V 4.1. For the Greek, *Plotini Opera*, eds., P. Henry and H. R. Schwyzer (Oxford: Oxford University Press, 1964-82), 3 vols. Unless otherwise noted, the translations cited here are Armstrong's. See also his *Cambridge History*, 236-49; E. Bréhier, *Philosophy of Plotinus*, 47-52; J. M. Rist, *Plotinus: The Road to Reality*, 66-83.

10. Rist 25-26.
11. See Bréhier, 134-35. The allusions to this phrase have two versions: (1) "the One is beyond being," and (2) "the One is beyond Intellect." See "Index Fontium," *Plotini Opera* **3**.357.
12. *Enneads* VI 8.13; Armstrong, *Plotinus*, 56.
13. See Armstrong, *Cambridge History* 241-43; Bréhier, 136-41; Wallis, 57.
14. *Enneads* V 4.1-2; V 1.6; V 2.1; cf. III 8.10, **5**.394, n. 1; see O'Meara, 42-44; Rist, 66-71; Wallis, 61-66. Wallis mentions Lovejoy's "Principle of Plenitude" on 64-65.
15. The text is problematic; see Armstrong on *Enneads* V 1.7, **5**.34, n. 1.
16. See *Elements*, 257-60 (Dodds' commentary); Wallis, 147-53. In one passage Proclus writes: "the One is prior to Intelligence." Prop. 20. But this passage occurs before the section in which he discusses the henads.
17. See, A.-R. Badawi, *La transmission de la philosophie greque au monde arabe* (Paris: Vrin, 1968), 46-73; Fakhry 32-44; J. Kraemer, "Neoplatonism," *Encyclopaedia Judaica* **12**.958-62; F. E. Peters, *Aristoteles Arabus* (Leiden: Brill, 1968), 56-57, 72-74. An English translation of the Arabic excerpts of the *Enneads* appears in Henry and Schwyzer, **2**; comparative tables of the Greek and Arabic are found at **2**.489-501.
18. See, I. R. Netton, *Muslim Neoplatonists: An Introduction to the Thought of the Brethren of Purity* (London: Allen and Unwin, 1982), 32-36; Ikhwān al-Ṣafā', *The Case of the Animals vs. Man before the King of the Jinn*, tr., Goodman, 57-58, 71, 110-12, 137-38, 171-75.
19. Arabic: *Avicenna's De Anima*, ed. F. Rahman (London: Oxford University Press, 1959), 16; Arabic and French: *Psychologie d'ibn Sina (Avicenne) d'après son oeuvre Aš-Šifa*, ed and tr. Ján Bakoš (Prague: Chekoslavak Academy of Sciences, 1956), 12-13. See also, *al-Shifā'*, De Anima V 7; Rahman, 225; Bakoš, 181. S. M. Afnan, 150-52; Goichon, 13-15.
20. Ed., G. C. Anawati, et al. (Cairo, 1960); tr., Avicenne, *La Métaphysique du Shifā*, (Paris: Vrin, 1978-85). For the essence-existence distinction, Afnan, 115-21; Goichon, 130-48; P. Morewedge, "Philosophical Analysis and Ibn Sina's 'Essence-Existence' Distinction," *JAOS* 92 (1972): 425-35; F. Rahman, "Essence and Existence in Avicenna," *Medieval and Renaissance Studies* 4 (London: Warburg Institute, 1958): 1-16, "Essence and Existence in Ibn Sina: The Myth and the Reality." For necessity and possibility, Afnan, 121-26; Fakhry, 142-56; Goichon, 151-80; G. Hourani, "Ibn Sina on Necessary and Possible Existence"; G. Smith, "Avicenna and the

Possibles," *New Scholasticism* 17 (1943): 340-57.

21. *Shifā'*, Metaphysics, IX 4, especially, Arabic: 405, l. 9 - 407, l. 8; French: 2.140-42.

22. Arabic: Algazel, *Tahāfot al-Falāsifat*, ed., M. Bouyges (Beirut: Catholic Press, 1927); English: largely in *Tahāfut al-Tahāfut*, tr., Van Den Bergh.

23. Bouyges, 110-30; cf. Van Den Bergh, 104-50. See Davidson, *Proofs*, 206-09; Kogan, "Averroes and the Theory of Emanation," 392-93 and n. 3; Goodman, "Did al-Ghazālī Deny Causality," *Studia Islamica* 47 (1978): 83-120.

24. See Stern's "Ibn Ḥasdāy's Neoplatonist: A Neoplatonic Treatise and its Influence on Isaac Israeli and the Longer Version of the Theology of Aristotle."

25. A. Altmann and S. M. Stern, *Isaac Israeli*; page references below are to their translation.

26. *Israeli*, xi-xiv.

27. *Israeli*, 151-58.

28. *Israeli*, 159-64.

29. For the *Fons Vitae*, Latin:  ed. C. Baeumker; Modern Hebrew translation from the Latin: J. Blaustein (Tel Aviv: Maḥbarot le-Sifrut, 1950). For the poem, *Keter Malkhut*, ed., I. A. Zeidman (Jerusalem: Mossad Harav Kook, 1950); *The Kingly Crown*, tr., Bernard Lewis (London: Vallentine, Mitchell, 1961); page references below are to the Lewis translation.

30. For a different reading of Ibn Gabirol's idea of Will, see J. Schlanger, *La Philosophie de Salomon ibn Gabirol*, 277-98.

31. Ibn Daud, *Ha-Emunah ha-ramah (The Exalted Faith)* II 4.3, Samuelson keyed to the pagination of the manuscript, as cited here; see also Samuelson's summary, 169-72.

32. See L. E. Goodman, "Three Meanings of the Idea of Creation."

33. A simplified version of the argument appears in Saadiah's *Emunot ve-De'ot*, I 3; ed., S. Landauer (Leiden, 1880), 46, ll. 8-12; ed. with modern Hebrew tr., J. Kafih (Jerusalem: Sura, 1969/70), 49; medieval Hebrew tr., Judah ibn Tibbon (Josefow, 1888; repr., Jerusalem: Maqor, 1962), 31b; tr., A. Altmann, in *Three Jewish Philosophers* (New York: Athenaeum, 1969), 67. The argument also appears in Judah Halevi's *Kuzari* IV 25, eds., D. H. Baneth and H. Ben-Shammai (Jerusalem: Magnes Press, 1977), 183-84; Hebrew: ed. A. Zifroni (Tel Aviv: Maḥbarot le-Sifrut, 1960), 267-68; tr., H. Hirschfeld (New York: Schocken, 1964), 238-39.

34. See *Guide*, I 56, 131; II 18, 300-01.

35. See *Guide*, II 22, 319-20. For this paragraph, see Hyman, "Maimonides on Creation," 54-59.

36. Davidson, "Averroes on the Active Intellect," 192-201.

37. Kogan, "Averroes on the Theory of Emanation," 384-404; *Averroes on the Metaphysics of Causation*, 248-255.

38. See H. A. Wolfson, "Plan for the Publication of a *Corpus Commentariorum Averrois in Aristotelem*," *Speculum* 38 (1963): 88-104; repr. in *Studies in the History of Philosophy and Religion*, 1.430-54.

39. Ed. M. L. Bisliches (Pressburg, 1837; reprinted in *Sheloshah Qadmonei Mefarshei ha-Moreh* Jerusalem, 1961). This edition as well as those of Ibn Kaspi's *'Amudei Kesef* and Narboni's Commentary on Maimonides' *Guide*, which appear in the same volume, are unsatisfactory and must be supplemented by manuscript materials.

40. Ed. S. Werbluner (Frankfurt a. M., 1848). On *'Amudei Kesef* in Kaspi's literary work, see B. Mesch, *Studies in Joseph Ibn Caspi* (Leiden: Brill, 1975), 52, n. 75. For another instance of Kaspi's indebtedness to Ibn Falaquera, see Mesch, 98, n. 99.

41. See *Moreh ha-Moreh*, 104-06. Ibn Falaquera's "quotation" from Porphyry is rather strange. It is probably based on Averroes' observation that Porphyry, who was not a very proficient philosopher, accepted the view that multiplicity came to be through intermediates. See *Incoherence of the Incoherence* III, Bouyges, 259-60; Van Den Bergh, **1**.154 and **2**.100 (note on 154.6). It seems likely that Ibn Falaquera used Averroes' comment to find an "ancestor" for the Farabian-Avicennian error. Cf. Badawi, *Histoire* **2**.814. How the late Medieval Jewish philosophers used their sources deserves further study. For a good example, see, A. J. Ivry, "Moses of Narbonne's 'Treatise on the Perfection of the Soul': A Methodological and Conceptual Analysis," *JQR*, N.S. 57 (1965-66): 271-79.

42. This argument consists of a literal translation of a small section of *Incoherence of the Incoherence* III, Bouyges, 175-76; Van Den Bergh, 105-06.

43. See, M. Steinschneider, *Die Hebräischen Übersetzungen* (Berlin:, 1893; Graz: Akademische Druck-und Verlaganstalt, 1956), 299-306. Albalag did not complete the translation; it was finished by Isaac ibn Pollegar. *Sefer Tiqqun ha-De'ot*, ed. G. Vajda (Jerusalem: Israel Academy of Sciences and Humanities, 1973). A French translation of most of the work appears in G. Vajda, *Isaac Albalag: Averroïst juif, traducteur et annotateur d'al-Ghazālī* (Paris: Vrin, 1960). Of the numbers cited parenthetically here, those before the semicolon refer to Vajda's edition; those after, to his translation.

44. Throughout his work, Albalag strives to show that the Averroean opinions he accepts are in harmony with Scripture and the sayings of the rabbinic Sages.

45. Albalag mentions the *Incoherence of the Philosophers* (96:7-8; 95) but never refers explicitly to Averroes' *Incoherence of the Incoherence.* He mentions only in passing that Averroes answered al-Ghazālī's attack on the Philosophers (5:9-10; 21). But Vajda in his *Isaac Albalag,* 34, mentions the influence of Averroes' *Incoherence of the Incoherence* on Albalag and cites examples in a number of notes.

46. Ed. J. Goldenthal (Wien, 1832). Corrections and additions to this edition are found in *Heḥaluṣ* 11 (1880): 76-91, esp. 84. References in parentheses are to the Goldenthal edition. I also used the following manuscripts: Paris 698, ff 49a-51a; see, M. Beit-Arié and C. Sirat, *Manuscripts médiévaux en caractères hébraïques* (Jerusalem-Paris: Israel Academy of Sciences and Humanities, 1979) 2.43; Paris 696.1, ff. 391-40b; see M. Zotenberg, *Catalogues des manuscrits hébreux et samaritains de la Bibliothèque Impèriale* (Paris, 1866), 110; Paris 697, ff. 149b-156a; ibid.

47. To the Averroean report that early Greek thinkers believed in two ultimate principles, Narboni adds a story concerning the founder of Manicheanism: Mani succeeded in attracting many people to his new religion, including Shapur [I], the king. Shapur invited Mani and important persons in his kingdom to a banquet. The important persons arrived first and the king commanded that they be hanged on trees in the garden of the palace. When Mani arrived, the king took him to the garden and explained that the god of evil had commanded him to do this deed. Telling Mani that the fate of his companions was also appropriate for him, the king commanded that Mani be hanged as well. For Mani in the Islamic literature, see *The Encyclopedia of Religion,* ed. M. Eliade (New York: Macmillan, 1987) 9.158-61.

48. There are some deletions of textual passages, but, characteristically, a Koranic verse (21:22) is also omitted. When Narboni's deletions occasion difficulties in understanding his comments, I use the fuller text in the *Incoherence of the Incoherence.*

49. Cf. *Incoherence of the Incoherence* III, Bouyges, 176-77; Van Den Bergh, 106.

50. Bouyges, 177, Van Den Bergh, 106-07. 'Anaxagoras' is the reading in *The Incoherence of the Incoherence.* Narboni has 'Pythagoras.'

51. According to Averroes, the celestial bodies are composed of form and matter, but not as terrestrial bodies are; 'form' and 'matter' are predicated of celestial and terrestrial bodies completely equivocally. See Averroes, *Ma'amar be-'Eẓem ha-Galgal (De Substantia Orbis),*

ed. A. Hyman (Cambridge-Jerusalem: Medieval Academy of America and Israel Academy of Sciences and Humanities, 1986) Hebrew: 13-14, 25, 27, 41-42, 50-51; English: 28-35, 39-43, 41 n. 6, 74-75, 82, 89-90, 110-11, 120).

52. Cf. *Incoherence of the Incoherence* III, Bouyges, 175-76; Van Den Bergh, 105-06.

53. Cf. Bouyges, 180-81; Van Den Bergh, 108.

54. Averroes is rather loose in applying this threefold distinction to the origins of various kinds of multiplicities. Narboni here has the reading 'matter'; Averroes, 'dispositions.'

55. On the matter of celestial bodies, see *Incoherence of the Incoherence* 2.94, on 142.8.

56. See Van Den Bergh 2.100, on 155.2.

57. See Van Den Bergh, 2.100, on 155.3.

58. See Van Den Bergh, 2.100, on 155.4. For a more extensive discussion of the influence of the twofold motion of the sun, see *Incoherence of the Incoherence* III, Bouyges, 188-89; Van Den Bergh, 113. The discussion has its origin in Aristotle's *On Generation and Corruption* II 10, 336a 23-336b 24. Averroes mentions this work; Narboni does not.

59. Cf. *Incoherence of the Incoherence* III Bouyges, 260-62; Van Den Bergh 154-55.

# Maimonides and Neoplatonism: Challenge and Response

## Alfred L. Ivry

The challenge of Neoplatonism is one that Maimonides tried to reject and could not. He could, however, pretend that he ignored the challenge, and he did. So successful has he been in this respect that few readers of the *Guide* over the centuries have been alert to the amplitude of the Neoplatonic dimensions of the work. That which it shares of this heritage with other medieval works, particularly its use of emanation and its concept of the One, is seen as part and parcel of the medieval Aristotelianism which incorporated such doctrines into its basic structures. It has not been recognized by and large that Maimonides' Neoplatonism could be a serious departure from Aristotelian doctrine, adduced only because that doctrine proved inadequate for him.

Maimonides tried to reject Neoplatonism because he found that it too was inadequate. He did not prove it inadequate, since he did not confront it openly, or philosophically, but his bias was towards Aristotle, and had been since his youth, as attested by his Treatise on Logic.[1] His letter to the Hebrew translator of the *Guide*, Samuel ibn Tibbon, recommending various authors, confirms this attachment and shows that Maimonides was disdainful of Neoplatonic authors.[2] Since the letter is silent about key works of Neoplatonic literature available and presumably known to Maimonides, the evidence from that source for Maimonides' involvement with Neoplatonic literature is inconclusive. More telling is the *Guide* itself, which shows its author adopting Neoplatonic ideas and perspectives repeatedly, although without arguing for them. In reconstructing Maimonides' argument, its Neoplatonic basis emerges clearly, and we can see why he was attracted to this philosophy, and why he could not bring himself to admit his dependence on it.

Maimonides had to be familiar with Neoplatonic teachings, since they were fairly ubiquitous in the intellectual circles of Islamic culture with which he was intimate. Particularly in twelfth-century Fatimid and immediate post-Fatimid Egypt, Shi'i theology, with its Neoplatonic leanings and borrowings, could not have escaped Maimonides' attention. He would have read or have heard of the teachings of Abū Ya'qūb al-Sijistānī (d. circa 971), Ḥamīd al-Dīn al-Kirmānī (d. circa 1021), and their disciples. We know that he met 'Abd al-Laṭīf b. Yūsuf al-Baghdādī, whose *Metaphysics* quotes and paraphrases part of the Theology of Aristotle. That treasure-house of Plotinian doctrine had circulated in the Islamic and Jewish world since the time of al-Kindī, the first philosopher of the Arabs. It was in fact part of the *Enneads* corpus. The tenth-century Ikhwān al-Ṣafā' had made use of its teachings in their encyclopedia, the *Rasā'il Ikhwān al-Ṣafā'*, a paraphrase of which, *al-Risāla al-Jāmi'a*, also circulated widely.[3]

Neoplatonic views thus surfaced in various guises in Islamic culture well before Maimonides' time and had become well known. In the writings of al-Fārābī, Avicenna, and even Averroes we see the inroads made by these teachings into supposedly Aristotelian territory. Maimonides' writing, in this area as in others, mirrors to a large degree that of his Muslim predecessors among the *falāsifa*. More than they, however, he seems to be struggling with this hybrid legacy.

The areas of Neoplatonic influence in the *Guide* are numerous, beginning with Maimonides' view of God as the One above all predication, of whom certain predicates are somehow still appropriate, particularly goodness, wisdom and will. Maimonides' God is the First Cause, who in knowing Himself knows the world and is responsible for the emanation of that world, or at least its ideal, intelligible aspect. God has no direct relation to matter, which is foreign to His nature, so He relates to the world through its universal forms, and does not relate directly to individuals as such. Providence, accordingly, is expressed in general and not particular ways. God is not responsible for the evil in the universe, which stems from the recalcitrance of matter and man's will. Both of these, matter and will, are loci of freedom. God's freedom, however, is inextricably bound up with the necessity of His being. It is to this God, finally, that we and all created being turn and return, our greatest felicity being knowledge of the divine and conjunction with it.[4]

Most of these ideas in the *Guide* are presented in disguised form, for they are hardly traditional and we can see that Maimonides struggled with them. The God revealed here is at least not apparently the God of revelation, and Maimonides is determined to maintain the validity of revelation as well as to keep faith with Aristotle. Aristotle's philosophy for Maimonides is the model of science and reasoned explanation, the ideal conjoining of logic and nature. He deviates from it only when compelled to do so. It is his declared admiration for the Stagirite which probably has blinded readers of the *Guide* to the extent of his actual deviations from his model. Most Maimonides scholars take his attachment to Aristotle as a given, and interpret the Master, ha-Rav, without serious concern for the Neoplatonic themes in his thought. They do so at peril to their interpretations.

The experience of Leo Strauss is instructive in this regard. His actual view of Maimonides' secret teachings is itself a pretty well-kept secret, as readers of his various studies of Maimonides' work can testify. His well-known, yet enigmatic introduction to Shlomo Pines' translation of the *Guide*, titled "How to Begin to Study *The Guide of the Perplexed*,"[5] has particularly puzzled, if not infuriated, scholars, to say nothing of the effect it must have on lay readers. This is not the place to undertake a full-scale analysis of that work, and I will restrict my remarks to the theme at hand. But Strauss' attitude toward Neoplatonism is critical, I believe, in his final assessment of Maimonides' beliefs. Strauss generally avoided discussing Neoplatonism in his writings on Maimonides and mentions it rather late in this introduction. He rightly views the initial theme of the *Guide* to be God's incorporeality, a notion critical in the fight against idolatry.[6] Idolatry is, of course, the *bête noire* of the Torah, and indeed of the Bible as a whole. Taken literally, idolatry entails corporeality, since an idol is a physical *eikon*, or likeness, of a god. Incorporeality thus removes the basis of idol worship.

Idolatry in Judaism, however, came to have a broader meaning, tantamount ultimately to denial of the law and synonymous with paganism, what Maimonides called Sabianism.[7] Polytheism is at the heart of Sabianism, and much of the *Guide* is devoted to the overthrow of this last vestige of pagan thought. In Maimonides' time, with the non-Jewish world of his cognizance divided between Islam and Christianity, one may well wonder which pagans Maimonides was attacking. Who were the real Sabians? For the historic Sabians were an obscure, essentially defunct polytheistic sect. The answer would seem to be that the "Sabians" Maimonides had in mind were Aristotle and his ilk, Maimonides' closest allies philosophically. Dwelling on the beliefs and rituals of the ostensibly historic Sabians may have served Maimonides' purposes in terms of justifying the establishment of the Mosaic law,[8] but it also distracts the reader from identifying Aristotle as Maimonides' main opponent and thus deters the reader from adopting a negative attitude to philosophy.

It is particularly Aristotle's belief in the existence of many unmoved movers,[9] known in the medieval tradition as the intelligences of the spheres, which struck Maimonides as inimical to monotheism. Not that Maimonides himself rejected the cosmological scheme whereby each sphere was informed by an intelligence of its own; but for him these intelligences and the heavenly bodies which are their physical counterparts are under God's ordinance, part of His created world, whereas for Aristotle the heavens in their entirety, intelligences and bodies alike, are co-eternal with God and in fact divine.[10] Aristotle's Nous is *primus inter pares*. The intelligences are incorporeal eternal beings, minor deities, it is true, yet gods nonetheless.

In inveighing against such a notion, Maimonides is protesting against a world view in which God plays essentially a mechanistic role, as the first mover, and in which the world runs itself, the heavens control themselves. Such a world holds no place for a personal God; it is a world governed by the strict dictates of logic; a naturalistic and scientific world in the most irreligious sense of the terms, at least when looked at from the traditional sort of viewpoint that Strauss believes Maimonides really holds.

Strauss notes that the argument against such a position cannot be based on the notion of divine incorporeality, since the intelligences of the spheres are themselves incorporeal. For Maimonides—though not, strictly speaking, for Aristotle—it is the argument for the unity of God, coupled with an argument for incorporeality, which ensures the validity of the monotheistic idea.[11] The main argument for divine unity, however, is taken from Aristotle, a premise of that argument being an eternal world which includes the eternal intelligences of the spheres.[12] Maimonides is thus left with the position, according to Strauss, in which he has to assert the creation of the world from nothing as the free act of the one God, in order to deny the existence of other eternal, hence divine, beings of any sort. But this assertion, in contrast to the belief in God's unity and incorporeality, is undemonstrable, and Maimonides knows it. It lacks, presumably, any scientific or natural premise of its own, and is based purely on a notion of logical possibility from which no necessary conclusions follow.[13]

The struggle against idolatry, which is the struggle against the Aristotelian naturalistic world view, is helped only partially by the arguments Maimonides adduces for the notion of divine incorporeality. For here, Maimonides is in danger of overkill, constructing through the *via negativa* an image of the one God which is practically devoid of any meaning, and certainly of any personal relationship to creation. Actually, Maimonides has two images of the divine incorporeal unity, and he alternates between them. The more problematic image, religiously, is the more Aristotelian, and it is that which identifies God as self-thinking intellect.[14] Intellect, as Strauss points out,[15] is the only term predicated of God which is not used equivocally, so that however little we may grasp of a being that is totally self-contained, we can yet comprehend it *qua* intellect and understand Maimonides' intention in identifying the notion of divine knowledge with the notion of life.[16]

We may understand Maimonides here, but we can barely believe that he is actually advancing such a radically deistic view in the name of Judaism. God as intellect is pure intelligence, without will or power. The existence, unity and incorporeality of God are established, but at great expense to the tradition. So it is not surprising to find Maimonides criticizing this view, which he himself supposedly endorsed. The critique is multi-faceted and need not detain us here.[17] Its thrust is to weaken if not destroy confidence in the Aristotelian and post-Aristotelian worldview, on which the identification of God as intellect is based. But the alternative to the logically flawed eternal world of Aristotle, sincerely offered according to Strauss and Maimonides' apparent teaching, a world created from nothing, lacks a scientifically, philosophically grounded conception of God.

Strauss is not deterred from this conclusion. Indeed he sees it as intrinsic to Maimonides' essentially anti-philosophical Jewishness. The unknown God of creation is not only one, existent and knowing, He also has will and power, however unaccountable to human reasoning. This assertion ties in neatly for Strauss with Maimonides' doctrine of attributes: While it is grossly inappropriate to predicate attributes of God in corporeal terms, and logically inappropriate in incorporeal terms, the negative moral of divine unity for Strauss is God's absolute uniqueness, a uniqueness which somehow tolerates its own set of unique attributes. As Strauss says, without demurral, "The meaning of the doctrine of attributes is that God is the absolute perfect being, the complete and perfectly self-sufficient good, the being of absolute beauty or nobility. . . . (S)ince we understand by God the absolutely perfect being, we mean the goodness of His creation or governance when we say that He is the 'cause' of something."[18] These attributes, Strauss emphasizes, are neither anthropomorphic nor discrete, but simply indicate divine perfection, a perfection which is an "unfathomable abyss."[19] Although unfathomable, this concept of God is considered by Strauss as an "appropriate expression of the Biblical principle" of the "hidden God who created the world out of nothing . . . in absolute freedom, and whose essence is therefore indicated by 'Will' rather than by 'Wisdom.'"[20]

Intellect and Will, then, emerge as emblems of the two images of God which Maimonides considers, the one supported by a scientific world view, however vulnerable; the other, carried aloft on the thin shoulders of a purely theoretical logic. Neither image is demonstrably true, it is realized, nor, presumably, is the combined image any the more demonstrable. In any event, Strauss feels that Maimonides' last word is not always the identity of intellect, or wisdom, and will in the divine being.[21] So, for Strauss, Maimonides never chooses rationally between the competing world views, but remains skeptical of ever attaining such knowledge. Strauss' own last word is one of perplexity, or rather perplexities, Maimonides' perplexities.[22] These perplexities are liberating, as Strauss sees it, and—although Strauss doesn't say so explicitly—they qualify Maimonides after all for the true philosopher's mantle, the skeptic's cloak.

However liberating Maimonides' perplexities may be, Strauss does not allow him the one model which could have resolved the impasse between intellect and will, eternity and creation, and governance and providence: the Neoplatonic model that challenged Maimonides. Strauss' avoidance of that challenge contributes largely to his image of Maimonides as a rational skeptic, or an agnostic believer. True, Strauss does not completely overlook Neoplatonism. When he finally gets to it, after describing the entailments of both models of the divine unity, he says that the "true state of things is somewhat obscured" by Neoplatonic teaching, which Maimonides' doctrine of attributes "restates."[23] For Strauss, however, Maimonides' use of Neoplatonic doctrine is unique here, although he fails to explain further. Evidently, Strauss considers this element in Maimonides' thought minor, restricting it to the doctrine of attributes, where it lacks the power to compete with the hidden God of revelation. Neoplatonism, then, does not seem to Strauss to be a weltanschauung that Maimonides seriously considered. But in underestimating it, Strauss may have fallen victim to the very literalism against which he campaigned.

The late and lamented Alexander Altmann may be the scholar who has most recently attested to a strong Aristotelian reading of the *Guide*, pronounced after a thorough and profoundly informed examination of the text.[24] Altmann, whose studies on Isaac Israeli and Jewish mysticism alerted him to the presence of Neoplatonism in medieval Jewish thought, did not find this presence predominant in Maimonides' philosophy. This reading is consistent with Altmann's earlier approach to Maimonides, and must be taken seriously. Nevertheless, I respectfully differ with his approach.

It is particularly Altmann's view of essence and existence in Maimonides' thought that I wish to consider. In an article published in 1953, which he saw fit to reprint in 1969,[25] Altmann refers to Maimonides' well-known definition of existence in *Guide* I 57, which he renders in English as "an accident (*'arad*) affecting (lit. happening to) that which exists (*mawjūd*), and therefore something (*ma'nā*) superadded to the essence (*māhiya*) of that which exists." Existence of this sort is restricted to caused beings, in contrast to the necessary, inherent existence characteristic of uncaused being, of which God is the unique example. Altmann observes that Maimonides' statement "reflects" Avicenna's theory concerning essence and existence, as has long been known, and that his medieval commentators took sides in interpreting Maimonides' remarks from an Avicennian or Averroean viewpoint, positing or denying the independent being of essences as "possible existents." Altmann questions whether Maimonides so understood Avicenna, whether in fact Avicenna should be so understood.

Altmann is influenced in his reading of Avicenna by the interpretation of the late Fazlur Rahman.[26] Both see their men as holding Aristotelian views of the subject, however un-Aristotelian the locutions may seem at first. The priority of actual to potential states of being, the view of potentiality as dependent upon prior actuality, where actuality is determined by the fact of existence, governs their understanding of Avicenna's treatment of necessary and possible existence. Altmann has no hesitancy in saying that Maimonides "stands solidly on Aristotelian ground" in his view of essence.[27] It is the form of an individual, definitive of it, and as such descriptive of the species to which the individual belongs. This account of essence in terms of species elevates it to the realm of universals, a realm which Maimonides, according to Altmann, considers logical, or conceptual, only. Quoting *Guide* III 18, Altmann tells us that for Maimonides, "it is an established fact that species have no existence outside our minds, and that species and other universals are concepts appertaining to the intellect, while everything that exists outside our minds is an individual or an aggregate of individuals." The constancy of forms, however, i.e., of essential forms or of the species, poses a problem for this interpretation of universal being; and, as Altmann says, "Maimonides does not further analyze the peculiar mode of being that attaches to essence or form as something existing only in concrete individuals and yet transcending them." Altmann, however, is sure that for Maimonides there is no mean between existence and non-existence.[28] This nominalist or conceptualist position is urged against the attempts of *Kalām* authors to find some middle ontological ground for divine attributes, neither real nor not-real. For Altmann, Maimonides is set against such attempts, on logical and scientific grounds, grounds which locate essences as true existents only in individual substances.

In clarifying the Aristotelian teaching of the relationship between essence and substance, in which the "primary substance," the concrete individual, is seen as inferior in being to the "secondary substance," its essence, Altmann appears to modify his stance. He acknowledges that, while essence "exists only in concrete things and never by itself, it has nevertheless being and unity in a higher degree than the concrete thing."[29] Altmann does not state immediately where this being comes from; the essence, like its existence, is seen to "happen," to come into being as the form of a particular matter, as the result of a causal process. It is, of course, the emanative process which for Maimonides would be the cause of the instantiation of a universal form.[30]

Yet Altmann does not go into this subject here, preferring to discuss the nature of existence as a function of God's Will, while relating essence to the divine Wisdom. Both are united in God's unique being;[31] but for us, Altmann argues, Wisdom stands for "essence which represents the realm of nature in the timelessness and constancy of being."[32] The temporal "happening" of essence is thus discrete from its timeless being, a state which Altmann identifies both with God's own Wisdom and with the realm of nature. This joint identification would place the essences of all things, their universal natures, into the Godhead in some form or other, with tremendous implications for Maimonides' teachings of the complete simplicity of the One. And this identification indicates as well the real nature of universals, subsisting timelessly within God. Altmann does not pursue the implications of his remarks directly, but at the end of the article makes the point that it is "remarkable that Maimonides refrained from using Aristotle's concept of the analogy of being (as al-Fārābī and Averroes did) but insisted on the homonymous nature of the term." Altmann says the reason for this is to be found in Maimonides' Neoplatonic orientation, "which he shared with Avicenna."[33]

Altmann invokes Neoplatonic doctrine, then, to account for the uniqueness of God's being in Maimonides' scheme, which reduced the "different shades of being . . . to one single level compared with the totally other Being of God." Neoplatonism here becomes a kind of functional synonym for a radical dichotomy between God and the world—a treatment which ignores the bridge which it offers between the two. Not only does emanationism provide such a bridge, but so too does the distinction between essence and existence, when that distinction is not forced into an Aristotelian mold. The little that Altmann explores of the entailments of this distinction is sufficient to draw attention to the problematic nature of essences for Maimonides. And a fresh look at Avicenna's understanding of possible existents—independent of Rahman's influential interpretation—suggests that possible existents are real, subsisting in a state of being prior to their actualization as "existent" beings. This, despite Avicenna's—and Maimonides'—ostensible claims to the contrary. The texts permit such a view, and the logic of possible existents *vis-à-vis* the Necessary Existent requires it. It is demanded, moreover, by the entire issue of God's relation to the world, conceived by both men in a way that preserves both necessity and freedom, for God and the world. Let us, then, explore Avicenna's famous doctrine in Avicenna's own terms, for only a complete understanding of the philosophical legacy that Maimonides inherited will permit us to understand his thought fully.

Avicenna followed al-Fārābī in distinguishing between God as the *wājib al-wujūd*, the "Necessary Existent" (literally, "Necessary of Existence"), and all the remaining substances of the world, each called *mumkin al-wujūd*, a "possible existent" (literally, "possible of existence").[34] Avicenna used this distinction primarily in his proof for the existence of God,[35] conceived as a unique being of utter simplicity. In contrast to all other beings, the essence of the Necessary Existent is simply its existence. It has no other nature. There are no other factors besides existence involved in the composition of the Necessary Existent, indeed it has no composition, no differentiating aspects which would require causal explanation. The Necessary Existent has no causes, it rather is the cause of all other existents. These others—all other existents in the world—are thus caused in a way the Necessary Existent is not: in regard to their existence. Their existence is not intrinsically part of their essence. Rather, it is conceived as extrinsic to their essence. The being of these other existents is composite, comprising an essence and a state of existence which is joined to the essence by an external cause. The actual joining of these two components renders these existents, which are possible existents in themselves, into necessary existents; the necessity, however, is extrinsic. Thus the existence of a possible existence, once it is brought into actual existence, is a necessary fact.[36]

Avicenna's argument for the existence of God affirms the contingency of all other beings in the world. But their contingency is theoretical only, evidently, since the extrinsically necessary existence which beings enjoy once realized renders them *de facto* necessary beings. Avicenna in a way had his cake and ate it, in claiming that possible existents are both possible *per se, bi-dhātihi*, and necessary per aliud, *bi-ghayrihi*. The world is seen as originally, continually and ultimately dependent on God, although it also functions in a necessary, continuous and predictable way.

We would seem, with this argument, to be back on the firm Aristotelian ground of a necessary universe, after having flirted with other conceptual schemes. Yet there are elements of this conception which are decidedly non-Aristotelian. This becomes evident when we closely examine Avicenna's formulation of the notion of the Necessary Existent. As we have said, this being is uniquely simple. Its entire being is its existence. In contrast, possible existents have an essence which is other than their existence. These essences are foreign to the nature of the Necessary Existent, by definition. They are the essences of particular objects, different from one another, each essence having a distinct identity of its own, classifiable within the divisions of being, a separate part of all that is. Yet the Necessary Existent can give these essences only what it has to give, which is what it is, existence pure and simple. It cannot give them their essences in any more defined or particularized a manner. For the Necessary Existent has no particular essence to give. As pure existence, the essence of the Necessary Existent is no doubt considered by Avicenna, and by Maimonides, to be the quintessential essence of all existents, its being comprising the essential element in all beings. Yet the dichotomy of necessary and possible existents which Avicenna has emphasized compels recognition of the "presence" or reality of essences independent of the existence and thus of the kind of being bestowed on them by the Necessary Existent. This being may be called existential being. It is critical for the existence of all beings but does not comprise the totality, or essential nature, of their being.

This raises the problem of determining the origin of the essences which in themselves are only possible existents. If these essences do not come from the Necessary Existent, where do they come from? Could they be independent entities with a reality of their own prior to being rendered necessary by God? This is a tempting suggestion, though it must be admitted that Avicenna nowhere entertains this possibility specifically. That is, he does not posit a primordial stage of "subsistence" for these essences "before" their being brought into "existence" by the Necessary Existent. He says that "quiddity before existence has no existence,"[37] by which he would appear to be intent on sticking to one world, the world of our experience, in which all possible existents are also necessary de facto. In this reading possible existents do not have a past history before they "enter into existence."

But the assertion that "quiddity before existence has no existence," may be no more than a tautology concerning existence as normally construed, repeating the distinction to which attention has been drawn between quiddity, or essence, and existence. Of course quiddities do not exist before they exist. Yet this does not preclude the possibility that quiddities may have some kind of subsistence, or reality, apart from their actual "existence," and beyond the mere potential which Aristotle allows. If possible existents cannot receive anything from God but actual existence, their essential natures remain unaccounted for. They cannot come from nothing on their own, haphazardly, and the Necessary Existent cannot create them in their particular natures. Rather, on this reading, the possible existents would be real in their own way, independently of the Necessary Existent, although dependent existentially upon it.

If this reading reflects Avicenna's true sentiments, it must be acknowledged, as admitted above, that he does not help the reader to realize it. Avicenna never speaks of a time in which the possible existents did not exist, or of a stage within God or within some universal hypostasis from which they "entered into existence."[38] The totality of their being includes their existence, which is bound up with the existence of their cause, the Necessary Existent, and always has been. Here we must remember that Avicenna, like al-Fārābī, believed in an eternal universe, with certain substances—the heavenly bodies and their formal and efficient principles, their intellects and souls—eternal in themselves.[39] He offers no endorsement in his presentation of metaphysics of a Platonic kind of creation. So

Avicenna must regard these eternal substances as *prima facie* refutations of the notion that an essence can have an identity other than the one it has, as known to us in its existential dimension. Even the sublunar world, which is not fixed in unchanging eternal structures, is locked into an eternal pattern of beings classified as species and genera. For Avicenna, as for Aristotle, universals are substances of a secondary sort, not existing independently of their individual members.[40] Yet these individual members are just that, particular expressions of a specific class. For Avicenna, this class, representing the essence of its potentially existent members, the possible existents in themselves, should have an ontological dimension. If so, though, Avicenna does not speak of it. Externally at least, he considers secondary substances separately from possible existents, and draws no inferences to the former from the putative nature of the latter.

Thus Avicenna would have us view the relation of potential and actual existence in an Aristotelian perspective. While any particular here may or may not be actualized, and thus qualifies as a possible existent in the literal sense of the term, such a potential existent does not have an independent existence as potential. It is tied to and caused by the prior actual existence of another member of its species, the existence of which was in turn assured by the prior actual existence of yet another member of the species. The sublunar world of generation and corruption thus has no more room for truly independent or anomalous possible existents than does the supralunar world of eternal beings. The contingency of beings on earth is a theoretical construct, as is the contingency of celestial substances, their being never existing other than as necessary, because of the eternal influence of the Necessary Existent upon them.

Avicenna has in this manner created a parallel structure, in the dichotomy of possible and necessary existents, to that of Aristotle's distinction between potential and actual substances. Yet our argument suggests that Avicenna should be prepared to posit (tacitly if not openly) the essentially independent nature of the beings of this world. Of course all beings owe their existence ultimately to God, the Necessary Existent, but this ultimate source of actual existence is just that, and the complex world of individual substances is foreign, in its very composition and multiplicity, to God's essence. Avicenna's Necessary Existent, like Aristotle's thought-thinking-itself, does not create this world in its entirety, does not in fact create it in any sense but one, although that is indispensable to the world's existence.

Avicenna's God like Aristotle's, then, is in the embarrassing position—for Avicenna—of not being the Creator of the universe in the fullest sense of the term. Since Avicenna defended an eternal universe this was to be expected. But the conceptualization of the Deity as the sole Necessary Existent and the *per se* contingent nature of all other beings tends to obscure this fact. Then too, as the Necessary Existent, Avicenna's God goes out to the world more directly than does Aristotle's Deity, an intelligence that actualizes and moves the world without ceasing to contemplate itself. But, for all its more active involvement in the world, Avicenna's God can in this construal no more know the world as it is than can Aristotle's deity, a situation which Avicenna would have found unbearable, presumably. For all their contingency, then, the possible existents constitute a real threat to divine omnipotence and omniscience; not in the *per se* contingency of their existence, but in the very nature of their being. There would indeed seem to be substances with which Avicenna's Necessary Existent interacts, beings which for want of a better term are called essences, and which appear in existence as the celestial substances and terrestrial species we know. The Necessary Existent "creates" them all, but only in one sense, by granting them existence. Their essential nature is their own.

If the forms of the world are an independent given for Avicenna, so too is its matter.[41] Matter is linked, of course, to that multiplicity which is foreign to the divine. The Necessary Existent, being simple in the extreme, has no shred of multiplicity, and hence no material dimension. It thus has no matter to give to the world. The matter of the world is its own reality, alien to God. As the Necessary Existent cannot give the world its forms, so the one immaterial God cannot endow the universe with its matter. In fact, God's relation to matter is even more remote than His relation to forms, since the existence bestowed upon a possible existent is bestowed directly only on its form. For the possible existent in itself is only form, or essence. It is true that the instantiation as actual existents of nearly all forms in this world (to exclude the intelligences of the spheres) entails the realization of their form in a material substratum. But this realization is part of the internal—dare we say autonomous—mechanics of the relation between matter and form. Presumably God does not deal directly with matter. It is too alien. God's role is to actualize the existence of possibly existent essences, without coming into direct contact with matter itself. The gift of existence is given directly to form, which is the principle of actuality in any event; and it is this actualized form which brings matter around, as it were, shapes it up and presents it as an existing being.

The distance between God and matter is expressed more explicitly by Avicenna when he comes to explain the emanation of the universe.[42] According to this well-known view of Avicenna's, the first being to issue from the One is the intelligence of the outermost sphere, that sphere which encompasses the entire world and defines its outermost limits. The definition of these limits, in a sense their creation, is the direct work not of God but of the first intelligence. Utilizing his distinction between possible and necessary existents, Avicenna says that this first intelligence generates the outermost sphere, which is the first body of the world, by thinking itself as itself, i.e., as a possible existent. Matter is thus introduced into the world as a function of its contingent nature; matter is, as it were, the embodiment of contingency.

God in this scheme is not directly responsible for the creation of matter, any more than He is for the ever-increasing multiplicity of beings. From God there eternally emanates only the one intelligent or formal principle, a single being which is presumed not to challenge the integrity of divine unity.[43] Multiplicity, like corporeality, is thought to enter the world through the activities of the first intelligence. Thus God can be held responsible for the totality of being only as its indirect cause, through the emanation of this first intelligence, and through the consequences of its activity.

The scheme which Ibn Sīnā elaborates ensures that God keeps far from matter, even while it affirms His role as the guarantor of the existence of all being. In the eternal rhythm of the emanative process, the intelligence of each sphere engenders the body of that sphere, as with the first, by regarding itself as a possible existent. By contrast, the intelligence of each sphere engenders the soul of that sphere and the intelligence of the subsequent sphere by reflecting, respectively, on the necessary aspect of its existence and on the intelligence from which it was itself engendered. Now necessary existence and intelligence are not dissociated from God. Thus the souls and intelligences in the heavens and their analogous formal appearances on earth are linked more directly to God than is the body of the world, its matter. Yet even they are not directly related to Him, since each intelligence and soul receives its nature from the preceding intelligence, not from God directly.

Looked at from another perspective the intelligences and souls of the spheres may be said to bear the imprint of God's presence. They are the result of the intelligence's apprehension of itself as a necessary existent, and this is the kind of existence which derives essentially from the Necessary Existent. The actual existence of heavenly souls and intelligences, as necessary existents, is thus testimony to God's direct presence in the world. That is, as we have learned already, God is present in the world directly through the actualization of its forms, both celestial and sublunar. As these forms are all related to matter, and in the sublunar sphere especially do not function apart from matter, God's presence, as the source of life, permeates matter too. Yet it permeates matter through the form with which that matter is associated, and does not relate to matter as such at all.

Matter, then, is like the possible existents in being separate from God's presence and knowledge. But in actual existence, matter is controlled by the forms with which it is always associated, and so brought within the divine purview. Separate or independent matter is itself another theoretical construct only. But we should not slight the significance of these constructs. For, however theoretical they may be, they are real ontologically in Avicenna's scheme, and serve a crucial purpose. Possible existents, as their name indicates, are not necessary in themselves. Matter, as the locus of potentiality, is indeterminate. Particularly sublunar matter, as the principle of motion and change, has to maintain its freedom from any necessary identification with one particular form. Yet matter and the possible existents represent respectively the indeterminate and non-necessary aspects of this world, that realm which God and man attempt to dominate, with mixed results.

The indeterminate, "free" status of matter, then, is not a positive value in Avicenna's scheme, and it is not surprising that the evil in the world is linked by him directly to matter:[44] Unlicensed, uncontrolled, unmodified (by form), matter is seen as a cause of evil in the world. Yet beyond this, the very presence of matter, as the symbol of potentiality and change, is antagonistic to all that God represents. That matter should yet be part of the emanative process which originates in God is accordingly a paradox, unless again we see the real origination of this process to be the work of the first intelligence.

The emanative scheme developed by Avicenna allows God to relate to the world in one way and keeps Him apart from it in another. He relates essentially to the forms of the world, not to their material counterparts, and even to the forms He is the giver of existence rather than the "donor of the forms" themselves. This may ensure God's unity and uniqueness, but it does not bring Him close to the world in the sense of being conscious of the particular natures of those beings for whose existence He is responsible. On this analysis God's knowledge of the world is very circumscribed. Indeed He knows no more of it than does Aristotle's First Mover. Such a conclusion is repugnant to Avicenna, and it would be ironic to have him adopt a Neoplatonic emanationist scheme in order to wind up with no closer relationship of God to the world than is found in Aristotle's metaphysics. So it is not surprising to find Avicenna often speaking of God's detailed knowledge of all the world's particulars, an expression as much of His omnipotence and providence as it is of His omniscience. Close analysis of these remarks, however, confirms the suspicion that such assertions of Avicenna's must be qualified, that God knows the particulars of this world in a universal way, even as He knows the many as one. Ultimately, one is forced back to the conclusion that God, for Avicenna, knows the world in knowing Himself, and that His self-knowledge is somehow transformed through emanation into the discrete entities which form this world.

The theories we have explored do not succeed in explaining this process, although they were clearly intended to relate God to the world more directly than Aristotle did. No more than Plotinus is Ibn Sīnā successful in bridging the gap from the One to the many, and like Plotinus, Ibn Sīnā too covers the inadequacies of his explanation with dogmatic statements which do rhetorically what logical argument cannot. Perhaps Maimonides realized this, and therefore drew back from utilizing the distinction between essence and existence more than he did. It was part of a heritage toward which he was profoundly ambivalent. His minimization of Avicenna's contribution to philosophy, in his letter to Samuel ibn Tibbon, may be taken as a negative judgment on Avicenna's Neoplatonic leanings. Compared to Avicenna, Maimonides makes little attempt to argue for the Neoplatonic doctrines he does hold. Yet he may well hold such views, despite his disinclination towards them, on the strength of the sort of arguments presented by Avicenna.

Maimonides' reticence in these matters has encouraged our predecessors to underestimate his full involvement with Neoplatonic doctrine and to minimize this dimension of his thought unduly. Alexander Altmann and Leo Strauss read Maimonides differently from one another, but on this point they seem to be in agreement, both relegating Neoplatonism to that supposed dimension of Maimonides' speculations in which faith in an unknown God and in His mysterious Will has replaced knowledge. The scientific and logical structure of Neoplatonic thought is thereby ignored. Perhaps Maimonides shared this attitude, and it prevented him from developing fully the ideas he borrowed from Neoplatonic sources. Yet the abundance of such ideas in the *Guide* shows that Maimonides did not dismiss this approach as cavalierly as some scholars have thought. It may be that Maimonides answered the challenge of Neoplatonism with a response that still awaits a response.

## Notes

1.    Ed. and tr., Israel Efros (New York, 1938); and his "Maimonides' Arabic Treatise on Logic," *PAAJR* 34 (1966): 155-60, Hebrew text, 9-42.

2.    See A. Marx, ed., "Texts by and about Maimonides," *JQR*, N.S. 25 (1934-35): 374-81; (Uncritical) English translation by L. Stitskin, *Letters of Maimonides* (New York: Yeshiva University Press, 1977), 130-36.    Cf. my appraisal in "Islamic and Greek Influences on Maimonides' Philosophy," in Pines and Yovel, *Maimonides and Philosophy*, 147 f.

3.    For further details, see Ivry, 144-46.

4.    See Ivry, "Providence, Divine Omniscience and Possibility: The Case of Maimonides," in T. Rudavsky, ed., *Divine Omniscience and Omnipotence in Medieval Philosophy*, 143-59, repr. in *Maimonides: A Collection of Critical Essays*, ed., J. A. Buijs (Notre Dame: University of Notre Dame Press, 1988), 175-91; "Maimonides on Creation," in *Creation and the End of Days: Judaism and Scientific*

*Cosmology*, Proceedings of the 1984 Meeting of the Academy of Jewish Philosophy, ed., D. Novak and N. Samuelson (Lanham: University Press of America, 1986), 185-214; "Neoplatonic Currents in Maimonides' Thought," in *Studies in Maimonides' Thought and Environment*, ed., J. Kraemer (Oxford: Oxford University Press, 1990), 149-74.

5.  xv-lvi.
6.  Strauss, xx f.
7.  See *Guide* III 29, p. 514 in the Pines translation, which will be used below.
8.  Cf. Pines' "Translator's Introduction: The Philosophic Sources of *The Guide of the Perplexed*," cxxiii f.
9.  Cf. *Metaphysics* XII 8 1074a 14.
10. See *Guide* I 72, 184 ff. and II 4-6.
11. See Strauss, xxii f.
12. *Guide* II 1, 245 f.
13. *Guide* II 17, 298; II 19, 303; cf. my "Maimonides on Possibility," in J. Reinharz et al., eds., *Mystics, Philosophers and Politicians* (Durham: Duke University Press, 1982), 67-84.
14. *Guide* I 68.
15. Strauss, l.
16. *Guide* I 53, 122.
17. See, e.g., *Guide* I 54, II 18, 19.
18. Strauss, xlviii f., and *Guide* I 35, 46, 53, 58, 59, 60 end; II 22.
19. Strauss, xlix.
20. Loc. cit.; cf. *Guide* III 13.
21. Strauss, liii.
22. Strauss, lvi.
23. Strauss, l.
24. See "Maimonides on the Intellect and the Scope of Metaphysics," in his *Von der mittelalterlichen zur modernen Aufklärung*, 60-129.
25. See "Essence and Existence in Maimonides," *Bulletin of the John Rylands Library* 35 (1953): 294-315; repr. in his *Studies in Religious Philosophy and Mysticism*, 108-27. References below are to the latter edition.
26. Altmann, 109, n. 5. Cf. Rahman's "Essence and Existence in Avicenna," in *Mediaeval and Renaissance Studies*, ed., R. Hunt et al., IV (London, 1958), 1-16; and "Essence and Existence in Ibn Sina: The Myth and the Reality."
27. Altmann, 109.
28. Cf. *Guide* I 51, 114. Maimonides actually puts the point as a question, which Altmann takes, apparently, as a rhetorical or stylistic device.

29. Altmann, 114.

30. See *Guide* I 58, 136; II 12, 279.

31. See *Guide* I 69, III 13.

32. Altmann, 117.

33. Altmann, 127.

34. Among the many studies, cf. still A.-M. Goichon, *La Distinction de l'Essence et de l'Existence d'après Ibn Sīnā*, 136-48; G. Verbeke, "Introduction Doctrinale" in S. Van Riet, ed., *Avicenna Latinus: Liber de Philosophia Prima sive Scientia Divina* I-IV (Louvain: Peeters, 1977), 42*-80*. George Hourani collected and translated the key passages in his "Ibn Sīnā on Necessary and Possible Existence."

35. See, e.g., *'Uyūn al-Masā'il, Al-Najāt* and *Al-Shifā'* in Hourani, 76, 81 and 83.

36. See the *Najāt* section in Hourani, 79.

37. As translated by Hourani, 78, from *Al-Risāla al-'Arshiyya* (Hyderabad, 1935), 4.

38. Ibn Sina's use of *dakhala fī* to describe the relation of possible existence to actual existence is misleading, and it would be better (*pace* Hourani, 85, n. 11) to translate it as "include in."

39. See, for example, I. Madkour et al., eds., *Al-Shifā', Ilāhiyyāt* (Cairo: Organisme Générale des Imprimeries Gouvernementales, 1960), 373 f.

40. See M. Marmura, "Avicenna's Chapter on Universals in the Isagoge of his *Shifa*," *Islam: Past Influence and Present Challenge*, A. Welch, P. Cachia, eds., (Edinburgh: Edinburgh University Press, 1979), 34-56, esp. 35.

41. See Avicenna's discussion of matter in the *Shifā'*, 175 ff.; and Goichon, 378-405.

42. See *Shifā'*, 402-09.

43. See Arthur Hyman's paper and others in this volume for the ramifications of this assumption.

44. In this Avicenna follows a distinctly Plotinian theme; see *Enneads*, I 8.3; J. Rist, "Plotinus on Matter and Evil"; A. Ivry, "Destiny Revisited: Avicenna's Concept of Determinism," in *Islamic Theology and Philosophy: Studies in Honor of George F. Hourani*, ed., M. Marmura (Albany: SUNY Press, 1984), 164.

# Maimonidean Naturalism

## L. E. Goodman

A telling criticism against the mechanistic tradition in science is made by Pierre Teilhard de Chardin in his celebrated cosmological meditation, *The Phenomenon of Man*:[1] Natural scientists have concerned themselves largely, perhaps exclusively, with just one of the two basic forms of energy of which we are aware, the outwardly directed or "tangential" energy by which bodies affect one another. The inwardly focused or "radial" energies by which things are centered and integrated in themselves and through which they are drawn, in seeming defiance of the second law of thermodynamics, towards ever higher levels of complexity and integration, have been neglected or ignored. All energy, Teilhard remarks, almost incidentally, must be assumed to be psychic in nature. But the radial sort, as the foundation of heightened complexity, is the prototype of consciousness.

Teilhard's two sorts of energy, radial and tangential, sustain a curious complementarity—mutually dependent, yet not reducible to each other's terms—as though locked in a sort of whirling dance, like twin rotating stars whose identity and distinctness are defined, for the moment, by one another's presence. Teilhard's terminology, in the nature of the case, is somewhat solecistic, and his thesis itself is rather opaque—perhaps, as he suggests, because science does not give us (as experience clearly does) a means of encountering consciousness. We cannot render subjectivity an object like other objects without eliminating all that makes it subjective. Still less does science hand us those inner dimensions of existence in inarticulate beings which are the prototypes—in medieval terms the "matter"—of consciousness.   Yet, despite its inherent difficulty, Teilhard's point needs perennially to be made, lest the drive toward completeness in our physical models of nature be mistaken to imply the comprehensiveness of mechanistic models, and a dimension be overlooked that runs through nature as pervasively as the "tangential energy" normally studied by the natural sciences. Without this "other energy," no finite thing would exist.   For none would have a determinate form.

Our penchant for seeking to objectify the unobjectifiable as energy runs back at least as far as the Stoic notions of *tonos* and *pneuma*.[2]  But we probably should drop that sort of naming, at least in its most familiar applications, where it encourages more confusions than it forestalls. Teilhard uses the term energy in a somewhat more generic, more Aristotelian sense than does our physical science. If we trace the concept back as far as the philosophy of Maimonides we find still functioning there the differentiated Aristotelian concepts of force or power (*dynamis, quwwa*) and task, act, work or function (*ergon, fi'l*), laid out in a Neoplatonic scheme as one variety of cause and effect.   Plotinus saw that a power is no mere passive receptivity.[3]   He was building on the pervasively teleological conception of causality pioneered by Aristotle, for whom *energeia* refers to that actuality which is both the goal of activity and the source of the powers that make action possible (*Metaphysics* VIII 8, 1049b 5, 1050a 9; 9, 1051a 4-5). Maimonides finds in Neoplatonism a means of fleshing out Aristotle's sketchy account and resolving some of its ambivalences between transcendent and immanent causation.   In the Torah he finds warrant for regarding the Neoplatonic view as congruent with the Biblical one and hints that enable him to correct the Neoplatonic view when it seems in jeopardy of falling short of its proponents' objectives.

Maimonides, like Teilhard, is persuaded by the weaknesses of mechanism and dualism to treat all forms of energy spiritually.[4] He takes to task the Neoplatonic Aristotelians for failing adequately to exploit the opening given them by the role of matter in their metaphysics for addressing the central problems of theology— finitude, privation, providence (its possibility and limitation)[5]— problems which Maimonides grouped together under the paradigmatic rubric of theophany, the Rabbinic issue of the chariot, manifestation of the Infinite in finite terms. By neglecting to apply the fundamental discovery of their own philosophy, that all actuality is form or spirit (and that prime matter, accordingly, is the mere principle of otherness), the Neoplatonic philosophers had made matter a realm apart and generated within their own system a dualism which made problematic (and needlessly so by their own premises) not only the relations of governance between mind and body, God and creation—but even the act of creation itself.[6]

Modern philosophers sometimes think of some form of Cartesian dualism as the ancestral or "background position" in philosophy. Even Plato, despite his equation of being with the Forms and his loyalty to the Parmenidean conception of the ultimate reality, is often assimilated casually to some form of dualism. And Aristotle too is treated as a dualist, despite his retention of the Platonic formula identifying *ousia* with forms—now brought down to earth.[7] So the problem of the ghost in the machine (and the related but larger problem of the larger but related Ghost beyond the natural machine) are made to appear much more pervasive (and medieval philosophers much more naive) than need be. The Neoplatonic synthesis is regularly overlooked. Yet its diverse monotheistic recensions for centuries afforded an integrated view of nature by locating the Platonic Forms as thoughts of an Aristotelian divine intelligence (thus obviating the Peripatetic worry about freestanding Forms[8]) and made those forms the mediating principles between the pure and absolute perfection of God and the partial and relative perfections found in material things. Neoplatonic forms remain principles of intelligibility, as in Plato, but are also principles of activity (energy), respecting the Aristotelian demand that explanatory principles exercise a causal role.[9]

The purpose of this paper is to explore the Maimonidean version of this classic way of integrating the cosmos within itself and with God.[10] Our aim, however, is not to uncover historic curiosities but to discover modes of thinking that might help us with some of our own persistent philosophic difficulties. Our task in that sense is one of critical appropriation. Curiously, but not surprisingly, we find Maimonides himself engaged in a similar task. For he couches his emanative naturalism in terms of a critical appropriation of the Biblical and Rabbinic idea of angels.[11]

## 1. Angels as Forms and Forces

Maimonides discriminates two kinds of angels: permanent and transitory. He warrants the distinction by the Rabbinic expedient of discovering an aporia in the dicta of the Sages. For traditionally angels are thought to be immortal (*hayyim ve-kayyamim*), but the Midrash relates, "Each day the Holy One blessed be He creates a band of angels, who sing their song before Him and go their way" (Genesis Rabbah LXXVIII; cf. *Hagigah* 14a). How is this dictum to be squared with the idea of immortal angels? "The answer would be that some are enduring and some transitory. And that is what is in fact the case. For particular forces come to be and perish continually, but the kinds of forces endure without disruption."[12] Maimonides' means of integrating the temporal with the eternal is appropriately Platonic. His suggestion that angels are forces and kinds of forces is borne out by another Rabbinic dictum: "No angel performs two missions, and no single mission is performed by two angels." This, he urges, lifting the passage from the midrashic idiom in which it is embedded, is an explicit avowal that angels are forces—as will be transparent to the wise, since they know that "every force has its own specific action (*fi'l*), and does not have two."[13] The *types* of forces, which are enduring by Maimonides' account, correspond to the angels construed as immortal beings. In Aristotelian parlance they are the disembodied intellects. Their message (for they remain intermediaries, as the Hebrew *mal'akh* implies) is the content of their thought; for they are thinking beings. Imparted one to the next and ultimately to the world, this thought is the objective, active, organizational form and force within things.[14] In us the corresponding form becomes the subjective answering rationality by which we apprehend the essences of things and thereby understand them.

God does not act upon the world directly but via natural forces. Paradigmatically, He burns things by means of flame. Thus, "God spoke to the fish and it vomited out Jonah," means that God imparted the volition to the fish, not that He made the fish a prophet![15] The ignorant do not understand that God's real majesty and might are manifested not in supernatural displays but in "bringing to be powers that act invisibly within a thing."[16] God is not "in" the created objects but acts through their instrumentality, as their Creator.[17]

Arguing from a famous midrash designed to promote consultation, a gloss on the use of the plural in Genesis 1:26 ("Let us make man in our own image"), Maimonides elucidates his equation of enduring angels with the Platonic forms. As the Sages gloss the passage: "The Holy One blessed be He, as it were, does nothing without consulting His supernal retinue." Maimonides marvels that the very word *consulting* was used as well by Plato for the Creator's resort to the eternal forms of things.[18] These forms are the celestial intellects themselves, the heavenly host; for forms do not exist alone.[19] The thoughts in the minds of the hypostatic intellects are identical with those intellects; for, as Aristotle made clear, the thought, the thinker, and the act of thinking are one and the same.[20] God's determination to "consult" the universal forms is the basis of creation, since these forms are the patterns of all things. And the world is created by God's thinking the forms that the supernal intellects contain. For the correspondence between God's thoughts and reality is not reflective like ours, but projective, inventive, productive, by way of emanation. Yet the intellects themselves are created as specifications of God's Perfection and Intention.[21] The disembodied intellects and souls of the spheres are the abiding intermediary hypostases, and the transient forces governing all natural events are the ephemeral causes.

Interpreting Psalm 94:6-9, "Will He who emplanted the ear not hear and He who formed the eye not see," Maimonides argues that the design in nature—manifest in the human frame—bespeaks an intelligence not present in nature itself but capable of governance through the characters it imparts, allowing vision by devising the appropriate character and arrangement in the aqueous and vitreous humors, membranes, nerves and sinews of the eye. One cannot think that such an arrangement of materials, each with a character and placement so ideally suited to its function, came about by chance. But God acts immanently, through the particulars in nature, the aqueous and vitreous humors and the like. One is not to suppose, Maimonides insists, that the "emplanting" of eyes was done *by means of eyes*, as though the argument were that "the Creator of the mouth must eat and the Creator of the lungs must shout." Rather, "the clear sense of the argument is that any maker of any sort of tool could not make it without conceiving the task for which it is to be used. The correct analogy is that a smith could not make a needle in the form needed for sewing adequately unless he had the concept and understood the nature of sewing."²² God's wisdom as a subject, unknowable in itself, can be inferred from the objective wisdom manifest in nature. But the linkage of God's wisdom to nature, classically known as governance, or more theologically as providence, is not on all fours with the processes of nature but operates through a higher order conceptualization analogous to that of a designer, who does not use the tools he makes but would not be able to devise them without an implicit understanding of their workings. God conceives the enduring forms of things and instantiates them in particulars. Indeed God knows, creates and governs the particulars and the ephemeral forms which are their energies through the same universal conceptual act.

> There is a great difference between a maker's knowledge of what he has made and someone else's knowledge of it. For if the product was made in accordance with the maker's knowledge, the maker simply followed his knowledge in making it as he did. But for anyone else who studies this artifact and comprehends it, the knowledge must follow the product. For example, the craftsman who made this case, with its weights moved by the flow of water to mark the passing hours of day or night, must know and understand the entire course of the water through it and each turning that it takes, every thread that must be pulled and every ball that must drop. But he does not know these movements by studying them now as they take place. Quite the contrary, these movements that now occur come to be only in accordance with his understanding. Not so with one who studies this instrument. For him each new movement he sees gives him new knowledge, and he continues to study and gradually to enhance and augment his knowledge until he has acquired an understanding of the instrument as a whole. If you were to suppose that the movements of this instrument were infinite, then the investigator would never understand it comprehensively, nor would he ever be able to know even one of its movements before it occurred. For whatever he knows is derived from what has occurred.
>
> This is just the situation with existence as a whole vis-à-vis our knowledge and God's. Whatever we know we know only through study of what exists. That is why our knowledge does not attach to the future or the infinite. Our sciences grow and vary with the objects from which our knowledge is derived. Not so with Him. His knowledge is not *a posteriori*, so that it should involve multiplicity and

change. Rather things follow His prior knowledge, which determines them to be as they are, whether as disembodied beings, as enduring material particulars, or as changeable beings whose pattern of change is undisrupted and invariant.[23]

Maimonides' emphasis on the specificity of the forms bespeaks his naturalism. The proof-texts he draws from Scripture to corroborate his interpretation of angels as forces or powers are earnest of the comprehensiveness of his project: When God shut the lions' mouths (Daniel 6:23), or made Balaam's ass halt (its speech was a subjective event in the consciousness of the prophet) He acted through an angel—that is, through natural forces in the animal. Strikingly, "even the elements are called angels: 'Who makest the winds His angels, the flaming fire His ministrants' (Psalms 104:4)."[24] When the Rabbis wonder how Judah could visit a prostitute (Genesis 38:15-16) and R. Yoḥanan reasons that the patriarch intended to pass by but for the intervention of "the angel appointed over lust," Maimonides seizes the usage to clinch his argument that any natural force or type of force can be called an angel—"this is the explicit teaching of all our Books. For you will find no reference to any act of God in them except by way of an angel, which you already know means a messenger. Thus anything appointed to a charge is an angel—even the motions of animals, including those that are inarticulate."[25] Every natural process or event stems from its Neoplatonic first principles via its own proper proximate causes, themselves intellectually disposed.[26]

Maimonides rejects the *kalām* occasionalist doctrine of God's immediate causation of each event on the theological grounds that such causation would render much of God's creation otiose. If our food is not necessary to nourish us or not sufficient in due measure to sustain us, then it was otiose for God to create it.[27] God does not, in fact, proceed directly to His goal (like an imperfect being impatient of perfection) but leads finite beings mediately to theirs. For the correct interpretation of the dictum that God created all things for His glory is that God created each thing for its own sake—to progress towards its goal: in the human case, realization of our inner likeness to God Himself.[28] As babes are fed on milk before achieving solid food, and as the Israelites were led through the wilderness rather than directly to the promised land, and enculturated through sacrificial worship before they learned to pray, and through prayer before they learned the silent contemplation of God's Perfection, so each thing requires its history. No step can be left out.[29]

Maimonides rejects the Epicurean claim that chance is an active force in nature. Natural events, as Aristotle argued, happen always or for the most part in uniform patterns. Such patterns require causal explanation. The name chance is therefore properly shifted, as it is in Aristotle, from the nonexistent realm of the uncaused to the realm of the unusual or unfamiliar. Chance is not an absence but a superfluity of causes,[30] an intersection of sequences not regularly associated because the causes normally operate independently. But even here there are causes, not only for the individual events but even for their juxtaposition. What we cannot analyze under the formal aspect of nature as an expression of God's wisdom, we refer to chance. But the notion, so applied, is purely subjective, referring—if Biblical parlance be taken seriously—to God's will, which is, in fact, by the arguments of radical monotheism, no different from His wisdom. All causal trains run back to the natural motions engendered by the rotations of the spheres and to the governance of the celestial intelligences, which contemplate God's perfection and manifest that contemplation by projecting the forms of things on nature.[31] All actions pursue the good, as constructed or construed by each being and type of being. Volitional actions are motivated ultimately by the pursuit of perfection, which articulate beings construe under the guise of some subjective good.[32]

The existence and the properties of natural objects are not necessary in absolute terms. For God was under no compulsion to create or to impart the natures we observe. But given that God did choose being over non-being for the world and did specify the characters of things as He did, there is a (relative and internal) necessity in the cosmos.[33] The whole is like a single organism[34] with its own settled order. And that order does not change essentially within itself, but things operate by the essences they are given: elements and their compounds and complexes, monovalently; animate beings, volitionally.[35] What emanates from God are the natural forms, including the souls of all living things (said to be in God's hand), and the rational soul of man—said to be in God's image.

Some of the "angels" that emanate from the divine are

conscious; others are not. Among the former, of course, Maimonides counts the disembodied intelligences and the souls of the spheres, but also the human soul. Even animal souls have some measure of awareness, although not rational thought and choice; for all animals, as in Aristotle, have perception and volition. The forms of inanimate things are not conscious. Their rationality is objective rather than subjective. But the forms in each being are the active, causal factors, existentiating each as an exemplar of its kind and founding the dispositional characteristics by which it expresses its nature.

In keeping with the Rabbinic exegetical practice, Maimonides embeds a small aporia in his own text on emanative naturalism, designed Socratically to prompt an inquiry and an inference: Among the Rabbinic texts he cites to warrant the claim that the principal parts of the cosmos include animate and intelligent beings entrusted, by delegation, with the governance of nature is one that oddly seems to warrant the quite un-Aristotelian and un-Maimonidean claim that the earth is intelligent as well as the spheres. For just as we read that "The heavens declare the glory of God" (Psalms 19:2), teaching us that "the spheres are living and rational," so at the beginning of *Genesis* we read that "the earth was *tohu* and *bohu*," which the Rabbis (in a gloss that Maimonides approves) interpret to mean "mourning and weeping." The earth bewailed the fact that although the heavens were created with her, they were alive and aware while she was dead.[36] The aporia lies in drawing the claim from the testimony of the earth itself. Comparable personifications only a few lines earlier were taken by Maimonides as proof that Scripture and the Rabbis assumed the heavens to be conscious and alive.

The resolution of the aporia arises from the equivocal status of matter, for earth is the paradigm of physicality. As a principle of otherness, prime matter is a mere abstraction, a concomitant, Maimonides argues, of finite being, but not a being itself—still less to be numbered among "the sons of God"—that is, the principles of being.[37] Yet "even the elements are called angels."[38] Matter becomes articulate to the extent that it is governed by form, that is, by the ideas that emanate from the Divine; relative to the heavens the elements are dead.[39] They are the most primitive actual instances of matter and achieve actuality by virtue of the specificity of form with which they are endowed. Elements are said to speak by a license beyond the poetic license of personification—a license which depends upon the fact that they have been assigned determinate characters and identities, that is, by virtue of the fact that they are not pure prime matter but actual existents.

Maimonides makes some remarkable claims in behalf of the celestial intelligences. Not only are they alive, intelligent, enduring beings, but also (unlike Islamic angels[40]) they outrank humanity in the scale of being—a crucial point in Maimonides' arguments for humility as a human virtue and against the notion that man is the goal and cynosure of creation.[41]   Moreover the disembodied intellects exercise a rather paradoxical sort of volition.  The spheres and intelligences apprehend their own actions, choose rationally and govern, but not as we choose and govern.  For all our choices and decisions address emergent events (*lākin laysa mithla ikhtiyārinā wa lā tadbīrinā, allādhi huwa kulluhu bi-'umūrin mutajaddidin*)—that is, new events about to take place, over which our choices and decisions will exercise a determining impact.  The angels, by contrast, are given no arbitrary discretion.  Thus the angel says to Lot: "I cannot do anything" (Genesis 19:22), and again (in Exodus 23:21), God's angel exercises no discretion, "for My name is in him."   Human beings are allotted choice and may choose wisely or unwisely; but the consciousness of the "angels," on which depend the motions of the heavens and operation of all natural processes—through these motions and through the forms imparted by the Active Intellect—is perfectly informed and chooses always "for the best," in accordance with the dictates of God's wisdom.[42]   Their "choices" are not immediate but eternal.

Clearly part of Maimonides' intention in speaking about angels is to demythologize:

> If you told one of those men who purport to be the Sages of Israel that the Deity sends an angel that enters the womb of a woman and then forms the foetus, that would impress him and he would accept it as an expression of God's greatness and power and an instance of His wisdom—although still convinced that an angel is a body of flaming fire one-third the size of the entire world—supposing all this perfectly possible for God.  But if you told him that God placed a formative power in the semen, by which the limbs and organs are shaped and demarcated, and that this is the angel, or if you told him that the forms of all things are the work of the Active Intellect

and that this is the angel constantly mentioned by the Sages as the magistrate of the world, he would bolt at such a view. For he does not understand the real meaning of greatness and power.[43]

The truth is that "all forces are angels"; and the Rabbis called an angel the third part of the world (Genesis Rabbah X) not to suggest its size, but to show the place of spiritual, intellectual, beings in the cosmic order: Angels, the bodies of the spheres, and the changing bodies of the sublunary world constitute the three types of created being. Only in the poetically charged imagination of the prophet is an angel actually envisioned.[44]  Angels are invisible because they are forces or powers, the generative forms that organize and enliven the natural world, differentiating it from mere chaos.  They are perceived from their effects, apprehended when we understand the structures of natural things and the characters and causes of natural processes.  Yet, if Maimonides' goal is to demythologize, why does he insist that "angels" are conscious, rational, volitional beings? Has he escaped the confines of Midrashic mythology only to ensnare himself in the myths of the Philosophers?

## 2.  Two Kinds of Volition

The forms, forces or angels that are permanent, as distinguished from those that are distributed in matter (divided with its divisions and dissolved when their work is finished[45]), are conscious, intelligent, rationally choosing beings.  They are delegated the governance of nature in accordance with their (invariant but inexorable) choices.  Clearly Maimonides' naturalism is not reductionistic in a physical direction.  His retention of the Biblical and Rabbinic language, referring to the powers that govern nature as angels, despite his vehement rejection of the mythic image of an angel, is far more than a mere *façon de parler* or shallow bow in the direction of tradition.  We gain an insight into his intentions from his insistence that the articulacy of the angels is not explicit but inner, like the silent consciousness of the meditative man who contemplates the Divine as he lies still upon his bed.[46]

Maimonides' treatment draws on a tradition that goes back to Plato's enunciation of Socrates' disappointment with the philosophy of Anaxagoras. Anaxagoras had promised to show that the world is governed by intelligence. If so, the young Socrates reasoned, one ought to learn from his book how all things are governed for the best, as intelligence requires: "Somehow it seemed right that mind should be the cause of everything, and I reasoned that if this is so, mind in producing order sets everything in order and arranges each individual thing in the way that is best for it. . . . I thought that by assigning a cause to each phenomenon separately and to the universe as a whole he would make clear what is best for each and what is the universal good." But Nous in Anaxagoras proved a fairly adventitious principle, lacking the power of governance for the good that Socrates expected.[47] Aristotle carries the same criticism further, arguing that the ultimate causal principles responsible for the cosmic order should not operate externally, like a *deus ex machina* in a bad play, but from within, through the inner dynamic of each player's actions.[48]

Both Plato and Aristotle devoted central attention in constructing their philosophies to emending the weaknesses they had found in Anaxagoras. Plato fused reality, causal power, rationality and goodness in his conception of the divine. Aristotle gave special emphasis to the immanence of divine causality by arguing that the being of a thing (the "what-it-is-for-a-thing-to-be") is specific to that thing and amounts to the nature each sort of thing develops and expresses in its actions in the world. All processes are teleological in the sense that they head toward a goal (completion), whether or not that goal is consciously articulated, and regardless of the fact that the endpoint of one natural process may be (must be) the initiation of another.[49] Platonically one can say that essences *specify* the universal idea of the Good. Aristotle renders the same conception dynamic and more pointedly causal by differentiating the material ground, telic goal and mediating formal and active principles that govern the action of all things in nature. For each species the pursuit of pure actuality and emulation of pure perfection are expressed by the interpretation of actuality or perfection in a specific natural mode of action or of life. Things realize themselves through their pursuit of goals. For no atemporal essence is ever wholly present in any particular at a given instant. And no single goal is ever comprehensive of all good.[50] God rules the world as He moves it, through the attraction towards divine perfection expressed in their diverse ways by the very essences which are the presence in each thing of that measure of pure actuality which properly belongs to each natural kind.

In the perspective of this tradition it becomes quite intelligible how Maimonides can claim that the Aristotelian (by which he means Neoplatonic Aristotelian) affirmation of consciously choosing intellects associated with the spheres is congruent with Biblical and Rabbinic views. To be sure, Aristotle is an eternalist and Maimonides is a creationist. But the means by which Maimonides will account for God's relation to the world—God's governance and even creation of the world—are the same emanationist means as those that the Neoplatonic philosophers had derived from their study of the metaphysics of Aristotle and Plato. Granted the world is distinct from God and the intelligences and forms are not to be deemed divine—still less the forces they induce in natural particulars—nonetheless, these forms and forces and the consciousnesses which represent the highest rung attained among imparted forms are "emissaries" of the divine. Like the breath of life that God breathed into Adam, they do God's will by imparting to things the power of acting for themselves.

In the role assigned to them the incorporeal intellects must be consciously choosing beings. For the specifications they determine are not exhaustive of the logical possibilities for finite being. Similarly, the intellects of the spheres must choose in order to govern—to steer and pilot the great ship entrusted to them.[51] Yet the choices made by the disembodied intelligences follow a consistent pattern. The cosmos will not take an alternative course—not because its motions are automatic but because the guiding intelligences choose always for the best.

This seems a strange admission for Maimonides, since he himself criticizes the Neoplatonic philosophers for purporting to assign to God the determination of the existence and character of all things yet simultaneously denying any real alternatives. The cosmos of the philosophers, as an eternal existent, becomes a necessary existent. Its character too is necessary. All things in nature must be as they are; and if the requirements of the Philosophers are taken strictly, change becomes impossible.[52] It is highly problematic, Maimonides argues, for the Philosophers to assign to God the authorship of the cosmos.[53] Al-Ghazālī argued, in the precedent for Maimonides' criticism, that it is contradictory for the Philosophers to ascribe the world's constitution to God's free act if the world would have had the same character regardless. What can be meant by God's choice if there were no real alternatives for it to range over?[54]

Now the same criticism might be applied to Maimonides himself. How does it make sense to say that natural events occur by rational choices of the angels (rather than automatically or mechanically) when the "choices" will never eventuate other than as they do and their outcomes are the same that any mechanist would predict as the regular outcomes of physical causes? There are two problems to clear up here, both hinging on the Rambam's curious insistence on applying the language of rational volition to the governance of nature: (a) Why is such governance called volitional at all, when by Maimonides' own standards volition must confront real alternatives? Why does he insist on volition when he is equally insistent in denying arbitrary discretion? Has he somehow abandoned the Aristotelian standards he uses throughout his discussion of human and divine volition: that voluntary choices are those which might eventuate in several different outcomes, whereas events in accordance with nature are distinguished by having only one outcome possible under given conditions?[55]     And (b) what function does cosmic volition play in Maimonidean nature when Maimonides is at pains to ensure that the system he describes would generate no event incompatible with natural science? If we can answer this pair of related questions, we come to the heart of Maimonides' naturalism, the distinctive basis of his dissatisfaction with mechanism and automatism.

(a) The theological-cum-modal question rests on a rather superficial confusion and is easily cleared up by logical considerations. God's choice does confront real alternatives: being or not being for the cosmos, this set of natural principles or that. Likewise with human choices. We confront the choices between life and death, the blessing and the curse.[56] The notion of alternative futures (implied in the very logic of the divine commandments and particularly in the ordinances that demand we take precautions against causing injury to others) does not imply the reality of alternative *actualities.*   Only one actuality will ever be real.   The other possibilities are virtual. There is no rabies on Oahu, there never has been, and perhaps there never will be. But to grant this is not to deny the possibility of rabies on Oahu and therefore abandon all precautions against its introduction. An event (*pace* Aristotle) is not to be called impossible merely because it will never occur. Accordingly, an option is not impossible merely because it will not be chosen. *To speak of choosing among alternatives is to acknowledge their possibility within a given framework of assumptions and to abstract from the assumptions that exclude or necessitate one alternative or another.* To speak of God's choosing to create the world or to create the world in a certain way is to abstract from the considerations (be they what they may) that actually govern God's choice and to make reference only to a looser framework of assumptions in which that choice is unconstrained. Perhaps God's choice to create the world was directed by His generosity and withholding of creation was excluded by God's grace. But when we speak of choice, we mean to abstract—as much as to say that leaving grace and generosity out of consideration, the world need not have existed.[57] The same analysis applies to any determinations, including human choices. When Maimonides says that human choices deal with emergent events or ephemera he addresses the contingency of outcomes. If Zayd makes a parapet on his roof,[58] he may forestall a particular catastrophe that might otherwise have occurred. If he fails to do so, an event that would otherwise have been impossible might become actual. But Zayd is the sort of being that can fail, through negligence, fatigue, distraction or forgetfulness.

What of the "choices" of the disembodied intelligences? God chooses to create, and were it not for His generosity might have chosen otherwise. Nothing in the nature of finite being determined Him to act, for it did not yet exist. Similarly, God chose the nature of the world. A variety of possible worlds are compatible with the logical requirements of internal coherence.[59] God chose this one, the one that operates by these natural principles. But these principles, according to Maimonides, are not abstract "laws" but determinants, disembodied intelligences, traditionally called angels, prime objects of creation. Their actions are invariant. Their "choices" are not irresolute, and their steadiness is the constancy of nature. The instances they govern are the forces that order and inform matter. They are purely intellectual (thus disembodied, fully actual, causally potent and conscious) forms. These intelligences choose in the same way that they were chosen: by delegating to what lies beneath them inwardly centered, natural control, for each thing, over its own motions and expressions, in accordance with the natures (rational or non-rational) chosen and imparted by the creative act of God.

The intelligences are said to act volitionally, then, because every natural juncture involves confrontation of alternatives. Things might have been determined so or so—not in the sense that, say, appetitive beings confront pragmatic vicissitudes, flexibly, prepared to alter our choices if our actions produce other than the expected outcomes, but determinatively, creatively, specifying the requirements of universal wisdom, with all but infinitely painstaking detail and care,[60] until all the myriad steps are traversed between the generalized idea of grace and the concrete particularity required for the instantiation of each natural kind and creature. In critically appropriating this idea, we would lay greater stress on the inner, evolutionary workings of natural choice at the junctures of contingency and none at all on the poetically personified hypostases. But the projection and pursuit of a good by each natural being remains as vital a supplement to mechanism as it was when Maimonides signalled the inadequacy of automatism in accounting for emanation, or when Socrates said that if all things are ruled by intelligence they would be directed toward the best. Volition in the "angels," even when they are construed as forms and forces, performs a specifying function that no mere automatism, whether mechanistic or intellectual, can achieve alone. Choice, specification of what need not have been, ensures that divine creativity and governance are not halted at the level of universals but actually reach the world of nature. For, as Aristotle himself taught, despite the Peripatetic denial of particular providence, nothing exists but particulars. There are no independent universals to be recipients of God's grace.[61]

(b)   What then of the cosmological point? If Maimonidean angels answer faithfully to the requirements of the good, obeying God's wisdom as each in its specificity perfectly but partially conceives it, faithfully replicating the very cosmos that would be expected on any rational scientific account, why are the angels retained at all? Why the emphasis on their intelligence and volition? Part of the answer has been already given. The rationalistic intellectualism that excludes voluntarism makes both the world and God's act necessary and eternal. At the same time it cuts off the world of particulars from the divine, as though universals were debarred somehow from governing their particulars. One more of the dangers of the exclusively intellectualist view, very obvious to us, is that it excludes empiricism—a failing marked both by Maimonides and by al-Ghazālī.[62] For it relegates to randomness what it cannot assimilate to wisdom and rational necessity, rather than leaving room for the kind of *a posteriori* recognition of necessity that discovers wisdom in nature even where we did not anticipate it. Maimonides' approach allows us to assimilate apparently random events to causal pattern without reducing them to matters of logical inevitability.

As for mechanism, its difficulties seemed obvious to Maimonides: It reduced the causal order to the play of chance. Even today mechanism tends to make necessity and chance indistinguishable. It thus has the effect of leaving nature unintelligible and causal regularities unexplained and inexplicable.[63] Where strict intellectualism carried rationalism too far, making God's choices themselves phenomena to be explained and treating all events as necessary categorically (as though logic were the sole and sufficient determinant of all natural determinacies), mechanistic materialism plainly did not go far enough. By debarring rational principles it made all natural events a mere series of inexplicable motions. Causes and effects became mere givens; every event, a pure positivity, with no principle of explanation to appeal to for understanding or prediction. We still confront the impact of this irrationalism when the positivistic heirs to the mechanism of Democritus attempt (rather lamely and inconsistently) to explain events in terms of natural laws and then turn the ledger to a bankrupt page when faced with the inquiry or the wonder why events should obey such laws.[64] Part of the strength of Maimonides' rationalistic naturalism lies in the very fact that its principles are not abstractions but concrete forces, intelligences that issue orders not as mere commands but through the inward natures and characters of things, which are, in fact, selected and designed—chosen—by the rational principles operative in nature.

Being determinative in their actions, the Maimonidean intelligences are not like ordinary mechanical forces. Yet the choice and consciousness assigned to the disembodied intellects are not like ours either. Their consciousness is of their own actions; and the choices they make, not dealing with contingent eventualities and ephemeral goals and patterns, are (as Socrates might have hoped) always for the best. This does not mean, of course, that the intelligences act as a kind of predestiny, charting the course of each finite being. On the contrary, such anthropomorphising notions of governance over nature treat the conduct of nature as though it were simply another pragmatic decision sequence manhandling contingent ephemera. Whereas in fact divine governance operates through the imparting of natural forms. Even in the human case, God's providence is expressed through the imparting of the human form and specifically, the rational soul or human intelligence.[65] Destiny is always causal, and in the human case it does not arise externally but through our own choices and actions.[66]

Nor are there any Panglossian implications to the Rambam's version of the idea that God governs for the best. For what is chosen by the hypostatic intelligences (from a diversity of alternative virtualities on Maimonides' account, which regards strict Neoplatonic emanation as too automatic to allow real differentiation and emergence of diversity and multiplicity[67]) is the pattern of nature at each step and stage of its elaboration. What God chooses is not the future of each being but the specificities of grace and nature by which each will freely manifest its own character in its milieu. In this specification, the divine wisdom is expressed in much the manner of a creative artist, where the wisdom is not fully articulated until it is instantiated. Thus the emanative generosity of God finds its meaning in the act of creation itself, not in its abstract virtuality. God, we can say, might not have created; but that would have been no act of grace. This fact is symbolized traditionally, both in the Neoplatonists and in the Psalms, by the representation of God's creativity as a fountain of light and life.[68] For light and life are not real until they are imparted; not imparted until they are real.[69] What is entailed in the notion that the intelligences of the spheres rule by conscious choice is that what we apprehend as an objective rationality in the cosmos has its roots in a higher, subjective rationality. It is to this matter that we must now turn—Maimonides' version of the answer to the mystery encapsulated in the famous words of Einstein: "The most incomprehensible thing about the universe is that it is comprehensible."

## 3. Inward Rationality and Choice in Nature

The Aristotelian spheres have fallen, and the Neoplatonic intelligences are dispersed. One might almost say that their work is completed. If God is to govern nature, He must do so without hypostases.[70] The age of vice-regents is past. But for that very reason the Aristotelian idea of immanence acquires a new and compelling force—although the Maimonidean value of distinguishing what is immanent from what is transcendent remains, as David Novak's paper makes very clear. But further, the Aristotelian natural forms have proved mutable—as a Plato or a Maimonides might have expected.[71] Indeed they are more mutable than Maimonides suspected. For he confined evolutionary change to the formative age of the cosmos and preserved the settled order of nature as an inner necessity against the supernaturalism of the superstitious. But we know that creation is not over and that natural laws are invariant at a rather higher level of abstraction than classical naturalists suspected. Seeming sports of nature prove to be causally significant in a process that may well be unrepeated; its outcomes, unexampled. The universe itself has a history. New meanings are discovered for the old ideas of Aristotle, Plato and al-Ghazālī, that time and space are relative to the things within them, or to the sensibilities of a percipient.[72] Even the idea of concreteness is profoundly altered with the discovery that matter is not what is ultimately conserved, and again with the recognition that the chemical atom is composed of parts made up in turn of particles whose properties are anything but homogeneous with those of the matter they compose.

If any natural object inherits the explanatory primacy of the Aristotelian spheres, it is the electron, or perhaps the quark. But electrons, like the spheres, no longer orbit. Their paths are not continuous curves—indeed they do not seem to be continuous. We can no longer even say in any very direct way of electrons—or of quarks—as once was proposed of the spheres, that their motions and locations determine events. Yet the curious status of our ultimate particles between matter and energy does somehow echo the character once assigned to the curiously non-material matter that Aristotle relied on as the substance of the spheres. And the ambiguous status of light, as wave or particle, seems to echo the ambiguous status of light in Neoplatonic systems, between matter and the ideal. Yet no one is likely to pretend that photons are alive. What possible meaning can be found for the Maimonidean scheme of angels as forces in a post-Aristotelian, post-Newtonian, post-Darwinian, even post-Planckian age? The beginnings of an answer are suggested in a passage cited by Averroes from Themistius, a philosopher well respected by Maimonides.[73]

Taking exception to an anti-Platonic argument in Aristotle's metaphysics based on the fact that man begets man—hence, that the human form comes to humans from their progenitors—Themistius argued that if "man is born only from man and horse from horse," spontaneous generation becomes inexplicable.[74] Now spontaneous generation is no more live an option today than are crystalline spheres. But the logic of spontaneous generation—by which species emerge from what they are not—is far more central to our evolutionary sciences than it was to Themistius, where it represented an odd countercase to Aristotelian naturalism, based on uncontrolled observation of marginal phenomena like the supposed generation of bees from dead cattle and hornets from dead horses. In an evolutionary context *all* species are taken to emerge from specifically and essentially different precursors, predecessors that lack the "form" of the emergent species. And all life is thought to derive from what was not alive.

Normally, in our science, such emergence is ascribed to the work of minute particles. Mendelian genetics has made good on the proposal of Epicurus that the causal principles behind natural selection lie not where Empedocles sought them, on the level of gross anatomy and function, but on the micro-level, in the germplasm, much cosseted from the environment, and capable, on the model laid out by Jacob and Monod and given biochemical configuration by Watson, Crick, Franklin and others, of organizing all the processes of life. But two assumptions common to most evolutionary schemes (whether their end products are living species or galaxies) call for closer examination in our Maimonidean framework than they usually receive: (a) The explanatory particles, at whatever level analysis ends and synthesis of higher order complexes is begun, move or spin or have a charge to impart, that is, they are still assumed to have distinctive, interactive characters, active dispositional properties, expressive of their natures. (b) In forming complexes or in other interactions, regardless how evanescent, the lower level particles engender higher order properties. The motion or spin or mass or other properties of "elementary" particles are taken as givens, and the higher order properties are treated as their resultants. To this familiar structure we must add two observations: The givenness of elemental properties is a contingent fact that can be explained only relative to *its* causes. And the emergence of "higher" properties from "lower" is a synthetic or creative act. For it takes the natural given beyond its givenness. The emergence of physical properties from, say electrical configurations or statistical regularities, of chemistry from physics, of biology from chemistry, of thought from life, at each stage generates dispositions and activities that could never be accounted for by the general laws describing the prior stages. Lower order properties in nature describe boundary conditions for the higher but neither predict nor explain them. For they do not even generate the categories necessary to describe them. Arithmetic will never "explain" geometry without the postulation of space, and chemistry will never explain psychology without the mention of thought.[75]

We cannot reduce biology to physics without remainder for the simple reason that what we note in physics abstracts away from all that is distinctive to biology. Physical laws are formulated to cover both living and non-living systems and attain their generality by ignoring the activities specific to living beings, which exploit the properties of matter, not "defying" them but *using* them to attain ends that matter considered *as* matter could never attain. Where science achieves generality by abstracting from the complexity and "thickness" of phenomena, it loses explanatory power over the specificities that are the quick of evolution. What emergence defies is not the general principles of nature but reduction to the terms of such general principles.

Mechanism ascribes the attainment of higher ends to complexity. But that is a clear case of disguising an abstract description of the effect as a reductive explanation of the cause, like saying that intelligence is a matter of problem solving or that opium acts through the *virtus dormitiva*. The explanatory power of reductive analysis rests on abstracting away from the thickness and complexity it seeks to explain, whereas here what we seek to explain is complexity itself, or rather, a certain kind of complexity—not turbulence or chaos, but a certain kind of order. In the emergence of life from non-living matter, higher order, organic ends are projected beyond the simple and immediate, elemental ends of the given. Matter exhibits such properties as impenetrability and inertia; compounds show acidity and basicity. But out of such properties as these new goals are constituted, by complexes capable not just of pursuing such goals but of projecting (and enlarging) a meaning for them: survival, reproduction, efflorescence, biological evolution.

Theorists of evolution who recognize the emergence of complexity tend to treat the fact not as a phenomenon but as a tautology: Of course the complex emerges from the simple. What else could it emerge from? Emergence represents not a tendency but the statistical exception to the general rule of breakdown. Stability, complexity, and higher order properties are not values pursued but mere names for what successfully persists, the delicate toy that rests glistening atop the slag heap of disordered wastes and failed attempts. Insensibly, iridescently, the claim that emergence is a tautology verges into the charge that emergence is a paradox. The notion of stability or success is bundled into a neutral-seeming package, masking the telic character that was present (and indeed presumed) from the outset, so that survival becomes an instance or at best a special case of inertia. Life and consciousness become fragments of a random walk rather than (as in Plotinus) a grand procession (*prohodos*) or (as in Maimonides) a cosmic panorama—nature passing before Moses in the panoply of its kinds (*Guide* I 38). By this means, emergence is assimilated to the random noise around it and ceases to stand forth as an achievement or a gift. And the value of the initial given, along with the values generated by evolving beings themselves in setting out their ends, is dismissed to grey facticity, the facticity that positivism acknowledges but cannot explain.

Simultaneous with the assimilation of the emergent to its background comes the paradoxical insistence on the ultimacy of disorder. It would take us too far afield to excavate the anthropomorphisms and projections latent in metaphysical applications of the idea of entropy, to urge reinstatement of the Aristotelian and Spinozistic insight that order and disorder, as value concepts, are *in our applications of them* (as Maimonides himself insists for all human applications of value notions—*Guide* I 2) necessarily tinged with subjectivity. We must await another occasion to attempt to re-enliven as a wholesome alternative to all anthropomorphising views of evolution and devolution the Aristotelian response to Empedocles' first falling foul of love and strife: the recognition that the breakdown of one thing is the build up of another.[76] What is pertinent here is the recognition that there is evolution in nature. To this we may add a recognition of ecological opportunism based very much on reading the Second Law of Thermodynamics in an Aristotelian spirit: Energy is not wasted in the cosmos if waste itself can be a resource—if a world as rich as ours can be sustained by the effluence of a middle class star like the sun.

Spinoza captures the dynamic of the two evolutionary assumptions far more forthrightly than most evolutionary theorists when he generalizes them to being at large. The essence of each thing is its tendency to preserve and promote its own being—not statically but through the expression of its own character and the elaboration of that character towards perfection. Here, despite (or perhaps because of) Spinoza's strictures against teleology of the anthropomorphising and anthropocentric type, we see the basis of a new yet properly Aristotelian teleology, in which all things in pursuing their own goals pursue perfection and by so doing, as Maimonides puts it, express the glory of God—or, as Spinoza puts it, express infinite being, each in its own way (*Ethica* I, def. 6). The means by which they do so, in Maimonidean language, are the essences imparted by God. For Maimonides is emphatic in maintaining that the disembodied intelligences from which forms stem are nothing apart from God, and matter itself is nothing but the condition of otherness by which God gives freedom or existentiation to finite particulars.[77]

In her efforts to rehabilitate Aristotelian teleology,[78] Martha Nussbaum is at pains to exclude as un-Aristotelian three doctrines which she plainly regards as damaging to the credibility of the Aristotelian approach in a modern scientific context: (i) "the idea of a universal teleology of nature"; (ii) the notion of mysterious, "non-empirical" strivings toward the realization of form; and (iii) the inclusion of non-organismic processes in teleology. She also objects to any effort to disengage matter from form or to see form as anything but the arrangement of matter. It is difficult to see in this context what would become of Aristotle's God, the pure Intelligence which is also pure Actuality, or how form is prevented from becoming always the secondary and passive, dependent variable, rather than the active and actualizing, ontically primary principle that Aristotle's metaphysics wants to make of it and requires it to be. But confining ourselves to the realm of nature and recognizing the indissolubility *here* of form from matter—for surely form cannot actualize when there is nothing in need of actualizing—we must recognize that Maimonides has followed an alternative line of interpretation to Nussbaum's in integrating the Aristotelian concepts of form, matter, telos and efficient cause—an alternative, closer to that of Joseph Owens, but not necessarily erroneous, and not necessarily as incompatible with the findings of our sciences as Nussbaum fears. There are good grounds for including non-organic processes in teleology, especially if we accept, as Nussbaum does, the distinction between objective and subjective ends. The goal of a process need not be conceptualized or envisioned by the actor in the process. Aristotle (like Spinoza) likes to speak in relative terms—of some actors as more articulate than others in reference to their goals. Clearly, in evolutionary terms, no integrated organic systems focused on (and thereby constituting) higher order goals are possible unless they could be built of components whose conatus is toward lesser, simpler, non-conceptualized goals.

The idea that such a conatus is a non-empiric "mysterious striving" towards the actualization of form is quite un-Aristotelian. To be sure, no ontic *élan* or thrust is to be detected by the senses. But Aristotelian induction makes it clear that a nisus in each thing towards the expression (and preservation, elaboration) of its character is the common theme in all finite being. There is nothing to save in Aristotelian teleology if we discard the notion of unconscious and inchoate goals. For the very essence of Aristotle's teleology is the distinction between ends, which all processes in nature have, and purposes, which only deliberating beings have. Speaking Spinozistically, we do not depart far from the thought of Aristotle if we say that the conatus of each thing is its essence, and that this is known from experience, although no conatus is a sense datum.

As for a general causal plan or universal teleology, Maimonides concurs with Nussbaum's suspicions, if the phrase "universal teleology of nature" intends the assignment of a single overall anthropomorphic purpose to God, as in the thesis which Maimonides anticipates Spinoza in rejecting: that God made all things for man and man that he might worship God.[79] Maimonides holds that God made all things in the first instance for their own sakes. Things glorify God in pursuing their own perfection. For in so doing they manifest, each in its own way, one aspect of the perfection of God. But, in this sense, on a meta-level, there *is* a general teleology of nature for Maimonides. The same is true, of course, for Aristotle. That is why the love and strife schematism of Empedocles must be rejected. It relies on separate principles to explain creation and destruction (order and entropy) instead of recognizing that in a single system of nature only one (but very general) principle is required, since build up and break down (like our oxidation and reduction) are the same process viewed from opposite perspectives. The single necessary principle is that of perfection.[80]

Each being in nature has an end or good of its own. It is for this reason in part that the term 'good' is systematically (*pros hen*) ambiguous for Aristotle. But there is no comfort for the relativism of the Sophists here. The recognition that finite beings have partial and partisan perspectives on the good does not entail that all differences in levels of perfection are subjective or that one segment of being is no better than another—the grub or speck of dust on a par with the inspired lawgiver and poet.[81] The notion of a universal good remains applicable by reference to the common orientation of each thing toward perfection—a specification of the pure perfection of God.

Nussbaum argues that Aristotle might have had a notion of a general or cosmic teleology had the concept of an ecosystem been available to him, but she denies that such a concept was accessible to Aristotle. Yet Aristotle has the idea of a single integrated cosmic system; and his distinctive use (against Empedocles) of the Heraclitean notion that "the way up is the way down" perfects that concept and allows for a characteristically Aristotelian ecology: Since the breakdown of one thing is the build up of another, energy in Aristotle's sense is not lost in the cosmos but systematically recycled by the action of the spheres and under the influence of the intelligences—there is no loss of complexity for the cosmos as a whole. It was for this reason in part that Aristotle's successors kept alive the ancient equation of the cosmos with an organism.

We cannot retain Aristotle's confidence in the absolute stability of the cosmic plan. But Maimonides, following the lead of al-

Ghazālī and Philoponus, long ago found excessive the Aristotelian claims for the stability of the cosmos. One of his greatest contributions was to disentangle the Aristotelian idea of the consistency of natural law from the metaphysical notion of an unalterable nature. As for ourselves, we expect neither unlimited cosmic "progress" nor necessarily (as in Philoponus) a universal cosmic endgame, but continued opportunities for evolution, accompanied by continued liabilities to decline—the two being by no means mutually exclusive.

Clearly, for Aristotle, if there were no integration of all causes in a single cosmos there would not be much point in taking Anaxagoras to task for failing adequately to integrate the rationality of Nous into the account of nature. Nor would it be clear why Aristotle should place Nous, at the helm (but not anthropomorphically) of his cosmic system, or why at the outset of the *Nicomachaean Ethics* (I 1) he should assume that means without an ultimate end have no end at all. Maimonides profits from the Neoplatonic recension of Aristotle's metaphysics by discovering in it a subtle account of how the form or essence of each thing can be both its project and its charge from God. It is here that he finds an affinity between the thinking of the Neoplatonic Aristotelians as to forms and ends and the Rabbinic, midrashically enunciated teachings and Biblical vignettes about angels. The astronomy of the scheme, of course, is quite secondary.

Maimonides is rather diffident toward the Aristotelian cosmology. He knows the weaknesses of Ptolemaic astronomy in accounting for the retrograde motion of the planets[82] and is skeptical of claims to knowledge about the celestial beings.[83] He echoes Plato's treatment of cosmology as "a likely story," arguing that the Aristotelian scheme is plausible but by no means established or even verifiable, and he stresses Ptolemy's treatment of astronomical theories as mathematical models designed to account for the observed phenomena, not necessarily to map the cosmos as it actually is.[84] In several passages he disclaims any intention of adding to the store of astronomical theory, and in one he urges that there are already enough books speculating on the correct number of the disembodied intellects.[85]

Yet despite these expressions of restiveness with classical astronomy and despite his explicit efforts to bracket the detailed claims of classical cosmology, Maimonides argues strenuously for the congruence of Biblical and Rabbinic angelology with Greek cosmology and outspokenly avows as general principles what he presents as its central theme: the existence of non-material intellectual beings superior in nobility to humanity and exercising volition in the governance of the cosmos.[86] I have argued that there is something of value here, to be disentangled from Ptolemaic astronomy, mythic angelology and even Aristotelian cosmology. Maimonides' efforts to articulate the insight he finds in quite non-Aristotelian idioms in Scripture and Midrash aid us in disentangling that insight and stating it in terms that do not sap our present scientific beachhead.

The quintessential spheres, slowed by retrogradation, breached by comets, and shattered by the laws of parallax that sent them careening into one another, were brought to the ground finally by the very demands of elegance that had erected them. It was no longer necessary to appeal to 55 or 47 or even 10 intelligences to account for the observed celestial motions when two impersonal forces— gravity and inertia—would suffice, given the adequacy of Newton's principles to account for Kepler's laws. The facts of relativity and the quantum relationships emerge from ambiguities in the behavior of light and its emanative cousins and cousins german— electromagnetism, gravity, and other sorts of forces that might be resident in a body or even propagated where no body is present to support them. The mechanistic materialism once taken as the message of Newtonian physics has given way (yet not entirely and consistently) to a variety of alternative metaphysical readings. Prominent among them are the Whiteheadian de-emphasis of substance in favor of events, and the phenomenalistic metaphysic that sometimes passes as radical empiricism or even bravely manifests its allegiance to the old materialism after which it still hankers, but sometimes openly or tacitly avows one form or another of idealism. For moody or disenchanted phenomenalists can still argue that appearances are nothing without subjects and thus that there are no facts without subjective apprehendors—that the very content of physics requires the positing of human subjects. Such arguments, regardless of where they are assumed to lead—whether to subjectivism, humanism, cultural relativism, mysticism, or some form of Buddhism—have no more in them today than they had before the advent of quantum physics. That observations are subjective is a tautology and cannot imply the metaphysically freighted denial that the world would not exist without an observer—a claim about the world which we have no evidence to support.

Both Process Philosophy and the many varieties of subjectivism that have claimed paternity in the new physics seem to rest their most convincing claims on the fact that what we study in physics (and thus what we know about nature) are intelligible patterns among things. This is what Heraclitus and Greek speakers after him, from Plato and Aristotle to Philo and beyond, called logos. It was not something subjective, at least not a figment of human thought alone. The tendency to read the intelligibility of nature as an artifact of human study is a symptom but not a demonstrated consequence of renaissance and enlightenment humanism. The projective/reflexive structure of such a claim is as indicative of its doubtfulness as is the same structure in any other anthropomorphism. We achieve some hope of overcoming subjectivism in our accounts of science by the same means that we find hope of objectivity in science itself: desisting from seeking in the cosmos (or in science) only images of ourselves. For the same distaste for narcissism that once taught us not to find an image of ourselves in the sky ought now to teach us not to seek that same image deflected to the sciences, but to cross-calibrate those sciences so that they reflect the world at large and not ourselves alone.[87] Accordingly, the intelligence that we detect in nature (and must detect in order to explain) must not be judged *as* intelligence by the extent of its approximation to a human mentality. Rather, we must recognize its wisdom in its own terms and learn what universal or absolute intelligence is from the inductive study of its work, not from the application to it of our own preconcerted notions.

The same idea, that we can triangulate from our diverse findings to generate some measure of objectivity in science, is expressed, with a slightly different (but still rather Pythagorean) emphasis when modern theorists say that mathematics is the language of physics. What they mean is that a scientific finding is one that answers to formal values such as comprehensiveness, symmetry, rhythm, harmony, and elegance. The exact character of such values cannot be specified *a priori*, just as there is no formal definition of a melody, a pattern, or a game. But in some measure, in specific circumstances, the appearance of such values is confirmable *a posteriori*, and the more we know of specific contexts and frameworks of operation, the more reliable we become in applying such notions consistently and communicating with others about where they arise and what forms they might be expected to take.[88]

No one could have predicted *a priori* that there were not four but over a hundred elements. Yet, given close observational experience and controlled experimentation with the patterns of behavior of many elements, it was possible in some measure to predict the character and even existence of others—even to generate the conditions in which new elements would arise. The same fact about the nature of science is expressed in Maimonidean terms by saying that scientists study the rationality embedded in nature; in Aristotelian terms, by saying that the sciences study why things must be as they are; in Platonic terms, by saying that they learn how intelligence governs all things for the best.

Explicitly or implicitly the standpoint remains teleological—explicitly in the medieval and classical formulations; tacitly, often surreptitiously, in our own. Standards of value are still used in framing viable hypotheses and in recognizing their confirming instances—which still answer to the description Aristotle gave: that in studying nature we will discover craftsmanship like that of the most skilled artistry.[89] The objective view clearly is not anthropocentric. But in our haste to avoid describing it as divine (for what is science if not the endeavor to understand the world in some small measure as God does and thereby transcend some of our human limitations) we conceal the character of the standards we apply, positivistically deny them (while still using them), or projectively displace them—as we do when we treat them as subjective—as though the order of the world (which in other contexts we feel free to criticize) could somehow be the work of our own minds.

The idea of forms[90] does not die as readily as that of spheres or sphere souls. For matter without form remains a mere virtuality, and all the principles we appeal to in the description or explanation of natural phenomena—forces, fields, charges, dispositions—remain formal characters in things. Nor does Aristotle's profound conception that the linkage between God and nature must be telic die with the gradual rusting of his all too material mechanism for that linkage, which Maimonides, Averroes, and Aristotle himself were more than prepared to bracket as a mere model of what must one day prove to be the case, and which Plato included most emphatically in what he called "a likely story." The ideal that beings strive for, the form they grope to realize as their own—conceptualizable as the orienting goal of their conatus—is, in its immediacy, neither hypostatic nor immanent. Rather, like Philo's Logos, it remains, through all changes in its conceptualization, a virtuality projected by each individual being, with a characteristic degree of articulacy, propinquity or remoteness.

The Maimonidean claim that the forces governing nature are not only rational but volitional, conscious and intelligent has some salvage value, then, in suggesting an alternative to the positivism that negates the categories of explanation we employ, and an alternative, for that matter, to the reactive subjectivism that romantically confounds those categories with artifacts of our cultures or figments of our psyches: (a) To invoke the notion of choice, as the Rambam does, is to imply that values are at stake, that the determinations we discover in nature are not made among neutral, equally valuable or valueless alternatives but involve a directionality that the conatus in all beings implicitly recognizes and participates in defining—not by assigning it an arbitrary direction but by specifying, composing, articulating and synthesizing. Something is better than nothing; a world in which evolution occurs is better than one in which no such process is possible—even though not every product of evolution will be concordant with *our* purposes.[91]   (b) To invoke the notion of intelligence is to make explicit the claim that a rationality is operative in nature that is answerable to our ideas of wisdom although far transcending them, since we at best anticipate the course of divine artistry and never know it *a priori.*

God governs by delegation in that God leaves all beings to the solution of their own problems, but not without means to address them. Human intelligence is a special case. Here the inner or self-focused energies of a being are brought to a pitch of articulation and integration that allows the conscious and communicable setting forth of values and the assignment of orders of priority among them. The inanimate and inarticulate achieve no such integration. Yet the lower is necessary to the higher, as finite minds cannot act without matter; and, for any action to take place or even the most elemental coordination to persist, some measure of integration is required. It is anthropomorphic to call integration among the elements purposive. But all beings have goals—create goals, we must say—in the very acts by which each being manifests persistence. The blind gropings necessary to the emergence of conscious purpose from its prototypes are referred to intelligence, by license, in the sense that they project a goal; but in earnest, in the sense that goal-directed and goal-constituting activity presupposes a directionality whose orienting pole is the pure intelligence and pure perfection of the Divine.

To find hallmarks of the intelligence that governs nature in the forms of things (not in the celestial bodies alone of course, but in all parts of the cosmos) is both to make that intelligence knowable and to deny that its apprehension depends on our projection. It is to locate in each thing the groping towards choice made by the conatus which is the being and the value of that thing. If the heavens are not alive, as Maimonides hoped, neither is the earth as dead as he supposed. The universe is rife with living beings and with the possibilities of life, light and consciousness. These come not from our perception but from things. They argue the governance of God with the same silent voice that bespeaks the possibility of science. When beings grope toward the definition of their future and the future of their kind they do not do so because we might say they do or as we might say they should. The values that direct their determinations are their own—most often fully articulated for the first time and thereby made actual in the very act of their selection. To understand the world is to see it not from our own perspective but from that of things themselves—that is, from the perspectives that the grace of God unselfishly, or to use Plato's term, unstintingly, imparts. Even the elements have their silent song to sing.

### Notes

1. London: Collins, 1959, 62-66.
2. See Shmuel Sambursky, *Physics of the Stoics* (London: Routledge Kegan Paul, 1959), 1-48.
3. See *Enneads* V 3.15; cf. III 8.10, 2; V 4.2, 38.
4. See Maimonides, *Guide* II 12; and cf. Ibn Ṭufayl's *Hayy Ibn Yaqzān*, Goodman, 125-27.
5. *Guide* III 16.

6. See *Guide* III 16; cf. I 17, 28, II 13. Maimonides follows Saadiah's lead in treating theodicy as one of the few legitimate problem areas in theology. He follows Aristotle himself, but more specifically the tradition we know as represented by al-Kindī and al-Āmirī, in assimilating First Philosophy to theology. See Dimitri Gutas, *Avicenna and the Aristotelian Tradition* (Leiden: Brill, 1988), 238-53; Everett Rowson, *A Muslim Philosopher on the Soul and its Fate*. Of the two major families of issues addressed in the *Guide to the Perplexed*—the Account of Creation and the Account of the Chariot—Maimonides treats the former as a special case of the latter. The problems of cosmology and cosmogony (philosophical "Physics") are a subset of the problems of theophany, God's manifestation in finite terms (metaphysics or theology). Rival schools of thought—creationism, interventionistic occasionalism, the laissez faire theology of the Epicureans and the eternalistic naturalism of the Aristotelians— accordingly lead to corresponding positions with regard to providence and creation. The idea that the principal problem of metaphysics is the emergence of the many from the one is, of course, neoplatonic, as Arthur Hyman's sketch of its history in this volume shows.

7. See Joseph Owens, *The Doctrine of Being in the Aristotelian Metaphysics*, 3rd ed. (Toronto: Pontifical Institute of Medieval Studies, 1978), 315-74.

8. Dillon traces the "intradeical" Forms as far back as the Middle Platonists and ultimately to Plato himself: *The Middle Platonists* 6, 95, 255, 410, with *Timaeus* 35A, *Laws* X. Plotinus fuses Aristotle's Nous with Plato's realm of forms, referring to the now content-filled thought-thinking-itself as Being. The other papers in this volume show the many uses found for the idea of Nous as a "one/many," in Plotinus's terms.

9. *Metaphysics* A 9, 991a 8: "Above all one might discuss the question what on earth the Forms contribute. . . . For they cause neither movement nor any change . . ."

10. Philo, heeding Platonic, Stoic, Rabbinic and Scriptural cues, is an architect of the approach, for his Logos partakes of both objective and subjective rationality and thus mediates between God's absoluteness and the particularity of the world. Like Maimonides, Philo calls the ideas powers, following *Sophist* 247DE; he makes them subordinate to God and active (*energoun*) organizing principles of nature. See *De Mutatione Nominum* 21, 122, *De Specialibus Legibus* I 8, 45-48 and Wolfson, *Philo*, 1.217-18; cf. David Winston, citing *Phaedo* 95E and Diogenes Laertius 7, 147 in *Logos and Mystical Theology in Philo of Alexandria*, 19.

11. The identification is not confined to the *Guide to the Perplexed*. See Maimonides *Code*, I, *Hilkhot Yesodei Torah* 2.7, ed. and tr. M. Hyamson (Jerusalem: Feldheim, 1974), 36a, where the highest echelon of angels, the scriptural *ḥayyot*, are called forms (*ẓurot*).

12. *Guide* II 6, Munk, **2**.17b, ll. 14-17.

13. *Guide* II 6, Munk **2**.17b, ll. 5-6. The usage which refers to emanative energies as forces or powers is precedented in Arabic in al-Fārābī's *Fī 'Aql (De Intellectu et Intellecto)*, ed., M. Bouyges (Beirut: Catholic Press, 1938); tr., A. Hyman, in Arthur Hyman and James Walsh, eds. *Philosophy in the Middle Ages* (New York: Harper and Row, 1967), 211-21.

14. *Guide* II 5, citing Psalms 19:2-4.

15. *Guide* II 4, Munk **2**.14ab; II 48, citing Jonah 2:2.

16. *Guide* II 6, Munk **2**.17b, ll. 1-3; cf. *De Generatione Animalium* II 3, 736b 26-737a 11.

17. Thus 1 Kings 19:11-12: ". . . and the Lord was not in the wind . . . the Lord was not in the earthquake . . . the Lord was not in the fire: and after the fire was a still small voice . . ." Maimonides cites the passage in *Guide* II 41 in justifying his account of prophecy, which neither reduces prophetic inspiration to a matter of subjective appearances nor treats it as a matter of divine indwelling but relies upon the (creationist) mediating scheme of (neoplatonic, intellectual/ formal) angels between God's Absoluteness and human intelligence.

18. *Guide* II 6, Munk **2**.16b-17a. The Rabbinic text Maimonides cites echoes Sanhedrin 38b but the verbatim citation is unknown. The celestial retinue are called God's *pamalya* (cf. the Latin *famulus*), servitors or ministrants, not peers. Plato speaks of the demiurge consulting the forms at *Timaeus* 28b-30c. The Platonic overtones of the Rabbinic dictum were of great significance in the Kabbalah, as Moshe Idel's paper in this volume shows.

19. See *Guide* III 18.

20. *De Anima* III 4, 429a 15-16, 430a 3; 5, 430a 17-20; *Guide* I 68, Munk **1**.86b; *Code* I, *Hilkhot Yesodei Torah* 2.10.

21. *Guide* I 48. Philo reaches a similar conclusion.

22. *Guide* III 19, Munk 3.40.

23. *Guide* III 16, Munk 3.43b-44a.

24. Cf. Saadiah on Job 28:34-25, in Goodman, tr., *The Book of Theodicy*, 331-33.

25. *Guide* II 6, Munk **2**.16-18.

26. Cf. al-Ghazālī, *Tahāfut al-Falāsifa*, The Incoherence of the Philosophers, ed. M. Bouyges (Beirut: Catholic Press, 2nd ed., 1962): "Our second point addresses those who grant that these events flow (or

emanate) from the First Principles of temporal events . . ."

27. *Guide* III 17, II 13; cf. III 31.
28. *Guide* III 13, I 1; "Eight Chapters" 5, echoing Plato's *Theaetetus* 176.
29. *Guide* III 32. Cf. Miskawayh, *The Refinement of Character*, tr. Constantine Zurayk (Beirut: American University, 1968), 81-83.
30. *Guide* II 20, citing *Physics* II 4-5; and *Guide* II 12, 48.
31. *Guide* II 3, 10, 12. For God's "will" and "wisdom," see my "Matter and Form as Attributes of God in Maimonides' Philosophy," 86-97.
32. See *Guide* I 2, II 4.
33. *Guide* II 17; cf. III 15.
34. *Guide* I 72, II 10.
35. Maimonides *Code* I, *Hilkhot Teshuvah* 5.2, 5.1, 5.4 viii, Hyamson, 86b-87b; cf. my "Determinism and Freedom in Spinoza, Maimonides and Aristotle." For animal vitality see *Guide* I 72, Munk 1.102b l. 17 - 103a l. 1.
36. *Guide* II 5, Munk 2.15ab. Maimonides emphasizes the inanimateness of the four elements in *Guide* I 72 and argues that if the elements were alive and the forces of nature exercised discretion, confining their actions only to what is necessary, there would be no natural evils.
37. See *Guide* III 22.
38. *Guide* II 6, Munk 2.16b l. 10.
39. *Guide* I 72, Munk 1.100b.
40. See Qur'ān 2:34 and the commentaries; for Shi'ite views, M. J. Kister, "Legends in *tafsīr* and *ḥadīth* Literature: the Creation of Adam and Related Stories," in Andrew Rippin, ed., *Approaches to the History of the Interpretation of the Qur'ān* (Oxford: Clarendon Press, 1988), 108-09.
41. *Guide* II, 11, III 12-14. The spheres, being composed of matter, are "impure" relative to the disembodied intellects; but even the spheres are nobler as bodies than human bodies are: They do not exist for our sake. For the nobility of the spheres and intellects, see Abraham Ibn Daud, *The Exalted Faith*, Samuelson, 120b.
42. *Guide* II 7, Munk 2.18b. Cf. Saadiah, on Job 1:6, *The Book of Theodicy*, 154-59.
43. *Guide* II 6, Munk 2.17ab.
44. *Guide* II 6, Munk 2.18b.
45. *Guide* II, Introduction, Premises 10-12. Natural forms are "forces in a body," but the substantial forms through which a body exists—soul and mind, for example—are not forces in a body or divided even *per accidens* with its divisions (cf. Aristotle, *De Anima* I 5, 411b 19-27). Maimonides accepts the premises of the Philosophers, except the

eternity of the world, which he treats as an isolable postulate of their system.

46. See *Guide* II 4, 5, 7, 8, esp. II 5, citing Psalms 19:4, Munk 2.15b.
47. *Phaedo* 97C-98E. Socrates assumed that in knowing how all things are governed for the best and thus what is best for each, he would know how human beings too should be governed. Cf. Maimonides on Moses' desire to learn God's ways, the laws of nature, so as to know how to govern the people: *Guide* I 54, glossing Exodus 33:13-20 and 34:6-7.
48. *Metaphysics* I 3, 984a 11-19, 985a 18; cf. *De Anima* I 2, 405a 14-17; *Poetica* 15, 1454b 1.
49. *Metaphysics* I 4, 985a 5-29.
50. Cf. al-Fārābī, *Kitāb Mabādī' ārā' ahlu 'l-madīnatu 'l-Fāḍila* (The Book of the Principles behind the Beliefs of the People of the Outstanding State) III 9, tr. R. Walzer as *Al-Farabi on the Perfect State*, 145-49.
51. *Guide* II 4.
52. *Guide* II 19.
53. *Guide* II 19, 21.
54. *The Incoherence of the Philosophers*, Discussions 3-4, 10; see my "Al-Ghazālī's Argument from Creation," *IJMES* 2 (1971): 67-85, 168-88; "Did al-Ghazālī Deny Causality?" *Studia Islamica* 47 (1978): 83-120; *RAMBAM*, 175-204.
55. See *Metaphysics* 1046b, 1048a 8-12, and Maimonides, *Guide* II 19; "Eight Chapters," 8; *Code*, I, *Hilkhot Teshuvah* 5.2, with 5.1 and 5.4 viii; see my discussion in "Determinism and Freedom in Spinoza, Maimonides, and Aristotle."
56. *Guide* III 17.5 and Deuteronomy 11:26.
57. To affirm an open future, I emphasize, is not to affirm the *actuality* of alternative futures but only the reality of alternative possibilities as possibilities—that is, their virtuality. Using the idea of emergence portended in Bergson's concept of duration or even in Spinoza's dynamic conatus, we can say that even if only one future will be actual, there are many alternative possibilities for it, since its nature does not become determinate until it exists, that is, until its causes make it actual.
58. Cf. "Eight Chapters," 8, citing Deuteronomy 22:8.
59. For the Maimonidean background of possible worlds, see my "Maimonides and Leibniz," with Leibniz' reading notes on the Latin *Doctor Perplexorum* (Basel, 1629).

60. I say *all but* infinitely painstaking care. Had infinite care been taken, the task could not have been completed and finite being could not have emerged. Finitude in the sense dealt with in David Novak's paper would have been overwhelmed.

61. *Guide* III 18. Maimonides stresses the Aristotelian origin of conceptualism, since the tradition of Alexander of Aphrodisias made Aristotle the champion of a denial of individual providence below the sphere of the moon. The worry that an Avicennan emanative naturalism excludes providence over individuals is answered by the recognition that providence cannot exclude the minds of human individuals, which are among the products of emanation. See *Guide* III 17. But no particular escapes *general* providence, since all are encompassed under their universals and thus under the universal governance of God's law.

62. See my "Three Meanings of the Idea of Creation."

63. *Guide* II 20.

64. Cf. my discussion of the incoherence of positivism in *Monotheism*, 61-69.

65. *Guide* III 25.

66. See Maimonides, "Eight Chapters," 8.

67. See Arthur Hyman's paper in this volume.

68. See *Guide* II 12, citing Jeremiah 2:13, Psalms 36:10; *Guide* I 68. The ideas of light, life, being and truth, come together in the Psalmist's fused image of a fountain of life which is the source of our enlightenment—the image in which Ibn Gabirol saw the affinity of Biblical poetry to Neoplatonic metaphysics. The elaboration of that intuition is the substance of Ibn Gabirol's metaphysics, as set forth in the papers of Professors Dillon, Mathis and McGinn.

69. Here, as in the analogies of the clock and the needle, Maimonides *did* develop the model of practical reason (cf. *Guide* III 21) as called for in David Burrell's paper, although it was not in the nature of Maimonides' project to make every move as explicit as we might prefer.

70. Cf. *Guide* I 23, 65.

71. For Plato insisted that all temporal things are mutable, and Maimonides urged that one cannot make a metaphysical canon of the observed stability of kinds in nature. See *Guide* II 17, 14; cf. the suggestive gloss of Genesis Rabbah XXI at *Guide* I 49: "Through this dictum they state clearly that the angels [sc. forms] are immaterial and have no fixed bodily form outside the mind." Munk 1.55b ll 2-4. For what is fixed, by Platonic standards must be ideal, and what is sensory, and so imaginable, must be mutable.

72. See Aristotle, *Physics* IV 2; al-Ghazālī, *Ma'ārij al-Quds* 203-04; *Tahāfut al-Falāsifa* (Incoherence of the Philosophers) Bouyges 2nd ed., 67; *Guide* I 52.

73. See *Guide* I 71, Munk 1.96a.

74. *Themistii in Aristotelis Metaphysicorum librum Lambda paraphrasis*, Medieval Hebrew translation, ed. S. Landauer, in *Commentaria in Aristotelem Graeca* 5.5 (Berlin, 1903): 8, cited in Herbert Davidson, "Averroes on the Active Intellect," 202.

75. See P. S. Schiavella, "Emergent Evolution and Reductionism," *Scientia* 108 (1973): 323-30.

76. Aristotle, *Metaphysics* Alpha 4, 985a 24.

77. See *Guide* III 18, 22; cf. I 68, and I 9, with Saadiah, *Book of Beliefs and Convictions*, II 13 ad fin., Kafah, 115; Rosenblatt, 136.

78. See her commentary on Aristotle's *De Motu Animalium* (Princeton: Princeton University Press, 1985), 60, 74, 93-98.

79. *Guide* III 13 with III 25.

80. Thus Maimonides' emphasis on the Aristotelian thesis, still employed by scientists, that the world forms a single system, and his further emphasis on the Saadianic point that the thesis of the world's singularity is vital to the central claim of monotheism. See *Guide* I 72.

81. See *Guide* III 17.

82. For Maimonides' rejection of epicycles and eccentrics see, *Guide* II 24; cf. I 71, Munk 1.96a; cf. F. J. Carmody, "The Planetary Theory of Ibn Rushd," *Osiris* 10 (1952): 556-86; A. I. Sabra, "The Andalusian Revolt against Ptolemaic Astronomy," in E. Mendelsohn, ed., *Transformation and Tradition in the Sciences* (Cambridge: at the University Press, 1984), 133-53.

83. *Guide* II 3.

84. *Guide* II 11. Plato's "likely story" account of science is not, of course, a skeptical rejection of the scientific enterprise, but an attempt to explain the nature and limits of what must pass for knowledge within the confines of a temporal, sensory world. See Anne Ashbaugh, *Plato's Theory of Explanation* (Albany: SUNY Press, 1988). Maimonides too is no radical skeptic. He accepts Saadiah's epistemology, and his most distinctive principle of method is the postulate that the possibility of doubt is *not* sufficient grounds for rejecting a claim.

85. *Guide*, II 2, 11. At II 8 Maimonides cites a passage now lost in Talmud texts, at *Pesahim* 94b, "The sages of the nations prevailed," to show that the Rabbis conceded the authority of secular science in astronomy and other natural sciences.

86.  *Guide* I 72, II 4-5. Averroes gives the same diffident approval of cosmic emanation that we find in Maimonides, bracketing such speculations as the work of "recent philosophers such as al-Fārābī," perhaps along with the ideas of Themistius and Plato, yet calling them "the most solid" notions we have to go on in these rather unsolid areas. Madrid Escorial Hebrew manuscript G1-14, fol. 103b, etc. cited in Davidson, "Averroes on the Active Intellect," n. 40. Al-Fārābī himself characteristically brackets metaphysical views which have an impact on cosmology as "beliefs of the people of the excellent state." See *Arā'*, and *Fuṣūl al-Madanī.*

87.  See my "Ordinary and Extraordinary Language in Medieval Jewish and Islamic Philosophy."

88.  See my "Why Machines Cannot do Science."

89.  See *De Partibus Animalium* I 5, esp. 645a 9.

90.  Cf. *De Partibus Animalium* I 1, 640b 30 ff.

91.  Here I refer to the profound insight articulated in Cynthia Ozick's story, "The Laughter of Akiva," in its original recension in the *New Yorker* 56 (November 10, 1980, et seq.): 50-60+.

# The Virtue of Faith

## Menachem Kellner

It is with apparent reference to the verse describing Abraham, "And he believed in the Lord and it was accounted to him as justice (*zedaqah*)" (Genesis 15:6) that Philo, who may well be considered the "father of Neoplatonism," calls faith a virtue, indeed, the "queen of virtues."[1] In his study of Philo's philosophy, Harry Wolfson explains that by 'faith' Philo means "two things: (1) belief in the unity and providence of God as well as in all the truths revealed directly by God, and (2) trust in God."[2] That faith which Philo held to be a virtue has cognitive (acquiescence to certain propositions) and non-cognitive (trust in God) elements.

This reading of faith as a virtue appears to be new in Philo. Wolfson says, "But in Greek philosophy prior to Philo neither faith in general nor faith in God in particular is spoken of as a virtue on a par with piety, the fear of God, and holiness."[3] This estimation is shared by John Passmore: "The path to perfection, as Philo envisages it, begins with faith, a faith in God comparable to Abraham's. This is a point at which Philo breaks sharply with the Greek tradition. There is nowhere in Greek thought any suggestion that faith is a virtue, let alone that it is 'the queen of virtues,' to quote only one of Philo's ecstatic descriptions of it."[4]

Philo's distinctive outlook finds a surprising echo in the writings of Moses Maimonides. In *The Guide of the Perplexed* (III 53) Maimonides calls faith (*al-imān*) a virtue (*faḍīlah*). In this paper I hope to explain why this is surprising and how an understanding of the claim that faith is a virtue can help us better to understand the place of ethics in Maimonides' thinking. Maimonides' claim about the virtue of faith comes up in the context of a discussion of three terms, *hesed* (loving-kindness), *mishpat* (judgment), and *zedakah* (righteousness). The last of these is defined as follows:

> The word *zedaqah* is derived from *zedeq*, which means justice; justice being the granting to everyone who has a right to something, that which he has a right to and giving to every being that which corresponds to its merits. But in the books of the prophets, fulfilling the duties imposed upon you with regard to others is not called *zedaqah* in conformity with the first sense. For if you give a hired man his wages or pay a debt, this is not called *zedaqah*. On the other hand, the fulfilling of duties with regard to others imposed upon you on account of moral virtue (*fadīlat al-khalq*), such as remedying the injuries of all those who are injured, is called *zedaqah*. Therefore it says with reference to the returning of a pledge:  And it shall be *zedaqah* unto you (Deuteronomy 24:13). For when you walk in the way of the moral virtues, you do justice unto your rational soul (*nafsika al-nāṭiqa*), giving her the due that is her right. And because every moral virtue is called *zedaqah*, it says:  And he believed in the Lord, and it was accounted to him as *zedaqah* (Genesis 15:6). I refer to the virtue of faith. This applies likewise to his dictum, may he be exalted:  And it shall be *zedaqah* unto us if we take care to observe, and so on (Deuteronomy 6:25).[5]

Maimonides here offers two definitions of justice. The first is giving to each his due; the second definition is Biblical and involves more than giving each his due.  It demands acting towards others in keeping with the requirements of the moral virtues.[6]  Maimonides uses the example of curing the hurts of those whom one has not injured.  He cites as a further example the Biblical obligation not to keep a pledge needed by its owner:  "When thou dost lend thy neighbor any manner of loan, thou shalt not go into his house to fetch his pledge.  Thou shalt stand without, and the  man to whom thou dost lend shall bring forth the pledge without unto thee.  And if he be a poor man thou shalt not sleep with his pledge; thou shalt surely restore to him the pledge when the sun goeth down, that he may sleep in his garment and bless thee; and it shall be *zedaqah* unto thee before the Lord thy God" (Deuteronomy 24:10-13).[7]

Maimonides gives another reason for calling the behavior demanded by moral virtue just: When we act morally we do justice to our rational soul, giving it its due. Maimonides here appeals to the first definition of justice in order to justify his second use of the term. But how does acting morally give our rational soul its due? The answer, I believe, involves Maimonides' claim that rational perfection cannot be attained without first achieving moral perfection.[8]

Maimonides now gives a third reason for calling moral behavior just: the fact that moral virtues are called *zedaqah*. As his example he cites the verse, "And he believed in the Lord and it was accounted to him as *zedaqah*." Realizing that this citation would not be transparent to his reader, Maimonides explains by saying, "I refer to the virtue of faith." This, then, is the context of Maimonides' claim that faith is a virtue.

The concordance shows that Maimonides did not have any other ready options if he needed a verse connecting a specific virtue with *zedaqah*. But his identification of faith as a virtue remains striking. For when he deals with questions of faith or belief it is almost always in what we would tend to call an intellectual as distinguished from a moral context. For example, he says of "belief" that it is not "what is said but rather what is thought when a thing is affirmed to be such as it is thought to be."[9] Maimonides reaffirms the point a bit further along in the same passage: "We cannot believe unless we think, for belief is the affirmation that what is outside the mind is as it is thought to be within the mind."[10] Belief, then, is not a matter of disposition, tendency, or relationship between persons. Rather it is the affirmation that what one represents to oneself does actually correspond to objective reality. Belief must then have specific cognitive content, and this content must be subject to proof or refutation. Put in other words, belief is the affirmation or denial of propositions which, at least in theory, must be such that they can be shown to be true or false.[11]

Maimonides in fact insists that the Torah commands the adoption of certain beliefs: first and foremost the existence of God. But all of the beliefs that Maimonides treats as commandments are matters which in his view are philosophically demonstrable.[12] So even in the area where Maimonides most strikingly affirms an obligation to believe, we see the concurrent assumption of the intellectual content of belief.

But if belief is a matter of the intellect, how can it also be a matter of moral virtue? Maimonides distinguishes the two realms and relates each to a different part of the soul. He subordinates the moral realm to the intellectual and insists that the sound morality is a prerequisite of intellectual perfection, but that the moral aspect of our personhood is less distinguished than the intellectual. He suggests that the importance of the moral side is primarily instrumental.

Maimonides uses two different Arabic terms, al-imān and al-i'tiqād, for what we call belief or faith. Avraham Nuriel has argued that Maimonides consistently distinguishes between them, reserving al-imān for what we would call "trust" and al-i'tiqād for intellectual acquiescence in the truth of a proposition.[13] In contemporary terms, we can say that Maimonides distinguishes between "belief in" and "belief that."[14]

Thus Maimonides' intellectualist definition of 'belief' in the Guide is a definition of i'tiqād, not of imān. In those Arabic texts where Maimonides commands belief, such as the first positive commandment in the Book of Commandments, he uses variants of i'tiqād, and not of imān. In their Hebrew parallels, such as "Laws of the Foundations of the Torah," I 1 in the Mishneh Torah, he uses variants of the Hebrew yedi'ah, knowledge, and not emunah, faith or trust. But when Maimonides calls faith a virtue he uses the term imān.[15] The text which prompts this study is a perfect example and is cited as such by Nuriel. That faith which is a moral virtue, then, is trust in God.[16]

Turning now to 'virtue,' we find that Maimonides takes up the issue in the first work he is known to have written, his treatise on logic.[17] He devotes the fourteenth chapter to the classification of the sciences,[18] among other sciences discussing political science, which he treats under four headings. Virtue is addressed under the first of these, self-government:

> Man's governance of himself is the science which enables him to develop good qualities and to free himself from bad qualities, if he has already acquired them. Moral qualities are dispositions which gradually become more and more fixed in the soul until they are formed into a habit by which actions are determined. Philosophers

describe moral qualities as either excellent or defective. Praiseworthy moral qualities are called virtues (*faḍā'il*); blameworthy moral qualities are called vices. Actions resulting from praiseworthy qualities are called good; those resulting from blameworthy qualities are called bad. [Similarly philosophers describe] reasoning (*al-nuṭq*), the act of conceiving ideas, as either excellent or defective. We thus speak of intellectual virtues and vices. The philosophers have many books on the moral virtues.[19]

Maimonides here follows Aristotle's distinction of two kinds of virtues: moral and intellectual. Moral virtues are praiseworthy moral qualities which can be "fixed in the soul," that is, strengthened by exercise. They can become habits which determine our behavior. Trust certainly is more appropriately thought of as finding expression in behavior than is intellectual acquiescence. One cannot truly claim to trust one's spouse, for example, if one acts inconsistently with such trust, say hiring private detectives to catch the spouse in acts of infidelity. But in most cases acquiescing to the truth of a proposition (that the earth revolves around the sun, for example, or that there exists a prime mover) has little immediate impact upon our behavior (and shouldn't if Hume is correct in saying that we cannot derive 'ought' from 'is'). Intellectual virtues relate not to dispositions which determine behavior, but to excellence in reasoning. They reflect either our skills in conceiving ideas or the soundness of the ideas we have conceived.

Maimonides affords more information about his conception of virtue in the second of his "Eight Chapters," where he analyzes the diseases of the soul. The title of the chapter is "On the Disobedience of the Soul's Powers and on Knowledge of the Part in which the Virtues and the Vices are Primarily Found." Once again, Maimonides distinguishes moral from intellectual virtue:

> As for the virtues, there are two kinds: moral virtues and rational virtues. Opposed to them are two kinds of vices. The rational virtues are found in the rational part [of the soul]. Among them are: (i) wisdom, which is knowledge of the remote and proximate causes and which comes after knowledge of the existence of the thing whose causes are being investigated; and (ii) intelligence, which includes (a) the theoretical intellect, I mean, the first intelligibles, which we have by nature; (b) the acquired intellect, but this is not the place for that;

and (c) brilliance and excellent comprehension, that is, excellent grasp of a thing quickly, in no time, or in a very short time. The vices of this power are the contrary of these or their opposite. The moral virtues are found only in the appetitive part, and the sentient part is in this case a servant of the appetitive part. The virtues of this part are very numerous: for example, moderation, liberality, justice, gentleness, humility, contentment, courage, and others. The vices of this part consist in being deficient or excessive with regard to these [things].[20]

Here Maimonides does not offer a definition of moral virtue, as he did in the "Treatise on Logic"; rather, he gives examples of the moral virtues, noting first that these virtues are found only in the appetitive part of the soul, which in this case is served by the sentient part. He relies on his discussion "of the soul of man and its powers" in the previous chapter, where we are told that the soul has five powers or functions, called parts for the sake of convenience, or even called different souls, although "the soul of man is a single soul." The five functions are the nutritive, sentient, imaginative, appetitive, and rational.[21] The nutritive part "consists in the power of attracting, retaining, digesting, excreting, growing, procreating its kind, and separating mixtures so that it isolates what should be used for nourishment and what should be excreted." The sentient part consists of the five senses. The imaginative part "is the power that preserves the impression of sensibly perceived objects . . . [and] puts together things it has not perceived at all and which are not possible for it to perceive." The appetitive part is

the power by which a man desires, or is repulsed by, a certain thing. From this power originate such actions as seeking something or fleeing from it, as well as being attracted to something or avoiding it; rage and agreeableness, fear and boldness, cruelty and compassion, love and hatred, and many such disturbances of the soul. This power uses all the organs of the body as instruments: for example, the power of the hand for hitting, the power of the foot for walking, the power of the eye for seeing, and the power of the heart for being bold or fearful. Likewise, the rest of the organs—both internal and external—and their powers are instruments for this appetitive power.

The last part of the soul, the rational, "is the power found in man by which he perceives intelligibles, deliberates, acquires the sciences, and distinguishes between base and noble actions."

The appetitive part of the soul, then, the locus of our desires and repulsions, is the seat of our moral virtues. One acquires moral virtues, accordingly, by training oneself to be attracted and repelled by the right things. A person who controls his or her appetites and acts in accordance with this self-discipline is said to possess moral virtue. The appetitive part of the soul, it is clear, should be guided by the rational part, since it "distinguishes between base and noble actions."[22]

In a note to their translation, Weiss and Butterworth maintain that "there probably was an additional virtue at this point in the original text, but it cannot be identified with certainty."[23] They do not explicate the basis for this view, but they do note that Ibn Tibbon's translation adds the virtue of emunah, faith. But the Arabic editions of Kafah and Wolff and the manuscripts examined by Weiss and Butterworth do not support Ibn Tibbon's reading.[24] Herbert Davidson's important study argues that in the "Eight Chapters" Maimonides makes heavy use of al-Fārābī's Fuṣūl al-Madanī (Aphorisms of the Statesman).[25] Davidson indicates that Maimonides' comments on the moral virtues in the second of the "Eight Chapters" follow section 7 of the Aphorisms.[26] But the passage from al-Fārābī does not list faith among the moral virtues. It reads:

> The virtues are of two kinds, ethical and rational. The rational virtues are the virtues of the rational part, such as wisdom, intellect, cleverness, readiness of wit, excellence of understanding. The ethical virtues are the virtues of the appetitive part, such as temperance, bravery, generosity, justice. The vices are similarly divided into two classes.[27]

So al-Fārābī's text settles nothing for us, and Ibn Tibbon's translation remains our only source for including faith in Maimonides' list of virtues in "Eight Chapters" 2, a rather thin reed to support the reading.

What we do learn from the "Eight Chapters" as it stands is that the moral virtues pertain to the appetitive part of the soul and are to be connected with the ethics of the mean, developed both here and in "Laws of Moral Qualities." For the moral vices involve excess or deficiency. So if faith is a moral virtue it should pertain to the appetitive part of the soul and the vices corresponding to it would be excessive or deficient faith. But what would a religious thinker mean by too much faith? The answer is not hard to provide if we follow Nuriel in defining 'faith' (*al-imān*) as 'trust.' Jewish tradition clearly acknowledges that trust in God may be exaggerated and warns against such exaggeration.[28]

Our discussion here, I think, allows us to correct the widely accepted view of Maimonides as a pure intellectual who ultimately prized nothing in the world of ideas or in the world of religion but intellectual perfection.[29] By emphasizing that there is a kind of belief that does not involve the cognition of the intelligibilia and is, in its own way, desirable we show that the faith of the non-philosopher, so long, of course, as it is not actually based on falsehood, is of moral value. At the same time we find a basis for criticizing the view that the ultimate perfection of the individual who has achieved a maximally perfected intellect is moral behavior.[30] For there is no doubt that Maimonides prizes knowledge of God over simple trust in Him.[31]

## Notes

1. See Philo, *On Abraham*, 270, *LCL*, **6**.133.
2. H. A. Wolfson, *Philo*, **2**.216-18.
3. Wolfson, 216.
4. John Passmore, *The Perfectibility of Man* (London: Duckworth, 1970), 61.
5. I quote here (and below) the translation of Shlomo Pines; here, 631.
6. Maimonides' distinction here is perhaps best summed up in the words of Steven Schwarzschild: "Jewish justice is different from the classic philosophic (Greek-Western) view of this concept. In the latter, justice is generally considered under the headings of 'distributive' and 'retributive.' These are, of course, also comprised in *zedakah*, but while 'distributive' and 'retributive' justice are essentially procedural principles (i.e., how to do things), Jewish justice is essentially substantive (i.e., what human life should be like)," "Justice," *Encyclopedia Judaica* (Jerusalem: Keter, 1971) **10**.476. Schwarzschild continues: "Substantive justice depends on an ultimate (i.e., messianic) value commitment."
7. See Maimonides, *Book of Commandments*, positive commandment 199, negative commandment 139; *Mishneh Torah*, "Laws of Lender and Borrower," III 5.

8.  See *Guide* I 34: "For it has been explained, or rather demonstrated, that the moral virtues are a preparation for the rational virtues, it being impossible to achieve true, rational acts—I mean perfect rationality—unless it be by a man thoroughly trained with respect to his morals and endowed with the qualities of tranquillity and quiet. . . . It is accordingly indubitable that preparatory moral training should be carried out before beginning with this science [metaphysics] so that man should be in a state of extreme uprightness and perfection" 76-7. For further details see my *Maimonides on Human Perfection* (Brown Judaic Studies, 1990).

9.  *Guide* I 50; here I follow tr. L. E. Goodman in *RAMBAM*, 77; cf. Pines, 111.

10. *Guide* I 50; Goodman, *RAMBAM*, 77-78; cf. Pines, 111.

11. See H. A. Wolfson, *The Philosophy of Spinoza*, **2**.147 and his "The Aristotelian Predicables and Maimonides' Division of Attributes," *Studies in the History and Philosophy of Religion*, **2**.163: "What Maimonides therefore means to say is that belief is that which can be expressed by a logical proposition."

12. See my essay, "Maimonides, Crescas, and Abravanel on Exodus 20:2—A Medieval Jewish Exegetical Debate," *JQR* 69 (1979): 129-57 and my *Dogma in Medieval Jewish Thought* (Oxford: Oxford University Press, 1986), 38-49.

13. See Abraham Nuriel, "Musag ha-Emunah ezel ha-Rambam," *Da'at* 2-3 (1978/79): 43-47.

14. See Kenneth Seeskin, "Judaism and the Linguistic Interpretation of Jewish Faith," *Studies in Jewish Philosophy* 3 (1983): 71-81, and my *Dogma*, 1-6.

15. Shalom Rosenberg claims that there are many examples of Maimonides' not distinguishing between *al-imān* and *al-i'tiqād*, but he mentions only one. See his "The Concept of Emunah in Post-Maimonidean Jewish Philosophy," in Isadore Twersky, ed., *Studies in Medieval Jewish History and Literature*, **2**.273-307, esp. 275. The present essay shows that in III 53 Maimonides does not use *imān* in the sense of intellectual acquiescence but means trust in God.

16. For the Rabbinic doctrine of faith as trust in God, see C. G. Montefiore and H. Loewe, *A Rabbinic Anthology* (New York: Schocken, 1974), 334-41.

17. Known as *Millot ha-Higayon* in Hebrew, this text was composed in Arabic and translated three times into Hebrew in the Middle Ages. Those portions of the Arabic text then known and the three Hebrew translations were edited and published with an English translation by Israel Efros as *Maimonides' Treatise on Logic* (New York: American

Academy for Jewish Research, 1938). The full Arabic text was discovered in Turkey and published there twice in 1960 by Mubahat Turker. Efros then published the complete text (in Hebrew characters) in *PAAJR* 34 (1966): 155-60 (English) and 9-42 (Hebrew). See Lawrence Berman, "Some Remarks on the Arabic Text of Maimonides' 'Treatise on the Art of Logic,'" *JAOS* 88 (1968): 340-42 and Israel Efros, "Maimonides' *Treatise on Logic*: The New Arabic Text and its Light on the Hebrew Versions," *JQR* 53 (1962-3): 269-73.

18. On this chapter see H. A. Wolfson, "The Classification of Sciences in Medieval Jewish Philosophy," *Hebrew Union College Jubilee Volume* (Cincinnati: Hebrew Union College, 1925), 263-315, repr. in *Studies in the History of Philosophy and Religion*, 1.493-545; cf. his "Note on Maimonides' Classification of the Sciences," *JQR* 26 (1936): 369-77, repr. in *Studies* 1.551-60; Leo Strauss, "Maimonides' Statement on Political Science," *PAAJR* 22 (1953): 115-30; Lawrence Berman, "A Reexamination of Maimonides' 'Statement on Political Science,'" *JAOS* 89 (1969): 106-11.

19. I follow Wolfson's translation, 538-39. Cf. Efros, 63-4 of his complete translation; and Ralph Lerner, tr., in M. Mahdi and Lerner, eds., *Medieval Political Philosophy* (Ithaca: Cornell University Press, 1972), 189-90.

20. Ed., Rabbi J. Kafaḥ, in *Mishnah 'im Perush Rabbenu Mosheh ben Maimon* (Jerusalem: Mossad ha-Rav Kook, 1963); I cite the translation (with some additions in brackets) of Raymond Weiss and Charles Butterworth, *Ethical Writings of Maimonides* (New York: New York University Press, 1975), 65.

21. See H. A. Wolfson, "Maimonides on the Internal Senses," *Studies* 1.344-70, esp. 364-66; Eliezer Schweid, *Iyyunim bi-Shemonah Perakim la-Rambam* (Jerusalem: Jewish Agency, 1969), ch. 2.

22. The quotations are from Weiss and Butterworth, 61-63.

23. Page 98, n. 7.

24. Kafaḥ, 377; M. Wolff, *Musa Maimuni's Acht Capitel* (Leiden: Brill, 1903), 5 (Arabic), 12 (German).

25. See Herbert Davidson, "Maimonides' Shemonah Perakim and Alfarabi's *Fusul al-Madani*."

26. Davidson, 38.

27. *Aphorisms of the Statesman*, Dunlop, 31.

28. The prevalent Rabbinic view is encapsulated in the maxim, "One is not to rely upon miracles" (Pesaḥim 64b). See R. J. Zwi Werblowski, "Faith, Hope and Trust: A Study in the Concept of *Bittaḥon*," *Papers of the Institute of Jewish Studies London* 1 (1964): 95-139, esp. 109-18, 125; Louis Jacobs, *Faith* (New York: Basic Books, 1968), ch. 10.

Cf. Saʿadiah's strictures against excessive reliance upon God in his *Book of Beliefs and Opinions* X 15, Rosenblatt, 395-97.

29. This view can be traced back to Samuel Ibn Tibbon, in his introduction to his Hebrew translation of Maimonides' Commentary on *Avot.* See Aviezer Ravitzky, "Samuel Ibn Tibbon and the Esoteric Character of the *Guide of the Perplexed*," *AJS Review* 6 (1981): 87-123. It is also the interpretation of Shem Tov ibn Falaquera. See Raphael Jospe, "Rejecting Moral Virtue as the Ultimate Human End," in William Brinner and Stephen Ricks, eds., *Studies in Islamic and Jewish Traditions* (Denver: University of Denver, 1986), 185-204. Recent upholders of the view include Isaac Husik, *A History of Medieval Jewish Philosophy* (New York: Macmillan, 1930), 299-300; and Alexander Altmann, "Maimonides' Four Perfections," *Israel Oriental Studies* 2 (1972): 15-24, repr. with additions in his *Essays in Jewish Intellectual History*, 65-76.

30. For this view see H. Cohen, "Charakteristik der Ethik Maimunis," in W. Bacher, ed., *Moses ben Maimon* (Leipzig, 1908) 1.63-134; J. Guttmann, *Philosophies of Judaism*, 200-3; Steven Schwarzschild, "Moral Radicalism and 'Middlingness' in the Ethics of Maimonides," *Studies in Medieval Culture* 11 (1977): 65-94. For a political variant, L. Berman, "Maimonides on Political Leadership," in D. J. Elazar, ed., *Kinship and Consent* (Ramat Gan: Turtledove Publishing, 1981), 113-25 and the studies by Berman cited there. For a halakhic interpretation, I. Twersky, *Introduction to the Code of Maimonides* (New Haven: Yale University Press, 1980), 511; D. Hartman, *Maimonides: Torah and Philosophic Quest* (Philadelphia: Jewish Publication Society, 1976), 26.

31. Just what Maimonides understands by knowledge of God and how such knowledge can inform our practical behavior is the central question of my monograph, *Maimonides on Human Perfection.* The key texts are *Guide* III 27 and III 54. See Shlomo Pines, "The Limitations of Human Knowledge According to Alfarabi, Ibn Bajjah, and Maimonides," in Twersky, ed., *Studies in Medieval Jewish History and Literature* 82-109; Warren Zev Harvey, "Bein Philosophiah Medinit li-Halakhah bi-Mishnat ha-Rambam," *Iyyun* 29 (1980): 198-212, esp. appendix; A. Altmann, "Maimonides on the Intellect and the Scope of Metaphysics," in his *Von der mittelalterlichen zur modernen Aufklärung*, 60-129.

# Why not Pursue the Metaphor of Artisan and View God's Knowledge as Practical?

## David B. Burrell, C.S.C.

While this question is put primarily to Moses Maimonides in the light of his praise for the artisan image as a way for us to render what lies quite beyond our comprehension—God's mode of knowing (III 21)—it must also be put to Aquinas, who boldly adopts the image as his master metaphor to render God's knowledge of the universe, yet fails himself to pursue it in any great detail. My focus, however, will be on Maimonides, with some help from his friendly commentator and critic after more than two centuries, Levi ben Gershom (Gersonides). And I shall put the question to his writings in both senses of its rhetorical impact: (1) why might he *not* have pursued the metaphor, what stood in the way? and (2) what might he have gained had he done so?

## 1. Maimonides' Model for Knowing

The answer to the first way of formulating our question seems relatively straightforward when we recall the Rambam's identification of the divine image (*zelem*) in us with "intellectual apprehension" (I 1) or the power by which "man distinguishes between the true and the false" (I 2).[1] In commenting on Genesis 3, he not only identifies the image of God with our capacity to possess a science "of necessary truths," but contrasts this with "the science of apparent truths (morals)" in which "right and wrong are the terms employed . . .: it is the function of the intellect to discriminate between the true and the false" (I 2). We have only to reflect that Aristotle makes his distinction between two "ways of arriving at truth" in the *Nicomachaean Ethics* (VI 3)—speculative and practical—as a preliminary step towards legitimizing ethical inquiry precisely by warding off objections that it cannot yield the certitude associated with science (i.e., the demonstration of essential properties as flowing necessarily from natures), to remind ourselves once again how beholden Maimonides is to Ibn Sīnā.[2]   In this sense, in fact, Maimonides' philosophy rightly belongs with "Islamic philosophy," since his cultural ambience is clearly "Islamicate."[3]

Maimonides argues that "*the* function of the intellect is to discriminate between the true and the false," not good and evil. Thus, "Adam possessed [understanding] perfectly and completely" but "was not at all able to follow or to understand the principles of apparent truths," until he had transgressed a command "with which he had been charged on the score of his reason." Only then did he obtain a knowledge of apparent truths. Maimonides bases this remarkable statement on the verse "and the eyes of both were opened, and they knew they were naked" (Genesis 3:7). The line is carefully parsed to reveal that Adam "received a new faculty whereby he found things wrong which previously he had not regarded as wrong" (I 2). Maimonides' sharp dichotomy between knowledge and opinion as applied to matters of fact and matters of morals is, of course, quite at variance with Aristotle, who speaks of one intellectual faculty whose distinct functions—knowing (speculative) and doing or making (practical)—are determined by the end in view (*Nicomachaean Ethics* VI 2).

So far as I know, Maimonides does not ever identify this "new faculty," although the natural place for him do so would be in the third part of the *Guide*, where he explains the place of the Torah in the life of men, insisting that "there is a reason for each one of the precepts . . . although there are commandments the reason of which is unknown to us, and in which the ways of God's wisdom are incomprehensible" (III 26). He contends that his belief in the law as manifesting God's wisdom—and not merely God's will—is shared by "the common people as well as the scholars," and he moves only to block speculation purporting to show the utility of the particular, detailed means of each of the 613 commandments of the law. Clearly, he argues, "the general object of the law is twofold: the well-being of the soul and the well-being of the body" (II 27). Thus the goal of Torah is a practical one, and its function for the people of God would be analogous to one of the roles Aristotle gives to practical reason: to discern right from wrong. So one might naturally have expected the relationship of God to God's people, as displayed in the bestowal of the Torah, to have offered Maimonides a model for the initial gift of existence and all that follows from it in creation. That he does not do so—so far as I know—offers another striking example of how much he was beholden to Ibn Sīnā's single-minded devotion to speculative reason as *the* paradigm for knowing and, correspondingly, for the relation between the universe and its source.[4]

But why then the encomium for "the knowledge which the producer of a thing possesses concerning it"? For such a model is suggested by the Rambam for the kind of knowledge God possesses of creation: "Note this well, for I think that this is an excellent idea, and leads to correct views; no error will be found in it; no dialectical argument; it does not lead to any absurd conclusion, nor to ascribing any defect to God" (III 21). It is difficult to imagine higher praise for a conception whose merits Maimonides has just noted: "our knowledge is acquired and increased in proportion to the things known by us. This is not the case with God. [Like the artisan,] His knowledge of things is not derived from the things themselves . . . on the contrary, the things are in accordance with His eternal knowledge." Yet this point of comparison is the only one to recommend the artisan image. When carefully examined, Maimonides' commendation proves to allow that the artisan image is conducive "to correct views" not in that it affords an adequate model for "this kind of knowledge [which] cannot be comprehended by us," but rather in the negative sense underscored by the modifiers following: that it will not mislead us.

So once again, the Rambam uses his dialectical skills to protect the God of Abraham, Isaac, and Jacob from a philosophic reason which can be relentlessly reductive when it tries to make human sense of God's ways. Yet here again I would ask whether the image cannot be pursued in a more fruitful, genuinely *leading* way. Was

Maimonides perhaps forestalled from doing just that simply by his Avicennan intellectualism?    For on such an account, the artist's knowing cannot be construed as real knowing; only the emanation of conclusions from premises—in the pattern of demonstrative reason— promises knowledge.    If God's knowledge will not conform to the speculative pattern, we must simply acknowledge that "the knowledge attributed to this essence has nothing in common with our knowledge . . . so we have no correct notion of His knowledge" (III 20).    We cannot look elsewhere in human knowing for a more acceptable model.    For there is nowhere else to look, since the "knowledge of the producer" (III 21) cannot claim to be knowledge at all.

Gersonides located the nerve of the Rambam's thesis of "sheer equivocity" regarding all divine attributes in his inability to reconcile God's knowledge of future contingents—notably free actions—with the free response demanded by the Torah.[5]    His own response, equally beholden to Ibn Sīnā, was to limit God's knowing to all that is "ordered and defined" (232), trying to persuade us that there is no more to know.    It is to Maimonides' credit that he could not take this tack, which he identified with Aristotle (III 17).    But let us explore the ways which could have opened to him had he allowed himself to pursue the image of the artisan.

## 2.  The Artisan's Knowledge

I have suggested that the Rambam was unduly influenced by Ibn Sīnā in accepting a deductive paradigm for knowing, Aristotle's pattern for science, which had inspired Ibn Sīnā's cosmological picture:    The universe emanates from the One in the way that conclusions in a syllogism follow logically from first principles.[6] Evidence for Maimonides' intellectualism abounds, notably in his treatment of prophecy (II 26) and of providence over individuals (III 17).    Yet it would seem that his treatment of the Torah (III 26-50) could have opened the way to making practical knowing more respectable, since observance of the law would account for human wellbeing (III 27).    In this respect, at least, the attunement to divine wisdom which aligns individuals with God's providential care could apparently be achieved by observance as well as by the "intellectual mysticism" one associates with Ibn Sīnā.[7]    Yet a concluding chapter of the *Guide* insists that "true worship of God is only possible when correct notions of Him have previously been conceived," since it is "the intellect which emanates from God unto us [that] is the link that joins us to God." The passive construction, to be sure, would allow that these notions could be passed on in various nonconceptual ways: through ritual or ethical practices. Yet it is this principle which encourages him to reassert "that Providence watches over every rational being according to the amount of intellect which that being possesses" (III 51).

There is a clear priority in favor of that "knowledge of God, i.e., true wisdom [which] demonstrates by proof those truths which Scripture teaches by way of tradition." This is "the only perfection which we should seek," since "having acquired this knowledge [we] will then be determined always to seek loving-kindness, judgment, and righteousness, and thus to imitate the ways of God." So the *Guide* ends where it began, identifying knowing with speculative knowledge, and clearly subordinating the formation of character to that "real wisdom [which] proves the truth of the law" (III 54). Accordingly, the manner in which the Torah shapes human life "to imitate the ways of God" will not emerge as a fruitful model for understanding divine "providence extending over His creatures as manifested in the act of bringing them into being and in their governance as it is" (II 54, Pines). Such understanding will only derive from that knowledge of God which Maimonides called "true wisdom" and which could *prove* the truths of scripture. Yet it was precisely that pattern of demonstrative reason which forced him to conclude that we can have no understanding of God's knowledge— that "only the words are the same" (III 20).

Let us examine the features by which he sets divine knowledge apart, to determine whether a more favorable ranking of practical knowing might have offered greater hope for modelling God's knowledge. The stakes are high since the speculative paradigm to which Maimonides is committed threatens his program with a double inconsistency. Authentic human perfection lies in "the knowledge of God [and] of His Providence" (III 54), yet such knowledge is denied us by his insisting that we cannot know God but only "qualities of actions emanating from Him" (I 60). And since the most perspicuously divine activity we can know would be God's bestowing of the Torah, practical knowing would seem to offer a model at the very point where speculative knowledge must fail. The ways in which God's "knowledge is distinguished from ours according to all the teaching of every revealed religion" are five: (1) it is one yet embraces many objects, (2) it applies to things not yet in existence, (3) it is infinite in comprehension, (4) it remains unchanged although comprehending changing things, (5) "according to the teaching of our Law, God's knowledge of one of two eventualities does not determine it, however certain that knowledge may be concerning the future occurrence of the one eventuality" (III 20).

By Gersonides' reading, it was the last of these which forced Maimonides to an agnostic position regarding all attributions of perfections to divinity. Yet in the chapter we are citing, he focuses on the fact "that God's knowledge is not different from His essence" and concludes that "as we cannot accurately comprehend His essence . . . so we have no correct notion of His knowledge" (III 20). The same applies to God's "management . . . and intention" (or perhaps better: *governance* and *purpose*). Such notions "are not the same when ascribed to us and when ascribed to God." Without recounting in detail Maimonides' arguments on equivocity (I 51-61), it should be clear that this generic observation will not suffice to render the discrepancy between divine and human knowledge so great as to prevent utterly our discoursing about divine knowledge. So Gersonides' reading must be sound. Maimonides must be shying away from comparisons of divine and human knowledge so as to avoid the conundrum of necessitation of contingent events by God's eternal omniscience. Now we ask, how could shifting to a practical paradigm for knowing help to overcome the apparently necessitating consequences of God's knowing "the future occurrence of the one eventuality"?

The main lines of a response are available in Aquinas, and in terms quite consonant with Maimonides' treatment, whose lineaments Aquinas generally followed, however critically.[8]  For Aquinas, nothing which has not yet occurred can be an object of knowledge for anyone, including God, for there simply is nothing to know. Not even God can know what is not yet present. At this point Aquinas invokes two devices: one which Maimonides neither invokes nor rejects, eternity; and the other which he praises, the practical knowing of an artisan. These must function together. For the mere mention of eternity, while presuming a speculative model for knowing, produces a mental cramp, or antinomy, when we try to ascertain how what has not yet occurred might nonetheless be *present* to God "in eternity."[9] But what has not yet taken place can certainly be present in the divine intention.

For God knows what God intends to do, as artisans know what they intend to do—without there being anything to know as the object of speculative knowing. Fourteenth-century Christian thinkers, following after Aquinas, began to fear this strategy, finding it too closely patterned on the pot-potter image, and so threatening to human freedom. Yet Aquinas remains serenely untroubled by any potential conflict with his forthright assertions about human freedom, since he finds no reason to understand freedom on the model of autonomy.[10] For like everything else in the created universe, human actions are dependent upon the Creator, whose proper effect is existence and the activity which follows upon existing.[11] Yet that apparently innocent formulation of the article of faith in God as creator embodies Aquinas' own invocation of the Rambam's insistence that a divine activity is utterly unlike its human counterpart. In this case, it is that "'to be made' or 'to make' are said equivocally in this universal production of things, and in other productions" (*In Phys.* 8.2, [1974]). Yet the fact that the term can be used formally, if not descriptively, rests on his identifying existence (*esse*) as neither a feature of things nor a substance, but the principle of anything's actually existing. This represents, of course, Aquinas' move beyond Aristotle, for whom *existence* is a concomitant of form, and forms are eternal. For Aquinas, however, God's creative activity has an effect proper to it, and the artisan image offers a model for divine knowing without pretending to tell us how God does it.

Sophisticated Rambam readers will remind us, of course, that Maimonides could not countenance such an analogous use of terms (cf. I 56), but I have argued elsewhere that he should have no substantive difficulties with an understanding of analogous terms which is as "negative" regarding descriptive features as Aquinas' is.[12] More conventional philosophers will profess to find both *analogy* and the *via negativa* incomprehensible, but at some point in our discourse about God incomprehensibility becomes a *desideratum* rather than a complaint. Then the question becomes a strategic one: why here, where Aquinas locates it, rather than there where Maimonides did? The answer is equally strategic. Aquinas' approach would allow us to exploit the expressly Biblical images of the artisan, which the Rambam praised. Moreover, adopting the model of knowing congruent with these images could have given him a way of formulating God's knowledge of what is to come, which would not appear so downright contradictory to our understanding of what it is to know. In fact, one might reconstruct Maimonides as advocating an account of divine knowledge whereby God knows the particulars *through* their ideas, i.e., through His intentions. This would not be incompatible with the proposal of practical reason nor contradictory to our ordinary ideas of knowledge. But developing that would involve integrating the practical model he proposes into his treatment in ways in which he does not actually do. Were he to have done so, the possibility of an analogous rather than an utterly equivocal account could have arisen—and that would certainly have fulfilled the goal of his project better than he was able to do with the paradigms available to him.

Indeed, Menachem Kellner offers us a way of so reading Maimonides,[13] and that is to regard the *Guide* itself as a journey. One may then read the final chapters, with their clear *halakhic* allusions, as the terminus of a gradual transition from Neoplatonic priorities regarding reason to a more distinctively Jewish understanding of *imitatio Dei*: becoming like God by acting as God would have us act. As we can know divine attributes of action, so we have been given to know how God would have us act to become Godlike. The Rambam's insistence even in these final chapters on the priority of reason would then be understood as our need to employ philosophy as a guide in undertaking this journey. We must put speculative reason in its proper place: indispensable, yet finally in the service of right action. That such a reading would be in tension with the opening chapters of the *Guide* itself would only highlight the point and purpose of the journey it outlines for us to take. Needless to say, I find this reflective reading attractive, chiefly because it places particular statements in the context of the whole work, read as the *Guide* it purports to be. My own proposal would then become the task of reading back onto Maimonides' accounts of providence and creation his concluding exaltation of practical reason, and so fleshing out the model he proposes (III 21) but does not actually develop.

## Notes

1. Unless otherwise noted *The Guide for the Perplexed* will be cited from the M. Friedlander tr. (New York: Dover, 1956), primarily because his terminology is more standardly philosophical than Pines'.

2. Maimonides' references to Aristotle (e.g., II 19) are often in fact allusions to Ibn Sīnā.

3. Marshall Hodgson introduces the term in *The Venture of Islam* (Chicago: University of Chicago Press, 1974) 1.39-45.

4. On Ibn Sīnā and the paradigm of speculative reason, see my *Knowing the Unknowable God* (Notre Dame: University of Notre Dame Press, 1986). The point is even stronger if Warren Zev Harvey's interpretation is correct: "A Third Approach to Maimonides' Cosmogony-Prophetology Puzzle," *Harvard Theological Review* 74 (1981): 287-301.

5. Norbert Samuelson, *Gersonides on God's Knowledge* [= *Wars of the Lord* III] (Toronto: Pontifical Institute of Medieval Studies, 1977), 204-09.

6. This is how I try to make the emanation scheme plausible in *Knowing* (note 4).

7. The phrase is Louis Gardet's in *La Pensée Religieuse d'Avicenne* (Paris: Vrin, 1956).

8. Cf. my "Aquinas and Maimonides: A Conversation about Proper Speech," *Immanuel* 16 (1983): 70-85; "Maimonides, Aquinas and Gersonides on Providence and Evil," *Religious Studies* 20 (1984): 335-51.

9. See Aquinas, *De Veritate* 2.12, *Summa Theologica* 1.14.13; cf. my "God's Eternity," *Faith and Philosophy* 1 (1984).

10. Cf. Joseph Incandela, "Aquinas' Lost Legacy: God's Practical Knowledge and Situated Human Freedom," Ph.D. dissertation, Princeton University, 1986.

11. Cf. my *Aquinas: God and Action* (Notre Dame: University of Notre Dame Press, 1979); for an approximation to this by Maimonides, see Lenn E. Goodman, "Determinism and Freedom in Spinoza, Maimonides, and Aristotle," in F. Schoeman, ed., *Responsibility, Character, and the Emotions*, esp. 144-48.

12. "Maimonides and Aquinas: A Dialogue about Proper Speech."

13. In his *Maimonides on Human Perfection* (Atlanta: Scholars Press, 1990).

# Matter as Creature and Matter as the Source of Evil: Maimonides and Aquinas

## Idit Dobbs-Weinstein

Throughout *The Guide of the Perplexed*[1] Maimonides presents two distinct accounts of matter, broadly characterizable as Neoplatonic and Aristotelian.[2] The first account is expressed in poetic language, presenting matter as the source of privation, evil, error, and all moral transgressions. The second is a scientific account, of matter as a principle underlying generation and corruption. Both accounts are based upon acceptance of creation *ex nihilo*, which Maimonides affirms in explicit opposition to Aristotle but finds to be consistent with Neoplatonic cosmology.[3]

The discussions are too prominent and recurrent in the *Guide* to permit us to explain away the conflicting accounts as an attempt at deliberate dissimulation. But the concurrent affirmations of matter as creature and as the source of evil seem to establish a causal relation between God and evil that militates against both the revealed and philosophical conceptions of the Deity. I see a genuine problem here, having concluded that the objections which may arise from an exoteric/esoteric distinction within the *Guide* are either invalid or render the text unintelligible *a priori*.[4]

After a brief outline of the problems inherent in the investigation of matter, I shall examine Maimonides' distinct accounts of matter critically and suggest a tentative resolution to the problem that can accommodate the tension between the two accounts without dismissing either as untrue or insignificant. Then, addressing the possibility of a harmonious synthesis between the God of revelation, the First Principle of Aristotle, and the One of Plotinus, I shall present Aquinas' account of matter as a successful attempt at such a synthesis.

The problem of a tension between matter and perfection is common to the philosophical and Scriptural traditions. Dante's tragic Aristotelian philosopher, who lives in longing without hope,[5] is no less affected by it than Plato's Er or the descendants of Adam. When prime matter is posited simply as a logical principle and distinguished from privation, the mutability of formed matter reflects merely the nature of all composite existence. As logical principles, form, matter, and privation render sublunar existence intelligible, but no more. To deny or lament these principles would be folly since their intelligibility is consequent upon the assent to necessary truths on which depends all our knowledge of the natural world. But when the very nature of matter is judged to be the cause of privation and evil, a serious and inescapable difficulty arises for any believing philosopher. For even if we exclude the issue of God's responsibility for evil, there remains the problem of attributing a qualification originating in practical reason to an ontological principle that is the proper object of speculative reason.

The least ambiguous doctrine conjoining ontological and ethical principles originates with Plotinus, for whom, as Rist points out, the scale of existence and the scale of value "are different ways of looking at the same metaphysical facts, for metaphysics in the *Enneads* is, strictly speaking, an indivisible synthesis of ontology and ethics."[6] Here, the "impotent potency" of prime matter renders it a real source of evil. By endowing matter with a real, albeit negative, ontological status, rather than merely a logical one, and by rejecting the Aristotelian dichotomy between ontology and ethics,[7] Plotinus, in effect, introduces an independent principle of evil into the realm of existence. Following the Plotinian tradition, and despite his repeated affirmations of the createdness of prime matter, Maimonides often posits matter as the cause of evil undermining the possibility of endowing it with a real positive role in existence.

Maimonides' distinct accounts of matter fall into his preliminary critiques of the *Mutakallimūn* and his exposition of his own doctrine; the former account is based upon Aristotelian principles, whereas the latter constitutes a critique of Aristotle. In his unsympathetic critique of the *Mutakallimūn*, Maimonides is an Aristotelian philosopher who faults the logic of *kalām*, whereas in his debate with Aristotle, he is a Neoplatonist who repeatedly points out the boundaries of demonstrative reasoning. The same division is visible in Maimonides' investigation of the status of prime matter either as a creature or as a co-eternal ontological principle, and again in his investigation of matter as a logical principle, one of the primary principles underlying natural science.

***

The focus of all investigations concerning prime matter is the possibility or impossibility of bringing something into being out of absolute non-being. According to Maimonides, this problem cannot be resolved by means of demonstration, a conclusion already reached by Aristotle.[8] Whereas inferences about necessity, possibility, and impossibility can be made about all things in the realm of generation and corruption, they cannot be extended to the principles rendering generation and corruption possible. The mistake of some philosophers and the *Mutakallimūn* was to infer what is possible about the creation of these ontological principles from the nature of what exists in its formed state. The philosophers inferred necessity and eternity, whereas the *Mutakallimūn* inferred the possibility of creation and, hence, the fact of creation from the state of the existing, formed universe. Maimonides denies the validity of both inferences, arguing that "a being's state of perfection and completion furnishes no indication of the state of that being preceding its perfection."[9] He argues that if one begins with the nature of what is, then Aristotle is correct in claiming that prime matter is subject to neither generation nor corruption. But for Aristotle the non-generated state of prime matter signifies eternity and necessity, whereas for Maimonides it designates the possibility of bringing something into existence out of absolute nonexistence, a possibility preceding generation and corruption and rendering it possible.[10] He further argues that his conclusions concerning inference can be derived from sensible experience inasmuch as even in the realm of generation and corruption the perfected, or actualized, state of a thing does not furnish the data required for inferring its purely potential state.[11] That is, since the laws comprising the logic of possibility are an abstraction from the repetitive regularity of the order of actual existence of which they are not the cause but rather the effect, they cannot govern the principles which make their derivation possible.[12]

Having cast sufficient doubt on the applicability of rules of logic to the investigation of the origin and status of prime matter, Maimonides can offer a Neoplatonic explanation as an alternative to both the Aristotelian and *Kalām* ones. Here, as in other metaphysical inquiries, he delimits the inquiry by two rules only, namely, that it should violate neither the nature of existing things (the error of the *Mutakallimūn*) nor intellectual judgments about God (the error of the Philosophers).

Maimonides first mentions the creation of prime matter in *Guide* I 28, when he explains the true meaning of Biblical terms referring to divine limbs that appear in the account of the apprehension of Moses, Aaron, and the elders of Israel. He states,

> For what they apprehended was the true reality of prime matter, which derives from Him, may He be exalted, He being the cause of its existence. . . . Accordingly their apprehension had as its object the first matter and the relation of the latter to God, inasmuch as it is the first among the things He <has> created that necessitates generation and corruption; and God is its creator ex nihilo.[13]

Although these statements do not constitute an explanation of prime matter, Maimonides' assumptions are quite clear and can help to elucidate the discussions of prime matter elsewhere in the *Guide*. The theses affirmed here are: (a) prime matter derives from God and from nothing else; and (b) it is the first created thing in the order of generation and corruption. Later statements make clear that prime matter is an essential condition for generation and corruption, and thus for natural possibility and impossibility. Accordingly it is also a condition for our derivation of the logical laws of possibility. Given Maimonides' affirmation of the created nature of prime matter, and given his claim that prime matter is *derived* from God, the nature of the condition obtaining prior to its creation can in no way require or necessitate the ontological actuality of anything other than God.[14] In fact, in my view, Maimonides denies such an actuality on the basis of an intellectual judgment about God, namely, that the affirmation of the eternal preexistence of anything whatsoever, be it understood as an ontological state, or a thing, circumscribes the divine will.[15]

Since Maimonides' formulations about any single topic are inconsistent and have given rise to diametrically opposed interpretations, it does not seem to be possible or productive to base our arguments strictly upon the language used. Rather I shall attempt to set forth an alternative solution to the problem of the status of prime matter which is based upon the hermeneutic principle that unless one is willing to grant that the author—in this case, the *teacher*—not only wished to communicate something true, but also wished that this knowledge be accessible to those who truly desire it, one would neither be able to understand the text nor to withhold judgment about it.

If we grant that Maimonides' affirmations reflect his true position, we have to accept the intelligibility of the following: (a) prime matter derives from God alone; (b) creation is a unique act entirely dissimilar to any natural activity such as making or producing; (c) prime matter is not subject to generation and corruption; and hence, (d) prime matter is primarily a metaphysical and ontological principle and only secondarily a physical and logical one.

In *Guide* II 17, Maimonides repeatedly affirms that prime matter was brought into existence out of nothing in a unique manner. Thus it is entirely dissimilar to any entity in the realm of generation and corruption. Once created and stabilized, it is one of the permanent conditions for composition, potentiality, actuality, in fact for the existence of all composite entities. Like time and motion, prime matter is everlasting. Only divine choice can compass its destruction. Despite his repeated references to it, Maimonides says little else about prime matter, except that "it does not exist devoid of form."[16] No doubt, it is difficult to conceptualize anything that is simultaneously everlasting and nonexisting. But I think that Maimonides is attempting to formulate a distinction between non-being proper and the nonexistence that pertains to any unactualized formed matter in the first instant of its composition. The difference is that in its first instant of existence, formed matter, or natural substance, is in a state of nonexistence which is already determined towards something. Formed matter is a privation of existence with respect to a specific form and the accidents proper to it; but prime matter is not a privation of any specific thing, precisely because it is absolutely undetermined. Privation is with respect to something; prime matter is not. Whereas privation designates the *dynamis* of some form or kind, or the lack of existence of an actuality determined by some actually existing form, no actuality corresponding to prime matter exists. In fact, properly speaking, neither prime matter nor form are existents, but rather each has an essence proper to it which in their conjunction renders existence possible. The difficulty in understanding and speaking of prime matter arises from the impossibility of predicating anything, even 'thingness,' of any unformed 'thing,' since it is not a thing. In the final analysis, apart from the term 'prime matter,' all that can be said about prime matter is by way of negating every predication. In my opinion, it is prime matter to which we could apply Ivry's attempt to explain that state prior to creation to which he refers as a certain ontological condition.

\*\*\*

In the first brief discussion of matter as one of the principles required for generation and corruption in *Guide* I 17, Maimonides presents a strictly Aristotelian account which first outlines three principles, matter, form, and "particularized privation," and then explains that precisely because privation is always conjoined with matter, the latter can receive form. He adds that the difficulties inherent in understanding the distinctions among the principles underlying natural science are the cause for the injunction against nonfigurative speech about the Account of the Beginning. For such univocal discourse is potentially dangerous insofar as it exceeds the apprehension of the multitude. In my opinion, this qualification is significant for understanding Maimonides' dual account of matter, and I shall return to it when I present a tentative resolution to this problem.

Maimonides' Aristotelian discussion of the distinction between matter and privation, the real meaning of privation, and its relation to evil is presented as a critique of the *Kalām* understanding of privation. According to Maimonides, the *Kalām* account is based upon two major errors: (a) The *Kalām* notion of privation, or non-being, recognizes only absolute non-being; and yet, (b) it treats privation as an existent thing. That is, although the *Mutakallimūn* did not distinguish between absolute and relative privation, although they limited privation to contrariety, and although, as a consequence, they maintained that privation did not require the act of an agent, nevertheless, they understood absolute non-being to correspond to an actual existing state, thus endowing it with an independent ontological status.

All the errors of the *Mutakallimūn* can be reduced to an ignorance of the nature of existence. Having failed to comprehend the distinction between essential and accidental characteristics, they concluded that accidents were in no way dependent upon the act of an agent; and, consequently, they were unable to account for them. Composite existence, on the contrary, requires both essential and accidental features, the former representing the real effects of the act of an agent, whereas the latter are related to that act as accidental effects. Only God, in the unique act of creation, brings something into existence out of *absolute* privation or non-being. All other agents produce a change from relative privations, which are absences of due perfections.

Maimonides' critique brings into sharp focus one of the major difficulties inherent in understanding privation in the Arabic tradition. This difficulty emerges again in the perennial difficulties encountered by scholars attempting to understand Maimonides. Since the Arabic term *al-'adam*, like the English term 'lack,' signifies both privation and non-being, the distinction between these concepts has to be read in terms of the specific context of discussion. For the sake of clarity, the interpreter or translator must supply a predicate signifying absolute or relative absence. Once this specification is supplied, it becomes clear that absolute non-being signifies a state prior to existence, or to the composition of matter and form, whereas relative non-being designates the absence of a specific form in a subsistent being. Nonetheless, it should be noted (a) that the only predication used by Maimonides is 'absolute,' and (b) that it has been argued that Maimonides may be inconsistent in his use of, or failure to use, this predicate.[17] Unlike the *Mutakallimūn*, Maimonides insists that all evils are relative privations (*'adam*). The failure to comprehend this proposition (evident in the teachings of the *Mutakallimūn*) occurs only in "one who does not distinguish between privation and habitus and between two contraries or one who does not know the nature of all things."[18] That is, rather than fault the art of *kalām per se*, Maimonides criticizes *Mutakallimūn* ignorant of philosophy.

Since no agent can be said to produce privation, or evil, essentially, it is ludicrous to assume that evil is something existing, let alone that God's unique act brought about the evils evident in the world. Given that God alone produces *only* being, and given that being is good by definition, all His acts produce absolute good. Consequently, all things which are understood as evil in this world, including matter, are essentially good and can be understood as evil only accidentally. In fact, understood in terms of their essence, all things existing in the universe without exception are, exist for, and promote being.

> Even the existence of this inferior matter, whose manner of being it is to be a concomitant of privation entailing death and all evils, all this is also *good* in view of the perpetuity of generation and the permanence of being through succession.[19]

Thus the distinction drawn by Maimonides between absolute and relative privation in his refutation of the teachings of the *Mutakallimūn* leads to the conclusion that, properly speaking, nothing is essentially evil, evil being merely a category imposed upon the object by human understanding. And, as Maimonides repeatedly points out throughout the *Guide*, "the Torah speaks in the language of the sons of men," and language is merely conventional, rather than natural.[20]

***

Thus far, Maimonides' accounts of matter provide a systematic synthesis of Aristotle and Plotinus. However, as soon as he discusses determinate matter, or matter's role in sublunar existence, he presents matter as the cause of evil. Although he uses Aristotelian physics in the account of matter and privation in Part III and, in fact, quotes

Aristotle's *Physics*, his repeated designation of matter as the source of evil, and the immediate succession of the discussion of generation and corruption by an explanation of evil sets the account far apart from Aristotle. Despite the fact that matter is necessary for substantial existence, it is never presented by Maimonides as an essential principle in the actualization of the human form; that is, man's is not an integrated composition. Rather than present matter as pure potentiality and, hence, as the possibility for human actualization, Maimonides underscores its role in corruption. In all these discussions, with one exception[21], he presents matter metaphorically as the feminine principle, even as a married harlot, who, never satisfied with her husband, seeks others continuously. "This is the state of matter. For whatever form is found in it, does but prepare it to receive another form."[22] The figurative accounts present form as powerless before the corruptive force of matter. Rather than emphasize the power of form over matter as the governing principle in a composite being, Maimonides presents composition primarily as the subjugation of potential form to matter, to such an extent that not only physical ills, but also all spiritual ills and sins are understood to result from corruptive matter. The language used to describe material existence is poetic rather than scientific and, if we are to avoid psychologizing, must be understood as a pedagogic device intended to bring about immediate assent to the premise which asserts that all corporeal desires are shameful and repulsive by definition.

The differences between Maimonides' neutral accounts of matter as an ontological category only and his loaded use of it as a category to which all evils can be ascribed are pronounced. Where the latter accounts collapse moral and ontological categories into one, the former not only distinguish between them but significantly circumscribe their meanings and applicability, implying that the attribution of evaluative categories to ontological entities is a result of the limitations of human knowledge.

Since evil, according to Maimonides, is a category imposed by man upon things, rather than something real existing in them, the discussion of evil in the *Guide* examines the three classes of things interpreted by man as evil. The two main premises upon which the discussion is based are: (a) Properly speaking, all evils are the result of ignorance, or "privation of knowledge,"[23] and (b) Teleological accounts that posit a final end of all existing things are erroneous, since a final end, *qua* end, implies privation and hence is meaningful only in the realm of generation and corruption.

The proliferation of the mistaken opinion that more evils exist in the temporal world than good is attributed by Maimonides to ignorance concerning the nature of evil which is exhibited not only by the multitude but also by some men of learning, all of whom follow their imagination rather than reason. This mistake, which violates the intellectual concept of God, implying that He is the cause of evil, results from the absurd assumption that all creation exists for the sake of man. Once the nature of existence is understood, however, and man's very limited portion in it becomes evident, it follows necessarily that all existence is a good consequent upon the divine will, or wisdom. Moreover, argues Maimonides, human existence is a very great good; in fact, it is a divine gift, since of all creatures subject to generation and corruption man alone was given the capacity to perfect himself so that he can overcome the necessary and natural limitations of sublunar existence. Consequently, evil is either a good which in our ignorance (itself an evil) we misconceive, or "we suffer because of evils that we have produced ourselves of our free will; but we attribute them to God, may he be exalted above this."[24]

***

Maimonides in my view deliberately declines to give matter an essential role in human perfection, thus drawing a radical dichotomy between the sub- and supralunar realms, and between intellectual perfection and all other human perfections. Rather than establish a closer relation between the two realms, requiring a more direct relation between the act of Being and natural corruption, Maimonides chooses to emphasize the distance between the changeable and the perfect. Since man is the only creature who belongs to both realms by nature, he is also the only creature whose existence and essence are not in natural harmony and cannot be harmonized naturally. Yet Maimonides insists that the created universe is perfect, containing no evil; and, further, that no divine act is vain or superfluous. That any being in the realm of change can achieve perfection is *ipso facto* evidence of divine munificence. But, as Maimonides points out, the repeated qualification 'good' used in the Torah to describe the various beings created by God is an expression used by man to refer to an object's conformity to its purpose; hence, the term 'good' instructs man that all that exists conforms to the particular purpose intended for it by the divine will, a purpose which, nonetheless, exceeds human apprehension, let alone demonstration. And, as pointed out by Maimonides, the limitations of human reason evident in man's inability to apprehend the distinctions between the primary principles of natural science and exhibited by both the vulgar and men of learning also sets limits to man's understanding of the nature of what exists so that we cannot even infer with certainty all of a natural being's potentialities from actual particulars.[25] Since the true nature of all that exists exceeds human knowledge, it also exceeds univocal discourse and renders necessary poetic accounts of determinate matter. Thus understood, the tension between the two accounts of matter is but a reflection of the tension constitutive of finite existence.

***

It is in his teachings about matter in general, and about the material substratum of human existence in particular, that Aquinas' philosophical doctrine differs most clearly from Maimonides'. Whereas Maimonides' metaphysics is, first and foremost, a metaphysics of the act of Being, that of Aquinas is *per prius et posterius* a metaphysics of the Good. For if Maimonides emphasizes the radical difference between corporeal and incorporeal existence, Aquinas underlines the unity of all existing things in virtue of their first and final cause—the Good, irrespective of composition. By focusing upon matter's relation to the Good and by arguing for its essential role in actualization, Aquinas establishes a continuity between sub- and supralunar existence which overcomes the Neoplatonic problematic of the relative independence of evil from the divine order. Indeed, it is significant that one of Aquinas' most integrated discussions of the relation between matter, privation, and evil occurs in a Neoplatonic text, his commentary on Pseudo-Dionysius' *De Divinis Nominibus*.[26] In the longest chapter, the one on the Good, Aquinas devotes about half of his discussion to dissociating the material principle of existence from evil and to relating it to the Good since it is one of the principles necessary for the perfection of rational souls. In fact, he maintains that to understand the procession of creatures from God, as the Good, we must begin with matter.

Although Aquinas is in general agreement with many principles of Neoplatonic metaphysics, he criticizes the understanding of matter as privation and non-being. Despite the criticism, he also underlines and praises the strength of the Neoplatonic system upon which he constructs his own metaphysics. He argues.

> [T]he causality of being does not extend except to beings. Thus, therefore, according to them, the causality of being did not extend to prime matter to which, nevertheless, the causality of the Good extends. The indication of this is that it desires the Good above all. Moreover, it is characteristic of an effect that it be turned towards its cause through desire. Thus therefore, the Good is a more universal and higher cause than being since its causality extends to more things.[27]

Upon reading *De Divinis Nominibus*, Aquinas' approbation of the Neoplatonists[28] becomes clear, since the recognition that the Good is a more universal cause than being makes it possible to encompass within it all the principles of existence. Moreover, as the exemplar and final cause of the universe, the Good is both the end sought by all things and the perfection which can render them similar to itself. Consequently, it is necessary that God be the cause of prime matter since it is "the first subject among the effects" and hence, "should be the effect of the first cause alone, which is the Good, while the causality of secondary causes does not reach as far as this."[29] That is, the entire chain of sublunar secondary causality depends upon prime matter, the principle of its operations, for its actualization. Thus, in contrast to Maimonides for whom the good is not a category of reason, let alone the final cause of all existing things, Aquinas argues not only that the Good is a proper object of the intellect, but also that we can know it as the first and final cause of all existence.

*De Divinis Nominibus* provides the best example of Aquinas' synthesis of Neoplatonic and Aristotelian principles, essential elements of which are brought together to form his own metaphysics.

He rejects the Neoplatonic interpretation of matter as "non-being because joined to privation"[30] in favor of an Aristotelian explanation, distinguishing matter from privation, and posits the latter as joined to matter *per accidens.* He then adds that like all caused things which are turned to their cause through desire, prime matter's desire for the Good as its cause "seems to be nothing other than privation and its ordering to actuality."[31]    In Aquinas' unique metaphysics the act of creation must be understood, first and foremost, as the manifestation of the Good since God, as the Good, is inseparable from His act, the effects of which can be nothing other than good.   Consequently, not only must prime matter be distinct from privation, but also it must have a positive, or real, function in the order of being, rather than merely a logical one.   For if the Good is the primary and more common principle of all creation, and if its extension is greater than that of being, an Aristotelian metaphysics of being cannot account fully for the whole of being.[32]

For Aristotle the desire for the Good *qua* the Good has a very limited function in the universal order.   But for the Neoplatonists and for Aquinas the desire for God, primarily as the Good, is the *ratio* of universal order.   For Aquinas, this desire is for the unifying principle into which all things return to the extent that they desire Him as an active principle, a conserving one, and an end.   Departing from both Aristotle and Pseudo-Dionysius, Aquinas maintains, as did Maimonides, that, rather than designating non-being, the seeming privation associated with prime matter is its desire for perfect being, or for its own actualization.   In addition, Aquinas disengages prime matter from its association with evil on the one hand, and on the other, attributes to it a real function in the order of existence, beyond both the epistemological and the ontological.   For Aquinas, prime matter is one of the necessary causes for the actual perfection of all created beings; privation, the cause of its hindrance.   Thus the main difference between Maimonides' and Aquinas' accounts of prime matter is not in their conception of prime matter as the substratum of natural existence, but rather in their understandings of (1) the moral categories and their relation to ontological categories and (2) the scope of human knowledge of causality.

Rather than view the indefinite potency which is prime matter as evil, Aquinas presents its role in existence as a manifestation of the Good.   Based upon the clear distinction between *non ens* and *non est*, Aquinas argues that the potency manifesting a privation of a particular form (*non est*), which seems to be an evil, is in fact a manifestation of matter's natural inclination, or desire, for the Good. Since the Good is the final cause of all existing things, and since no being can be said to desire nonexistence *per se*, neither can privation be said to be essentially evil, nor can any thing be understood as utterly evil. In fact it is precisely because no being can desire evil that evil neither can be caused nor be the cause of anything *per se* and, hence, rather than subsisting *per se*, it must be caused by the Good *per accidens*. Thus Aquinas argues not only that nothing is essentially evil, but also that what is understood as evil can only be an absence of a good which can be possessed, a goodness which properly belongs to the nature of the thing as the effect of the Good cause.

One of the most striking features of Aquinas' exposition of the *De Divinis nominibus* is his ability to dissociate matter entirely from any evil designation in a commentary on a Neoplatonic text which exhibits all the tensions inherent in the Plotinian understanding of matter. He repeatedly argues that change in the natural universe, the principle of which is matter, in no way may be understood as a defect or an evil. Following Aristotle, he argues that natural corruption is the source of further generation and therefore is required for the perfection of the universe, a perfection which must comprise all grades of existence. Given Aquinas' distinctions between *non ens* and *non est*, and between matter and privation, it would be more accurate to explain his understanding of natural corruption as a decay into particular nonexistence which makes further existence possible, rather than into non-being.

Diversity of effects, the material cause of evil, cannot be attributed necessarily to a natural agent, which does one thing only, but rather, to a rational willing agent. In fact, the distinction between good and evil can be found only in the will, the proper object of which is the Good,

> since it is characteristic of that which is contrary to virtue to be evil, and it is not found in any other genus that certain species be distinguished through a difference between good and evil, except in the virtuous and wicked *habitus* of the soul.[33]

If the natural universe is perfect, then evil cannot be attributed to a natural inclination or appetite so long as these conform to the natural order. Consequently, only an intellectual being can choose evil; that is, only an active principle of the natural universe can choose to act contrary to nature. But, when acting in opposition to the natural order, man desires nonexistence *per accidens*, insofar as he acts against the principle of his self-preservation.

By rejecting the Neoplatonic theory of Forms and by replacing it with the Aristotelian doctrine of universals, Aquinas is able to establish an all-inclusive continuity between the sub- and supralunar realms of a kind clearly rejected by Maimonides.[34]    While he concurs with Dionysius' (and Maimonides') assertion that evil is found in particular rather than universal nature, Aquinas rejects the premise that universal nature is something separate, arguing that forms exist in matter as principles of action and consequently, have to be understood as "the active force of a first body which is first in a genus of natural causes."[35]    Natural universal principles, such as prime matter and form, according to Aquinas, do not have existence *in se*, but only *in alio*; they can be said to exist only as particulars consubsisting in nature. Natural powers, *qua* natural, depend upon the natural order for their actualization, are never independent of it and, hence, cannot act entirely against it. Consequently, evil is a particular act *praeter* rather than *secundum naturam*. Aquinas adds that since Dionysius himself excludes the possibility of positing the body as the cause of the corruption of the soul, the particular act manifest as actual sin makes evident that the evil of the soul originates in free choice, which uses corporeal things. For, if matter, *qua* natural potency, were posited as the cause of the corruption of the soul (form), not only would it follow that it is independent of it in some essential way, but more significantly, the corruption of the human soul would occur necessarily, "for an effect follows upon a posited cause out of necessity unless something should impede it."[36]

In emphasizing the essential relation between natural universal principles and natural particulars, and arguing that forms constitute the active principles in subsistent existents, Aquinas is arguing against the understanding of any particular matter as a hindrance to the perfection of the particular composed of it.[37]    Consequently, neither can any instance of natural corruption, such as ill health, be understood as evil, except *per accidens*, nor can it inhibit the true perfection of any natural being. Moreover, *qua* natural power, matter can only act *secundum naturam* and, hence, it can never be argued that a corrupt matter exists, nor that any matter whatsoever constitutes an obstacle to the perfection of the soul. As Aquinas points out, were it the case that any matter corrupts its form or acts independently of it in any way, the corruption of that form would follow necessarily.

***

For Maimonides the act of creation is a communication of actual being only and cannot extend to anything in potency.[38]   But for Aquinas, the act of creation is, first and foremost, the active communication of being through its most extensive manifestation—the Good and, hence, can extend to beings still in potency.   Since Maimonides denies that a final end can be posited to things and argues that their only purpose is actual existence, the predication 'good' can be assigned to things only subsequent to and in proportion with their proper act.   Consequently, Maimonides circumvents the problem of natural universals existing only *in alio* by affirming neither agency proper nor goodness or evil in them.   Although Aquinas concurs that, properly speaking, the object of the intellect is the universal and, thus, the true and the false, he also argues that good and evil are distinctions pertaining to modes of particular objects; potential existence is a good, whereas evil is a privation of a due perfection which (1) can be known[39] and (2) should and could be possessed.   As the unifying principle of all existing things, the Good is their final end; and, thus, it is also their impetus to act, which must extend beyond actual being.   Consequently, Aquinas can attribute causal agency and goodness to natural universals as well as to particulars.

Since Aquinas' metaphysics is, first and foremost, a metaphysics of the Good and is one of act only as a consequence, it succeeds in dissociating matter from evil and overcomes the tension between sub- and supralunar existence.   Maimonides minimizes the active role of matter in perfection and denies inherent goodness to all corporeal beings, rendering perfection beyond the reach of most individuals. Aquinas, by contrast, translates the seeming privation inhering in matter into its desire for the Good, thus providing a consistent account of the relation between particular goods and the final good and rendering perfection a universal possibility.

## Notes

1. All translations will follow Pines.
2. The broad juxtaposition of Neoplatonic and Aristotelian thought in this paper is not meant to suggest that Neoplatonism is free of Aristotelian elements, nor to imply that the two philosophical schools are inherently antagonistic. To facilitate discussion, I present the Neoplatonic doctrine of matter as a unified one, although it presents as many distinct doctrines as there are thinkers who adopt the Plotinian cosmology of emanation or the procession of the many from the One.
3. My argument suggests that whereas creation *ex nihilo* is always inconsistent with an Aristotelian cosmology, it can be consistent with Neoplatonic cosmology. But (1) *ex nihilo* does not preclude *de Deo*, and (2) my claim here is limited to the question of *ex nihilo* and does not encompass the question of time, which will be discussed later.
4. See Idit Dobbs-Weinstein, "Medieval Biblical Commentary and Philosophical Inquiry as Exemplified in the Thought of Moses Maimonides and St. Thomas Aquinas," in E. Ormsby, ed., *Moses Maimonides and His Times* (Washington: The Catholic University Press of America, 1987), esp. iv.
5. See *The Divine Comedy, canto* iv, *Inferno*, l. 42, tr., Charles Singleton (Princeton: Princeton University Press, 1970).
6. John Rist, "Plotinus on Matter and Evil," 160.
7. See *Nicomachaean Ethics* X 8-9. 1178a8-1181b23, and Ross' introductory essay in *The Nicomachaean Ethics of Aristotle* (London: Oxford University Press, 1954).
8. Aristotle, *Topica*, I 1, 104b14-18, tr., H. Tredennick (Cambridge: Harvard University Press, *LCL*, 1960).
9. *Guide*, II 17, 297-98.
10. *Guide*, II 17, 296-98. For a full discussion of the possibility of creation and the status of prime matter see, Idit Dobbs-Weinstein, "The Concept of Providence in the Thought of Moses Maimonides and St. Thomas Aquinas," Ph.D. Dissertation, University of Toronto, 1987, Chap. 3, esp., 141-77.
11. *Guide*, II 17, 295.

12. See Emil Fackenheim, "The Possibility of the Universe in Al-Farabi, Ibn Sina and Maimonides," *PAAJR* 16 (1947): 39-70 and the discussion in my dissertation.

13. *Guide,* I 28, 61.

14. In "Beri'at ha-'Olam le-fi ha-Rambam," (forthcoming in a Festschrift honoring S. Pines, Jerusalem: Hebrew University Press), Alfred Ivry suggests that to resolve the logical impossibility of *ex nihilo* we must interpret the expression "absolute privation" to connote a certain ontological actuality which "serves as a passive cause for that which appears subsequently, in all its stages."

15. Rist provides a similar argument for Plotinus' major objection to the Gnostics: "Plotinus on Matter and Evil," 161.

16. *Guide,* II 17, 297.

17. See Ivry passim. I do not think that we can evaluate Maimonides' consistency without a thorough semantic study of the texts and manuscript traditions. A comparative study of the terms in the Arabic philosophical tradition is also a desideratum.

18. *Guide,* III 10, 439.

19. *Guide,* III 10, 440.

20. See *Guide,* II 30, 358.

21. *Guide,* III 8, 433. In his gloss on Proverbs 31:10: "A woman of virtue who can find?" Maimonides presents the good woman not only as the most excellent matter but, in fact, as a *"divine gift."* This type of matter, however, is so exceptional that it is most similar to angelic matter, least similar to the human. I do not think that I overstate the case when I propose that the class of individuals who possess this type of matter may be limited to one, namely, Moses. For an alternative interpretation of the relation between matter as the "married harlot" and as the "woman of virtue," see L. E. Goodman, "Matter and Form as Attributes of God in Maimonides' Philosophy."

22. *Guide,* III 8, 431; cf. I 6, 7, 14.

23. *Guide,* III 11, 440.

24. *Guide,* III 12, 443.

25. Since we cannot infer the final cause(s) or purpose(s) of natural entities, and since we do not know the quiddity of their first cause, our knowledge of them does not constitute "science" in the strict Aristotelian sense.

26. *In librum Beati Dionysii "De Divinis Nominibus" Expositio* (Turin and Rome: Marietti, 1950). The translations from the Latin are my own.

27. *De Divinis Nominibus,* 3.1.226.

28. See especially the *proemium* to *De Divinis Nominibus.*

29. *De Divinis Nominibus,* 4.2.296.

30. *De Divinis Nominibus*, 4.2.295.
31. *De Divinis Nominibus*, 4.2.296.
32. It seems clear to me that Aquinas realized that an Aristotelian metaphysics of the act of Being necessarily leads to a denial of sublunar providence.
33. *De Divinis Nominibus*, 4.15.486.
34. Since Maimonides, like Aquinas, rejected the Neoplatonic theory of Forms, he could have established a greater continuity between the two realms had he been willing to include the good among the most universal manifestations of the act of creation (like will and wisdom) even if not the most extensive. But contrast the view of Goodman in "Matter and Form . . ."
35. *De Divinis Nominibus*, 4. 21. 550. Cf. *In I Sententiarum*, d. 8, q. 5, a. 1; *Quaestiones de Anima*, 1, ad 2; J. Owens, "Diversity and Community of Being," *Mediaeval Studies* 22 (1960): 257-302.
36. *De Divinis Nominibus*, 4.21.566.
37. See Owens, "Diversity and Community" and "The Unity in the Thomistic Philosophy of Man," *Mediaeval Studies* 25 (1963): 54-82.
38. Despite the difficulties inherent in the interpretation of Maimonides' statements about prime matter, it should be emphasized that, being subject neither to generation nor to corruption after creation, it must be understood to possess actual being of a unique kind.
39. It is important here that for Aquinas practical reason possesses its own primary principles. See *Summa Theologiae*, Ia, IIae. Q. 90, a. 1 and esp., Q. 94, a. 2, where he argues that the first principles of practical reason are *propositiones per se nota* and that *bonum* is to practical reason what *ens* is to theoretical reason.

# Divine Unity in Maimonides, the Tosafists and Me'iri

## J. David Bleich

The writings of medieval Rabbinic authorities reflect two, or possibly three, distinct theological positions with regard to Christianity. These positions are not merely theoretical or attitudinal in nature. Rather, they yield disparate halakhic rulings governing the conduct of Jews with regard to interpersonal relationships between members of the different faith-communities as reflected in many aspects of commercial and social conduct.

An entirely negative theological view of Christianity is expressed by Maimonides (1135-1204) both in his *Commentary on the Mishnah* and in his *Mishneh Torah*. The Mishnah, in the opening statement of Tractate *Avodah Zarah*, prohibits various forms of commercial intercourse with idolaters during the three days preceding their days of religious observance. The concern is that an idolater, pleased by the success of a commercial enterprise, may, in the course of the impending religious celebration, give thanks to his pagan deity for his good fortune. Jews are admonished not to be involved even vicariously in acts of idolatry and may not even indirectly cause an idolatrous act to be performed. The Mishnah (1:3) goes on to enumerate a number of such days of religious observance. Maimonides declares the references to be to days of Christian observance, although the days named are not readily identifiable as known holy days of the early Christian calendar:[1]

> These feast-days herein mentioned were well known at that time among the Christians[2] and those who cleave to them. . . . And know that all the various sects of this Christian people who profess the claim of the Messiah, all of them are idolaters . . . and one must conduct oneself with respect to them with regard to all [the laws of] the Torah in the manner in which one conducts oneself vis-à-vis idolaters.

Maimonides proceeds to declare that Sunday is to be regarded as a day on which commercial traffic with "believers in the Messiah" is forbidden. This principle is codified in his *Mishneh Torah, Hilkhot Avodat Kokhavim* 9:4:

> Edomites are idolaters, and Sunday is their day of religious observance. Therefore, in the Land of Israel, it is forbidden to do business with them on Thursday and Friday of each week. It need not be stated that on Sunday it is forbidden in every locale.[3]

In some censored editions of the *Mishneh Torah* the term "Canaanites" is substituted for "Edomites"; in others the entire section, including the numeral introducing the section, is omitted, so that the published version proceeds from section 3 to section 5, with the total elimination of section 4. Maimonides' position is substantiated by manuscript readings of *Avodah Zarah* 6a and 7b, as cited by Rabbi R. N. Rabbinovicz, *Dikdukkei Sofrim*, X, 15. As will be noted, the texts of *Avodah Zarah* eliminated by the censor pose a formidable problem for those authorities who differ with the Maimonidean categorization of Christianity.

Maimonides reiterates his view in the *Mishneh Torah* in a second context. He rules that it is forbidden to derive any benefit whatever from wine that has been handled by an idolater. But the rule about wine handled by a non-Jew who is not an idolater is somewhat different. Such wine may not be consumed by a Jew but there is no prohibition against deriving other benefits from it, e.g., it may be sold to a non-Jew.[4] In *Hilkhot Ma'akhalot Assurot* 11:7, Maimonides declares that "the Ishmaelites," i.e., Muslims, are non-idolatrous gentiles, but that Christians are idolaters, and hence no benefit may be derived from any wine touched by them. In censored editions of the *Mishneh Torah* the word *nozrim* is deleted and replaced with the phrase *'otan ha-'ovdim 'akum.*

A somewhat different view of Christianity is ascribed to the Tosafists (12-13th centuries) in their comments on *Sanhedrin* 63b and *Bekhorot* 2b.[5] A literal reading indicates that they hold that acceptance of a doctrine of *shittuf* (association) is permitted to non-Jews. The doctrine involves a belief in the "Creator of the heavens," but links a belief in the Creator with a belief in some other being or entity. The term *shittuf* is not uncommon in medieval philosophical literature and connotes plurality in the Godhead.[6] The *Tosafot* refer explicitly to the gentiles of their day, and the most obvious example of *shittuf*, clearly the doctrine which the *Tosafot* seek to legitimize for non-Jews, is Trinitarianism.

However, this interpretation of the *Tosafot* is by no means universally accepted. The *Tosafot* state only that one may administer an oath to a Christian even though he swears in the name of the Trinity. This ruling is justified by the *Tosafot* with the declaration that nowhere is there recorded a prohibition against causing gentiles to "associate" or to "incorporate" another deity in an oath invoking the Divine Name. R. Ezekiel Landau[7] understands the *Tosafot* as carefully distinguishing between *shittuf* or Trinitarianism as a professed doctrine and the swearing of an oath in the name of the Trinity. *Noda' bi-Yehudah* declares the former to be idolatry and, as such, forbidden to Jew and gentile alike, since idolatry is forbidden by the Noahidic Code. Swearing an oath in the name of a pagan god does not constitute an act of worship or adoration but is forbidden in the commandment "and in His Name shall you swear" (Deuteronomy 10:20). That commandment, however, is addressed only to Jews. Although this reading of the *Tosafot* does not at all strain the plain meaning of the text and is followed by a number of later authorities,[8] it is probably correct to say that the majority of latter-day authorities interpret the *Tosafot* more broadly as declaring that *shittuf* does not constitute idolatry for Noahids.[9]

The conventional analysis of the *Tosafot* must be understood as distinguishing between the denial of polytheism and the upholding of Divine Unity. In proscribing the worship of foreign gods, the Noahidic Code binds gentiles to the acceptance of a monotheistic belief. That concept, however, entails only the rejection of *shetei reshuyot*, i.e., a multiplicity of powers each capable of independent action. The full doctrine of Divine Unity requires much more than abjuration of such a primitive notion. Indeed, Maimonides, in formulating the second of his Thirteen Principles, affirms that God's unity is unique:

1. Mankind, for example, is a single species, a unity composed of all individual men. God, however, is not such a collective unity; He is not to be construed as a genus composed of distinct beings or powers. The unity of God is not the unity of a collectivity.

2. The unity of God is not the unity of an aggregate. God is not a compound. His unity is not the unity of a composite divisible into its component parts.

3. Merely to say that God's unity is not the unity of a compound does not exclude the possibility of a nature analogous to that of even the smallest corporeal substance, which, at least in principle or conceptually, may be further divided or broken down. God's unity, however, is not the unity of magnitude. It cannot admit of any division whatsoever. A "simple substance," not composed of parts, cannot be broken down. Since destruction involves the division of an entity into component parts, it follows that God, who is a perfect unity, is not susceptible to destruction.

For Maimonides, renunciation of polytheism is not a separate principle or doctrine standing alone. It flows rationally and necessarily from the notion of Divine Unity and is part and parcel of a sophisticated conception of the unity unique to God. Since rejection of polytheism and acceptance of Divine Unity are but two sides of the same coin, it follows that Noahids, who are commanded to renounce idolatry, are *ipso facto* commanded to accept the doctrine of Divine Unity.[10]

According to this analysis, the *Tosafot* posit that Noahids are required only to renounce the notion of multiple, independent deities. This is expressed in the statement that contemporary gentiles recognize the "Creator of the heavens," by which the *Tosafot* undoubtedly intend to ascribe to Christians a belief in a single Creator who continues to exercise providence over His creatures. The highly sophisticated belief that the Deity is an absolute unity is demanded of Jews but is not a requirement placed upon non-Jews. So worship of a triune God by Christians is not tantamount to idolatry or to polytheism, since they do not ascribe independent powers to the members of the Trinity.

Support for a distinction between rejection of polytheism and acceptance of the doctrine of Divine Unity may, almost paradoxically, be found in a source that formulates this distinction only to reject any difference that might arise therefrom. In describing the obligations of non-Jews, *Hullin* 92a speaks, not simply of the Seven Commandments of the Sons of Noah, but of thirty commandments "accepted" by Noahids:

> "And I said to them, if ye think good, give me my hire; and if not, forebear. So they weighed out for my hire thirty pieces of silver" (Zechariah 11:12). Ulla said, "These are the thirty commandments which the Sons of Noah accepted upon themselves, but they observe only three [of them]: (i) they do not draw up a *ketubah* for males; (ii) they do not weigh flesh of the dead in the market; and (iii) they respect the Torah."

Rashi, in his commentary, indicates that the identification of these thirty commandments is unclear.[11] But Samuel ben Hofni (d. 1034), the last Gaon of Sura, does provide a complete enumeration of these commandments and lists belief in the unity of God among them.[12] Although he posits an obligation binding Noahids to accept the doctrine of Divine Unity, Samuel ben Hofni clearly recognizes it as an obligation quite distinct from acceptance of the monotheistic principle which prohibits polytheistic worship. For Samuel ben Hofni the two beliefs are distinct; but, since both are binding upon Noahids, this is a distinction without a difference. Yet once it is accepted, as against the view of Maimonides, that the two are distinct notions and not mutually entailed, it is much less surprising to find that the *Tosafot* recognize acceptance of Divine Unity as a belief incumbent only upon Jews, while for non-Jews renunciation of polytheism is sufficient.

The belief in a single "Creator of the heavens" sharing the divine essence with another being, or with other beings, ascribed by the *Tosafot* to the Christians of the day, is an accurate depiction of a conception of relative unity developed by the Apologists to reconcile Christian belief in a triune God with the inherited Jewish belief in one God. The Apologists accepted the concept of Divine Unity as an expression of the concept of unity of rule, i.e., the concept of a single absolute ruler of the universe. To them, however, the Deity was not an absolutely simple being but consisted of three beings inseparably united. Thus, for example, Tatian speaks of Christianity as accepting the "rule of one" as opposed to Greek polytheism which acknowledges "the dominion of many,"[13] and Athenagoras describes God, the Logos, and the Holy Spirit as "united in power."[14] This doctrine is also formulated in the writings of Tertullian who declares, "I am sure that monarchy has no other meaning than single individual rule; but, for all that, this monarchy does not, because it is the government of one, preclude him whose government it is, either from having a son . . . or from ministering his own government by whatever agent he will."[15] Tertullian describes the members of the Trinity as "three, however, not in status, but in degree; not in substance, but in form; not in power, but in species; yet of one substance, and of one status and of one power."[16] The terms "monarchy" and "united in power" clearly express the notion of rule.[17] Reflected in each of these citations is a clear renunciation both of a multiplicity of powers and of the notion that Divine Unity demands absolute simplicity. Later Church Fathers formulate the concept of triunity in terms of Aristotelian notions of species, genus and substratum. Statements expressing such concepts do not at all negate the fundamental concept of unity of rule.

A far more positive view of Christianity is expressed by R. Menaḥem Me'iri (1249-1306). In a number of statements scattered throughout his commentary on the various tractates of the Talmud, Me'iri unequivocally rules that Christians are not idolaters.[18] His most explicit ruling occurs in his commentary on the opening Mishnah of *Avodah Zarah*, where he holds that the restrictions on commercial intercourse with idolaters on their feastdays are not applicable "in these times." He takes pains to note that the uncensored text of the Talmud, *Avodah Zarah* 6a and 7b, refers explicitly to the "*Noẓri*" as an idolater. But Me'iri dismisses that text by declaring that the reference is to an ancient people mentioned in Jeremiah 4:16, whose appellation is derived from the name Nebuchadnezzar. He depicts that people as sun-worshipers who observe the first day of the week as a day of religious devotion because it is regarded as the day of the sun's dominion.

Theologically, Me'iri's most positive statement concerning Christianity is his unequivocal declaration that "they believe in God's existence, His unity and power, although they misconceive some points according to our belief" (*Bet ha-Behirah, Gittin* 62a, p. 258). This citation is far more significant for determining Me'iri's theological assessment of Christianity than are his frequent and oft-quoted references to "*umot ha-gedurot be-darkei ha-datot*—nations restrained by the ways of religion."[19] Me'iri's employment of such phraseology is invariably in the context of jurisprudential and interpersonal matters. Hence his comments might well be understood as reflecting the thesis that halakhic distinctions between Jews and gentiles regarding such matters are predicated upon the principle that the advantages enjoyed by Jews, e.g., restoration of lost property, depend on reciprocal respect for property rights and the welfare of others. Hence Jews owe such obligations only to fellow Jews who reciprocate in kind, but not to gentiles "not restrained by the ways of religion," who feel no legal or moral obligation to comport themselves in a similar manner. On such an analysis, Me'iri might well be understood as asserting that law-abiding and benevolent adherents of religions which make similar demands of their devotees are entitled to the same benefits, privileges and protection as Jews. But from such a position nothing can be deduced as to the status of the theological beliefs of the members of such religions. Such a distinction is bolstered by Me'iri's ruling that, unlike a heretic, an apostate Jew is to be accorded the rights and privileges of members of his adopted faith in all matters pertaining to jurisprudence.[20]

Jacob Katz' analysis of Me'iri's stance toward Christianity is flawed by insensitivity to the role of the distinction between positive juridical/moral institutions and valid theological doctrines. Katz characterizes Me'iri's theological comments on Christianity as something that "Ha-Me'iri sometimes adds to the characteristics of the contemporary nations."[21] But Me'iri's references to Christian beliefs are neither an afterthought nor mere theological gilding of the lily of morality. They are formulated in those contexts precisely in which the halakhic issues hinge upon belief and are omitted in discussions of halakhic issues predicated upon juridical and moral institutions and comportment. Thus there is no support for Katz' conclusion that "Ha-Me'iri's positive evaluation of Christianity stems in the main from his esteem for the maintenance of legal institutions and moral standards of society." Me'iri's evaluation is, of necessity, twofold: moral and theological; but there is no entailment between these two evaluations.

Me'iri's theological assessment of Christianity is unique in Rabbinic literature. Katz' assertion that "independently of him, a similar line of reasoning was followed by certain seventeenth-century scholars, among them Moshe Rikves . . ."[22] is simply erroneous. R. Moshe Rikves in his glosses to the *Shulḥan Arukh* bearing the title *Be'er ha-Golah* does indeed posit an obligation to rescue gentiles from danger, and, moreover, to pray for their welfare.[23] And he does express a positive theological attitude toward Christianity, but it is the attitude of the *Tosafot*, not of Me'iri. *Be'er ha-Golah* correctly ascribes to Christians a belief in God as Creator of the universe and author of providence, as evidenced by the phenomena of the Exodus, and adds that "their whole aim and intent is toward the Creator of the heaven and earth, as the codifiers have written." The expression "aim and intent" refers to acts of worship and adoration and is equivalent to the formulation used by the *Tosafot* with regard to Christianity as *shittuf*. The phrase "as the codifiers have written" is clearly a reference to the treatment of the doctrine of *shittuf* advanced by the *Tosafot*, for that is the only positive categorization of Christianity found in the writings of codifiers of Jewish law.

Moreover, it is extremely difficult to determine whether the comments of *Be'er ha-Golah* are to be taken as an expression of normative Halakhah or whether they were penned with an eye to the censor or otherwise intended to dispel anti-Semitic enmity. Phrases such as "the gentiles in whose shadows we live and under whose wings we shelter" and "hence we stand on guard to pray continually for the welfare and success of the kingdom and the ministers" have a ring that is not halakhic, but can be characterized as almost servile in tone. Certainly, the citation of Maimonides' qualification of R. Joshua's dictum (*Sanhedrin* 105a) that the pious of the nations enjoy a portion in the World to Come is imprecise and indeed may have been appended as a means of divulging to the discerning reader that the entire statement is hyperbole. Maimonides maintains that the pious of the nations of the world are entitled to a portion in the

World to Come only if they obey the Noahidic Code because they accept it on the basis of divine revelation. A Christian who believes that the Sinaitic covenant has been abrogated but adheres to the provisions of the Noahidic Code because he accepts them on the basis of natural law, on general humanitarian grounds, or for some other reason, is excluded by Maimonides from the category of the "pious of the nations of the world." If *Be'er ha-Golah* did not accept the limitation Maimonides places upon the concept "the pious of the nations of the world," he might simply have cited the dictum of R. Joshua without reference to Maimonides. So it seems likely that *Be'er ha-Golah*'s citation of Maimonides was intended as a clue to the nature of the entire statement.

But Me'iri does not merely distinguish Christianity from polytheism. He makes the far more positive statement that Christians accept Divine Unity. The tenor of his comment about the "misconceptions" of Christianity gives the impression that any doctrinal error on the part of the Christians is not tantamount to a denial of Divine Unity. Nowhere in his categorization of the beliefs of contemporary religions does Me'iri suggest a distinction between idolatry as prohibited to Jews and idolatry as subsumed in the Noahidic Code.

Me'iri's position has long been a source of puzzlement to Rabbinic scholars. Indeed, there is a strong feeling in some Rabbinic circles that these comments are either falsely ascribed to Me'iri or were inserted for fear of the censor. *Hatam Sofer,* citing the comment of Me'iri quoted by *Shitah Mekubezet, Baba Kamma* 113a, declares, "It is a *mizvah* to erase it for it did not emerge from his holy mouth."[24] I am inclined to believe that statements concerning financial and interpersonal relations were introduced into the text with an eye to the censor but that the statements concerning Christian theology constitute Me'iri's considered opinion. My reasons for accepting the censor thesis in part and rejecting it in part are twofold:

Only the hovering presence of the censor can elucidate the remarks of Me'iri in his commentary on *Yevamot* 98a.[25] The Talmudic rule is that no paternal relationship exists among gentiles. The principle regarding paternal relationship is thus analogous to that governing determination of animal species, regarding which "there is no concern whatsoever with the seed of the sire." The practical halakhic application of this principle is that no levirate obligations are attendant upon converts. Me'iri qualifies the discussion by inserting a statement that this status includes "every idolater who is not within the pale of the religions." The implication is that levirate obligations do devolve upon Christians who convert to Judaism. There can be no question that the qualifying phrase was introduced by Me'iri as a means of obscuring a statement the censor was bound to find offensive. If, as is obvious, this passage was emended for the sake of the censor, there is reason to assume that similar liberties may have been taken with other potentially offensive passages.

Moreover, discrepancies among the manuscripts of *Bet ha-Behirah, Yoma* 84b, discussing rescue of a gentile on *Shabbat*, clearly reflect the handiwork of the censor. The edition published in Jerusalem in 1885 contains the phrase "the idol-worshippers of antiquity . . . since they have no religion and are also unconcerned with the detriment of human society." This phrase is absent in the Parma manuscript which is the basis of the Jerusalem, 1975 edition edited by Joseph ha-Kohen Klein.[26]

However, Me'iri's remarks regarding Christian theology in his commentary on *Avodah Zarah* cannot be understood in the same light: Relaxation of the rule against commercial intercourse with idolaters on their feastdays was not born of a desire to appease the censor. Certainly, a distorted theological perspective was not required to justify suspension of that rule. The *Tosafot* and other early authorities had no difficulty in justifying the departure from previous practices without attempting to flatter the censor. Moreover, Me'iri's elucidation of the term *Nozri*, unless sincerely held, is entirely gratuitous. He could simply have ignored the term in his commentary. To sustain the "censor thesis," it would be necessary to argue that these comments were inserted, not simply as a means of assuring that Me'iri's work would not be suppressed, but were expressly intended to curry favor with Christian authorities for reasons having nothing to do with dissemination of the volumes in which they occur.

Even more baffling is Me'iri's assertion that adherents of the Trinity are believers in the doctrine of Divine Unity. Orthodox Christian views of the Trinity are certainly incompatible with the monotheistic beliefs of Judaism. It appears likely that Me'iri, in formulating his views regarding Christianity, assumed that Christians professed a view of the Trinity which, although erroneous, did not do violence to the doctrine of Divine Unity. Such views did exist within the Church, particularly during its infancy, only later to be branded as heretical by various Church councils. A number of possible views that are theologically compatible with Me'iri's characterization should be examined:

1. The original Jewish adherents of Christianity conceived of the founder of that nascent faith as a mere human being. This doctrine, known as Ebionism, viewed Jesus of Nazareth as the promised Messiah upon whom rested "the spirit of the Lord" (Isaiah 11:2). Somewhat later a form of neo-Ebionism evolved which understood the notion of the incarnation of the Logos in the person of Jesus in much the manner that the Divine Presence may be said to rest upon any righteous and exemplary man. However, in this instance, that phenomenon was posited as an act of grace and the presence of the Logos was attributed to a miraculous event associated with Jesus' birth or baptism.[27]

2. Docetism represented a diametrically opposing view introduced by pagan converts to Christianity. Adherents regarded Jesus as God, who only appeared in human form. This doctrine could certainly have been understood as affirming a perfectly monotheistic notion of God and as explaining all corporeal references found in the Gospels as reports of phenomena which exist only in the mind of man. Thus the second-century figure Simon the Gnostic, displaying a thorough consistency, spoke not only of the merely human appearance of the son but also of the mere appearance of his suffering, stating "thus he was thought to have suffered in Judea, when he had not suffered."[28]

Wolfson notes that a literal reading of the Pentateuch provides a source for belief in the phenomenon of God appearing to man in the form of a human being.[29] Genesis 18:1 records that "the Lord appeared" to Abraham and thereupon informs us that Abraham "lifted up his eyes and, lo, three men stood by him" (Genesis 18:2). Maimonides asserts that the entire incident occurred in a dream.[30] He clearly denies that man can perceive the Deity in a waking state.[31] And the *Midrash ha-Gadol*, commenting on the verse, assumes that such an appearance is possible only in a prophetic vision. Nevertheless, a literal reading of the text suggests precisely a waking appearance. Such an understanding of the text may be completely erroneous, but there is no indication even in Maimonides' comments (whose position on this matter is the most extreme in Judaism) that a literal reading of this Biblical narrative would be heresy or a fundamental doctrinal error:  Belief in even repeated appearances of the incorporeal God to man in the guise of a corporeal being is no more than the belief that God has repeatedly chosen to generate an optical illusion or mirage.  Accordingly, Docetism, if understood as ascribing no substantive reality to the persons of the Trinity, is entirely compatible with a pure monotheistic belief.

Various forms of Ebionism and of Docetism were found among the Gnostics, and a number of forms of neo-Ebionism and neo-Docetism were condemned as heresies by Church councils, including those of Nicaea in 325, Constantinople in 381, Ephesus in 431, and Chalcedon in 451.  Condemnation of these doctrines was confirmed by the Council of Constantinople in 556.  Thus, any form of Ebionism or Docetism that could conceivably be regarded as monotheistic seems to have disappeared by the middle of the sixth century.

3.   The early Christian Apologists made various attempts to present a monotheistic formulation of the notion of the Trinity by describing the members of the Godhead as names, predicates or attributes, rather than discrete entities.  Jewish philosophy was later to struggle with the notion of divine attributes precisely because of its belief that multiplicity of attributes, as conventionally understood, is at variance with the doctrine of God as a simple unity.  But attributes are ascribed to the Deity by Scripture, and such ascription could well abide explanation.  The notion of divine attributes required careful elucidation, a task that commanded the attention of all medieval Jewish philosophers.  But what Judaism was to regard as a problem, for some early Christian theologians, became the solution. The "heresies" of Praxeas, Noetus and Sabellius involved a categorization of the distinction among the members of the Trinity as nominal rather than real.  If the terms Father, Son and Holy Spirit are regarded as mere names or attributes, devoid of reality, the unity of God is preserved.  This view is closely related to Modalism as described by Origen.  Modalism regards the Logos as having no reality as a being distinct from God, but as a power of God, a mode of His manifestation to man.  This conceptualization of the Trinity

was condemned by Justin Martyr and does not appear to have been accepted by any later source.[32]

4. At roughly the same time, other Christian theologians seeking to reconcile the notion of the Logos as endowed with reality with strict Divine Unity formulated a position known as Creationism. They conceived of the Logos as created by God either *ex essentia Dei* or *ex nihilo*. As a created being, the Logos could not be regarded as a Deity in any real sense. This view proved attractive to some and preferable to Modalism in that it permitted acceptance of the Logos, not simply as a power in God, but as a real being outside of God. According to both Philo and Justin Martyr, the Logos originally existed only as a power in God but became a real being outside of God.[33]

The Apologists maintained that the Logos, in its second stage, was generated by God out of His own essence before the creation of the world.[34] Later, Arius adopted a view similar to that of Philo, asserting that the Logos was created by God "out of things nonexistent."[35] Such a Logos cannot be regarded as God. Naturally, the Arian Logos is intimately associated with Jesus of Nazareth. The role of the Logos in that context is, for Arius, roughly equivalent to that of the divine spirit in Philo's description of prophetic experience. Philo speaks of the mind being evicted and replaced by the divine spirit during prophecy and of the return of the mind at the conclusion of the prophetic experience.[36] The Arian Logos, in effect, performs the same function that Philo ascribes to the divine spirit. According to Arius, however, Jesus had no other rational soul; hence, the Logos became immanent in him in a manner analogous, in Philonic terms, to a person continually endowed with a prophetic state, by virtue of the constant immanence of the divine spirit.[37]

Although Arianism was repeatedly condemned by Church councils during the fourth century and ceased to be a power inside the Roman Empire subsequent to the Council of Constantinople in 381, it remained the faith of the barbarian invaders. Despite the fact that Arianism was suppressed by a series of civil decrees, Roman law was binding upon Romans only; no attempt was made by the Roman emperors to interfere with the beliefs of their Gothic soldiers, who remained "privileged heretics in the midst of the orthodox Empire."

With the Teutonic conquest of the West in the fifth century, Arianism became dominant in Italy and Spain.[38]

5. Although Arianism declined rapidly in the ensuing period, a related theological tenet gained currency towards the end of the eighth century in the form of Adoptionism. The adherents of this idea held the relationship between the Deity and the founder of Christianity to have resulted from God's adoption of a son rather than as flowing from a natural, existential state. Among the Adoptionists, the Cerinthians taught that Jesus became the adopted son of God by virtue of wisdom, virtue and purity; the Basilidians held that Jesus was arbitrarily selected and purified through his baptism to serve as the medium of revelation. The primary focus of the various forms of Adoptionism was insistence upon the humanity of Jesus. Indeed, some historians point to concepts apparently expressed in a letter written in 783 by one of the leaders of this movement, Felix, Bishop of Urgel, to Elipandus, Archbishop of Toledo, as designed to pave the way for a union between Christians and Muslims. The Muslims, of course, would have rejected out of hand any theology in which monotheistic principles were compromised. The doctrines expressed by Felix received wide currency in Spain and France but were repeatedly condemned by Church Councils in the last decades of the ninth century. With the death of Felix in 818 Adoptionism was eclipsed, but similar views are ascribed to Ecumenius in the tenth century and to Euthymius Zigabenus and others in the twelfth. References to, and rejections of, these views appear in the writings of the Schoolmen, including Peter Lombard, Thomas Aquinas and Duns Scotus, suggesting that the positions continued to enjoy a certain currency, even though they were not widely held. Particularly interesting is the fact that Duns Scotus, although he rejected the theory of adoption, was prepared to allow the use of the term with certain modifications and explanations.

Given the fact that neo-Arianism and various forms of Adoptionism did not become entirely extinct during the medieval period, it is not farfetched to hypothesize that the Christianity about which Me'iri made positive comments was not an orthodox Trinitarianism but a Christianity that espoused a theology branded heretical by the Church. Of course, if this is the case, Me'iri must have been misled in assuming that these were the beliefs accepted by the Church as a whole. How this occurred, one can only conjecture.

It may be that he lived in the midst of one of the lingering pockets of neo-Arianism or Adoptionism or had conversations with Christian clerics who, in their desire to influence a prominent Jewish scholar, purposely presented Christian theology in a manner most likely to evoke a sympathetic response. Or perhaps Me'iri's information came from a manuscript or manuscripts which, unknown to him, emanated from these "heretical" circles and did not represent mainstream Christian teaching. Since little is known of the circumstances of Me'iri's life and since details of Church history during that period are also obscure, there is little likelihood of finding a "smoking gun" to confirm this thesis.

### Notes

1. The names seem to be those of celebrations associated with the pagan cults of Roman deities. See *Tiferet Yisra'el*. Moreover, manuscript versions include "Saturnalia" rather than an alternative reading found in the published editions of the Mishnah. Curiously, R. Joseph Kafaḥ incorporates the "Saturnalia" reading in his edition of Maimonides' *Commentary on the Mishnah* (Jerusalem, 1963) without remarking on its incongruity with Maimonides' comments.

2. The Arabic term used in Maimonides' original version is correctly rendered as *"ha-nozrim"* in the Kafih translation of the *Commentary on the Mishnah*. Published versions of the Ibn Tibbon translation, reflecting the handiwork of the censor, render the term *"ha-akum."*

3. This distinction between the Land of Israel and the Diaspora is formulated by the Gemara, *Avodah Zarah* 11b. Rashi, *ad loc.*, explains that in the Diaspora these restrictions are relaxed during the three-day preparatory period (1) because in the Diaspora the burden of desisting from commercial intercourse for an extended period would be onerous, since Jews in the Diaspora are entirely dependent on commercial relations with non-Jews for their livelihoods and (2) because of "fear." *Lehem Mishneh, Hilkhot Avodat Kokhavim* 9:1, avers that the distinction is not geographic but socio-economic; hence, in an age when Jews residing in the Land of Israel lack political and economic independence, these restrictions are relaxed in the Land of Israel as well. However, Maimonides' codification does not accommodate such a conclusion. *Lehem Mishneh* asserts that, according to Maimonides, the distinction lies in the fact that gentiles "in the Diaspora are not idolaters and therefore only the feast-day is forbidden." *Lehem Mishneh* presumably means to suggest that non-

Jews in the Diaspora are not staunch in their convictions and observances: lacking the zeal of their counterparts in the Land of Israel, they are unlikely to perform acts of devotion to their deities for beneficences other than those immediately experienced. *Lehem Mishneh*'s distinction undoubtedly relies on the dictum recorded in *Hullin* 13b, "Gentiles in the Diaspora are not idol worshippers; rather they adhere to the practice of their forebears." In context, this statement refers only to diminished dedication and zeal on the part of idolaters in the Diaspora. But *Lehem Mishneh*'s use of this dictum to explain Maimonides' codification is problematic. For, regardless of the nature of idolatrous zeal during the Talmudic period, there is no reason to assume that twelfth-century Palestinian Christians were more zealous than their co-religionists in other countries. Thus, just as the distinction between residents of the Land of Israel and Diaspora is not hard and fast according to Rashi, it should not be absolute according to the thesis advanced by *Lehem Mishneh*.

4.    Wine handled by an idolatrous gentile is forbidden lest the idolater had intended to perform an idolatrous libation. All benefit is forbidden from any item used in conjunction with idolatrous worship. The wine of non-idolatrous gentiles is forbidden by virtue of a later Rabbinic decree *"mishum benoteihem,"* literally, "because of their daughters": intimacy born of drinking wine with gentiles may lead to intermarriage.

5.    Parallel statements also appear in Rosh, *Sanhedrin* 7:3; Rabbenu Yeruham, *Sefer Adam ve-Havvah* 17:5.

6.    See David Kaufmann, *Geschichte der Attributenlehre* (Gotha, 1877), 460, n. 148.

7.    *Teshuvot Noda' bi-Yehudah, Mahadurah Tinyana, Yoreh De'ah,* no. 148.

8.    *Sha'ar Efrayim,* no. 24; *Me'il Zedakah,* no. 22; *Teshuvot ve-Shev ha-Kohen,* no. 38; *Teshuvot Hadashot le-Rabbeinu Akiva Eger* (Jerusalem, 5738), 164-66; *Pri Megadim, Yoreh De'ah, Siftei Da'at* 65:11; idem, *Orah Hayyim, Eshel Avraham* 156:2; and *Mahazit ha-Shekel, Orah Hayyim* 156:2.

9.    See Rema, *Orah Hayyim,* 156:1; *Darkei Mosheh* 151; *Shakh, Yoreh De'ah* 151:1 and 151:7; *Derishah* and *Bah, Hoshen Mishpat* 182; *Teshuvot Havot Ya'ir,* nos. 1 and 185; R. Ya'akov Emden, *Mor u-Kezi'ah* 224; *Mishnat Hakhamim, Hilkhot Yesodei ha-Torah;* Rabbi Zev Boskowitz, *Seder Mishnah, Hilkhot Yesodei ha-Torah* 1:7 and *Shoshan Edut* (commentary on *Eduyyot*), 188; *Teshuvot ve-Shev ha-Kohen,* no. 38; Rabbi A. Vermeiz, *Me'orei Or* IV 8a, 13a, V, 111b; *Revid ha-Zahav, Parshat Yitro; Yad Sha'ul, Yoreh De'ah* 151;

*Teshuvot Sho'el u-Meshiv, Mahadurah Tinyana* I nos. 26, 51; R. Zevi Hirsch Chajes, *Kol Sifrei Maharaz Hayes*, I 489-90; *Ha-Ketav ve-ha-Kabbalah*, Deuteronomy 4:19; and *Pithei Teshuvah*, *Yoreh De'ah* 147:2.

10. Maimonides does refer to polytheism as a belief to be abjured, in the *Mishneh Torah, Hilkhot Yesodei ha-Torah* 1.7. That reference is both appropriate and necessary in its context, a succinct specification of the requirements of the commandment, "I am the Lord your God," rather than in a discussion that is primarily philosophical in nature.

11. See, however, sources cited by *Maharab Ranshburg, Hullin* 92a.

12. See Aaron Greenbaum, *The Biblical Commentary of Rav Samuel ben Hofni Gaon* (Jerusalem, 1978), 617.

13. *Oratio ad Graecos*, 14.

14. *Supplicatio pro Christianis*, 24.

15. *Adversus Praxeam*, 3.

16. *Adversus Praxeam*, 2.

17. For unity of rule as a rejection of polytheism, see Wolfson, *The Philosophy of the Church Fathers*, 312-22.

18. See Me'iri, *Bet ha-Behirah, Avodah Zarah*, ed., Abraham Schreiber (Jerusalem, 1944) 2a (p. 4), 6b (p. 9), 15b (p. 39), 20a (p. 46), and 22a (p. 53); *Baba Kamma*, ed., Kalman Schlesinger (Jerusalem, 1963) 113a-b (p. 330); *Gittin*, ed., Kalman Schlesinger (Jerusalem, 1964) 62a (p. 258). See also the comments of Me'iri cited by R. Bezalel Ashkenazi, *Shitah Mekubezet, Baba Kamma*, 38a, 113a, and *Asifat Zekenim*.

19. See *Bet ha-Behirah, Pesahim*, ed., Joseph ha-Kohen Klein (Jerusalem, 1966) 21b (p. 67); *Ketubot*, ed., Abraham Sofer (Jerusalem, 1947) 15b (pp. 67 f.); *Kiddushin*, ed., Abraham Sofer (Jerusalem, 1963) 17b (p. 108); *Baba Kamma* 113a-b (p. 330); *Baba Mezi'a*, ed., Kalman Schlesinger (Jerusalem, 1963) 59a (p. 219); *Avodah Zarah* 13b (p. 29), 20a (p. 46), 22a (p. 53).

20. See *Bet ha-Behirah, Horiyot*, ed., Abraham Schreiber (Jerusalem, 1969), 11a (p. 274) and *Avodah Zarah*, 26b (p. 61).

21. *Exclusiveness and Tolerance* (Oxford, 1961), 121.

22. *Exclusiveness and Tolerance*, 164.

23. *Be'er ha-Golah, Hoshen Mishpat* 425:5.

24. See the responsum of *Hatam Sofer* published in R. Baruch Frankel-Teumim's *Ateret Hakhamim*, no. 14, repr. in *Kovez She'elot u-Teshuvot Hatam Sofer* (Jerusalem, 5733) no. 90. See also R. David Zvi Hillman, "Leshonot ha-Me'iri she-Nikhtevu le-Teshuvot ha-Minim," *Zefunot* 1 (5749): 65-72.

25.  Ed. Samuel Dickman (Jerusalem, 1962), 354.
26.  See 212, nn. 229, 237
27.  See Wolfson, *Church Fathers*, 602-04.
28.  Iranaeus, I 23, 3; Hippolytus, VI 9, 6; *Church Fathers*, 591-92.
29.  *Church Fathers*, 518.
30.  *Guide* II 42; cf. 45.
31.  *Guide* II 45.
32.  See *Church Fathers*, 580.
33.  *Church Fathers*, 192-93 and 582.
34.  *Church Fathers*, 292-94.
35.  *Church Fathers*, 586.
36.  Philo, *Quis Rerum Divinarum Heres* 53, 265.
37.  *Church Fathers*, 593-94.
38.  See Henry M. Gwatkin, *The Arian Controversy* (New York, 1891), 165 and his *Studies in Arianism*, 271-72.

# Platonic Themes in Gersonides' Doctrine of the Active Intellect[*]

## Seymour Feldman

### I

The second-century Platonist philosopher Numenius is reported to have said, "What else is Plato but Moses speaking Attic Greek."[1] It would certainly be excessive to say of Gersonides that he is Plotinus writing in medieval Hebrew. Yet in several important respects he and many other medieval philosophers were as much influenced by Plotinus as they were by Aristotle. By virtue of the efforts of many scholars we recognize now that Plotinus' philosophical ideas were available and absorbed throughout the Middle Ages. But in the Middle Ages many of these doctrines were attributed to Aristotle, the Greek philosopher whom the medievals knew best and to whom the title "the Philosopher" was applied, even though this famous name may have been originally applied to Plotinus.[2] To be sure most of the medieval philosophers worked within a broad Aristotelian framework and wrote in a philosophical language that was unmistakably Aristotelian in provenance and meaning. Yet the spirit of Plotinus often hovers over, behind, and

* I am thankful for the comments of all the participants in the conference on Neoplatonism and Jewish Thought, and for a suggestion made to me by Zev Warren Harvey of the Hebrew University.

beneath the letter of Aristotle. This is especially true in the theory of mind and intellection.[3]

The late John Randall was fond of describing Aristotle's theory of knowing set forth in *De Anima* III 5, as "a Platonic wild oat coming home to roost."[4] In this obscure but fecund passage Aristotle mysteriously alluded to a philosophical persona that was to play an enormous role in the later philosophical stories about intellection and cosmology. Looking for an active cause of cognition—for, like sensation, cognition involves both active and passive factors—Aristotle fell back upon Plato's myth of a power that "illuminates" the mind and enables it to know. Just as the sun enlightens all physical reality and makes sensation possible, so some supraphysical cause enlightens mental reality and causes knowledge. As Randall suggested, Aristotle does "turn Platonist in the end."[5] *De Anima* III 5, then, ought to be read as a variation on a theme originally stated in Plato's *Republic* VI. Plotinus will incorporate both passages in his own philosophy, and medieval thinkers will read Aristotle through Platonic spectacles, forged by philosophical artisans some of whom were not wholly aware of the sources of their materials.

In *On the Generation of Animals* 736b, 27-29, it might be said again that a Platonic wild oat took root. Here Aristotle discusses when and how the soul emerges in the course of biological development. The question is particularly important for Aristotle in the case of those living things with the highest form of soul, the rational soul, *nous* (*he psyche he noetike*). Aristotle is quite clear here that the purely physical apparatus of the body is not sufficient to account for man's intellectual activities; an external cause must be introduced to explain the presence and operations of the human intellect. This is the "external intellect" (*nous thyrathen*), which acts upon the human body and is divine (*theion*). This external intellect produces that part in man which is immortal, or separable. It is not, I believe, too speculative to suggest that this passage shows the influence of both Plato's *Republic* and Aristotle's own *De Anima* III 5. In the hands of the later commentators, most notably Alexander of Aphrodisias, this notion of an external, divine intellectual power, responsible for the rational soul in man, had an enormous influence. Indeed, I would like to suggest that it was this passage in *De generatione animalium* that led Alexander to claim that the active catalyst anonymously referred to by Aristotle in *De anima* III 5 is a *transcendent* divine power, which he now dubbed "the Active Intellect" (*ho nous ho poietikos*).[6] It was this conception of the Active Intellect as a "divine intellect from without," that was to have a powerful impact upon the philosophical tradition of al-Fārābī, Ibn Sīnā, Maimonides and Gersonides[7]—but again not without Plotinian mediation. For Plotinus too was to insist upon a supernal intellectual force responsible for human cognition and for the natural order. By the time Gersonides made his entry the stage had been well set and several acts of the drama had been played.

In telling this story I shall adopt the favorite genre of medieval philosophical prose: the commentary. But since Gersonides himself was deeply influenced by Averroes, both in form and in content, I shall adapt one of Averroes' more original contributions to this philosophical prose form, the epitome. I shall begin by citing, with only brief comment, some key passages from Plotinus pertinent to the topics of intellection and generation. Then I shall write a Gersonidean epitome of these passages, in which Gersonides' own doctrines will be developed from a Plotinian perspective. My aim is to show both the similarities and the differences between these two thinkers. Like all medieval philosophers, both were the students of an Aristotle who occasionally at least sang a Platonic tune, and of a Plato who sometimes anticipated an Aristotelian aria.

## II

Plato himself suggested the question, '*Where* are the Forms?' But he did not give a clear-cut answer.[8] His later followers, now usually called Middle Platonists, claimed that the Forms are in the divine mind, fusing the theories of Plato and Aristotle into one philosophical doctrine: Aristotle's First Intellect, or God, eternally thinking of itself, thinks of the Platonic Forms. This is a common theme in late Hellenistic philosophy and appears explicitly in Philo of Alexandria, whose Logos theory, at least in some of its formulations, is an answer addressed to this central Platonic question.[9]

So is Plotinus' theory of Nous. But unlike Aristotle's First Intellect, or God, and Plato's Form of the Good, Plotinus' Nous is not the ultimate reality. It is the second hypostasis in his ontology, inferior to the One, or the Good, although superior to everything else. Nous eternally *emanates* from the One,[10] a non-temporal production that Plotinus usually describes in metaphors. Plotinus' theory of Nous is rich and complex, since Nous for him is quite active. Two of its functions are paramount: Nous is the primary factor in cognition, and it is a generative cause. Let us begin with cognition.

Following in the footsteps of the Middle Platonists, Plotinus places the ultimate objects of knowledge, Plato's Forms, within Nous. Like Philo, Plotinus calls Nous an "intelligible world" (*kosmos noetos*) in which the objects of knowledge (*ta noeta*) reside.[11] Here Plotinus modifies Plato's idea of the *Timaeus*, where the divine *demiourgos* or craftsman consults the Forms in making the physical world. For Plotinus the Forms are *not* external to but in Nous. The key text is found in the Fifth Ennead, 5, titled: "That the objects of knowledge are not outside of Nous." Consider the following passages:

1.     If one grants that the objects of thought are as completely as possible outside Intellect (*ton noun*) . . . then it cannot possess the truth of them . . . but will only get images of them. . . . One must not then look for the intelligibles outside.[12]

2.     But if this is so [the *noeta* are not outside], the contemplation (*theorian*) must be the same as the contemplated (*to theoreton*), and the Intellect (*ton noun*) the same as the intelligible (*noeta*). . . . In this way, therefore, Intellect and the intelligible are one. . . . The first Intellect which possesses the real beings (*ta onta*), or rather is the same as the real beings . . . (*Enneads* V 3.5, 22-29)

3.     . . . for this Intellect is not potential, nor is it one and its intellection another: for in this way again its substantiality would be potential . . . it is one and the same with its actuality. . . . All together are one: Intellect, intellection and the intelligible. (V 3.5, 40-44)

The first passage argues that the knowables are *essentially inherent* to Nous. I use this phrase to connote the *necessary interiority* of the objects of knowledge in Nous. Thus its knowledge is originative, whereas our knowledge is acquired. The second passage insists on the *identity* of Nous with its objects. Plotinus reaches this conclusion by applying one of Aristotle's epistemological principles: Where the knower is non-physical, and hence utterly actual, the knower is identical with what it knows.[13] The third passage stresses the absence of potentiality in Nous: It is separable (*choristos*), to use Aristotle's language, and thus completely actual (*on energeia*).[14]

Nevertheless, this identity of the knower and the known in Nous is *not* absolute. For Plotinus it is a fundamental postulate that all thinking involves some kind of diversity or plurality.[15] Even thought at its most perfect and pristine, as Nous, exhibits some otherness. For there are different Forms: Justice is not identical with Beauty; Equality is not the same as Courage. Accordingly, in Nous the objects of knowledge are diverse. This theme is clearly sounded in the following passages:

4. . . . for [Nous] is not only one but it is one and many (*Enneads* IV 8.3, 10).

5. Let it be granted, then, that Intellect is the real beings, possessing them all not as if [they were in it] as a place, but possessing itself and being one with them. "All things are together there, and none the less they are separate. . . . Intellect is all things together and also not altogether because each is a special power. But the whole Intellect encompasses them as a genus does its species . . ." (V 9.6, 1-4, 8-11)

This otherness, or diversity, in Nous distinguishes it fundamentally from the One, where there is no interior plurality of any kind. Only the One is absolutely simple. Indeed the One is even beyond thought.[16] This essential difference between the One and Nous was to be quite vexing and would have important ramifications in medieval thought. For how can that which is many directly emanate from that which is utterly simple?[17]

In a way Plotinus anticipates this question and answers it. Nous is composite in that it encapsulates many Forms, but it is *one* insofar as it constitutes a unified system of Forms. What it produces, after all, is an intelligible cosmos, that is, as the term *kosmos* connotes, order and system. Here we come to one of our main themes: Plotinus' Nous, despite its irreducible compositeness and plurality, is the ground of order and lawfulness in the physical universe. For in

Nous the diverse genera and species are so ordered and integrated that a complete plan of reality results:

> 6.    And just as in our [physical world] composed of many parts all these parts are linked together . . . so there [in the intelligible world] it is even more proper that all the parts be linked together, each to each other and each to the whole. (VI 7.2, 30-37)

The order and regularity of our world is prefigured, indeed brought about, by the transcendent Nous, where all the Forms which are exemplified corporeally exist in a "separable" mode of reality. Here we have a clear and early statement of an important theme in medieval philosophy: exemplarism.[18]

Nous, then, is an intelligible world containing in unity all the objects of knowledge and paradigms of the natural order. It has a causal role both in human cognition and in the production of nature. In human cognition:

> 7.    [Nous] gives vision to the one who sees . . . (*Enneads* VI 6.18, 25, my tr.)
> 8.    The cognitions of the objects of Nous, which are truly cognitions [are derived] from Nous and *come into* the rational soul . . . (*Enneads* V 9.7, 4-5, my tr.)

These two passages express the causal role of Nous in human cognition, reflecting how Plotinus absorbed Aristotle's Active Intellect into his Nous. The same process of assimilation occurs where Plotinus speaks of Nous as generative.

> 9.    It is not possible then for being to exist if Nous has not generated (*energesantos*). (*Enneads* VI 7.13, 28-29, my tr.)
> 10.   Intellect . . . the true maker and craftsman. Intellect provides [the Soul] with the forming principles. (*Enneads* V 9.3, 27-32)
> 11.   Being a power for generation Nous generates from itself, and its activity is substance. . . . And this very first activity generated reality (*hypostasin*). (VI 7.40, 18-19, my tr.)

The emergence of form in the physical world is an effect of the formal structure present in Nous. Plotinus' Nous has taken over the job, at least in part, of Aristotle's transcendent divine intellect responsible for the generation of terrestrial life, which Alexander had identified with the Active Intellect.[19]

The texts from Plotinus provide us with the background for a favorite medieval theme—the *dator formarum*. The idea is usually attributed to Avicenna, but clearly its provenance is in Plotinus.[20] The cognitive and generative functions that Aristotle had assigned to the Active Intellect are in Plotinus given over to Nous. Like Philo's Logos, Plotinus' Nous is not only the "place of the Forms," the "intelligible world" containing the rational order exemplified in nature, but it is also the efficient cause of cognition and generation in the physical world. Aristotle's criticism that the Forms have no real causal efficacy has been answered, indeed dissipated by Plotinus.[21]

## III

Turning now to Gersonides' epistemology, I preface my exposition with the cautionary remark that like most philosophers in the Arabic and Hebrew medieval orbit, Gersonides did not write on epistemology as such. His epistemological discussions are scattered throughout his writings. Some are found where one might expect to find them, in his super-commentaries on Averroes' commentaries on Aristotle's *De Anima* and *Parva Naturalia*. But *The Wars of the Lord* and some of the Biblical commentaries prove even more useful. The commentary on *Song of Songs* is quite important, since Gersonides reads this set of love poems as a philosophical allegory of the Active Intellect and the human intellect.

Gersonides' epistemology begins on an Aristotelian theme: *nihil in intellectu quod prius non fuerit in sensu*. Seemingly rejecting any Platonism in epistemology, Gersonides is committed to the empiricist claim that knowledge begins with sensory data. This theme is sounded throughout his writings.[22] It is a theme found in most medieval thinkers of an Aristotelian bent. But, as Aristotle acknowledged, mere sensation is not sufficient for knowledge; sensation provides us only with *particular* information, and knowledge is, strictly speaking, of *universals*.[23] Another "Platonic wild oat coming home to roost." But Aristotle doesn't say too much on *how* the idiosyncratic material of sensation is transformed into universal truths, just as he doesn't say much about the role of the

Active Intellect in cognition. Later commentators must fill in the gap, and by the thirteenth century a fully developed theory was in fashion: the doctrine of abstraction.[24] In different authors abstraction assumes diverse interpretations, but several common ideas can be isolated. First, there is the initial role of sensation. Second, a return to Platonism insofar as knowledge is claimed to imply the existence of Forms, however they may be interpreted. Third, the Active Intellect is introduced to account for the universalization of the sense data. I want now to spell out Gersonides' version of this general doctrine.

Following Alexander's reading of *De Anima* III 5, Gersonides interprets the human, or material, intellect as initially a mere capacity, or disposition (*hakanah*) for knowledge, not an independent incorporeal substance, as in Themistius and Averroes. Again like Alexander, Gersonides sees the Active Intellect as a transcendent intellectual force that acts upon the material intellect "from without." He rejects "immanentist" interpretations of *De Anima* III 5 like those found in Themistius, Averroes and Aquinas. In this respect he follows the tradition of al-Fārābī, Avicenna and Maimonides.[25] For cognitive material the human intellect relies upon the sensory impact of external physical objects. He calls the inputs "sensory forms" (*zurot muhashot*) and the bodies, "sensory objects" (*muhashim*). The sensory data are images of the sense objects that cause them, so they preserve the very particularity that knowledge must overcome. Thus we have to move to a "higher" stage.

This more advanced stage is dominated by the theme of *dematerialization*. At the level of sense, the cognitive givens literally *affect* the sense organs: The sense organ is physically changed. In modern terms, in seeing an oak tree in the field I receive visual impressions that cause an electro-chemical reaction on the retinas of my eyes, which in turn is transmitted to the brain, where all kinds of bio-physical processes take place *in* the cells and nerves. If the visual impression is too strong, the sensory organ can be harmed. Averroes and Aquinas call sensation a process that involves alteration (*immutatio*), or change, in the organ.[26] For the sense-organ is a material thing and the sense object is a material object. Here Hume's term "impressions" is appropriate, and Gersonides' term '*rishumim*' similarly expresses the idea of a physical impact.[27]

But the data do not remain at the level of sense. They are quickly "elevated" to the level of imaginative forms (*zurot dimyoniyot*), objects of the faculty of imagination, which has the dual role of storing the data (*ha-koah ha-shomer*) and re-producing, or re-presenting, them *ad libitum* (*ha-koah ha-zokher*). This level is more "spiritual" (*ruhaniyyi*), for the material impact of the original sense-datum has disappeared. Stored in the imagination or reproduced, the image no longer affects the imaginative power in such a way that the latter literally "suffers," as in sensation. (The Greek and Latin words *pathema* and *passio* express this idea better than the Hebrew or Arabic *hipa'alut* and *munfa'il*.) On the level of sensation the perceiver suffers; imagination is free of this consequence of our materiality. As Hume was to insist later, ideas are less vivid than impressions. But we have not yet left the world of materiality entirely behind. Imagination is corporeal insofar as it still reproduces the particularity of the material domain. A further spiritualization is needed before we can say that we have attained knowledge proper. Here the Active Intellect must enter the process.

So far Gersonides is following a commonplace medieval account.[28] But his understanding of the Active Intellect makes his version noteworthy. He accepts Alexander's doctrine of the Active Intellect as an external, supernal intellect acting upon the material, or human, intellect, but he develops this familiar theme in a striking Platonic, indeed Plotinian, fashion. In any of the medieval theories, the Active Intellect can act upon our mind and enable us to acquire knowledge because it *has* this knowledge. Like Plotinus' Nous, Gersonides' Active Intellect comprises in itself intelligible forms, or patterns. Thus Gersonides frequently calls it "the intelligible order" (*ha-siddur ha-muskal*). Plotinus and Gersonides here reproduce Philo's notion of an *intelligible world* (*ho kosmos noetos*), which serves both as a cosmological blueprint and as a necessary condition of human cognition. The intelligible world can function in this capacity because it exemplifies and contains the rational structure embodied in nature. In the Active Intellect this structure is of course found at a higher level of abstraction and perfection than in particulars. In nature the intelligible order is literally *in* matter, for the material object instantiates the universal law, and thus the intelligible form is embodied (*enulon*) and individualized. In the

Active Intellect these forms exist unencumbered with matter (*a'ula*) in absolute generality. They are perfect in abstraction, unity and harmony. Like the Plotinian Nous, the Gersonidean Active Intellect is a unity and a plurality. It is a system of intelligible forms ordered as a unity. The plan exhibits variety insofar as it is a plan for and of a domain containing many items of diverse natures, yet the plan is itself a *systemic* ordering of the forms of these natures.

Repeatedly Gersonides insists on the contrast between man's knowledge of nature and the knowledge possessed by the Active Intellect. Human knowledge is cumulative and successive, thus subject to quantitative and qualitative imperfection; but the knowledge of the Active Intellect is perfect. Just as Boethius' God knows everything simultaneously and wholly (*simul et tota*),[29] the Active Intellect contains the intelligible order "all at once and entirely."[30] True, the Active Intellect is not an *absolute* unity, since it comprises a system of many and diverse formal structures; yet it is one system. Like Plotinus' Nous, the Active Intellect is a "one-many"[31] by its very nature. The human intellect is, however, a many that can become one; but, even when it does, it is never complete.

There is one important difference between Plotinus' Nous and Gersonides' Active Intellect. Nous for Plotinus comprises an absolutely complete plan of all reality. Here Plotinus follows in the footsteps of Plato and Philo. The Active Intellect for Gersonides, however, is only a partial plan. It comprises the intelligible order only of the sublunar world.

It is because the Active Intellect comprises the intelligible order of the terrestrial world that it can help the human intellect acquire knowledge of nature. Just as Nous "lends" its cognitive capital to what is lower on the ontological ladder, so the Active Intellect "endows" the human intellect with information. The word 'information' is telling. For Gersonides the Active Intellect literally imparts intelligible Forms to the human mind. Gersonides uses the terminology of Avicenna, referring to the Active Intellect as the giver of forms (*noten ha-ẓurot*).[32] Once en-formed, the human intellect is capable of distinguishing the essential from the accidental, the universal from the particular in the sense images it has accumulated. Having acquired these universal concepts, it can formulate universal propositions true of all members of a species or genus. This is knowledge proper.[33]

Although the general outline of Gersonides' account of abstraction is straightforward, some of the important details are not clearly or consistently delineated. In some texts the "material intellect" of the individual seems to be assigned an active role; in others it is almost entirely passive. Thus in the *Commentary on Song of Songs* and the supercommentary on *Averroes' Epitome of De Anima* Gersonides describes the material intellect as a power or disposition residing in the imagination, or in the imaginative forms themselves, stimulated (*mit'orrer*) to abstract general concepts from these forms by the external action of the Active Intellect.[34] Here the latter functions primarily as a catalytic agent, as appears to have been Aristotle's original intent. Both the Active Intellect and the images provided by sensation are necessary (and together sufficient) to afford us ordinary knowledge—knowledge not communicated through prophecy. On this account, intellection is a capacity, like vision. Just as vision is a disposition of the eyes to receive sensory inputs from external objects, given the medium of light, and to transmit them to a central synthesizing subject, so intellection is the power of the imagination to abstract the general nature embedded in many idiosyncratic images, a power brought into action by the Active Intellect. This dynamic account seems quite close to Aristotle and Alexander.

Yet in other texts, chiefly in *The Wars of the Lord*, a very different account appears. Gersonides still mentions the need for sensory data, but his main concern here is to magnify the role of the Active Intellect, and he does so at the expense of the imagination. It is not just that the latter is not sufficient to generate knowledge; this was a medieval commonplace. Rather, now the Active Intellect as "the giver of forms" has become virtually the *sole agent* in cognition. Gersonides insists that the Active Intellect does *not* directly work upon the imaginative forms; nor do the latter work upon, or move, the material intellect. The role of the imagination is now reduced considerably. The Active Intellect, Gersonides claims, acts *directly* upon the material intellect and renders it capable of apprehending the general concept present *in potentia* in the individual images produced by sensation. Since the Active Intellect possesses these general concepts *a priori*, it can "endow" the material intellect with them, but it does so successively. So the knowledge of the material intellect is essentially fragmentary. In ordinary human cognition we still need sensation to give us the appropriate data. These data will of necessity be incomplete and acquired accumulatively; this is the human condition.[35] But if the Active Intellect is the "giver of forms" and moves the material intellect to receive the general concept, why do we need the sensory data at all? Since Gersonides stresses the fact that the Active Intellect can give us knowledge, even of ordinary things, without our having the relevant sense data, e.g., in mathematics, his usual empiricist orientation seems here to be abandoned in favor of a Plotinian-Avicennan model of knowledge. Aristotle has given way to Plato. Human cognition is now more a matter of external illumination than of the mind's own abstraction of concepts. It would seem that our knowledge is more a gift than an acquisition achieved by one's own hard work.

A comparison with Aquinas will be useful. He too sees the process of acquiring concepts as one of giving by the Active Intellect and receiving by the "possible intellect." But the Active Intellect for Aquinas is a part or function of the human mind, not a separate, transcendent force that acts upon us "from without." That is the basic difference between Aquinas' account of abstraction and Gersonides'. By internalizing the Active Intellect, Aquinas was, I believe, more successful in making clear what goes on in abstraction. The process becomes no more puzzling than the operation of the heart. Just as one part of the heart pumps the blood coming in from the veins to another part, which pumps the blood into the lungs, so one part of the human mind abstracts the general concept and another part receives and stores it. Aquinas admits that the human intellect is not altogether autonomous and requires the help of some separate, transcendent power, but this is God, not some lesser supernal intellect, as in Gersonides.

Aquinas explicitly rejects the Avicennan theory of the *dator formarum*, which was adopted by Gersonides. His major criticism is virtually the same as the one I just raised against Gersonides' account of abstraction: If the Active Intellect imparts the general concepts to the material intellect, a view that Aquinas characterizes as Platonistic, then there is no need for sense data. What is most curious is that

Gersonides criticizes Avicenna on the same grounds, yet falls to the same charge.[36] I suspect that his desire to permit extra-sensory cognition to enter the domain of knowledge led him to this more Platonic, indeed Plotinian, account. Since the Active Intellect was needed to explain prophecy, it became tempting to hand over to it the responsibility for the whole cognitive process. But it is surely fallacious to argue that since *some* knowledge needs to be given us as a finished product, *all* knowledge is given to us in this way.

In Gersonides' defense it could be argued that sense data would in most cases still be needed as cues for the human apprehension of the intelligible forms. The Active Intellect possesses these forms and does provide them to the human intellect, but we cannot receive them "naked," or neat; the mind needs images to prepare itself to receive the endowment of the Active Intellect. Here both Plato and Aristotle agree. Plato acknowledged the role of sense data as stimuli for the recollection of the Forms; Aristotle insisted upon the need for images in thinking.[37] We all know, sometimes to our chagrin, that it is not easy to think abstractly; we often prefer literally to "fantasize" and reify our concepts. Our inevitable involvement with sense images while we are *in statu isto*, i.e., in our bodies, was a common theme in Latin Scholastic thought. Scotus and Ockham, for example, both distinguished between the cognitive conditions operative in this world and the state when man is no longer attached to sense. In the latter state we shall no longer need sense images to acquire and to retain knowledge. But as long as we are in the former condition, these images are needed for knowledge.[38]

Perhaps Gersonides shared this opinion, at least in part. It is, he insisted, of the nature of the *material* intellect to need sensory data. The cause of cognition is the Active Intellect, but while we are embodied we need images to "dispose" us to receive the influence of the Active Intellect. In the emphasis he put upon the Active Intellect, Gersonides was close to the Augustinian tradition represented by Bonaventure, Henry of Ghent and Matthew of Aquasparta—all of whom believed that human knowledge *in statu isto* is possible only through supra-natural illumination. And, of course, Plotinus was Augustine's philosophical mentor.[39] Yet Gersonides retained Aristotle's psychology, in which human thought necessarily involves *imaging*. Thus Platonic and Aristotelian elements tug at one another in his epistemology.

If Gersonides' epistemology is somewhat unsatisfactory on this score, his analysis of cognitive statements is much better. Taking the paradigm of an epistemic claim to be an affirmative universal statement of the form 'All S is P,' Gersonides argues that although such statements are true precisely because there is in the Active Intellect a formal structure corresponding to and grounding each statement, the statement is not true of *universalia in rebus*. In this claim echoes of both Plato and Aristotle are made to harmonize. With Aristotle, Gersonides denies that there exist independently existing universals. Yet, each species corresponds to a formal structure or pattern in the Active Intellect. In the Active Intellect the intelligible order exists in its pristine state; in nature it exists embodied in the individuals we encounter in perception. The form is the exemplar or paradigm for the particular. As Plotinus had maintained, the earthly man that talks to us is an embodiment of a supernal exemplar in Nous.[40]  But this Platonic Realism is not transferred to the analysis of universal propositions. An affirmative universal judgment is analyzed into a set of particular statements about individuals:  The statement 'All dogs are mammals' is true because it applies to each particular dog in our world.

Like his contemporary William of Ockham—who was Gersonides' coresident in Avignon for a few years—Gersonides calls for a "descent to particulars" in the analysis of universal propositions. In this sense, but only in this sense, he too can be called a nominalist.  Universal affirmative judgments do *not* denote a universal entity in nature, since in nature there are only individuals. Yet each individual exemplifies a formal pattern in the Active Intellect which constitutes the order of nature. Thus the Gersonidean version of the famous Avicennan formula would be that universals exist *ante rem* insofar as they exist in the Active Intellect; they exist *in rebus* only insofar as each individual in nature instantiates a formal structure found in the Active Intellect; they exist *post rem* insofar as the human intellect can come to know this intelligible order by abstraction.[41]  Unlike Ockham Gersonides is still wedded to the Platonic model of knowledge, whereby to know is to apprehend a universal form. True, this form is embedded in concrete individuals, as Ockham would insist; but each individual exemplifies a paradigm in the Active Intellect.  Without it the particulars of our sensory experience would be void of intelligibility and order.

## IV

In Book 5 of the *Wars of the Lord* the generative role of the Active Intellect is spelled out in detail. Here our passage from Aristotle's *On Generation of Animals* is especially relevant. Giving a very general interpretation to it, Gersonides claims that *all* living species are guided by the Active Intellect, or "the divine intellect from without," in their cycles of development and growth. The soul of each organism is its form,[42] and the Active Intellect is the form of the terrestrial world, responsible for the presence and development of all form in this world. The cycles of biological development on earth not only mirror the intelligible order in the Active Intellect but are brought about by it. Each embodied form emanates from the formal structure in the Active Intellect, which is the "giver of forms." In Plotinian terms, the formal structure of our sensible world is isomorphic with the intelligible world, which is Nous, the Active Intellect in Gersonides' interpretation.[43]

Gersonides' Plotinian account of generation is consciously contrasted with Averroes' more naturalistic reading of Aristotle's theory of generation. As Herbert Davidson has shown, Averroes' views on this topic shifted from an early Platonistic understanding to a more physicalistic interpretation.[44] This is exactly how Gersonides read Averroes. He too distinguished different views in Averroes but saw him as ultimately advocating a naturalistic account of biological development, except in the case of the human soul.[45] But Gersonides departs from his philosophical teacher. He urges that *On Generation of Animals* be taken literally. All biological development is to be accounted for in terms of some transcendent intellectual force. Gersonides' general counter-argument to Averroes is that a purely naturalistic theory, one that aims to explain life in terms of physical entities and processes alone, cannot account for the hierarchical-telic structure exhibited in nature. All the arguments he marshals against Averroes are based on the same disjunction: Generation is either attributable to chance or to a purposive agent. Since everyone admits that chance cannot be the cause of orderly telic phenomena, we must posit a purposive agent. The question is whether this agent is corporeal and immanent or incorporeal and transcendent. Averroes claims that the agent is of the former type— e.g., the seed in the animal produced by its parents and the heat coming from heavenly bodies. As Aristotle claimed, a human being is produced by another human being and the sun. Here Averroes uses Galen to interpret Aristotle: in the seed there is a "formative power" (*dynamis diaplastike*) that is the formative and efficient cause behind the generative process. There is no need to appeal to anything else.[46]

Averroes' account of generation is false, Gersonides argues, because natural generation is not a discontinuous or piecemeal operation. Even today, when teleological biology is certainly not fashionable, we still talk of biological and ecological systems. Averroes' biological perspective, Gersonides claims, is too narrow. He looks at the generation and development of one organism or one species without taking the rest into account. But a more holistic framework is precisely what we need. A certain species of worm, for example, develops within a context defined by the generation of other organisms, birds, plants, *et alia*. Within any subsystem each member is "directed" toward the others. All these microsystems are parts of a comprehensive macrosystem "directed" toward one unified goal: maximum telic perfection. Nature exhibits a definite tier-structure, with the various genera and species ordered hierarchically, such that one level is "the form and perfection of another." The whole system, Gersonides argues, must be directed by an external agent. For if the agent were within the system, it would be part of it and would itself need to be directed, leading to a vicious regress. The whole macrosystem, then, is governed by a transcendent intentional agent that "sees to" the orderly, telic development of terrestrial life. This is the power Aristotle referred to in his *Generation of Animals*; it is the very power described by Themistius, speaking on behalf of Aristotle, that emanates from the heavenly bodies. It is the Active Intellect.[47] Or, in Plotinian language, it is the force emanating from Nous via the Universal Soul that governs the natural order.[48] Gersonides rejects Averroes' naturalistic reading of Aristotle in favor of a literal reading of *On the Generation of Animals* and a Plotinian understanding of the Active Intellect.[49]

Gersonides' defense of a supranaturalistic account of biological development needs to be completed by a more comprehensive discussion of the place of the Active Intellect in this process, relative to the other separate intellects. Gersonides undertakes this task in the concluding chapters of Book V, Part 3 of *The Wars*. His problem here is essentially twofold: to differentiate the Active Intellect from the separate intelligences other than God, and to differentiate it from God. Plotinus made a sharp distinction between the One and Nous, on the one hand, and Nous and Universal Soul, on the other. In the emanation theory espoused by the Muslim *falāsifa*, al-Fārābī and Ibn Sīnā, the Active Intellect is placed at the lowest level of the incorporeal world. It emanates from the ninth intelligence, which is the specific mover of the lunar sphere and is therefore nearest to the terrestrial domain, of whose natural processes it is the proximate supranatural agent. The Active Intellect emanates directly from the intelligence above it, and the latter from the intelligence above it, and so up to the First Intellect, or God, from whom all the intelligences, directly or indirectly, emanate.[50] Gersonides modifies this model in several respects.

Gersonides' Active Intellect emanates from *all* the separate intelligences that are the movers of the celestial spheres. Insofar as a separate intelligence is the mover of a particular sphere it is the cause of the influence of that sphere here on earth; but it is the cause of *this* influence alone. For example, the intellect governing the sun is responsible for the solar influence of light and heat, and that is all. The Active Intellect, however, is the generative cause of the *whole* sublunar domain; as such it must transmit *all* the influences emanating from the whole celestial world. The separate intelligence for each celestial sphere is only a partial emanative force, but the Active Intellect is a universal power for generation on earth, a "synthesis" (*qibbuz*)[51] of all the influences emanating from the movers of the spheres and the spheres themselves. In this "synthesizing" role the Active Intellect is the cause of the order prevailing on earth. For example, if the force emanating from Mars were to reach us unmediated by the Active Intellect, we would constantly be subjected to wars and conflict. Fortunately, the irenic influence from Jupiter is "mixed in," and peace occasionally occurs. The mixing or filtering is the work of the Active Intellect. Like Plotinus' Nous, the Active Intellect exemplifies a general scheme for the domain under its governance and influence. It achieves generality by integrating the particular and sometimes opposing forces emanating from the heavenly domain.

Gersonides mentions that the philosophers, the Torah and the Rabbis agree that the Active Intellect is the lowest (*shafel*) of the separate intellects, because it is attached to the matter of the "lower world," the domain of generation and corruption.[52] But I do not believe that this appeal to authority does justice to the logic of Gersonides' own position. Insofar as the Active Intellect represents a *general* plan for the sublunar world it is superior to the partial representations possessed by the individual separate intellects that move the heavenly spheres. He says that the Active Intellect is in this respect like God, whose intellectual representation of reality is also general. Indeed in the very next paragraph Gersonides quotes a passage in which the Rabbis say of the chief member of the angelic court, the Metatron, "its name is like the name of its Master."[53] The Rabbis, Gersonides assumes, were referring to the Active Intellect. If the Active Intellect is the Metatron, it cannot be the least of the cosmic intellects. Because of the generality of its plan and its generative role, the Active Intellect is like God and bears His name. This Rabbinic hint is supported by Gersonides' interpretation of Proverbs 30:4. There the Biblical author (like Job 28) expresses the difficulty of our understanding the mysteries of nature: "Who has ascended heaven and come down . . . who has gathered up the wind (*ruah*) in the hollow of his hand? Who has established all the extremities of the earth? What is his name or his son's name . . .?" Gersonides identifies the spirit in this passage as the Active Intellect, or the soul that emanates from the spheres. This force is called "son" because it is the effect of another cause, God. Indeed, God created the human species with the aid of the Active Intellect, and it creates individual humans by means of the male and female seeds.[54] It is evident, I think, that the Active Intellect is far more important in its causal efficacy than any or perhaps all of the separate intellects of the spheres. Thus it is duly described in metaphorical terms as "God's son." Here Gersonides approximates Philo's habit of calling the Logos the divine son.[55]

But if the Active Intellect bears the general schema for the sublunar world and is the cosmic power responsible for this domain, how is it different from God, "its master"? For God too represents the whole scheme of nature. In Plotinus the problem of distinguishing Nous from the One is easier, since Plotinus' One is beyond thought and being. Gersonides' God, however, needs to think and to be; otherwise it cannot be said to act. Accordingly, Gersonides has to find another way to distinguish sharply between the two separate intellects whose representational and causal range is general.

This problem is handled in two steps. First, opposing Averroes, Gersonides denies that God is the mover of a particular sphere, specifically the sphere of the fixed stars. Here again he is closer to Avicenna, who also "detached" God from any particular sphere, and to the Neoplatonic tradition that permeated Avicenna's cosmology.[56] If God were the mover of a particular sphere, His influence would clearly be limited. Second, since the Active Intellect is the force that governs the sublunar sphere, its illumination is restricted to this domain. Even though the influence coming from both God and the Active Intellect is general, the scope of the intelligible order in God is therefore wider than that in the Active Intellect. In God the intelligible order is the plan for the whole universe, celestial and terrestrial.[57]

Gersonides' emanation model, then, like the Plotinian and Avicennan models, is a vertical ontic flowing forth from an ultimate reality to lower levels of existence. Yet his doctrine of the Active Intellect incorporates functions that Plotinus assigned either to Nous or to the Universal Soul. These functions are so important that the Active Intellect is no longer just one among many separate intellects each with a circumscribed role, as it is for Avicenna; instead, it has become a general transmitting agent whose synthesizing capacity is responsible for the order of the sublunar world. For Gersonides the emanative flow begins with a universal agent, God; it then disperses among a plurality of separate intellects, the emanative force of each one of which is restricted to a particular sphere; finally, all these productive powers are integrated by the Active Intellect. The initial unity of the original intelligible order in God is preserved, even though it is particularized as it descends the ontological ladder. It is the Active Intellect that preserves that original unity and order, serving literally for Gersonides as God's chief agent for the sublunar world.

## Notes

1.  Quoted in F. E. Peters, *The Harvest of Hellenism* (New York: Simon and Schuster, 1970), 585.
2.  F. E. Peters, *Aristotle and the Arabs* (New York: New York University Press, 1968), 10, 15. André Neher holds that the first mention of Plotinus in Hebrew was in Abravanel's *Commentary on Genesis* 1:16 (New York: Reprint, 1959) 1.24b; *Jewish Thought and the Scientific Revolution* (Oxford: Oxford University Press, 1986), 221. I am skeptical of this claim.
3.  See P. Merlan, *Monopsychism, Mysticism, Metaconsciousness.*
4.  J. H. Randall, Jr., *Aristotle* (New York: Columbia University Press, 1962), 102.
5.  Randall, 99.
6.  Alexander of Aphrodisias, *Commentary on De Anima*, ed., I. Bruns, Supplementum Aristotelicum 2 (Berlin, 1887): 88-89, 112. P. Moraux, *Alexander d'Aphrodise: exégète de la noétique d'Aristote* (Liege, 1942). P. Merlan, *Monopsychism*, section 2.
7.  Themistius, an early fourth-century commentator, gave a different interpretation to *De Anima* III 5, holding that the Active Intellect is in one respect *immanent* in the human intellect. Averroes was influenced by this interpretation, as was Aquinas. Themistius, *In libros Aristotelis de anima paraphrasis*, ed., R. Heinze (Berlin, 1899), 99-105; O. Hamelin, *La théorie de l'intellect d'après Aristote et ses commentateurs* (Paris, 1953); S. Feldman, "Gersonides on the Possibility of Conjunction with the Agent Intellect," *AJS Review* 3 (1978): 99-120; A. Ivry, "Averroes on Intellection and Conjunction," *JAOS* 86 (1966): 76-85; Herbert Davidson, "Al-Farabi and Avicenna on the Active Intellect," "Averroes on the Material Intellect."
8.  *Phaedrus* 247C-E.
9.  See H. A. Wolfson, *Philo*, ch. 4; J. Dillon, *The Middle Platonists*, 155-64.
10. *Enneads* V 6 4, 14-16.
11. *Enneads* III 2.1; IV 8.3, 8; Philo, *De Opificio Mundi* IV-V.
12. *Enneads* V 5.1, 51-56 and V 5.2, 1. I use Armstrong's translation except where noted.
13. Aristotle, *Metaphysics* XII 7, 1072b 21-23; *De Anima* III 7.
14. *Metaphysics*, loc. cit.; *De Anima* III 5, 430a 18.
15. *Enneads* VI 7 13; VI 9 2.
16. *Enneads* VI 7.41, 35-38.
17. See Maimonides, *Guide* II 22 and Arthur Hyman's paper in this volume.

18. Augustine, *De Gen. ad. litt.* 5, 15, 33; Bonaventure, *Quaestiones disputatae de scientia Christi*, q. 4, in J. Wippel, *Medieval Philosophy* (New York: Macmillan, 1969), 314-17.
19. T. Szlezak, *Platon und Aristoteles in des Nuslehre Plotins* (Basel, 1979), 135-43.
20. J. Moreau, *Plotin* (Paris, 1970), 43 ff.; H. Davidson, "Al-Farabi and Avicenna on the Active Intellect," 121-23, 159-60; F. Rahman, *Avicenna's Psychology*.
21. Aristotle, *Metaphysics* I 6, 9. See the English translations of *Plotinus Arabicus* in the Henry and Schwyzer edition of the *Enneads*, 2.67-68, 91, 231, 235, 241, 247, 263, 275, 291, 309, 375, 411, 415.
22. *Commentary on the Megillot, Song of Songs*, 2d, 8a-10a (Riva di Trento, 1560); *The Wars of the Lord*, tr., S. Feldman (Philadelphia: JPS, 1984) I, chs. 6, 9, 10. See the Brandeis dissertation of J. Mashbaum, *Chapters 9-12 of Gersonides Super-commentary on Averroes' Epitome of De Anima: The Internal Senses* (Ann Arbor: University Microfilms, 1981).
23. Aristotle *De Anima* II 5, 417b 22-27; *Posterior Analytics*, I 31, II 19.
24. In *Posterior Analytics* II 14 Aristotle appears to allude to the abstraction of universal concepts; Alexander develops the theme further. See Merlan, 42-46.
25. See my "Gersonides on the Possibility of Conjunction," 103; Davidson, "Al-Farabi and Avicenna on the Active Intellect," 109-78; Alexander Altmann, "Maimonides on the Intellect and the Scope of Metaphysics" in *Von der Mittelalterlichen zur modernen Aufklärung*, 60-91.
26. Mashbaum, 94-96. Thomas Aquinas, *Summa Theologiae* I q. 78, a. 3.
27. *Commentary on Song of Songs*, 8a-10a.
28. F. Rahman, *Avicenna's Psychology*, chs. 7, 11; Aquinas, q. 85, articles 1 and 2.
29. *The Consolation of Philosophy*, V 6, 10.
30. *Wars* I, ch. 6; V, pt. 3, chs. 5, 13.
31. *Enneads* VI 7.13, 7.17.
32. *Wars*, I, ch. 6, 156.
33. The activity of abstraction, or concept-formation, is *ziyyur*; the activity of judgment, or verification, is *'imut*. See *Wars* I, ch. 4. Mashbaum, 45, 62, 86. C. Touati, *La Pensée Philosophique et Théologique de Gersonide* (Paris: Éditions de Minuit, 1973), 411-31.
34. *Commentary on Song of Songs*, 2d, 9b.
35. *Wars*, I, ch. 6, 150, 161; ch. 10, 204-07. Davidson, "Al-Farabi and Avicenna . . .," 162 ff.

36. Aquinas, *Summa Theologiae*, I qq. 79, 84, 85; esp. q. 84 a. 4. *Wars,* I, ch. 6, 148, 161, 207.

37. Plato, *Phaedo*, 73c-d; Aristotle, *De Anima* III 7. Mashbaum, 56.

38. John Duns Scotus, *Oxford Commentary on the Four Books of the Sentences*, Book I, Distinction 3, question 1; in A. Hyman and J. Walsh, *Philosophy in the Middle Ages*, 602. William of Ockham, *Reportatio*, Book II, Question 15; in Hyman and Walsh, 678.

39. Augustine, *On Free Will*, II, chs. 12-17; *Soliloquies* I 6. Bonaventure, *Quaestiones disputatae*, in Wippel, 314-17. Matthew of Aquasparta, *Ten Disputed Questions on Knowledge*, in R. McKeon, *Selections from Medieval Philosophers* (New York, 1930) 2.240-302.

40. *Enneads* VI 7.6 and 8.

41. *Wars*, I, ch. 10; Touati, *La Pensée*, 413-23; Julius Guttmann, "Levi ben Gersons Theorie des Begriffs," *Festschrift zum 75-jahrigen Bestehen des Judisch-Theologischen Seminars* (Breslau, 1929) 2.131-49; William of Ockham, *Philosophical Writings*, tr., T. Boehner (Indianapolis: Hackett, 1964) II, sections 4-8; IV, section 4.

42. Aristotle, *De Anima* II 1-4.

43. *Wars*, V, pt. 3, chs. 3-4; cf. I, ch. 6. *Enneads* V 8.9, VI 7.7 and 7.12. The Philonic overtones are clear.

44. Davidson, "Averroes on the Active Intellect as a Cause of Existence"; Touati, "Les Problemes de la Generation et le Role de L'intellect Agent chez Averroes," in *Multiple Averroes* (Paris, 1978), 157-64.

45. *Wars*, V, pt. 3, ch. 3.

46. Aristotle, *On Generation and Corruption*, II 10; Galen, *On Natural Faculties* 1, 5-6; *Wars* I, ch. 6, 153, n. 17; V, pt. 3, ch. 3. Davidson, "Averroes on the Active Intellect as a Cause of Existence," 214-22.

47. *Wars* I, ch. 6; V, pt. 3, ch. 3. Themistius, *In Aristoteles Metaphysicorum Librum Lambda Paraphrasis*, ed., S. Landauer (Berlin, 1903), Hebrew 8, Latin 9.

48. *Enneads* VI 7.15, 14-23; VI 9.3, 25-26.

49. In his *Tahāfut al-Tahāfut*, which Gersonides did not know, Averroes attributes this Platonistic theory to "the philosophers." His attitude toward it here is at least neutral, perhaps even positive; tr., Van Den Bergh, Third Discussion, para. 217-18.

50. Maimonides, *Guide* II 4, 6, 11. Davidson, "Al-Farabi and Avicenna . . .," 135 ff.

51. Instead of following the printed editions, reading '*qibbul*,' I have adopted the reading of '*qibbuz*,' found in the Vatican, Bodleian and one of the Parisian manuscripts.

52. *Wars*, I, ch. 6; V, pt. 3, chs. 8 and 13.

53. *Wars* V, pt. 3, ch. 13, citing *Sanhedrin* 38b, referring to Exodus 24:1. See also Gersonides' *Commentary on the Torah* (Venice, 1547) 201c.
54. Gersonides, *Commentary on Proverbs*, 30:4; *Commentary on the Torah*, 12d-13a.
55. Philo, *De agricultura*, 12, 51; Wolfson, *Philo*, 1.234, n. 43.
56. *Wars*, V, pt. 3, ch. 11; cf. Davidson, passim.
57. *Wars*, V, pt. 3, ch. 12.

# Utterance and Ineffability in Jewish Neoplatonism

## Steven T. Katz

### 1. Apophatic Claims and their Problems

Neoplatonism, generally, and Jewish Neoplatonism in particular, presents a familiar yet profound problem. According to its declared premises, verbal descriptions of the ultimate realities are not possible. Language operates upon and within a given categorical structure and is of limited applicability to those realia that lie outside its constructive schema. Philo, the forerunner of Jewish Neoplatonism, tells us that "the companions of the soul, who can converse with intelligible incorporeal natures, do not compare the Existent to any form of created thing, but dissociate Him from every quality." They allow "the conception of existence only, without investing it with any shape."[1]  Philo argues that "it is wholly impossible that God according to His essence should be known by any creature."[2]  The Divine is "unnameable and ineffable."[3]  Whether Philo was the first Platonist to insist upon God's ineffability, and whether or not he did so more for Biblical than Platonic reasons as Wolfson contended,[4] his position becomes a given for the Church Fathers. And the same view had no less powerful an impact on Plotinus and Proclus and their heirs.

Plotinus, in a well known passage (*Enneads* V 5.6) argues: "the One must be without form.  But if it is without form, it is not a substance; for a substance must be some one particular thing, and something, that is, defined and limited; but it is impossible to apprehend the One as a particular thing: for then it would not be the Source but only that particular thing which you said it was. But if all things are in that which is produced by the One, which of the things in it are you going to say the One is? Since it is none of them, it can only be said to be beyond them: but they are beings and Being; it therefore transcends Being. This phrase 'beyond Being' does not mean that it is a particular thing—for it makes no positive statement about it—and it does not say its name, but all that it implies is that it is 'not this.'"[5] Plotinus' radical insistence on this point is well known, and through Proclus' systematization the Plotinian position becomes a cardinal doctrine of all later Neoplatonic theory. As Proclus writes in his Commentary on the *Parmenides*: "the most glorious One is neither expressible nor knowable."[6]

By the medieval era the ineffability of the One was taken as an indisputable axiom both by mystics and by Neoplatonic philosophers. Among Jewish Neoplatonists it was a premise of Zoharic and post-Zoharic Kabbalah as well as in the philosophical constructions of such thinkers as Solomon Ibn Gabirol and Baḥya Ibn Paquda. Its influence is prominent even among Aristotelians like Maimonides, whose insistence on it overarches everything else he has to say about God and our attempts to comprehend and relate to Him.[7]

Isaac the Blind, the early medieval Kabbalist, refers to the Ultimate as "that which is not conceivable by thinking (*mah she-ain ha-maḥshevah moseget*)." This, as Gershom Scholem reminds us, "sounds like a paraphrase of the Neoplatonic *akataleptos*,"[8] as does the later Kabbalistic term *yitron*, which appears to be a Hebrew rendering of the Neoplatonic term *hyperousia*, or "superfluity" (or, perhaps better, "beyond being").[9] Later the *Zohar* accepts the same principle, beginning its depiction of the ontological descent of the cosmos by insisting that the *sefirot* irradiate from the One, called the *'Eyn Sof*, literally, "the Infinite." There is no comprehension of the *'Eyn Sof per se*: "For all binding and union and wholeness are secreted in the fastness that cannot be grasped or known . . . the *'Eyn Sof* does not abide being known."[10]

Ibn Gabirol had described this clearly: "To know the veritable nature of Substance . . . is impossible . . . because it is above all things and is infinite."[11]   And the twelfth century Jewish Yemeni Neoplatonist Nethanel ben al-Fayyūmī, in his *Bustān al-'Uqūl*, declaimed: "nothing is like unto Him; He created all things out of nothing. Unto him we cannot apply definition, attribute, spatiality or quality. He has no throne that would imply place nor footstool that would imply sitting. He cannot be described as rising up or sitting down, as moving or as motionless, as bearing or being born, as having characteristics or as in any way defined. . . . His essence is indescribable and cannot be grasped by means of the attributes."[12]

If we take these claims for apophatic theology seriously, two problems, one philosophical the other theological, arise: Philosophically the issue is how can the "x of x's" retain any meaning given the embargo on content for all predications about the ultimate. Theologically the concern is how can God, conceived so radically apophatically, be the object, or subject, of covenantal relationship, the revealer of Torah and *mizvot*, the Judge or Redeemer of souls, the One to whom one addresses prayers and supplications?

## 2. Responding to the Difficulties of the Apophatic Idea

There are three classical responses to these elemental questions:

*i. The Strict Constructionist.* In response to the demand that divine transcendence be respected we are encouraged to take the utter ineffability of God's true nature in its maximal and literal sense. The "x of x's" then drops out of our vocabulary. Strictly speaking, once we have denied the possibility of linguistic ascription nothing more can or should be said. In some models of theological and philosophical language about ultimates, such as God, Atman, and the like, some system of analogical predication comes into use, allowing or putatively allowing an asymptotic relationship. That is, the operative predicative language continues *ad infinitum* to approach its object but never reaches it. But here, where the Neoplatonic axiom of ineffability is taken in too strong a sense, there is no asymptote. The One cannot be indicated. For, in al-Fayyūmī's phrase, it is beyond "definition and the attributes of spatiality or quality." We are unable to construct any line that will approach the Ultimate, which thus becomes undefinable as an asymptote. It becomes impossible to say which of all linguistic forms is appropriate to the One, for all language is equally inappropriate. To distinguish some language as "more appropriate" would require standards of judgment and adequacy, criteria of meaning and verification, that have been ruled out by the basic claim.

This may seem no more than what the Neoplatonist wishes to assert. But the curious implication of the position is that it becomes impossible to claim that such predicates as 'good,' 'loving,' 'providential,' 'caring,' 'wise,' 'gracious,' and 'merciful' are more appropriate than 'evil,' 'hateful,' 'uncaring,' 'foolish,' and the like. Metaphysical attributes like unity or coherence similarly cannot be preferred to notions such as multiplicity or randomness.

R. T. Wallis claims that "In contrast to Plato, Plotinus's treatises exhaust the resources of language in endeavoring to attain successively closer approximations to what remains finally inexpressible."[13]  But, on the strict interpretation of the ineffability standard, Wallis' description becomes nonsensical.  How can Plotinus' language "attain successively closer approximations" to anything, given the collapse of the asymptotic model.  And what is true of Plotinus is true of his heirs, insofar as they follow his apophatic lead.  Not surprisingly, we observe that, even against their express declamations, Jewish Neoplatonists without exception self-contradictorily use apophatic discourse as well as the language of attributes and essence.  They speak of the One in ways that carry content, even if only implicitly and connotatively, by reference to the larger conceptual context that informs everything they say.[14]

*ii.  The Logician's Critique.*  The second response to the difficulties raised by apophatic claims is to argue that the ineffability thesis is either self-contradictory or meaningless.  The thesis holds: 'For any attribute q, x is not q.'  But this predicates 'not-q' of x and thus contradicts itself.  Here again claims to strict ineffability destroy the contrast between the "sayable" and the "unsayable," rendering both apophatic and cataphatic discourse devoid of content.

Some recent scholars propose to rescue the Neoplatonic schema from inconsistency through recourse to Cantor's,[15] or Kurt Gödel's[16] set-theory.  The proposals are ingenious and suggestive. It is argued that we should treat x in the proposition 'For any q, x is not q' as logically similar to Cantor's *Aleph* or Gödel's U, the universal class that itself is not a member of any class but which contains all sets. This approach opens up new lines for investigation. But I believe that to employ these revolutionary logical insights we will have to forego strict ineffability. For neither Cantor's nor Gödel's axioms will operate if strict apophasis is required.

Still, given the genius of the Neoplatonic tradition, merely to dismiss it out of hand on the logicist ground of self-contradiction is shortsighted and conceptually unsatisfying.

*iii. The Universalist-Comparativist.* In this widely advocated third option the claim is advanced—for example by W. T. Stace, before him by William James, and more recently by Ninian Smart and many others—that ineffability and the experience of transcendence that it mirrors indubitably point to a common experience available to all humanity once we escape the conceptual fetters of language. "In Mystic States," James writes, "we both become one with the Absolute and we become aware of our oneness. This is the everlasting and triumphant mystical tradition hardly altered by differences of clime or creed. In Hinduism, in Neoplatonism, in Sufism, in Christian mysticism, in Whitmanism, we find the same recurring note, so there is about mystical utterances an eternal unanimity which ought to make a critic stop and think, and which brings it about that the mystical classics have . . . neither birthday nor native land. Perpetually telling of the unity of man with God, their speech antedates language and they do not grow old."[17]

Walter Stace, writing in a more contemporary idiom, after constructing his typology of mystical states, concludes by affirming that "In [the] general experience of unity which the mystic believes to be in some sense ultimate and basic to the world, we have the very inner essence of all mystical experience."[18] Criticizing R. C. Zaehner, Ninian Smart writes: "Phenomenologically mysticism is everywhere the same."[19] The basis for these claims of comparability, even uniformity, is the contention that, on close inspection, all significant mystical reports reveal a common type marked by a sense of unity that is (a) paradoxical and (b) ineffable.

Still we must ask: Do the elements identified as "common"— ineffability and paradoxicality—allow an inquiry into the suggested identity of mystical experiences or even exploration of their comparability? For the terms 'paradox' and 'ineffable' do not inform us about the content of any experience or state of affairs. Rather they cloak experience from investigation and hold mysterious whatever ontological commitments or remarkable experiences one has. The terms 'paradox' and 'ineffable' do not provide *data* for comparability but rather eliminate the possibility of the comparisons altogether. Thus, for example, a Neoplatonic description of ecstasy cannot be taken as evidence for a Jamesian or Stacian (or other) phenomenology or typology of mystical experience, when the experience in question is said to be ineffable and paradoxical. It is a *non sequitur* to infer, as James, Huxley, Stace and many others do, that if two mystics claim that their experiences are paradoxical and ineffable, they are describing like experiences.

This criticism leads to a related question: 'What ontological or logical grounds require that there be only one experience that is ineffable or paradoxical?' If mystic experiences are accurately described as paradoxical and ineffable, they are removed from all possibility of definition or description and thus, also, from comparability. No other result can follow. If these terms mean anything, they cancel out all descriptive claims, undermining all attempts at a phenomenological typology of mystical experience.[20] X is canceled out of our language. The frequent comparisons of mystical states break down. Among the rubble one will find Stace's comparison of Neoplatonism and Kabbalah and Emile Brehier's comparison of Plotinus and Advaita,[21] a false parallel widely circulated earlier by Rudolf Otto[22] and D. T. Suzuki, among many others.

Now if this analysis is correct, if the three standard responses to the problems of apophatic claims present insuperable linguistic and cognitive difficulties, how does Neoplatonism operate so successfully? How does it happen that Neoplatonism, despite these primal philosophical conundrums, is one of the seminal, enduring intellectual traditions of Western theological and metaphysical thought? The answer to this important question is to be found in the fact that Neoplatonists, consciously or unconsciously, but universally, recognize the conceptual cul de sac that absolute faithfulness to an apophatic hermeneutic entails and use language and thought that contradict their elementary epistemological commitments.

## 3. Affirmation Despite Negation

Philo insists on the utter transcendence of God and the impossibility of speaking of Him. He draws upon Pythagorean ideas of the One as the transcendent Nous, on Platonic doctrines of the One adumbrated in the *Parmenides*, and on the Middle Academy's distinction between *hyparxis* (unqualified being) and *poiotēs* (qualified being) to substantiate his claims. Yet in depicting the Absolute and His primordial activity in bringing that which is into being, Philo contradicts his negative theology as often as is necessary to his exegesis. Among the small but telling cluster of attributes that the Philonic Deity ultimately possesses we find:

1. Being *per se* as compared to Being *per accidens*. We might even say "necessary Being," although such a gloss bears Anselmian and Scholastic associations that could confuse the issue. Philo asserts: "God alone has true being" (*Quod Deterius Potiori Insidiari Soleat*, 44, 160).

2. Being is One. Philo means not only numerically one but simple and unified and, arguably, indivisible.[23]

3. Being is the First Principle (*De Vita Contemplativa* 2; *Quaestiones et Solutiones in Exodum* II 68).

4. Being is immaterial. This becomes a "content" claim, although it originates in apophatic assertions where God is said repeatedly to be beyond space, time and the Aristotelian categories (*Quod Deus Sit Immutabilis* II; *Quis Rerum Divinarum Heres*, 187).

5. Being is "unchangeable" (*Legum Allegoria* II 9, 33, 24).[24]

6. Being is *Mind*, absolute or universal Intelligence. The Forms are God's thoughts (*De Opificio Mundi* 17-19); their "place" is the Logos of God (*De Opificio Mundi*, 20; *De Cherubim*, 49).[25]

7. The Forms are the cosmic blueprint. They become actualized through the Divine Will rather than by necessity as emphasized by Plato (with some ambiguity in the *Timaeus*) and Aristotle and then Plotinus and his pagan disciples.

8. God's freedom of action is connected to the deeply held premise that "It is the property (*idion*) of God to act" (*De Cherubim*, 24, 77). Impelled by the Biblical account, Philo insists that: "It is impious and false to conceive of God in a state of complete inactivity. We ought . . . to be astounded at His powers as maker and Father" (*De Opificio Mundi*, 2, 7).[26]

9.  Moreover, as "Maker and Father," God acts "benevolently" (*Legum Allegoria*, III, 68) and out of His "goodness" (*Legum Allegoria*, I, 15; *De Abrahamo*, 268).

This much then is clear, the principle of ineffability is certainly elastic. Unless one wishes to crush Philo in a logical vise, it must be taken nonliterally.

Beyond this, the exegesis of Philo's large corpus reveals something still more philosophically fecund. His God, however "ineffable," is rooted conceptually in a matrix that is both Greek and Jewish. Philo is at his most philonic in his valiant struggle to do justice to both traditions and in his effort to show their ultimate harmony and congruence. Thus his "apophatic" readings are highly colored, fundamentally shaped, by the inherited problematics of Middle Platonism as they had developed in the Hellenistic age—in particular by the problems of eidetic causation and participation. Yet, simultaneously, Philo's *Weltanschauung* demands the centrality of the Torah, although, conversely, the sinaitic revelation must conform to the truths discerned by the immortal Plato. Thus there is no disjunction between the God of the philosophers and the God of Abraham, Isaac and Jacob. The Philonic One, to use the Platonic/Plotinian terminology, must be understood as a response to specific ontological problems, Greek and Hebraic. The notions of Being, Will, and Necessity that Philo wrestles with come to him with a history and a rich penumbra of meanings. So it was not "being" or "necessary being" in some neutral sense that Philo predicated of the God of Israel, but "Being" understood in a well-defined, channelized philosophical tradition oriented by distinctive conceptions, say of limit and form. And his rendering of God as a subject is consciously and critically shaped by his effort to adjudicate between the Aristotelian principle of necessity and the Biblical insistence on Divine Freedom.

The Jewish Neoplatonists who came after Philo would continue to struggle with their dual inheritance of necessity and freedom. One sees the contradictions resulting from the attempt in Isaac Israeli's obscure, confused and confusing treatment in *The Book of Elements*.[27] Israeli seeks to reconcile the conceptual obligations imposed by the scriptural claims for God's will with the canonical theory of Neoplatonic emanation by distinguishing between the One's willed creation of the first two simple substances and the "necessary" emanation of all further things. Whether, as Alexander Altmann proposed, this entailed a dual theory of creation—the first two substances and then emanation for the rest—or, as Harry Wolfson contended, a dual theory of emanation, need not detain us.[28] What is significant for our argument is that the One of Israeli, the first important medieval Jewish Neoplatonist, is the resultant of a historical development that decisively influenced its nuanced formulation, even while Israeli claimed the inability to comprehend this God.

Given the prominence of the issue and Israeli's failure to treat it adequately, it is not surprising that Solomon Ibn Gabirol returns to it in his *Mekor Hayyim* (II 17-20), arguing for an emanationist theory while maintaining the Hebraic volitional imperative by attributing the creation of form to the Divine Will and the creation of matter to God's essence, i.e., necessity. Given Ibn Gabirol's close affinity to the mainstream of pagan Neoplatonism,[29] his positing of a Divine Will is striking.[30] Yet Ibn Gabirol, like the Ikhwān al-Safā', the Muslim Sincere Brethren (tenth Century),[31] rejects the Plotinian doctrine of "spontaneous necessity"[32] and the versions of this teaching widely circulated, for example in the *Theology of Aristotle* and its Arabic forms. He opts instead for the reality and repercussive significance of the Divine Will at the origin of the emanative process. Even in the Latin, the *Mekor Hayyim* makes abundantly clear that "The creation of things by the Creator, the going out of the forms from the prime source, is from the will (*voluntate*)."[33] One has only to compare this to Plotinus' treatments of the same stage in the creative process to appreciate its Biblical resonances. Plotinus writes: "There is in everything the act of the essence and the act of going out from the essence: the first act is the thing itself in its realized identity, the second act is an *inevitably* following outgo from the first, an emanation distinct from the thing itself."[34] I am not dissuaded from seeing here a sharp disjunction between Ibn Gabirol and Plotinus, despite Rist's nondeterministic reading, which seems to me anachronistic.[35]

It is illuminating to trace these two 'traditions,' the Philonic and Plotinian, a stage further, among the post *Bahir*-Kabbalists. Those influenced more heavily by the tradition stemming from Plotinus, Proclus, and Pseudo-Dionysius argued not only for the absolute transcendence and ineffability of the *'Eyn Sof,* but also for its impersonality. Others, like Philo before them, were more sensitive to the scriptural imperatives affecting the doctrine of the One. They sought to "personalize" the One, referring to *ha-'Eyn Sof,* the Infinite, rather than just *'Eyn Sof,* that which is "Endless" or "Boundless." Both formulations appear in the *Zohar,* but it certainly seems to favor the Philonic view, at least with regard to the question of God's freedom to create. The position was later taken up by Moses Cordovero in his Commentary on the *Zohar* and by Isaac Luria in his remarkable teaching that the first movement of creation was made possible by God's willed self-contraction (*zimzum*).[36] The supernal reality that the *Zohar* calls the *Attika Kadisha* ("the Holy Ancient One") indeed is more than pure negation possessing Will. The exact relation of *'Eyn Sof* or *ha-'Eyn Sof* to the *Attika Kadisha* is the subject of widespread debate, but there is no question that the *Tikkunei Zohar* specifically and clearly teaches that the two are identical: "It is called *'Eyn Sof* internally and *Keter Elyon* externally."[37] Yet, paradoxically, even as these assertions are being argued over, all the Kabbalists agree that nothing can be known or said about *'Eyn Sof.*

Given this philosophical and mystical tradition, we can make two generalizations: (1) 'God,' or the 'One,' or the 'Absolute,' is not only a name, an arbitrary verbal sign, a cipher, but also and necessarily in all meaningful contexts, at least, a "disguised description." The many Philonic excursuses on God's names, especially the Tetragrammaton, and the theurgical power of the NAME, of such great importance to Kabbalists, should be reconsidered in light of this recognition. (2) Even the One about whom one can offer only negations, who transcends all predicates, is a definite individual: the 'disguised descriptions' establish a meaning-giving context that shapes the content of their descriptiveness. Thus, for example, in Philo, in the Plotinian tradition,[38] in the Spanish Jewish Neoplatonists, and in the *mekubbalim* (masters of the Kabbalah), there is agreement that the negation of all attributes is *not* an indication of negativity *per se,* of nothingness or meaninglessness. Nor is it an indication that at the center of being there is only randomness and chaos. Rather, in contradistinction to a negative reading of negation, it must be recognized that the One is intrinsically good, as both Plato (*Republic* VI 509C) and Scripture taught. This Good is *the* creative origin and designing *telos* of all that is. All comes from and returns to the One/Good.

Thus, Isaac Israeli attributes creation-emanation to the One's goodness alone. The identity of the One is informed by the meaning-giving context of a tradition which imputes goodness to the One. The co-incidence of the One with the Good as the Source of creation is a profoundly charged and content-ful *assumption* of classical Western thought. In no way is it an assumption that is necessary *a priori*. Certain Buddhist schools and certain modern scientistic accounts attribute no such positive status to the One that they posit as the point of cosmic origination.

Ibn Gabirol expresses this affirmative presumption with paradigmatic clarity in his *Keter Malkhut*. At the end of stanza 3 he proclaims the apophatic dogma:

> Thou existeth, and Thy secret is hidden, and who shall attain to it?
> *Attah nimza', ve-sodkha ne'elam; u-mi-yasigenu.*
> So deep, so deep, who can discover it?
> *'Amok 'amok, mi yimza'enu?*

Yet in stanza 6, the *Eḥad*, the One of stanza 2, is, as the God of Israel must be, the One "Who forbearest long with sinners" (*ta'arikh l'hata'im*) and Whose "mercies are upon all thy creatures, yea upon all of them" (*rahamekha 'al kol beru'ekha, khulam*). The secret and hidden One is not only existent but knowably concerned with human sin, forbearing, ultimately forgiving, and merciful to all. These attributions of grace and mercy are positive construals of the Goodness of the One, despite the obligatory negations entailed by the mature Neoplatonic schema. And this movement from ineffability to positive attribution is no mere poetic image suitable to the *Keter Malkhut* but inapposite in the more rigorous domains of Neoplatonic philosophy. For in the rigorously philosophical *Mekor Hayyim* Ibn Gabirol calls the One *ha-Po'el ha-ri'shon ve-ha-kadosh* ("First Author, sublime and holy").

A third conclusion about the work of most Jewish and other Neoplatonists, inextricably connected with what I shall call the logic of emanation, appears warranted as well. This conclusion follows from the logical, ontological and linguistic implications of the process of emanation and the relationship of the One to the realities that flow from It and can be summarized as follows: Given the definition of emanation there is a particular and informative reciprocity between the One and the many. For example, Philo can point to the outcome of Divine action, creation, as affording some inferential awareness of Him. Likening the Platonic Forms to Biblical "causes," i.e., to Divine Action, he argues, glossing Moses' prayer in *Exodus*, that "He himself alone is incomprehensible—but He may come to be apprehended and known by the powers that follow and attend Him." Philo immediately adds the qualification: "These make evident not His essence but His existence,"[39] but his remark is especially provocative given the ontological implications of an emanationist metaphysics, i.e., that cause and effect are in some primal and definitive sense the same.

Plotinus tells us, despite all his negations, that the central concept of ontic participation unfolds against the background of the emanationist principle: "The One is all things and no one of them; the source of all things is not all things; and yet it is all things in a transcendental sense, all things, so to speak, having run back to it; or more correctly, not all as yet are within it, they will be."[40] Thus, "The One remains intact . . . since the entities produced in its likeness . . . owe their existence to no other." "Just as there is, primarily or secondarily, some form or idea from the monad in each of the successive numbers—the later still participating though unequally, in the unit—so the series of Beings following upon the first bear, each some form or idea derived from the source."[41] Thus things incorporate, reflect and reveal that from which they derive. Indirectly, then, insofar as we can speak of 'things' we are describing or naming something of the One. Plotinian emanation implicates the One cataphatically as a consequence of its ontological choreography.

Similarly, R. Azriel of Gerona, explaining the emanation of the *Sefirot*, writes:

> I have already informed you that *'Eyn Sof* is perfect . . . that the agent which is (initially) brought forth from Him must also be perfect. Thus the dynamic of emanation is fittingly the beginning of all creation, for the potency of emanation is the essence of all things.

And extending this exegesis he affirms:

> The One is the foundation of the many, and in the many no
> power is innovated—only in Him . . . although this first is the dynamic
> order of the other . . . the metaphor for this is the fire, the flame, the
> sparks . . . they are all of one essence.[42]

The emanation of the *Sefirot* is a process within the Godhead, not a
descent into space-time, but R. Azriel's description does lead us to
ask what it is that we may potentially come to know, to say, of the
*'Eyn Sof*. Given that "that potency of emanation is the essence of all
things" and that the *Sefirot* (by definition) "are all one essence" with
the One (*'Eyn Sof*) does it not follow that our unquestioned ability to
know the *Sefirot* entails that we can in some sense know the *'Eyn
Sof*? As Gershom Scholem writes, "The hidden God in the aspect of
the *'Eyn Sof* and the God manifested in the emanation of the *'Eyn Sof*
are one and the same viewed from two different angles."[43]
Analogously, among later Kabbalists, whatever the hermeneutical and
metaphysical ambiguities, there emerges a Kabbalistic consensus that
the emanative process continues downward and is responsible for the
sublunary and material worlds. So these lower realms also participate
in and reflect the *Sefirot* from which they emerge. Even if at a
remove, they are continuous with the *'Eyn Sof*. Even in the *'alma
de-peruda*, the world of separation, when things are seen mystically,
i.e., properly, "everything is revealed as One."[44] As a consequence,
at a far lower level, we can learn about the *'Eyn Sof* (through the
mediation of the *Sefirot*) by way of the things in our world. By
knowing and naming these we know and name the *'Eyn Sof*,
obliquely but authentically. Moses de Leon, the author of the *Zohar*,
notes in his *Sefer Ha-Rimmon*:

> Everything is linked with everything else down to the lowest ring
> of the chain, and the true essence of God is above as well as below,
> in the heavens and on the earth, and nothing exists outside of him. . . .
> Meditate on these things and you will understand that God's essence
> is linked and connected with all worlds, and that all forms of existence
> are linked and connected with each other, but derived from His
> existence and essence.[45]

Correspondingly, the inherent dialectic of return to the Source,
seeking felicity by reversing the ontic process of differentiation and

procession that is central to both Kabbalah and philosophical Jewish Neoplatonism, is rooted in the metaphysical unity of all things from above to below. The elemental doctrines of *nizozot* (sparks), *bittul ha-yesh* (annihilation), *hithpashtuth* (egression), and *histalkuth* (regression) are all connected with and to be deciphered by reference to the primordial participation of all that is in the *'Eyn Sof* through the "mediation" of the *Sefirot,* which are manifestations of the Godhead itself. In this way the theory of regress, the inversion of the metaphysics of emanation, like emanation itself, raises profound ontological, linguistic and logical questions. For it casts new light, perhaps some would say shadows, over the status of the *'Eyn Sof*'s transcendence of all conceptual and linguistic forms.

The regressive accessibility of the One allows the possibility of *devekut* or union beyond intellection or language, of which the Kabbalists and philosophers speak. The recommendation and the hope which seeks this end are predicated on the assumption that ultimately there is a commonality, a shared ontic nature, that will become apparent and dominant once linguistic and categoreal restraints have dropped away in the ascent, or return, of the soul to its source. In the Neoplatonic expression of R. Ezra: "Everything issues from the first cause and everything returns to the first cause"; or, in a more messianic form, in the end we will experience "*hashavat kol ha-devarim le-havvayatam*" ("the restoration of all things to their original being.")[46] Given the possibility of *devekut* and of the return of the *Sefirot* to *Ayin,* can we say that we know nothing and can say nothing of *'Eyn Sof*?

Similarly, the doctrine of emanation has profound implications for Jewish and other Neoplatonic moral theories that, like Bahya's and Ibn Zaddik's, and even more like Ibn Gabirol's in his *Tikkun Middot ha-Nefesh* (*Improvement of the Moral Qualities*),[47] presume that the human capacity for ethical perfection resides in our derivation from the One through the creative devolution operative in the universe. Once again, then, more is "sayable" about the essential Goodness of Being than the overt declarations of the Neoplatonists would suggest. Insofar as moral theories implicate and depend upon anthropological conceptions—including the much favored doctrine of the microcosm—for all the qualifications they would introduce at this juncture, the Neoplatonic moralists point to still further venues in which the *'Eyn Sof*/One, incarnate in men, is available to cognitive scrutiny and linguistic description.

Still more generally, the emanationist model presumes a hierarchial descent from the *'Eyn Sof* and correspondingly relates "degrees of being" to one's place in the hierarchy: the "higher" and closer to the *'Eyn Sof*, the more "spiritual"; the "lower" and further from the *'Eyn Sof*, the more "material." This scheme is unescapably conceptual and linguistic. It depends for its cogency upon an order of beings, "beyond which," although somehow related, is the One. The egress of meta-Being/*'Eyn-Sof* to Being/*Sefirot*, i.e., the emanation of *'Olam ha-azilut*, down to the emanation of material beings in the *'Olam ha-'asiyyah*, our terrestrial world, and the regress from *'Olam ha-'asiyyah* to the Sefirotic realm and then to *Ayin* is a process that is, in a real sense, cataphatic. This is evident, for example, in the first systematic use of the notion of *'Eyn Sof* by R. Isaac the Blind. In his teachings on the first *Sefirah*, i.e., his views relating to *mahshavah* (thought) as co-incident with *'Eyn Sof* and *mahshavah* as the desired, and potentially available, object of contemplation and relation, the following expressible connection is described: Through *hitbonenut*, mystical contemplation, one proceeds from the isolated things of the *'olam ha-nifradim* to the *Sefirot*, up to *hokhmah*, and from there to *mahshavah*, which is inseparable from *'Eyn Sof*.[48] For all his restraint, that is, R. Isaac is here deconstructing and reconstructing the egress-regress spiral of the *Sefirot*, and their inherent ontic connection with *'Eyn Sof*, in a form that is both intelligible and informative. A similar 'truth,' in poetic form, is likewise expressed in the following formulation from the *Keter Malkhut*:

> Thou art the God of Gods, and the Lord of Lords,
> Ruler of beings celestial and terrestrial,
> For all creatures are Thy witnesses
> And by the glory of this Thy name, every creature is bound to Thy
>     service
> Thou art God, and all things formed are Thy servants and worshippers
> Yet is not Thy glory diminished by reason of those that worship aught
>     beside Thee,
> For the yearning of them all is to draw nigh Thee . . .

But Thy servants are as those walking clear-eyed in the straight path,
Turning neither to the right nor the left
Till they come to the court of the King's palace.
Thou art God, by Thy Godhead sustaining all that hath been formed,
And upholding in Thy unity all creatures.
Thou art God, and there is no distinction 'twixt
Thy Godhead and Thy Unity, Thy pre-existence and Thy existence,
For 'tis all one mystery.
And although the name of each be different,
"Yet they are all proceeding to one place."[49]

Ibn Gabirol, now through the tropes and magic of poetry, conveys the essential Neoplatonic piety, shared with R. Isaac:  God and His creation are one.  The *mekubbal* or philosopher may not know how the transcendental ontic interactions occur, but he does seem to know at least that they take place.  And in knowing this he knows more of the "x of x's" than would at first seem possible given the systematic negations of Neoplatonic epistemology.

## 4.  Concluding on a Positive, if Paradoxical, Neoplatonic Note

Let me conclude by congratulating the Jewish Neoplatonists of all schools, mystical and philosophical, for their "inconsistency." They intuited, despite the intellectual fashions of their day, that the One of classical pagan Neoplatonism could not be the God of Israel. It might serve as a formal limit to an infinite regress, linguistic and otherwise, but it could not serve the religious and existential requirements of Jews and Judaism.  To redeem the negations-of-negations that are Neoplatonism, to instill into these denials the breath of life and meaning, Jewish, Muslim and Christian Neoplatonists, like Plotinus himself in his more intuitive moments, sought, however contradictorily, to recreate the asymptotic approximation that a literal reading of Neoplatonic apophatic theory renders impossible.  At the same time, they did learn the epistemic lesson that Neoplatonism teaches, that the God of Israel must always be more than we can say—although this does not require repeating the error of the Neoplatonists in supposing that we can say nothing of the Absolute.  In the expressive phrase of the Kotzker Rebbe:

*"Pfui,* I am not interested in a God that any Tom, Dick or Harry can understand!"

**Notes**

1. Philo, *Quod Deus Sit Immutabilis,* 11, 55-56.
2. *De Posteritate Caini,* 48, 167.
3. *De Somniis* I 11, 67. See also *De Mutatione Nominum* 2, 11; *Legum Allegoria* III, 206; *De Posteritate Caini* 16; 168.
4. See his *Philo,* 2.110-15.
5. Tr. after Armstrong, with some phraseology of Stephen McKenna (London: Warner, 1917-30) 5 vols.
6. *Plato Latinus* III, *Parmenides usque ad finem primae hypothesis nec non Procli Commentarium in Parmenidem, pars ultima inedita,* eds., R. Klibansky and C. Labowsky (London: Warburg Institute, 1953), 71.
7. *Guide* I 52-53; I 54: "His essence cannot be grasped as it truly is." See A. Nuriel, "The Torah speaketh in the language of the sons of man in the *Guide of the Perplexed,*" in Moshe Hallamish and Asa Kasher, eds., *Religion and Language: Philosophical Essays* (Tel Aviv: Tel Aviv University Press, 1981), 97-103 (in Hebrew); Shlomo Pines, "The Limits of Human Knowledge according to Al-Farabi, Ibn Bajjah and Maimonides," in Twersky, ed., *Studies in Medieval Jewish History and Literature,* 82-109; and Wolfson's many studies in Twersky, ed., *Studies in the History of Philosophy and Religion.*
8. *Major Trends in Jewish Mysticism,* 353, n. 10.
9. G. Scholem, *Kabbalah,* 89.
10. *Zohar* 3:26b.
11. *Fons Vitae* I 5.
12. Tr., D. Levine as *The Garden of Wisdom* (New York: Columbia University Press, 1908), 1.
13. R. T. Wallis, *Neoplatonism,* 41.
14. J. N. Findlay is notable among those interested in Neoplatonism and mysticism in recognizing the need for positive attributions to the One. See his *Ascent to the Absolute* (London: Allen and Unwin, 1970), and "The Logical Peculiarities of Neoplatonism," in R. Baine Harris, ed., *The Structure of Being,* 1-10.
15. See Robert Brumbaugh, *Plato and the One* (New Haven: Yale University Press, 1961); and "Cantor's Sets and Proclus' Wholes," in R. Baine Harris, ed., *The Structure of Being,* 104-13.

16. Carl Kordig criticized and extended Brumbaugh's discussion, using Gödel's notation, in "The Mathematics of Mysticism: Plotinus and Proclus," in R. Baine Harris, ed., *The Structure of Being*, 114-24.

17. *Varieties of Religious Experience* (New York: Mentor, 1958), 321; cf. 292-94.

18. Walter T. Stace, *Mysticism and Language* (London: Macmillan, 1961), 132. See his full discussion in ch. 2, "The Problem of the Universal Core," 41-133.

19. Ninian Smart, "Interpretation and Mystical Experience," *Religious Studies* 1 (1965): 87.

20. Cf. my paper "Language, Epistemology and Mysticism" in Steven T. Katz, ed., *Mysticism and Philosophical Analysis* (New York: Oxford University Press, 1978), 54-56.

21. *The Philosophy of Plotinus*, 123 ff.

22. *Mysticism East and West* (New York: Macmillan, 1932).

23. The theme is constantly invoked by later Jewish Neoplatonists, cf., for example, Solomon Ibn Gabirol, "The Royal Crown" (*Keter Malkhut*), section 2; and Bahya Ibn Paquda *Hovot ha-Levavot*, Chs. 8 and 9. Augustine, another classical Neoplatonist caught in the same theological tension as Philo, says of God *est per essentiam suam* ("He exists by His own essence"). See his *Comments on Psalms*, 134:4; cf. *City of God*, 8.6, and 12.2.

24. See also *De Cherubim*, 19; and *Quaestiones et Solutiones in Genesin*, I 93.

25. See here Augustine's use of this notion in his *Book of Eighty Three Questions*, q46, 1-2, in Migne, *Patrologia Latina* 33.29-31.

26. I am indebted here to Wolfson's *Philo* 1.131-35. Philo appears to argue here that God produces the Logos eternally and that His creative activity is continuous and eternal. Yet this continuous creativity is not the result of some blind necessity. See also Winston's paper in this volume.

27. *Sefer ha-yesodot* (*Kitāb al-Ustuqussāt*), tr. in Altmann and Stern, *Isaac Israeli*, 79-105.

28. See Altmann's, "Creation, Emanation and Natural Causality," in Altmann and Stern; Wolfson's reply in "The Meaning of *Ex nihilo* in Isaac Israeli," *JQR* N.S. 50 (1959): 1-12, repr. in Twersky, ed., *Studies in the History of Philosophy and Religion* 1.222-23; cf. Altmann's "Isaac Israeli's 'Chapter on the Elements' (Ms Mantua)," *Journal of Jewish Studies* 7 (1956): 31-57. In "Creation and Emanation in Isaac Israeli: A Reappraisal," Altmann maintains his position. See also Stern's "Ibn Hasday's Neoplatonist."

29. See the papers of Dillon and Mathis in this volume.

30. Cf. Judah Halevi's critique of the Neoplatonic and Aristotelian position in *Kuzari* II 6.
31. *Rasā'il Ikhwān al-Ṣafā'* (Beirut: Dar Sadir, 1957), 3.38; but cf. the ambiguous analysis in 3.518.
32. I use this locution in light of A. H. Armstrong's reminder that: "Though this production or giving out is necessary in the sense that it cannot be conceived as not happening, or as happening otherwise, it is also entirely spontaneous: there is no room for any binding or constraint, internal or external, in the thought of Plotinus about the One. The One is not bound by necessity; it establishes it. Its production is simply the overflow of its superabundant life, the consequence of its unbounded perfection." *Cambridge History of Later Greek and Early Medieval Philosophy*, 241.
33. *Fons Vitae* V 41, Baeumker, 330 ll. 17-20, cited in Altmann, "Creation and Emanation in Isaac Israeli," 33, n. 25.
34. *Enneads* V 4.2, cited in Altmann, "Creation and Emanation," 24; cf. V 3.12.40; V 1.6; V 3.16.
35. See *Plotinus: The Road to Reality*, 27. Rist proposes that VI 8.19 is meant to "deter the reader from supposing there is any necessary production of the hypostases." Even recognizing the nuances introduced by Armstrong, I find Rist's position extreme, not allowing sufficient weight to Plotinus' 'inevitability.'
36. See David Novak's essay in this volume.
37. *Tikkunei Zohar*, end of *Tikkun* 22.
38. See, for example, Proclus, *Elements of Theology*, Prop. 7.
39. *De Posteritate Caini* 48, 169.
40. *Enneads* V 1, tr. McKenna.
41. *Enneads* V 5.5., tr. McKenna.
42. R. Azriel of Gerona, *Perush 'Eser Sefirot*, "Explanation of the Ten Sefirot," found as a prolegomenon to Meir Ibn Gabbai's *Sefer Derekh Emunah* (Warsaw, 1850), 3-9.
43. *Kabbalah*, 98.
44. *Zohar* I, 241a.
45. Moses de Leon, *Sefer Ha-Rimmon*, cited in Scholem, *Major Trends*, 223; 402, n. 4. The work is now critically edited in Elliot Wolfson's Brandeis dissertation, 1986.
46. R. Isaac, *Perush 'al Sefer Yeẓirah*, ch. 3 end; cited in Scholem, *Origins of the Kabbala*, 300.
47. Tr. Stephen S. Wise.
48. See Isaac's *Commentary on Sefer Yeẓirah* in the appendix to Scholem's *Kabbalah ba-Provence* (Jerusalem: Hebrew University, 1963).

49.  *"Keter Malkhut,"* tr., Israel Zangwill in *Selected Religious Poems of Solomon Ibn Gabirol* (Philadelphia: Jewish Publications Society, 1973), Stanza 8, 86-87.

# Self-Contraction of the Godhead in Kabbalistic Theology*

## David Novak

### 1. Kabbalah and Rabbinic Theology

In the mid-sixteenth century, when Kabbalah had already become a staple in Judaism, the leading Jewish legal authority in Egypt, Rabbi David ibn Abi Zimra (Radbaz, d. 1573), was asked whether there was any basis in the classical Jewish sources for the relatively new practice of putting on *tefillin* (phylacteries) at home and wearing them into the synagogue, as opposed to the usual practice then of wearing them only in the synagogue itself. He answered as follows:

> One of the later sages wrote in the name of Rabbi Simon ben Yoḥai of blessed memory [traditional author of the *Zohar*] that since one must say when entering the synagogue, "I bow towards Your holy sanctuary in awe of You" (Psalms 5:8), if there are no *tefillin* on his head, where is the reverence? It is as if he were testifying falsely about himself. . . . Anywhere you find that the books of the Kabbalah

---

\* All translations, unless otherwise noted, are by the author. The author wishes to thank Prof. Lenn E. Goodman for his critical reading of the first draft of this paper and for his suggestions, which led to important revisions in this final draft.

run counter to the ruling of the Talmud (*pesaq ha-gemara*), follow the Talmud and the codes. But anywhere it does not dispute them, as in this case, which is not mentioned either in the Talmud or in the codes, I have seen fit (*'ani ra'iti*) to rely on the words of the Kabbalah.[1]

This responsum epitomizes the deep inroads Kabbalah made into Rabbinic Judaism over the centuries. For Kabbalah presented itself as a deeper manifestation of Rabbinic Judaism, not as an innovation that might challenge it. In the case at hand, *tefillin* were worn, at least by scholars, outside the synagogue, certainly during the early Rabbinic period. The Kabbalistic practice, then, could be seen as a return to purer Rabbinic practice and higher piety. Kabbalah asserted its authority where the Rabbinic sources were silent or ambivalent, and by so doing deeper into common Jewish practice and belief than did the rationalistic theology of the medieval Jewish Neoplatonists and Aristotelians. It rarely presented its problematic in general philosophical terms, and was quite circumspect especially in exposing the influence of Neoplatonism on its development. As a result, for many Jews, Kabbalah was seen as a solely Jewish doctrine, indeed, as Judaism's most profound and original manifestation. In fact, one could argue convincingly that the waning of the hold of Rabbinic Judaism on the allegiance of modern Jews and the waning of the hold of Kabbalah on their imagination were almost simultaneous.

The important Kabbalistic doctrine of *zimzum*, what Gershom Scholem called *Selbstverschränkung Gottes*, "the self-contraction of God,"[2] has significant Rabbinic precedents upon which Kabbalah built. There may also be some affinity with Neoplatonic modes of addressing the problem of the One and the many, but I shall argue that the affinity is real only at one particular point in the development of this doctrine in the theology of Rabbi Isaac Luria (Ari, d. 1572). The main body of the doctrine, held by virtually all Kabbalistic thinkers was at odds with what Plotinus and his followers thought about the relation of the One and the many. This paper cannot cover all the various ways the doctrine of *zimzum* was enunciated in Kabbalistic literature. Rather, I shall try to represent a single synthetic theory of *zimzum*.

Rabbinic theology is much more loosely constructed than Rabbinic law. So here Kabbalah found significant openings for its own doctrines. The most important issue for Rabbinic theology is God's giving the Torah to the Jewish people and their acceptance of it. And it was about the problem of revelation that the Kabbalists were most persistently concerned. The doctrine of *zimzum* plays a crucial role in the Kabbalistic metaphysics of revelation.

The earliest Rabbinic use of the term *zimzum* seems to be in a midrash about revelation as a relationship that involves active giving and active receiving:

> You find that when the Holy-One-blessed-be-He gave the Torah to Israel, had He come to them with His full strength, they would have been unable to endure, as it says in Scripture, "If we continue to hear [the voice of the Lord our God anymore, we shall die]" (Deuteronomy 5:22). So He only came upon them according to their strength, as it says in Scripture, "the voice of the Lord in strength" (Psalms 29:4). It does not say "in His strength" (*be-kokho*), but "in strength" (*ba-koah*): according to the strength of each of them.[3]

In the Torah, Israel's inability to bear the voice of God in its full strength is addressed by the people's proposing Moses as their intermediary and God's acceptance of this compromise (Deuteronomy 5:24-25). But in the midrash, God limits His own power. Where Scripture invokes an intermediary external to God, the midrash perceives God's reflexive Self-confinement. The midrash develops this idea as follows:

> When the Holy-One-blessed-be-He said to Moses, "make for Me a sanctuary" (Exodus 25:8), he was amazed and said, "The glory of the Holy-One-blessed-be-He fills the heavenly and earthly realms, yet He says 'make for Me a sanctuary'?!" . . . Said the Holy-One-blessed-be-He, "I do not think as you think . . . but I shall descend and contract (*ve'azamzem*) My presence (*Shekhinati*) within the cubits of the sanctuary."[4]

From this text and others like it, it can be inferred that there are two aspects of the divine life: One relates to what lies beneath it; the other transcends all relations.[5]

According to other midrashim, God's concentration and descent are needed because without His direct involvement the Jewish people would inevitably misinterpret the Torah.[6]   In effect, God has descended to the human level by giving the Torah as a human possession, binding Himself to what is now humanly interpreted and adjudicated law.  As one seminal aggadah put it:

> Rabbi Eleazar said that ordinarily (*be-noheg she-ba'olam*) a king of flesh and blood makes a decree (*gozer gezerah*), and if he wants to keep it he does; if not, it is kept by others.  But with the Holy-One-blessed-be-He it is not so.  Rather, He makes a decree and He Himself keeps it first.  Thus it is written in Scripture, "Before the aged shall you rise and you shall honor the elderly, and you shall fear the Lord" (Leviticus 19:32).  I am the One who first kept the commandment to stand before the aged.[7]

The Palestinian Talmud asks, "What is the basis of this?  'And they shall keep My charge (*mishmarti*); I am the Lord' (Leviticus 22:9), that is, I am He who kept the commandments of the Torah first."[8]  This motif runs through Rabbinic literature from the tannaitic period on.  A famous tannaitic aggadah expresses the point vividly:

> Rabbi Eliezer said to them again, "If the law is according to my view, Heaven will so attest."  A heavenly voice (*bat qol*) came forth and declared, "Why do you hold a position against that of Rabbi Eliezer?  The law is according to him!"  Rabbi Joshua rose to his feet and said, "It is not in heaven!" (Deuteronomy 30:12). . . . Rabbi Jeremiah said that the Torah was given at Mount Sinai already and we do not regard a heavenly voice as authoritative, for You already wrote at Mount Sinai, "Incline after the majority" (Exodus 23:2).  It happened that Rabbi Nathan met Elijah. He said to him, "What did the Holy-One-blessed-be-He do at that time?"  He said to him that He smiled and remarked, "My children have vanquished Me indeed (*nizhuni*)."[9]

All of this opened up the possibility for the subsequent metaphysical development of the theme of divine dependence on Israel by the Kabbalists.[10]

## 2. The Post-Rabbinic Problematic

From these representative texts it is clear that the rabbis regarded the price of active divine involvement in human affairs to be a bifurcation of divinity into a nonrelational priority and a relational posteriority. God, for them, was conceived as both *Deus absconditus* and *Deus revelatus*. God's accessibility is actively and freely initiated by God Himself and freely accepted by Israel. God's absolute oneness and absolute transcendence are thus modified by divine and human freedom. Plotinus addressed the corresponding problem in a radically different way:

> So if there is a second after the One it must have come to be without the One moving at all, without any inclination or act of will (*oude boulethentos*) or any sort of activity on its part. How did it come to be, then, and what are we to think of as surrounding the One in its repose (*peri ekeino menon*)? It must be a radiation (*perilampsin*) from it while it remains unchanged, like the bright light of the sun which, so to speak, runs round it, springing from it continually while it remains unchanged. . . . If anything comes into being after it (*met' auto ginetai*), we must think it necessarily (*anangkaion*) does so while the One remains continually turned towards itself.[11]

The contrast between these two views of the divine-human relationship can be seen best when the different verbs and prepositions used by the rabbis and Plotinus are contrasted. The rabbis use transitive verbs like "gave" (*natan*) and "came" (*ba*). They use prepositions like "to" and "for" (both expressed by the prefix *le*). The transitive verbs clearly indicate God's relational activity, which entails temporal succession. The prepositions suggest an active and free mutuality between God and His human creatures. Plotinus, on the other hand, denies that such prepositions pertain to the One: "Everything which is moved must have some end to which it moves (*pros ho kineitai*). The One has no such end, so we must not consider that it moves."[12] Here the key prepositions are "after" (*meta*) and "around" (*peri*). Such relations can involve no reciprocity or mutuality. The many *relate* themselves to the One; the One does not relate itself to the many. The many accept their lower ontological status (*meta*) and situate themselves in the orbit (*peri*) of the One, an orbit compared to the splendor of the sun. The One, however, simply (*ex haplou*) remains (*menon*) as it has always been "because it seeks nothing (*to meden zetein*), has nothing and needs nothing."[13] Because there is no temporal succession, there is no active freedom; the One and the many have always been so related. Their relation could not be otherwise. Verbs suggesting temporality such as *ginetai*, "came to be," and *pepoieken*, "made," are used only metaphorically.

In view of the contrast between Rabbinic theology and Neoplatonic philosophy, one can see why Jewish thinkers of late antiquity and the Middle Ages, who were seriously committed to the cosmological paradigm of their pre-Galilean age, had a vexing problem with the actively relational God of Rabbinic theology and its closely connected theme of the primacy of *praxis* over *theoria*. The paradigm of Aristotle, Ptolemy and Plotinus regarded the heavens to be of superior substance and activity to anything beneath the moon. Circular orbit was deemed superior to locomotion, intransitive action superior to transitive action, *theoria* superior to *praxis*, and metaphysics superior to ethics.[14] To many Plotinus' model of the relationship of the One and the many looked a good deal more attractive than that of the Rabbis. Indeed, Plotinus claimed that his problematic was not born of his own particular vision, but was, as he put it, "the question repeatedly discussed also by the ancient philosophers, how from the One (*pos ex henos*) . . . anything else . . . came into existence (*hypostasin eschen*) . . . which we think it right to refer back to the One."[15]

Although the Kabbalists were immensely successful in concealing whatever philosophical sources they used in the construction of their own theology, it seems that they accepted the general problematic of Neoplatonism concerning the One and the many. But then they reinterpreted Judaism, not according to a Neoplatonic solution of this problem, as did most of the rationalist theologians, but as bearing a superior solution. The Kabbalists attempted this daring project through their development of the closely related doctrines of the divine multiplicity (*sefirot*) and divine self-contraction. The problem remains whether Rabbinic Judaism can bear the stretching of its categories this far. But the influence of Neoplatonism here is much less direct than it is in the openly philosophical approach of many of the rationalist theologians.

Capitulation to philosophy cannot readily be charged against Kabbalah. For the appropriation of Neoplatonic themes is covert, and the philosophic mode of argument and exposition remain external to the Kabbalistic texts. In fact, in the early days of its appearance, Kabbalah was not accused of being too philosophical but of resembling Christian trinitarianism.[16] Yet, unlike rationalistic theology, Kabbalah was adopted by many Rabbinic authorities. So the criticisms were mostly muted even at the beginning and gradually disappeared almost entirely. In the great controversy between the Hasidim and their opponents (*mitnagdim*) in the late eighteenth century, the two leading Rabbinic antagonists, Rabbi Elijah of Vilna and Rabbi Shneur Zalman of Liadi, were both Kabbalists.

If the Kabbalists accepted the general problematic of Neoplatonism, they had to deal with the following questions: (1) What is it within the Godhead (*'Elohut*) that makes possible for it an active relationship with finite beings? (2) Does the relational theology of Rabbinic Judaism seem to make God ultimately dependent on His human creatures? The irony is captured in the Talmudic phrase, "the native-born is on earth and the sojourner is in heaven?!"[17] In other words, is not the proper hierarchy essentially reversed? (3) How can God be bound by (or even involved with) the commandments revealed to Israel in the Torah when most of them seem to address quite mundane issues? This concern parallels Parmenides' challenge to Plato's theory of Forms: "And are you undecided about certain other things, which you might think rather ridiculous (*geloia dokseien*), such as hair, mud, dirt, or anything else particularly vile and worthless? Would you say that there is an idea (*eidos*) of each of these . . . things . . . or not?"[18] Yet the Torah is concerned with the hair of the Nazirite (Numbers 6:18), the mud of an afflicted house (Leviticus 14:42), and even dirt, as in the ordeal of the Bitter Waters (Numbers 5:17).

### 3. The Foundation in the *Zohar*

It is often pointed out that the doctrine of *zimzum* as such is not found in the *Zohar*.[19] Yet one can see it as a logical development of the *Zohar's* doctrine of the *Sefirot*, the exfoliation of the Godhead from solitary infinity (*'Eyn Sof*) to its ten supernal manifestations. The difference between the realm of the *'Eyn Sof* and that of the *Sefirot* is pointedly expressed in this passage from the *Zohar*:

> Behold in one word everything is connected, and that mystic word (*ve-raza de-millah*) is I AM (*'ehyeh*, Exodus 3:14). This includes all. When the highways are closed and are not spread out (*ve-la mitparshan*) but are together in one place, He is called I AM. Everything is sealed (*satim*) and not revealed (*'itgalayya*). But after the beginning (*shayruta*), when that river has been impregnated to draw everything forth, then He is called WHAT (*'asher*) I SHALL BE. This means, therefore (*'al ken*), I SHALL BE (*'ehyeh*). I will be prepared for the future (*zamin*) to draw forth and give birth to everything. I AM means, now (*hashta*) I am He who includes everything as an undifferentiated whole (*kellala*) without any parts (*perata*). WHAT I SHALL BE means that the 'mother' will be impregnated and be prepared for the future to bring forth all the particulars and to reveal the exalted Name.[20]

The *Zohar* finds a finitizing element in the word *'asher*—'what.' This *what* marks the transition from absolute transcendence to transcendent relationality in God. The process of emanation (*'azilut*) is a preparation for the act of creation (*beri'ah*). For it is in creation that the relationality of God will find the objects which it intends and in which it will become immanent.

The distinction between *Deus absconditus* and *Deus revelatus* is especially clear in the following passage from the *Zohar*:

> He (*hu*) is concealed and not revealed, for the Torah comes from the upper world (*me'alma 'ila'ah*) and in every place He is the upper world which is not revealed. . . . That is why He is called "He" and not "You" (*hu ve-la 'attah*). . . . Everywhere there are two worlds: that which is revealed and that which is concealed (*ve-da b'itkasya*). And we indeed declare God blessed in these two worlds, as it says in Scripture, "blessed be the Lord God of Israel from world to world" (*me'olam 'ad 'olam*, Psalms 106:48). For the upper world we call "He" and the lower world we call "You."[21]

This passage builds upon a peculiarity of Hebrew, especially the liturgical Hebrew of the rabbis. For a blessing (*berakhah*) begins in the second person, as a direct address: "blessed are You, Lord" (*barukh 'attah, Ha-Shem*), but concludes in the third person, as an assertion, for example: "who has (*'asher*) given the true Torah to us."[22]  On this peculiarity, it seems as though the author of the *Zohar* has built a major theological point: that the human response to God's blessedness intends both divine relationality and divine aseity.  For it is clearly in the world of creation alone that God allows Himself to be addressed as "You," that is, He allows human creatures to be related to Him and thus brings Himself into a relationship with them.[23]  But human worshippers must always be aware that God is never exhausted by this relationship.[24]  Paul Tillich (d. 1965) analyzed the same theological question as it appears in the metaphysical thinking of the West, from which Kabbalah cannot be divorced:

> Theological criticism of these attempts is easy if the concepts are taken in their proper sense, for then they make God finite, dependent on a fate or accident which is not himself. . . . But this is not the way in which these concepts should be interpreted.  They point symbolically to a quality of divine life which is analogous to what appears as dynamics in the ontological structure. The divine creativity, God's participation in history, his outgoing character, are based on this dynamic element.  It includes a "not-yet," which is, however, always balanced by an "already" within the divine life.[25]

Tillich's distinction between the "not-yet" and the "already" in the divine life can be useful, it seems to me, in analyzing the Kabbalistic distinction between God as *'Eyn Sof* and God as *Sefirot*.

### 4.  Finitization and Freedom

Some Kabbalists saw a basic opposition between divine effusion (*hitpashtut*) and divine contraction (*zimzum*). But others saw the two as complementary aspects of the divine descent into relationality.[26] For any differentiation entails limitation.  Such inner divine preparation for relationship with human creatures is described by the sixteenth-century Safed Kabbalist Rabbi Moses Cordovero:

Through ten utterances, that is, *sefirot*, was the world created. The Holy-One-blessed-be-He caused ten *sefirot* to emanate, and He combined within them the effusion of revelation (*shef'a gilluy*) of His splendor in the most complete unity (*bi-takhlit ha-yihud*) to create the world through them. By means of them [He created] all the worlds and the creatures which are limited and determined (*ba'alei gevul ve-takhlit*). And the ten *Sefirot* of emanation shine and are linked together (*u-mishtalshalot*) . . . for creation, formation (*yezirah*) and making (*'asiyah*), through a mighty *zimzum*. For if between the Source-of-emanation-blessed-be-He and the world there were not the order (*seder*) of the *Sefirot*, it would be impossible for the world, because of its lowliness (*pehituto*) to be led by the *'Eyn Sof.*[27]

Here *zimzum* seems to take place not between the *Sefirot* and the *'Eyn Sof,* but between the *Sefirot* and creation.[28] The *Sefirot* are not the result of a process of *zimzum* above them. Rather they themselves perform a process of *zimzum* in relation to what is beneath them, namely, the created world. But even here the differentiation and separation are already present in the process of emanation between the *'Eyn Sof* and the *Sefirot.* Thus the early sixteenth-century Kabbalist Rabbi Meir ibn Gabbai spoke of the realm of the *Sefirot* as "the power (*ha-koah*) stored and sealed to go forth from potentiality to actuality (*'el ha-po'el*)."[29] If the actuality to be achieved is relationship, then a *zimzum* is present even before creation. For relationship presupposes the limitation of the ego.

In the theology of Rabbi Isaac Luria in sixteenth-century Safed *zimzum* was definitely seen within the Godhead itself. It was not just a condescension required for the process of emanation to lead into finite creation. Rather, it became the very foundation of emanation from the *'Eyn Sof* into the ten *Sefirot.* Luria's disciple, Rabbi Hayyim Vital expressed his master's theory as follows:

The essence of this *zimzum* is to reveal the root of judgments, in order to place the attribute of divine judgment (*middat ha-din*) in the worlds. . . . And after this *zimzum*, it seems to me that there remains a vacant place (*meqom he-hallal*), an open and empty space within the light of the *'Eyn Sof* itself. It seems to me that this indeed was originally (*kevar*) a place where the emanations, and the created beings, and the beings formed, and the beings made, exist.[30]

The primordial process of finitization was the making of vessels (*kelim*) to hold the diminished light of the emanations. "For in the beginning the light needed to be condensed (*zimzum*) and diminished (*ve-mi'uto*), and by means of this the existence of the vessel would be revealed . . . so that the vessel would be able to subsist and not be destroyed."[31]

For Kabbalists there is no real difference between creation and revelation. Creation is itself an act of revelation. It is not the bringing into existence of something really external to God, but rather God's making room within His own being for a greater diversity. In the theology of Luria and those who followed him, the "vessels" in which God's self-contraction allowed some of His light to be contained are seen primarily as the commandments (*mizvot*) of the Torah. God's ineffable Name is differentiated and finitized in the Torah as divine self-revelation. Thus God's binding Himself to the commandments of the Torah, as it were, does not entail a reduction of God to the control of humans or His confinement within the categories of our world. On the contrary, this binding is now an inner divine act prior to the creation of the world. Our keeping of the commandments with proper intention (*kavvanah*) elevates us as active participants in the inner divine drama. The commandments, despite their mundane phenomenality, are in truth symbols pointing to and participating in a transcendent reality. Here the Kabbalists revived the ancient Rabbinic interest in "the reasons of the commandments" (*ta'amei ha-mizvot*) with a powerful new impetus.[32] By introducing the doctrine of the ten *Sefirot* and the seemingly endless possibilities of relation among them, the Kabbalists multiplied without limit the possibilities for interpreting what the various commandments of the Torah truly intend.

The concern with the inner, spiritual meanings of the commandments is present in Kabbalah from its earliest manifestations. But Luria's theology focused appreciation of the commandments as acts of concentration and spiritual discipline by stressing their cosmic significance on the grandest scale. Rabbi Isaiah Ha-Levi Horowitz, a late sixteenth-century Safed Kabbalist who did much to spread Kabbalistic teachings among a wider mass of Jews, speaks about the significance of the commandments in the same vein:

And the Torah, which is light, subsists through knowledge of the reasons of the commandments and their inner mysteries (*ve-sodeihen*) . . . for the intention of the commandment (*kavvanat ha-mizvah*) is His mysterious Name, may He be exalted. For were it not for this, there would be no connection (*devequt*) of the material aspects of the act to spirituality (*le-ha-ruhaniyut*). . . . And it is evident in the *Zohar* and in the sages of the Truth [that is, Kabbalah] that from the material aspects of the commandment (*me-gashmiyut ha-mizvah*), the Torah and prayer . . . there is no taking hold of (*'ahizah*) and connection to the higher Garden of Eden . . . except through the intentions of the mystic knowledge of His names, may He be exalted.[33]

In the theology of the Hasidic masters, beginning in the eighteenth century, these Kabbalistic doctrines took hold of the imagination and devotion of the largest masses of Jews, those in Eastern Europe. The doctrine that the life of the commandments involves a real participation in the life of God gave an enormous incentive to increased observance and deeper piety. And the doctrine of *zimzum* developed by Luria and his immediate disciples played a key role in this explication of the commandments. We see this in a passage from the writings of one of the most important of the first generation of Hasidic masters in eighteenth-century Poland, the Maggid of Mezeritch:

What it means is that the Holy-One-blessed-be-He contracts Himself and makes Himself manifest (*shoreh*) in this world by means of the Torah and the commandments, which are here in contracted form (*be-zimzum*) and subject to various limiting conditions (*she'urin*). . . . Just as a father who loves his son even though very far from him, concentrates his mind and imagines as though his son's image stood before him, so, as it were (*ki-ve-yakhol*), the Holy-One-blessed-be-He contracts Himself.[34]

By insisting that God, the '*Eyn Sof*, transcends all particularity yet relates Himself to all things through the *Sefirot*, the Kabbalists preserve the Scriptural and Rabbinic theme that all God's acts are freely performed. God's self-contraction to make room for multiplicity is a free act. The relative non-being of *zimzum* is not something eternally existent like Aristotle's relative non-being (*me on*), which is potentiality (*dynamis*) in relation to actual being (*to on*).[35] Both the relative non-being of *zimzum* and the actual being of creatures (*nivra'im*) are the results of God's free will. Vital (presumably following Luria, his teacher) does assert that it was "necessary" (*mukhrah*) for God to bring His potential goodness into actuality by creating the world. But he also asserts that this is an act of God's will (*ke-she'alah bi-rezono*). Hence one might say that although God has a compulsion to give forth of His plenitude, it is still His choice *how* and *when* to exercise it. But it must be admitted that Luria and his school, of all the Kabbalists, came closest to the Neoplatonists in their metaphysical qualification of God's freedom.

The Kabbalistic continuation of the classical Jewish doctrine of God's absolute freedom sustains a corresponding doctrine of human freedom of choice. Where Luria saw God as limiting His omnipotence to make *space* for created being, later Kabbalists saw God as limiting His omniscience as well. The eighteenth-century Kabbalist Rabbi Hayyim ibn Attar saw this as a *temporal* limit. For human freedom is the capacity to act into an open future. That future cannot be known in advance, even by God, or it would not be the future—it could not be other than it *already* is known to be. Knowledge follows its object; it does not produce it. Even God can know objects only *after* He has created them. The doctrine of human freedom assumes that God does not create human actions *before* we actually perform them; therefore, even God cannot know them in advance. Present knowledge presupposes an existing object. So the future as such cannot be an object at all. Having no presence/existence (*mezi'ut*, "foundness") the future *cannot be found*. Thus it is determined by action, not vice-versa.

At this level there seems to be an antinomy between divine omniscience and divine freedom.[36] With their new metaphysical doctrine of *zimzum*, the post-Lurianic Kabbalists had a way out of the apparent antinomy of human freedom versus divine omniscience:[37] It is not that God cannot know the future; rather, God wills not to know the future—so as to allow human freedom, lest the open future collapse into an "eternal now." As Ibn Attar writes:

> For I inform you that the Lord is able to cancel (*lishlol*) knowledge that His intellect apprehends, that is, not to know it, when the Lord so wills. Human beings do not have the capacity to do this. . . . Now we can say that at the time of the creation of human beings,

the Lord canceled from His knowledge the [future] sins of man . . . so
that the contention of the wicked would have no basis, when they say
that God's knowledge necessitates (*makhrahat*) that what it knows will
be—Since He already knew that this person would sin as he did, it
was necessary (*yithayyev*) that it be so.[38]

Although Ibn Attar uses the term *shellilah* (cancellation) rather than
the Lurianic term *zimzum*, *shellilah* is the temporal equivalent of
spatial *zimzum*. God limits His power for the sake of creation,
especially of human beings, and He limits His knowledge for the sake
of human freedom. Divine freedom and human freedom are not just
posited, they are correlated in a nexus of complementarity within the
Kabbalists' metaphysical articulation and elaboration of Scriptural and
Rabbinic themes.

A problem remains in Ibn Attar's formula. Literally, he states
that God *had* omniscience and *then* canceled it for the sake of human
freedom and responsibility. How does anyone choose to *not-know*
what he had previously known? If what is known must be existent,
even if the knower chooses to forget the object of knowledge, that
object does not cease to exist just because it was forgotten. Even to
posit that God's knowledge is *praxis* and not *theoria*, treating it as
knowledge *before* the act rather than after it,[39] would not solve Ibn
Attar's problem. For such *practical* knowledge can only be that of
the actor. For God to have such *practical* knowledge of human acts
would require that He, not man, be their author. God's omniscience
as theoretical knowledge eliminates the futurity which human
freedom presupposes; it makes what must be essentially future past.
But God's omniscience as practical knowledge even more directly
eliminates human freedom by denying that man is the author of *his
own* acts.

I can only suggest the following solution to Ibn Attar's
difficulty. One cannot assume that God was omniscient, then created
the world, and then chose not to be omniscient about it. But one can
say that God chose not to be omniscient *before* He created man in
order for man to have the authorship of his own acts and the open
future required by freedom and responsibility. In terms of *zimzum*,
this would mean that God chose to cancel potential rather than actual
knowledge of human action. Power rather than actual deeds is what
can be restrained in advance.

## 5. *Zimzum* and Platonic Teleology

I have attempted to show that the Kabbalistic doctrine of *zimzum*, although sharing in the general Neoplatonic problematic of the One and the many, expresses Scriptural and Rabbinic doctrines of divine and human freedom and God's relation to creation. These distinctive Jewish doctrines are at variance with what Plotinus taught. They imply that God's covenantal relationship with His creatures is a good, not a detriment to be overcome or an embarrassment to be explained away. The initial concern is with God's relation to His creatures and, then, correspondingly, with how this relation enables creatures to relate themselves back to God. For Plotinus the ultimate end of this relationship is that it be overcome, that relationality lead to identity, and the many become absorbed into the One. He says:

> The One is all things and not a single one of them: it is the
> principle (*arche*) of all things, not all things, but all things have that
> other kind of transcendent existence (*ekeinos*); for in a way they do
> occur in the One (*hoion endrame*); or rather they are not there yet
> (*oupo estin*), but they will be (*estai*).[40]

For Plotinus, all things do not come from the One in the sense that the One created them. Rather, "a great multiplicity flowed from it as that which is seen to exist in beings, but which we think it right to refer back to the One (*anagein de auto pros ekeino*)."[41] All things are related *to* the One in the sense that they do not truly exist and cannot be understood outside this relation. But the One is not itself related *to* all things in that way at all. It does exist apart from them and in no way requires their existence. The relation is wholly nonreciprocal; there is no genuine interaction between the parties: One side is solely absolute and the other solely contingent. We see much the same in Plato. In the *Timaeus*, the Demiurge creates the cosmos in order to relate unintelligible matter to the intelligible Forms. But the Forms, not the Demiurge, are ultimate reality, and they do not relate themselves actively or reciprocally to anything beneath them.[42] The same can be said of the God of Aristotle, who is not an efficient cause in the Aristotelian scheme.[43]

Some Kabbalists seem to have accepted this Platonic-Aristotelian-Plotinian teleology. They asserted that the purpose of all human striving is the overcoming of multiplicity and limitation. For Rabbi Hayyim Vital, Luria's chief disciple, the ultimate purpose of all human striving, through the commandments properly intended, is the return of human souls to their pre-*zimzum* union with God.[44] But acceptance of this teleology poses a severe problem for Jewish theologians. For if God created finite multiplicity, why is it His and our goal to overcome it? Did God make a cosmic mistake? Is creation not really good after all, as the Gnostics maintained? Why should God have created it in the first place? Subordinating present relationality to future unification seems to negate the original goodness of God's act of creation and to cancel the worth of created beings.[45] If creation is good, why should it be returned to its source? If creation is to be overcome, why create at all? Why should God have not left everything in its primordial unity? The challenge of Gnosticism is particularly telling for the Neoplatonism of Jews, Christians or Muslims, since their traditional theologies affirm *creatio ex nihilo*. When Kabbalah comes to share the same teleology, which animates so much of medieval theology, more theological problems arise than are solved. It is the demand for a return to pristine unity, I would argue, whether in Kabbalah or in the rationalist theology it attempted to surpass, that must now be set aside or bracketed as a failed experiment.[46] Once this is done, perhaps Kabbalah can be returned to its own true origins as a development of the tradition of Scripture and the rabbis.[47]

## Notes

1. *Responsa Radbaz* (Warsaw, 1882), 4, #1111. Cf. #1151. In #1315 Radbaz calls this the practice of "the sages of Safed," the great center of Kabbalah in his time. I have been unable to find the exact statement in any of the writings ascribed to R. Simon bar Yohai, but the practice seems to be implied in *Zohar*: Shelah, 3:175b. See also, R. Moses Isserles, *Darkhei Mosheh* on *Tur*: *'Orah Hayyim*, 25, #2, quoting R. Menahem Recanti's *Commentary on the Torah*: Shelah, end; R. Abraham Gumbiner, *Magen 'Avraham* on *Shulhan 'Arukh*: *'Orah Hayyim*, 25.1, referring to the practice of R. Isaac Luria (Ari). For the Rabbinic practice of scholars wearing *tefillin* all day, see B. Megillah 28a; Maimonides, *Hilkhot Tefillin*, 4.25 and R. Joseph Karo, *Kesef Mishneh* ad loc. The usual reasons given for now wearing

*tefillin* only during weekday morning prayers are as follows: the need for great bodily cleanliness precludes their continual wear by most people (B. Shabbat 49a); *tefillin* were worn by certain charlatans to trick people into believing that they were pious and honest (ibid., Tos., s.v. *k'Elisha*); when wearing *tefillin* one's mind was not to be distracted from their sanctity (R. Nissin Gerondi, *Ran* on *Alfasi*: Shabbat, ch. 4, ed. Vilna, 22b, s.v. *garsinan* and *u-me-d'amar*, quoting B. Sukkah 26ab; *Tur: 'Orah Hayyim*, 37, and R. Joseph Karo, *Bet Yosef* ad loc. Cf. B. Berakhot 30b. Louis Ginzberg in his *Payrushim ve-Hiddushim Bi-Yerushalmi* on Y. Berakhot 2.3/4d (New York: Jewish Theological Seminary of America, 1941) 1.257-63 suggests very plausibly that the practice ceased to be so public because of Jewish fears of Roman persecution. For later halakhic considerations, see R. Obadiah Yosef, *Yabi'a 'Omer* 1, #36, sec. 15 (Jerusalem: n.p., 1954) 1.127; Jacob Katz, *Halakhah ve-Kabbalah* (Jerusalem: Magnes Press, 1984).

2. "Schöpfung aus Nichts und Selbstverschränkung Gottes," *Eranos Jahrbuch*, 25 (1956): 90 ff.

3. *Shemot Rabbah* 34.1. See *Shir ha-Shirim Rabbah* 6.3, quoting Psalms 29:4 and 19:8; *Pesiqta Rabbati*: Qorbanei Lahmi, ed. Friedmann, 84b.

4. *Shemot Rabbah* 34.1. See *Pesiqta Rabbati*: 'Aharei-Mot, 190a; B. Sanhedrin 7a and Rashi, s.v. *"le-ba-sof."*

5. See my *Halakhah in a Theological Dimension* (Chico: Scholars Press, 1985), ch. 9.

6. *Pesiqta de-Rab Kahana*: Rosh Hashanah, ed., Mandelbaum, 2.337.

7. *Vayiqra Rabbah* 35.5.

8. Y. Rosh Hashanah 1.3, 57b. See Y. Bikkurim 3.3, 65c; *Pesiqta Rabbati*: Ba-Yom ha-Shemini, 7b; *Tanhuma*: Ki Tissa, printed ed., number 33.

9. B. Baba Mezia 59b. See B. Pesahim 119a ad Psalms 13:1 and Rashbam ad loc.

10. For divine dependence on Israel, see, e.g., B. Berakhot 7a; cf. note of R. Jacob ibn Habib in *'Ayn Ya'aqov* ad loc. The theme was much developed in Kabbalah, especially in the concept of *zorkhei Gavoha* (divine needs). See, e.g., R. Meir ibn Gabbai, *'Avodat ha-Qodesh* (Venice, 1566) 2.2 ff.

11. *Enneads*, V 1.6, Armstrong, 5.30-31.

12. 5.28-29.

13. V 2.1, 5.58-59.

14. See Martin Heidegger, "Modern Science, Metaphysics and Mathematics," tr., W. B. Barton, Jr. and V. Deutsch, in D. F. Krell,

ed., *Heidegger: Basic Writings* (New York: Harper and Row, 1977), 265 ff.

15. *Enneads*, V 1.6, **5**.28-29.

16. See *Responsa Ribash* (Constantinople, 1547), number 157; *Zohar*: Bereshit, 1:22b, and I. Tishby, *Mishnat Ha-Zohar* (Jerusalem: Mosad Bialik, 1961) **2**.279-80.

17. B. Yoma 47a and parallels.

18. *Parmenides*, 130CD, tr., H. N. Fowler (Cambridge: Harvard University Press, 1926), 210-11.

19. See Gershom Scholem, *On the Kabbalah and Its Symbolism*, 110-11.

20. *Zohar*: 'Aharei-Mot, 3:65ab as emended by Tishby, *Mishnat ha-Zohar*, 2nd ed. (Jerusalem: Mosad Bialik, 1957) **1**.195. Cf. my *Law and Theology in Judaism* (New York: KTAV, 1974) **1**.147-48.

21. *Zohar*: Vayeze, 1:156b and 158b. See R. Joseph Gikatila, *Sha'arei 'Orah*, sec. 5, ed. Y. Ben-Shlomoh (Jerusalem: Mosad Bialik, 1971) **1**.189 and sec. 10, **2**.115. Cf. M. Berakhot, end.

22. Cf. the dialectic between prayer as direct petition (*baqashah*) and prayer as less direct praise (*hoda'ah*). See B. Berakhot 31a; B. 'Avodah Zarah 7b-8a; *Zohar*: Vayeze 1:155b (sitrei Torah); Vayishlah 1:169a; Vayehi 1:243b-244a.

23. See R. Moses di Trani, *Bet 'Elohim* (Venice, 1576), Sha'ar ha-tefillah, ch. 5; he explains that the second person part of the blessing intends God as revealed (*nigleh*) and the third person part intends God as concealed (*nistar*); cf. Sha'ar ha-yesodot, chs. 32-33. See also Nahmanides ad Exodus 15:26; Rabbenu Bahya, *Shulhan shel 'Arba*, sec. 1 in *Kitvei Rabbenu Bahya*, ed. C. B. Chavel (Jerusalem: Mosad Ha-Rav Kook, 1970), 467.

24. The relational aspect of Jewish piety was most profoundly explicated by Martin Buber in *I and Thou*, pt. 3. Cf. Paul Tillich's oblique criticism of the reduction of God to "Thou," *Theology of Culture* (New York: Oxford University Press, 1959), 62.

25. *Systematic Theology* (Chicago: University of Chicago Press, 1951) **1**.246. Tillich was greatly influenced by Schelling. For Schelling's remarkable affinities to Kabbalah, see Gershom Scholem, *Major Trends in Jewish Mysticism*, 3rd ed., 412, n. 79.

26. For an emphasis on the opposition, see, e.g., R. Shne'ur Zalman of Liadi, *Tanya* (New York: Kehot, 1967), Sha'ar ha-yihud, ch. 4, 6; R. Abraham Joshua Heschel of Apt, *Torat 'Emet*: Bereshit, quoted in I. Werfel, *Sefer ha-Hasidut* (Tel Aviv: Leinman, 1947) 50a.

27. *Tomer Deborah* (New York: n.p., 1974), intro., 213. See M. Avot 5.1. For early modern discussion of this Jewish doctrine in the light of idealistic philosophy, especially that of Schelling, see R. Nahman Krochmal (d. 1840), *Moreh Nevukhei ha-Zeman*, sec. 17, ed., S. Rawidowicz (London: Ararat, 1961), 306-11.

28. See *Pardes Rimmonim* (Jerusalem: n.p., 1962) 1.2.1; also Y. Ben-Shlomoh, *Torat ha-'Elohut shel Rabbi Mosheh Cordovero* (Jerusalem: Mosad Bialik, 1965), 98-100.

29. *'Avodat ha-Qodesh* 1.1. See, also, R. Abraham ha-Mal'akh, *Hesed l'Abraham*: Terumah, quoted in Werfel 21a.

30. *'Ez Hayyim* (Jerusalem: n.p., 1910) 1.11b. See S. A. Horodetzki, *Torat ha-Kabbalah shel 'Ari ve-Rabbi Hayyim Vital* (Tel Aviv: Ha-Hevrah le-Mif'alay ha-Sifrut, 1947), 35 ff.; Adin Steinsalz, *The Thirteen Petalled Rose*, tr., Y. Hanegbi (New York: Basic Books, 1980), 21-24.

31. *'Ez Hayyim* 1.13a.

32. A whole Kabbalistic literature developed on this subject, one of the most popular books in it being R. Menahem Recanti's *Ta'amei ha-Mizvot* (Basel, 1580). An early and seminal version of this new interest is found in Nahmanides (d. 1267), an important precursor of the *Zohar* and subsequent Kabbalah. See, e.g., his comment on Exodus 29:46.

33. *Shenei Luhot ha-Berit* (Jerusalem: n.p., 1963), 2b.

34. *Maggid Devarav le-Ya'aqov* (Satmar: n.p., 1905), 26, 29.

35. See Aristotle, *Metaphysics* 1089a 25.

36. *'Ez Hayyim* 1.5a, 11a. See Horowiz, *Shenei Luhot ha-Berit* 14a; Scholem, "Schöpfung aus Nichts und Selbstverschränkung Gottes" 100, 117. For the history of this basic issue in Western philosophy, see A. O. Lovejoy, *The Great Chain of Being* (Cambridge: Harvard University Press, 1936), 48 ff.

37. The tendency to present divine omniscience and human freedom as forming an antinomy is seen as early as M. Avot 3.18 (see Maimonides ad loc.). It was later expressed most explicitly by Maimonides in his *Commentary on the Mishnah:* "Eight Chapters," 8, end, ed., Kafah (Jerusalem: Mosad Ha-Rav Kook, 1965) 2.265-66; *Hilkhot Teshuvah* 6.5; *Guide* III 20. Cf. L. E. Goodman, "Determinism and Freedom in Spinoza, Maimonides, Aristotle."

38. *'Or Hayyim* ad Gen. 6:5. In medieval Jewish philosophy, *shellilah* has a stronger negative force than Ibn Attar gives it here: It has the force of absolute negation (*ouk on*; see Aristotle, *Metaphysics* 1089a 15-30). See Maimonides, *Guide* I 58.

39. Cf. David Burrell's paper in this volume.

40.  *Enneads* V 2.1, 5.58-59.

41.  *Enneads* V 1.6, 5.28-29.

42.  See *Timaeus*, 29E ff.; D. Novak, *Suicide and Morality* (New York: Scholars Press, 1975), 33-35.

43.  See *Metaphysics* 1072a 25 ff.; W. D. Ross, *Aristotle* (New York: Meridian, 1959), 177 ff. Cf. Henri Bergson, *Creative Evolution*, tr., A. Mitchell (New York: Random House, 1944), 350-53.

44.  See *'Eẓ Ḥayyim* 2.66b; also, Gershom Scholem, *Sabbatai Sevi*, tr., Werblowsky, 15 ff.

45.  In Scriptural-Rabbinic anthropology, the human person is essentially mortal (see 1 Chronicles 29:15), whereas rationalist and Kabbalistic anthropology assign the soul a potentiality for immortality. Death is real and an inherent liability in created goodness (see *Bereshit Rabbah* 9.5 ad Genesis 1:31). Even the Rabbinic doctrine of the resurrection does not imply any human potential for immortality. We do not return to some infinite divine origin. Being embodied, the human person has no such potentiality; see Genesis 3:19. Rather, resurrection manifests God's grace (*Targum Yerushalmi* ad Genesis 30:22; B. Berakhot 34b ad Isaiah 64:3; B. Ta'anit 2ab; B. Sanhedrin 91b ad Deuteronomy 32:39). The life of the world-to-come portends God's power even over death, not man's.

46.  For modern Jewish attempts to interpret *zimẓum* more psychologically than metaphysically, see Joseph B. Soloveitchik, "The Community," *Tradition* 17 (1978): 15; M. Rotenberg, *Dialogue with Deviance: The Hasidic Ethic and the Theory of Social Contraction* (Philadelphia: Jewish Publication Society, 1983), esp. 8-16.

47.  For a contemporary philosophical argument that divine contraction and divine creativity entail each other, see Robert Neville, *God the Creator* (Chicago: University of Chicago Press, 1968), 83.

# Jewish Kabbalah and Platonism in the Middle Ages and Renaissance

## Moshe Idel

### I. Plato in the Kabbalah: An Overview

At the end of the twelfth century Jewish thought underwent several radical changes. The regnant Neoplatonism expressed in the work of such philosophers as Isaac Israeli, Solomon ibn Gabirol, and, in a less explicit manner, Moses and Abraham ibn Ezra and Abraham bar Ḥiyya, lost its dominance in favor of more Aristotelian ways of thinking like that of Maimonides and Abraham ibn Daud. Later European Jewish philosophy progressed under the aegis of Maimonidean Aristotelianism. But concomitantly with Maimonides' floruit, another speculative trend in Jewish thought began its career as a historical factor, the Provençal Kabbalah. In Provence, the stronghold of this incipient movement, the *Guide of the Perplexed* was translated into Hebrew and began to exercise its impressive influence over Europe. But the nascent Kabbalah was simultaneously emphasizing the Platonic elements in medieval philosophic texts, holding the Maimonidean version of Aristotelianism religiously suspect. The fiery controversy around the Maimonidean writings in Provence and Spain centered on non-philosophical, Halakhic and theological issues.[1] But a need was clearly felt for an alternative to Maimonidean Aristotelianism, and the main, indeed unique, speculative alternative in the environment of the Maimonidean controversy in Europe was the early Kabbalah, a fountainhead of Neoplatonic concepts, imagery, and mystical cum mythical speculations.[2] The early Kabbalists welcomed ideas explicitly rejected by Maimonides, but even exploited the *Guide* itself to lend credence to a Platonic view actively combatted by Maimonides. R. Ya'akov ben Sheshet, a Catalan Kabbalist, wrote:

> God was contemplating the Torah[3] and saw the essences (*havvayot*)[4] in Himself, since the essences were in Wisdom (*Hokhmah*) and discerned that they are prone to reveal themselves. This tradition I heard in the name of R. Isaac son of R. Abraham, of blessed memory.[5] And this was also the opinion of the Rabbi [Moses Maimonides], the author of [*The Book of*] *Knowledge*, who said that He, in knowing Himself, knows all existent creatures.[6] Yet the Rabbi was astonished in Part II, ch. 6 of the *Guide*, at the dictum of our Sages that God does not do anything before He contemplates His retinue (*Pamalia*), and he quoted there the dictum of Plato, that God, blessed be He, does contemplate the intellectual world and causes to emanate therefrom the emanation [which produces] reality.[7]

The Kabbalist here juxtaposes two discussions of Maimonides: in the *Mishneh Torah* the author presents his view, stemming ultimately from Themistius, about God containing the forms of all existents and thus knowing them by way of self-knowledge;[8] discussing a different issue in the *Guide*, Maimonides sharply opposes a simplistic interpretation of the Midrashic dictum that God created the world by contemplating the Torah as the blueprint of reality. To the Kabbalist the two views seem to be equivalent. Thus his surprise at Maimonides' inconsistency in accepting the first while rejecting the second. Since the position of R. Isaac the Blind, cited before Maimonides' views, must be the truth for Ben Sheshet, Maimonides' critique is implicitly rejected, and the Platonic view mentioned in the *Guide* is deemed correct. R. Ezra of Gerona was similarly anxious about "misinterpretation" of Maimonides' Midrashic view.[9] The Ben Sheshet passage, to which we shall return, illustrates the eagerness of the Kabbalists to exploit the hierarchical structure of Neoplatonism in mediating between the divine and the lower realms.

The Aristotelian transcendent theology of Maimonides is unwelcome in view of these motivations.

Concurrently with the rise of the early Kabbalah, Neoplatonic themes were exerting their influence on the mystical movement that developed in Ashkenazi esoteric theology, although penetrating through channels that escape modern scholarship.[10] The geographic areas of the two centers of Jewish learning in which Neoplatonism reverberates are not remote from each other. Perhaps some influences penetrated before the Ashkenazi and Provençal types of Jewish mysticism went their separate ways.[11] But the two movements independently underwent further Neoplatonic influences.

As Maimonidean thinking spread in Spain, fears about its implications fostered a more negative attitude toward Maimonides and his source, Aristotle. From the thirteenth century examples can be collected in which Aristotelian views adopted in the *Guide* were criticized obliquely, attributed only to Aristotle or to Maimonists like Samuel ibn Tibbon.[12] If Epicurus was the *bête noire* of the ancient sages, conservative medieval Jews conceived of Aristotle as the root of theological errors. This image of the Stagirite opened the way for the positive reception of Plato. At the beginning of the fourteenth century we find an adaptation of a legend dealing with the history of Greek medicine,[13] in which the Italian Kabbalist R. Menahem Recanati inserts the name of Aristotle:

> There are several testimonies as to persons burned by the "path of the turning sword," and all of them were masters of the ancient philosophy. Most of their sayings were close to those of our sages, of blessed memory. And since then [the burning] they disappeared, and Aristotle came with his wicked disciples, and deviated completely from the way of the Torah, following their own speculations and demonstrations, which the masters of Kabbalah recognized as illusory (*ahizat 'eynayyim*).[14]

The ancient philosophers are anonymous and forgotten; the watershed is Aristotle, who is responsible for the ruin of knowledge.

By the end of the first third of the fifteenth century, Greek philosophy was epitomized among the Kabbalists in a manner highly sympathetic to Plato:

The views of the ancient philosophers like Plato seem to be close to the views of the Torah, but those who came later did not understand his thinking. For they were as insignificant as the heretics of our nation.[15]

Like his fourteenth-century predecessor Menaḥem Recanati, R. Shem Tov ben Shem Tov, who formulated this admiring view of Plato, was clearly anti-Aristotelian. He relates that he became acquainted with Plato through followers of Aristotle,[16] whose views diverge from Plato's. But Plato's thought was seen as consonant with Jewish piety, not through a profound study of the Platonic corpus (which was unavailable to Jews in the West, as it was to their Christian contemporaries), but precisely because Plato's works (unlike those of Aristotle) were inaccessible and therefore, according to R. Shem Tov, could not possibly have influenced Kabbalistic thought. From an anonymous hand in the generation of the Expulsion from Spain, we read:

> those books [the *Sefer Yeẓirah* and *Sefer Enoch*] in their entirety fell into the hands of the Greeks, who took them from the academy of Solomon in Jerusalem. And the sayings of the early Greeks, up to Plato, were almost religious views, taken from there. In vain did they attribute every science and tradition to their own investigations. In fact they found them written in these books. Then came Aristotle and his companions and they plagiarized them in their flattering language, and all the world followed them.

Aristotle was seen by R. Shem Tov and by the anonymous author just quoted as the source of a pernicious shift in Greek thought: The ancient Greek sages held views close to those of the Torah, and Plato is the paragon of sound theology.

With the coming of the Renaissance and the translation of the bulk of the Platonic and Neoplatonic corpus, Platonic philosophy became a live option for the elite. Christians and Jews alike could now enjoy the writings of the ancient philosopher, who moved to the center of intellectual life in many circles all over Europe. The impact of this Platonic revolution shaped European thought for more than a century, but Jewish intellectuals in close contact with the Florentine thinkers were the chief catalysts. The main body of Jewish thought underwent only a tangential influence from the luxuriant growth of Neoplatonic literature now available in Latin or Italian. Steeped in the medieval Aristotelianism that was already constitutive to the speculative patrimony of Judaism, most philosophically inclined Jews remained relatively indifferent to the disclosure of the authentic Plato. The Neoplatonic corpus translated by Marsilio Ficino remained untranslated into Hebrew. In a period when Jews were key translators of Aristotelian material into Latin, as with the translations of Eliahu del Medigo, Abraham de Balmes, and Jacob Mantino, the Jewish elite were only rarely interested in the Neoplatonic trend of thought that was expanding its influence among Christian intellectuals.

But at the close of the fifteenth century the pejorative mentions of Platonism common among Jewish Aristotelians gave way to much more positive attitudes. R. Yehudah Messer Leon, a committed Aristotelian, compared Platonism contemptuously to Kabbalah. But his son was interested in Kabbalah and described Plato as the divine master, just as his Christian contemporaries did.[17] The number of printed quotations by Jews from the Latin Platonic corpus in the last quarter of the fifteenth century is minuscule. But there was another type of influence of Ficino's translations: If direct quotations from the Latin are rare, the interest in medieval Jewish and Arabic Neoplatonism was incomparably greater, and was paralleled and supported by heightened interest in the Kabbalah.[18] Derided by the Aristotelian intellectual establishment of the fifteenth century, the Kabbalah gradually became the center of Jewish culture. The same trend is evident in Christian thought in Florence, where the deep interest in Neoplatonism was coupled with the introduction of Kabbalah as an exotic graft onto Christian theology. The Christian interest marks a sharp departure from medieval reticence about pagan philosophy and magic on the one hand and Jewish mysticism on the other.[19] Among Jews the renewed interest in the Neoplatonic legacy is a return to the medieval tradition, at least partially motivated by the Christian rediscovery of Platonic thought.

Why the slight response, then, to the translations of Ficino? Jews active in Florence, close to the circle of Ludovico de Medici, deliberately refrained from immersing themselves in the new world cultivated by their neighbors. Apparently, late fifteenth-century Jews retained a certain medieval selectivity about the sources they would quote explicitly. They openly cite the Arabic authors, who provide the problematic and background of medieval Jewish philosophy. But they tend not to mention Christian philosophy, even when it influences them. This hypothesis was proposed by Shlomo Pines in discussing the use or abuse of scholastic thought by medieval Jewish thinkers, and mooted again in the case of Leone Ebreo,[20] to whom we shall return. I propose to expand this point to the relationship of Renaissance Jewish thinkers in general to the Platonic, Neoplatonic and Hermetic literatures and the related writings of Pico and Ficino. The material quoted explicitly may be rare, but the impact of the intellectual movement is profound. Rather than focus only on explicit materials, I propose to work inductively to assay the influence of Christian thought on Jews in the first stages of the Renaissance.

Strangely enough, Plato, the philosopher who for some medieval Kabbalists seemed closest to the Jewish religion, became suspect in the eyes of most of the Renaissance Jews who could benefit from study of his works. Evidently he was much more welcome as a legendary representative of lost Greek lore than as a philosopher to be openly cultivated. But an important exception is the famous *Dialoghi d'Amore* of Leone Ebreo, the key exponent of Renaissance Jewish Neoplatonism, whose influence on the Renaissance in general was wide and profound. More than any other Jewish thinker Leone Ebreo profited from Renaissance Christian Neoplatonism.[21] So consideration of his response to Plato may contribute to a more nuanced description of Jewish Renaissance Neoplatonism. Pines emphasizes the medieval Arabic philosophical sources of the theory of love enunciated by Ebreo, and I have suggested another possible Arabic source.[22] I find much less openness to the Christian Neoplatonists than is often supposed, and Arthur Lesley has come to similar conclusions.[23] Ebreo knew Florentine Neoplatonism but did not consider it the apex of philosophy, and, as I shall show elsewhere, he criticized Ficino's handling of some Platonic issues. Following medieval Jewish sources, Ebreo saw Plato as dependent on Mosaic revelation and even as a disciple of the ancient Kabbalists; Aristotle was a disciple of Plato who did not understand clearly all that his mentor had learned from his Jewish masters.[24] The story is reminiscent of Kabbalistic treatments.

With the establishment of Neoplatonism as a major focus of

European thought, from the beginning of the sixteenth century, its influence on the interpretation of Jewish Kabbalah becomes more and more visible. By the end of the sixteenth century and the beginning of the seventeenth, Neoplatonic speculations dominate the thinking of many Italian and other European Kabbalists, eager to quote substantially from Platonic and Neoplatonic sources, ancient, medieval and contemporary.[25] Let me explore one point of impact of Neoplatonic thought on Kabbalah during the medieval and Renaissance periods.

## II. The *Sefirot* and Hebrew Letters as Neoplatonic Ideas

### A. *Neoplatonic Influences in the Early Kabbalah*

A key source of Kabbalistic theosophy and cosmology is the short treatise known as the *Sefer Yezirah*. Tantalizing its many commentators for centuries, the work remains an enigma for modern scholarship. At the very beginning of the work Kabbalists found reference to two basic elements necessary to the creation of the world: the ten *Sefirot*, originally ten mythic numbers, and the twenty-two letters of the Hebrew alphabet. According to the medieval Kabbalists, these elements are important not only as instruments of the act of creation, but also, perhaps especially, in constituting the Kabbalistic *Deus revelatus*, God revealed as and through the pleroma of the ten *Sefirot*. The mystic numbers preceded creation and were crucial not only to the world's emergence but also to its continued existence. In the early Kabbalah the *Sefirot* and letters were active forces appointed over the universe and susceptible to influence by human activity. The events of their dynamic formed the life of God.[26] The history of Kabbalistic theosophy is to some extent the history of various understandings of the *Sefirot* and the letters. The fortunes of the *Sefirot* are an index of the growth of Neoplatonism in the Kabbalah.[27]

The view of R. Isaac the Blind cited by Ben Sheshet affirms the existence of all essences in the second *Sefirah*, *Ḥokhmah*, which plays the role of the divine intellect and thus comprises the world of ideas. The same Provençal master is quoted elsewhere by Ben

Sheshet about the nature of the *havvayot*: "The beginning (*hathalat*) of the *havvayot* is one."[28] 'Beginning' here points to the first *Sefirah*, referred to by Ben Sheshet as a subtle and fine *havvayah*. Thus, passage from the first to the second *Sefirah* is passage from unity to multiplicity, although the multiplicity is realized fully as such only in the third *Sefirah*, *Binah*. Ben Sheshet thus places the essences or ideas in a container that is neither wholly "extradeical" nor wholly "intradeical." For the second *Sefirah* is identical with God's thought, yet distinct from the Highest phase of the divine, the *'Eyn Sof* or Infinite. According to the Kabbalist, Maimonides is perfectly right to agree that God contemplates all things by an act of Self-knowing. But the "great eagle" was wrong to oppose the recognition of a certain distance between the contemplator and the realm of the ideas.[29]

Ben Sheshet's conception of the second *Sefirah* as the container of the essences is part of a broader Neoplatonic scheme. Explaining the word *'Ayn*, nothingness, he writes:

> *Alef* points to the Will, which [reaches] the *'Eyn Sof*. . . . *Yod* points to *Hokhmah* . . . and the *Nun*, to the emergence of things from *Hokhmah*.[30]

So the divine will is the starting point of emanation, the *alpha* of the whole process of expansion in the divine world; it is identical to the first *Sefirah*. The *Yod*, pointing to *Hokhmah*, symbolizes the intellectual; the third letter refers to the multiplicity that emerges from the essences comprised in the second *Sefirah*. Although the text does not state it explicitly, the numerical value of the Hebrew letters hints at the emergence of multiplicity from unity: *Alef* (one) is unity; *Yod* (ten) is the decad of primary essences in *Hokhmah*, and *Nun* (fifty) stands for the full fledged multiplicity of the third *Sefirah*, *Binah*, traditionally connected to this number in a long series of texts. Ben Sheshet writes:

> This is the statement of the philosopher who arranged four [things]: the Intellect, the Will, the spiritual (*ha-nafshi*), and the natural (*ha-tiv'i*). The Will is the divine will; under it is the Intellect, that is, the Active Intellect; under that, the Soul, i.e., the intellective soul; under it, the natural. We see that *Alef* in our terms (*bi-*

*leshonenu*) corresponds to the divine Will in their terms, and *Yod* in our terms corresponds to the Active Intellect in theirs, etc.[31]

Thus the Kabbalist was aware of a philosophical position paralleling his own and quite like the Plotinian scheme of the Arabic Long Version of the *Theology of Aristotle*, with the divine will placed above Nous.[32] The scheme is reinterpreted in Kabbalistic terms, with Will as the first *Sefirah*, Intellect as the second, Soul apparently identified with the third, and Nature consigned to the lower *Sefirot*. This Kabbalist is well aware of the foreign source of the doctrine and acknowledges the difference in terminology but remains convinced that the concepts correspond. A similar view is found in Ben Sheshet's compatriot and contemporary R. Azriel:

> The words of the wisdom of the Torah and the words of the aforementioned masters of investigation (*ba'alei ha-mehqar*) are as one (*sheneihem ke'ahat*). Their way is one, and there is no difference between them but the terms alone, since the investigators did not know enough to give the proper name to every part.[33]

Only the Kabbalists, R. Azriel urges, who received traditions from the Prophets, know how to designate each entity appropriately. But the philosophers are not to be cast aside—at least not all of them. Aristotle and Plato approximated the wisdom of the Kabbalists.[34] The views quoted in their names are, of course, purely Neoplatonic and have little to do directly with the actual teaching of the two Greek philosophers.[35] The stance of the two Geronese Kabbalists as to the congruence of Kabbalah and Neoplatonism is not found earlier. But a similar cosmology surfaces in the theosophy of R. Azriel. He too conceptualizes the *Sefirot* in a distinctly Plotinian manner. At the highest level is an Unseen or Invisible world (*'Olam ha-Ne'elam*), paralleled in Ben Sheshet and elsewhere in Azriel, by the divine Will.[36] Next comes the Intellectual World (*'Olam ha-Muskal*); then, the sensory (*'Olam ha-Murgash*), paralleling the world of the Soul in the Plotinian scheme; and finally, the Natural World (*'Olam ha-Mutba'*).[37] In postulating the existence of all the worlds in the divine realm, these Kabbalists seem to intend the idea that all perfections are contained in the divine and then displayed in the emanative process.

By identifying *Hokhmah* with the Universal or Active Intellect, Ben Sheshet is assuming that all the forms, or ideas, exist there. Yet he rejects the Neo-Aristotelian view of the Active Intellect as given charge over the sublunar world and places it on a higher level, as in the Plotinian cosmology. The second *Sefirah* is identical with the Torah and God's Throne, the essence of which is grasped intellectually.[38] Thus the second *Sefirah* is an intellectual entity, and a conscious one, the object of its thought being the *dimyonot*—visions, images, archetypes, or forms.[39] Here the last may be the best rendering: The divine intellect thinks the forms, much as the human mind does. In a passage reminiscent of Ben Sheshet, R. Azriel, explains:

> The 32 wondrous paths of *Hokhmah* are the ten *Sefirot* of *Belimah* and the 22 letters. Each has its own distinctive path, and their beginning is the Will, which precedes everything. Nothing is outside it, and it is the cause of Thought (*Mahashavah*). The *Sefirot* and the paths, and all that will be created out of them in the future—everything—is hidden in the *Mahashavah* and revealed in its paths: in the paths of Speech (*Dibbur*) and the paths of Deed (*Ma'aseh*). 'He contemplates the Torah' means that He contemplated the *Mahashavah*—the paths included in it, and drew each one from the beginning . . . and in the forms (*dimyonei*) of that *Mahashavah* the words and deeds were prefigured (*niztayyru*), since the *Mahashavah* is the root.[40]

The pre-existence of the roots of speech and deeds in divine thought is compared by R. Azriel with the pre-existence of form and *hyle* in divine thought according to the Neoplatonic sources he quotes. But the philosophers deal only with entities; the Kabbalist is concerned as well with speech and deeds as dynamic processes comprehended in the *Mahashavah*. The verb *niztayyru* means both figured and imagined. The same root occurs again, along with the term *dimyon* in relation to deeds, in the work of another Geronese Kabbalist who might have known the work of R. Azriel, R. Moses ben Nahman, the famous Nahmanides:

Whatever occurred to the Fathers is a sign to the sons (Genesis Rabbah 40, 8). When Scripture expatiates on the story of their travels, the digging of wells, and other events, one may think it redundant or otiose, but all is there to teach of the future. For whenever something happens to a prophet or the three Patriarchs, he may understand from it what is predestined for his progeny. Know that every divine decision, wherever it turns from the potentiality of a decree into the actuality of a *dimyon*, will be fulfilled, regardless of the circumstances. ... Thus God kept [Abraham] in the land [of Israel] and created for them *dimyonot* of whatever He purposed to do to his progeny.[41]

Here the destiny of the Patriarchs is linked to a *dimyon*, just as deeds were connected to a *dimyon* by R. Azriel. The root *z-y-r* is used again in a similar context in Nahmanides:

Scripture here concludes the Book of Genesis, which is the Book of Formation, concerning the creation of the world and all created things, and the events in the lives of the Fathers, which were formative for their progeny—for all their experiences are prefigurations (*ziyyurei devarim*) that hint and presage all that will come to pass in the future.[42]

Here, as in R. Azriel, everything is contained in the Torah, an assumption of which Ben Sheshet was especially fond.[43] Nahmanides does not elaborate on the relation between future events and the creation but leaves obscure just how the acts of the Fathers determine the fate of their progeny. Amos Funkenstein proposes that the Christian term *figura*, indicating the prefiguration of later events by earlier ones, is the basis of Nahmanides' *ziyyur*. He gives 'similitude' as the correct translation of *dimyon*.[44] But since the metaphysical background of Nahmanides' usage is corroborated in the discussions of his compatriots and contemporaries Rabbis Azriel and Ben Sheshet, I think we should understand his terms and views in the light of their discussions. The *Sefirah* of *Hokhmah*, or *Mahashavah* in Azriel's text, includes the forms not only of the things to be created but also of all future deeds and words. The specifically Kabbalistic conception of prefiguration would be underlyingly Neoplatonic, although the Neoplatonism is of a distinctive type. It involves not only the classical correspondence of terrestrial objects to ideas, but also the prefiguration of acts and utterances in the divine intellect. Naḥmanides supplies an example from the realm of deeds.

Turning to the realm of speech, we find that Ben Sheshet interpreted the *intellecta* of *Ḥokhmah* as the roots of the Hebrew letters:

> *Ḥokhmah* emerges from the Nothingness (*me-'Ayn*),[45] and *Binah* from the *Alef*, and the *Alef* points to a subtle entity (*Ḥavvayah daqqah*) out of which the *Ḥokhmah* comes into existence . . . it is the beginning of all the essences (*ḥavvayot*) . . . the *Yod* points to the *Ḥokhmah*, which is the Beginning. . . . And out of the *Ḥokhmah*, the letters were emanated and engraved in the spirit of the *Binah*, and the essence of the letters is that they are the forms of all creatures, and there is no form which has not a likeness in the letters or in the combination of two or three of them or more.[46]

The Plotinian ideas are the essences of all things, existing in an intellectual container, the second *Sefirah* according to the Kabbalists, and are identical with the roots of the Hebrew letters. Moreover, these letters, as forms, have an important Neoplatonic characteristic: Following the view of R. Isaac the Blind, Ben Sheshet indicates that "each letter comprises all the others."[47] This formulation is reminiscent of the Proclean view applied to the Platonic ideas, that "all is in all."[48] The view of the letters as the ideas in *Ḥokhmah* harmonizes with the view, expressed several times in Ben Sheshet's writings, that identifies the second *Sefirah* with the Torah, which is in turn conceived as containing all the sciences.

R. Ya'akov ben Sheshet and R. Azriel of Gerona do not mention each other, but their work seems to be distinctive in the Geronese Kabbalah—distinct even from the thinking of R. Ezra of Gerona and Naḥmanides. The latter were less interested in philosophy in general and in Neoplatonism in particular; they lack the fourfold cosmology and do not mention an affinity between philosophy and Kabbalah. Ben Sheshet need not have innovated these views, but the integration of the scheme may result from his work, perhaps together with that of R. Azriel. The view that *Ḥokhmah* includes the letters that contain each other can be reconstructed from the writings and fragments of R. Isaac the Blind. So we may assume that the Plotinian view of the second *Sefirah* and of language as a prototype was already present in the Provençal Kabbalah. A similar view is found in a text of R.

Asher ben David, nephew of R. Isaac the Blind: "for the power of one (*Sefirah*) is in the other, since each *middah* is contained in the other."[49] Thus it seems that the principle of Proclus is applied, at the very inception of the Kabbalah, not only to the letters but also to the *Sefirot*.

The affinity between Neoplatonic and Kabbalistic conceptions, then, reaches far beyond the residues of Neoplatonism found in the nascent Kabbalah. For we see it in the adaptation of philosophical terminology in the writings of at least two important Kabbalists. Both R. Azriel and Ben Sheshet were innovative authors who openly exposed Kabbalah, apparently for the first time, to an audience beyond that of immediate disciples.[50] Perhaps they were ready to acknowledge the correspondence between Kabbalistic and Neoplatonic concepts because of their commitment to propagating the Kabbalah. Again, an author who believed that an ancient philosopher acknowledged the same ontological structure as the Kabbalah may have been less inclined to keep to himself the previously esoteric doctrines. What was disclosed would not be wholly novel to his audience.[51] Thus the first author to mention the affinity between the Platonic ideas and the *Sefirot* was R. Yehudah Romano, an Italian thinker well acquainted with scholastic theology and so with the Platonic ideas.[52]

## B. Platonic Ideas and Renaissance Kabbalah

Faced with the more elaborate Platonic views presented in the translations of Ficino and his followers, the Kabbalists' response is less positive than that of R. Ya'akov and R. Azriel at the beginning of the thirteenth century. These compared one view of Plato, as quoted by Maimonides, with a central doctrine of the most important early Kabbalist, in the case of Ben Sheshet, or with the analogous treatments drawn from authentic Neoplatonic texts, in the case of R. Azriel, and they did so without disparagement of Plato. On the contrary, it was Maimonides who was criticized for resisting the Platonizing notion of archetypal essences in divine thought. R. Eliahu del Medigo, a late fifteenth-century Aristotelian who rejected both Platonism and Kabbalah, sees the Platonic background of Kabbalistic thinking as a detriment. His commentary on *De*

*Substantia Orbis* reports on the Kabbalistic doctrine of the *Sefirot* and concludes that, "These opinions were taken from the propositions of the early philosophers, particularly from Plato." On this basis, he questions the orthodoxy of Kabbalah and the legitimacy of its provenance as Jewish lore.[53] A more balanced appraisal is found in Isaac Abravanel:

> For of necessity things exist as a figuration[54] in the mind of the agent before they come into being. Indubitably this image is the world of the *Sefirot* mentioned by the Kabbalistic sages of true wisdom, [who said] that the *Sefirot* are the divine figurations with which the world was created. Thus they said that the *Sefirot* are not created but emanated, and that all of them are united together in Him, blessed be His name, for they are the figurations of His loving-kindness and His willing what He created. In truth, Plato set down the doctrine of separate universal forms not as Aristotle understood them.[55]

The affinity between Plato's "separate universal forms" and the *sefirot* is presented without any historical claims. The similarity is simply observed. But Isaac Abravanel believed that Plato studied with Jeremiah in Egypt and received his knowledge from the prophet.[56]

As long as a Kabbalist could present Plato as a more venerable alternative to the pernicious doctrine of Aristotelianism, Plato served as a valuable foil, paralleling and in a way corroborating Kabbalistic themes. But when the Platonic corpus becomes a potential rival to traditional views, Jewish authors begin to stress not Plato's affinity to Kabbalah but his discipleship of a prophet. Rather than allow for two independent sources of knowledge, Mosaic and Greek, they preferred to see the truth and the highest insights as one, stemming ultimately from the Mosaic revelation, accepted by Plato, but distorted by Aristotle. Aristotelianism, in any case, was less influential among Renaissance Jews than among their medieval forebears, and so less threatening. R. Yoḥanan Alemanno, a companion of Pico della Mirandola, writes:

> The ancients believed in the existence of ten spiritual numbers.
> . . . It seems that Plato thought that there are ten spiritual numbers of
> which one may speak, although one may not speak of the First Cause,

because of Its great concealment. However, [the numbers] approximate its existence so closely that we may call these effects by a name that cannot be ascribed to the movers of corporeal bodies. Indeed, in the opinion of the Kabbalists, one may say this of the *Sefirot. . . .* This is what Plato wrote in the work *Ha-'Azamim ha-'Elyonim*, as quoted by Zechariah in the book *Imrei Shefer*.[57] From this it follows that in Plato's view the first effects are called *Sefirot* because they may be numbered, unlike the First Cause, and therefore he did not call them movers.[58]

Alemanno here links the terms *Sefirot* and *Misparim*, numbers. Both were considered "separate," i.e., spiritual, beings, so he could assume that their apparent common root was no accident. The passage implies that "Plato" (sc., Proclus, in the *Liber de Causis*, quoted here in an otherwise unknown translation) presented a doctrine of disembodied numbers similar to the Kabbalistic *Sefirot*, and that he held these views independently. But elsewhere Alemanno repeats the view that Plato studied with Jeremiah.[59]

Alemanno is interested in the *Sefirot* mainly for cosmological reasons. In a roundnote of his in the margin of a quotation from the commentary of R. Yehudah Ḥayyat, a Spanish Kabbalist, on *Ma'arekhet ha-Elohut*, we read:

> They said that the *Sefirot* are intermediary between the world of the eternal rest that is *'Eyn Sof*, and the world of motion, that is, the world of the spheres. This is why they are sometimes in a state of rest and sometimes in motion—as is the nature of the intermediary, composed as it is from the extremes.[60]

The Spanish Kabbalist copied by Alemanno held a dynamic view of the *Sefirot*, as linked to human activity and the fulfillment of the commandments. But Alemanno preferred to see the *Sefirot* as intermediary, their motion caused by their ontic status and not influenced by human acts.

In the works of R. Yeḥiel Nissim of Pisa, whose grandfather was Alemanno's patron, and whose uncle, R. Isaac of Pisa, was Alemanno's student, we find a similar stance, but with a peculiar emphasis:

The upper creatures are a model for the lower. For every lower thing has a superior power, from which it came into existence. This resembles the relationship of the shadow to the object that casts it. . . . Even the ancient philosophers such as Pythagoras and Plato taught and expounded about this. But the matter was not revealed to them clearly; they walked in darkness and attained but did not attain (*noge'a ve'eino noge'a*), since the universals and the forms indicated by Plato only hinted at this. . . . And since they did not receive the truth as it is but groped like the blind in darkness, such were their speculation and their sayings. But we shall hold to the words of our ancient sages, which are true and were received from the prophets, blessed be their memory. And we shall conclude that if this is so, and the lower things need the higher, this being a strict necessity, and the higher beings need the lower, to a limited extent, the entire world proves to be one individual (*ke'ish ehad*), and in this manner each particular thing will be attributed to the ten *Sefirot*, as if you were to say that a particular creature were to be attributed to a certain *Sefirah*.[61]

The nexus between the *Sefirot* and lower beings is seen as similar to that proposed in the Platonic and Neopythagorean theories of ideas and numbers. But the pagan philosophers did not receive the clear truth but a dim glimmering, inferior to the vision of the Jewish sages and prophets. The limited dependence of the upper on the lower is the obvious difference: The *Sefirot* need human acts of worship to function perfectly, a view that is alien to Plato. R. Yehiel ascribes the possibility of influencing the supernal powers to the anthropomorphic structure of the Sefirotic realm. Man reflects this structure in his shape and so can influence it by his deeds. This central claim of the theosophical-theurgical Kabbalah is elaborated by the Italian Kabbalist in the discussion that follows the passage just quoted. Elsewhere R. Yehiel soundly portrays the affinity and the distance between the two types of thought:

From the words of Plato it seems that he is close to the view of the Sages, of blessed memory, when he says that the lower and corporeal world is in the likeness and image of the upper world. He also said that there are forms in the divine mind called universals (*kelalim*), which resemble the individuals. Still it seems to me that he did not penetrate deeply enough to know truly the profound sense of the Torah and her sages, blessed be their memory, but remained outside the court: He attained and he did not attain. Thus he and the other ancients could not know the true quintessence of things, although they came close, as it was said in the *Midrash ha-Ne'elam*: They are close to the path of truth.[62]

Here too there follows a lengthy discussion on the centrality of man in ensuring the unity of the world. The deepest knowledge is not the awareness of the paradigmatic relations but the grasp of the dynamic influence on the higher world of religious acts fulfilling the *mizvot*. Plato knew the starting point of Kabbalah, the structural parallel of the higher to the lower, but the ultimate significance of the parallelism in practical and religious life escaped him. It is as though the Kabbalist were locating Plato in the cave, as one who had not received the clear revelation of the truth from its source. He is still dependent on the shadows, unlike the Kabbalists, whose knowledge of the truth is complete. Thus the reference to the palace of Maimonides' *Guide* (III 51), indicating that Plato lacks the inmost secrets of theology.

The dynamic interaction characteristic of Jewish theurgical mysticism disappears in another comparison of the Platonic ideas with the *Sefirot*, in R. Abraham Yagel's encyclopedic *Beit Ya'ar ha-Levanon*:

> And the power that is in the lower beings is found in the upper worlds in a subtler, more exalted and sublime way. It is found in great purity and clarity in the holy, pure *Sefirot*, which are the truth, the *ideae* for all things.[63]

Yagel does not pursue the historical significance of the relation between the Ideas and the *Sefirot*. But elsewhere he does represent Plato as dependent on the Mosaic tradition. No major difference is mentioned. The Renaissance theory of *prisca theologia* and multiple sources of truth influenced him, and the older notion of a Jewish source for Plato's teachings was still active. R. Joseph del Medigo of Kandia, a younger contemporary of Yagel's, seems to hold this theory of Plato's Jewish instruction. In his *Mazref la-Hokhmah* he contests the view of his ancestor, R. Eliahu del Medigo, who had contemptuously compared Kabbalah with the teachings of the ancient philosophers rejected by the moderns:

> My heart does not concur, since the ancient philosophers spoke more truly than Aristotle, who aimed to blame them only to vaunt himself alone. This is obvious to anyone who has read what is written on the philosophy and principles of Democritus, and especially on Plato, the master of Aristotle, whose views are almost those of the Sages of Israel, and who on some issues almost seems to speak from the very mouth of the Kabbalists and in their language, without any blemish on his lips. And why shall we not hold these views, since they are ours, inherited from our ancestors by the Greeks, and down to this day great sages hold the views of Plato and great groups of students follow him, as is well known to anyone who has served the sage of the Academy and entered their studies, which are found in every land.[64]

Del Medigo repeatedly quotes from the whole Neoplatonic corpus as disseminated by the Renaissance translations. He considers the Neoplatonic treatment of the Ideas as fully in accord with the Kabbalistic theory of *Sefirot*, and he calls attention to other congruences between the two systems.

Quite different is the attitude of Simone Luzzato, the Venetian rabbi who wrote at the beginning of the seventeenth century. In his treatise on the Venetian Jews he writes:

> The second part [of the Kabbalah] is more speculative and scientific; it deals with the dependence of the physical world on the spiritual world, the supersensory world being the paradigm. They assume all corporeal things are grounded in primary roots and seeds which are like inexhaustible wells from which springs the power of the divine *dynamis* directed toward our material world as if through channels and pipes. This is the function of the ten [*Sefirot*]. . . . These ten *Sefirot* are somewhat similar to the Ideas posited by Plato, but in my opinion the reasons that influenced the theory of the Kabbalists are different from those of Plato.[65]

According to Luzzato, Platonic thought addressed an epistemological problem: how to comprehend the changing world. The ideas afford stability and so ensure the possibility of knowledge. The Kabbalists were seeking to explain the transition from the complete spirituality of God to the corporeality of the world. The *Sefirot*, viewed as "the Ideas of the Kabbalists," are differentiated from one another by their functions and by their spirituality. Luzzato mentions the four worlds of the Kabbalists, each composed of ten *Sefirot,* which enable a gradual transition to the lower world. This cosmological role, widely assigned to the *Sefirot,* was emphasized by Yagel, who reinterprets the four worlds in Neoplatonic terms.

A contemporary of Luzzato, R. Abraham Cohen Herrera,[66] was deeply immersed in Neoplatonic thought and offered a speculative interpretation of the Lurianic Kabbalah according to Neoplatonic and scholastic principles. He proposes to understand the formative elements of the *"malbush"* or divine garment of the Kabbalah of R. Israel Sarug, by reading its Hebrew letters as pointing to Platonic Ideas. According to his special version of the Sarugian Kabbalah, the garment is not transcendent and does not precede the Primordial Man, *Adam Kadmon,* but is identical with him.[67] The Platonic Ideas refer to the elements that constitute the anthropomorphic archetype of all the worlds. R. Menasseh ben Israel, writing at the same time and also in Amsterdam, regards the Ideas as numbers and letters:

> Plato recognized that the world . . . was not produced by chance. . . . It was formed by wise understanding and intelligence. . . . So these plans of the universe, which pre-existed in the divine mind, are termed by him Ideas. . . . Now these ideas or plans . . . are the letters [of the divine language]. This is treated in various ways in the *Sefer Yezirah.* . . . R. Joseph ben Carnebol explaining in his *Sha'arei Zedek* . . . Nahmanides . . . in the *Sefer ha-Bitahon.* . . . R. Barachiel in his *Perakim.*[68]

Early Renaissance authors were reticent toward Plato, even when perceiving the affinity between the Kabbalah and the theory of ideas, or they attributed a Jewish teacher to him. But by the last third of the sixteenth century, Plato and his Renaissance followers like Pico, Ficino and Cornelius Agrippa of Nettesheim became part of the spiritual patrimony of Jewish thinkers who were ready to accept the Platonists' influence even though they recognized its clear independence of Judaism. Perhaps the caution evident in the earlier Kabbalists reflects concerns lest there be a reduction of the Jewish mystical tradition to a mere recapitulation of Platonic views. But the impassivity of the Ideas, even in their Neoplatonic metamorphoses, restrained a more positive reception—even as the Kabbalah matured and continued to integrate Platonic, Neoplatonic, and Neopythagorean thinking. The earlier Kabbalists were interested in the Platonic ideas at the level of the second *Sefirah* alone. But in the Renaissance the interest was more general, comparing the whole Sefirotic system to the realm of the Ideas. Renaissance Jews confronted an articulate Neoplatonic philosophy that could deeply affect the inner structure of Kabbalistic theosophy, and they absorbed, rejected, or responded critically in a fashion informed by awareness of that fact.

The most extreme expression of anti-Platonic feelings is found in the answer R. Yehudah Arieh of Modena, that is, Leone Modena, addressed to a Christian correspondent:

> E se Philone ha troppo Platonizato in questa et altra grave materia, per
> cio non e stato accettato da noi, ne mai sono stati tradotti in hebreo.[69]

One of the fiercest anti-Kabbalists, Modena says that the deep influence of Plato is the reason for the rejection of the theology of Philo by the Jews. His statement sums up the concern of Jewish theologians not to permit too great an influence to Greek philosophy. The same concern may help to explain why Kabbalists like Yagel and Herrera, who did absorb a deep influence from the Greeks, remained outside the mainstream of the Kabbalah. But Modena's anti-Kabbalistic attitude was stronger than his anti-Platonism. For he uses a text of pseudo-Dionysius as a counterforce to the Kabbalistic view of prayer.[70]


## III. Negative Theology and Kabbalah

Medieval Jewish thought produced two major types of negative theology: the philosophical, which has both Neoplatonic and Aristotelian expressions, and the Kabbalistic. The former was formulated in the two classics of medieval Jewish philosophy, the *Fons Vitae* and the *Guide of the Perplexed*. The negative theology of the philosophers was not completely novel but was influenced by Islamic philosophies, which in turn were influenced by Greek Neoplatonic sources. In the Kabbalah, the major realm described in negative terms is the *'Eyn Sof*, the source of the ten *Sefirot*. The affinity between the Kabbalistic views of the *'Eyn Sof* and the Neoplatonic theology was emphasized by Gershom Scholem, who understood some of its expressions in purely Neoplatonic terms.[71] He did not accept the view of some earlier scholars that the term *'Eyn Sof* originated as a translation from the Greek[72] but envisioned it as a semantic mutation of the adverbial phrase, *'ad 'eyn sof.*[73] Yet he still tended to present the concept as basically Neoplatonic in nature, finding nothing antagonistic to philosophical negative theology in the Kabbalistic understanding of the *Deus absconditus.* He saw clashes between the Biblical and Plotinian concepts of God, but was inclined to see them in terms of an opposition between philosophical and Scriptural modes of thought.

I would like to qualify Scholem's diagnosis by emphasizing some of the more positive conceptions of the Kabbalistic Infinite— the anthropomorphical rather than philosophical-theological concepts connected to the *'Eyn Sof.* I believe that Neoplatonic negative theology was presented by some Kabbalists as an exoteric theory, while an anthropomorphic theology of the *'Eyn Sof* was in their eyes more esoteric and thus closer to the truth.

In one of the texts of R. Azriel of Gerona's *Commentary on Sefer Yeẓirah* we learn of the possibility of contemplating the *'Eyn Sof:*

> Here he mentioned that all is from the *'Eyn Sof,* and although the entities (*devarim*) have a measure and size, and they are ten, that attribute which they possess is infinite (*Eyn lah sof*). For the natural (*ha-muṭbbaʿ*) emerges from the sensory (*murgash*) and the intellectual from the heights of the Hidden (*Rom ha-neʿelam*), and the Hidden is infinite. Thus even the natural and the sensory and the intellectual are infinite, and the attributes (*middot*) were made in such a manner as to allow contemplation through them of the *'Eyn Sof.*[74]

R. Azriel is one of the most important exponents of the early Neoplatonizing Kabbalah. But his reliance on the *via negativa* in some writings[75] does not preclude his assigning a material content to the concept of the Infinite. The gist of the above text is that infinitude is conceivable through the *Sefirot,* which actually preserve some of its infiniteness. Later in the same commentary R. Azriel applies the name 'Unique Lord,' *Adon Yaḥid* to the *'Eyn Sof,* a description far removed from purely negative theology,[76] and he refers to the *'Eyn Sof* as the *Dynamis* of the *Causa causarum* (*Koaḥ*

*'Illat ha-'illot*), another positive characterization of the Infinite.[77]

R. Azriel grounds the contemplative process in meditation upon the structure of the human body, which corresponds to the ten *Sefirot*: Contemplation of the revealed and manifest (*ha-galui*) leads to the unseen—"You must contemplate from the manifest to the Hidden."[78] The anthropomorphic starting point leads, strikingly, to the *Sefirot*. Is anthropomorphism relevant there too? The answer is not simple. The *middot*, that is, *Sefirot*, were created to aid the contemplation of the *'Eyn Sof*, just as the human body was made to enable us to contemplate the *Sefirot*. R. Azriel's colleague, R. Ezra of Gerona, states that emanation had a beginning, whereas the essences, the *havvayot*, are preexistent.[79] It is not clear whether these primordial essences are arranged in a human form, but the possibility cannot be neglected. A detailed analysis of the texts may clarify the situation. In any case, the influence of the Neoplatonic negative theology is far less important in the early Kabbalah than modern scholarship has supposed. Positive views of the Neoplatonic worlds and the theory of the letters and *Sefirot* as ideas are much more prominent, as we have seen.

Clearly in some late thirteenth-century Kabbalists there is an esoteric theosophy of the *'Eyn Sof*, reliant on an anthropomorphic structuring of ten entities that are supernal, static roots of the ten dynamic *Sefirot*, the *Deus revelatus*.[80] The static nature of these roots seems to counter the personalistic tendency of some Zoharic anthropomorphic discussions of the highest level of the divine world. The post-Zoharian Kabbalists sometimes call the static entities *Zahzahot, Zihzuhim*, or inner *Sefirot*.[81] Such a theology seems to represent an attempt to maintain the ancient Jewish notion of the *Shi'ur Komah*, the anthropomorphic body of the deity as spoken of in the Heikhalot literature, by projecting it into the deepest divine realm in Kabbalistic theosophy. Here we can hardly speak of a dominant influence of Neoplatonic negative theology. It is hard to say how central the anthropomorphic theosophy may have been, since it was treated as especially esoteric and has only recently been analyzed in scholarly studies. In time we may discover more instances of a "deeper" positive understanding of the *'Eyn Sof*, and the relationship of Kabbalistic theosophy to Neoplatonic negative theology may undergo some significant changes.

The anthropomorphic conception of the *'Eyn Sof* was surely influential in the *Zohar* and later on, especially in the works of R. David ben Yehudah he-Ḥasid, who wrote under the profound influence of this book. He located an anthropomorphic configuration in the bosom of the *'Eyn Sof*: ten *Zaḥzaḥot* which seem to found, for him or his sources, an esoteric interpretation of the *Shi'ur Komah*.[82] Yet immediately after the appearance of the *Zohar*, another type of Kabbalistic theosophy emerged, which strove to purify the highest realm of the divine from all anthropomorphic attributes. Using the term *Causa causarum*, *'Illat kol ha-'illot* in the case of the author of the *Tikkunei Zohar*, or *'Illat ha-'illot* alone in the case of R. Menaḥem Recanati, these Kabbalists employed explicitly negative attributes to reinterpret the theosophy of the *Zohar*.

After the expulsion from Spain, the concept of super-*Sefirot* within the *'Eyn Sof* was propagated by the exiles. A clear expression of this view is found in the commentary of R. Yehudah Ḥayyat on *Ma'arekhet ha-Elohut*. The latter work, an anonymous classic of the early fourteenth century contains one of the most explicit statements of negative theology in the Kabbalah, arguing that the *'Eyn Sof* is not mentioned in the Torah because there is no way even to hint at Him.[83] The commentator, an exponent of classical, post-Zoharic Spanish Kabbalah, uses the term *Ziḥzuḥim* to designate the super-*Sefirot* in the bosom of the *'Eyn Sof*.[84] The Italian Kabbalist R. Elḥanan Sagi-Nahor echoes this approach.[85] But in time this type of theosophy disappears from the Italian Kabbalah, probably eclipsed by the negative theology accepted by Italian Jews from medieval Neoplatonism and corroborated by the work of Renaissance Christian thinkers influenced by the translations of Marsilio Ficino.

We find an example of the elimination of a reference to the roots of the *Sefirot* in the *'Eyn Sof* in Yoḥanan Alemanno's summary of the stance of R. Yehudah Ḥayyat:

| Ḥayyat[86] | Alemanno[87] |
|---|---|
| Although you will find in the *Tikkunei Zohar* in several places that the name *Yud He Vav He, Yud Hi Vav Hi* refers to the *'Eyn Sof*, it is to be understood as | It is said in the *Zohar*[88] and in the *Sefer ha-Tikkunim* that the name *Yud He* is said of the *'Eyn Sof*. But He has no known name because if He had a known name |

explained above: these ten letters are the ten *zihuhim* hidden within Him, and they are the ten *Sefirot,* comprised in the name YHVH. But He has no known name. This is hinted at by Elijah, of blessed memory . . . that You have no known name, since you fill all the names, and You are the perfection of all of them, etc. The meaning of this is that if He had a name that can be known He would be limited to that name alone, and it would be impossible to take Him away from it, and He would emanate only to that name.

which designates His essence, He would operate only according to that name.

Here and elsewhere where he might have used Hayyat's view of the supernal *Sefirot, zihzuhim* as roots of the traditional *Sefirot* in the *'Eyn Sof,* Alemanno suppresses the words of his source. Study of the way Alemanno quotes Hayyat's Zoharic sources shows that the exclusion is not accidental. Moreover, the terms Alemanno uses to describe the First Cause or *Causa causarum* are plainly taken over from the *Liber de Causis* in its Hebrew translation.

The theosophy of the *Zahzahot* was likewise rejected by R. Moses Cordovero, who accepted only the view that there are three *Zahzahot* in the *'Eyn Sof,* which are not understood anthropomorphically. However, R. Isaac Luria was influenced by the doctrine of the ten supernal *Sefirot,* which in his system became the *Adam Kadmon,* placed above the *Sefirot.*[89] While it was not identical with the *'Eyn Sof,* it was called by that name, to point to the exalted status of the figure above all other things.

At the beginning of the seventeenth century, the negative theology disseminated in Renaissance translations and original writings made a deep impression on many Kabbalists. R. Abraham Yagel,[90] R. Menasseh ben Israel,[91], and R. Joseph del Medigo bear testimony to the depth of penetration of the Neoplatonic negative theology. Although pursuing discussions that began in the medieval Kabbalah and continued in the Renaissance,[92] the seventeenth-century authors owe much to the Christian and pagan sources, as they openly acknowledge.

The attenuation or even obliteration of that trend of theosophy which attributes anthropomorphic characteristics to the *'Eyn Sof* represents a retreat from the dynamic and mythical Kabbalah prevalent in the Spanish tradition and the cultivation of a much more philosophical theosophy consonant with the Christian Neoplatonism of the Renaissance. The shift is paralleled by a new willingness to interpret the *Sefirot* in Platonic terms. After reducing the mythical elements inherent in the dynamism of the *Sefirot*, there was no need to look for static roots beyond or behind them. The *via negativa* preoccupied Jewish authors in the first half of the seventeenth century much more than in previous periods, as is evident from the writings of Herrera, Menasseh ben Israel, and Joseph Shelomo of Kandia. There is evidence that R. Joseph Shelomo devoted a treatise to negative theology, which he planned to print. The printer of his *Novelot Hokhmah*, R. Shemuel ben Yehudah Leib Ashkenazi, noted in publishing the latter work:

> The Rabbi the author wrote a treatise to show that there is no name which reflects the essence of the *'Eyn Sof*, and I plan to print it, if God so decree.[93]

Unfortunately the plan was not carried out.

It seems that in the whole history of the Kabbalah negative theology never enjoyed the interest among Kabbalists that it had in the period when Renaissance Neoplatonism was already in decline, at the beginning of the seventeenth century. For some Italian Kabbalists, the more mythic the Kabbalah they encountered (as in various versions of Lurianic Kabbalah), the more they inclined to accentuate the mythic elements by imposing a philosophical significance upon the authentic Kabbalah of Safed. It was in Italy, the stronghold of the Neoplatonism of the Renaissance, that the Kabbalah underwent the most powerful impact of negative theology.

But negative theology found its way into Kabbalah from another source as well: Ismā'īlī theology. Following up on the assumption that God is wholly beyond the reach of the human mind, this Islamic sectarian school treated the "first creature" as the being to be addressed in worship. Any attempt to direct one's thought to the

Transcendent was regarded as heresy.[94]     God was described as beyond existence and non-existence.[95]  By the thirteenth century we find the theory of the "first creature" playing an important role in the religious life of the Kabbalah, alongside the view that God transcends both existence and non-existence.[96]  A reverberation of the negative theology implicated with the concept of the "first creature" is heard in the works of a Kabbalist who wrote in Spain before the expulsion and later in Jerusalem, R. Abraham ben Eliezer ha-Levi.  He writes that higher than the ten *Sefirot* there is an entity different from the First Cause, called "the first Simplicity," *Peshitut Rishon.*[97]  In other writings he calls it "the first creature" or three lights higher than the *Keter* and lower than the First Cause.  These, he says, are beyond the comprehension of anyone.  The assumption that anything below the level of the First Cause is incomprehensible seems to reflect the Ismāʿīlī emphasis upon negative theology.  The Kabbalist was apparently acquainted with concepts or fragments of the *Theology of Aristotle*, the medieval abridgement of Plotinus' *Enneads*.  For he describes Aristotle, in his "later" period as almost a Kabbalist, who received his doctrine from R. Simeon the Righteous.  According to this late Aristotle, the ancient philosophers believed in a deity who coexisted with an eternal world, but he himself, Aristotle the Kabbalist, knew that above that deity was a higher deity who is the source of the lower one.[98]  The lower deity, connected to the world through the act of emanation, would be the Ismāʿīlī "first creature," mediating between the First Cause and the *Sefirah* of *Keter*.

To sum up our findings: In the medieval Kabbalah the influence of the Neoplatonic theory of Ideas is easily traced, and the positive ideas of Neoplatonism recur in Renaissance Kabbalah.  But the influence of negative theology is marginal in medieval Kabbalistic texts.  It comes to the fore by the end of the fifteenth century and reaches its apogee in the seventeenth.  Neoplatonic reinterpretations of the Kabbalah, especially those of the early seventeenth century Kabbalists, mediated its penetration into European culture, through the translations of Knorr von Rosenroth, as Professor Popkin's paper illustrates.

## Notes

1. For the controversy, see Bernard Septimus, *Hispano-Jewish Culture in Transition* (Cambridge: Harvard University Press, 1982), 39 ff., 147 n. 1; Gershom Scholem, *Origins of the Kabbalah*, 393-414.
2. See my "Maimonides and the Kabbalah," in I. Twersky, ed., forthcoming.
3. Cf. Genesis Rabbah I 2 and my "The *Sefirot* above the *Sefirot*," *Tarbiz* 51 (1982): 265, n. 131 (Hebrew).
4. For the term, See Scholem, *Origins*, 281; Idel, "*Sefirot*," 240-49.
5. For this important early master, see Scholem, *Origins*, 248 ff.
6. See *Hilkhot Yesodei Torah* II 10.
7. *Sefer ha-Emunah ve-ha-Bitahon*, ch. 18, ed., C. B. Chavel, *Kitvei ha-Ramban* (Jerusalem: Mossad Ha-Rav Kook, 1964) 2.409; cf. Idel, "*Sefirot*," 265-67; cf. S. O. Heller-Wilensky, "Isaac ibn Latif— Philosopher or Kabbalist?" in A. Altmann, ed., *Jewish Medieval and Renaissance Studies* (Cambridge: Harvard University Press, 1967), 188-89, esp. n. 26.
8. Cf. Shlomo Pines, "Some Distinctive Metaphysical Conceptions in Themistius' Commentary on Book Lambda and their Place in the History of Philosophy," in J. Wiesner, ed., *Aristoteles Werk und Wirkung: Paul Moraux Gewidmet* (Berlin: De Gruyter, 1987), 177-204, esp. 196-200.
9. Cf. my "Maimonides and Kabbalah."
10. See Scholem, *Major Trends*, 116-17.
11. See my "*Sefirot*," 243, 280.
12. See Georges Vajda, *Recherches sur la philosophie et la Kabbale dans la pensée juive du moyen âge* (The Hague: Mouton, 1962), 33-113.
13. On the origins and evolution of this legend, see my "The Journey to Paradise," *Jerusalem Studies in Folklore* 2 (1982): 7-16 (Hebrew).
14. *Commentary on the Pentateuch* (Jerusalem, 1961 repr.) fol. 15a.
15. R. Shem Tov ben Shem Tov, *Sefer ha-Emunot* (Ferrara, 1556) fol. 27ab.
16. Cf. Meir Benaiahu, "A source of the Spanish Exiles in Portugal and their Exit to Saloniki after the Decree of 1496," *Sefunot* 11 (1971-78): 264 (Hebrew).
17. See Solomon Schechter, "Notes sur David Messer Leon," *REJ* 24 (1892): 122.
18. See my "The Magical and the Neoplatonic Interpretations of the Kabbalah in the Renaissance," in B. D. Cooperman, *Jewish Thought in the Sixteenth Century* (Cambridge: Harvard University Press, 1983), 216-42.

19. See Frances Yates, *Giordano Bruno and the Hermetic Tradition* (Chicago: University of Chicago Press, 1964), 1-116.

20. See Pines' "Medieval Doctrines in Renaissance Garb? Some Jewish and Arabic Sources of Leone Ebreo's Doctrines," in B. Cooperman, 390-91.

21. W. Melczer, "Platonisme et Aristotélianisme dans la pensée de Léon L'Hebreu," in *Platon et Aristote à la Renaissance* (Paris, 1976), 293-306.

22. See Pines' "Medieval Doctrines," and my "The Sources of the Circle Images in *Dialoghi d'Amore*," *Iyyun* 28 (1978): 156-66 (Hebrew).

23. See his "The Place of the *Dialoghi d'Amore* in the Contemporaneous Jewish Thought," in *Ficino and Renaissance Neoplatonism*, in University of Toronto Italian Studies 1 (1986): 69-86.

24. See my "Kabbalah and Philosophy in R. Isaac and Yehudah Abravanel," in M. Dorman and Z. Levy, eds., *The Philosophy of Leone Ebreo* (Tel Aviv: Ha-Kibbutz Ha-Meuchad, 1985), 79-86 (Hebrew).

25. See my "Magical," 224-29 and "Differing Conceptions of Kabbalah in the Early 17th Century," in I. Twersky and B. Septimus, eds., *Jewish Thought in the 17th Century* (Cambridge: Harvard University Press, 1987), 138-41, 155-57.

26. See my *Kabbalah: New Perspectives* (New Haven: Yale University Press, 1988), chs. 8-9; and "Reification of Language in Jewish Mysticism," in S. Katz, ed., *Mysticism and Language* (Oxford: Oxford University Press, 1991).

27. Cf. H. A. Wolfson, "Extradeical and Intradeical Interpretations of the Platonic Ideas," in *Religious Philosophy, A Group of Essays*, 27-68; W. Norris Clarke, "The Problem of Reality and Multiplicity of Divine Ideas in Christian Neoplatonism," in Dominic O'Meara, ed., *Neoplatonism and Christian Thought*, 109-27.

28. *Sefer ha-Emunah ve-ha-Bitahon*, 364.

29. I emphasize that the essences in the *Sefirah* of *Hokhmah* are not identical with the *Sefirot* in general, which for most Kabbalists are dynamic entities quite unlike the static Platonic ideas. As paradigms of all creatures, the essences are found only in *Hokhmah*, and the other *Sefirot* behave quite differently from Platonic ideas.

30. *Sefer ha-Emunah ve-ha-Bitahon*, loc. cit.

31. *Sefer ha-Emunah ve-ha-Bitahon*, 386. See Scholem, *Origins*, 429, pointing out the affinity of this peculiar view of the Active Intellect to Neoplatonism. The Kabbalistic discussion of the *'Ayn* as a symbol of the highest triad is reminiscent, as Professor John Dillon has kindly pointed out to me, of the view attributed by Proclus to Theodotus of Asine. Note the correspondence of the *spiritus asper* and the *Alef*.

See Proclus, *Commentaire sur le Timée*, tr., A.-J. Festugière (Paris, 1967) 3.318; Asi Farber, "On the Sources of Rabbi Moses de Leon's Early Kabbalistic System," in J. Dan and J. Hacker, eds., *Studies in Jewish Mysticism, Philosophy, and Ethical Literature, presented to Isaiah Tishby* (Jerusalem, 1986), 96, n. 65 (Hebrew). R. Isaac the Blind, following an even earlier tradition, interpreted *Eḥad*, One, similarly as suggesting the *Sefirot*: *Alef=Keter, Ḥet=Eight Sefirot*, and *Dalet=*the last *Sefirah*; see my "The *Sefirot*," 279-80.

32. See S. Pines, "La Longue recension de la théologie d'Aristote dans ses rapports avec la doctrine ismaelienne," *Revue des Études Islamiques* 22 (1954): 7-20.

33. *The Commentary on the Talmudic Aggadot*, ed, I. Tishby (Jerusalem: Magnes Press, 1945), 83.

34. *Commentary*, 820.

35. See Alexander Altmann, "Isaac Israeli's 'Chapter on the Elements' [MS Mantua]" *JJS* 7 (1956): 31-57.

36. See Scholem, *Origins*, 418, 436-39. The emergence of the Will as the highest divine manifestation in the works of these two Kabbalists and to a lesser degree in those of R. Asher ben David, the nephew of R. Isaac the Blind, preceded the similar development in the writings of R. Isaac ben Abraham ibn Latif, who seems to have been influenced both by the Neoplatonic sources and by the Ismāʿīliyya; see Heller-Wilensky.

37. See R. Azriel's *Shaʿar ha-Shoʾel* in Meir ibn Gabbai's *Derekh Emunah* (Berlin, 1850) fol. 3a. On the early Kabbalistic views of the spiritual worlds, see Scholem's important essay, "The Development of the Doctrine of the Worlds in the Early Kabbalists," *Tarbiz* 2 (1931): 415-42; 3 (1932): 33-66 (Hebrew). The source that influenced R. Azriel's view seems to echo the Neoplatonic terms *cosmos noetos* and *cosmos aisthetos* reflected in Azriel's use of *ʿOlam*. Thus Scholem may overstate the impact of the Gnostic *aion* as the basis of the Kabbalistic pleroma; 416-17. He inclined to minimize the influence of Neoplatonic sources on early Kabbalah as to this issue.

38. See his *Sefer Meshiv Devarim Nekhoḥim*, ed., G. Vajda (Jerusalem: Israel Academy of Sciences and Humanities, 1969), 78, 100-101.

39. See Israel Ta-Shema, "On the Commentary on the Aramaic Piyyutim from the Maḥzor Vitry," *Qiryat Sefer* 57 (1982): 707-08 (Hebrew).

40. *Commentary*, 82; for the ontic division of *Maḥashavah, Dibbur*, and *Maʿaseh*, 110, where also the origins of the *Sefirot* are located in the Divine Will; cf. Scholem, *Origins*, 438-39. At *Commentary* 108 the second *Sefirah* is called the "beginning of Speech."

41. Nahmanides on Genesis 12:6, ed., C. B. Chavel, 1.77; cf. Amos Funkenstein, "Nahmanides' Symbolical Reading of History," in Dan and Talmage, 136-37.
42. *Commentary on Exodus*, ed., Chavel, 179; cf. Funkenstein, 136.
43. See e.g., *Meshiv Devarim Nekhohim*, 78-79.
44. Funkenstein, 137-38.
45. See Job 28:20.
46. *Meshiv Devarim Nekhohim*, 150; cf. my "Reification." *Binah* is conceived by ben Sheshet as the "World of the letters."
47. *Sefer ha-Emunah ve-ha-Bitahon*, 387.
48. *Elements of Theology*, Prop. 176, ed. Dodds, 155.
49. See *Sefer Ha-Yihud*, ed., Hasidah, 18; cf. Scholem, *Origins*, 284.
50. There is even a theory that the writings of ben Sheshet are not full fledged Kabbalistic works and therefore do not disclose esoteric views. See J. Dan, *Jewish Mysticism and Jewish Ethics* (Seattle: University of Washington Press, 1986), 37.
51. Cf. my "Particularism and Universalism in Kabbalah: 1480-1650," forthcoming.
52. See Giuseppe Sermoneta, "Jehuda ben Moshe Daniel Romano, Traducteur de Saint Thomas," in *Hommage à Georges Vajda*, G. Nahon and C. Touati, eds., (Louvain: Peeters, 1980), 246. Romano's remark is brief and apparently not influential; it is not mentioned by later authors.
53. MS Paris BN 968, fol. 41r. For the context, see my "The Magical," 219. For the historical critique of the Kabbalah, cf. Leone Modena, discussed in my "Differing," 155-57.
54. *Ziyyur*. The Geronese Kabbalists addressed the content of the second *Sefirah*, but Abravanel envisions the whole Sefirotic realm as the content of the divine mind.
55. *The Answers of R. Isaac Abravanel to R. Sha'ul ha-Cohen* (Venice, 1574) fol. 12d. On the comparison of the third *Sefirah* to the Platonic deas, see Abravanel's *Mif'alot Elohim* (Lemberg, 1863) fol. 58d. Cf. R. David Messer Leon, who also posits the *Sefirot* as Ideas in the divine mind; see Hava Tirosh-Rothschild, "*Sefirot* as the Essence of God in the Writings of David Messer Leon," *AJS Review* 7-8 (1982-83): 413-25.
56. See my "Kabbalah and Philosophy," 77-79.
57. On this work of Abulafia, his quotation from the *Liber de Causis*, and its reverberations, see my "The Magical," 216-17, 220-23. Neoplatonic influences are more dominant in the theosophico-theurgical Kabbalah than in the ecstatical Kabbalah. But some Neoplatonic motifs came to the fore in the second stage of the

development of the latter school, in the works of R. Isaac of Acre and the anonymous *Sha'arei Zedek*. They are negligible in the writings of the founder, Abraham Abulafia, where the Aristotelian influence is regnant.

58. *Hesheq Shelomo*, MS Berlin 832, fol. 83ab.
59. See my "The Study Program of R. Yohanan Alemanno," *Tarbiz* 48 (1979): 325, 331-32, and nn. 55-56 (Hebrew).
60. MS Oxford 2234, fol. 159a.
61. MS New York, JTS Rabb. 1586, fol. 126b. This text was copied in the various versions of the *Commentary on the Ten Sefirot* written by R. Yehiel Nissim and his circle; see my "The Magical," 227 and n. 233.
62. *Minhat Qenaot*, ed., D. Kaufmann (Berlin, 1898), 84, cf. 49, 53. For the *Midrash Ne'elam*, see my "The Journey," 12-13.
63. MS Oxford 1304, fol. 10b. For the context, see my "The Magical," 224-26. Yagel's formulation is conspicuously influenced by Proclus as represented in the *Liber de Causis*.
64. Ch. 25. See my "Kabbalah, Platonism, and *Prisca Theologia*: The Case of R. Menasseh ben Israel," J. Kaplan et al., eds. *Menasseh ben Israel and his World* (Leiden: Brill, 1989), 86-87.
65. See François Secret, "Un texte malconnu de Simon Luzzato sur la Kabbale," *REJ* 118 (1959-60): 25.
66. See the discussion of his role in Professor Popkin's paper in this volume.
67. See Alexander Altmann, "Lurianic Kabbalah in a Platonic Key: Abraham Cohen Herrera's *Puerta del Cielo*," *HUCA* 53 (1982): 339-40.
68. *Conciliador*, tr., E. H. Lindo (London, 1842) 1.108-09.
69. See Cecil Roth, "Leone da Modena and the Christian Hebraists of his Age," *Jewish Studies in Memory of Israel Abrahams* (New York, 1027), 400. Cf. Henry More's similar stance in differentiating Kabbalah from Neoplatonism; see A. Coudert, "A Cambridge Platonist's Kabbalist Nightmare," *Journal of the History of Ideas* 35 (1978). Thanks to Prof. Richard Popkin for this reference.
70. See my "Differing," 176-78.
71. See especially his *Kabbalah* (Jerusalem, 1974), 88; *Origins*, 441, and the important essay "La Lutte entre le Dieu de Plotin et la Bible dans la Kabbale Ancienne," in *Le Nom de Dieu et les symboles de Dieu dans la mystique juive*, tr. M. Hayoun and G. Vajda (Paris: Le Cerf, 1983), 17-53.
72. See Christian Ginzburg, *The Kabbalah* (London, 1865), 105.
73. *Kabbalah*, 88; *Origins*, 265-71, 431-34.

74. *Commentary on Sefer Yezirah*, attributed in print to Naḥmanides, in C. B. Chavel, *Kitvei ha-Ramban*, 2.454. The four terms: 'natural,' 'sensory,' 'intellectual,' and 'hidden' recur in other writings of R. Azriel, but not in all of them; see 455. These writings may form a later layer in the literary activity of this Kabbalist, who could have become acquainted with this Neoplatonic sequence after completing his *Commentary on the Talmudic Aggadot* and *Commentary on the Daily Prayers*. Such a development may be related to the affinity of R. Azriel's thought to that of R. Ya'akov ben Sheshet. The issue deserves further study.

75. See his *Sha'ar ha-Sho'el*, fol. 2b.

76. *Commentary on Sefer Yezirah*, 455.

77. *On Sefer Yezirah*, 453.

78. *On Sefer Yezirah*, 453-54.

79. See my "The Sefirot," 241-44.

80. See my "The Image of Man above the *Sefirot*," *Daat* 4 (1980): 41-55, and "Kabbalistic Material from the School of R. David ben Yehudah he-Ḥasid," *Jerusalem Studies in Jewish Thought* 2 (1983): 170-93 (Hebrew), esp. 173; and "The Sefirot," passim.

81. See my "The Image," 41-43, 47; "Kabbalistic Material," 171-73, 179-81.

82. See "The Image," 44, 48, 53.

83. See Scholem, *Kabbalah*, 89.

84. *Minḥat Yehudah* (Mantua, 1556) fol. 13a, 18a, 44ab, 46a.

85. See Ephraim Gottlieb in J. Hacker, ed., *Studies in Kabbalistic Literature* (Tel Aviv: Tel Aviv University Press, 1976), 424-25, 463-68, 470 (Hebrew).

86. *Minḥat Yehudah*, fol. 44b.

87. MS Paris BN 849, fol. 125ab.

88. This is a mistake; the view presented is found only in the *Tikkunei Zohar*.

89. See "The Image," 48-50.

90. See David Ruderman, *Kabbalah, Magic and Science in the Cultural Universe of a Jewish Physician* (Cambridge: Harvard University Press, 1989), 147.

91. See Altmann, "Lurianic Kabbalah," 350.

92. The *Liber de Causis* was quoted by Alemanno, Abravanel, and Yagel on negative theology.

93. Basel, 1631, fol. 122b.

94. See Husayn F. al-Hamdani, "A Compendium of Ismā'īlī Esoterics," *Islamic Culture* 11 (1937): 212-13.

95. See Georges Vajda, *Juda ben Nissim ibn Malka, philosophe juif marocain* (Paris, 1954), 65. For the formula, "God is beyond existence and non-existence," see my "Franz Rosenszweig and the Kabbalah," in Paul Mendes-Flohr, ed., *The Philosophy of Franz Rosenszweig* (Hanover, N.H.: University Press of New England, 1988), 244, n. 24.

96. See Sarah Heller-Wilensky, "R. Isaac ibn Latif."

97. See *Masoret ha-Ḥokhmah*, published by Scholem in *Qiryat Sefer* 2 (1925/6): 129 (Hebrew).

98. *Ma'amar ha-Yiḥud* MS Jerusalem 8' 154, fol. 146ab; see my "Philosophy and Kabbalah," 80-81.

# Love and Intellect in Leone Ebreo: The Joys and Pains of Human Passion

## Reflections on his Critical Panpsychism and Theory of "Extraordinary Reason"[*]

### Hubert Dethier

Ordinary (practical) reason fluctuates between extremes, its goal being the preservation of life; extraordinary (contemplative) reason disregards the normal conventions of prudence and often leads to alienation and self-sacrifice. Comprising both disinterested love and the desire to "acquire" or "attain" the beloved, its ambivalence is personified in the figure of Sophia, the reluctant mistress of the *Dialogues*. The ordinary reasonableness of the day to day world is challenged here by the radical intransigence of a higher love, which bears with it a higher standard of reason. This philosophically exalted blend of love and desire is the source of Philo's paradoxical desire to both live and die.

* I am deeply indebted to Lenn Goodman for his critical reading of an earlier draft of this paper and for suggesting a number of pertinent revisions and improvements. The responsibility for any remaining shortcomings lies with the author. My thanks are also due to Mrs. Margaret Lee for her help in preparing the typescript.

## 1. The Achievement of Leone Ebreo

Leone Ebreo's achievement resides in his effort to present a syncretic philosophy elaborated in all aspects, from metaphysics to ethics, in a truly coherent and systematic manner. Philosophy in his view seeks to give the soul an awareness of its higher destiny, an assurance of its ultimate union with God. This "*pia philosophia*" affirms the identity of rational and religious truth, the harmony of the logical-metaphysical order with the testimony of Revelation. The focus of this paper is Leone Ebreo's encounter with the theories of Avicenna and Averroes on the interactions of human and divine intelligence. For here he recaptured the profound inner sense of Platonic idealism, and, through his rediscovery of Plato and Plotinus, brought to life a pantheistic aspect of the thinking of Averroes, discovering an interdependence of God and man within a higher unity. Of course not just any kind of unification of the cosmos is tantamount to pantheism. It is the particular strategy that Ebreo adopts in behalf of his project of unifying the cosmos that will justify our characterization of his philosophy as pantheistic.

In his introduction to the Italian *editio princeps* of the *Dialoghi*, Carl Gebhardt characterizes the unitive perspective that attracted Leone Ebreo as follows: In itself, the Intellect—potential as well as actual—is of no specific sort, but is identical with the totality of things, which are here potential, there actual. In its actuality, however, the intellect comprises all grades of Being in perfect unity and simplicity.[1]  From this Neoplatonic thesis, Leone draws an inference long latent in Averroism and one which has often led to his rejection as a heretic: He identifies the *intelletto attuale* (actual intellect) with the Deity and thus reaches a Pantheism or, more precisely, a Panlogism. For he had already identified the Intellect with the totality of things: "The idea of the world does not really exist in the divine understanding, but is the divine understanding and the divine spirit itself. For the idea of the world is the highest wisdom, through which the world was made. And the divine wisdom is the Word" (III, 121a). Although the Word here still appears to differ somewhat from God, Leone's reading of Logos as Nous urges complete identification of God with His wisdom. Gebhardt cites *Dialoghi*, III, 122b-123a: The first Intellect in Aristotle's sequence of disembodied Intelligences, is one and the same with the highest God and in no way different, except verbally. The essence of the Divine is nothing other than the highest wisdom and intelligence. As the purest and simplest Unity, God/Intellect produces the universe with all its parts, which are ordered into a whole; and, in producing it, He knows the whole and all its parts, and the parts of its parts in a supremely simple act of knowing. Knowing Himself, as the highest wisdom, on which everything depends as image and likeness, He is, while remaining one in Himself, the knower, the known, the knowing and the wisdom—the one who understands, the act of understanding, and the thing understood. This is the most perfect knowledge of the whole universe and of all created things, far superior, far more perfect and far more definite than knowledge drawn from things. For that knowledge is caused by the things known and so is divided, manifold and imperfect. But this knowledge is the ultimate cause of all things and so is free of the deficiencies of mere effects. The unity and simplicity of the Intellect allows infinite and supremely perfect knowledge of the whole universe.

The pantheism of the Vedanta argues that since God is All and One, what is many must be illusory. The pantheism and near pantheism characteristic of the European Middle Ages evolved, by contrast, from the view that because God alone truly is, all that is must in some sense be God. The ancestry of this view is Platonic or Neoplatonic, relying on the notion of true being. It would be misleading to call Neoplatonism itself pantheistic, although it conceives the material world as an emanation of the Divine. For the fallen and radically imperfect character of this world is always emphasized. Yet the translation of Neoplatonic themes of emanation into Christian terms by John Scotus Eriugena (ca. 810 - ca. 877) led to condemnation of his work as heretical precisely because of its apparent break with monotheism. Eriugena may not seem to be completely pantheistic, in that he does not treat every aspect of nature as being part of the divine in the same way and to the same degree. But by this criterion no thinker could ever be judged a pantheist! In every medieval case after Eriugena, the imputation of pantheism is at best inconclusive. It is only since the sixteenth century that genuine pantheism has become a familiar European phenomenon. Yet we shall argue that Ebreo resorts to a kind of pantheism, that is, the identification of God and nature, in order to ensure God's access to nature as Knower and as Creator. A prototype of this approach is clearly present in Eriugena.

According to Eriugena, the whole, "natura," consists of four species of being:

> what creates and is not created
> what is created and creates
> what is created and does not create
> what is not created and does not create.

The first is God as Creator; the last, God as that to which all created beings return. The second and third comprise the created universe, which is passing from God in His initial form to God in His final form. Eriugena states that each class of beings belongs to a different phase in a historical flow, but he also views this expression as a misleading, if necessary, figure of speech. "Natura" is eternal; the whole process is eternally recurrent; and everything is a theophany, a manifestation of God.

## 2. Resistance to the temptations of pantheism

Suzanne Damiens[2] argues that Leone Ebreo resisted the temptation of pantheism inasmuch as he preserved the relative independence of created beings. Thus the work of salvation, which is open to the most intelligent creatures, acquires a sense of personal conquest or achievement, and one can conceive God in more personal terms than in, say, Spinoza. God's love will not be strictly necessary, but will represent "a grace and benevolence more in keeping with the scriptural images of God as father and king." Further, what motivates creatures for Ebreo is final causes, which stimulate their desires and lead them to their ultimate perfection. This view is hardly in keeping with a necessitarian pantheism. Yet there is a pantheistic tendency in Abarbanel which recalls and in some ways exceeds the pantheism of the Stoics! For even Marcus Aurelius, when he addressed the Universe as a deity, did not simply address all that is, but rather the ordering principle (*hegemonikon*) that informs all that is.

The pantheism of the Stoics, like that of Eriugena or Bruno, is founded on the view that the universe must be a single, all-inclusive system, if it is to be intelligible. Thus their pantheism is derived from their ideal of explanation. Leone Ebreo similarly derives his metaphysical unity from purely intellectual premises:

1. Every being, especially every intelligent being, is united and unites itself with the world in such a way that it is in harmony with all other creatures.[3] Thus the world forms a single, harmonious system, reflecting the harmony of the intellectual world.

2. Thus, the perceptible world is emblematic of the intelligible world. This correspondence is fraught with pantheistic significance. Causally, the intelligible world is the unity that underlies the observable unity of nature. But from an experiential point of view the phenomenal unceasingly bears witness to its divine source. Since the phenomenal and the intelligible are counterparts, "Natura" is eternal, the whole process is eternally present, and everything, as in Eriugena, is a theophany.

3. Ebreo moves away from Stoic materialism, for instance when he objects to the notion of harmony as a "matter of dimension" and states that it is "formal grace." But he does not give a purely Platonic account (III 4). Rather he offers an almost Baconian view of the perceptible, remarkably expressed in the language of Platonism: Physical beauty is a mere shadow or image of the intellectual "splendor" of the underlying Forms or Ideas. But such shadows are necessary, since Ideas are first known as images of sensible objects, just as the concept in the mind of an artist is known through the work of art.

4. If Ideas are the original patterns of all created things, do they not, perforce, share the enormous diversity and even, to some extent, the multiplicity of these things? Leone answers this objection by recalling two Plotinian premises:
   a. an effect is always inferior to its cause, and
   b. corporeal substance is caused by intellectual matter.

So, Leone returns to the idea of the universe as an organic whole, its many parts unified in a single body. In the mind of the divine artist the multitude and diversity of his creation is "pure unity and true identity." The unity-in-multiplicity of Ideas is appropriate to their intermediate position between the artist and his work. Reliance on the Plotinian notion of the unity of the Ideas as thoughts of the divine is what makes Ebreo a pantheist. For such a view intentionally blurs the distinction between the One and the many.

For Ebreo's relation to Stoic materialism, Dialogue Two is of great importance. It expands the discussion to cosmological scope by showing that love is a principle that governs the entire created universe: the world below the heavens, the heavens themselves, and the disembodied intellects or angels. In the crucial final section Ebreo shows how love is the force, or principle of interaction and unification connecting these three levels. Such unity or love between higher and lower is imitated in lower beings as well, proving that without love the universe as a whole and all the creatures in it would not exist.

The closing section of Dialogue Two discusses love among the heavenly intelligences. Here Leone addresses what is perhaps the critical problem of his entire system: How does one explain the love of a superior for an inferior? Why would the intelligences care to move the lower spheres; why would a perfect God love a sinful world? Leone explains that a generous love is better than a selfish love. A father loves his son in order to improve him, not for any personal benefit. Moreover, a defect in creation implies a defect in the Creator. The immediate inference would be that God loves and blesses His creation for the sake of His own perfection, which does not contradict His loving it for its own sake. But the further implication is that human sin may adversely affect God himself. Leone frequently returns to the view that God himself depends on man's righteousness, a notion common to many Kabbalistic writers and often based on the saying that the Just Man is the foundation of the universe (Proverbs 10:25).[4] Not wanting to distress religious sensibility by the boldness of this concept, Leone prefers to emphasize the positive side of the argument: that the mutual love between superior and inferior leads to their union, which is "the principal end of the highest Maker and Sovereign God in the production of a world of ordered diversity and unified plurality."

After a brief discussion of the love of the intelligences for God, the author elaborates on his theme of the universe as a single organism:

> The entire universe is like an individual or person, and each of
> these corporeal and spiritual or eternal and corruptible things is a
> member or part of this great individual, the whole and each of his
> parts having been produced by God for the common end of the whole,
> together with an end proper to each of its parts. . . . The end of the
> whole is the unity and perfection of the entire universe . . . and the
> end of each of the parts is not only that it be perfect in itself but that
> it may thereby contribute to the perfection of the whole; and this
> universal end is the prime intention of the Deity.[5]

The argument, also found in Bernard Silvestris' *De universitate
mundi* or *Cosmographia* (circa 1143),[6] seeks in part to legitimize a
compromising of the intellect's crucial contemplative activity. For
the proper act of the Intellect is to know itself and thus all things
within itself, as the divine essence shines within its clear vision like
the sun in a mirror. But Intellect must also consent to "move a
material heavenly body, an act extrinsic to its own true essence."[7]
A corollary for the human case is the recognition that the joys of
contemplation may best be enjoyed after death.

It is love that imparts the unity at each level and thus explains
the existence and active functioning of each thing in the universe and
each level of the celestial hierarchy: Just as God is united with His
creation through love, the angels join with the celestial bodies, the
world soul with the sphere of generation, and the intellectual soul
with the human body. The poles of these syzygies are familiar:
upper and lower, spiritual and physical, active and passive, light and
darkness—and, especially meaningful in a discourse on love, male
and female. We are now prepared for Ebreo's broaching of the
Kabbalistic insight that "all creation is female with respect to God the
Creator" and for the next Dialogue, which will elaborate on the
mystic theme of the cosmic union of God with His creation.[8]

## 3. Noesis

Leone maintains that only the intellect in man is eternal and
capable of approaching the Divine. He discerns five levels of
intellect, each of which reflects the divine beauty according to its
own nature or capacity: (1) human intellect *in potentia*, (2) human

intellect *in actu,* (3) human intellect coupling or in "conjunction" (cf. Ibn Bājjah) with pure or angelic intellect, (4) angelic, and (5) divine intelligence. Man's quest is for union with the Active Intellect. The Philosophers regard it as the lowest of the angelic intellects, but true believers identify it with God Himself.[9]  The two views are complementary rather than contradictory according to Leone. The first describes the limits of man's natural reason, but the second describes the glory conferred by divine grace, the angelic vision of God.

Great difficulties are involved in the notion of an Active Intellect separated from the minds it actualizes and able to actualize them only through such human faculties as memory, imagination and abstraction. But Leone succeeds in reconciling the transcendence of the Active Intellect with its action upon the individual intellects of angels and men. His detailed commentary on the functioning of "*noein*" places him among the Neoplatonic commentators of Aristotle's *De anima* and with Alexander of Aphrodisias' *On Intellect*.[10]  Intellection, in its imperfect, human form, cannot be explained without recourse to that which is absolutely perfect. The transcendent intellect is what the human mind thinks, because that intelligence both thinks and creates the human mind. But even the distinction between the two is misleading. For in the intelligence in the act of thinking, the object of thought and the act itself are one. The words are Aristotle's in the *De Anima* (III 5). But Leone's Neoplatonic idealism carries their implications far beyond what Aristotle envisioned when he enunciated them as a psychological and epistemological insight.

Ebreo cleaves to the Neoplatonic tradition in holding that forms are the determinants of nature and thus that genera are conceptually and ontologically *richer* than species. That his inspiration is from Plato and Plotinus is evident in the role he ascribes to light, both literally and symbolically. For physical light symbolizes the operation of the Active Intellect which makes us understand and allows us to become what we understand. This higher light makes us intelligent beings in the "exercise of our essence." The idea of the good is the sun of the intelligible world. It accounts for the harmonious organization of the universe as the ontological and epistemological principle of the Ideas, ordering all by logic and finality. The highest genera of Being emerge from the Idea of the

One or the Good, whose truth does not require conformity to any other object. For that truth is not *secundum rem*. Rather, as Plotinus would say, "Intellect provides it (the soul) with the forming principles, as in the souls of artists the forming principles for their activities come from their arts."[11] The same Neoplatonic position had been held by Maimonides.[12] As Plotinus himself explains: "Intellect therefore really thinks the real beings, not as if they were somewhere else: for they are neither before it nor after it; but it is like the primary lawgiver, or rather is itself the law of being. So the statements are correct that 'thinking and being are the same thing' and 'knowledge of immaterial things is the same as its object' and 'I searched myself' (as one of the real beings); so also are 'recollections,' for no one of the real beings is outside, or in place, but they remain always in themselves and undergo no alteration or destruction: that is why they are truly real."[13] In the same vein, Leone remarks that in a single act of intellection, if it is sufficiently complete, knowledge of all things can be comprised (*Dialoghi* I 41).

Although God is perfectly one and simple, a mysterious multiplication occurs within Him. Just as Eve is said to have sprung from the body of Adam, the original active entity, God's beauty or simply essence, produces a feminine entity. Thus we can distinguish: (1) God's beloved, beauty or goodness, (2) His wisdom or intellect, the active lover, (3) the love that arises between the two. Since the beloved is always superior, Leone concludes that God the beloved is superior to God as lover, contradicting the Christian view that Father and Son are equal. Yet, since God is pure act, beloved, lover and love are identical in Him—an interesting extension of the traditional Aristotelian notion of the identity of knower, known and knowledge in the act of knowing.[14]

Beyond his original, intrinsic love, God also loves extrinsically. For, in loving himself, God also desires to reproduce his beauty. Thus God has two loves: (1) the first towards himself, (2) the second towards his images or creatures. The crucial role is played here by the divine Intellect, which, in addition to loving God in perfect contemplation, also contains all the Ideas or patterns of creation. The emanative process, as described here differs slightly from Bernard Silvestris' description in *De universitate mundi*. In the *Dialoghi*, the Intellect is female in its love toward God, but active or male in its love towards creatures. The original dialectic of love is repeated on this lower level: The divine Intellect contemplates itself as well as God, and from this contemplation a female entity is produced, again on the pattern of Eve from Adam. This new female element is chaos or Prime Matter. These two, Intellect and Chaos, are conceived as male and female, Prime Form and Prime Matter, the original parents of creation. From their mutual love emerges all generation.

### 4. Leone Ebreo and Spinoza

Leone's description of the intellectual love of God and his differentiation of five levels of intellect, each of which reflects the divine beauty according to its own nature or capacity (III, third question) leads us to inquire after connections between Spinoza's conception of intellectual love of God and Leone's related Neoplatonic conception. In both philosophers the link between man and God is intellectual, critically dependent on knowledge. Yet in Leone Ebreo awareness of a lack is central. In Spinoza the intellectual love of God involves a recognition of necessity, not of the order of causes outside us, but of the sequence of causes affecting us. To attain true love, we must know ourselves and the affections of our soul insofar as these follow from the necessity of the eternal essence of God. But in both philosophers attainment of the love of God involves knowing our own essence in God and the essence of all things. It is by knowing the immensity of God that we can love Him, actualizing our essence as a part of the infinite essence of God.

For both philosophers the intellectual love of the soul for God is the very love by which God loves himself. In Spinoza this is because the human soul, insofar as it is the idea of the body under the form of eternity, i.e., insofar as it has knowledge of the second and third kinds, forms a part of the Idea of God. It "understands in God, and does so through the very intelligence of God." It is therefore the very joy of God, apprehending the plenitude of his being in the logical sequence of his infinite modes:

> it is apparent that our mind, in so far as it understands, is an eternal mode of thinking, which is determined by another eternal mode of thinking, and this again by another, and so on to infinity: so that

together they all constitute the eternal and infinite intellect of God. (*Ethics* V, Prop. 40)

The joy of the soul taken up in God is a finite mode of the joy of God and is taken up for ever, the part identifying itself with the whole. Thus the famous corollary of Proposition 36 in Part V of the *Ethics*:

> Hence it follows that God, in so far as he loves himself, loves men, and consequently that the love of God for men and the mind's intellectual love towards God are one and the same thing.

Here we find under another guise the famous circle of Leone Ebreo: The arc of "reductive" loves, that turn back to God, can exist only by virtue of the original arc of "productive" loves.

For Spinoza, however, the unitive knowledge of the soul yearning towards God is not knowledge of a lack that commands aspiration toward sovereign perfection. Rather our upward reaching only expresses in duration what we are in fact throughout eternity. For we are always in God and through God. Duration for Spinoza is only an appearance. So the intellectual love of God is not a kind of progress but an inner nature constituted for all eternity. It is for us to enter it, or rather find it. But it is a kind of intellectual grace that cannot be withheld.

In both philosophies, there is a way for man to achieve beatitude, and this is above all through the transformation of knowledge. To conceive this achievement as a kind of personal adventure is far more difficult in Spinoza than it is in Leone Ebreo, because Spinoza holds time to be only an appearance; and an individual personality, merely a transitory mode. This contrast may seem a bit unfair to Spinoza, because it presses his monism too hard, ignoring his seriousness about the drama of the moral life and equally ignoring, for example, the opening passage of *De Intellectus Emendatione*. Nevertheless Suzanne Damiens argues that in the framework of Spinoza's intellectualism the reactions of a will that would respond to the circumstances of an individual destiny so as to achieve self-mastery, while unceasingly challenged by the solicitations of an animal nature, are hardly conceivable. The source of our salvation in Spinoza is the act of understanding in a certain way, a task of pure intellection, which detaches us from an inadequate apprehension of the actuality of things and ourselves and brings us at once the experience of eternity:

> We conceive things as actual in two ways: either insofar as we conceive them to exist in relation to a certain time and place, or insofar as we conceive them to be contained in God and to follow from the necessity of divine nature. But the things we conceive in this second way as true or real we conceive under a certain aspect of eternity, and to that extent their ideas involve the eternal and infinite essence of God, as we showed in Prop. 45, Part II.[15]

It is from this that Spinoza goes on to argue: "Insofar as the human mind knows itself and its body under the aspect of eternity, it necessarily has knowledge of God, and knows that it exists in God and is conceived through God" (*Ethics,* V, Prop. 30).

It is only through the realization of our intellectual capacity to see things in God that we experience eternity. So everything seems to happen as though, on the level of the intellection of the second and third kinds, a radical change takes place in man. We suddenly become independent of the sensory. The third kind of knowledge takes over, dependent on the mind as its formal cause insofar as the mind is eternal (*Ethics* V, Prop. 31). The progress of the soul towards beatitude does not find its true cause in the effort itself from which it seems to result or in the desire to attain a greater perfection or power, since in the long run this effort expresses only what we are throughout eternity, in God and through God. It is for this reason that Spinoza can affirm: "Blessedness is not the reward of virtue, but virtue itself; nor do we enjoy it because we restrain our lusts; on the contrary, because we enjoy it, we are able to restrain our lusts."[16] In Spinoza, as Victor Delbos remarks, it is always the knowledge of our rational union with God that is the means of salvation, "and not the pretension of our will to exceed what we are by relying on the transitory modalities of our present life."[17]

It is easier in the perspective of a creationism like Leone's to account for the love that moves us from awareness of our imperfection to the appeal of an ideal that arouses us. Here we dramatically envisage real progress toward beatitude. Yet while progress in time cannot define ultimate felicity, Spinoza does see temporal duration as a means to the achievement of happiness. It seems he arrives at this possibility in two ways: (1) through the notion of the anteriority of an intelligible nature,[18] (2) through conferring an ontological status upon the tendency (*conatus*) to be and to persist in being, the desire for power which truly manifests itself only in the realization of our intellectual nature, and yet which is the common principle of all life, whether in those who are not wise men or in those who are wise and have found the intellectual way of living in God. The first of the two alternatives privileges the attribute of thought over that of extension; the second discloses the common basis of the affections which are passions and those which are no longer passions but actions, because they are caused in man by the rational sequence of his ideas. It is perhaps not too brash to consider that it was the reading of the *Dialogues of Love* that enabled Spinoza to develop his conception of the dialectic of the salvation of man.

Spinoza is akin to Leone and through him to Neoplatonism in his mistrust of Aristotelian abstraction. The universal idea drawn from experience of the multiplicity of things is not the purest reality. The generic representation of the secant is not the essence of the secant, for this depends on the relation of the secant to the circle. The essence of the tangent is not all the common characteristics of all tangents but the definition of the tangent as limit of the secant. The essence of man is not the general idea drawn from the individuals met in experience; rather it is determined in the relation of the individual mode to God. In Spinoza, as Léon Brunschvig has clearly shown, reality is totality, envisaged not as a whole depending on its parts but as a unity that bears the reason for its existence within itself.[19] This totality is the ultimate source of determination in all that is. As Spinoza makes clear, a being does not exist by virtue of its limit, which is only an extrinsic definition, but through its inner principle, which gives it being and the force to persevere in its being.[20] Thus: "Every idea of every body or individual thing actually existing necessarily involves the eternal and infinite essence of God."[21] Here in Spinoza's distinctive application of Neoplatonism we find a clear parallel with the thought of Ebreo. The point that needs to be emphasized is that it is from the supreme intelligible that the finite modes of infinite substance derive their determination.

## 5. The intellectual love of God in Leone Ebreo

In the Neoplatonic scheme of Leone Ebreo, the One, in its infinite energy, sends forth a radiation that brings forth the second substance, the Intelligence. This in turn brings forth another, lesser being, the Soul. The Soul, unlike the Intellect, is capable of moving towards things other than itself. It too can contemplate itself; and, through the intermediacy of the Intelligence, it can recognize the light of the One. But when it produces a reflection of itself, the outcome is a still lower being, an animated body. In producing it, Soul acquires the desire and the power to incline towards it and provide for its sustenance. As a result Soul diverges from Intelligence.

Leone takes up the Neoplatonic formula: 'The soul is formed from the same and the other.' Its movement towards the intelligible is invisible. But its other movement is visible; it is the motive force of the physical. The human soul and the world soul are a mixture of spiritual intelligence and bodily change. Both are needed to animate body (III 179). Its movement, now towards the intelligible essences, now towards corporeal things, reveals the figure of the circle.

Following Plotinus,[22] Leone compares the intellect to the sun and the soul to the moon, the intermediary between the sun and the earth. The celestial comparisons that seem to fascinate him fit the taste of the time. They are found as well in Marsilio Ficino and Pico della Mirandola and recur often in the iconography of the Renaissance, in stained-glass windows, painting and sculpture.[23] Leone represents all the movements of the soul in terms of the relations of the moon to the sun and earth. The moon sometimes turns a lit-up face to the sun and darkness to the earth. Its light is borrowed. The soul similarly reflects the clarity of the intellect, and is now full of the light of the intellect, now deprived of it, but most often, a mixture of intellectual radiance and corporeal darkness. We shall not examine in detail Leone's comparison of the phases of the moon to the movements of the soul. But two examples should be given: When the soul is wholly preoccupied with matter and oblivious to contemplation, it is like the full moon, full of light for us earthdwellers, but full of darkness towards heaven. At the eclipse of the moon, the face of the moon, darkened by the interposition of the earth between moon and sun, corresponds to the loss of consciousness of the soul. This occurs when sensuality places itself between the intellect and our soul. The soul loses all the light it receives from the intellect, not only in its superior part, but also in its inferior, active and corporeal part. It becomes comparable to the soul of wild beasts and brutes (III 194). It is no longer truly human.

Even in a solar eclipse the sun is never deprived of its light, as the moon can be; when the soul receives the light in its intellectual part only, and its lower part is wholly deprived of light, the body loses its being: "This is the happy death caused by the coupling of the soul with the Intellect, which our blessed ancestors Moses and Aaron tasted, as well as those of whom the Holy Scriptures speak saying that they died through the mouth of God by the kiss of God."[24]

Since Soul receives the light of Intellect, it too radiates and produces a reflection inferior to itself, the body it animates. If it inclines too far towards the body, soul can break away from its moorings and lose itself. But if it turns completely inward and towards its principle, it will reject the care of its body and endanger its survival. We find the source of Leone's analogy in Plotinus:

> The First, then, should be compared to light, the next (Nous), to the sun, and the third (Psyche), to the celestial body of the moon, which gets its light from the sun. For Soul has intellect as an external addition which colors it when it is intellectual, but Intellect has it in itself as its own, and is not only light but that which is enlightened in its own being; and that which gives it light is nothing else but a simple light giving Intellect the power to be what it is.[25]

Leone has told us that the soul can turn in two different directions. How does it choose which way to turn? Here we confront the question of love. The cause of the changes of the moon lies in the local movement of the moon. But the ground for all the changes of the soul resides in the love inherent in it. Leone discerns a double aspiration of the soul. As an effect of the divine intellect it seeks the Beautiful beyond the sensible, and when it encounters intellectual beauty, it actively desires it: "It falls in love with this sovereign intellectual beauty, its higher source, as an imperfect woman falls in love with the man who makes her perfect." But the soul is also seized "by another love, linking the soul to the corporeal world beneath it, like the love of the male for the female, seeking to make the corporeal world perfect, by imprinting on it the beauty which it derives from the Intellect by way of the first love."[26] This conception of twofold love echoes Plato's references in the *Symposium* to the heavenly and vulgar Aphrodite. By combining the two aspects of love, Leone seeks to protect what is unique in beauty, which is a reflection of what is above, and what is unique in that other love, which, even when it is led astray into carnal union, still finds a means to attain Form, drawn from above, to imprint it on matter:

> just as the soul, made great by the beauty of the intellect, desires to engender it [this beauty] in the corporeal world and either gathers the seed of this same beauty to make it germinate in the body or, like an artisan, gathers specimens of intellectual beauty to sculpt them from life, in bodies.[27]

Since the love of the soul is twofold, it is sometimes more inclined toward intellectual beauty, to the point of leaving the body in "the happy death of coupling." But in other cases the opposite occurs. The soul is more inclined towards the body and loses sight of the higher beauty. Most often, however, reason comes to a compromise with sensuality, inclining perhaps towards the body or perhaps towards the intellect, as in the waxing and waning of the moon. Here one can differentiate the man who is merely chaste from the man who is temperate. Chastity is the lesser virtue. In temperance, the activity of the intellect can be discerned more clearly. Conversely, unchastity is a less serious fault than intemperance. Each soul must use its potentialities to work out what balance it will strike between the intellectual and the sensuous.

In such a scheme, does destiny depend on the external forces that bestow our faculties and sensibilities, or on ourselves? Does Leone leave room for individual freedom? All depends on his conception of God's love for his creatures. This love is not the recognition of a lack. Rather God's immense perfection makes Him love and desire his creatures, allowing them to reach the highest degree of their own perfection, and, once they possess it, to enjoy it eternally (III 215). Divine love is the principle that explains both creation and the sustenance of creation. Without love no father would beget or provide for the preservation of his offspring. Similarly, no master would tirelessly impart science and wisdom to his pupil, and no friend would act to make another happy.

Man must pass through two stages to gain happiness: (a) the attainment of virtue and the moral life, and (b) the work of the understanding, dianoetic activity, which finds its highest fulfillment in contemplation. The first stage demands an ascesis which Leone depicts as a sequence like the phases of the moon. Only the temperate soul lives well. But virtue cannot be defined through temperance alone. Like Aristotle, Leone characterizes virtue as the exercise of a faculty or disposition appropriate to every situation, and as a means towards achieving the universal goal of felicity.

Every being belongs to a whole, and the perfection of the whole is the highest good (Dialogue Two, 162). But in realizing its proper perfection, every being serves the perfection of the whole:

> It follows that the more the whole and the parts are perfect and happy, the more correctly and completely will they follow the duties to which they are subjected by the divine artisan. The ultimate end for all is the unified perfection of the whole universe, designed by the divine architect. So the aim of each part is not only the perfection of that part in itself, but that it thereby directly contribute to the perfection of the whole, which is the universal goal, the prime intent of the Deity. It is for this common goal, rather than solely for its own sake that each part was made, destined and dedicated. . . . So a part failing in such service, in acts pertaining to the perfection of the universe, would be more at fault and would become more unhappy than if it had failed in its own act.[28]

Virtue so understood has two main effects:

1. It contributes to the continued creation of the universe and to the order of the world as a whole:

> Since our soul is only spiritual and intellectual, nothing occurring in the corporeal, ephemeral and corruptible state could benefit it more than its own pure intellectual act already does; but it applies to our body only for the love and service of the Sovereign Creator of the world, drawing life and knowledge and the divine light of the higher eternal world towards the inferior corruptible, lest this lower part of

the world be deprived of divine grace and eternal life, and so that this great animal shall have no part which is not alive and intelligent like the whole.[29]

2.    Secondly, virtue maintains the existence of love in the world in both senses: both the yearning toward higher perfection and the impetus to give light to the lesser. The soul which is inclined towards the intellect that can perfect it has no less love for the body which it desires to perfect. Twofold virtue in the service of the whole sustains love in the world and thus strengthens the unity of the world:

> For the more being there is in the world and the things in it, the more united and joined together are the world and all its members, like the limbs of an individual. Otherwise the disharmony would cause its total perdition. And just as nothing unites the universe with all its various realities, except love, it follows that this love is the cause of the being of the world and all its realities.[30]

Just as the soul must gain the ethical virtues to acquire happiness, it must make itself beautiful by the exercise of its intellectual faculties to open up the dianoetic way. There are two intellectual faculties: *dianoia*, which uses rational discourse to reach clear knowledge of the forms and their interrelations, and intellection:

> The first "aspect" of the soul towards the Intellect is intellectual reason, with which it discourses by way of a universal and spiritual knowledge which abstracts the forms and intellectual essences from particular sensory bodies, constantly converting the corporeal world into the intellectual. The second "aspect," which is turned towards the body, is sense perception, particular knowledge of corporeal things.[31]

For each of these two ways of knowing a different form of love is engendered. The love of sensible things alienates the soul, by subjecting it to multiplicity. Only spiritual love leads man to happiness. The universal, spiritual knowledge of *dianoia* is assimilated to the world soul. For "all abstract forms in the unitive order are found spiritually in the world soul of which our rational soul is the image" (III 331). Thus discursive intelligence, using the knowledge of the forms, attains comprehension of the ideal archetype, upon which the world is founded. As a result, the order of the universe is represented in our souls under the form of the ordered relations of the ideas. The highest degree of such intellection is intuitive intelligence, which is compared to the ineffable vision of the One, itself, the consummation of all rational knowledge.

That the intuition of the forms should be tantamount to the beatific vision is not surprising, for in the Divine Intellect we find the ideal essences of all things in a unique and perfect union:

> The pure intellect which shines in us is at the same time the image of the pure divine Intellect, marked by the unity of all the ideas. At the end of all our discursive reasonings, it reveals the ideal essences in a unique and utterly abstract intuitive knowledge, when our well-trained reason so deserves.[32]

Leone adds:

> Once we can see with the eyes of the intellect, we can see in one single intuition the sovereign beauty of the first intellect and the divine ideas: and seeing it we are delighted and we love it; and with the eyes of our rational soul, with its ordered discourse, we can see the beauty of the soul of the world and in it the whole system of forms whose beauty delights us again greatly and moves us to love.[33]

Before specifying how Leone envisages this intellectual love, we note his acknowledgement of the inequality of souls in attaining knowledge—a result of the unequal obedience of bodies to souls (III 329). Leone describes in Platonic terms the situation of souls which appear to enjoy corporeal beauties but fail to discern true beauty or formal grace, sensing only physical pleasure or utility. If in the end we find sensual pleasures or utilitarian profits inadequate, we have only the imperfection of our desires to blame. For sensuous pleasures rob us of higher goals that could bring real satisfaction, and sensuous desires disturb our quiet contentment by succumbing to "restless matter, the mother of sensory beauties" (III 332 f.). Leone stigmatizes those who favor lasciviousness, because they fail to find spiritual beauty in corporeal things. Such persons turn the accessory into the essential, prefer shade to light. At the end of the third dialogue, Sophia is advised by her lover not to take delight, as Narcissus did, in a mere image of beauty, losing sight of the original, and drowning in its reflection. It is in the realization of our intellectual essence that the highest form of love occurs, when rational intuition grasps the essences latent in the divine wisdom.

The love of God for his sovereign wisdom is the primal love that produces the world, holding forth the first beauty, toward which the loving God draws in the first expression of love, through which the world was ordered out of chaos. But this primal love is identical with the love of creatures that leads this world to its final perfection. The perfection or virtue of a glass is that it is made in likeness to the form and design in the mind of the maker. But its final perfection is that it be used for the proper purpose for which it was made. We recognize here an Aristotelian distinction, applied by Leone to the universe at large.[34]

Sophia asks: "What then are the activities that contribute to perfecting the generated universe?" Philo answers that many such acts are found in the universe at diverse levels. The ultimate perfection is the most perfect, and the rest are only means of attaining it. These means are physical actions, but by rising through them to the purest intellectual acts one can discover and communicate to the world what leads to the ultimate perfection for the world. The highest of the intellectual acts is that of understanding, which has as its goal the divine essence and its sovereign wisdom,

> For this level includes and comprehends every intellectual matter and every degree of intellection; and this is what can make the potential intellect wholly actual and the other produced intellects actual in the highest degree of their perfection?[35]

The ultimate perfection is achieved by means of three acts: thought, love, and unitive pleasure. Sophia asks Philo if thought uses any act other than understanding once it reaches love and unitive pleasure. Philo answers: "No, love at the intellectual level is in essence no different from thought itself." Love and intellection remain one, and it is only "according to reason" that they are distinct. Unitive pleasure is the highest and most perfect thought, because the more perfect an intellectual act is, the more perfect is the union of the intellect that understands and the matter understood.[36]

The intuitive knowledge of divine wisdom is love. For it is knowledge of the sovereign beautiful and good and this knowledge is as much a prerequisite of love as an outcome of it. Indeed, if it were the kind of knowledge that implies desire, this desire would disappear with the possession of the object and pleasure would not endure! But there is a love beyond desire, which has recognized its object and united with it. To understand this we must refer to an illustration that Leone uses as early as the first Dialogue: He who has no child longs for one; but he who has one does not desire one, but loves and enjoys the offspring he has. Another comparison is used in the third Dialogue:

> A certain knowledge precedes the wish for food, but once the food has been enjoyed, the perfect knowledge of nourishment that is unitive, creates a love which is no longer caused by the lack of union, but by a desire to preserve it.

God's paternal love for his creatures, which corresponds to the order of production of the universe, is answered by "the reductive love" of his creatures resulting from the realization of their essence in virtue, the highest phase of which is intellectual virtue. The counterpart of the half-circle of loves from the Perfect to the imperfect is that which runs from the least perfect to the most perfect.[37] Leone's image of the circle from God to the least of creatures and back, by the road of love, to God in his supreme intelligible and intellectual perfection, like Marsilio Ficino's, was doubtless inspired by the Alexandrian mystics and such thinkers as Dionysius the Areopagite. Ficino writes:

> If God fills the world with delight and the world is filled with delight by him, there is a certain continual attraction between God and the world which begins in God and passes through the world and finally ends in God, as a circle returns to where it began. So there is one single circle that runs from God to the world and from the world to God and is named in three ways: insofar as it begins in God and has power of attraction: beauty; insofar as it is transferred to the world and fills it with delight: love; insofar as it returns to the Creator and unites his works: delight. So love starting from beauty ends in delight. . . . And it is necessary that love is good: born from the Good, it will return to the Good.[38]

The circle represents the pattern of outflow and return, dear to all Neoplatonists. Marsilio says:

> The Sovereign Creator, God, first created all things, secondly filled them with delight in himself, thirdly gave them perfection. God is therefore beginning, middle and end.

Leone takes over this formula almost completely. In union with the divine principle, we encounter the goal of all love. Indeed, without love and the yearning for sovereign beauty, it would have been impossible for things to emanate and become detached from the Deity. And it is precisely for this reason that love and the desire to return to their divine origin manifest themselves under the form of a desire for and a love of the beautiful which leads them toward their ultimate perfection.

Sophia, in the presence of this great conception, raises three objections:

1. How is it possible for delight to be the goal of intellectual love, since delight is a passion, and the intellect, being separated from the matter, is not susceptible to passions?
2. Can delight be the goal of productive love? Does it not seem impossible to rejoice while approaching the non-beautiful or the less beautiful?
3. Is it not difficult to admit that the love that leads the universe to its perfection is the reductive love of creatures for sovereign beauty, and not the productive love of God for the world He produced?

Leone answers:

1. Intellectual delight is not a passion in the intellect. Thus there can be a delight that is not a passion. It is an intellectual act and nothing else.
2. Delight can be the goal of productive love: God rejoices in His works, as many texts from the Torah confirm. True, neither sadness nor joy are found in God. But the delight here is "the agreeable fitness of the perfection of the effect, and the sadness is privation on the part of the effect."[39] Divine delight consists in the union of the not beautiful or the less beautiful with what makes them beautiful. It is not a union of the sovereign beautiful with the not beautiful or the less beautiful.

3.  There is no difficulty in admitting that the love that leads the
    world and God to their perfection is the "reductive" love rather
    than "the productive love of God." For there is no beauty or
    perfection that does not grow when it is communicated; the fruit-
    bearing tree is always more beautiful than the sterile one.

The universe was produced by God "not just to keep it in its primal
state of production but also and more truly to lead it to its ultimate
perfection through its happy union with sovereign beauty."[40]

> Indeed, there is no doubt that our eyes and visual powers with
> the desire of perceiving the light lead us to see the light and the body
> of the sun in which we rejoice. And their knowledge and enjoyment
> would not exist if our eyes were not at first illuminated by the sun and
> by the light.[41]

Our intellectual love, which is the highest form of love for the
sovereign beauty in the universe and which leads us to unite with it,
would never be capable of such a union "if our intellectual faculty
were not assisted and illuminated by the sovereign beauty and by the
love God has for the universe. It is this love that rouses and revives
the love of the universe. It illuminates the intellectual faculty of the
human soul to lead it to happiness in union with sovereign
beauty."[42]  Hence a true reciprocity is established between the
"productive" love of God which conditions the order of existence and
the "reductive" love which leads the universe and God himself to
ultimate perfection. Here Leone Ebreo comes very close to Marsilio
Ficino, who writes in the second book of Letters: "to be enraptured,
you would never have desired it if He had not desired it." God's
love for his creatures is the original force and the impetus that
sustains each being and imparts the intelligence to understand and to
love God.

Victor Delbos observes, "It is possible that Spinoza borrowed
from Leone Ebreo and his *Dialogues of Love* his formula on the
relation of knowledge and love, at the source of which we find Plato
and Neoplatonism; but the formula was widespread in the language
of the philosophers."[43]  I think that Spinoza must have been struck
by the pertinence of Leone's writing concerning the intellectual love
of God, the objections of Sophia and the answers the Jewish
philosopher gave to them. In the *Short Treatise* he wrote:

> As man is in God together with all that is, he cannot have love
> for anything else, since all that is forms just one single thing, God
> himself. (chap. 14)

And in the *Ethics*:

> God is free from passions, nor is he affected with any emotion
> of pleasure or pain (V, Prop. 17).

and

> He who loves God cannot endeavor to bring it about that God
> should love him in return (V, Prop. 19).

Yet the difficulties adumbrated in such propositions are not
insurmountable. Leone could aid Spinoza by showing that neither in
God nor in a man who loves intellectually is love a passion, since it
is the act of the intelligence. With this aid Spinoza can conclude the
*Ethics* by stating that God does love Himself and man, since there
necessarily exists in God an idea of His own essence and of all that
necessarily follows from this essence (*Ethics* II, Prop. 3). This idea,
constitutive in the infinite intellect, ensures that God knows Himself
through an eternal and infinite mode of His thought. As a result,
there can be a love of God for Himself. For the infinite perfection
in which God conceives Himself goes hand in hand with the idea of
Himself as cause of Himself and this perfection. But that formula,
of course, answers to the definition of love. Thus: "God loves
himself with infinite intellectual love" (*Ethics* V, Prop. 35).

As for God's love of man: every soul is defined as "the idea of
a body." But insofar as our soul uses the knowledge of the second
and of the third kinds, the soul understands itself as an eternal
essence linked to the eternal essence of God, thus a part of the idea
of God. Accordingly, one can understand the intellectual love of
souls for God as a part of the infinite love of God for Himself (*Ethics*
V, Prop. 36 and corollary).

Here once again we find the famous circle of Marsilio Ficino,
but made more explicit by Leone Ebreo. It is through the elaboration
of God's infinite essence that the soul exists as a finite mode. But
it is only insofar as God can unfold Himself through the essence of

the human soul that he loves Himself. As Victor Delbos remarks: "There is truly no love of God for himself except insofar as finite beings, which are part of his Being, love him."[44] It would be right to add: insofar as these finite beings think of themselves *sub specie aeternitatis*, that is, in the light of the dependence of their essence on the essence of God. But in drawing this conclusion Leone lays the emphasis elsewhere. For after it has completed the dianoetic path, our intellection results in the intuition of our intimate union with God. If there is a kind of mysticism in Leone, it in no way represents a state which exceeds reason, unless on account of the joy or infinite delight of one who ultimately knows God.[45]

In Plotinus the ecstatic intelligence that conjoins with the One is a power the mind possesses eternally, although it seldom uses it: "because it is intelligence (*oti esti nous*) it contemplates the first principle, by means of what in it is not intelligence (*tō eautou mē nō*)." The full text is:

> Since the substance generated [from the One] is form—one could not say that what is generated from that source is anything else—and not the form of some one thing but of everything, so that no other form is left outside it, the One must be without form. But if it is without form it is not a substance; for a substance must be some one particular thing, something, that is, defined and limited; but it is impossible to apprehend the One as a particular thing: for then it would not be the principle but only that particular thing which you said it was. But, if all things are in that which is generated [from the One], which of the things in it are you going to say that the One is? Since it is none of them, it can only be said to be beyond them. But these things are beings, and being: so it is beyond being. (*Enneads* V 5.6, Armstrong, 173)[46]

In Leone Ebreo we find nothing of this kind[47]—an intelligence that attains what is beyond itself and which contemplates the first principle by means of what in itself is not intelligence as such, does not exist. Still it is this conception which Proclus, in the footsteps of Plotinus, outlines in his *De providentia et fato*.[48] He calls this ecstatic intelligence the apophatic intelligence as opposed to the normal, cataphatic intelligence. It is Leone Ebreo's more rational and pertinent method of approaching ecstatic intelligence that, it seems to us, renders his intellectualism much more marked than that of his predecessors in antiquity, and brings it nearer to that of a philosopher like Spinoza.[49]

## Notes

1.  Leone Ebreo, *Dialoghi d'Amore: hebraeische Gedichte*, tr., Carl Gebhardt (Frankfurt a.M.: Curis Societatis Spinozanae, 1929), 55 ff., citing *Dialoghi*, I, 26a-b. This edition is a revision of Leone Ebreo, *Dialoghi d'amore, poesie hebraiche*, Ristampati con introduzione di Carl Gebhardt (Heidelberg: C. Winter; Gravenhage: Nijhoff; London: Oxford University Press, 1924). We have also consulted Léon Hébreu, *Dialogues d'amour* (Lyon, 1551; tr. Pontus de Tyard) ed. T. Anthony Perry (Chapel Hill: University of North Carolina Press, 1974), which is of particular interest for its introduction. The Italian edition of Ebreo's work to which we refer throughout is the Santino Caramella edition of *Dialoghi d'amore* (Bari: Laterza e figli, 1929). Beyond its well known influence on such diverse figures as Montemayor, Giordano Bruno, Cervantes, Spinoza and Schiller, Leone Ebreo's *Dialoghi d'Amore* has enjoyed a relatively recent resurgence of interest, judging from the translations in Spanish, German, English and Hebrew and re-edition in Italian. E. Friedberg-Seeley and J. H. Barnes translated it into English as *The Philosophy of Love* (London, 1937); this was not available to me in Belgium, and the translations here are my own. The classic study was H. Pflaum, *Die Idee der Liebe* (Heidelberg, 1926); cf. now Suzanne Damiens, *Amour et Intellect chez Léon l'Hebreu* (Toulouse: Edouard Privat, 1971) and Alfred Ivry's splendid "Remnants of Jewish Averroism in the Renaissance," in B. Cooperman, ed., *Jewish Thought in the Sixteenth Century* (Cambridge: Harvard University Press, 1983), 243-65. Ivry shows the infusion of Averroian and Averroist thought (distinguishing the thought of Averroes from that of his interpreters) not only in works of admitted and obvious disciples but also in the compositions of their major intellectual adversaries, the Platonists of the period.
2.  Suzanne Damiens, *Amour et intellect chez Léon l'Hébreu*.
3.  *Dialoghi* III 385 f.
4.  See Gershom Scholem, *Les origines de la kabbale* (Paris: Payot, 1966), 165. Similarly, according to the ancients (probably the Kabbalists), "le juste rend la splendeur divine parfaite, et elle est par le méchant tâchée" (144). The world is perfect, not sinful. From this we might infer that God's love is not diminished by its manifestation

in the world but preserved, so that the world remains in some sense divine or an expression of the divine.

5.  II 162-63: "Tu hai altra volta inteso da me, o Sofia, che tutto l'universo è un individuo, cioè come una persona, e ognuno di questi corporali e spirituali, eterni e corruttibili, è membro e parte di questo grande individuo, essendo tutto e ciascuna de le sue parti produtta da Dio per uno fine commune nel tutto, insieme con uno fine proprio in ognuna de le parti. Séguita che tanto il tutto e le parti sono perfetti e felici, quanto rettamente e interamente conseguono gli offizi ai quali sono indirizzati dal sommo opifice. Il fine del tutto è l'unita perfezione di tutto l'universo, disegnata dal divino architettore, e il fine di ciascuna delle parti non è solamente la perfezione di quella parte in sé ma che con quella deserva rettamente a la perfezione del tutto, che è il fine universale, primo intento de la divinità." Cf. Maimonides, *Guide* I 72, II 10. Maimonides called the indirect way through which nature attains its goals a "gracious ruse" of God and his wisdom; he may have taken the expression from Alexander of Aphrodisias' *Principle of the All* (extant only in Arabic translation; see A. Badawi, *La Transmission de la philosophie grecque en monde arabe* (Paris: Vrin, 1968); J. M. Rist, "On tracking Alexander of Aphrodisias," *Archiv für Geschichte der Philosophie* 48 (1966): 82-90; J. van Ess, "Über einige neue Fragmente des Alexander von Aphrodisias . . .," *Der Islam* 42 (1966): 149-54; F. W. Zimmermann and H. V. B. Brown, "Neue arabischen Übersetzungstexte aus dem Bereich der spätantiken Griechischen Philosophie," *Der Islam* 50 (1973): 313-24; P. Thillet, "Un traité inconnu d'Alexandre d'Aphrodise sur la Providence dans une version arabe inédite," *Actes du 1er Congrès international de philosophie medievale* (Louvain, 1960). The idea is suggestive of Hegel's "cunning of Reason."

6.  Bernard Silvestris, ed., Peter Droncke *Cosmographia* (Leiden: Brill, 1978). See also *The Cosmographia of Bernardus Silvestris*, tr., Winthrop Wetherbee (New York: Columbia University Press, 1973); see also Brian Stock, *Myth and Science in the Twelfth Century: A Study of Bernard Silvester* (Princeton: Princeton University Press, 1972).

7.  II 162: "In questo alto debbe consistere la sua felicità e il suo ultimo fine, non in muover corpo celeste che è cosa materiale e alto estrinseco de la sua vera essenzia."

8.  The view that sperm is produced by the entire body is found in the *Zohar*, II 150 b, 82, tr. H. Sperling, M. Simon and P. Leverhoff (London, 1933-34), 5 vols.; *Sepherha Zohar (Le livre de la splendeur) Doctrine ésotérique des Israélites*, tr., Jean de Pauly, ed., Émile

Lafuma-Giraud (Paris: Leroux, 1906-1911), 6 vols; *Le Zohar*, tr., Charles Mopsik, (Albertville: Verdier, 1981). See also Gershom Scholem, *Les grands courants de la mystique juive* (Paris: Payot, 1960); *Jewish Gnosticism, Merkabah Mysticism, and Talmudic tradition* (New York: JTS, 1960); *Zur Kabbala und ihrer Symbolik* (Zürich: Rhein-Verlag, 1960); Z'ev ben Shimon Halevi (i.e., Warren Kenton), *Adam and the Kabbalistic Tree* (London: Rider, 1974) and François Secret, *Le Zohar chez les kabbalistes chrétiens de la Renaissance* (La Haye: Mouton, 1964).

9. See the important passage on Avicenna and Averroes in the *Dialoghi*, ed., Caramella 283-85, corresponding to 231-39 in the Anthony Perry ed. of the French translation of Pontus de Tyard (1551). That the active intellect is the lowest of the angels was maintained in Italy by such Jewish Neo-Aristotelian philosophers as Yehudah Romano (b. 1292). Its identification with God was defended especially by Christians, including Thomas Aquinas. See Joseph B. Sermoneta, *La dottrina dell' intelletto e la "fede filosofica" di Jehudah e Immanuel Romano* (Spoleto: Ateneo, 1965). On intellection in Leone, see Suzanne Damiens.

10. Alexander of Aphrodisias, *On Fate*, ed. and tr., R. W. Sharples (London: Duckworth, 1983); *Traité du destin*, ed., Pierre Thillet (Paris: Belles Lettres, 1984); Paul Moraux, *Der Aristotelismus bei den Griechen, von Andronikos bis Alexander von Aphrodisias: Die Renaissance des Aristotelismus* (Berlin: De Gruyter, 1973).

11. *Enneads* V 9.3; Armstrong 5.293.

12. *Guide* III 2.

13. *Enneads* V 9.5; Armstrong 5.299. This passage affords an excellent example of Plotinus' practice of collecting texts of varied significance in their original contexts to support his own doctrine: Cf. Parmenides frg. B3, Diels; Aristotle *De anima* III 4, 430a 3-4 and 7, 431a 1-2; Heraclitus frg. B101, Diels; and (for example) Plato, *Phaedo* 72E 5-6.

14. Alexander Altmann credits this doctrine to the Islamic Aristotelians, and credits Maimonides (*Guide* I 68; *Hilkhot Yesodei-ha-Torah* 2.10) for its currency among Jewish philosophers; see his "Moses Narboni's Epistle on Shi'ur Qoma," *Jewish and Medieval Renaissance Studies* 4, ed., A. Altmann (Cambridge: Harvard University Press, 1967), 265. Cf. Carl Gebhardt, 55 f.: "Mit dieser Lehre von Der Identität Gottes und der Welt als des göttlichen Denkinhalts steht Leone in der Tradition jüdischer Philosophie. Aus des Aristoteles Bestimmung der Gottheit als der noesis noeseos (Metaph. XII, 9) hatten die arabischen Peripatetiker den Satz geformt: Gott ist das Denken, der Denkende und das Gedachte. Ihnen folgend lehrt Abraham ibn Esra im 12.

Jahrhundert: Er ist allein Verstehender, Verstand und Verstandenes, und im 13. Jahrhundert übernimmt Maimonides die Identitätslehre in de *Yesodè-ha-Torà* un den *More Nebukhim*: Er ist Verstand, Verstehendes und Verstehbares und diese drei sind in Gott nur ein und dasselbe Ding, in dem es keine Vielheit gibt, und er findet die Einheit nicht nur im Schöpfer, sondern in jedem actualisierten Verstand. Auch die Mystiek der Qabbala hat sich die Identitätslehre nicht entgehen lassen; im 16. Jahrhundert ist Mose Corduero ihr Vertreter. Und wie die Mystik des Mittelalters in Meister Eckhart das Auge darin ich Gott sehe, in eines setzt mit dem Auge, darin mich Gott siehet, so kündet Leone die gleiche Identität: Der Verstehende, das Verstandene und der Verstand sind geschieden, sofern sie potentiell sind, und sind vereinigt, sofern sie actuell sind (III, 57a). In Gott ist der Erkennende und das Erkannte und die Erkenntnis selbst alles ein und dasselbe." (III, 56a. References to editio Carl Gebhardt: Heidelberg, 1924).

15. *Ethics* V, Prop. 29, scholium, tr., after E. Curley, *The Collected Works of Spinoza* (Princeton: Princeton University Press, 1985), 610.

16. *Ethics* V, Prop. 42; cf. *Short Treatise* II, Ch. 26.

17. *Le Spinozisme* (Paris: Vrin, 1916), 171. Such a reading might encourage the notion that because Spinoza writes *more geometrico* he must conceive human life as a geometric deduction. But *Short Treatise* II, ch. 26 shows how aware Spinoza was of the human moral drama; and when he says there are no demons but only our own weaknesses, he echoes Heraclitus' *ethos anthropoi daemon*—hardly a cold or overly monistic point.

18. Of this Victor Delbos asks if it is not the imperfect substitute, but a substitute nonetheless, for the idea of predestination, *Le Spinozisme*, 166 ff.

19. Léon Brunschvig, *Spinoza et ses contemporains* (Paris: Alcan, 3rd edition, 1923); see also his "Le Platonisme de Spinoza," *Chronicon spinozanum* 3 (1923).

20. *Ethics* III, Prop. 6, 7; cf. Def. 6; IV, Props. 3, 5.

21. *Ethics* II, Prop. 45.

22. "Again, just as in the number two there is a one and another, and it is not possible for this one with another to be the number one, but it is necessary for there to be a one by itself before the one with another; in the same way it is necessary that, when a thing has immanent in it something simple along with something else, the simple thing should be simple in and by itself, having nothing in itself of all that it has in its association with other things. For what could make it something else in something different, if there was not something before it from which this something else comes? For the simple could not derive

from something else, but that which is many, or two, must itself depend on something else." *Enneads* V 6.4; Armstrong, 5.209.

23. Cf. Edgar Wind, *Pagan Mysteries in the Renaissance* (London: Faber and Faber, 1968) and *Le soleil à la Renaissance: Science et mythes* (Bruxelles, Paris: Presses universitaires de Bruxelles/Presses universitaires de France, 1965) the proceedings of a colloquium held in April 1963 which include Francesco Negri Arnoldi, "L'iconographie du soleil dans la Renaissance italienne," 519-38, and Francois Secret, "Le soleil chez les kabbalistes chrétiens de la Renaissance," 211-40. See also George Francis Hill, *A Corpus of Italian Medals of the Renaissance before Cellini* (London: British Museum, 1930).

24. III 19: "E questa è la felice morte che causa la coppulazione de l'anima con l'intelletto, la quale hanno gustata i nostri antichi beati Moisé e Aron, e gli altri de quali parla la sacra Scrittura che morino per bocca de Dio baciando la divinità (come t'ho detto)."

25. *Enneads* V 6.

26. III 195: "(l'anima) . . . s'innamora di quella somma bellezza intellettuale sua superiore origine, come s'innamora la femmina imperfetta del maschio suo perficiente, e desidera farsi felice ne la sua perpetuata unione. Con questio si giunta un altro amore gemino de l'anima al mondo corporeo a la inferiore, come del maschio a la femmina, per farlo perfetto imprimendo in lui la bellezza che piglia da l'intelletto mediante il primo amore."

27. III 195: ". . . come che l'anima, ingravidata de la bellezza de l'intelletto la desidera parturire nel mondo corporeo, o veramente piglia la semenza di essa bellezza per farla germinare nel corpo, ovvero come artifice piglia l'esempli de la bellezza intellettuale per sculpirli al proprio ne'corpi."

28. II 163: "Séguita che tanto il tutto e le parti sono perfette e felici, quanto rettamente e interamente conseguono gli offizzi ai quali sono indirizzati dal sommo opifice. Il fine del tutto è l'unita perfezione di tutto l'universo, disegnata dal divino architettore, e il fine di ciascuna delle parti non è solamente la perfezione di quella parte in sè, ma che con quella deserva rettamente a la perfezione del tutto, che è il fine universale, primo intento de la divinità. E per questo comun fine, più che per il proprio, ogni parta fu fatta, ordinata e dedicata. Talmente che, mancando parte di tal servitù negli atti pertinenti a la perfezione de l'universo, le sarebbe maggiore difetto e più infelice verebbe a essere, che se li mancasse il suo proprio atto."

29. II 164: "Ché l'anime nostre essendo spirituali e intellettive, nissun bene da la società corporea, fragile e corruttible lor potrebbe occorrere, che non stessero molto meglio col sua atto intellettivo intrinseco e

puro; ma s'applicano al nostro corpo solamente per amore e servizio del sommo creatore del mundo, traendo la vita e la cognizione intellettiva e la luce divina dal mundo superiore eterno a l'inferiore corruttibile, acciò che questa piú bassa parte del mondo non sia anch'ella priva de la grazia divina e vita eternale, e perché questo grande animale non abbia parte alcuna che non sia viva e intelligente come tutto lui."

30. II 165: "Però che tanto il mondo e le sue cose hanno essere, quanto egli è tutto unito e collegato con tutte le sue cose a modo di membra d'uno individuo: altrimenti la divisione sarebbe cagione de la sua totale perdizione; e siccome niuna cosa non fa unire l'universo con tutte le sue diverse cose, se non l'amore, séguita che esso amore è causa de l'essere del mondo e di tutte le sue cose."

31. III 331: "La prima faccia, verso l'intelletto, è la ragione intellettiva, con la quale discorre con universale e spirituale cognizione, estraendo le forme ed essenzie intellettuali da li particulari e sensibili corpi, convertendo sempre il mondo corporeo ne l'intellettuale; la seconda faccia, che è verso il corpo, è il senso, che è cognizione particolare de le cose particulari corporee, aggiunta e mista la materialità de la cose corporee conosciute."

32. III 326: "E il puro intelletto che riluce in noi è similmente immagine de l'intelletto puro divino, disegnato de l'unitê di tutte le idee, il quale in fine de'nostri discorsi razionali ne mostra l'essenzie ideali in intuitiva unica e astrattissima cognizione, quando il merita nostra bene abituata ragione."

33. III 326: "Si che noi con gli occhi de l'intelletto possiamo vedere in uno intuito la somma bellezza del primo intelletto e idee divine: vedendola ne diletta, e noi l'amiamo; e con gli occhi de l'anima nostra razionale con ordinato discorso possiamo vedere la bellezza de l'anima del mondo e in lei tutte l'ordinate forme, la quale ancora grandemente ne diletta e move ad amare."

34. III 372: "Cosi ne l'universo prodotto il primo fine del producente e la prima perfezione di quello consiste ne la perfezione de l'opera divina, essendo proprio simulacro de la divina sapienzia, ma l'ultimo fine suo e l'ultima perfezione di quello consiste in esercitarsi esso universo ne l'atto e opera per il quale fu prodotto, il quale è fine di esso operato però che l'essere de l'operato è fine de l'operante, e l'opera de l'operante è fine de l'esser suo."

35. III 373: "Però che in questo (come gía altrove t'ho detto) consiste e si comprende ogni cosa intelletta e ogni grado d'intellezione; e questo è quello che può redurre l'intelletto possibile secondo tutta la sua essenzia in intero atto, e gli altri intelletti prodotti attuali nel sommo

grado de la sua perfezione."
36. III 374: "Però che quanto più perfetto è l'atto intellettivo, tanto è maggiore e più perfetta l'unione de l'intelletto intendente e de la cosa intelletta."
37. For a clear analysis of the grand reconciliation of these opposites in cyclical activity and of the final synthetic vision that crowns the *Dialoghi*, see *Dialogues d'amour*, tr., Pontus de Tyard, Perry, Introduction, 22 ff.
38. Quoted in Festugière, *La philosophie de l'amour de Marsile Ficin et son influence sur la littérature française* (Paris: Vrin, 1947), 34.
39. III 383: "Ma in effetto nè la tristezza nè la letizia son passione in lui, ma la dilettazione è grata correspondenzia de la perfezione del suo effetto e la tristezza privatione di quella da la parte de l'effetto."
40. III 384: "Però che non è alcuna perfezione nè bellezza che non cresca quando è communicata ché l'arbore fruttifero sempre è più bello che'l sterile, e l'acque emananti e correnti fuora sono piú degne che le raccolte e ritenute in le sue vivagne. Prodotto l'universo, fu prodotto con lui l'amore di Dio a esso, come del padre nel figlio giá nato: Il qual non solamente fu per sostentarlo nel primo stato de la sua produzione, ma ancora e più veramente per condurlo ne la sua ultima perfezione con la sua felicitante unione con la divina bellezza."
41. III 384: "Non è dubio che li nostri occhi e virtù visiva col desiderio di sentire la luce ne conduce a vedere la luce e corpo del sole, nel quale ci dilettiamo: niente di manco, se gli occhi nostri non fussero prima illuminati da esso sole e da la luce, noi non potremmo mai arrivare a vederlo, però che senza il sole impossibile è che il sole si veda, perche col sole il sol si vede."
42. III 385: "Né l'amor nostro né suo sarieno mai capaci di simile unione, né sufficienti di tanto alto grado di dilettevole perfezione, se non fusse la nostra parte intellettuale auitata e illuminata de la somma bellezza divina e de l'amore che esso ha a l'universo; quale avviva e solleva l'amore de l'universo illuminando la parte sua intellettiva, acciò che'l possa condurre a la felicità unitiva de la sua somma bellezza."
43. *Le Spinozisme*, 165.
44. *Le Spinozisme*, 166; cf. Descartes, *Lettre à Chanut* (1er février 1647), *Oeuvres*, ed., Charles Adam and Paul Tannery (Paris: Le Cerf, 1897-1913) **4**.607, or Geneviève Rodis-Lewis, ed., *Correspondance avec Arnaud et Morus* (Paris, 1953); tr. in part by Leonora D. Cohen in *Annals of Science* 1 (1936): 48-61. Henry More, *Enchiridion-Ethicum*, IX 13-18 in *Opera philosophica* (1678), tr., Edward Southwell (New York: Facsimile Text Society, 1930); cf. John Hoyles, *The waning of the Renaissance, 1640-1740: Studies in the thought and poetry of*

*Henry More, John Norris and Isaac Watts* (The Hague: Nijhoff, 1971); *Philosophical poems*, ed., Geoffrey Bullough (Manchester: University Press, 1931); cf. Serge Hutin, *Henry More: essais sur les doctrines théosophiques chez les Platoniciens de Cambridge* (Hildesheim: Olms, 1966).

45. Cf. the idea of rational mysticism in L. E. Goodman, Ibn Tufayl's *Ḥayy Ibn Yaqẓān*, 30-49.

46. Cf. Plato *Republic* VI 509: "The Sun, I presume you will say, not only furnishes to visibles the power of visibility but it also provides for their generation and growth and nurture though it is not itself generation. . . . In like manner, then, you are to say that the objects of knowledge not only receive from the presence of the good their being known, but their very existence and essence is derived to them from it, though the good itself is not essence but still transcends essence in dignity and surpassing power," tr., Paul Shorey.

47. As Goodman suggests, it is not impossible that the sense of hunger and lack Leone speaks of corresponds to this, and so to Diotima's genealogy of love in the *Symposium* as an offspring of *poros* and *penia*. But we must remain cautious here. The opening statement of the *Dialoghi* places the entire work under the sign of a Platonic and rationalistic theory of love. Love (like desire) is always based on knowledge. If love is based on knowledge, the latter in turn can only be of what is; the beloved object must have real existence. The proposition that love expresses a relationship between a subject and an object both real and lovable rigorously follows Socrates' own conclusions in the *Symposium* (200e-201b). Socrates' further observation that one can love or desire only what one does not have, however, seems unacceptable or at least requires clarification. The objection is raised by the quick-witted Sophia apparently to divert the ardor of her suitor's bold opening declaration: How can Philo claim to feel both love and desire? Philo counters with the example of a man's affection for his wife, which may be described as both love and desire.

48. Proklos Diadochos, *Über die Vorsehung, das Schicksal und den freien Willen an Theodoros, den Ingenieur (Mechaniker)*, ed., Theo Borger, tr., Michael Erler (Meisenheim am Glan: Anton Hain, 1980).

49. Love is seen as following upon knowledge and stimulating it in turn. Love and desire are means of raising us from imperfect knowledge to the perfect union which is their true end. For the reciprocal relation of love and knowledge, see Ivry's essay, cited above, n. 1. Analyzing Ebreo's remark, "As we know His perfection, so we love and enjoy Him in the most perfect union of knowledge possible to us," Ivry

comments: "The phrase 'possible to us' is a conventional qualification expressing the concern to maintain God's transcendence, a belief Ebreo holds in uneasy alliance with the conviction of His immanence. . . . Ebreo goes further towards uniting man directly with God than do most medievals. Once he even identifies God with the Agent Intellect of our World, its formal principle, with which individual intellects may conjoin" (247).

# Spinoza, Neoplatonic Kabbalist?

## Richard Popkin

In the first history of the Jews written after Josephus, the French Huguenot Jacques Basnage wrote, "There is among the *Jews* a third Opinion about the Creation, which Spinoza has reduced to a System. In truth that *Jew* had borrow'd the foundation of his Iniquity from the Rabbis of his Nation, who were known to him; rather than the *Chineses,*[1] or the Heathen Philosophers. He has never cited the *Cabalists* as his Vouchers, because that Man was so extreamly jealous of the immortality of his Name, that he designed to pass for an Original, and an Inventor of his Opinions. The *Cabalists*, no less greedy of glory than *Spinosa*, might have claimed a Discovery which belonged to them, and gloried in that which has made Spinosa immortal; but his Name was become too odious to enter into a Society of Atheism with him. In short the *Jews* rose up against him."[2]

Basnage went on, "The *Cabalists* for this long time have been as it were allow'd and authorized to throw about their Extravagances, and make themselves to be admired by some Persons who love to run after shadows and trifles, things of nought: But this comes about by their having the Art and Dexterity to veil themselves under a Mystical Language. They produce their Dreams and Visions as Explications of Scripture, and spiritual Conjectures rather than as decisions of Faith. *Spinosa*, on the contrary, has made a System, and has endeavoured to prove it. He has kept very well to part of the obscure and Mystical Language of the *Cabalists*, and therefore those who confute him are often accused of not understanding him; and his Disciples affirm, that all those who have attacked him, have not thoroughly comprehended his true thoughts."[3]   Spinoza, Basnage insisted, was a disciple of the Cabalists, had taken his principles from them, but went further than they did until he undermined the foundations of Judaism.

This strange interpretation of Spinoza is similar to one that appears in another work of the time, *Den Spinozismus im Judenthums, oder, die von dem heutigen Judenthumb und desen Geheimen Kabbala* (*Spinoza and Judaism, On Present Day Judaism and the Secret Kabbala*), by Johann Georg Wachter.[4]   Considering that Spinoza is usually seen as the most rational and non-mystical of philosophers, and one who treated Kabbalistic readings of Scripture with complete disdain, it does seem, *ab initio* implausible that Spinoza was a secret Kabbalist, who drew his philosophical system from the mystical one of the Kabbalists.   In fact, Spinoza said, "I have read and known certain Kabbalistic triflers, whose insanity provokes my unceasing astonishment."[5]   What I shall try to do in this paper is to explore why such an interpretation was offered by two serious intellectuals in the generation after Spinoza, and whether there may have been any justice in their reading of Spinoza.

By now we all know that Spinoza developed his views from Cartesianism, rational Jewish medieval thinkers, and from Renaissance Neoplatonists like Leone Hebreo.   What is so obvious now that Spinoza has been put in his place by the German idealist historians of philosophy and by scholars of Jewish intellectual history, was not so obvious when Spinoza's *Opera Posthuma* was published in 1677.   The central work, *The Ethics demonstrated by geometrical method*, gave no clue as to what tradition it came from or how one was supposed to read it.[6]   Spinoza had published only two seemingly unrelated works previously, *The Theological-Political Tractatus* and *The Principles of Descartes' Philosophy.*[7]

Forty years earlier, when Descartes produced his strikingly novel works, *The Discourse on Method* and *Meditations on First Philosophy*, the author was alive and only too willing to explain to anyone interested what was revolutionary and true in his philosophy. So Descartes left us a large legacy of published and epistolary explanations and justifications of his views.[8]   Spinoza unfortunately was dead when the *Ethics* was published. The few letters printed by his disciples provided scant explanation of the majestic work. Spinoza's radical friends, who accepted his attacks on established religion, like St. Evremond, Col. J.-B. Stouppe and Henriquez Morales (Henri Morelli), just indicated that they agreed with him.[9] Others who had discussed and disputed Spinoza's early views, like Henry Oldenburg, the secretary of the Royal Society, gave no guidance about the import of *The Ethics*. Leibniz, who had apparently leaned towards Spinoza's views, shied away from association with them as soon as they were denounced. The early reading was that Spinoza was "the first to reduce atheism to a system"[10] or that as a consistent Cartesian he perforce became an atheist.[11] Clearly he was exotic, perhaps some kind of Oriental philosopher.[12]

Bayle and Spinoza's early biographer, Colerus, had portrayed the heroic Spinoza as a bright Jewish lad who could not abide the rigidity and aridity of the Synagogue school. He got himself expelled, *then* studied Latin, read Descartes, became a Cartesian, and, as Henry More might have predicted, by being consistent, became an atheist.[13] This picture of Spinoza's development was to become the standard one in the histories of philosophy of the eighteenth and nineteenth centuries.

It is, of course, difficult to put oneself back into the intellectual world of the late 1670s and early 1680s, when Spinoza became an important figure. He provided no introductory material, no intellectual biography. He left no disciples who were ready and able to explain it all. The situation would have been analogous to the appearance of Ludwig Wittgenstein's *Tractatus Logico-Philosophicus* without Bertrand Russell's preface. (The fact that so many publishers turned down Wittgenstein's masterpiece *before* Russell wrote the preface indicates the problem.) How would Spinoza's contemporaries have known what to make of the strangely presented text or what school of philosophy to put it in? The difficulty in assessing what Spinoza was up to, even when there were living students and contacts of Spinoza to ask for guidance, is attested by Bayle's enormous article on "Spinoza" in the *Historical and Critical Dictionary*.[14] Where would a contemporary look for some explanation? The texts of Basnage and Wachter show that they looked in a work published the same year, the *Kabbala Denudata,* and accepted the clues offered by a strange figure, Moses Germanus.

The *Kabbala Denudata,* an immense compilation and Latin translation of major Zoharic and Lurianic Kabbalistic texts, with explanations and discussions, was put out by Christian Knorr von Rosenroth (1636-1689), a mystical Christian Kabbalist and follower of Jacob Boehme. He studied the Hebrew language and Jewish texts with rabbis in Amsterdam and obtained from them many manuscripts of works of Isaac Luria and his followers, including many that had not been published in any language. Gershom Scholem mentions one manuscript which is now known only through Knorr von Rosenroth's Latin translation.[15]  The manuscripts were published in the *Kabbala Denudata* in two volumes, in 1677 and 1684.[16]

The editing and translating was done by Knorr and some of his friends such as the Cambridge Platonist Henry More; More's student, Lady Anne Conway; her doctor, Francis Mercurius van Helmont; their Rabbinical consultant, Isaac Abendana, then reader in Hebrew at Cambridge; and Moses Germanus. The last was a Catholic student of the Jesuits who became a Pietist associate of the Protestant leader Jacob Spener and then converted to Judaism, becoming rabbi of the Spanish-Portuguese Synagogue in Amsterdam, and leader of a new Messianic movement after the collapse of the Shabtai Zvi movement in Holland.[17]

The declared purpose of the *Kabbala Denudata* was to make the Kabbalistic texts, especially the newer Lurianic ones, available to Christian Europeans.  Learned Christians would then see what wisdom and enlightenment were to be found there.  As Henry More had remarked, "there is pretious gold in this Cabbalisticall rubbish."[18]  Further, making these texts more widely known would help in the great Millenarian mission of converting the Jews, by making their secret books available, and thus enabling right-minded Christians to show Jews that the inner message of their Kabbalistic books is that of Christianity.  Knorr von Rosenroth makes it clear from the beginning to the end of the *Kabbala Denudata* that the work serves as an important part in a program to convert the Jews, as a prelude to the Millennium.  Thus the last item in volume 2 is a brief tract by Van Helmont on the *Christian* Kabbalah, spelling out the view that the application of the doctrines of the Hebrew Kabbalists will help lead to the conversion of the Jews.[19]   Knorr von Rosenroth's achievement was used by European Christians for about two centuries.  Locke, Newton and Leibniz, among others, all knew it.  The German idealists used it, and it was partially translated into English.[20]

Since volume 1 of the *Kabbala Denudata* and Spinoza's *Opera Posthuma* appeared in the same year, many prominent intellectuals read both.  Although it has not yet been investigated, Knorr von Rosenroth and Spinoza must have had quite a few friends or discussants in common.  They both knew Leibniz.  Knorr was involved with the Behmists in the Netherlands, a group that included at times Van Helmont, Peter Serrarius, Benjamin Furly, Adam Boreel and other radical Protestants who also knew and associated with Spinoza.  Spinoza's publisher also published the works of Jacob Boehme and his disciples.  So some of the same people would have read Spinoza, Boehme, and the work of their friend and associate Knorr von Rosenroth.

Even before Moses Germanus pointed it out, some readers must have noticed a striking similarity between Part I of Spinoza's *Ethics* and the first chapters of the Latin abridgement of Abraham Cohen Herrera's *Gate of Heaven*, which appeared as an appendix in volume 1 of the *Kabbala Denudata*.  Abraham Cohen Herrera (ca. 1570-1635 or 1639), born Alonso Nunez de Herrera in Florence, was the scion of a prominent New Christian family who lived as Catholics in Florence and Venice, doing international business for the Duke of Tuscany and the Sultan of Morocco.  The son apparently mastered the Florentine Neoplatonism of Ficino and Pico and studied the Kabbalah with a disciple of Isaac Luria, Israel Sarug, at Dubrovnik.  Herrera became an agent for the Sultan of Morocco, went to Spain on business for him, and was captured by the English in the Earl of Essex's raid on Cadiz in 1595.  He languished under house arrest in England for a few years until released as a result of pleas by the Sultan.  Some time later, Herrera went to Amsterdam, where he was one of the first members of the Sephardic Jewish community that came together there.  He died in Amsterdam in the mid-1630s, when Spinoza was very young.[21]   His great work, *Puerta del Cielo*, written in Spanish, was not published in the original, but a Hebrew translation by one of Spinoza's teachers, Isaac Aboab, was published in 1655, and Knorr von Rosenroth abridged the Hebrew text and translated and published it in Latin in 1677-78.[22]

Herrera set out first to formulate the message of Lurianic Kabbalism in the Neoplatonic idiom. The first several chapters contain no peculiarly Hebrew terms or concepts but lay out the underlying philosophical basis of Lurianic Kabbalism in didactic and demonstrative form. Much of the first part of the text might be interchangeable with portions of Spinoza's first book of the *Ethics*. This is not to say that Spinoza read Herrera. He could have read the Hebrew translation, he could have heard of it in school, he could have learned of it from someone like Knorr von Rosenroth. Or he could have worked out independently a similar Neoplatonic theory of the nature of God and the relation of all kinds of existence to God. It has been suggested by Dunin-Borkowski, a leading Spinoza scholar, that Spinoza did know Herrera's work. Others have questioned this claim.[23] But whether Spinoza knew of Herrera's writings or learned from them, his work was immediately associated with Herrera's ideas. Moses Germanus, Wachter and Basnage all cite similarities.

Gershom Scholem discussed Wachter's interpretation at length in his introductory essay to the German translation of Knorr von Rosenroth's Latin condensation of Herrera's work, and more briefly in his last public lecture at the 1984 Spinoza Symposium at Wolfenbüttel.[24] But Wachter, in fact, mainly dealt with the views of Moses Germanus on Spinoza, on Judaism, on pagan religion, and with the views of Herrera. He said very little about Spinoza, despite his title.[25] Basnage, who is mentioned only in passing by Scholem,[26] has not been examined thoroughly, but his discussion is much more detailed in relating Spinoza's views to those found in the *Kabbala Denudata*.

Basnage devoted thirty pages to Spinoza in the fourth book of his *Histoire des Juifs*, arguing for the true, Kabbalistic origin of Spinozism.[27] Basnage began with Spinoza's view that there is in the universe only a unique substance, God, and that all other beings are only modifications of this. For a substance cannot engender another substance, and nothing can be created out of nothing. *Ex nihilo nihil fit*, Basnage said, was a principle borrowed from the Kabbalists.[28] Those who deny it, according to the Kabbalists, we are told, oppose not only reason but the wisdom and power of God.

A reference is given here to Henry More's *Fundamenta Cabbalae*, which appears in volume 2 of the *Kabbala Denudata*.[29] Basnage was well aware that the *ex nihilo nihil fit* doctrine was articulated by the Epicureans, but he claimed it was taken over by others, including the Kabbalists.

Spinoza's principle that there is only one substance, agrees with the teaching of the Kabbalists, except that Spinoza made this substance material, while for the Kabbalists it is spiritual.[30] Basnage contended, however, that both views came down to the same thing— that there is only one substance, and everything is a modification of it. Basnage again cited More as his authority for saying this.[31] The difficulties for Spinozism will be greater than in "la Theologie Cabbalistique," but both systems will have problems explaining how anything other than the one substance exists.[32] Basnage went on to explore the Kabbalistic Neoplatonic emanation theory and Spinoza's notion of modes. After showing how strange and blasphemous Spinoza's theory could become, Basnage restated his thesis that the foundations of Spinozism lie in Kabbalistic theology: All that Spinoza had done was to dress it up in Cartesian terms, leading to his materialistic characterization of the one substance.[33] Basnage preferred the Kabbalistic spiritualistic version, and he tried to show that Spinoza's materialistic formulation ran into all sorts of special problems.[34] But "the great difficulty of Spinoza, and the Cabbalists before him, is that nothing can come from nothing. If that is so, God has produced nothing outside of himself. Then all parts of the universe must necessarily be parts of the One only substance."[35] Basnage insisted that this was implausible. Far more plausible is the belief that God made the material world by His infinite power, even if we do not know how this could be done. The refutation of particulars in Spinoza's theory Basnage left to his friend, Pierre Bayle.[36]

In the next chapter Basnage went on to deal with other Jewish theories of creation.[37] Here he plunged into the Kabbalistic writings in the *Kabbala Denudata*, Luria's work, More's response, and Abraham Cohen Herrera's work.[38] Strikingly, Basnage disavowed the claim of various Christian Kabbalists who found Jesus, the second person of the Trinity, in the Kabbalistic explanation of how the world was generated from God.[39] Exposing the mistake of the Christian Kabbalists, who find what they want in the obscure expressions of the

Jewish exegetes, Basnage said: "Cohen Irara, a Portuguese Cabbalist who wrote at the end of the last century, has shown us how to understand the thought of the Cabbalists."[40]   He then outlined Herrera's emanation theory.

Basnage gave no source for his reading of Spinoza as a Kabbalist or for taking Abraham Cohen Herrera's text as the clearest statement of the Kabbalistic emanation theory. He made no mention of Wachter's book.   But Basnage read a vast amount of Jewish literature for his *Histoire des Juifs*, mostly in Latin or modern language editions (although he cited some texts in Hebrew). He did not have access to the manuscripts of the Jewish anti-Christian polemics written in Holland until some were sold in the auction of his son-in-law's library in 1715.[41]   This would indicate that he did not have deep connections in the Dutch Jewish world. He did not even have access to the sort of Kabbalistic manuscripts that Knorr von Rosenroth edited.   But he knew a lot of gossip and rumor about the Jews of his day, some of which looks as if it came from Jewish informants rather than books.[42]   He did not name people he might have talked to.  He went to Holland himself after Spinoza was dead. He knew of Orobio de Castro; but, unlike Locke or Philip van Limborch, he does not seem to have known him personally.[43]

Johann Georg Wachter, on the other hand, knew at least one Amsterdam rabbi, namely Moses Germanus. He had known him first as Johann Peter Speeth (or Spaeth), a disciple of Jacob Spener, and collaborator of Knorr von Rosenroth in the *Kabbala Denudata*. Speeth went through a series of spiritual gyrations in the 1680s and 1690s, going back to Catholicism, then becoming involved with Quakers, Mennonites and Socinians, studying Hebrew and Kabbalah, and finally in 1697 becoming a Jew in Amsterdam and a rabbi of the Portuguese Synagogue, with the name Moses Germanus. Wachter came to visit him and derived his ideas about Spinozism and Kabbalism through this personal contact and through letters from Moses Germanus.[44]

A, or *the*, central issue in relating Spinoza to the Kabbalah for Wachter was the centrality in Spinoza, Moses Germanus, and Abraham Cohen Herrera of the principle, *ex nihilo nihil fit*—the problem of articulating a satisfactory emanation theory. It seems too great a coincidence that both Basnage and Wachter saw this as a central issue in Spinoza, unless the two had a common source.

Wachter spoke of the issue as to whether Spinozism was a Kabbalist theory or came from Kabbalism as the latest controversy going on in Holland.[45] Like Basnage, he related the thesis of Moses Germanus and of "Judaism" that "dass alles Wesen Gott sey," with the "rabbinical" and Kabbalistic principle, *ex nihilo nihil fit*[46] and contended that these two theses lie at the heart of Spinoza's view. In this form there is a similarity between Spinoza's, Herrera's and Moses Germanus' formulations, especially if one leaves out the dimension Basnage made all-important, the material aspect of Spinoza's God—and if one ignores the differing conceptions of Divine Causality.

I should like to consider three questions about these early readings of Spinoza: (a) could Spinoza have drawn his views from Kabbalistic sources? (b) is the similarity stressed by Basnage, Wachter and Moses Germanus significant? and (c) do the differences between Spinoza's views and those of the Kabbalah make the similarities of little importance?

Given Spinoza's statement in the *Tractatus Theologico-Politicus* that he read and knew "Kabbalistic triflers," "whose insanity provokes my unceasing astonishment," it remains to be asked whether Spinoza adopted any of the Kabbalistic outlook. Wachter and Moses Germanus were struck by Spinoza's remark in one of the last letters to Henry Oldenburg, at the end of 1675, where Spinoza said, "For I hold that God is of all things the cause immanent, as the phrase is, not transient. I say all things are in God and move in God, thus agreeing with Paul, and perhaps with all the ancient philosophers, though the phraseology may be different: I will even venture to affirm that I agree with all the ancient Hebrews, in so far as one may judge from their traditions, though some are in many ways corrupted."[47] Wachter and Moses Germanus took this as a confession by Spinoza to his close friend, Oldenburg, that his views preserved the tradition of the Jewish Kabbalah in a kind of Jewish Neoplatonism.[48]

Spinoza could have learned something about the Kabbalah while a student at the Synagogue. He was a student of Aboab while the latter was translating Herrera's work. He could have read the published Hebrew version. After the excommunication, Spinoza was close to many Christian mystics among the Quakers, Collegiants and Mennonites. People whom Spinoza knew—like Adam Boreel, the leader of the Collegiants, who took in Spinoza in 1656—knew Van Helmont, the close associate of Knorr von Rosenroth. Van Helmont was *au courant* in Kabbalistic studies, and his work on the Hebrew language was itself a major Kabbalistic work.[49]  So Spinoza's known circle of mystical non-denominational Christians overlapped with the Van Helmont-Knorr von Rosenroth one; Spinoza could have known their views, and they his.  Knorr von Rosenroth studied Hebrew and Kabbalah with rabbis in Amsterdam for several years. He was there while Spinoza was alive.  He was editing the *Kabbala Denudata* by 1670 and published the first volume in the year of Spinoza's death.  A manuscript at the Herzog August Bibliothek in Wolfenbüttel tells of a trip Knorr von Rosenroth took to Amsterdam in the 1660s.  He did not name many of the people he saw there, but he met many scientifically inclined intellectuals and religious figures.[50]  In the preface to the *Kabbala Denudata*, he states that he got the impressive collection of manuscript material he used from an unnamed rabbi who was then denounced by the Jewish community. All sorts of troubles descended on the rabbi and his family, he reports, for giving him the material, and on Knorr and his family for receiving it and making it available.[51]

Boreel too, who edited the Hebrew text of the *Mishnah* with the aid of rabbis Judah Leon Templo (who lived and ate in Boreel's house), Menasseh ben Israel, and Isaac and Jacob Abendana, complained about how secretive the Jews were about their religious documents.[52]  Yet Boreel and Menasseh apparently agreed to take part in a College of Jewish Studies to be established in London to publish the texts of the Jewish mysteries in Hebrew and in translation.[53]  The English Deists found it impossible to obtain the Jewish anti-Christian documents by leaders like Haham Saul Levi Morteira, Orobio de Castro and others, until they suddenly turned up in the sale of Basnage's son-in-law's library in 1715.[54]  Previously the only indication that these works circulated outside the Jewish community is a note by Orobio on one of his manuscripts, saying he did not publish it for fear of causing scandal, but he showed it to the Jesuits in Brussels, who liked it.[55]

Presumably the Jewish community would be even more guarded about Kabbalistic documents by Luria, Hayyim Vital, Israel Sarug and others, many of which were not published in Hebrew until the late nineteenth or early twentieth centuries.  The fact that a renegade rabbi gave this material to Knorr von Rosenroth is quite interesting. I do not know who the rabbi was—maybe Moshe Idel or Yosef Kaplan can shed light on the question. Perhaps the unknown rabbi was disillusioned by the debacle of the Sabbatian movement, which was so strong in Amsterdam, tossed away his mystical manuscripts, and left for a new life in America.

At any rate, the Kabbalistic material passed into Christian hands in Amsterdam in the 1660s or early 1670s. Knorr von Rosenroth obviously showed it to Van Helmont, and it probably became known amongst the philosemitic mystical Christians like Boreel, Serrarius, Furly, Dury (who was Oldenburg's father-in-law), and others, many of whom regularly attended Synagogue services and interacted with the Jewish community.[56] Peter Serrarius, Spinoza's patron, was the leader of the Christian followers of Shabtai Zvi and did some Kabbalistic studies with Amsterdam rabbis on the matter.[57] Spinoza could easily have come to know of the materials available to these Christians.

Contrary to the accepted story, Spinoza knew some Jews in the twenty-one years after his excommunication. He knew the son-in-law of Rabbi Benjamin Musafia of Copenhagen, and he was a close friend of the Egyptian Jew Henriquez Morales (Henri Morelli), the physician of the libertine poet Charles St. Evremond.[58] He may have known others, especially if they were not members of the Amsterdam synagogue. From the Jews he knew he may have learned some things about the Jewish intellectual interests of the time. Oldenburg asked him what he knew about the appearance of the King of the Jews (Shabtai Zvi) and what the Jews of Amsterdam thought about this.[59] Regrettably, the answer (if there was one) is missing, but we have Serrarius' answer. And Serrarius was the point of contact between Spinoza in Holland and Oldenburg and Robert Boyle in England, receiving and transmitting their mail. He was clearly involved with the Amsterdam Jewish Sabbatians and sent copies of Shabtai Zvi's letter to the Amsterdam Jews to John Dury in Switzerland. Thus *he* had access to such a document![60]

Spinoza, then, had Christian and Jewish contacts who could have given him access to the Kabbalistic ideas and materials being studied in the Jewish community. Further exploration of Spinoza's Christian Millenarian contacts and his Jewish ones may reveal more about Spinoza's knowledge of what was going on in the Jewish world, and about knowledge among Jews of Spinoza's activities. But even what we know now shows us that Spinoza could have used Kabbalistic sources or ideas. The view stated by Basnage is not preposterous; it is even genuinely possible. Spinoza could have been a secret Kabbalist trying to assert his own originality.

Whether or not Spinoza drew from Kabbalistic sources and ideas, is there enough similarity between his views and Kabbalistic ones to be of any importance? Here I think one has to distinguish between the detailed Kabbalistic system, with the 'Eyn Sof, the Adam Kadmon, and other elements unmentioned by Spinoza, and a metaphysical system such as that presented by Abraham Cohen Herrera as a basis for, or prelude to, Kabbalism. There are some striking similarities between Part I of the *Ethics* and the first five chapters of Herrera's *Porta Coelorum*. A detailed study would, I think, show that Spinoza and Herrera held to similar views about the status and nature of being or substance and its relation to supposedly created objects. They both had, for want of a better term, a Neoplatonic conception of the One, or Substance. Herrera probably came by his views from the Florentine Platonists. Both men had to hold some kind of emanation theory to account for other existences without allowing for independently caused or produced entities. Both have the basic problem of explaining how and why there is something other than just Being as such. If these features are taken as central, then Spinoza and Herrera have similar metaphysical commitments, which can be described as Basnage, Moses Germanus and Wachter did, as exhibiting the consequences, in a Neoplatonic metaphysics, of accepting either Spinoza's theory of causality, or Herrera's theory of necessary existence, or *ex nihilo nihil fit*.[61]

Interesting as this may be for the ontology of Part I of the *Ethics*, it does not come to grips with either Spinoza's theory or Herrera's of what the world is like and how it operates. The Kabbalistic orientation may have helped fix Spinoza's and Herrera's starting place, but it does not reveal where their respective theories led. Given the purposes of the early interpreters, Basnage, Moses Germanus and Wachter, however, the characterization of the initial orientation may have been enough.

If Moses Germanus originated the interpretation of Spinoza as a secret Kabbalist, as Leibniz claims in the *Theodicy*,[62] we have reason to believe, from a letter of Moses Germanus to Van Helmont in 1696, that Moses was opposing both Spinoza and Kabbalism in order to advance his own idiosyncratic version of Judaism.[63] Having gone through so many religious and theological turnings, from Catholicism to mystical pietistic Protestantism, back to Catholicism, to the radical Protestantism of the Quakers, Mennonites and Socinians, Moses Germanus became a Jew. As he explains, he became convinced that the Jewish people were the suffering servant of *Isaiah* 53, and Van Helmont urged him to convert to Judaism and move to Amsterdam.[64] What appears in his Amsterdam years indicates that he had developed an extremely Jewish version of Christianity and saw the presence of the actual Jewish Messiah as a historical reality of his time. He claimed to oppose Spinoza's ahistorical and irreligious views and the Kabbalah's obfuscations. What the Jewish people really yearned for, he insisted, was the Messianic Redeemer. Jesus, a rabbi of Roman times with fine moral teachings, was, like other Jews, hoping for and expecting this Redeemer. Around 200 of the Common Era, he was grossly and deliberately misinterpreted as presenting himself as the redemptive Messiah. A conspiracy of sinister forces established Christianity and maintained it up to the Reformation. Then one could again see the New Testament for what it was, the life of a pious rabbi conjoined with some inspirational literature, and some dastardly addenda that created a pseudo-Messianic movement around Jesus of Nazareth after his death.[65] This Judaizing version of Christianity (later adopted by some German Bible critics) was coupled with a Messianic Judaism centered on the person of Oliger Pauli, a Dane who had a Jewish grandfather. Moses Germanus and Pauli caused a great deal of stir and agitated the rulers of Europe to join them in liberating Palestine, reestablishing the Jewish people there, and rebuilding the Temple.[66]

It appears that Moses Germanus rejected Spinoza's irreligion along with the Christian reading of the Kabbalah, which he had known first hand as a worker with Knorr von Rosenroth on the *Kabbala Denudata*, in order to advocate his own brand of Messianism. His ground for rejecting both would be the same: their common metaphysical assumptions as reflected in their handling of the problem of emanation. Evidently, for him, this single common theme provided sufficient grounds for rejecting the two systems, as well as for linking them, regardless of what other views Spinoza, or Herrera, or other Kabbalists might hold.

Wachter visited Moses Germanus in Amsterdam shortly after he settled there. As a result of conversations and letters he received, Wachter grew deeply disturbed by Moses Germanus's anti-Christianity. He saw Amsterdam Judaism as being in ferment because of Spinozism and because of Moses Germanus' views. Wachter published his exchange with Moses Germanus, in which the latter attacked Christianity as modern paganism.[67]   One aspect of Wachter's counterattack was to contend that Moses Germanus' theory was, all protestations notwithstanding, just Spinozism and Kabbalism. Much of the evidence he offered was to show that Moses Germanus and Spinoza held the same views as Herrera, especially regarding Being, *ex nihilo nihil fit*, and emanation.[68]   A substantial part of Wachter's response is an analysis of Herrera's text in the *Kabbala Denudata*.[69]   Wachter hoped to undermine Judaism, whether in the form it took in Moses Germanus or as represented in Herrera. Part of his tactics was to lump these thinkers together with the notorious heretic Spinoza.

Basnage offers a more interesting interpretation than Moses Germanus' of Spinoza as a Kabbalist, first because he deals more directly with Spinoza, and secondly because Basnage saw that Spinoza's emanation theory was a materialistic rendition of Cartesianism, a modern scientific account of the world. Basnage himself was involved with a kind of Calvinist Cartesianism, and so could see Spinoza in both the Cartesian and Kabbalistic traditions.[70]

Basnage undertook his massive *Histoire des Juifs* from Roman times to the present, not just out of curiosity. He knew that Menasseh ben Israel had planned such a work, a continuation of Josephus, as evidence that Jewish history is Providential History.[71] Basnage was a Millenarian, concerned to show, through Jewish history, that God is active in history, and in His Actions towards the Jews is bringing about the climax of human history, the Thousand Year Reign of Christ, which Basnage foresaw as starting in the early eighteenth century. Jewish history illustrates God's power, God's concern, God's wrath, and God's redemptive action. In studying Jewish history, the true and believing Christian will have his faith reinforced, and the Jew may be enlightened to see that he has to overcome Jewish myopia and recognize the fulfillment of Judaism in Christianity.[72]

Basnage's work is quite tolerant, especially when compared with what German experts on Judaism, like Wagenseil, Spitzel and others, were turning out.[73] Basnage tried to be objective and to get the facts from reliable sources. He studied Jewish texts and apparently collected a lot of oral history from people in the Netherlands. He often defended the Jews from false anti-semitic accusations. And he was unimpressed with the efforts of those who tried to convert the Jews through force or arguments. Force had backfired in Spain and Portugal, creating the Marrano situation; and Jews usually won the arguments.[74] So, Basnage advised letting God do the actual converting.[75] But a learned, well-intentioned Christian could see that what kept intelligent Jews in their blindness was their philosophy—Kabbalism. Basnage had read the *Kabbala Denudata* and other sources and saw the Kabbalah as the central ideology of Judaism. He devoted a large section of his study to the history of the Kabbalah and explanation of its doctrines.[76] For he was convinced that once the Jews saw the faults and flaws of their Kabbalistic theosophy, they would be prepared for conversion.

Bringing Spinoza into the discussion of Kabbalism was a way of indicating what was wrong with Spinoza and of showing that the roots of Spinoza's atheism lie in Kabbalism. If one could show (a) that Spinoza was a Kabbalist in metaphysics, and (b) that he was an atheist, then his Kabbalism would seem to imply his atheism. Revealing Spinoza's hidden sources in the Kabbalah would destroy his claim to originality. At the same time, Spinoza's sacrilegious results would explain why the Kabbalists were not anxious to claim him as their heir.[77]

All this I presume Basnage got first, second, or third hand from Moses Germanus. But Basnage did see and emphasize the critical difference between Spinoza's emanation theory and the Kabbalistic one, that for the Kabbalists all derivative being is spiritual. For Spinoza, Basnage contended, all derivative being is material. "The Cabbalists agree further with Spinoza in recognizing only one unique Substance, but this impious one makes this substance material, in order to make God corporeal and to annihilate the spirituality of this being."[78] Basnage saw Spinoza's materialism as allowing him to take over Cartesian science but leaving a host of problems, such as how to explain mental or spiritual events and how to explain contrary or conflicting modifications of the one substance. Basnage contended that the only novelty in Spinoza's theory was in his use of the term "modification."[79] But having done this, he argued, Spinoza had left himself open to the problems that fill dozens of pages in Pierre Bayle's rather amazing article on Spinoza. Basnage was a close friend of Bayle's and cited the text in which Bayle tried to make hash out of Spinoza's views by identifying modifications with substance and arguing that for Spinoza "God is hot" and "God is cold" simultaneously.[80] In short, Basnage sought to push Spinoza back to a Jewish Kabbalistic world and to make his theory a mass of contradictions, discrediting both Spinoza and his Kabbalistic roots. Elsewhere Basnage sought to show that Spinoza's Bible criticism and its impious conclusions came from Jewish sources.[81]

To picture Spinoza as a Kabbalist taking over Jewish views then appearing in the *Kabbala Denudata* was natural for Moses Germanus, Wachter and Basnage. In terms of the interest each had in Judaism, such an interpretation was not far-fetched. From their perspective, Spinoza's metaphysics at its core looked the same as Herrera's. It was certainly possible that Spinoza had known of Herrera's views and used them. Anyone who bought the *Kabbala Denudata* and Spinoza's *Opera Posthuma* in 1677 might have thought them related works, at least until reaching the exposition of Spinoza's Cartesianism or discovering the details of real Jewish Kabbalism.

Seeing how Spinoza's contemporaries could read him as a Kabbalist helps us understand, I think, the milieu in which his ideas appeared. He was connected with many mystical non-denominational Christians, followers of the pantheism of Jacob Boehme. He was also involved with freethinkers. But there is little in his correspondence or writings that shows he was involved with Cartesians, that is, living followers of Descartes. He was interpreted by some as a Kabbalist, and his metaphysics may reflect a synthesis of Cartesianism and Kabbalism. Our received view of Spinoza's thought as growing out of the Cartesian ferment has dulled us to the much richer, more exciting intellectual world in which he flourished. If we can see him as some of his contemporaries did, we may discover that in spite of all the difficulties that dogged his intellectual career, and in spite of his ongoing polemical attacks on Judaism and the Jewish community in which he was reared, Spinoza may have still derived a central part of his philosophy from a vital part of his heritage—the Kabbalism then being studied in Holland. Perhaps he was trying to utilize the Neoplatonized Kabbalism of Herrera as a way of integrating the new science and the rational/spiritual mysticism of his time. If we can suspend disbelief in Spinoza as a Kabbalist, we may find him a much more exciting and excited thinker.

## Notes

1. The possibility that Spinoza drew his philosophical theory from Chinese thought was raised in the article "Spinoza," Rem. B, in Pierre Bayle's *Dictionnaire historique et critique.*

2. Jacques Basnage, *The History of the Jews from Jesus Christ to the Present Time: Containing their Antiquities, their Religion, their Rites, the Dispersion of the Ten Tribes in the East, and the Persecutions this Nation has suffer'd in the West. Being a Supplement and Continuation of the History of Josephus* (London, 1708) Book IV, ch. vii, 294. The work originally appeared in French in 1707, with the second, greatly enlarged edition in 1716.

3. Loc. cit. Pierre Bayle was among those accused of not understanding Spinoza when he criticized his philosophy. See Remark DD of Bayle's article "Spinoza."

4. Johann Georg Wachter, *Den Spinozismus im Judenthums, oder, die von dem heutigen Judenthumb und dessen Geheimen Kabbala, vergotterte Welt, an Mose Germano sonsten Johann Peter Spaeth von Augsburg geburtig befunden under widerleget* (Amsterdam, 1699).

5. Benedictus de Spinoza, *Theological Political Tractatus,* chap IX, ed., R. H. M. Elwes (London, 1883; repr. New York: Dover, 1951), 140.

6. Cf. Harry Wolfson, *The Philosophy of Spinoza,* ch. 1.

7. Yirmiahu Yovel, in "Bible Interpretation as Philosophical Praxis: A Study of Spinoza and Kant," *JHP* 11 (1973): 189 ff., discusses what people might have made out of Spinoza's views if only these two works had survived.

8. We have Descartes' replies to the objections to the *Meditations,* a great deal of correspondence with and about various critics, as well as Descartes' *Conversations with Burman,* where he answered some very direct questions about what he thought he was doing.

9. See Gustave Cohen, "Le séjour de Saint-Evremond en Hollande," *Revue de Littérature comparée* (1925-26); R. Ternois, "Saint-Evremond et Spinoza," *Revue d'Histoire littéraire de la France* 1 (1965): 1-14; K. O. Meinsma, *Spinoza et son cercle* (Paris: Vrin, 1983), ch. xii; and R. H. Popkin, "Serendipity at the Clark: Spinoza

and the Prince of Condé," *The Clark Newsletter* 10 (1986): 4-7, and "Some Seventeenth Century Interpretations of Spinoza's Ideas," in C. Augustijn et al., *Essays on Church History Presented to Jan van den Berg* (Kampen: J. H. Kok, 1987), 63-74.

10. Bayle, "Spinoza" at the beginning.

11. This was Henry More's diagnosis when he heard about Spinoza's views. See More's letter to Robert Boyle, December 4 [1670?], in *The Works of the Honourable Robert Boyle* (London, 1772) **6**.514.

12. This was Bayle's view in "Spinoza," Remark B.

13. See Bayle, "Spinoza" and Jean Colerus, *La Vie de B. de Spinosa* (La Haye, 1706).

14. See Rems. CC, DD, and EE.

15. Gershom Scholem, "Knorr von Rosenroth," *Encyclopedia Judaica* **10**.1118.

16. Christian Knorr von Rosenroth, *Kabbala Denudata* (Sulzbach, 1677, 1684).

17. On the editing of the *Kabbala Denudata*, see Allison Coudert, "A Cambridge Platonist's Kabbalist Nightmare," *Journal of the History of Ideas* 35 (1975): esp. 635-39, 645-52. On Moses Germanus, see under Spaeth, Johann Peter (Moses Germanus) in the *Jewish Encyclopedia* **11**.483-84, *Encyclopedia Judaica* **15**.219-220, and Hans Joachim Schoeps, *Philosemitismus im Barok* (Tübingen: Mohr, 1952), 67-81.

18. Quoted in Brian P. Copenhaver, "Jewish Theologies of Space in the Scientific Revolution: Henry More, Joseph Raphson, Isaac Newton and their Predecessors," *Annals of Science* 37 (1980): 522-23.

19. See the preface of vol. 1 by Knorr von Rosenroth, and the appendix to vol. 2, Francis M. Van Helmont, "Adumbratio Kabbalae Christianae, Id est Syncatabasis Hebraizans, sive Brevis Applicatio Doctrinae Hebraeorum Cabbalistimme ad Dogmata non foederis; pro formanda hypothesi, ad conversionem Judaeorum proficia."

20. The *Kabbala Denudata* was cited frequently for over a century after its publication. It was partially translated by S. L. MacGregor Mathers, *The Kabbalah Unveiled* (London, 1887). I own a fifth printing from 1938. I have been told that the pages of Newton's copy, given to him by Van Helmont, are uncut.

21. On Herrera's amazing life, see the introduction by Gershom Scholem to the German edition of his *Pforte des Himmels* (Frankfurt: Suhrkamp, 1974) and the article on Herrera in the *Encyclopedia Judaica*, which differs from Scholem's account in some important regards.

22. The original Spanish text has now been edited for the first time by K. Krabbenhaft: Abraham Cohen Herrera, *Puerta del Cielo* (Fundacion Universitaria Espanola, 1987). This edition has a long introduction giving biographical and bibliographical information. The title page of the Latin abridgement and translation has the subtitle: *In quo Dogmata Cabbalistica de AEn-Soph, Adam Kadmon, Zimzum, Aziluth, Briah, Jezirah, Asiah, Nomine Tetragrammato, Revolutionibus Alphabethicis, Avvir Kadmon. . . . Philosophica Platonica conservatur.*

23. Cf. Stanislaus von Dunin-Borkowski, *Der junge De Spinoza* (Münster, 1910), 188-89; Scholem, "Einleitung," 41-46.

24. Gershom Scholem,"Einleitung," 41-46, and "Die Wachtersche Kontroverse uber den Spinozismuss und ihre Folgen," in K. Grunder and W. Schmidt-Biggemann, *Spinoza in der Frühzeit seiner religiosen Wirkung, Wolfenbütteler Studien zur Aufklärung* 12 (Heidelberg: Lambert Schneider, 1984): 15-25.

25. Wachter discussed Spinoza only occasionally, as on pp. 5v, 3, 4 and 34, and in the last part of his work.

26. Scholem, "Einleitung," 61; "Wachtersche Kontroverse," 23.

27. Basnage, *Histoire des Juifs* (La Haye, 1716) Livre IV, ch. V, 4.128-158; in the English folio edition of 1708, the chapter on Spinoza is 294-99.

28. Basnage, French ed., 131-32; English ed., 294.

29. French ed., 132 and note; English ed., 294.

30. French ed., 132-35; English ed., 295.

31. French ed., 137-8; English ed., 295.

32. French ed., 136-9; English ed., 295-6.

33. French ed., 140-41; English ed, 297.

34. French ed., 141-2; English ed., 297.

35. French ed., 149-50; English ed., 297.

36. French ed., 156-7; English ed., 298.

37. French ed., Livre IV, ch. viii, "Creation du Monde par voie d'Emanation," 158-84; English ed., 299 ff.

38. French ed, Livre IV, chap. xiii, sec. 3-15.

39. Sec. xv, 174-6.

40. French ed., 175.

41. See R. H. Popkin, "Jacques Basnage's *Histoire des Juifs* and the Biblioteca Sarraziana," *Studia Rosenthaliana* 21 (1987): 154-62. See the "Table des Auteurs qu'on a citez dans cet Ouvrages," at the beginning of the *Histoire des Juifs*, xlix-lxxxvi, which contains many Jewish authors.

42. Quite a bit of the material on sixteenth and seventeenth-century developments in Jewish communities does not seem to have come from books—at least no citations are given.

43. Basnage discussed Orobio in his section on seventeenth-century Jews in Holland, Livre IX, ch. xxxvii, sec. 13-16. He learned of Orobio's unpublished anti-Christian writings from the manuscripts sold in the Sarraz auction in 1715.

44. See Wachter, *Den Spinozismus im Judenthums*, "Vorrede," *5-*5v.

45. Wachter, *5: "Wir praesentiren der hier *Geneigter Leser*, die allerneuesten Controversien von Holland."

46. Wachter, *5v-*6v.

47. Letter to Oldenburg, Epistola LXXIII.

48. Wachter, 34.

49. Francis Van Helmont's *Kurtzer Entwurff des eigenthielen Natur-Alphabets der Heiligen Sprache* (Sulzbach, 1667). Allison Coudert is preparing an edition of this work.

50. The Herzog August Bibliothek at Wolfenbüttel has a great many of Knorr von Rosenroth's papers including correspondence and materials used in the *Kabbala Denudata*. The account of his trip is MS. Extrav. 253.1.

51. See Knorr von Rosenroth, "Lectori Philebraeo Salutem," *Kabbala Denudata*, 1.18-19. The passage is translated in Allison Coudert, "A Cambridge Platonist's Kabbalist Nightmare," 695.

52. John Dury reported that Boreel was having difficulties with the rabbis about the Spanish translation of the *Mishnah* "by reason of the iealousie & envious spirit wch in yt Nation to hinder all strangers from the knowledge of their law and way." Letter of John Dury to Samuel Hartlib, Amsterdam 5/15 July 1661, Hartlib Papers, Sheffield University MS. 4/4/26. On the Jewish-Christian project to edit the *Mishnah*, see R. H. Popkin, "Some Aspects of Jewish-Christian Theological Interchanges in Holland and England, 1640-1700," in J. van den Berg and E. G. E. van der Wall, eds., *Jewish-Christian Relations* (Dordrecht: Kluwer, 1988), 3-32.

53. See R. H. Popkin, "The First College of Jewish Studies," *REJ* 143 (1984): 351-64.

54. See Popkin, "Jacques Basnage's *Histoire des Juifs* and the Biblioteca Sarraziana," 156. Anthony Collins complained that Jews "are forbid, under pain of excommunication" to lend these documents to Christians, *A Discourse of the Grounds and Reasons of the Christian Religion*, (London 1724), 82n-83n.

55. This note appears on the flyleaf Hs. 48 E 42 of the Ets Haim, Amsterdam collection, presently at the National Library of Israel. The Portuguese text is reproduced in L. Fuks and R. G. Fuks-Mansfeld, *Hebrew and Judaica Manuscripts in Amsterdam Public Collections*, 2 (Leiden: Brill, 1975).

56. See Popkin, "Some Aspects of Jewish-Christian Theological Interchanges."

57. Serrarius described a Kabbalistic discussion with "quelque Juif" in 1664 in a letter to Dury, Zurich Staatsarchiv Ms. E. II. 457d, fol. 421(659). On Serrarius see E. G. E. van der Wall, *De Mystieke Chiliast, Petrus Serrarius (1600-1669) en zijn Wereld*, (Dordrecht: ICG, 1987); and R. H. Popkin, "A Note on Serrarius," in K. O. Meinsma, *Spinoza et son cercle* (Paris, 1983), 277-79, n. 62.

58. Cf. Michael Petry and Guido van Suchtelen, "Spinoza and the Military: A Newly Discovered Document," *Studia Spinoziana* 1 (1985): 361-69; and R. H. Popkin, "Serendipity at the Clark: Spinoza and the Prince of Condé," *The Clark Newsletter* 10 (1986): 4-7.

59. Letter of Oldenburg to Spinoza, London, 8 December, 1665, in Marie Boas Hall and A. Rupert Hall, eds., *The Correspondence of Henry Oldenburg*, letter 467 (Madison: University of Wisconsin Press, 1965) 1.633-37.

60. Serrarius to Oldenburg, 5 July 1667, in Oldenburg Correspondence, letter 652, **2**.446-47. Letter 493, **2**.48-51, a report from Oldenburg to Robert Boyle about what was happening in Shabtai Zvi's affairs, is probably based on information from Serrarius. Dury's letter to Ulrich, January 25, 1666, Zurich Staatsarchiv MS. E. II. 457e, fol. 747; and van der Wall, *Mystieke Chiliast, Petrus Serrarius*, esp. Hoofdstuck X.

61. Neither Spinoza nor Herrera used the formula *ex nihilo nihil fit*, but it is equivalent to Spinoza's axioms 1, 2, 3 and 7, and to Herrera's, "Quod entia vel omnia sint necessaria, vel omnia contingentia." cap. I.

62. Leibniz was taken in the eighteenth century as the authority on this. He said, in the *Théodicée*, sec. 9, "Un certain Allemand natif de la Suabe, devenu Juif il y a quelques années et dogmatisent sous le nom de Moses Germanus, s'étoit attache au dogmes de Spinoza, a cru que Spinoza renouvelle l'ancienne Cabale des Hebreux; et un savant homme [Wachter] qui a refute ce proselyte Juif, paroit etre de meme sentiment." Leibniz knew both Wachter and Van Helmont personally.

63. See Wachter, end of "Vorrede"; and H. J. Schoeps, *Philosemitismus im Barok*, 67-81.

64. See "Spaeth," *Jewish Encyclopedia* 11.484; and Johann Jacob Schudt, *Judische Merckwurdigkeiten* 1.273, 4.194.

65. "Spaeth," *Encyclopedia Judaica* **15**.219-20; Schoeps, 67-80, and Schoeps, *Juden, Christen und Judenchristen* (Bern: Francke, 1965), 83-91.

66. See Schoeps, *Philosemitismus im Barok,* chapters on Pauli and Moses Germanus, 51-81, and articles "Spaeth" and "Pauli, Holger (Oliger)," *Jewish Encyclopedia,* **11**.483-84 and **9**.563.

67. Wachter published Moses Germanus' "Gegensatz der Judisch und Heydischen Religion" in German and Latin at the beginning of his book, along with his own answer to it.

68. Wachter, passim.

69. Wachter, 81-101. The third part of Wachter's work is directed against Spinoza.

70. On Basnage's career and interests, see Gerald Cerny, *Theology, Politics and Letters at the Crossroads of European Civilization: Jacques Basnage and the Baylean Huguenot Refugees in the Dutch Republic* (Dordrecht: Kluwer, 1987). On Calvinist Cartesianism, see Michael Heyd, *Between Orthodoxy and Enlightenment, Jean-Robert Chouet and the Introduction of Cartesian Science in the Academy of Geneva* (The Hague: Nijhoff, 1982).

71. Basnage referred to Menasseh's project several times. In his discussion of Menasseh, he gave the intended title as *Historia y Continuacion de Flavio Josepho hasta nuestros Tiempos, Histoire des Juifs,* Livre IX, chap. xxxvi, Tome XV, 1001.

72. Basnage, *Histoire des Juifs,* Livre I, ch. 11; and Cerny, ch. 5.

73. As Cerny points out, "The Huguenot historian was profoundly repelled by Christian persecution of the Jews," and he admired the Dutch toleration of the Jews; 198-99. He did not support any of the blood libels that appear in the writings of Wagenseil and others.

74. See Cerny, 182-200, for Basnage's objectivity. In the last chapter, Livre IX, chap. xxxix, Basnage evaluated the attempts to convert the Jews.

75. Basnage, *Histoire des Juifs,* Livre IX, chap. xxxix, 1140: "Dieu seul connoît le tems auquel il rappellera cette Nation elue. Cette Réfléxion engage les Chrétiens à prier Dieu pour eux, au lieu d'emploier les Moiens violens qui les oppriment, & ne les convertissent pas."

76. The Kabbalah is discussed throughout the work. Livres III and IV offer a very detailed discussion of Kabbalistic doctrines. All sorts of Jewish and Christian sources were used.

77. This seems to be the point of Livre IV, ch. vii, where Spinoza is treated as a secret Kabbalist.

78. Basnage, *Histoire des Juifs*, Livre IV, ch. vii, sec. 5, 136 in the French edition. The English edition, 295, reads "that Wretch" for "impious one."
79. Basnage, 137-38.
80. Bayle, "Spinoza," Remarks N and DD.
81. Basnage, *Histoire des Juifs*, Livre V, ch. i, sec. ix. He also includes a biography of Spinoza in the section on Jews in Holland, Livre IX, ch. xxxvii, sec. vii-xii, which is quite critical.

# The Psychodynamics of
# Neoplatonic Ontology

Robert B. McLaren

It is a commonplace that analytical psychology is concerned with dynamic "integrative principles" that preserve the self intact.[1] These principles include orientation toward need-satisfying goals.[2] Among the followers of Freud it has been a basic tenet that the striving to achieve these goals is psychosexual in nature. Religion, as one integrative strategy, is not less psychosexual than the rest and arises from the effort to identify with a projection of one's earthly father after discovery of his limitations.[3]

It may be argued that the psychodynamic approach is inadequate for, if not irrelevant to, the study of Neoplatonic ontology. Freud addressed himself primarily to the monotheism of Judaism and Christianity, while Neoplatonism proposes not a paternal deity but an Ultimate Reality, *ontos on*, the ineffable One, who transcends being, and is clearly unrelated to anything so crude as a Father-figure-in-the-sky.

Three responses may be proffered before entering on our main line of argument. First, the Freudian interpretation of the father-projection has not met with universal acceptance even among analysts. It is certainly foreign to the religious experience of many who have sought understanding, from the Hebrew prophets to Maimonides, to Maslow and Einstein. Indeed the earliest conception of YHWH was that of One who is Ultimate Being, yet no mere being: *ehyeh asher ehyeh*—I AM THAT I AM (Exodus 3:14), whose very name was not to be pronounced lest it suggest finitude. Lenn Goodman points out that "Maimonides advised parents from the earliest age (in marked contrast to Plato) to inform their children that God is not a person or a thing."[4] Einstein echoed this idea, placing blame for present-day conflicts between science and religion on the concept of a personal God, "which we must have the stature to give up."[5] Yet both Maimonides and Einstein, like others who rejected personifications of the deity, believed YHWH to be personal in essence—approachable and responsive.[6]

Second, the eagerness with which the Neoplatonic concept of the *ontos on* has been embraced by thinkers outside the Neoplatonist tradition, when traditional religious notions have been found wanting, is most appropriate and interesting for psychological study.

Third, while the psychosexual element of religious experience seems (at least on the surface) wholly lacking in Plotinus' discussion of the One, the Neoplatonist trend in later mysticism produced remarkably vivid sexual content, which has not escaped the notice of even those furthest removed from Freudian interpretation. Perle Epstein notes: "A favorite theme for meditation among Spanish Kabbalists is the *Matrone*, or female aspect of God's face. In Kabbalah the very presence of the living God in the world is female. Rabbi Joseph, a thirteenth century mystic, writes in his *Sefer Tashak*: 'She so pervades the lower world that if you search in deed, speech, thought and speculation, you will find *Shekhinah*, for there is not beginning nor end to her. . . . Her hair, like the Father's beard, is black and curly.' The thirteenth century Castilian Kabbalist Rabbi Joseph's erotic motif presents the cosmos in the form of a grand sexual embrace."[7] Alexandre Safran, commenting on the Kabbalah, notes that Israel is herself "female," and that every Israelite shares in a mystical, communal soul which is at one with God.[8]

In a world where betrayed trusts, estrangements, warfare and death have so often overwhelmed persons and whole communities, and the comforts of traditional faiths have seemed illusory, the desperate need for spiritual security has driven many to seek alternatives. The search has sometimes led to a First Hypostasis, an Allsoul or Oversoul, the One, or to a rejection of any "ground of being" at all. Whether, as R. M. Martin has suggested, the logic of Neoplatonism leads to "a kind of Principle of Pan-psychism" or to sheer atheism,[9] the gauntlet to investigate is down.

## I

A falling away from the faith of the forefathers in times of disaster, when the gods or Providence seem impotent or absent is not new to human history. Thus the taunt of Elijah to the dismayed worshippers of Baal: "Cry aloud, for he is a god; perhaps he is asleep and must be awakened" (1 Kings 16:27). The Hebrew people themselves were often so disheartened by circumstances as to neglect the faith, while indulging themselves (Haggai 1:4-7) or redoubling their efforts to placate the Deity they thought had forsaken them by multiplying their ceremonies—to the neglect of justice and acts of charity, as their prophets charged (Isaiah 1:11-17; Amos 5:21-24). Sometimes they squabbled over whose worship was most acceptable to the Lord (Ezra 4:1-3) or abandoned YHWH in favor of other deities: "Whoring after other gods" (Deuteronomy 31:16; Ezekiel 23:30). Indeed many of the nineteen major and minor prophets of Scripture excoriated their fellow Jews for apostasy in terms so blistering as to be exiled or martyred.

After the tragic years of the Temple's destruction, the generation of Babylonian captivity, occupation by the Greeks and brutalization by the Romans, many of the more sophisticated Jewish scholars, particularly in Alexandria, were attracted to the mystical aspects of Platonic and Pythagorean thought. In the region of Jerusalem, Hellenization was extensive. "Palestinian Judaism," Jacob Neusner points out, "and the Pharisaic sect in particular, are to be seen as Jewish modes of a common international cultural style known as Hellenism. Some of the most important terms of Rabbinic Biblical exegesis have been borrowed from the Greek. This is basic; the existence of such borrowing can be explained only by a period of profound Hellenization."[10] It is was a characteristically Hellenistic trait to demand precise readings and interpretations of texts (a tendency that persists today among Fundamentalist Christians) and to insist that every word of Scripture be literally applied. Some scholars argue that it was Jesus' comparative liberalism that sparked the conflict between himself and the Pharisees, rather than opposition to Phariseeism *per se.*[11]

Amid the political, social and cultural decay of the Roman empire, there was a readiness, especially among intellectuals, to accept the exile and seek comfort in Neoplatonism. It replaced the rigors of the old Phariseeism and the pessimism of the Sadducees with mystical elements, theurgics, and a soteriology of ultimate union with the *en kai pan.* Psychologically, the appeal appears to have been to turn away from the "almighty" god who had commanded obedience to a host of laws and regulations, but who failed to defend them as he had promised, and to embrace a concept of a transcendent, holy, yet impersonal, One.[12] It was both intellectually and emotionally satisfying to contemplate the utter transcendence of the One and to ponder how from this apparent non-Being, goodness and perfection may emanate—for goodness and perfection themselves were to be expected only beyond the phenomenal world.[13]

Next to our hunger for spiritual security in a providential God, perhaps our most primitive spiritual impulse, a root both of religion and philosophy,[14] has been the human eagerness to identify with an earthly monarch who could embody the Logos, the spirit and wisdom of Deity. Thus Stobaeus wrote: "To look at the king should put one in order like the music of a flute."[15] In Jewish experience kings rarely justified such a description. Yet the dream persisted and can be found even in Philo,[16] and in the pagan Neoplatonist Proclus, whose antipathy to Christianity arose at least in part from Christians' refusal to bend the knee to earthly powers. Yet many Jews had had enough of kings and high priests. Those who could embrace the One, in preference to the God of their fathers, could find in Neoplatonism freedom from dependence on impermanent thrones as well as on traditional faiths.

This is not at all to suggest that these Neoplatonists had become impious or had rejected all loyalty to civil society. Indeed their piety was enhanced by the conception that all persons, objects and virtues are emanations from the One, and that in what Plotinus calls *epistrophe* all things yearn to return to the Source. The longing to recover oneness with the One is the highest expression of religious faith. And because Neoplatonists believed all souls are ultimately one, having originated in the One, they could see human society as comprised of a brotherhood of persons who must share concern for one another's well being.[17] Although "the Soul is evil by being infused with the body,"[18] and all mortals share in the debility of sin,[19] we still have freedom to act, to improve by keeping our eyes on the perfection of the One. This focus on the Ideal, *the Intellectual Principle*, is seen on three orders: the merely material ("those who adopt this as their philosophy are like birds who are so weighted down they cannot fly"); the moderately transcendent; and "the third order—those godlike men who, in their mighty power, in the keenness of their sight, have clear vision of the splendor above and rise to it from among the clouds and fog of earth and hold firmly to the other world."[20]

It was this third quality of life that had such appeal to the religious expatriates of both Judaism and Christianity in the early centuries of the common era. The concept of humanity united with the Ultimate Being through contemplation, provided a philosophical vantage point from which to view the storms of life with a measure of serenity. This certainly played a major role in the production of Boethius' book, *The Consolation of Philosophy*, one of the most popular writings in Western Europe soon after its appearance in 524. His experience affords an apt illustration for psychodynamic study. When still a child he lost his father, whom he worshipped; he was raised by foster parents, received a good education and achieved some social prominence, but was arrested and imprisoned on political grounds. In disgrace and awaiting execution, he reached beyond conventional religion for solace. He described the inspiration for his book: "While I silently pondered, and decided to write down my wretched complaint, there appeared standing above me a woman of majestic countenance whose flashing eyes seemed wise beyond the ordinary wisdom of men." As the scholarly prisoner dried his tear-stained face with her robe, the apparition introduced herself as Lady Philosophy.[21] Her rival, Lady Fortune, is presented as the personification of prosperity and adversity which so easily entraps the earthly-minded. From a psychoanalytic viewpoint, such use of female figures as both saviors and seducers (whether Lady Philosophy, the Holy Virgin, or the numerous goddesses that populate mythology), would seem to support the claims about the psychosexual nature of our commitments. Boethius' acceptance of consolation from Lady Philosophy is in terms of turning to the unknown and unknowable God, who, he hopes can make sense of the pain of life: "O God, whoever you are who joins all things in perfect harmony, look down upon this miserable earth."[22]     Boethius' imprisonment and the female visitors become metaphors for every mortal's struggle from bondage to freedom, from sickness to wholeness: "Happy is he who can look into the shining spring of good; happy is he who can break the heavy chains of earth."[23] Unity with that "shining spring of good," is the only goal worthy of striving.

Boethius adds a caveat of special interest for psychodynamic analysis. At the end of Book Three (Poem 12), in words reminiscent of the story of Lot's wife (Genesis 19:26) and of Jesus' warning against those who look back being unfit for the Kingdom (Luke 9:52), Boethius reminds us that when Orpheus sought to rescue Eurydice from hell, he was warned not to look back.   His disobedience cost them both their lives, and perhaps their souls. This fable, he writes, "applies to all who seek to raise your minds to sovereign day.  For whoever is conquered and turns his eyes to the pit of hell . . . loses all the excellence he has gained."

"Love is a law unto itself," Orpheus insisted, and in failing to repress the pleasure-principle of *libido*, forfeited the goal of the ego, lost the integration of the desires of the id with the demands of the superego, failed, if the symbols be resolved psychodynamically, at the synthesis of happiness with goodness.  In terms of Neoplatonism, since "the Good is that on which all else depends, towards which all Existences aspire,"[24] the disobedience of Orpheus made impossible the achievement of that union with the Good which is the path to salvation.[25]

It is probable, as R. Baine Harris reminds us, that no "pure Neoplatonists" can be found after about 500 C.E., "since most of those who might be labeled as Neoplatonists have actually held Neoplatonic views in combination with other commitments."[26] After the collapse of Rome, amid the chaos of competing tribes and kingdoms trying to dominate Europe, popular literature continued using psychosexual metaphors and quasi-Neoplatonic elements of mysticism.  Lady Nature appears in Alan of Little's *Complaint of Nature*; the female figure of Reason features in *Roman de la Rose*; the "Holy Grail" theme figures in the growing legend of King Arthur by the seventh century.[27]     Dante will introduce both "Lady

Philosophy," and Beatrice; Holy Church and Lady Meed are both seen as feminine figures in *Piers Plowman*, and presiding over the consciousness of Christendom is Mary, "Queen of Heaven," almost the Ultimate Reality as "Mother of God."

Here indeed is grist for the Freudian mill, suggesting that the ontology of the Neoplatonists and of the mystic visionaries they inspired is a creation of the human *libido*. Contemplation of an utterly transcendent One, from which all reality emanates and to the serenity of which we all must return, would be part of what Freud called "the grand illusion." But it is well to remember the caution of one of Freud's colleagues, that "Freud's beliefs concerning religion were his own, and did not necessarily reflect the scientific findings of the process of psychoanalysis which he developed."[28]

Dynamic psychologists who seek the conjunction of the psychosexual with mystical elements will find little to satisfy their expectations when they examine the works of such men as the Muslims al-Kindī (ca. 801 - ca. 867) and al-Fārābī, who was called a second Aristotle (870-950); or the Christian John the Scot, called Eriugena (ca. 810-870); or the Jewish philosopher Solomon ibn Gabirol (ca. 1021-1058). Rather than the playing out of libidinal and counter-libidinal fantasies and symbolisms, a dynamic of a much more profound nature is discovered, where "deep calls unto deep," and the being of each person seeks communion with Ultimate Being.

"If you will imagine the structure of the whole," writes Solomon ibn Gabirol, "that is, the universal body and the spiritual substances that contain it, consider the formation of man and take that as an image. For the body of man corresponds to the universal body, and the spiritual substances that move it correspond to the spiritual substances that move the universal body, and among these spiritual substances the inferior substance obeys the superior and is submissive to it until the motion reaches the substance of the intelligence. You will find that the intelligence orders and dominates these substances, and you will find that all the substances that move the body of man follow the intelligence and obey it while it perceives them and judges them."[29] In this hierarchy of lower levels dominated and judged by the higher, Avicebron makes it clear that in wisdom, the lower will seek communion with the higher: "Know too that this is the path that leads to perfect happiness and allows us to obtain true delight, that is our end."[30]

It is true that a pantheistic variety of Jewish Neoplatonism evolved, and that one aspect of it led to the development of the Kabbalah. The mystical and sensual aspects of the Kabbalah cannot be denied, but the focus is on the spiritual: "Corresponding to every natural, physical function of each human organ is a spiritual function which is governed by the appropriate *Mitzvah*. Even the structure of the human soul is modeled on that of the *Torah*. Therefore the soul and body constitute a unity: Man is a unified being."[31] And "main-line" Judaism did not follow the most extreme doctrines and images of the Kabbalah but remained grounded in the Mosaic tradition. Maimonides recognized certain "drawbacks which the timelessness of emanation and apparent necessity of its flowing forth represented," but nevertheless found emanation "an admirable model for the relation of the divine to the world."[32]

Meanwhile, "mainline Christendom" was organizing into a vast power-structure, which took into itself many strains of philosophical thought. Neoplatonism, made available through the translation of a number of books by John the Scot, made its impress on numerous scholars, including Thomas Aquinas, Meister Eckhart, and Dante. Aquinas' handling of the relation of Being and the Good, and of Being and Truth, profited greatly from the Neoplatonic synthesis.[33]

## II

Modern Neoplatonists can probably be traced to that convulsive era of the Renaissance and Reformation when again many of the faithful found diminished confidence in established dogmas and rituals. The founders of the Florentine Academy (ca. 1462) were people of prominence in the political and religious institutions of their day. But George Gemistus Pletho and Cosimo di' Medici had already come to regard the powers of both State and Church with disdain. Preferring philosophy to theology, they found in Neoplatonism both a haven and a stimulus to creative work. In seventeenth century England the Cambridge Platonists worked to blend the new Anglican Christianity with Neoplatonic ideas. On the Continent, the legacy of Meister Eckhart (1260-1327) and Gerhard Groot (1340-1384) found a ready audience for both mystical contemplation and liberal interpretations of Scripture among the

Humanists.[34] Jacques LeFevre published three volumes in 1514 reflecting his position within Neoplatonism, the full importance of which was made clear in the lives of Giordano Bruno, Leibniz, and the German Idealists.

Bruno (1548-1600) makes a particularly poignant case for study, having been raised the son of an often absent father who was a professional soldier. He dabbled in magic and Greek philosophy and joined the Dominican order at seventeen. Suspected of heresy, he was nevertheless ordained a priest but soon thereafter was on trial and fled to Rome, only to be tried again and excommunicated. Sickened by the St. Bartholomew's Day Massacre of some 30,000 Protestants, he identified, in sympathy, with the Calvinists, but his unorthodox publications led to his expulsion from Geneva. At Oxford his writings and lectures took on an increasingly Neoplatonic tone: God, as the principle of unity, is known to us in the unfolding patterns of nature. Here Bruno reveals his awareness of Proclus' dictum that emanations from the One are horizontal as well as vertical. It is the evolving patterns which give the appearance of purpose, hence the notion that God is a transcendent personality. Facing death, Bruno wrote, "we may hope that our purposeful natures may be reunited with that eternal aspect of nature we call God, and of which we were originally a part."[35]

Like his quixotic contemporary Cervantes, Bruno was caught in the corridor between the Renaissance and the Age of Reason by Inquisitors who belonged to neither age. Unlike Cervantes, he was executed; and his death, like that of others who had challenged orthodoxy, turned many away from the familiar traditions. One may question whether the numerous failures of Christendom's primary institutions to be "Christian enough" was the major cause of the disenchantment, or whether it was a combination of the corruption of the humane ethic of the Gospels by some of its leaders and the rise of the sciences in the seventeenth and eighteenth centuries challenging the credibility of the Biblical cosmology. But it is clear that much of the "back to nature" movement which followed "the Age of Reason" and evoked a reawakened interest in Neoplatonism was the product of an emotional reaction. Lenn Goodman expressed this (though without direct reference to Neoplatonism): "The disappointment professed by fideists and agnostics . . . is expressive of the still undissolved entanglement of their thoughts in the mythic level of religion. Hume, Bayle, Voltaire, and the numberless flotsam which drifts in the currents set up by the fall of such giants from naive faith, were convinced that the God of true religion is the God of simple faith. Failing to find that God, they believe that they (meaning religion) have failed absolutely. Their pose of melancholy loss is communicated to the Bertrand Russells and Walter Lippmanns of the twentieth century, with some loss of erudition, and stylistic verve but no loss of the essential ingredient, a true Rousseauvian introspective (if not narcissistic) angst." He adds: "These men who weep for the lost God of their childhood seem rather to be mourning childhood, which indeed they will never recapture, rather than God."[36]

## III

From the vantage point of dynamic psychology, these observations are highly suggestive. Certainly the loss of childhood faith, whether in one's earthly parents or in the cosmic projection of them (as Freud suspected), or in the whole matrix of family-community-religious institution-state, has often sent the despairing subject in quest of a believable substitute. But the effort to understand the Ultimately Real is not always the product of emotional distress. It is well to recall the words of Avicebron: "This is wisdom: to know the First Essence." The writer of Proverbs placed such a value on wisdom as to insist: "Wisdom is the principal thing; with all your getting, get understanding" (Proverbs 4:7). If the gaining of wisdom is the major dynamic of one's life, then comprehending the goal of such knowledge, "the First Essence" is not an exercise of neurosis but of mental health.

Historically, Neoplatonism, with its distinctive ontology, has provided an alternative to the religious traditions which seemed no longer viable to their adherents. But this fact cannot be used to infer that Neoplatonism is that and no more. Indeed its concept of the One remains as challenging today as ever, and can be found in the Pragmatic philosophies of Charles Sanders Peirce[37] and William James as well as in the Process philosophy of Alfred North Whitehead[38] and the convictions of physicists like Schrödinger[39] and Arthur Holly Compton.[40] It is in Whitehead particularly that we find a conjunction of ideas between Neoplatonism and dynamic psychology. He subscribes to the emanation concept of the coming-to-being of substances, but notes that "science can find no aim in nature . . . creativity. It finds mere rules of succession" suggesting no external purpose.[41] He notes the *appearance* of purposes but insists these are purblind: "Blind prehensions, physical and mental, are the ultimate building blocks of the universe."[42] This conclusion fully accords with what psychoanalysts have maintained about the *libidinal* urgencies, which Gordon Allport described as "goal seeking,"[43] and Brown discussed as "vectors in the psychobiological field."[44]

It may be questioned whether there is not a non sequitur in the Neoplatonic effort to move from the proposition that the Ultimate One has no personal attributes, to the proposition that the vast array of complex objects of the familiar universe, especially purposing beings who can love and create, have emanated therefrom. Purpose is a higher order, not a lower order of reality than purposelessness, and the capacity to love is almost universally acknowledged to be the "highest" attribute of personality. Whitehead sensed this and departed from the Neoplatonic position in holding that God both transcends and guides His creation. "God is unique in the sense that He provides for the organization and relevance of eternal objects, and 'saves' them by absorbing them into His enduring life."[45] Salvation, then, is not achieved by returning to an impersonal One, relinquishing all that is highest and noblest in personality, but by identifying with that which is still higher.

What is of greatest importance to dynamic psychology is not to test the truth or even the reasonableness of Neoplatonic formulations, but to ask whether they have answered the need of human personalities for some sense of Being in which they can ground their own beings and which cannot be exhausted by the stresses of life. If so, they have served the psycho-integrative purposes which Freudian thought requires of any religious or philosophical system. Erich Fromm said it well: "The problem of religion is not the problem of God, but of men; religious formulations and religious symbols are attempts to give expression to certain kinds of experience. What matters is the nature of these experiences. The symbol system is only the cue from which we can infer the underlying reality."[46]

Persuading the followers that the "underlying reality" is truly present and adequately expressed in such symbol systems as sacred writ, sacraments, or reasoned argument about becoming one with the All is the task of the religion or philosophical system in question. Meanwhile, because we are unavoidably psychosexual creatures for whom even such concepts as love, justice and compassion for the naked and hungry have quite physical implications, Neoplatonism in both its Jewish and Christian forms has more Freudian aspects than is generally admitted. Both are deeply concerned with questions of our destiny, and thus of our becoming.

Wayne Oates listed what he calls "the spiritual goals of man's becoming: meaningfulness, direction, balance, community, maturity in love, and integration."[47] If the Neoplatonic ontology can provide what Whitehead calls "the vision of something which stands beyond, behind and within the passing flux of immediate things; that gives meaning to all that passes," it will have proved to be more than a mere substitute for religion. It will qualify for the definition in the oldest sense of the term: *re-ligio*: to bind back (to the Source). Such a vision, as Whitehead reminds us, is "the one element in human experience which persistently shows an upward trend (and) is our one ground for optimism."[48] It has thus also satisfied the interests of dynamic psychology.

## Notes

1. Edoardo Weiss in Franz Alexander, ed., *Dynamic Psychiatry*, (Chicago: University of Chicago Press, 1953), 44: "The forces operating within the mind are subjected to what we call 'the integrative principle' which characterizes biological processes. The organism and its structural parts form a coherent unity manifesting the tendency to preserve itself."
2. J. F. Brown, *The Psychodynamics of Abnormal Behavior* (New York: McGraw-Hill, 1940), 20.
3. Sigmund Freud, *The Future of an Illusion* (New York: Liveright, 1928), 76 f.
4. L. E. Goodman, *Monotheism* (Totowa, New Jersey: Allanheld Osmun, 1981), 23.
5. Albert Einstein, *Out of my Later Years* (New York: Philosophical Library, 1954), 27.

6.  God's self-disclosure to Moses is treated at some length in *Guide* I 63; see the discussion in Lenn Goodman's *RAMBAM*, 102-18. Einstein's personalist conviction is quoted in an interview: "I believe in a personal God," in Fredrick Rikter, *Can a Scientist Believe in God?* (Oslo, 1958), quoted by Gustaf Stromberg, *All Church Press*, January 8, 1960, 4.

7.  Perle Epstein, *Kabbalah* (New York: Doubleday, 1978), 47.

8.  Alexandre Safran, *The Kabbalah* (New York: Feldheim, 1975), 20.

9.  R. M. Martin, "On Logical Structure and the Platonic Cosmos," in R. Baine Harris, ed., *The Structure of Being*, 23.

10. Jacob Neusner, *From Politics to Piety: The Emergence of Pharisaic Judaism* (Englewood Cliffs, New Jersey: Prentice-Hall, 1973), 9-10.

11. The Pharisees were perceived by Jesus as making compliance with Jewish law a stifling affair, while many of them took such liberties with it as to require denunciation. See Matthew 23:13, 13, 23, 24; 24-25; Luke 18:11; Paul Ramsey, *Basic Christian Ethics* (New York: Scribners, 1953), 59. It is probable that Jesus considered himself to be in the Pharisaic line. Certainly the Pharisees were highly respected for urging "The service of God calls for the human heart. Love for Him and fellow man must undergird all our actions." Leo Trepp *Judaism, Development and Life* (Belmont, California: Wadsworth, 1966), 20.

12. In the *Fifth Ennead* Plotinus writes of the One as "The First" which is "without form, and, if without Form, then it is not Being."

13. Yet the trans-ontological character of the One is held in balance in the *Sixth Ennead*, where Plotinus insists that the Good can only be found within the realm of Being: "since it is never a Non-Being." Power, *energeia*, is also inherent in the One (VI 8.7), a distinctly ontological concept. *Enneads*, tr., Stephen MacKenna in Great Books of the Western World (Chicago: University of Chicago Press, 1971) **17**.231, 346.

14. Einstein held that religion, the sciences, philosophy and the arts are all "branches of the same tree." A deep human yearning to make sense of the universe and to discover our place in it gives rise to all of these studies: *Out of My Later Years*, 9.

15. Stobaeus, *Anthologium* IV 265, quoted in Erwin Goodenough, *The Psychology of Religious Experiences* (New York: Basic Books, 1965), 49.

16. *De Specialibus Lebibus* IV 30, 157; and the discussion in Wolfson, *Philo*, **2**.325-37; Erwin Goodenough, *An Introduction to Philo Judaeus* (New York: Barnes and Noble, 1963), 68-71.

17. *Enneads* IV 9.1.

18. *Enneads* I 2.3.

19. *Enneads* I 8.1-5.

20. *Enneads* V 9.1.

21. Boethius, *Consolation of Philosophy*, tr., R. Green (New York: Bobbs-Merrill, 1962), 3 f.

22. *Consolation* I, Poem 5.

23. *Consolation* I, Poem 12.

24. *Enneads* I 8.2.

25. In psychodynamic terms "goodness" is generally defined with reference to societal demands rather than cosmic or metaphysical concerns. Yet, see Carl Jung's discussion in *Psychology and Religion* (New Haven:  Yale University Press, 1938), 112 f. Cf. Paul W. Pruyser, *A Dynamic Psychology of Religion* (New York: Harper and Row, 1968), 305-17.

26. *The Significance of Neoplatonism* (Norfolk: International Society for Neoplatonic Studies, 1976), 12.

27. Christopher Hibbert, *The Search for King Arthur* (New York: Harper and Row, 1969), 15.

28. Louis Thorpe, *The Psychology of Mental Health* (New York: Ronald Press, 1960), 514.

29. *Fons Vitae*, tr., H. E. Wedeck (London:  Peter Owen, 1963), 131.

30. *Fons Vitae*, tr. Wedeck, 132.

31. Safran, *The Kabbalah*, 20.

32. Goodman, *RAMBAM*, 346.

33. *Summa Theologica*, Part I, Q. 3, a 2, 4, 7; Q. 12, Q. 54, a. 3.

34. Williston Walker, *A History of the Christian Church*, 3rd ed. (New York:  Scribners, 1970), 291.

35. See Herbert Butterfield, *The Origins of Modern Science* (London: Bell, 1962), 57 f., and my treatment of Bruno in *The World of Philosophy* (Chicago:  Nelson-Hall, 1983), ch. 3.

36. *Monotheism*, 23.

37. "I recognize three universes; one of these embraces whatever has its being in itself alone. I denominate the objects (of this Being) *Ideas*, or *Possibles*." The second, Peirce found to be objects and facts about them. The third consisted of the co-being of whatever is in its nature *necessitant*, "that is, a law or something expressible in a universal proposition." *Values in a Universe of Chance* (Stanford:  Stanford University Press, 1958), 404.

38. Whitehead, like the Neoplatonists, held that purposes in nature arise from consciousness as a subjective form; *Process and Reality* (New York: Macmillan, 1929), 470. In *Modes of Thought* (Cambridge:  at

the University Press, 1938) he described "aim" as the essential characteristic of life, a theme familiar both to Neoplatonism and to dynamic psychology.

39. *What Is Life?* (Cambridge: at the University Press, 1947). Schrödinger's identification of Atman=Brahman with the *Deus factus sum* of medieval mystics in the epilogue to his tightly structured discourse on purely biological concerns climaxes with his affirmation of the imperishable, indwelling self. Cf. *Enneads* IV 7.

40. "A Modern Concept of God," in *Man's Destiny in Eternity*, The Garvin Lectures (Boston: Beacon Press, 1949), 19 f.

41. *Modes of Thought*, 211. "Science," he adds, "only deals with *half* the evidence provided by human experience."

42. *Process and Reality*, 470.

43. *Personality: A Psychological Interpretation* (New York:4 Holt, 1937), 108, 112-14.

44. *Psychodynamics of Abnormal Behavior*, 8-21.

45. *Process and Reality*, 224.

46. *Psychoanalysis and Religion* (New Haven: Yale University Press, 1950), 113.

47. *The Religious Dimensions of Personality* (New York: Association Press, 1957), 249-70.

48. *Science and the Modern World* (New York: Macmillan, 1946), 275.

# Bibliography*

Altmann, Alexander, *Studies in Religious Philosophy and Mysticism* (Ithaca: Cornell University Press, 1969).

————, *Essays in Jewish Intellectual History* (Hanover, NH: University Press of New England, 1981).

————, "Creation and Emanation in Isaac Israeli: A Reappraisal," in I. Twersky, ed., *Studies in Medieval Jewish History and Literature*; repr. in *Essays in Jewish Intellectual History*.

————, *Von der Mittelalterlichen zur modernen Aufklärung* (Tübingen: Mohr, 1987), 60-91.

————, and Samuel M. Stern, *Isaac Israeli: A Neoplatonic philosopher of the early tenth century* (Oxford: at the Clarendon Press, 1958).

Armstrong, A. H., ed., *The Cambridge History of Later Greek and Early Medieval Philosophy*, (Cambridge: at the University Press, 1967).

---

\* Multiply-cited texts and studies are referenced here and cited only in brief form in the notes to the individual papers.

427

Armstrong, A. H., ed., *Classical Mediterranean Spirituality* (New York: Crossroad, 1986).

Bréhier, Émile, *The Philosophy of Plotinus*, tr., Joseph Thomas (Chicago: University of Chicago Press, 1958).

Brunner, Fernand, *De Jamblique a Proclus* (Geneva: Entretiens Hardt 21, 1975).

————, *Platonisme et Aristotelisme. La critique d'Ibn Gabirol par saint Thomas d'Aquin* (Louvain-Paris: Beatrice-Nauwelaerts, 1965).

Cantarino, Vincent, "Ibn Gabirol's Metaphysic of Light," *Studia Islamica* 26 (1967): 49-71.

Ibn Daud, Abraham, *The Exalted Faith (Ha-Emunah ha-Ramah)*, ed. and tr., Norbert Samuelson; tr. edited by Gershon Weiss (Rutherford: Fairleigh Dickinson University Press, 1986).

Davidson, Herbert, "Al-Farabi and Avicenna on the Active Intellect," *Viator* 3 (1972).

————, "Alfarabi and Avicenna on the Active Intellect as a Cause of Existence," *Viator* 18 (1987).

————, "Averroes on the Material Intellect," *Viator* 17 (1986): 91-137.

————, "Averroes on the Active Intellect as a Cause of Existence," *Viator* 18 (1987): 191-225.

————, "Maimonides' Shemonah Perakim and Alfarabi's *Fusul al-Madani*," *PAAJR* 31 (1963).

————, *Proofs for Eternity, Creation and the Existence of God in Medieval Islamic and Jewish Philosophy* (New York: Oxford University Press, 1987).

Dillon, John, *The Middle Platonists* (London: Duckworth, 1977).

*Al-Farabi on the Perfect State: Abū Naṣr al-Fārābī's Mabādi' Arā' Ahl al-Madīna al-Fāḍila*, ed. and tr., R. Walzer (Oxford: Oxford University Press, 1985).

————, *Fuṣūl al-Madanī (Aphorisms of the Statesman)*, ed. and tr., D. M. Dunlop (Cambridge: at the University Press, 1961).

Ibn Gabirol, *Avencebrolis Fons Vitae ex Arabico in Latinum translatus ab Iohanne Hispano et Domenico Gundissalino*, ed., Clemens Baeumker (*Beiträge zur Geschichte der Philosophie des Mittelalters* 1.2-4 (Münster: Aschendorff, 1892-5).

————, *The Improvement of the Moral Qualities (Tikkun Middot ha-Nefesh)*, tr., Stephen S. Wise (New York: Columbia University Press, 1902; repr. AMS, 1966).

Goheen, John, *The Problem of Matter and Form in the "De Ente et Essentia" of Thomas Aquinas* (Cambridge: Harvard University Press, 1940).

Goichon, A.-M., *La Distinction de l'Essence et de l'Existence d'après Ibn Sīnā* (Paris: Brouwer, 1938).

Goodman, L. E., "Determinism and Freedom in Spinoza, Maimonides and Aristotle: A Retrospective Study," in F. Schoeman, ed., *Responsibility, Character and the Emotions* (Cambridge: at the University Press, 1987).

————, "Did al-Ghazālī Deny Causality?" *Studia Islamica* 47 (1978): 83-120.

————, "Al-Ghazālī's Argument from Creation," *International Journal of Middle Eastern Studies* 2 (1971): 67-85, 168-88.

Goodman, L. E., "Maimonides and Leibniz," *Journal of Jewish Studies* 31 (1980): 214-36, with Leibniz' reading notes on the Latin *Doctor Perplexorum* (Basel, 1629).

―――, "Matter and Form as Attributes of God in Maimonides' Philosophy," in Ruth Link-Salinger, ed., *A Straight Path: Studies in Medieval Philosophy and Culture—Essays in Honor of Arthur Hyman* (Washington: The Catholic University Press of America, 1988), 86-97.

―――, "Ordinary and Extraordinary Language in Medieval Jewish and Islamic Philosophy," *Manuscrito* 11 (1988): 57-83.

―――, "The Greek Impact on Arabic Literature," *The Cambridge History of Arabic Literature* (Cambridge: Cambridge University Press, 1983) 1.460-82.

―――, "Three Meanings of the Idea of Creation," in D. Burrell and B. McGinn, eds., *God and Creation*, (Notre Dame: University of Notre Dame Press, 1990).

―――, "Why Machines Cannot do Science," in D. DeLuca, ed., *Essays on Creativity and Science* (Honolulu: HCTE, 1986), 269-82.

Guttmann, Julius, *Philosophies of Judaism* (Garden City, N.Y.: Doubleday, 1966).

Harris, R. Baine, ed., *The Structure of Being* (Albany: SUNY Press, 1982).

Hourani, George, "Ibn Sīnā on Necessary and Possible Existence," *Philosophical Forum* 4 (1972): 74-86.

Ikhwān al-Safā', *The Case of the Animals vs. Man before the King of the Jinn*, tr., L. E. Goodman (Boston: Twayne, 1978).

Kogan, Barry S., "Averroes and the Theory of Emanation," *Medieval Studies* 43 (1981): 384-404.

———, *Averroes and the Metaphysics of Causation* (Albany: SUNY Press, 1985).

Maimonides, Moses, *Dalālat al-Ḥā'irīn*, (Guide to the Perplexed), ed. with French tr. as *Guide des Égarés*, S. Munk, 3 vols. (Paris, 1856-66; repr. Osnabrück: Zeller, 1964); English, *The Guide of the Perplexed*, tr., Shlomo Pines (Chicago: University of Chicago Press, 1963); selections tr. with commentary in L. E. Goodman, *RAMBAM: Readings in the Philosophy of Moses Maimonides* (New York: Viking, 1976).

Merlan, Philip, *From Platonism to Neoplatonism* (The Hague: Nijhoff, 1960).

———, *Monopsychism, Mysticism, Metaconsciousness* (The Hague: Nijhoff, 1963).

O'Meara, Dominic, ed., *Neoplatonism and Christian Thought* (Albany: SUNY Press, 1982).

———, *Structure Hierarchique dans la pensée de Plotin* (Leiden: Brill, 1975).

Philo's works are cited from *LCL*, ed., F. H. Colson and G. H. Whittaker (Cambridge: Harvard University Press, 1929-1962), where a key to the abbreviations of titles is provided.

Pines, Shlomo and Yirmiyahu Yovel, eds., *Maimonides and Philosophy* (Dordrecht: Nijhoff, 1986).

Plotinus, *Enneads*, tr., A. H. Armstrong (Cambridge: Harvard University Press, *LCL*, 1984).

Proclus, *Elements of Theology* (Oxford: Oxford University Press, 1963).

Rahman, Fazlur, "Essence and Existence in Ibn Sina: The Myth and the Reality," *Hamdard Islamicus* 4 (1981): 3-14.

Rist, John M., *Plotinus: The Road to Reality* (Cambridge: at the University Press, 1967).

————, "Plotinus on Matter and Evil," *Phronesis* 6 (1981): 154-66.

————, *Stoic Philosophy*, (Cambridge: at the University Press, 1969).

————, ed., *The Stoics* (Berkeley: University of California Press, 1978).

Rowson, Everett, *A Muslim Philosopher on the Soul and its Fate al-Āmirī's K. al-Amad 'alā 'l-abad* (New Haven: American Oriental Society, 1988).

Rudavsky, Tamar, "Conflicting Motifs in Ibn Gabirol's Discussion of Matter and Evil," *The New Scholasticism* 52 (1978): 54-71.

————, ed., *Divine Omniscience and Omnipotence in Medieval Philosophy*, (Dordrecht: Reidel, 1985).

Ibn Rushd, *Tahāfut al-Tahāfut (The Incoherence of the Incoherence)*, Arabic ed., Maurice Bouyges (Beirut: Catholic Press, 1930), tr., Simon Van Den Bergh (London: Luzac, 1954).

Saadiah Gaon al-Fayyūmī, *K. al-Mukhtār fī 'l-Āmānāt wa 'l-I'tiqādāt (Select Book of Beliefs and Convictions)*, II 13 ad fin., ed. J. Kafaḥ (Jerusalem, 1970); tr. Samuel Rosenblatt (New Haven: Yale University Press, 1948; repr., 1967).

————, *The Book of Theodicy* (translation and commentary on the Book of Job), tr. with commentary, L. E. Goodman (New Haven: Yale University Press, 1988).

Schlanger, Jacques, *La Philosophie de Salomon Ibn Gabirol: Étude de d'un Neoplatonisme* (Leiden: Brill, 1968).

Scholem, Gershom, *Kabbalah* (New York: Schocken, 1974).

————, *Major Trends in Jewish Mysticism*, 3rd rev. ed. (New York: Schocken, 1961).

————, *On the Kabbalah and Its Symbolism*, tr., R. Manheim (New York: Schocken, 1969).

————, *Origins of the Kabbala* (Princeton: Princeton University Press, 1987).

————, *Sabbatai Sevi: The Mystical Messiah*, tr., R. J. Z. Werblowsky (Princeton: Princeton University Press, 1973).

Sirat, Collette, *A History of Jewish Philosophy in the Middle Ages* (Cambridge: at the University Press, 1986).

Stern, Samuel M., "Ibn Ḥasdāy's Neoplatonist—A Neoplatonic Treatise and its Influence on Isaac Israeli and the Longer Version of the *Theology of Aristotle*," *Oriens* 13-14 (1961); repr. in S. M. Stern, *Medieval Arabic and Hebrew Thought*, ed., F. W. Zimmermann (London, 1983), 58-120.

Ibn Ṭufayl, *Hayy Ibn Yaqzān*, tr., L. E. Goodman (New York: Twayne, 1972; repr., Los Angeles: Gee Tee Bee, 1983).

Twersky, Isadore, ed., *Studies in Medieval Jewish History and Literature* (Cambridge: Harvard University Press, 1979).

Wallis, R. T., *Neoplatonism* (London: Scribner, 1972).

Whittaker, John, *Studies in Platonism and Patristic Thought* (London: Variorum Reprints, 1984).

Winston, David, *Logos and Mystical Theology In Philo of Alexandria* (Cincinnati: Hebrew Union College Press, 1985).

Wolfson, Harry A., *Philo* (Cambridge: Harvard University Press, 1948), 2 vols.

————, *The Philosophy of Spinoza* (Cambridge: Harvard University Press, 1934), 2 vols.

————, *The Philosophy of the Church Fathers* (Cambridge: Harvard University Press, 1964).

————, *Religious Philosophy: A Group of Essays* (Cambridge: Belknap, 1961).

————, *Studies in the History of Philosophy and Religion* (Cambridge: Harvard University Press, 1973, 1977), 2 vols.

# The Contributors

**J. David Bleich** is Herbert and Florence Tenzer Professor of Jewish Law and Ethics at Yeshiva University, where he also serves as Professor of Law in the Benjamin N. Cardozo School of Law and Professor of Talmud and *Rosh Kollel le-Hora'ah* at the Rabbi Isaac Elchanan Theological Seminary. He is the author of *Contemporary Halakhic Problems* (3 vols.), editor of *With Perfect Faith: The Foundations of Jewish Belief*, and coeditor with Fred Rosner of *Jewish Bioethics*.

**David Burrell**, C.S.C., is Theodore M. Hesburgh Professor at Notre Dame, where he teaches philosophy and theology. He is currently exploring Jewish, Christian and Muslim philosophical ideas about divine and human freedom in the context of the idea of creation. His most recent book, *Knowing the Unknowable God: Ibn Sina, Maimonides and Aquinas,* is a comparative study of philosophical responses to a shared problem of the monotheistic traditions.

**Hubert Dethier** is Ordinary Professor at the Free University of Brussels and Senior Lecturer in the philosophy of culture at the University of Amsterdam. He specializes in medieval and modern philosophy, textual theory and the history of religions and is particularly interested in the interactions of medieval and renaissance philosophy.

**John Dillon** is Regius Professor of Greek at Trinity College, Dublin. He is the author of *The Middle Platonists* and editor/translator of the

Fragments of Iamblichus' commentaries on Plato, and Dexippus on Aristotle's *Categories*. He collaborated with David Winston on *Two Treatises of Philo Judaeus* and with Glenn Morrow on Proclus' Commentary on the *Parmenides* of Plato.

**Idit Dobbs-Weinstein**, a 1987 Ph.D. in Medieval Studies from the University of Toronto is an Assistant Professor of Philosophy at Vanderbilt University. She has written several articles on Maimonidean themes in philosophy and exegesis and on allied topics.

**Seymour Feldman** is Professor of Philosophy at Rutgers University, the State University of New Jersey. He is the translator of Gersonides' *The Wars of the Lord* and editor of the translation of Spinoza's *Ethics* recently published by Hackett, as well as the author of numerous essays on the history of philosophy in the Middle Ages and Late Antiquity.

**Lenn Goodman** is Professor of Philosophy at the University of Hawaii and author of *Monotheism: A Philosophic Inquiry into the Foundations of Theology and Ethics*. He has written on Maimonides, Saadiah, Bahya Ibn Paquda, and most of the major Muslim philosophers. His translation and commentary on Saadiah's Arabic treatment of the Book of Job appeared in the Yale Judaica Series, and he recently completed a new philosophical study entitled *On Justice*.

**Arthur Hyman** serves as University Professor of Philosophy at Yeshiva University and as Visiting Professor of Philosophy at Columbia University. The author of essays on medieval Jewish and Islamic philosophy, he was the co-editor of *Philosophy in the Middle Ages* and editor and translator of the Hebrew version of Averroes' *De Substantia Orbis*. He has served as a visiting professor at the Hebrew University of Jerusalem, UC San Diego, and Yale.

**Moshe Idel** is Professor of Kabbalah in the Department of Jewish Thought at the Hebrew University in Jerusalem and has served as Centennial Scholar in Residence at the Jewish Theological Seminary in New York. His books include *Kabbalah: New Perspectives*, from

Yale University Press, and two books from SUNY Press: *The Mystical Experience in Abraham Abulafia*, and *Studies in Ecstatic Kabbalah*.

**Alfred Ivry** is Skirball Professor of Modern Jewish Thought at New York University and teaches medieval Jewish and Islamic philosophy in the graduate programs of NYU's Skirball Department of Hebrew and Judaic Studies and Department of Near Eastern Languages and Literatures. He is the editor/translator of *Kindī's Metaphysics* and *Averroes' Middle Commentary on Aristotle's De Anima*.

**Steven Katz** is Professor of Jewish Studies and Chairman of the Jewish Studies Program at Cornell University. His books include *Post-Holocaust Dialogues* from NYU Press, and he is the editor of three volumes on comparative mysticism published by Oxford University Press. His new three-volume work, *The Holocaust in Historical Perspective*, will be published by Harvard University Press.

**Menachem Kellner** holds the Sir Isaac and Lady Edith Wolfson Chair in Jewish Thought at the University of Haifa. His books include *Dogma in Medieval Jewish Thought* from Oxford University Press and *Maimonides on Human Perfection* in Brown Judaic Studies. He is the translator of Isaac Abravanel's *Principles of Faith* and author of numerous other scholarly studies.

**Bernard McGinn** is Professor of Historical Theology and the History of Christianity at the Divinity School of the University of Chicago, where he also directs the Institute for the Advanced Study of Religion. He is a specialist in medieval Christian mysticism and philosophy and has published studies and translations of Lactantius, Meister Eckhart, Isaac of Stella, Adso of Montier en-Der, Joachim of Fiore, Savonarola, and other masters of western spirituality.

**Robert McLaren** is Professor of Human Development at California State University, Fullerton. The author of four books, he is a frequent contributor to interfaith dialogue in such publications as *Christian Century*, *Darshana International*, and the *Bulletin of Atomic Scientists*. He is President of the Pacific Peace Prize Foundation and

Vice President of the Academy of Jewish, Christian and Islamic Studies.

**C. K. Mathis II** is a graduate of California State University, where he now works in the Learning Resource Center. Deeply committed to Neoplatonic Studies, Mr. Mathis is currently investigating the evidence for linkages between the philosophy of Damascius and the Christian thought of pseudo-Dionysius.

**David Novak** is Edgar M. Bronfman Professor of Modern Judaic Studies at the University of Virginia in Charlottesville and the author of numerous studies on Jewish law and theology. His book on the Noahidic Laws, *The Image of the Non-Jew in Judaism*, and his subsequent volume from Oxford University Press, *Jewish-Christian Dialogue*, are milestones in interfaith exploration.

**Richard Popkin** is Professor Emeritus of Philosophy of Washington University in St. Louis and Adjunct Professor of History and Philosophy at UCLA. For many years he served as editor of the *Journal of the History of Philosophy*, and he is the author of numerous books and articles including *The High Road to Pyrrhonism* and *The History of Scepticism from Erasmus to Spinoza*. His most recent book is a study of the philo-semitic author of the Prae-Adamite theory, Isaac La Peyrère.

**David Winston** is Professor of Hellenistic and Judaic Studies at the Graduate Theological Union in Berkeley. He is the author of the Anchor Bible commentary on the Wisdom of Solomon and has written several books on Philo. He is also associate editor of *Studia Philonica Annual*.

# INDEX

Abendana, Isaac 390
Abendana, Jacob 396
Aboab, Isaac 391, 395
Abraham ben Eliezer ha-Levi
 344
Abravanel, Isaac 332
Abravanel, Judah. *See* Leone
 Ebreo
Abstraction 165, 173, 175, 220,
 262–66, 268, 360, 365
*'Adam* 223–24
*Adam Kadmon* 337, 342, 398
Adoptionism 250–51
*Akataleptos* 23, 280
Albalag, Isaac 124–26
Albert the Great 86, 96;
 critique of Ibn Gabirol
 97–99
Alemanno, Yohanan 332–33,
 341–42
Alexander of Aphrodisias
 256–57, 260, 262–63, 265,
 360
All is in all 330
*'Alma de-peruda* 291
Altmann, Alexander 67, 72, 86,
 118, 143-46, 154, 287

al-Āmirī, Muhammad b. Yūsuf
 67
Angels 26-27, 159, 182, 358-
 60; choices 166–67,
 170–72; composition 95;
 invisible 167; natural
 forms and forces 160–65,
 167, 176; permanent and
 transitory 160, 167
Anthropomorphism 23, 178,
 182, 184, 340; Leone
 Ebreo 354; Philo 23,
 285–86, 288
Antipater 26
*Apatheia/eupatheia* 24, 32
*to Apeiron, to Aoriston* 47
*Apoios* 21
Aquinas, Thomas 85, 96, 98,
 262, 266; artisan image
 207, 213; cognition 256;
 creation 220; esse 207;
 God's knowledge 207; the
 Good 227; matter 218–22
*'Arad* 143
Archaenetus 63
psuedo-Archytas 63
Arianism 249-51

439

Aristotle  47, 56, 68, 97, 112,
    123, 125, 137–39, 148,
    150, 153, 159, 161,
    164–65, 169, 171–72,
    175–76, 179–80, 184–85,
    199, 208–13, 217–19,
    224–25, 229–30, 255–60,
    265–68, 270, 304, 310,
    313, 321–22, 354, 360,
    369; cognition 256, 261;
    good 181; and the
    Kabbalists 324, 327, 332,
    336, 344; matter 43, 44,
    87; Nous 140, 168, 182,
    256; as a pagan naturalist
    139–42, 269–70; soul
    256; substance 119, 149,
    175; teleology 158, 180,
    181
pseudo-Aristotle, *Theology* 51,
    54, 56, 69, 115, 287, 327,
    344
Artisan image  207, 209–10,
    213
Asher ben David  331
Atheism  387, 389, 401, 413
Athenagoras  242
*Attika Kadisha*  288
Augustine  85, 93, 95, 267
Averroes (Ibn Rushd)  97,
    123–24, 126–28, 138, 145,
    176, 185, 257, 261–62,
    265, 269–70, 273, 354
Avicebrol.  *See* Ibn Gabirol
Avicenna (Ibn Sīnā)  81, 86–7,
    93–4, 97, 111–12, 115–16,
    118, 121, 123–24, 137–38,
    144–54, 208–10, 257,
    261–62, 264, 266–68, 271,
    273, 354; Active Intellect
    257, 261–62, 264, 266,

    268, 271, 273; argument
    for the existence of God
    116, 146–47; emanation
    111–112, 116, 123, 153,
    210, 273; essences  144,
    147–50; forms  150, 152,
    264; God's knowledge
    153, 210; matter  150–152;
    Necessary Existent  121,
    146–151; potential and
    actual existence  149;
    universals  145, 148–49,
    264, 268
Azriel of Gerona  290–91,
    327–31, 339–40
*Azilut*  293, 306

Baeumker, Clemens  71
al-Baghdādī, 'Abd al-Laṭīf  138
Balbus  28
*Basilike dynamis*  22, 29
Basnage, Jacques  387–89,
    392–96, 398, 400–02;
    *Histoire des Juifs*  392,
    394, 400
Bayle, Pierre  389, 393, 402,
    420
Behmists  391
Being  69, 70, 85–86, 89, 120,
    145, 226–27, 280, 285–86,
    290, 292–93, 354, 360,
    377, 398, 400, 412,
    414–415, 417–18, 421
Bertola, Ermengildo  86
*Bet ha-Behirah*  243, 246
*Binah*  326, 330
Blessing  170, 306
Boehme, Jacob  390–91, 402
Boethius  85, 93, 264, 415–16
Bonaventure  94, 267
Boreel, Adam  391, 395–97

*Boulesis* 26, 29
Brehier, Emile 284
Brotinus 63
Bruno, Giordano 419
Brunschvig, Léon 365
Bürgel, J. C. 67

Cantor, Georg 282, 283
Causality 72, 84–85, 91, 111,
 122, 158, 168, 228–29,
 395, 398
Cervantes, M. 419
*Chara* 26–30
Chartres, School of 93
Chastity 368
Chrysippus 28
Cicero 28–29, 31
Cleanthes 28
*Codex Brucianus* 63
Cognition 23, 115, 202;
 Aquinas 267; Aristotle
 256, 262; Gersonides 263,
 265–66; Plotinus 257–58,
 260–61
Coinherence principle 82–85,
 89, 97
Colerus, J. 389
Commercial relations 237–38,
 242, 246
Communion 417
Complexity from simplicity 178
Contingency 95, 113, 147,
 149–51, 171–72
Conway, Lady Anne 390
Cordovero, Moses 288, 307,
 342
Creation 70, 94, 97–98, 126,
 141–43, 148, 151, 159,
 161, 163, 166, 169, 171,
 174–75, 181, 209, 214,
 217, 219–23, 226, 232,
 249, 287–90, 306–9,

311–14, 325, 329, 357–59,
 361, 368–69, 387, 393,
 417; Aquinas 220, 229,
 232; distinct from Creator
 84, 86, 124, 151, 421; Ibn
 Gabirol 84–91, 94,
 120–21, 294; Isaac Israeli
 118–19, 289

*ha-davar ha-pashut* 112
Damascius 62, 64–65, 67, 69,
 71, 73, 438; *De Primis*
 *Principiis* 64
Damiens, Suzanne 356, 363
*Dator formarum* 261, 266
David ben Yehudah20
 he-Hasid 341
David ibn Abi Zimra (Radbaz)
 299
Davidson, Herbert 113, 123,
 201, 269
De Wulf, Maurice 95
Delbos, Victor 364, 375, 377
Dematerialization 262
*Deus revelatus* 303, 306, 325,
 340
*Devekut* 292
Development, biological 178,
 256, 269, 270
*Dianoia* 370
Diogenes Laertius 26, 28
Docetism 247, 248
Drummond, J. 21
*Dynamis* 158, 222, 310, 336,
 339; *Dynamis diaplastike*
 270

Ebionism 247–48
Eckhart, Johannes (Meister
 Eckhart) 98–99, 418, 437
Einstein, Albert 174, 411–12
Elhanan Sagi-Nahor 341

*Eleos* 30–32
Eliahu del Medigo 323, 331, 335
Elijah Gaon of Vilna 305
Elipandus, Archbishop of Toledo 250
Emanation 52, 54, 73, 84, 119–21, 125, 146, 161, 286–87, 289–93, 306, 308–9, 320, 326, 340, 344, 355, 393–94, 398–401, 414, 419, 421; of Active Intellect 271–73; Averroes 123; Avicenna 111, 116, 118, 123–24, 151, 153, 271, 273; cause of multiplicity 114, 116–17; Ibn Daud 118; al-Fārābī 111, 116, 118, 123–24, 271; Ibn Falaquera 70; Gersonides 271, 273; al-Ghazālī 116–17, 122–23; Maimonides 111, 117, 122, 137–38, 153, 169, 172, 174, 210, 418; *Mimekha noba'at* 120; Plotinus 113–14, 153, 271, 273, 290; Proclus 115
Emotion, rational 25, 27
Empedocles 52–55, 176, 179, 181
psuedo-Empodocles, *Book of Five Substances* 52–53, 67
*Emunah* 198, 201
Endress, Gerhart 55
Energy, "radial"/"tangential" 157–58
Epictetus 25, 29, 65
*Epistrophe* 414

Epstein, Perle 412
*Ergon* 158
Eriugena, John. *See* Scotus
Essences 85, 126, 144–48, 150–51, 160, 164, 168, 179, 320, 325–26, 330–31, 340, 366, 370–72
Eternity, experiencing 364
*Eulabeia* 26, 29
*Eunoia* 26
*Eupatheiai* 25–26, 29–30
Evil as privation 11, 217–18, 222, 224–25, 227, 230
Evolution 177–179, 182, 186
*Ex nihilo nihil fit* 392–395, 398, 400
Exemplarism 260
Existence 21, 24, 45, 48–49, 52, 62, 71, 73, 80–81, 93–94, 114–15, 122, 128, 140, 153, 158, 162, 213, 218, 220–23, 228–31, 243, 262, 273, 279, 290–91, 294, 304, 309, 311, 313, 325, 327, 330, 333–34, 344, 349, 365, 370, 375, 392, 413; Maimonides' definition 141, 143–47, 169, 183, 185, 197, 199, 209, 219, 224–27, 232; potential and actual 147–49, 152, 221, 232; necessary/possible 112, 116, 121, 144, 146–47, 150–51, 164, 222, 398
*Exousia* 22
*'Eyn Sof* 280, 288, 290–93, 306–8, 310, 326, 333, 338–43, 398; personal conception 326; *ha-'Eyn Sof* 288

*Faḍā'il* 199
Faith 62, 77, 139, 154, 195–98,
  201–2, 213, 243, 247, 249,
  387, 400, 413–14, 420
al-Fārābī 97, 112, 115, 118,
  124, 127, 138, 145–46,
  148, 201, 262, 417; Active
  Intellect 257, 271;
  emanation 111, 123–24
Felix, Bishop of Urgel 250
*Fi'l* 158, 160
Ficino, Marsilio 323–24, 331,
  337, 341, 366, 373,
  375–76, 391
Form(s) 21, 23–24, 44–50,
  52–56, 63–65, 67–73,
  79–96, 98, 113, 116–17,
  119–22, 124–28, 139,
  144–45, 150–53, 158–67,
  169, 171–72, 174–76,
  179–80, 182, 185–87, 213,
  218, 221–23, 225, 230–32,
  242, 247, 257–70, 279,
  285–87, 290–92, 305, 313,
  320, 328–30, 332, 334,
  340, 356–57, 360, 362,
  370–72, 377; angels 95,
  121, 159–61, 163–67, 172,
  182; diffusion 84; *forma
  animae, forma mundi* 81;
  Leone Ebreo 357, 368,
  371; as limit 47–48, 53,
  56, 64, 70–71, 73, 89, 280,
  286, 377; prime form 67,
  70, 72, 231, 287, 362; and
  soul 45, 50, 53–55, 81,
  83, 94, 116–17, 152, 161,
  164–65, 174, 185, 231–32,
  269, 370–71; three types
  80–81; universal 43, 70,
  73, 80–84, 87–91, 97,
  118–21, 138, 145, 161,

  268, 332, 334
Freedom 139, 142, 146, 152,
  179, 213, 285–86, 288,
  303–4, 307, 311–13,
  414–16; Leone Ebreo 368
Freud, Sigmund 411–12, 417,
  420–22
Fromm, Erich 421
Funkenstein, Amos 329
Future contingency 171, 174,
  210

Gebhardt, Carl 354
Generation 47, 63, 72, 84–85,
  128, 149, 176, 217,
  219–22, 224–26, 230, 257,
  260–61, 269–72, 322, 359,
  362; spontaneous 176; *to
  genikotaton* 22
Germanus, Moses (Johann Peter
  Speeth) 390–92, 394–95,
  398–402
Gersonides (Levi ben Gershom)
  207, 255, 257, 272–73;
  Active Intellect 257,
  262–73; cognition 257,
  263, 265–68; epistemology
  261, 267–68; human
  intellect 261–64, 266–68;
  knowledge of God 207,
  210–12; material intellect
  262–63, 265–67; universals
  268
al-Ghazālī 118, 121–25, 169,
  173, 175, 182; arguments
  against necessary
  emanation 116–17, 122,
  125; *Incoherence of the
  Philosophers* 116,
  122–23, 125
Gilson, Étienne 95
Gnostics 248, 314

God 1–3, 5–10, 13–15, 21–32, 46, 48, 63–69, 71, 73, 81–84, 86, 89–93, 97–98, 111–12, 116–27, 138–54, 159–66, 168–69, 171–72, 174–75, 179–82, 185–87, 195–98, 202, 209, 211–14, 217–18, 220–21, 223–24, 226–27, 240–42, 244, 247–50, 257–58, 264, 271–73, 279–81, 283, 285–289, 291, 293–95, 300–307, 309–14, 320, 325–26, 329, 336, 339, 343–44, 354–56, 358–68, 372–77, 392–93, 395, 400–402, 412, 414, 416–17, 419–21; Aquinas 95, 207, 212–13, 218, 228–29, 266; attributes 15, 23, 26, 28–29, 32, 69, 118, 120–22, 124, 142–44, 210, 214, 248, 281, 285, 288, 421; *Causa causarum* 339, 341–42; choice 170–71, 173–74, 221, 311; contraction 288, 300, 304, 307, 309–10; Creator 26, 53, 68–69, 80, 84, 86, 90–91, 94, 117–18, 126, 150, 160–61, 213, 220, 239–41, 244, 287, 356, 358–59, 369, 373–74; dependence on Israel 301–302, 334; the Fons Vitae 65, 68, 75; governance by delegation 165, 167, 171, 186; guarantor of being 151; in history 307, 400; incorporeality 139–41; joy 26–28, 362–63, 374, 377; knowledge 80, 90, 125, 139, 141, 152–53, 162–63, 202, 207, 209–12, 214, 264, 311–12, 320, 355, 361, 364; mercy 30–32, 289; omniscience 150, 153, 212, 311–12; rationality 24, 25, 28, 168; self-thinking 141; transcendence 21, 81, 87, 95, 120, 281, 285, 303, 306, 414; unity 64, 68–71, 73, 89, 117, 141–43, 151, 153, 195, 239–43, 245–49, 273, 283, 294, 308, 354–55, 359, 419; unknowable 48, 68, 162, 416

Goheen, John 68, 71, 73
Good 23, 63, 65, 97, 113, 115, 168, 227–30, 232–33, 258, 289, 361, 373, 416, 418; Aquinas 227–30, 232, 418; Aristotle 168, 229; beyond being 85, 280, 377. *See also* the One
Gundissalinus, Dominicus 78, 93–94, 97; translator of Ibn Gabirol 78, 93

*Hakanah* 262
Happiness 23, 27, 365, 369–70, 375, 416–17
Harris, R. Baine 416
Ḥasidim 305
*Ḥatam Sofer* 245
*Ḥavvayot* 320, 326, 330, 340
Ḥayyat, Yehudah 333, 341–42
*Ḥefeẓ, Ḥefeẓ mezuman* 120
Hellenism 413

Henry of Ghent 267
Herrera, Abraham Cohen
  337–38, 343, 391–95,
  398–400, 402–403; and
  Spinoza 391–92, 394–95,
  398–400, 402–403; *Puerta
  del Cielo* 391
Ḥesed 196
Hispanus, Johannes 78
Ḥokhmah 120, 293, 320,
  325–26, 329–30
Holistic 270
*Hormai* 25, 29
Horowitz, Isaiah ha-Levi 274
*Hyle* 43, 122, 328; *hylé noété*
  44
Hylomorphism 64, 87–88,
  93–94, 97–98; Ibn Gabirol
  87, 94, 98; implications
  88; Proclus 64
*Hyparxis* 285
*Hyperousia* 280; hyperousian
  72
*Hypodoche* 43
*Hypokeimenon* 47, 55

Iamblichus 48, 50, 52, 61–62,
  64–73; influence in Islamic
  lands 67; *peras/apeiron*
  48, 64–65, 71, 73
Ibn Attar, Ḥayyim 311–12
Ibn Daud, Abraham 71, 118,
  121–22, 319
Ibn Falaquera, Shem Tov 66,
  69, 78, 123–26;
  emanationism 123
Ibn Gabirol (Avicebrol) 43–56,
  61–64, 66–73, 77–99,
  118–22, 280, 287, 289,
  292, 294, 319, 417;
  coinherence principle

82–85, 97; creation 70,
  84–91, 94, 97–98, 118,
  120–21, 287, 294; *Fons
  Vitae* 43, 46, 48, 51,
  65–68, 71, 73, 79–80, 83,
  86–89, 92–94, 96, 119–21,
  338; hylomorphism 64,
  87–88, 93–94, 96–98;
  ineffability 69, 279–83,
  286, 288–89; influence
  48, 52, 63, 78, 92–95, 99,
  121, 280, 287; Intellect
  46, 52–53, 67, 69–73, 84,
  86–87, 89, 98, 118–19,
  121; intelligible substances
  composite 45–47, 49, 53,
  72; introduction to
  Scholastics 95; life 53,
  120; lost works 66; matter
  43–56, 61, 63–64, 67–73,
  79–91, 94–95, 97, 118–22,
  287; matter/form
  contrariety 72; matter
  prior to form 71, 89;
  mediation 54, 79–82, 85,
  97; nine levels of
  subsistence 80; principal
  elements of system 67;
  the soul is complex 50;
  sources 43, 48, 51–52, 54,
  56, 62, 66, 78, 95, 119;
  Will 51–52, 67–71, 79,
  82–92, 97–98, 120, 287
Ibn Hasday's Neoplatonist 53,
  67
Ibn Ḥazm 67
Ibn Kaspi, Joseph 123
Ibn Sīnā. *See* Avicenna
Ibn Tibbon, Samuel 137, 154,
  201, 321
Idolatry 139–41, 237, 239–40,
  245

Ikhwān al-Ṣafā' 138, 287
al-Imān 195, 198, 202
Indefinite Dyad 43–44, 46–47, 56
Ineffability 69, 279–83, 286, 288–89; Philo 279, 286; Proclus 279, 287
Infinity 71, 306, 362
Intellect 46, 50, 52–54, 56, 67, 69–73, 85–87, 89, 98, 112–14, 116, 118–19, 121–22, 124–26, 141–44, 148, 160–61, 166, 169, 173, 182, 198–202, 208, 211, 228, 232, 256–73, 311, 325–28, 330, 354–55, 358–63, 366–68, 370–72, 374, 376; Active 166, 257, 260–73, 326–28, 360; Aristotle 56, 89, 111–12, 141–42, 161, 199, 208, 256–58, 260–61, 265, 267–70, 354, 360; and cognition 202, 257, 260–63, 265–67; compared to light 50, 54, 366–67; composed of matter and form 48–49, 54, 87, 121–22, 124; First 73, 87, 89, 112, 118, 122, 257–58, 271, 354, 371; generative 258, 260–61, 269–72; human 116, 256, 261–62, 264, 266–68, 359–60; Ibn Gabirol 46, 50, 52–54, 67, 69–73, 84, 86–87, 89, 98, 118–19, 121; *intelletto attuale* 354; Leone's five levels 359–362; Maimonides 112, 122, 141–44, 161, 171–73,

198–99, 202, 207–10, 257, 262, 326, 362; material 262–63, 265–67; *nous thyrathen* 256; and the One 46, 52, 70, 73, 85–86, 114, 116, 258–59, 271, 273, 361, 366, 371; Plotinus 45–46, 52, 85, 87, 114, 255–61, 263–64, 267–68, 271–73, 360–61, 366–67
Intellectual love of God 362–63, 366, 375–76
Intelligence 73, 83, 87–87, 111–12, 114–17, 122, 124, 126–28, 140–41, 150–53, 159, 161, 164–66, 168–69, 171–75, 177, 179, 181, 183–87, 199, 271, 285, 337, 354–55, 358, 360, 362, 366, 370–71, 375–77, 417; apophatic/cataphatic 377; intuitive 115, 371
Intelligences, disembodied 165, 169, 171, 179, 355
Intelligible order 263–64, 268–69, 273
Isaac Israeli 53–54, 67, 72, 118–20, 143, 286–87, 289, 319; *Book of Substances* 54, 118–19; creation 118–19, 287, 289; sources 54, 66, 119
Isaac the Blind 280, 293, 320, 325, 330–31; *'Eyn Sof* 280, 293
al-I'tiqād 198

James, William 283–84, 420
Joseph del Medigo of Kandia 335, 342

Judah Leon Templo 396
Justice 195–97, 200–1, 259,
    413, 422

Kabbalah 280, 284, 288, 292,
    299–300, 305, 307,
    309–10, 314, 319–21, 323,
    325, 327, 330–32, 334–44,
    390–91, 394–96, 399, 401,
    412, 418; Christian 390;
    *Kabbala Denudata*
    390–94, 396, 399–402;
    Lurianic 337, 343, 390,
    392; and Platonism 323,
    331, 338; texts 303, 305,
    319, 326, 331, 340, 344,
    390, 394, 396, 401
*Kalām* 144, 163, 219–20,
    222–24
Katz, Jacob 243–44
*Keter Elyon* 288
al-Kirmānī, Ḥamīd al-Dīn 288
Knowledge 23, 49, 52, 80, 84,
    90–91, 115, 120–21, 125,
    139, 141, 143, 152–54,
    162–63, 182, 198–99, 202,
    207–12, 214, 218, 221,
    225, 227, 229, 256,
    258–68, 310–12, 320–21,
    332, 335–36, 355, 361–64,
    369–71, 373, 375–76, 420;
    Divine 125, 141, 211–12,
    214
Kogan, Barry 113, 123
*Kosmos noetos* 47, 258, 263

Landau, Ezekiel 239
Leon, Yehudah Messer 323
Leone Ebreo 324, 354–69,
    371–77, 388; anthropo-
    morphism 350; essence of
    the Divine 35, 359, 372;

five levels of intellect
    359–62; forms 357, 360,
    370–71, 376; freedom
    368; intellectual delight
    374; intellectual love of
    God 362–63, 366,
    375–76; love 324, 356,
    358–59, 361–65, 367–77;
    movements of the soul
    366; prime matter/prime
    Form 362; role of
    philosophy 354; and
    Spinoza 356, 362–65,
    375–76, 378
Leone Modena 338
Libido 416–17
Light imagery 50, 54, 65–66,
    70, 85, 113, 119, 121, 174,
    303, 360, 366–367, 375;
    sun and moon 366–67
Limit 22, 47–48, 52–54, 56, 64,
    70–71, 73, 89, 151, 286,
    294, 301, 311–12, 365
Logos 22, 29, 46, 51, 90–92,
    97, 120–21, 184, 186, 242,
    247–49, 257, 261, 272,
    285, 354, 414; Arius 249
    constitutive principles 22;
    divine son 272;
    knowledge of 91, 121;
    Philo 22, 29, 51, 184,
    186, 249, 257, 261, 272,
    285, 414
Love 25, 53–54, 118, 179, 181,
    200, 324, 353, 356,
    358–59, 361–64, 367–77,
    416, 421–22; among the
    heavenly intelligences
    358; beyond desire 373;
    God's self Love 361–63,
    376–77; imparts unity
    359;

Love (cont'd) intellectual/
spiritual 362–63, 370–71,
374–76; intrinsic and
extrinsic Divine love 361;
intuitive knowledge of
divine wisdom 373;
"productive"/"reductive"
363, 373–75
Luria, Isaac 288, 300, 308–12,
314, 342–43, 390–93, 396
Lust 163, 364
Luzzato, Simone 336–37

*Ma'nā* 144
*Māhiya* 144
Maimonides 90, 98–99,
111–12, 117–18, 122–23,
137–47, 153–54, 158–61,
163–67, 169–76, 178–83,
185, 187, 195–202,
207–14, 217–29, 231–32,
237–38, 240–41, 244–45,
247–48, 257, 262, 280,
319–21, 326, 331, 335,
361, 411–12, 418; artisan
image 207, 209, 213;
attributes 111, 122,
142–44, 210, 214, 248;
belief 139–41, 197–98,
202, 208; chance 161,
164, 173; on Christianity
237–38; composition 112,
221, 223, 225, 227;
creation 141–43, 159,
161, 163, 166, 169, 171,
174–75, 209, 214, 217,
219–21, 226, 232;
definition of existence
143; and emanation 111,
117, 122, 137–38, 146,
161, 169, 172, 174, 210,
320, 418; evil 139, 208,
217–18, 222, 224–29, 231;
faith 139, 154, 172,
195–98, 201–02; force
160–61, 163–64, 167, 169,
171–73, 175–76, 183,
185–86, 225, 231, 257,
262; intellectualism
172–73, 210; Intellect
112, 122, 141–42, 166,
257, 262, 361;
intelligences 111, 122,
140–41, 164–66, 169,
171–75, 179, 181, 183;
justice 196–97, 200–201;
knowledge, human and
Divine 141, 211–12, 225,
227, 229; matter 90, 118,
138–39, 145, 158–59,
165–67, 171, 174–75,
179–80, 185–86, 197–98,
217–29, 231–33;
mechanism 158, 170,
172–73, 177, 185; and
Neoplatonism 118, 137,
139, 143, 145, 154, 158,
320–21; occasionalism
163; and the One 137–38,
145, 153, 210, 218; parts
of the soul 200; prime
matter 159, 165–66,
218–22, 228–29, 231;
privation 158, 217–18,
221–30, 232; unity of God
141, 240–41, 248; virtue
113, 122, 165–66,
195–201; Will 142, 145,
154
Marius Victorinus 69
*Matrone* 412
Matter 21–22, 43–56, 61,
63–64, 67, 73, 79–91,
94–95, 97, 116–22, 124,

Matter (cont'd) 126–29,
    138–39, 145, 150–53,
    158–59, 165–67, 171, 175,
    177–80, 185–86, 217–33,
    263–64, 272, 287, 313,
    334, 357, 362, 366, 368,
    371–72, 374; and
    contingency 95, 151;
    essentially good 224; and
    evil 152, 217–18, 222,
    224–25, 227–30, 232;
    intelligibility 218, 221
    intelligible matter 22,
    44–46, 48–49, 51–52,
    55–56; Maimonides 138,
    165, 179–80, 217–22,
    224–26, 229, 231;
    metaphorically feminine
    225; and multiplicity
    44–45, 47, 70, 117, 119,
    121, 127–28, 150, 357;
    prime matter 53, 159,
    165–66, 218–22, 228–29,
    231, 362; prime matter
    manifestation of the Good
    229–30; priority to form
    89; properties of universal
    87–88; receptacle 43, 56,
    71; separate from God's
    Knowledge 152; source of
    substantiality 88;
    universal 43, 48, 70, 73,
    80, 82, 84, 87–89, 91, 97,
    118–21
Matthew of Aquasparta 267
*Mawjūd* 144
Mechanism 158, 170, 172–73,
    177, 185; Maimonides
    158, 170, 172–73, 185
Mediation 54, 79–82, 85, 97,
    117, 121, 257, 291–92;
    Law of 79–80; *Sefirot*

291–92
Meir ibn Gabbai 308
Menaḥem Me'iri 242–47,
    250–51
Menasseh ben Israel 337,
    342–43, 396, 400
Mercy, Divine 30–32
Metaphysics 63, 80, 82, 89, 97,
    148, 153, 158, 169, 176,
    180, 182, 218, 227–29,
    232, 290, 292, 301, 304,
    354, 398, 401–2;
    Iamblichus 61–62; Ibn
    Gabirol 62, 82, 89, 97;
    Pseudo-Archytas 63
Metatron 272
*Middot* 339–40
Midrash 160–61, 183, 247, 301,
    320, 335
*Mishpat* 196
*Mitnagdim* 305
*Miẓvot* 281, 335; *kavvanat ha-
    mitzvah* 310; *ta'amei ha-
    mitzvot* 309
Modalism 248–49
Moon 28, 304, 366–69
Morales, Henriquez 389, 397
More, Henry 389–90, 393
Morteira, Haham Saul Levi 396
Moses ben Naḥman. *See*
    Naḥmanides
Moses of Narbonne (Narboni)
    126–29
*Muhashim* 262
*Mumkin al-wujūd* 146
Munk, Solomon 78
*Mutakallimūn* 218–20, 223–24.
    *See also Kalām*
Mysticism 78, 143, 183, 210,
    283, 321, 323, 335, 377,
    403, 412, 416; intellectual
    210

Naḥmanides 328–30, 337
Naturalism 159, 163, 165, 167, 170, 173, 176; Maimonides 159, 163, 165, 167, 170, 173
Necessary Existent 146–52, 169; in itself/through another 150
Neoplatonism 55, 68, 78–80, 82, 85–86, 88, 92–93, 97–98, 115, 118, 137, 139, 143, 145, 154, 148, 195, 279, 283–84, 287, 292, 294, 300, 304–5, 314, 319–21, 323–25, 327, 329–31, 341, 343–44, 355, 365, 375, 391, 395, 411, 413–14, 416, 418–22; and dynamic psychology 419–22; Maimonides 118, 137–39, 143, 145, 154, 158, 280, 320, 331
Nethanel ben al-Fayyūmī 281
Neusner, Jacob 413
*Noten ha-ẓurot* 264. *See also Dator formarum*
Numenius 63, 82, 255; *De Mundo* 63
Nuriel, Avraham 198, 202
Nussbaum, Martha 179–81

Oaths 239
Objectivity 184
Occasionalism 163
Oldenburg, Henry 389, 395, 397
Olympiodorus 67
Omniscience and human freedom 311–12
One, the 22, 44, 46–48, 52, 55–56, 62–66, 69–73, 82, 85–86, 90, 94, 113–16, 120, 137–38, 145, 151, 153, 210, 218, 258–59, 271, 273, 279–82, 285–94, 300, 302–4, 313, 358, 361, 366, 371, 377, 393, 398, 412, 414–15, 419–20; and the Dyad 46–47, 56, 64, 71; Eudorus of Alexandria 63; from the One only one can come 86; *ho haplos hen* 64, 66; Maimonides 137–38, 145, 153, 280, 361, 411–12; and Nous 52, 63, 72, 85–86, 90, 114–15, 258–59, 271, 273, 285; Plotinus 22, 46–48, 52, 62–63, 85, 89–90, 113–15, 153, 218, 258–59, 271–73, 279–80, 282, 290, 300, 303–4, 313, 361, 377, 412, 414; *to hen on* 64–65, 73
One-many 72, 85–86, 264
*Ontos on* 411–12
Origen 248
Orobio de Castro 394, 396
Orpheus 416

Panlogism 354
*Pantelos arrheton* 64, 68
Pantheism 354–57, 402; Eriugena 355–57; Leone Ebreo 354–58; Stoics 356–57
Pauli, Oliger 399
*Peras* 22, 47–48, 64–65, 71, 73
Peratae 63
Perfection as a goal 164, 179, 181, 363–64, 369
Philo 21–32, 51, 63, 77, 89,

Philo (cont'd) 184, 186, 195, 249, 257–58, 261, 263–64, 272, 279, 285–86, 288, 290, 338, 353, 372, 414; anger of God 23, 30, 32; anthropomorphism 23, 184; attributes of God 23, 27–28, 285, 288; being 22–23, 26, 29, 249, 285–86, 288; faith 195; generation 63, 261; ineffability 279–84, 286, 288; joy of God 23, 26–28; Logos 22, 29, 51, 186, 249, 261, 272, 285, 414; mercy/pity of God 30–32; rationality of God 24–25, 28; transcendence of God 21, 285

Philolaus 63

Phylacteries 299

Pines, Shlomo 139, 211, 324

Pity 31–32

Plato 22, 25, 43–44, 52, 56, 63, 66, 79, 89, 113, 126, 159, 161, 167–69, 175, 182, 184, 186–87, 218, 255–58, 264, 266–68, 282, 285–86, 289, 305, 313, 320–24, 327, 331–38, 354, 360, 368, 375, 412; conception of the Divine 168; matter 43–44, 56, 127, 218; mediation 79

Plotinus 22, 44–52, 56, 62–63, 80, 82, 85, 87, 89, 113–15, 153, 158, 178, 218, 224, 255–61, 263–64, 267–68, 271–73, 279–80, 282, 284–85, 287, 290, 294, 300, 303–4, 313, 344, 354, 360–61, 366–67, 377, 412,
414; cognition 115, 257–58, 260–61, 263, 267; compositeness of *logoi* 46; emanation 113–15, 290; *epistrophe* 414; Forms 44, 47, 258–61; Intellect 46, 52, 86, 114, 258–61, 263–64, 267, 270–71, 273, 361, 367; intelligible matter 22, 44–46, 49, 51–52; Nous 22, 52, 63, 85–87, 89–90, 114–15, 258–61, 263–64, 268–71, 273, 285, 327, 367; the One 22, 46–48, 52, 62–63, 85, 89–90, 113–15, 153, 218, 258–59, 271–73, 279–80, 282, 290, 300, 303–4, 313, 361, 377, 412, 414; prime matter 218

*Pneuma* 28, 158

*Poietike dynamis* 22

*Poiotēs* 285

Polytheism 140, 239–42, 245

Prefiguration 329

Prime Matter 53, 159, 165–66, 218–22, 228–29, 231, 362; distinct from privation 218, 222–23, 229–30; Maimonides 165, 218–21, 229

*Primum Esse* 67

Privation 158, 217–18, 221–30, 232, 374

Proclus 22, 48, 54–55, 64, 67, 71–73, 80, 114–15, 279–80, 287, 331, 333, 377, 414, 419; emanation 115, 419; hylomorphism 64; ineffability 279–80, 288;

Proclus (cont'd) intelligibility
    of matter 55; mediation
    80
*Pros hen* equivocity 181
Psychology, dynamic 411,
    420–22

*Quwwa* 158

Radbaz. *See* David ibn Abi
    Zimra
Rahman, Fazlur 144, 146
Reason, ordinary/extraordinary
    353; *he psyche he noetike*
    256
Recanati, Menahem 321–22,
    341
Receptacle 43, 56, 71
Revelation 139, 143, 218, 245,
    250, 286, 301, 308–9, 324,
    332, 335, 354
Rikves, Moshe, *Be'er ha-Golah*
    244–45
*Rishumim* 262
Rist, John 71, 218, 287
Roland of Cremona 95–96
Romano, Yehudah 331
Rowson, Everett 67

Sabianism 67, 140
Safran, Alexandre 412
Salvation 356, 363–65, 416,
    421; female saviors 415
Samuel ben Ḥofni 241
*Sapientia* 92, 120
Sarug, Israel 337, 391, 396
Scholem, Gershom 280, 291,
    300, 338–39, 390, 392
Scotus (John Eriugena) 67,
    355–57, 417; four species
    of being 356; pantheism

355–57
*Sefirot* 280, 290–93, 304–10,
    325, 327–28, 331–44; and
    Platonic Ideas 330–31,
    335, 337–38
Seneca 25–26, 28, 31–32;
    God's joy 28
Set-theory 282
Shaw, Gregory 64–65
*al-Shay al-basīṭ* 112
*Shekhinah* 412
Shephard, Ann 71
*Shittuf* 239, 244
*ha-Siddur ha-muskal* 263. *See
    also* Intelligible order
al-Sijistānī, Abū Yaʿqūb 69,
    138; attributes of God 69
Silvestris, Bernard 359, 361
Simon the Gnostic 247
Simon, Heinrich 66
Sincere Brethren of Basra. *See*
    Ikhwān al-Ṣafāʾ
Smart, Ninian 283
Shneur Zalman of Liadi 305
*Soterion eleon* 30
Soul 24–27, 29, 45, 50–51,
    53–55, 66–67, 81, 83–84,
    94, 112, 116–17, 122, 148,
    151–52, 161, 164–65, 174,
    185, 196–202, 209, 228,
    230–32, 249, 256, 260,
    269–73, 279, 281, 292,
    314, 326–27, 354, 359,
    361–64, 366–71, 375–77,
    412, 414–16, 418;
    Aristotle 165, 256,
    269–270; complex 50
    like the moon 366–68;
    Maimonides 165,
    197–200, 361; Universal
    Soul 270–71, 273

Speusippus 44, 50, 63;
multiplicity 44
Spinoza 179–80, 356, 362–65,
375–76, 378, 387–89,
391–403; *Ethics* 363–64,
376, 388–89, 391–92, 398;
evolution 179–80; and
Herrera 391–95, 398–400,
402–3; and Kabbalah 388,
391–403; knowledge of
God 364; and Leone 356,
362–65, 375–76, 388;
*Tractatus Theologico-
Politicus* 388, 395
St. Evremond, C. 389, 397
Stace, W. T. 283–84
Stobaeus 414
Stoics 24–26, 28–32, 51, 56,
158, 356–58
Stouppe, J.-B. 389
Strauss, Leo 139–43, 154
Subjectivism 183–84, 186
Substance 48–50, 52–56, 63,
71, 73, 80–86, 88–89, 92,
95, 116–17, 119, 122, 126,
128, 145–46, 148–50, 175,
183, 213, 221, 240, 242,
260, 262, 280, 287, 304,
357, 365–66, 377, 392–93,
401–2, 417, 421
*Substantia media* 81, 83
Syrianus 63–64, 71, 73;
*apeiron* 71, 73

Tardieu, Michel 67
Tatian 242
Teilhard de Chardin, Pierre
157–58
Teleology 179–81, 313–14;
Aristotelian 179–80, 313
Temperance 201, 368–69
Tertullian 242

Tetragrammaton 288
Themistius 176, 262, 270, 320
Theology 85, 93, 118, 138,
158, 245–46, 250–51, 281,
285, 300–01, 304–5,
308–10, 314, 321–23, 327,
331, 335, 338–44, 393,
418; analogy 189;
anthropomorphic 23–25,
339–40; apophatic
281–82, 284–86; Ismāʿīlī
343–44; rabbinic 237,
244–45, 299–302, 304–5,
310, 312–13
Theon of Smyrna 72
*Tonos* 28, 158
Torah 121, 139, 158, 197–98,
208–11, 224, 227, 237–38,
241, 272, 281, 286, 301–2,
305–7, 309–10, 320–22,
327–30, 334, 341, 374,
418
Tosafists 239
Transcendence 21, 81, 87, 95,
120, 281, 283, 285, 288,
292, 303, 306, 360, 414
Transmission of texts 51, 55
Trinity 90, 239–40, 242,
246–48, 393

Ultimate particles 175
Universals 144–45, 149,
172–73, 231–32, 261, 268,
334; Gersonides 268. *See
also* Form

Van Helmont, Francis Mercurius
390–91, 396–99
Vedanta 355
Verbum 91, 120
*Via negativa* 23, 141, 213, 339,
343

Virtue 26-29, 113, 122, 166, 195–201, 227, 230, 250, 364, 368–70, 372–73, 414; Maimonides 113, 122, 165–66, 195–201
*Virtus agendi* 84
Vital, Hayyim 308, 311, 314, 396
Von Rosenroth, Christian Knorr 344, 390–92, 394, 396–97, 399

Wachter, Johann Georg 388–89, 392, 394–95, 398, 400, 402
*Wājib al-wujūd* 146
Wallis, R. T. 282
Whitehead 183, 420–22
Will 26, 29, 51–52, 54, 67–71, 79, 82–92, 97–98, 118, 120–22, 138–39, 141–43, 145, 154, 161, 164, 169, 208, 221, 226–27, 230, 285–88, 303, 311, 326–28, 364; and creation 70, 84, 91, 97–98, 118, 120–21, 142, 287–88; and form/matter 52, 54, 67–71, 79, 82–84, 89, 91, 118, 120–21, 287; Ibn Gabirol 51–52, 67–71, 79, 82–88, 90–92, 97, 120–21, 287; Maimonides 122, 138, 142–43, 154, 208, 226–27
William de la Mare 95
William of Auvergne 94, 96–97
William of Ockham 268
Wine 238
Wisdom 28, 91, 118–21, 138, 142, 145, 162, 164, 166, 172–74, 184, 186, 199, 201, 208, 210–11, 226,

250, 320, 327, 332, 354–55, 361, 369, 372–73, 390, 392, 414–15, 417, 420
Wolfson, Harry 21, 67, 195, 247, 279, 287
World Soul 81, 359, 366, 370

Ya'akov ben Sheshet 320, 325–31
Yagel, Abraham 335, 337–38, 342
*Yedi'ah* 198
Yehiel Nissim of Pisa 333
Yehudah Arieh of Modena 338
*Yitron* 280

Zahzahot, Zihzuhim 340–42
Zedaqah 195–97
Zimzum 288, 300–1, 305, 307–14
Zohar 280, 288, 291, 299, 305–07, 310, 341
*Zurot muhashot* 262
Zvi, Shabtai 390, 397